ISNM 90:
International Series of Numerical Mathematics
Internationale Schriftenreihe zur Numerischen Mathematik
Série internationale d'Analyse numérique
Vol. 90

Edited by
K.-H. Hoffmann, Augsburg; H. D. Mittelmann, Tempe;
J. Todd, Pasadena

Birkhäuser Verlag
Basel · Boston · Berlin

Multivariate Approximation Theory IV

Proceedings of the Conference at the Mathematical Research Institute at Oberwolfach, Black Forest, February 12–18, 1989

Edited by

C. K. Chui
W. Schempp
K. Zeller

1989

Birkhäuser Verlag
Basel · Boston · Berlin

Editors

C. K. Chui
Center for Approximation Theory
Department of Mathematics
Texas A & M University
College Station, Texas 77843
USA

W. Schempp
Lehrstuhl für Mathematik I
Universität Siegen
Hölderlinstrasse 3
D–5900 Siegen

K. Zeller
Mathematisches Institut der
Universität Tübingen
Auf der Morgenstelle 10
D–7400 Tübingen 1

CIP-Titelaufnahme der Deutschen Bibliothek

Multivariate approximation theory . . . : proceedings of the conference at the Mathematical Research Institute at Oberwolfach, Black Forest. – Basel ; Boston ; Berlin : Birkhäuser, 1989
Teilw. mit d. Erscheinungsorten Basel, Boston, Stuttgart
NE: Mathematisches Forschungsinstitut <Oberwolfach>
4. February 12–18, 1989. – 1989
(International series of numerical mathematics; Vol. 90)
ISBN 3-7643-2384-1
NE: GT

Printed in Germany on acid-free paper
ISBN 3-7643-2384-1
ISBN 0-8176-2384-1

Contents

PREFACE

Multivariate Approximation Theory forms a rapidly evolving field in Applied Mathematics. The reason for its particular current interest lies in its impact on Computer Aided Geometric Design (CAGD), Image Processing, Pattern Recognition, and Multidimensional Signal Processing. Multivariate Bernstein polynomials and box splines, for example, play an important rôle in CAGD. Conversely, the highly important filter bank design problem of signal processing, for instance, gives rise to a new family of multivariate approximating functions, the Gabor wavelets, with interesting technological and biological applications.

The conferences on Multivariate Approximation Theory held at the Mathematical Research Institute at Oberwolfach, Black Forest, in 1976, 1979, 1982, 1985 and 1989 reflect the progress made in this area and related fields. The present volume which is a continuation of the preceding volumes

Constructive Theory of Functions of Several Variables, Lecture Notes in Mathematics **571** (1977)

Multivariate Approximation Theory, ISNM **51** (1979)

Multivariate Approximation Theory II, ISNM **61** (1982)

Multivariate Approximation Theory III, ISNM **75** (1985)

is based on the conference held on February 12-18, 1989. It includes most of the lectures presented at the Oberwolfach meeting and reveals the wide spectrum of activities in the field of multivariate approximation.

The organizers are grateful to the Director of the Oberwolfach Mathematical Research Institute, Professor Dr. M. Barner, and his staff for providing the facilities, and to Dr. G. Baszenski, Professor Dr. F.J. Delvos, Dr. H. Nienhaus, and Dr. K. von Radziewski for their valuable cooperation during the preparation of the meeting.

July 1989

C.K. Chui (College Station, Texas)

W. Schempp (Siegen)

K. Zeller (Tübingen)

International Series of
Numerical Mathematics, Vol. 90

A RECURSION FORMULA FOR THE DIMENSION OF SUPER SPLINE SPACES OF SMOOTHNESS r AND DEGREE $d > r2^k$.

Peter Alfeld and Maritza Sirvent

Department of Mathematics, University of Utah

Abstract

We consider super splines of global degree of smoothness r, polynomial degree d, in a general number k of independent variables, defined on a k-dimensional triangulation $\mathcal{T}$ of a suitable domain Ω, which are $r2^{k-m-1}$-times differentiable across every m-face $(m = 0 \ldots k-1)$ of a simplex in $\mathcal{T}$. For the case $d > r2^k$ we give a recursion formula for the dimension of these super spline spaces.

1. Introduction

Let $\mathcal{V} \subset \mathbb{R}^k$ be a given set of N distinct points, let Ω denote the convex hull of $\mathcal{V}$ and let $\mathcal{T}$ be a set of k simplices defining a triangulation of Ω, note that a μ-face of a simplex in $\mathcal{T}$ is itself a μ-dimensional simplex. We denote by $\mathcal{S}_\mu$ the set of all μ-faces of the simplices in $\mathcal{T}$ $(\mu = 0 \ldots k-1)$ and let $\mathcal{S} = \bigcup_{\mu=0}^{k-1} \mathcal{S}_\mu$. On the triangulation $\mathcal{T}$ we define a multivariate spline space $S_d^r(\Omega)$ as usual by

$$S_d^r(\Omega) = \{s \in C^r(\Omega) \ : \ s|_\tau \in \mathcal{P}_d^k \ \forall \tau \in \mathcal{T}\}$$

where $\mathcal{P}_d^k$ is the $\binom{k+d}{d}$-dimensional linear space of all k-variate polynomials of total degree less than or equal to d.

The area of multivariate spline spaces has seen a great deal of research activity in recent years, culminating in a book [5] devoted to the subject. Much of the activity has been centered around the surprisingly difficult problem of calculating the dimension of bivariate spaces where $k = 2$ (see e.g., [2] and the references quoted there), and significant progress has been made. The dimension (and a basis) is known if the polynomial degree d

is sufficiently large relative to the degree of smoothness r. Much less has been accomplished in analyzing spline spaces where $k > 2$. It turns out [3] that, for given $r > 0$, understanding the dimension of S_d^r even just for sufficiently large d implies the understanding of bivariate spaces for *all* values of d. Obtaining for example the dimension of S_2^1 with $k = 2$ appears to be unlikely in the foreseeable future, and thus there seems to be little hope at present to obtain a dimension formula for the general space S_d^r in the case $k > 2$, independent of the size of d. In this situation, the usual approach taken in the finite element technique, and more generally by Chui and others [6], [7], [10], is to consider subspaces of S_d^r obtained by increasing the smoothness requirements across faces of the underlying simplices.

More precisely, the (super spline) space $\mathbb{S}_d^r(\Omega)$ is a subspace of $S_d^r(\Omega)$ which is defined as follows:

$$\mathbb{S}_d^r(\Omega) = \{s \in S_d^r(\Omega) \ : \ s \text{ is } \rho\text{-times differentiable across } \sigma \ \ \forall \sigma \in \mathcal{S}\},$$

where $\rho = r 2^{k - \dim \sigma - 1}$.

In this paper we give a recursion formula to compute the dimension of $\mathbb{S}_d^r(\Omega)$ whenever $d > r2^k$.

2. The Generalized Bézier-Bernstein Form

Crucial to analyzing the dimension of spline spaces on triangulations is the Bézier-Bernstein form of a multivariate polynomial. In the case $k \leq 2$ this form is used widely and is well known. A review of the Bézier-Bernstein form for a general number of variables is in [4]. In this paper, we use a notation that is particularly suitable for our purposes. However, generalized barycentric coordinates and global control nets have also been proposed in [1] and [4].

We use $\mathcal{V}$ as an index set and denote by $\mathbb{N}$ the set of non-negative integers. For vectors $\mathbf{I} = [i_v]_{v \in \mathcal{V}} \in \mathbb{N}^N$ and $\mathbf{a} = [a_v]_{v \in \mathcal{V}} \in \mathbb{R}^N$ we define

$$|\mathbf{I}| = \sum_{v \in \mathcal{V}} i_v,$$

$$\mathbf{a}^{\mathbf{I}} = \frac{|\mathbf{I}|!}{\prod_{v \in \mathcal{V}} i_v!} \prod_{v \in \mathcal{V}} a_v^{i_v},$$

where

$$0^0 := 1.$$

We also use the notation

$$\sigma(\mathbf{I}) = conv\{v \ : \ i_v > 0\}, \ \ \sigma(\mathbf{a}) = conv\{v \ : \ a_v \neq 0\}.$$

We now define *generalized barycentric coordinates* as cardinal piecewise linear functions $b_v \in S_1^0(\Omega)$ by the requirement

$$b_v(w) = \delta_{vw} = \begin{cases} 1 & \text{if } v = w \\ 0 & \text{else} \end{cases} \quad \forall v, w \in \mathcal{V}.$$

Clearly, in each k-simplex $K \in \mathcal{T}$ the functions b_v, where v is a vertex of K, reduce to the ordinary barycentric coordinates. Globally, i.e., for all $x \in \Omega$, they satisfy

$$\sum_{v \in \mathcal{V}} b_v = 1, \ \ b_v \geq 0 \ \ \forall v \in \mathcal{V}, \, and \ \ x = \sum_{v \in \mathcal{V}} b_v(x) v$$

For a given polynomial degree d, we use the *domain index set*

$$\mathbf{I}_d = \{\mathbf{I} \in \mathbb{N}^N \ : \ |\mathbf{I}| = d \ \ and \ \ \sigma(\mathbf{I}) \in \mathcal{S}\}$$

Letting

$$\mathbf{b} = \mathbf{b}(x) = [b_v(x)]_{v \in \mathcal{V}}$$

it is clear that every function $s \in S_1^0(\Omega)$ can be written as

$$s(x) = \sum_{\mathbf{I} \in \mathbf{I}_d} c_{\mathbf{I}} \mathbf{b}^{\mathbf{I}}$$

The coefficients $c_{\mathbf{I}}$ are the *Bézier ordinates* of s.

Remark. *Customarily one uses the domain points*

$$P_{\mathbf{I}} = \sum_{v \in \mathcal{V}} \frac{i_v}{|\mathbf{I}|} v$$

The points $(P_{\mathbf{I}}, c_{\mathbf{I}}), \mathbf{I} \in \mathbf{I}_d$, are then called the Bézier control points of s, and the set of all control points is the control net of s. However, for our purposes it is preferable *to use the domain indices $\mathbf{I} \in \mathbf{I}_d$ directly since then we can define subsets in terms of algebraic relations satisfied by the components of* $\mathbf{I}$.

For each simplex $\sigma \in \mathcal{S} \cup \mathcal{T}$ let $\rho = r2^{k-\dim\sigma-1}$ as before; we define two sets of domain indices recursively by

$$\overline{\mathcal{D}}(\sigma) = \left\{ \mathbf{I} \in \mathbf{I}_d \ : \ \sum_{v\in\sigma} i_v \geq d - \rho \right\}$$

and

$$\mathcal{D}(\sigma) = \overline{\mathcal{D}}(\sigma) \setminus \bigcup_{\tau \prec \sigma} \mathcal{D}(\tau)$$

where $\tau \prec \sigma$ denotes that τ is a proper face of σ.

3. A Minimal Determining Set of $\mathcal{SS}_d^r(\Omega)$

Definition. *A set $D \subset \mathbf{I}_d$ is a determining set of $\mathcal{SS}_d^r(\Omega)$ if, for all $s \in \mathcal{SS}_d^r(\Omega)$*

$$c_{\mathbf{I}} = 0 \ \ \forall \mathbf{I} \in D \Longrightarrow s \equiv 0.$$

D is a minimal determining set if there is no determining set with fewer elements than D.

The following theorem is proved in [3]:

Theorem 1. *Let $r \geq 0$, $d > r2^k$ and let $\mathcal{A}(\sigma) = \mathcal{D}(\sigma) \bigcap K$ where $K \in \mathcal{T}$ is a k-simplex so that σ is a face of K. Then*

$$\mathcal{A} := \bigcup_{\sigma\in\mathcal{S}\cup\mathcal{T}} \mathcal{A}(\sigma)$$

is a minimal determining set of $\mathcal{SS}_d^r(\Omega)$.

Corollary. $\dim \mathcal{SS}_d^r(\Omega) = \sum_{\sigma\in\mathcal{S}} |\mathcal{A}(\sigma)|$.

4. A Recursion Formula for $\dim \mathcal{SS}_d^r(\Omega)$

In view of the above Corollary to compute $\dim \mathcal{SS}_d^r(\Omega)$ we need only to know the cardinality of $\mathcal{A}(\sigma)$ for every $\sigma \in \mathcal{S}$. Clearly $|\mathcal{A}(\sigma)|$ only depends on $m = \dim\sigma$. Let us assume first that $0 < m < k$. The following Theorem is the central result of this paper:

Theorem 2. *$dim S_d^r(\Omega) = \sum_{m=0}^{k} \phi(m) f_m$, where f_m is the number of m-simplices of $\mathcal{S} \bigcup \mathcal{T}$, and for $m = 0 \ldots k$, $\phi(m) = \phi_m^k(0)$; where $\rho_m = r2^{k-m-1}$ and $\phi_q^m(p)$ is recursively defined as:*

$$\phi_q^m(p) = \sum_{j=0}^{\rho_q - p} \binom{j+m-q-1}{j} \left[\binom{d-p-j+q}{q} - \sum_{i=0}^{q-1} \binom{q+1}{i+1} \phi_i^q(p+j) \right]$$

if $0 < q < m$,

$$\phi_0^m(p) = \sum_{j=0}^{\rho_0 - p} \binom{j+m-1}{j} = \binom{\rho_0 - p + m}{m}$$

and

$$\phi_k^k(0) = \binom{d+k}{k} - \sum_{m=0}^{k-1} \binom{k+1}{m+1} \phi_m^k(0).$$

We may and will assume that $\mathcal{T}$ is the k-simplex

$$K = \{\mathbf{I} = (i_0, \ldots, i_k) \colon i_0 + \ldots + i_k = d,\ i_j \geq 0\ \forall j\}$$

and that

$$\sigma = \{\mathbf{I} \in K : i_{m+1} = \ldots = i_k = 0\}.$$

Define the ball and the sphere with center σ and radius p to be the sets

$$B_p(\sigma) = \{\mathbf{I} \in K : i_{m+1} + \ldots + i_k \leq p\}$$

and

$$S_p(\sigma) = \{\mathbf{I} \in K : i_{m+1} + \ldots + i_k = p\}$$

respectively.

Note that if $\rho_m = r2^{k-m-1}$, then

$$\mathcal{A}(\sigma) = B_{\rho_m}(\sigma) \setminus \bigcup_{\xi_j \prec \sigma} B_{\rho_j}(\xi_j)$$

where ξ_j is a j-dimensional proper face of σ. Also $B_{\rho_m}(\sigma) = \bigcup_{p=0}^{\rho_m} S_p(\sigma)$.

Let $Y = \bigcup_{\xi_j \prec \sigma} B_{\rho_j}(\xi_j)$ then

$$\mathcal{A}(\sigma) = \bigcup_{p=0}^{\rho_m} (S_p(\sigma) \setminus Y).$$

Let $\bar{a} = (a_{m+1}, \ldots, a_k)$ be an ordered partition of p, i.e. $a_i \geq 0$ and $a_{m+1} + \cdots + a_k = p$. Define

$$\Delta_{\bar{a}} = \{\mathbf{I} \in K : i_{m+1} = a_{m+1}, \ldots, i_k = a_k\},$$

$\Delta_{\bar{a}}$ should be thought of as an m-simplex parallel to σ at distance p.

Now, $\mathcal{A}(\sigma) = \bigcup_{p=0}^{\rho_m} [\bigcup_{\bar{a}} (\Delta_{\bar{a}} \setminus Y)]$ and so

$$|\mathcal{A}(\sigma)| = \sum_{p=0}^{\rho_m} \sum_{\bar{a}} |\Delta_{\bar{a}} \setminus Y|.$$

Next, is easy to see that, for fixed p, the number $|\Delta_{\bar{a}} \setminus Y|$ is independent of the ordered partition $\bar{a}$; hence, since there are $\binom{p+k-m-1}{p}$ different partitions,

$$|\mathcal{A}(\sigma)| = \sum_{p=0}^{\rho_m} \binom{p+k-m-1}{p} |\Delta_{\bar{a}_p} \setminus Y|$$

where $\bar{a}_p$ is a fixed partition of p, say $\bar{a}_p = (0, \ldots, 0, p)$.

Therefore, to compute $|\mathcal{A}(\sigma)|$ we need to know $|\Delta_{\bar{a}_p} \setminus Y|$. Now, $\Delta_{\bar{a}_p}$ can be identified with the m-simplex

$$\sigma' = \{(i_0, \ldots, i_m) : i_j \geq 0,\ i_0 + \ldots + i_m = d'\},\ d' = d - p.$$

With this identification in mind, we can write

$$|\Delta_{\bar{a}_p} \setminus Y| = |\sigma' \setminus \bigcup_{\xi_i \prec \sigma'} \mathcal{A}(\xi_i)|$$

where again we have

$$\mathcal{A}(\xi_i) = B_{\rho_i'}(\xi_i) \setminus \bigcup_{\eta_l \prec \xi_i} B_{\rho_l'}(\eta_l)$$

and $\rho_i' = \rho_i - p$.

So, we have reduced the problem of finding $|\mathcal{A}(\sigma)|$ to finding $|\mathcal{A}(\xi_i)|$ where now $\mathcal{A}(\xi_i)$ is the determining set for an i-simplex, ξ_i, contained in an m-simplex, σ', where the degree is d' and the radii are ρ_i'.

To be more explicit:

$$\begin{aligned}
\left|\sigma' \setminus \textstyle\bigcup_{\xi_i \prec \sigma'} \mathcal{A}(\xi_i)\right| &= \binom{d-p+m}{m} - \left|\sigma' \cap \left[\textstyle\bigcup_{\xi_i \prec \sigma'} \mathcal{A}(\xi_i)\right]\right| \\
&= \binom{d-p+m}{m} - \left|\textstyle\bigcup_{\xi_i \prec \sigma'} [\sigma' \cap \mathcal{A}(\xi_i)]\right|. \\
&= \binom{d-p+m}{m} - \textstyle\sum_{\xi_i \prec \sigma'} |\sigma' \cap \mathcal{A}(\xi_i)|
\end{aligned}$$

k	r	d	$\phi(0)$	$\phi(1)$	$\phi(2)$	$\phi(3)$	$\phi(4)$
2	1	5	6	1	0		
2	1	6	6	3	1		
2	2	9	15	3	1		
2	2	10	15	6	3		
2	3	13	28	6	3		
2	3	14	28	10	6		
3	1	9	35	8	7	4	
3	1	10	35	14	13	10	
3	2	17	165	40	46	56	
3	2	18	165	55	64	84	
3	3	25	455	112	142	216	
3	3	26	455	140	178	282	
3	4	33	969	240	320	544	
4	1	17	495	105	111	205	325
4	1	18	495	140	151	288	490
4	2	33	4845	990	1145	2701	6965
4	2	34	4845	1155	1345	3217	8305

Table 1: Some Dimensions

For each $q < m$, let $\phi_q^m(p) := |\sigma' \bigcap \mathcal{A}(\xi_q)|$, and using the fact that there are $\binom{m+1}{q+1}$ q-simplices in an m-simplex, we obtain:

$$\sum_{\xi_q \prec \sigma'} |\sigma' \bigcap \mathcal{A}(\xi_q)| = \sum_{q=0}^{m-1} \binom{m+1}{q+1} \phi_q^m(p).$$

Therefore

$$|\mathcal{A}(\sigma)| = \phi_m^k(0) = \sum_{p=0}^{\rho_m} \binom{p+k-m-1}{p} \left[\binom{d-p+m}{m} - \sum_{q=0}^{m-1} \binom{m+1}{q+1} \phi_q^m(p) \right]. \blacksquare$$

Example 1. *For $k = 2$ we recover the formula given by Chui and Lai [8] and also by Schumaker [10]:*

$$\dim \mathcal{S}_d^r(\Omega) = (r+1)(2r+1)f_0 + \frac{(r+1)(2d-7r-2)}{2} f_1 + \frac{(d-3r-1)(d-3r-2)}{2} f_2.$$

Example 2. *For $k = 3$ and $r = 1$ we obtain*

$$\dim S_d^1(\Omega) = 35f_0 + (6d - 46)f_1 + (d^2 - 13d + 43)f_2 + \frac{d^3 - 18d^2 + 107d - 210}{6} f_3.$$

Example 3. *Table 1. lists some additional coefficients obtained by the above recursion formula.*

References

1. Peter Alfeld, A trivariate Clough-Tocher scheme for tetrahedral data, Computer Aided Geometric Design **1** (1984), 169--181.
2. Peter Alfeld and L.L. Schumaker (1989), On the dimension of bivariate spline spaces of smoothness r and degree $d = 3r + 1$, submitted for publication.
3. Peter Alfeld and Maritza Sirvent (1989), The Structure of Multivariate Spline Spaces of High Polynomial Degree, submitted for publication.
4. C. de Boor (1987), B-Form Basics, in G.E. Farin, Geometric Modeling: Algorithms and New Trends, SIAM Publication, 131--148.
5. Charles K. Chui (1988), Multivariate Splines, SIAM Publication.
6. Charles K. Chui and He (1987), On the dimension of bivariate super spline spaces, CAT Rpt. 141, Center for Approximation Theory.
7. Charles K. Chui and M. J. Lai (1985) On bivariate vertex splines, in Multivariate Approximation Theory III, W. Schempp & K. Zeller (eds.), Birkhäuser, Basel, 84-115.
8. Charles K. Chui and M. J. Lai, 1987 On Multivariate Vertex Splines and Applications, in C.K. Chui, L.L. Schumaker, and F.I. Utreras, Topics in Multivariate Approximation, Academic Press.
9. A. Kh. Ibrahim and L. L. Schumaker, 1988, Superspline spaces of smoothness r and degree $d \geq 3r + 2$, preprint.
10. L.L. Schumaker (1989), On super splines and finite elements, SIAM J. Numer. Anal., to appear.

Acknowledgments.

This work was supported by the National Science Foundation with Grant DMS-8701121.

Department of Mathematics
University of Utah
Salt Lake City
U.S.A.
Alfeld@Science.Utah.Edu
(801) 581--6851

International Series of
Numerical Mathematics, Vol. 90

APPROXIMATION WITH BARYCENTRIC COORDINATES
THE HILBERTIAN CASE

M. ATTEIA
Laboratoire d'Analyse Numérique
118 route de Narbonne
31062 Toulouse Cedex

0. Introduction

In this paper, we present a unified approach for the construction of a large class of piece-wise functions (which contain classical finite elements, polynomial and polyhedral splines). This approach is based on a general formalism which proceeds from algebraic topology and theory of Hilbertian Kernels. Here we can give only an overview of that technique.

1. The primal problem

Let $\mathcal{C}$ (resp. W) a simplicial complex in $\mathbf{R}^k$ (resp. $\mathbf{R}^\ell$), $k \leq \ell$, with vertices $A_0,\ldots,A_m$ (resp. $B_0,\ldots,B_n$, $n \geq m$) and :

$$I(\mathcal{C}) = (0,1,\ldots,m) \text{ (resp. } I(W) = (0,1,\ldots,n)).$$

We denote by T (resp. W) the set of points of $\mathbf{R}^k$ (resp. $\mathbf{R}^\ell$) belonging to some simplex of $\mathcal{C}$ (resp. W), and by ch(T) (resp. ch(W)) the convex hull of T (resp. W).

Definition 1.1. Let $X \in ch(T)$. Then :

$$X = \sum_{j \in I(\mathcal{C})} \lambda_j A_j \quad , \quad \lambda_j \geq 0, \quad \sum_{j \in I(\mathcal{C})} \lambda_j = 1.$$

We define ψ by setting that : $\psi(X) = \sum_{j \in I(\mathcal{C})} \lambda_j B_j$ and $\psi(T) = \{\psi(X) \ ; \ X \in T\}$.

Conversely, let $Y \in \psi(T)$. Then :

$$Y = \sum_{j \in I(W)} \lambda_j B_j \quad , \lambda_j \geq 0, \quad \sum_{j \in I(W)} \lambda_j = 1,$$

and there exists only one element $\varphi(Y) \in ch(T)$ such that :

$\varphi(Y) = \sum_{j \in I(W)} \lambda_j A_j$.

Example 1.1.

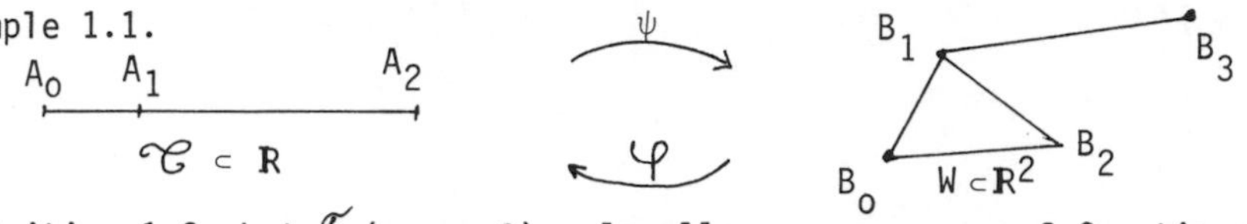

Definition 1.2. Let $\mathcal{F}$ (resp. $\mathcal{G}$) a locally convex space of functions or distributions on ch(T) (resp. ch(W)). If $f \in \mathcal{F}$, $X \in T$ (resp. $g \in \mathcal{G}$, $Y \in \psi(T)$) we denote :

$$(pf)(Y) = (f \circ \varphi)(Y) \quad (\text{resp. } (rg)(X) = (g \circ \psi)(X)).$$

The following problem "*given* $g \in \mathcal{G}$, *characterize* rg" *will be called the primal problem.*

2. The primal problem for splines : Hilbertian representations of a simplicial complex.

Assume that $\mathcal{G}$ is a linear subspace of $\mathbf{R}^{ch(W)}$ with continuous injection and $\mathcal{H}$ a Hilbertian subspace of $\mathcal{G}$ with Hilbertian kernel H.

We denote by $(\cdot|\cdot)$, (resp. $\|\cdot\|$) the scalar product (resp. the norm) of $\mathcal{H}$. Then : $\forall\, h \in \mathcal{H}$, $\forall\, Y \in ch(W)$, $h(Y) = (h|H\,\delta_Y) = h|H(\cdot,Y))$.

Definition 2.1. Given $\beta \in \mathbf{R}^{ch(W)}$, let e_W such that :
$\forall\, Y \in ch(W)$, $e_W(Y) = \sum\limits_j H(Y,B_j)\,\beta(B_j)$.

Then, $e_T = r\,e_W = e_W \circ \psi$ is the solution of the primal problem for e_W.

e_W (resp. e_T) will be called a *Hilbertian representation* of W(resp. T).

Remark 2.1. e_W is a spline function solution of the following problem :

Inf $\{\|h\|$; $h \in \mathcal{H}$, $h(B_j) = \gamma_j$, $j \in I(W)\}$ for convenient γ_j, $j \in I(W)$.

Remark 2.2. To the geometrical simplicial complex W we associate the abstract simplicial complex with vertices $H(\cdot,B_0),\ldots, H(\cdot,B_n)$

A *fundamental case* (cf. [1], [2])

W is the simplex of $\mathbf{R}^{m+1}$ with vertices : $B_j = (0,\ldots,0,\underset{\substack{\uparrow\\ j}}{1},0,\ldots,0)$, $0 \le j \le m$.

Let K be a Hilbertian subspace of $\mathbf{R}^{[0,1]}$ with Hilbertian kernel K such that : $\forall\, t \in [0,1]$, $K(0,t) = 0$.

Given $Y \in W$, denote by $\lambda_0(Y),\ldots, \lambda_m(Y)$ the coordinates of Y.

We suppose that $\mathcal{H}$ is the Hilbertian subspace of $\mathbb{R}^W$ with Hilbertian kernel H such that :

$$\forall\ Y_1, Y_2 \in W,\quad H(Y_1,Y_2) = (m+1)\cdot \sum_{j=0}^{m} K(\lambda_j(Y_1), \lambda_j(Y_2)).$$

Example 2.1. $\mathcal{K} = \{f \in H^2(0,1)\ ;\ f(o) = 0\}$ equipped with the scalar product : $(f_1,f_2) \to f_1(1)\cdot f_2(1) + \int_0^1 f''_1 \cdot f''_2 \ dt$. Then :

$$K(t,s) = \frac{1}{6}[(s-t)_+^3 + (t-1)s^3 + (t^3 - 3t^2 + 8t)s\ ,\ t,s \in [0,1].$$

Example 2.2. $\mathcal{K} = \{f \in H^1(0,1)\ ;\ f(0) = 0\}$ equipped with the scalar product : $(f_1,f_2) \to \int_0^1 (f'_1 \cdot f'_2 - f_1 \cdot f_2)dt$. Then :

$$K(s,t) = \begin{cases} \sin t \cdot \cos(1-s)\cdot(\cos 1)^{-1} & \text{if } t \le s \\ \sin s \cdot \cos(1-t)\cdot(\cos 1)^{-1} & \text{if } t > s \end{cases}$$

3. Elementary operations with Hilbertian representations

Below, we shall define only basic operations.

These definitions will be written in the following condensed form which is equivalent to the definition 2.1 :

$$\mathcal{C} \xrightarrow[\psi]{} W \to (e_j\ ;\ j \in I(W)) \subset \mathcal{G} \to e_T = \sum_{j \in I(W)} (e_j \circ \psi) \in \mathcal{E}$$

where : $e_j = H(\cdot,B_j)\cdot\beta(B_j)$, $j \in I(W)$ and $\mathcal{E} \subset \{rg\ ;\ g \in \mathcal{G}\}$

3.1. Cartesian product :

$$\mathcal{C}_1 \xrightarrow[\psi_1]{} W_1 \begin{matrix} \nearrow (e_j^{11}) \subset \mathcal{G}^1 \\ \searrow (e_j^{21}) \subset \mathcal{G}^2 \end{matrix}\ ,\quad \mathcal{C}_2 \xrightarrow[\psi_2]{} W_2 \begin{matrix} \nearrow (e_k^{12}) \subset \mathcal{G}^1 \\ \searrow (e_k^{22}) \subset \mathcal{G}^2 \end{matrix}$$

$$\mathcal{C}_1 \times \mathcal{C}_2 \xrightarrow[\psi_1\times\psi_2]{} W_1 \times W_2 \to \begin{pmatrix} (e_j^{11}) & (e_k^{12}) \\ (e_j^{21}) & (e_k^{22}) \end{pmatrix}$$

$$\to \left[(X_1,X_2) \to \begin{pmatrix} e^1_{T_1\times T_2}(X_1,X_2) = \sum_j (e_j^{11}\circ\psi_1)(X_1) + \sum_k (e_k^{12}\circ\psi_2)(X_2) \\ e^2_{T_1\times T_2}(X_1,X_2) = \sum_j (e_j^{21}\circ\psi_1)(X_1) + \sum_k (e_k^{12}\circ\psi_2)(X_2) \end{pmatrix}\right]$$

We obtain *direct sum* when $e_k^{12} = 0$, $e_j^{21} = 0$.

3.2. Tensor product

$$\mathcal{C}_i \xrightarrow[\psi_i]{} W_i \to (e_j^i,\ j \in I(W_i)) \subset \mathcal{G}^i\ ,\ i = 1,2.$$

$$\mathcal{C}_1 \otimes \mathcal{C}_2 \xrightarrow[\psi_1 \otimes \psi_2]{} W_1 \otimes W_2 \to (e_j^1 \otimes e_k^2\ ;\ (j,k) \in I(W_1) \times I(W_2)) \subset \mathcal{G}^1 \otimes \mathcal{G}^2$$

$$\to \left[(X_1,X_2) \to e^{\otimes}_{T_1 \times T_2}(X_1,X_2) = \sum_{j,k} \mu_{j,k}\ ((e_j^1 \circ \psi_1)(X_1) \cdot (e_j^2 \circ \psi_2)(X_2))\ .\right.$$

Restriction on the diagonal of $T_1 \times T_2$:

$$X \to e^{\otimes}(X) = \sum_{j,k} ((e_j^1 \circ \psi_1)(X) \cdot (e_j^2 \circ \psi_2)(X)).$$

3.3. Image

$$\mathcal{C}_1 \xrightarrow[\psi_1]{} W_1 \quad , \quad \mathcal{C}_2 \xrightarrow[\psi_2]{} W_2\ .$$

τ is a simplicial map from W_1 into W_2 such that : $\tau(B_j^1) = B^2_{\tau(j)}$. ω is a linear map from $\mathcal{G}^1$ into $\mathcal{G}^2$ such that : $\omega e_j^1 = e_j^2$. Let : $u = \tau \times \omega$. Then :

$\to (u\ e_{T_1})(X_2) = \sum_j ((\omega e^1_{\tau(j)}) \circ \psi_2)(X_2)$.

With the three elementary operations above, we can construct all the classical finite elements or polynomial splines and many other piece-wise functions. (Cf. [1], [2])

4. The dual problem

With the same hypotheses and notations as in definition 1.2, assume that p is a (linear) continuous map from $\mathcal{F}$ to $\mathcal{G}$. Let us denote $<\cdot,\cdot>_1$ (resp. $<\cdot,\cdot>_2$) the duality bracket between $\mathcal{F}$ (resp. $\mathcal{G}$) and its topological dual $\mathcal{F}'$ (resp. $\mathcal{G}'$).

Definition 4.1. Let $g^* \in \mathcal{G}'$. Then : $\forall\ f \in \mathcal{F}$, $<pf,g^*>_2 = <f,\ {}^t pg^*>_1$.

The following problem :"*Characterize* ${}^t pg^*$" *will be called the dual problem.*

Application 4.1. Generalized polyhedron spline

Assume that $\mathcal{F}$ is a linear subspace of $C°$ (ch T) with continuous injection. Let $\mathcal{A}$ be a Hilbertian subspace of $\mathcal{F}$ and A its Hilbertian kernel.

If $<\cdot|\cdot>$ denotes the scalar product of $\mathcal{A}$, then :

$$\forall\, f \in \mathcal{A},\ \forall\, X \in ch(T),\ f(X) = <f \mid A(\cdot,X)> .$$

Let P be a polyhedron of $\mathbb{R}^{\ell}$. Then :

$$\forall\, f \in \mathcal{A},\quad \int_P (f \circ \varphi)(Y)dY = \int_P <f|A(\cdot,\varphi(Y))>\, dY.$$

With regularity conditions satisfied in all classical cases :

$$\int_P <f|A(\cdot,\varphi(Y))>\, dY = <f \mid \int_P A(\cdot,\ (Y))dY > .$$

Definition 4.2. $\int_P A(\cdot,\varphi(Y))dY$ will be called : *Generalized polyhedron spline.*

From basic operations defined in the above section, we can easily deduce basic operations on generalized polyhedron splines.

Using duality between chains and differential forms it is possible to define another dual problem as in the following application :

<u>Application 4.2. Generalized divided differences</u>

Let $K = \{(u_0,u_1)\ ;\ u_0 \geq 0,\ u_1 \geq 0,\ u_0 + u_1 \leq 1\}$,

$(u_0,u_1,u_2) = a_0u_0 + a_1u_1 + a_2u_2,\ u_0 + u_1 + u_2 = 1$. Then :

$(u_0,u_1,u_2) = a_2 + h_0u_0 + h_1u_1$, with $h_0 = a_0 - a_2$, $h_1 = a_1 - a_2$.

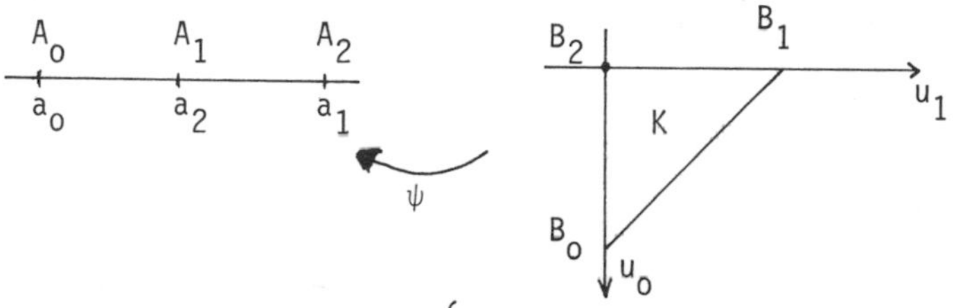

Let us consider the integral $\int_K (f'' \circ \varphi)du_0du_1$, where : $f \in C^2\,[a_0,a_1]$.
It is easy to prove that :

$$2(f'' \circ \varphi)(du_0 \wedge du_1) = d\omega,\ \omega = \frac{1}{h_0}\,(f' \circ \varphi)du_1 - \frac{1}{h_1}\,(f' \circ \varphi)du_0.$$

Then : $\int_K (f'' \circ \varphi)du_0du_1 = <K,\ d\omega> = <\partial K,\ \omega>$.

But : $<\partial K,\omega> = <B_0B_1,\ d\omega_{01}> + <B_1B_2,\ d\omega_{12}> + <B_2B_0,\ d\omega_{20}>$

$$=[\{\omega_{01}(B_1) - \omega_{01}(B_0)] + [\omega_{12}(B_2) - \omega_{12}(B_1)] + [\omega_{20}(B_2) - \omega_{20}(B_0)]$$

$$= \frac{1}{2h_0 h_1} \{f(a_1) - 2f(a_2) + f(a_0)\}.$$

With the same notations as in application 4.1 and convenient assumptions we have :

$$\int_K A(\cdot, \varphi(u))du_0 du_1 = \frac{1}{2h_0 h_1} [A(\cdot,a_1) - 2A(\cdot,a_2) + A(\cdot,a_0)].$$

In the same way as above, we obtain automatically generalized divided differences formulas in the multidimensional case.

5. Further developments

The strategy described in the above sections can be extended by

(i) Replacing Hilbertian kernels by Hermitian or Banachic kernels.

(ii) Considering simplicial complex with an infinity of vertices.

(iii) Developing a homology theory.

Bibliography

[1] M. ATTEIA : Fonctions "spline" et méthodes d'éléments finis, RAIRO, 1975, pp. 13-40.

[2] M. BOATTIN : Approximation en coordonnées barycentriques généralisées. Thesis January 1989 (Université Paul Sabatier Toulouse).

[3] W. DAHMEN and C.A. MICHELLI : Recent progress in multivariate splines, in Approximation Theory IV, eds. C.K. Chui, L.L. Schumaker, J.D. Ward, Academic Press, 27-121, 1983.

International Series of
Numerical Mathematics, Vol. 90

A Discrete Fourier Transform Scheme for Boolean Sums of Trigonometric Operators

G. Baszenski and F. J. Delvos

1. Introduction

We consider bivariate square-summable functions $f(s,t) \in L_2(J)$ defined on the region $J = [0, 2\pi] \times [0, 2\pi]$. These functions have an associated Fourier double series expansion

$$f(s,t) \sim \sum_{k \in \mathcal{Z}} \sum_{l \in \mathcal{Z}} \widehat{f}_{k,l}\, e_k(s)\, e_l(t) \tag{1.1}$$

where $e_k(s)$, $e_l(t)$ are the exponential functions of imaginary argument

$$e_k(s) = e^{iks}, \quad e_l(t) = e^{ilt}$$

and $\widehat{f}_{k,l}$ are the Fourier coefficients of $f(s,t)$:

$$\widehat{f}_{k,l} = \frac{1}{(2\pi)^2} \iint_J f(\sigma,\tau)\, \overline{e_k(\sigma)}\, \overline{e_l(\tau)}\, d\tau\, d\sigma.$$

Interesting subclasses of L_2 for deriving error estimates are the Korobov spaces

$$E^\alpha(J) = \{f \in L_2(J) : |\widehat{f}_{k,l}| = \mathcal{O}(|kl|^{-\alpha}), |k|, |l| \to \infty\}$$

which are defined for positive real parameters α.

If $f \in E^\alpha$ with $\alpha > 1$ then the Fourier series of f converges uniformly and, more generally, smooth functions with periodic derivatives are contained in Korobov spaces in the following way

$$C^{(m+1,m+1)}(J) \cap C^{(m-1,m-1)}_{2\pi,2\pi}(J) \subset E^{m+1}(J), \qquad m \in \mathcal{N}_0.$$

The Krylov-Lanczos method provides a means for constructing functions in these classes [3].

We have shown in earlier work [1,2,3,4] that hyperbolic Fourier partial sums yield good approximations in L_2 and L_∞ norm to functions from a Korobov space and that the asymptotic order of the error remains the same if the Fourier coefficients $\widehat{f}_{k,l}$ are replaced by discrete Fourier coefficients:

1.1 Theorem. *Let* $f \in E^\alpha(J), \alpha > 1$. *Then*

$$\Big\| f(s,t) - \sum_{|kl|<N}\sum \widehat{f}_{k,l}\, e_k(s)\, e_l(t) \Big\|_\infty = \mathcal{O}\Big(\frac{\log N}{N^{\alpha-1}}\Big) \quad \text{as } N \to \infty \tag{1.2}$$

$$\Big\| f(s,t) - \sum_{|kl|<N}\sum f^*_{k,l}\, e_k(s)\, e_l(t) \Big\|_\infty = \mathcal{O}\Big(\frac{\log N}{N^{\alpha-1}}\Big) \quad \text{as } N \to \infty \tag{1.3}$$

where

$$f^*_{k,l} = f^*_{k,l;N,N} = \frac{1}{(2N)^2} \sum_{h=0}^{2N-1} \sum_{j=0}^{2N-1} f(t_h, t_j)\, \overline{e_k(t_h)}\, \overline{e_l(t_j)}$$

with $t_j = 2\pi j/2N \quad (j = 0, \ldots, 2N-1)$.

While approximation (1.2) is simpler to derive theoretically, it is obvious that (1.3) is better suited for practical computations.

The hyperbolic approximations with discrete tensor product coefficients as in (1.3) do not have all the properties one might want to have when comparing with univariate discrete Fourier expansions: the bivariate approximant is in general not interpolating, $\mathcal{O}(N^2)$ data values of $f(s,t)$ are required to compute $\mathcal{O}(N \log N)$ coefficients $f^*_{k,l}$, and the only obvious way to apply one of the usual discrete Fourier transform algorithms in order to compute the coefficients $f^*_{k,l}$ is to use an $2N \times 2N$ point scheme and to disregard the unneeded of the resulting coefficients. If N is a power of 2 then the operation count of the Fast Fourier transform algorithms is $\mathcal{O}(N^2 \log N)$ for this approach.

In the following we will construct a discrete bivariate Fourier approximation scheme which resolves all the problems mentioned. It is interpolating at $\mathcal{O}(N \log N)$ knots, it yields an L_∞ error bound of asymptotic order $\mathcal{O}(\log N/N^{\alpha-1})$ for functions $f(s,t) \in E^\alpha(J)$, and its coefficients are computable with $\mathcal{O}(N(\log N)^2)$ floating point operations if N is a power of 2.

The scheme is obtained by an Nth order Blending construction. Therefore, we first discuss the univariate interpolation projectors to be used. Then we introduce parametric extensions and Tensor products of the projectors and finally we carry out the Blending scheme, derive a representation formula, error estimates and discuss how to organize an algorithm to compute the coefficients of the Blending interpolant.

2. Univariate Trigonometric Interpolation at $2N$ Points

The univariate interpolation projectors the construction is based on are defined by trigonometric interpolation at an even number of points. For Fast Fourier Transform algorithms an even number of interpolation knots is preferable and, besides the technical requirement of the transform algorithms, subsequent doubling of knots yields the simplest chain of interpolation projectors. These chains are a crucial necessity for the Blending approach.

2.1 Definition. *For $N \in \mathcal{N}$ and $f(t) \in E^{\alpha}[0,2\pi]$, $\alpha > 1$ let $T_N f(t)$ be defined as*

$$\begin{aligned} T_N f(t) &= \sum_{k=-N}^{N}{}' f^*_{k,N}\, e_k(t) \\ &= \frac{1}{2}\Big(f^*_{-N,N}\, e_{-N}(t) + f^*_{N,N}\, e_N(t)\Big) + \sum_{k=-N+1}^{N-1} f^*_{k,N}\, e_k(t) \end{aligned}$$

with

$$f^*_{k,N} = \frac{1}{2N} \sum_{j=0}^{2N-1} f(t_j)\, \overline{e_k(t_j)} \tag{2.1}$$

where $t_{j,N} = 2\pi j/2N$ $(j = 0, \ldots, 2N-1)$, and $e_k(t) = e^{ikt}$.

2.2 Remark. *a) T_N is the interpolation projector with knots*

$$\operatorname{prec} T_N = \{t_{j,N} : j = 0, \ldots, 2N-1\}$$

and with range

$$\begin{aligned} \operatorname{Im} T_N &= \operatorname{span}\{e_{-N+1}(t), \ldots, e_{N-1}(t), e_{-N}(t) + e_N(t)\} \\ &= \operatorname{span}\{1, \cos t, \ldots, \cos Nt, \sin t, \ldots, \sin(N-1)t\} =: \widetilde{\Pi}_N \end{aligned}$$

(here we have used the fact that $f^*_{-N,N} = f^*_{N,N}$).

b) $\operatorname{prec} T_N \subseteq \operatorname{prec} T_{2N}$, *and* $\operatorname{Im} T_N \subseteq \operatorname{Im} T_{2N}$, *thus*

$$T_1 \leq T_2 \leq T_4 \leq \ldots \leq T_N \leq T_{2N} \leq \ldots$$

is a chain of projectors (where the order relation $A \leq B$ is defined as $AB = BA = A$.

The remainder associated with $T_N f$ can be expanded into a Fourier series as follows:

2.3 Lemma. *(Aliasing) Let $f(t) \in E^\alpha[0, 2\pi]$ where $\alpha > 1$. Then*

$$f^*_{k,N} = \sum_{\nu \in \mathcal{Z}} \widehat{f}_{k+2N\nu}. \tag{2.2}$$

Proof: In the definition (2.1) of $f^*_{k,N}$ expand $f(t_j)$ into a Fourier series. This series converges uniformly. A discrete orthogonality argument concludes the proof.

A direct consequence is:

2.4 Theorem. *For $f(t) \in E^\alpha[0, 2\pi]$, $\alpha > 1$, we have the following Fourier expansion for the remainder of trigonometric interpolation:*

$$T^c_N f(t) = f(t) - T_N f(t) = \sum_{k \in \mathcal{Z}} c_k \, e_k(t)$$

where

$$c_k = \begin{cases} -\sum_{\nu \in \mathcal{Z}^*} \widehat{f}_{k+2N\nu} & \text{if } |k| < N \\ \frac{1}{2}\widehat{f}_k - \frac{1}{2}\sum_{\nu \in \mathcal{Z}^*} \widehat{f}_{k+2N\nu} & \text{if } |k| = N \\ \widehat{f}_k & \text{if } |k| > N. \end{cases} \tag{2.3}$$

2.5 Corollary. *Let $f(t) \in E^\alpha[0, 2\pi]$ with $\alpha > 1$. Then*

$$\left\| f(t) - T_N f(t) \right\|_\infty = \mathcal{O}(N^{-\alpha+1}) \quad \text{as } N \to \infty.$$

Proof: With c_k as in (2.3) we have

$$\begin{aligned} \|f(t) - T_N f(t)\|_\infty &\leq \sum_{k \in \mathcal{Z}} |c_k| \\ &\leq \sum_{|k| \geq N+1} |\widehat{f}_k| + \sum_{|k| \geq N} |\widehat{f}_k| \\ &\leq C \int_{N-1/2}^{\infty} \frac{dk}{k^\alpha} \\ &= C(\alpha - 1)^{-1}(N - 1/2)^{-\alpha+1}. \end{aligned}$$

3. Parametric Extensions and Tensor Product Interpolants

For bivariate functions we define parametric extensions of the interpolation projector T_N in the following way:

3.1 Definition. *Let $f \in E^\alpha(J)$ be given, $\alpha > 1$. Let $M, N \in \mathcal{N}$. Then parametric extensions of T_M, T_N are defined by*

$$T'_M f(s,t) = \sum_{k=-M}^{M}{}^{\cdot}\, f^*_{k,M}(t)\, e_k(s)$$

with

$$f^*_{k,M}(t) = \frac{1}{2M} \sum_{h=0}^{2M-1} f(t_{h,M}, t)\, \overline{e_k(t_{h,M})},$$

and

$$T''_N f(s,t) = \sum_{l=-N}^{N}{}^{\cdot}\, f^{**}_{l,N}(s)\, e_l(t)$$

with

$$f^{**}_{l,N}(s) = \frac{1}{2N} \sum_{j=0}^{2N-1} f(s, t_{j,N})\, \overline{e_l(t_{j,N})}.$$

$T'_M f(s,t)$ interpolates $f(s,t)$ along the lines $s = t_{h,M}$ $(h = 0, \ldots, 2M-1)$, $0 \le t \le 2\pi$ and $T''_N f(s,t)$ interpolates $f(s,t)$ at $0 \le s \le 2\pi$, $t = t_{j,N}$ $(j = 0, \ldots, 2N-1)$.

Using the tensor product notation for operators, these two interpolation projectors can be characterized as $T'_M = T_M \otimes I$, $T''_N = I \otimes T_N$ where I is the identity operator.

3.2 Remark. *The parametric extensions T'_M and T''_N commute and yield the tensor product interpolant:*

$$\begin{aligned} T'_M T''_N f(s,t) &= T''_N T'_M f(s,t) = T_M \otimes T_N f(s,t) \\ &= \sum_{k=-M}^{M}{}^{\cdot} \sum_{l=-N}^{N}{}^{\cdot}\, f^*_{k,l;M,N}\, e_k(s)\, e_l(t) \end{aligned} \tag{3.1}$$

where

$$f^*_{k,l;M,N} = \frac{1}{4MN} \sum_{h=0}^{2M-1} \sum_{j=0}^{2N-1} f(t_{h,M}, t_{j,N})\, \overline{e_k(t_{h,M})}\, \overline{e_l(t_{j,N})}.$$

The range and precision set of $T_M \otimes T_N$ are

$$\operatorname{Im} T_M \otimes T_N = \widetilde{\Pi}_M \otimes \widetilde{\Pi}_N$$

$$\operatorname{prec} T_M \otimes T_N = \{(t_{h,M}, t_{j,N}) : h = 0, \ldots, 2M-1,\ j = 0, \ldots, 2N-1\}.$$

An analogue to the univariate aliasing formula (2.2) expresses the parametric coefficients $f^*_{k,M}(t), f^{**}_{l,N}(s)$ as Fourier series:

3.3 Lemma. *For $f \in E^\alpha(J)$, $\alpha > 1$ we have*

$$f^*_{k,M}(t) = \sum_{l\in\mathcal{Z}} \sum_{\mu\in\mathcal{Z}} \widehat{f}_{k+2M\mu,l}\; e_l(t),$$

$$f^{**}_{l,N}(s) = \sum_{k\in\mathcal{Z}} \sum_{\nu\in\mathcal{Z}} \widehat{f}_{k,l+2N\nu}\; e_k(s).$$

For the Blending construction we need error estimates for products of the remainders of T'_M, T''_N. In order to get these we expand the interpolation remainders into double series:

3.4 Lemma. *If $f \in E^\alpha(J), \alpha > 1$ then*

$$T'^{\,c}_M f(s,t) = f(s,t) - T'_M f(s,t) = \sum_{k\in\mathcal{Z}} \sum_{l\in\mathcal{Z}} c_{k,l}\, e_k(s)\, e_l(t)$$

with

$$c_{k,l} = \begin{cases} -\sum_{\mu\in\mathcal{Z}^*} \widehat{f}_{k+2M\mu,l} & \text{if } |k| < M \\ \frac{1}{2}\widehat{f}_{k,l} - \frac{1}{2}\sum_{\mu\in\mathcal{Z}^*} \widehat{f}_{k+2M\mu,l} & \text{if } |k| = M \\ \widehat{f}_{k,l} & \text{if } |k| > M \end{cases}$$

and

$$T''^{\,c}_N f(s,t) = f(s,t) - T''_N f(s,t) = \sum_{k\in\mathcal{Z}} \sum_{l\in\mathcal{Z}} d_{k,l}\; e_k(s)\, e_l(t)$$

with

$$d_{k,l} = \begin{cases} -\sum_{\nu\in\mathcal{Z}^*} \widehat{f}_{k,l+2N\nu} & \text{if } |l| < N \\ \frac{1}{2}\widehat{f}_{k,l} - \frac{1}{2}\sum_{\nu\in\mathcal{Z}^*} \widehat{f}_{k,l+2N\nu} & \text{if } |l| = N \\ \widehat{f}_{k,l} & \text{if } |l| > N. \end{cases}$$

As in the univariate case in Corollary 2.5 we can now give error estimates for products of the parametrically extended trigonometric interpolation projectors:

3.5 Corollary. *If $f(s,t) \in E^\alpha(J)$ with $\alpha > 1$ then*

$$\left\| T'^{\,c}_M f(s,t) \right\|_\infty = \mathcal{O}(M^{-\alpha+1}) \quad \text{as } M \to \infty$$

$$\left\| T''^{\,c}_N f(s,t) \right\|_\infty = \mathcal{O}(N^{-\alpha+1}) \quad \text{as } N \to \infty$$

$$\left\| T'^{\,c}_M T''^{\,c}_N f(s,t) \right\|_\infty = \mathcal{O}((MN)^{-\alpha+1}) \quad \text{as } M, N \to \infty.$$

4. The Boolean Sum Trigonometric Interpolant

From Remark 2.2 we have that

$$T'_{2^0} \le T'_{2^1} \le T'_{2^2} \le \ldots \le T'_{2^n}$$

and

$$T''_{2^0} \le T''_{2^1} \le T''_{2^2} \le \ldots \le T''_{2^n}$$

are chains of projectors. Their Boolean sum is defined by

$$B_n = \bigoplus_{r=0}^{n} T'_{2^r} T''_{2^{n-r}} \tag{4.1}$$

(where $A \oplus B = A + B - AB$ by definition) and an ordinary sum representation for this Boolean sum is known to be [7]

$$B_n f(s,t) = \sum_{r=0}^{n} T'_{2^r} T''_{2^{n-r}} f(s,t) - \sum_{r=0}^{n-1} T'_{2^r} T''_{2^{n-r-1}} f(s,t). \tag{4.2}$$

Inserting (3.1) for the tensor product terms yields a finite trigonometric double sum for $B_n f(s,t)$.

The range of the Boolean sum operator and its interpolation knots are given by

$$\operatorname{Im} B_n = \sum_{r=0}^{n} \operatorname{Im} T'_{2^r} T''_{2^{n-r}} = \sum_{r=0}^{n} \widetilde{\Pi}_{2^r} \otimes \widetilde{\Pi}_{2^{n-r}},$$

$$\operatorname{prec} B_n = \bigcup_{r=0}^{n} \{(t_{h,2^r}, t_{j,2^{n-r}}) : h = 0, \ldots, 2^r - 1, j = 0, \ldots, 2^{n-r} - 1\}.$$

(see [9]).

Figure 1 shows a graphical representation of the range of the operator B_4. An integer grid point with coordinates (k,l) is marked as

$\cdot$ if $\cos ks \cos lt \in \operatorname{Im} B_n$

$|$ if $\cos ks \cos lt, \cos ks \sin lt \in \operatorname{Im} B_n$

$-$ if $\cos ks \cos lt, \sin ks \cos lt \in \operatorname{Im} B_n$

$+$ if $\cos ks \cos lt, \sin ks \cos lt, \cos ks \sin lt \in \operatorname{Im} B_n$.

$*$ if $\cos ks \cos lt, \sin ks \cos lt, \cos ks \sin lt, \sin ks \sin lt \in \operatorname{Im} B_n$.

Figure 1 exhibits a pseudo-hyperbolic structure of the grid points corresponding to the frequencies of the trigonometric functions which span $\operatorname{Im} B_n$. The step sizes are powers of 2 while the summation method outlined in Theorem 1.1 yields a hyperbolic structure (see [1,2]).

The interpolation knots for B_4 are shown in figure 2 in the order in which they are located in the domain J and in figure 3 they are shown with their indices arranged in bit-reversed order where the same pseudo-hyperbolic structure as in figure 1 can be observed.

Since B_n is formed with chains of projectors there is the following ordinary sum representation for the associated remainder [7]:

$$\begin{aligned} B_n^{\mathrm{c}} f(s,t) = T_{2^n}''^{\,\mathrm{c}} f(s,t) &+ \sum_{r=0}^{n-1} T_{2^r}'^{\,\mathrm{c}} T_{2^{n-r-1}}''^{\,\mathrm{c}} f(s,t) + T_{2^n}'^{\,\mathrm{c}} f(s,t) \\ &- \sum_{r=0}^{n} T_{2^r}'^{\,\mathrm{c}} T_{2^{n-r}}''^{\,\mathrm{c}} f(s,t). \end{aligned} \tag{4.3}$$

Together with the tensor product error estimates derived in Corollary 3.5 this yields an asymptotic error bound:

4.1 Theorem. *Let $f \in E^\alpha(J)$ and $\alpha > 1$. Then*

$$\left\| B_n{}^{\mathrm{c}} f(s,t) \right\|_\infty = \mathcal{O}\Big(\frac{n}{(2^n)^{\alpha-1}}\Big) \quad \text{as } n \to \infty.$$

Finally we want to discuss the operation counts when Fast Fourier Transform algorithms are used to compute the coefficients of the interpolant $B_n f(s,t)$ to given data.

4.2 Theorem. *The number of floating point operations (i. e. real additions and real multiplications) to compute $B_n f(s,t)$ grow as $\mathcal{O}(n^2 2^n)$ if $n \to \infty$, when it is assumed that all necessary trigonometric values $\sin kt_{h,M}$, $\cos kt_{h,M}$ are precomputed already.*

Proof: The operation count for a univariate Fast Fourier Transform of 2^r data values is known to be $\mathcal{O}(r2^r)$ [5,14], for Tensor product discrete Fourier transforms of $2^r \times 2^s$ data values it is $\mathcal{O}((r+s)2^{r+s})$. Assume now that all Tensor products in (4.2) are evaluated separately without further optimization. Then the bound of $\mathcal{O}(n^2 2^n)$ is attained already.

The data of the tensor products with negative sign in (4.2), $T_{2^r}' T_{2^{n-r-1}}'' f(s,t)$, are subsets of the data for the positive terms $T_{2^r}' T_{2^{n-r}}'' f(s,t)$, therefore their discrete Fourier transforms occurr as intermediate results in the recursion when $T'_{2^r} T''_{2^{n-r}} f(s,t)$ are transformed. Moreover, there are overlaps in the data sets of $T'_{2^r} T''_{2^{n-r}} f(s,t)$ when r varies from 0 to n so that more intermediate results could be reused in the computation. The asymptotic behaviour of the operation count would not be improved by these effects, however.

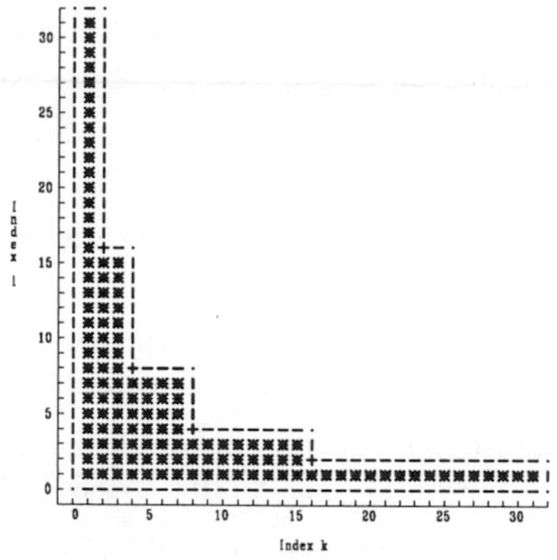

Figure 1.

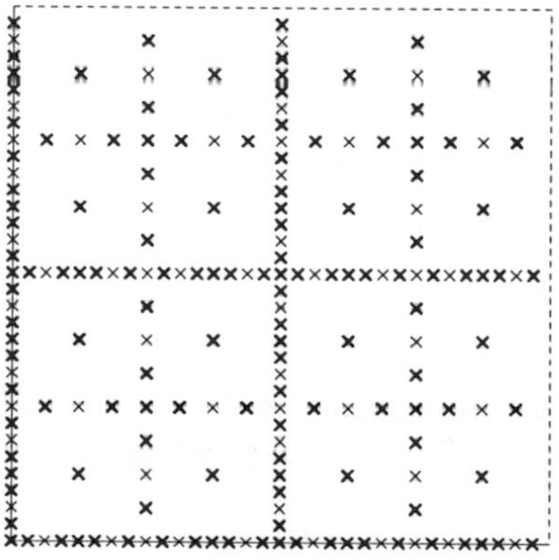

Figure 2.

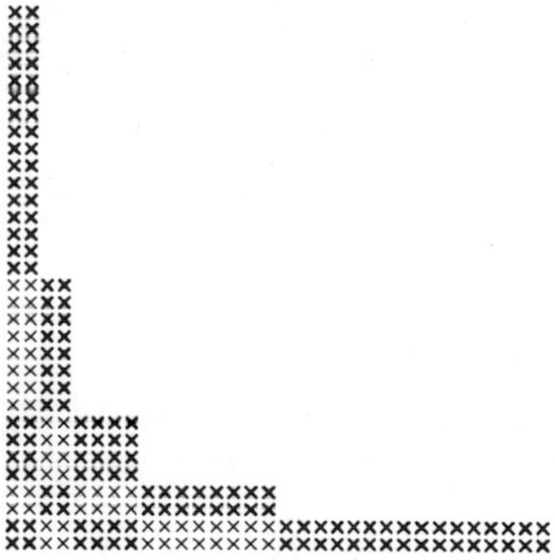

Figure 3.

References

1. Baszenski, G., *Zur Konvergenzbeschleunigung von Orthogonal-Doppelreihen.*, Dissertation, Universität Siegen 1983.

2. Baszenski, G., Delvos, F.-J., Accelerating the convergence of bivariate Fourier expan-

sions. In *Approximation Theory IV* (Eds.: C.K. Chui, L.L. Schumaker, J.D. Ward), Academic Press, New York 1983.

3. Baszenski, G., Delvos, F.-J., Boolean methods in Fourier approximation. In *Topics in Multivariate Approximation* (Eds.: C. K. Chui, L. L. Schumaker, F. I. Utreras), Academic Press, New York, 1987, 1–12.

4. Baszenski, G., Delvos, F.-J., A variant of the Krylov-Lanczos method for bivariate trigonometric interpolation. In *Constructive Theory of Fuctions '87* (Eds.: Bl. Sendov et al.), Publishing House of the Bulgarian Academy of Sciences, Sofia, 1988, 33–39.

5. Cooley, J. W., Tukey, J. W., An algorithm for the machine calculation of complex Fourier series. Math. of Comput. 19 (1965), 297–301.

6. Delvos, F.-J., Fourier series and right invertible operators. Math. Nachr. 122 (1985), 99–108.

7. Delvos, F.-J., Posdorf, H., *N*th order Blending. In *Constructive Theory of Functions of Several Variables* (Eds.: W. Schempp, K. Zeller), Springer-Verlag, Berlin, 1977, 53–64.

8. Gordon, W. J., Blending function methods of bivariate and multivariate interpolation and approximation. SIAM J. Numer. Anal. 8 (1971), 158–177.

9. Gordon, W. J., Cheney, E. W., Bivariate and multivariate interpolation with non-commutative projectors. In *Linear Spaces and Approximation* (Eds.: P.L. Butzer, B. Sz.-Nagy), Birkhäuser, Basel, 1977, 381–387.

10. Hlawka, E., Firneis, F., Zinterhofer, P., *Zahlentheoretische Methoden in der numerischen Mathematik.* R. Oldenbourg Verlag, Wien 1981.

11. Hua Lookeng, Wang Yuan, *Applications of Number Theory to Numerical Analysis.* Springer-Verlag/Science Press, Bejing 1981.

12. Lanczos, C., *Discourse on Fourier Series*, Hafner, New York 1966.

13. Tasche, M., Zur Konvergenzbeschleunigung von Fourier-Reihen. Math. Nachr. 90 (1979), 123–134.

14. Vetterli, M., Nussbaumer, H. J., Algorithmes de transformations de Fourier et en cosinus mono et bidimensionnels. Ann. Télécommun. 40, No. 9–10 (1985), 466–476.

Dr. Günter Baszenski
Ruhr-Universität Bochum
Rechenzentrum
Universitätsstraße 150 NA
4630 Bochum 1
W. Germany

Prof. Dr. F.-J. Delvos
Lehrstuhl für Mathematik I
Universität Siegen
Hölderlinstraße 3
5900 Siegen
W. Germany

International Series of
Numerical Mathematics, Vol. 90

A LOCAL BASIS FOR CERTAIN SMOOTH BIVARIATE PP SPACES

Carl de Boor*
Center for the Mathematical Sciences
University of Wisconsin-Madison
Madison WI USA

Abstract

An earlier argument for the approximation order of certain smooth bivariate pp spaces is shown to provide a simple proof of the existence of a local basis for these spaces. The argument also shows the uniform stability of such bases, except for triangulations with many near-singular vertices.

The argument in [**BH**] is unusual in that it establishes the exact approximation order from certain smooth bivariate pp spaces without the (explicit) construction of an approximation scheme. Nevertheless, all the work for constructing such a scheme giving the approximation order proved, i.e., all the work needed to show the existence of a stable local basis for those spaces, has already been done in that paper, as I pointed out in [**B**]. The recent papers [**H**], [**CL88**] and [**IS**] make it interesting to explain this claim in minute detail.

The argument in [**BH**] (to which the reader is referred for any detail left unexplained here) is based on the observation that it is possible to identify the space

$$S_0 := \pi^0_{k,\Delta}$$

of all continuous piecewise polynomial functions of degree $\le k$ on the triangulation Δ with the space of 'sequences' or mesh-functions on the discrete set

$$U := V_k = V_{k,\Delta}$$

by identifying any function f in S_0 with its **Bernstein-Bézier**- or **B-net** b_f. Here, $V_k := \bigcap_{\delta\in\Delta} V_{k,\delta}$, with $V_{k,\delta} := \{(u\alpha(u) + v\alpha(v) + w\alpha(w))/k : \alpha:\{u,v,w\} \to \mathbb{Z}_+, |\alpha| = k\}$ for the triangle δ with vertices u, v, w, and $f = \sum_{|\alpha|=k}(\xi_u,\xi_v,\xi_w)^\alpha b_f(\alpha)$ on δ, where, e.g., ξ_u is the linear polynomial which is 1 at u and 0 at v and w. The map

$$S_0 \to \mathbb{R}^U : f \mapsto b_f$$

* supported by the National Science Foundation under Grant No. DMS-8701275 and by the United States Army under Contract No. DAAL03-87-K-0030

is 1-1 and onto and is bi-continuous if we choose the max-norm for both function spaces. The map is also **local** in the sense that, for each triangle $\delta \in \Delta$, $(b_f)_{|\delta} = b_{(f_{|\delta})}$. This means that, for all intents and purposes (except the actual use in approximations), we can think of S_0 as the **discrete** space $\ell_\infty(U)$. In particular, we can think of the space $\ell_1(U)$ of all mesh-functions on U with the 1-norm as imbedded in the *dual* of $S_0 \subset C(\mathbb{R}^2)$.

In [**BH**], this setup is exploited in a study of the smooth subspace

$$S := \pi^{\rho}_{k,\Delta}$$

of all ρ times continuously differentiable functions in S_0, with $k \geq 3\rho + 2$. This subspace is characterized within S_0 as the kernel of a collection T of *smoothness conditions* τ, i.e.,

$$S = \operatorname{span}(\mathrm{T})_\perp.$$

A major impetus for the use of the B-nets in [**BH**] was the fact that these smoothness conditions take a particularly simple and geometrically significant form when expressed in terms of B-nets. Each $\tau \in \mathrm{T}$ has its support somewhere in the mesh quadrangle whose mesh-diagonal is provided by the edge to which the condition τ belongs.

Since we can think of S_0 as $\mathbb{R}^U$, we think of T as a **matrix**, with each row one of the τ's, and each column corresponding to some point in U. Then, looking for a basis for S is the same as looking for a basis for $\ker \mathrm{T}$.

With this, we organize the conditions and the points as follows. In [**BH**], we associated with each edge e of the mesh a set U_e of points from the two triangles sharing that edge. This was done in such a way that (i) the set T_e of all smoothness conditions having some support on U_e is linearly independent over U_e, and that (ii) the remaining smoothness conditions fall into sets T_v, one for each vertex v in the triangulation, and so that the union U_v of the supports of the smoothness conditions in T_v is disjoint from $U_{v'}$ for $v \neq v'$.

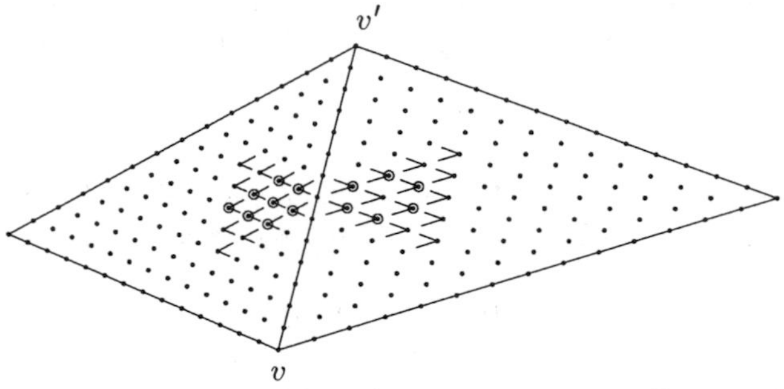

Figure 1. U_e and T_e

The construction is illustrated in Fig.1. This figure shows T_e and U_e for a particular edge e. More explicitly, the two triangles sharing this edge and all the meshpoints within these triangles are shown. The meshpoints in U_e are circled. Each smoothness condition in T_e is indicated by the two tips of its support diamond. The figure also suggests the ready split of the remaining smoothness conditions across that edge e into the two classes T_v and $\mathrm{T}_{v'}$ according to which vertex they are closer to, as well as the disjointness from $U_{v'}$ of the union U_v of the supports of the conditions in T_v; see also Fig.2 below. Finally, the set U_e being asymmetric, there is a certain arbitrariness here which could be settled by ordering the vertices of Δ, thereby providing an orientation for all edges and then choosing, e.g., to have more points of U_e on the left side of the edge.

Now organize U in the following way. Take first U_0, then U_V and, finally, U_E, with V and E the vertices, resp., edges of the triangulation Δ, and

$$U_0 := U \backslash (U_V \cup U_E), \quad U_V := \cup_v U_v, \quad U_E := \cup_e U_e.$$

Similarly, organize T to have first the conditions T_v for each $v \in V$ and then the conditions T_e for each $e \in E$. The matrix T then takes on the following block shape in which the zero blocks are denoted by 0 while the possibly nonzero blocks are denoted by X, Y or Z, except for those known to be invertible which are denoted by I:

$$\text{(1)} \qquad \mathrm{T} = \begin{pmatrix} \mathbf{O} & \mathbf{X} & 0 \\ \mathbf{Y} & \mathbf{Z} & \mathbf{I} \end{pmatrix} := \begin{pmatrix} 0 & X & 0 & \dots & 0 & 0 & 0 & \dots & 0 \\ 0 & 0 & X & \dots & 0 & 0 & 0 & \dots & 0 \\ \vdots & \vdots & \vdots & \ddots & \vdots & \vdots & \vdots & \ddots & \vdots \\ 0 & 0 & 0 & \dots & X & 0 & 0 & \dots & 0 \\ & & & & & & & & \\ Y & Z & Z & \dots & Z & I & 0 & \dots & 0 \\ Y & Z & Z & \dots & Z & 0 & I & \dots & 0 \\ \vdots & \vdots & \vdots & \ddots & \vdots & \vdots & \vdots & \ddots & \vdots \\ Y & Z & Z & \dots & Z & 0 & 0 & \dots & I \end{pmatrix}.$$

Since the block $\mathbf{I}$ is invertible, while the block above it is 0, there is a 1-1 correspondence between $\ker \mathrm{T}$ and the kernel of the block matrix $B := [\mathbf{O}\ \mathbf{X}]$. For, the restriction to $U_0 \cup U_V$ maps $\ker \mathrm{T}$ into $\ker B$, while the extension

$$\text{(2)} \qquad \varphi \mapsto \psi := \begin{cases} \varphi & \text{on } U_0 \cup U_V; \\ -\mathbf{I}^{-1}[\mathbf{Y}\ \mathbf{Z}]\varphi & \text{on } U_E \end{cases}$$

maps $\ker B$ into $\ker \mathrm{T}$ and has that restriction as (left) inverse.

The first block in B is the zero matrix, hence provides elements for a basis for $\ker B$ (hence for $\ker \mathrm{T}$) in a trivial way: Each point $u \in U_0$ gives rise to a basis element, viz. the mesh-function $\varphi_u := e_u$ which is one at u and zero at all other points. The remaining basis elements come from the kernel of $\mathbf{X}$. Since $\mathbf{X}$ is block-diagonal, $\ker \mathbf{X}$ is the direct sum of the kernels of the diagonal blocks X. The typical such diagonal block $X = X_v$ is associated with some vertex v. Take any basis for $\ker X_v$, and extend each of its elements to all of $U_0 \cup U_V$ by setting it to zero wherever it is not already defined (thus retaining the direct sum nature). Finally, extend it to U_E in the unique way dictated by $\mathbf{I}$, i.e., as described in (2).

The resulting basis is local in the strong sense that the support of each element contains at most one vertex in its interior. This is immediate for the basis elements derived from a point u in the support of no smoothness condition; their support as mesh-functions consists of that one point only (in the interior of a triangle), hence, as piecewise polynomials, they are supported on just one triangle. For the remaining basis elements derived from **O**, we start off at some meshpoint u in some triangle and then extend it via (2). The resulting meshfunction has support only at u and at the unique U_e associated with it in the sense that some smoothness condition has u as well as (part of) U_e in its support. The corresponding piecewise polynomial has as its support the two triangles sharing that edge. For the remaining basis elements, we start out with a mesh-function supported on U_v for some vertex v and then use **I** to extend it to an element of $\ker \mathrm{T}$. In this extension process, the mesh-function is determined on U_E from its values elsewhere and from the condition that it should satisfy all the conditions in $\mathrm{T}_E := \cup_e \mathrm{T}_e$. Since, away from U_E, the function has support only on U_v for some v, it will receive non-zero values only on U_e with e having v as one of its endpoints. Hence the support of the extended mesh-function is restricted to the cell Δ_v of triangles sharing the vertex v. In Chui's parlance [**CL85**], all the elements in our basis are **vertex splines**.

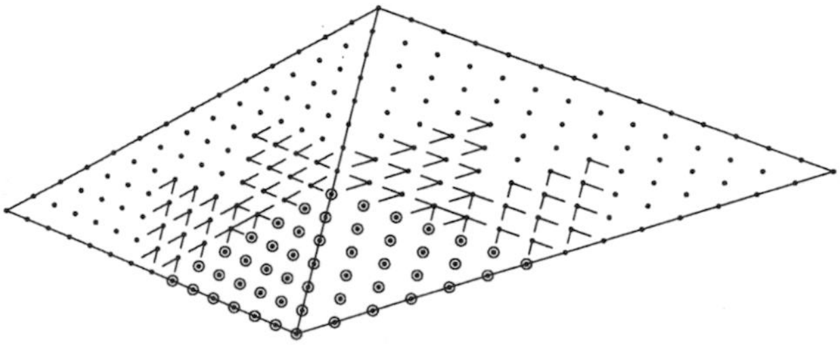

Figure 2. U_v

This proves the existence of a local basis for S, as claimed in [**B**], but does not explicitly construct a basis. It does give a recipe, though, that could (and, in effect, has been) followed. For, it reduces the actual construction of such a basis to the local problem of constructing a basis for the kernel of each of the matrices X_v. This is entirely equivalent to finding a basis for the spline space $\pi^{\rho}_{k^*,\Delta_v}$, with Δ_v the **cell** formed by all the triangles in Δ containing v, and $k^* := \lfloor (k-1)/2 \rfloor$ the "diameter" of U_v; see Fig.2. For, the matrix X_v depends only on ρ and not on k (other than that the polynomial degree should be large enough to accommodate all the smoothness conditions occurring in X_v; the minimal such degree is k^*). In any case, the dimension of this space was determined by Schumaker [**S79**] some time ago; see also [**S89**].

[**H**], in effect, follows this recipe. He identifies a particular choice of the free variables in the homogeneous linear system $X_v = 0$. In the terms used here, he identifies, for each v, a subset U_v^* of U_v which is minimally total for $S_{|U_v}$. In other words, he constructs a basis for $\ker X_v$ consisting of mesh-functions each supported at one point only. [**IS**] follow that construction, but extend it to the **'super' vertex** spline space $\pi^{\rho,\mu}_{k,\Delta}$. This is the subspace of $S = \pi^{\rho}_{k,\Delta}$ consisting of those functions which are C^{μ} at all vertices. In effect, one adds to the conditions T all those of order $\le \mu$ which have a vertex in their support diamond. The effect of this enlargement on the above construction is minimal, as long as the smoothness conditions added around the vertex v have their support diamond entirely within U_v. For then, all this amounts to is the enlargement of X_v by additional rows, thus reducing its kernel. In particular, the kernel becomes very simple when μ is chosen as large as possible, i.e., when $\mu = k^*$. In that case, $\pi^{\rho,\mu}_{\mu,\Delta_v}$ is just π_μ. This particularly simple case is treated by Chui & Lai [**CL88**] because it leads to a very simple approximation scheme which, at least generically, still gives the full approximation order of S since the subspace $\pi^{\rho,\mu}_{k,\Delta}$ still has a local basis (and still contains π_k).

But now **stability** is of concern when one wants, as do [**CL88**], to use the basis for the construction of quasi-interpolants giving the full approximation order from S.

For this, one has to look at the above construction in a little more detail. The stability constant of any normalized basis is boundable by the biggest norm of an element in some (suitable) dual set for that basis. In fact, such a dual basis to a local basis provides a good quasi-interpolant if it is also local.

For this, we now choose the basis for $\ker X_v$ carefully. We know from Auerbach's Theorem that we can find a basis for $\ker X_v$ with condition number $\le \dim\ker X_v$. More explicitly, we can find a sequence $\Phi_v = (\varphi)_{\varphi\in\Phi_v}$ of mesh-functions of max-norm ≤ 1 with support in U_v whose restriction to U_v spans $\ker X_v$, and a corresponding sequence $\Lambda_v = (\lambda_\varphi)_{\varphi\in\Phi_v}$ of mesh-functions, whose support is also in U_v, whose 1-norm is $\le \dim\ker X_v$, and which is dual to Φ in the sense that $\lambda_{\varphi'}\varphi = \delta_{\varphi'\varphi}$. The extension of such a φ to an element of $\ker \mathrm{T}$, i.e., an element of S, will change these facts in only one respect: The modification on U_E may change the norm of φ. By (2), $\varphi_{|U_E} = -\mathbf{I}^{-1}[\mathbf{Y}\ \mathbf{Z}]\varphi$. Fortunately, [**BH**] provides a bound

$$\|I^{-1}\| \le \mathrm{const}_\Delta \tag{3}$$

for the inverses of the matrices $I = I_e$ which make up $\mathbf{I}$, a bound which depends on the actual mesh Δ only slightly: it depends on the smallest angle in any triangle of the mesh (but see the final paragraph). This bound is obtained there under the normalizing assumption that all the smoothness conditions $\tau \in \mathrm{T}$ have unit 1-norm. This implies that $\|[\mathbf{Y}\ \mathbf{Z}]\| \le 1$ and therefore provides the uniform bound

$$\|\varphi\| \le \mathrm{const}_\Delta \|\varphi_{|U_V \cap U_E}\| \le \mathrm{const}_\Delta \tag{4}$$

for the properly extended elements φ of the basis Φ_v of $\ker X_v$.

The same argument shows that the basis functions φ_u corresponding to $u \in U_0$ have max-norm $\le \mathrm{const}_\Delta$ since they start from the unit mesh-functions e_u. They have the convenient dual sequence $\lambda_u := e_u$.

The resulting basis $\{\Phi_v : v \in V\} \cup \{\varphi_u : u \in U_0\}$ for $S = \ker \mathrm{T}$ has condition number $\le \mathrm{const}_\Delta \sup_v \dim\ker \mathrm{T}_v$ since its elements have max-norms no bigger than const_Δ while the elements of its dual set $\{\lambda_\varphi : \varphi \in \Phi_v, v \in V\} \cup \{\lambda_u : u \in U_0\}$ have 1-norms no bigger than $\sup_v \dim\ker \mathrm{T}_v$. For fixed degree k, this latter number is also boundable in terms of the smallest angle in (any triangle in) Δ, since it is trivially boundable in terms of the number of points in a k-ring, i.e., the number of points from U in the triangles sharing a vertex.

Finally, a sobering remark. While the claim in [**BH**] is that the constant in (3) can be made to depend only on the smallest angle, the argument offered there does not fully support this. The difficulty arises from the fact that the matrices I_e constructed in the

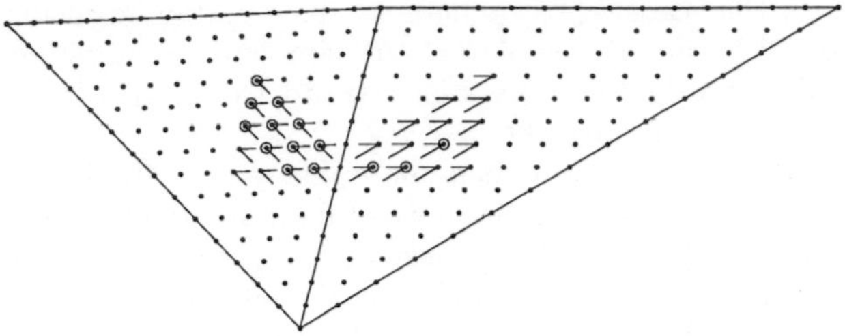

Figure 3. An alternative choice for U_e

generic case have some of their rows vanish when the two other edges (of the two triangles sharing e) meeting at one of the vertices of e are parallel. This means that, near such a configuration, $\|I_e^{-1}\|$ becomes unbounded. The remedy proposed in [**BH**] is ultimately unconvincing. It is possible to deal with the difficulty by choosing U_e differently near such a configuration, for example as shown in Fig.3. The resulting I_e is invertible at the exceptional configuration, hence uniformly invertible near it and can therefore safely be used in that circumstance. The resulting $\mathbf{I}$, though, will now fail to be block-diagonal. This, too, is no real problem, except when e is one of four edges sharing the same vertex and each parallel to an opposing edge. Such a vertex is called **singular**. For a singular vertex, the modified construction produces a noninvertible $\mathbf{I}$. If the singular vertex is isolated, then this difficulty can be overcome by treating the singular vertex and its four neighbors as one 'super'-vertex. But that still leaves certain meshes untreated by this approach.

References

[**B**] Letter dated July 31, 1987, to Bruce Piper.

[**BH**] C. de Boor and K. Höllig, Approximation Power of smooth bivariate pp functions, *Math.Z.*$\mathbf{197}$ (1988), 343–363.

[**CL85**] C.K. Chui and M.J. Lai, On bivariate vertex splines, in *Multivariate Approximation III*, W. Schempp and K. Zeller eds., Birkhäuser, Basel, 1985, 84–115.

[**CL88**] C.K. Chui M. Lai, On bivariate super vertex splines, *CAT Report #164*, March 1988, Texas A&M University, College Park TX.

[**IS**] Adel Kh. Ibrahim and Larry L. Schumaker, Super Spline Spaces of Smoothness r and Degree $d \geq 3r + 2$, ms, (1988).

[**S79**] L.L. Schumaker, On the dimension of spaces of piecewise polynomials in two variables, in *Multivariate Approximation Theory*, W. Schempp & K. Zeller eds., Birkhäuser, Basel, 1979, 396–412.

[**S89**] L.L. Schumaker, Dual bases for spline spaces on cells, CAGD, to appear.

Carl de Boor, Center for the Mathematical Sciences, 610 Walnut St., Madison WI 53705, USA.

International Series of
Numerical Mathematics, Vol. 90

POLYNOMIAL IDEALS AND MULTIVARIATE SPLINES

Carl de Boor * & Amos Ron

Center for the Mathematical Sciences
University of Wisconsin-Madison
Madison, WI U.S.A

Abstract

The well-established theory of multivariate polynomial ideals (over $\mathbb{C}$) was found in recent years to be important for the investigation of several problems in multivariate approximation. We illustrate this point.

1. The issue

An **exponential** is, by definition, any function of the form $\sum_{\theta\in\Theta} e_\theta p_\theta$, with Θ a finite subset of the set $\mathbb{C}^s$ of complex s-vectors, with each $p_\theta \in \pi\backslash 0$, i.e., a (nontrivial) polynomial in s variables, and with $e_\theta : x \mapsto e^{\langle\theta,x\rangle}$ the **pure exponential for the frequency** θ. We call the pointset Θ the **spectrum** of the exponential $\sum_{\theta\in\Theta} e_\theta p_\theta$. We take the spectrum of a function space to be the union of the spectra of all exponentials in that space. We think of exponentials as defined on $\mathbb{C}^s$ or merely on $\mathbb{Z}^s$, depending on the situation. In the latter case, we treat the frequency θ of e_θ as an element of $\mathbb{C}^s/2\pi i\mathbb{Z}^s$, since $e_\theta = e_\xi$ on $\mathbb{Z}^s$ whenever $\theta = \xi \bmod 2\pi i\mathbb{Z}^s$. We also use $e^x := (e^{x(1)}, \ldots, e^{x(s)})$.

Let ϕ be a distribution in the space $\mathcal{E}'(\mathbb{R}^s)$ of all compactly supported complex-valued s-dimensional distributions. Let C be the space of all sequences defined on the lattice $\mathbb{Z}^s$. Define the operator $\phi*$ on C by

$$\phi* : c \mapsto \phi * c := \sum_{\alpha\in\mathbb{Z}^s} c_\alpha E^{-\alpha}\phi, \tag{1.1}$$

where E^α is the shift operator $E^\alpha : f \mapsto f(\cdot+\alpha)$. The range of $\phi*$ is denoted here by $S(\phi)$, i.e., $S(\phi)$ is the space spanned by the integer translates of ϕ. Important subspaces of $S(\phi)$ are the space $H(\phi)$ of all exponentials in $S(\phi)$ and its polynomial subspace $\pi(\phi) = S(\phi)\cap\pi$. The study of these spaces, or, more generally, any subspace $F \subset S(\phi)$, is facilitated once we know the preimage $(\phi*)^{-1}(F)$

* supported by the National Science Foundation under Grant No. DMS-8701275 and by the United States Army under Contract No. DAAL03-87-K-0030

of F. Since $H(\phi)$ and $\pi(\phi)$ are both shift-invariant (i.e., closed under integer translates), their preimage is too. Moreover, since these spaces are finite-dimensional, their preimage is closed under pointwise convergence. For that reason, we equip $\mathcal{C}$ with the topology of pointwise convergence (which makes it into a Fréchet space), and equip $S(\phi)$ with the topology induced by $\phi*$, i.e., the strongest topology that makes $\phi*$ continuous. The main result of this note is as follows.

(1.2) Theorem. *Let F be a closed shift-invariant subspace of $S(\phi)$. Then there exists a finite set $\Theta \subset \mathbb{C}^s/2\pi i\mathbb{Z}^s$ and polynomial spaces $\{P_\theta\}_{\theta\in\Theta}$ such that the (sequence) exponential space $\bigoplus_{\theta\in\Theta} e_\theta P_\theta$ is dense in $(\phi*)^{-1}(F)$.*

We note that this theorem supplies also information about the **kernel** of $\phi*$, which corresponds to the choice $F = 0$.

In case $F = H(\phi)$, F is also finite-dimensional. For a finite-dimensional F, more can be said.

(1.3) Theorem. *Let F be a finite-dimensional shift-invariant subspace of $S(\phi)$. Then there exists an exponential subspace G of $(\phi*)^{-1}(F)$ which is mapped bijectively onto F. Furthermore, G can be so chosen that, for every θ in its spectrum and every $\alpha \in \mathbb{Z}^s$, $e_\theta(\alpha)$ is an eigenvalue of $E^\alpha{}_{|F}$.*

The proof of the above results uses the validity of spectral synthesis in $\mathcal{C}$ (i.e., the fact that every closed shift-invariant subspace of $\mathcal{C}$ contains a dense exponential space) and makes essential use of polynomial ideal theory. In section 2, we review some analytic aspects of polynomial ideals, and in section 3 discuss the kind of ideal that appears in our context. Lefranc's [L] proof of the validity of spectral synthesis in $\mathcal{C}$ is provided (in a slightly modified version) in section 4. In section 5, we prove the above theorems and apply them to the special choices $F = H(\phi)$, $F = \pi(\phi)$. An example concerning box splines is then examined in the last section.

We now make more explicit the connection between $\mathcal{C}$ and polynomial ideals, showing that each closed shift-invariant subspace of $\mathcal{C}$ is characterized by a corresponding ideal. The dual of $\mathcal{C}$ is given by $\mathcal{P}$, the space of all sequences with finite support, with the natural pairing

$$\mathcal{P} \times \mathcal{C} \to \mathbb{C} : (p, c) \mapsto \langle p, c\rangle := \sum_{\alpha\in\mathbb{Z}^s} p_\alpha c_\alpha.$$

In particular,

$$C\perp := \{p \in \mathcal{P} : \langle p, c\rangle = 0, \ \forall c \in C\} \tag{1.4}$$

is the **annihilator** of the subspace C of $\mathcal{C}$, while the annihilator of a subspace $P \subset \mathcal{P}$ is the analogously defined subspace of $\mathcal{C}$. It is a consequence of the Hahn-Banach theorem that every closed subspace $C \subset \mathcal{C}$ satisfies $C\perp\perp = C$. Furthermore, in case $P \subset \mathcal{P}$ is shift-invariant, it is determined by its subspace P_+ of all elements supported on $\mathbb{Z}^s_+$. Also, a shift-invariant subspace $C \subset \mathcal{C}$ is orthogonal to the shift-invariant $P \subset \mathcal{P}$ if and only if it is orthogonal to P_+. We thus conclude

(1.5) Proposition. *Let S and C be shift-invariant subspaces of $\mathcal{C}$. Then their closures coincide if and only if*

$$S\bot_+ = C\bot_+.$$

Polynomial ideals enter in this way, since each $p \in \mathcal{P}_+$ can be identified with the polynomial $p\check{} := \sum_\alpha p_\alpha()^\alpha$, while the shift-invariance of P implies (yet is not equivalent to) the fact that $P_+\check{}$ is an ideal of π. Further, with this identification, $p\check{}(e^\xi) = \langle p, e_\xi \rangle$, hence the point $\theta = e^\xi$ lies in the variety of the ideal $C\bot_+\check{}$ if and only if the pure exponential e_ξ lies in C.

2. Polynomial ideals

Let I be a polynomial ideal in the ring π of all polynomials in s variables (over $\mathbb{C}$). Associated with I is its **variety**

$$\mathcal{V}_I := \{v \in \mathbb{C} : \; q(v) = 0, \; \forall q \in I\}. \tag{2.1}$$

The fundamental result in polynomial ideal theory is Hilbert's Nullstellensatz which says that a power of $p \in \pi$ lies in I whenever p vanishes on $\mathcal{V}_I$.

An ideal is **primary** if some power of p must lie in it whenever the product pq lies in it and q does not. The importance of primary ideals in ideal theory is primarily due to the classical fact that every ideal I is the intersection of finitely many primary ideals. The primary decomposition is, in general, not unique even when assuming irredundancy. Yet, the **prime components** of $\mathcal{V}_I$, i.e, the varieties of the primary ideals in an irredundant decomposition of I, are uniquely determined by I. Furthermore, every primary ideal which corresponds to a maximal prime component is also determined uniquely by I.

The primary decomposition can be used to show that a *polynomial ideal I is characterized by its* **multiplicity spaces**

$$I\bot_v := \{p \in \pi : \; p(D)q(v) = 0, \; \forall q \in I\}. \tag{2.2}$$

Here, $p(D)$ is the differential operator with constant coefficients induced by the polynomial p. As the notation indicates, we think of $I\bot_v$ as the annihilator of I with respect to the pairing

$$\pi \times \pi \to \mathbb{C}^s : (p, q) \mapsto p(D)q(v).$$

$I\bot_v$ is nontrivial exactly when $v \in \mathcal{V}_I$. Since I is an ideal, $I\bot_v$ is D-invariant, i.e., closed under differentiation. Conversely, for any D-invariant polynomial space P and any $v \in \mathbb{C}^s$,

$$P\bot_v := \{q \in \pi : p(D)q(v) = 0, \forall p \in P\}$$

is an ideal.

(2.3)Theorem. *If I is a primary ideal, then $I = I\perp_v\perp_v$ for any $v \in \mathcal{V}_I$.*

Outline of the proof of (2.3)Theorem([L]): Assume without loss that $v = 0$ (which can always be achieved by a translation). The ideal I_A generated by I in the ring A of formal power series is closed (in the natural topology of A as a local ring, i.e., f_n converges to f iff, for every k, all terms of order $< k$ of $f - f_n$ are zero eventually; cf., e.g., [N;Proposition 2 on page 85]), yet $I_A\perp_0 = I\perp_0$, therefore $I_A = I\perp_0\perp := \{f \in A : p(D)f(0) = 0 \ \forall p \in I\perp_0\}$, using the fact that the pairing

$$\pi \times A \to \mathbb{C}^s : (p, f) \mapsto p(D)f(0)$$

makes it possible to identify π with the continuous dual of A and A with the dual of π. Cn the other hand, since I is primary, the Noether-Lasker Theorem (cf., e.g., [K;p.61]) ensures that $I = I_A \cap \pi$. ♠

The primary decomposition available for an arbitrary polynomial ideal provides the following

(2.4)Corollary. *Let $I = \cap_i Q_i$ be a primary decomposition for the ideal I. Then, for any V which intersects each $\mathcal{V}_{Q_i}$,*

(2.5) $$I = \cap_{v \in V} I\perp_v\perp_v.$$

Indeed, with $v \in \mathcal{V}_{Q_i} \cap V$, we have $I\perp_v \supset Q_i\perp_v$ since $I \subset Q_i$, hence $I\perp_v\perp_v \subset Q_i\perp_v\perp_v = Q_i$ by (2.3)Theorem. This shows that the right side of (2.5) is contained in I, while the opposite inclusion is trivial.

3. q-ideals

If the linear subspace P of $\mathcal{P}$ is shift-invariant, then $P_+\check{}$ is an ideal, but not every ideal in π arises in this way. A polynomial ideal I is of the form $P_+\check{}$ for some shift-invariant subspace P of $\mathcal{P}$ if and only if it satisfies the condition

(3.1) $$p \in I \Longleftrightarrow ()^\alpha p \in I$$

for every $\alpha \in \mathbb{Z}_+^s$. This condition is equivalent to the requirement that

(3.2) $$p \in I \Longleftrightarrow qp \in I$$

for the polynomial $q := ()^{1,1,\ldots,1}$. Provided I is non-trivial, we call such an ideal a **q-ideal**. We define the **q-reduced variety** $\mathcal{V}_I^q$ of I by

$$\mathcal{V}_I^q := \{\theta \in \mathcal{V}_I : \ q(\theta) \neq 0\}.$$

An **E-ideal** corresponds to the choice $q = ()^{(1,\ldots,1)}$, hence its reduced variety becomes $\mathcal{V}_I^* := \mathcal{V}_I \cap \mathbb{C}_*^s$, where $\mathbb{C}_*^s := (\mathbb{C}\backslash 0)^s$.

(3.3) Proposition. *If I is a q-ideal and the polynomial p vanishes on $\mathcal{V}_I^q$, then a power of p lies in I.*

Indeed, if p vanishes on $\mathcal{V}_I^q$, then pq vanishes on $\mathcal{V}_I$. Therefore, by the Nullstellensatz, $p^k q^k \in I$ for some k, and repeated application of (3.2) then yields $p^k \in I$.

The following theorem is a special case of [N;Thm. 6, p. 23]:

(3.4) Theorem. *An ideal I is a q-ideal if and only if it admits a primary decomposition $I = \cap_i Q_i$ with $\mathcal{V}_{Q_i}^q \neq \emptyset$ for all i.*

Proof: Assume first that I is a q-ideal, let $\cap_i Q_i$ be a primary decomposition of I and suppose that for some j, $\mathcal{V}_{Q_j}$ lies in the zero set of q. Then $J := \cap_{i \neq j} Q_i \supset I$. On the other hand q vanishes on $\mathcal{V}_{Q_j}$, hence $q^n \in Q_j$ for some n, and therefore $q^n J \subset Q_j J \subset Q_j \cap J = I$. Since I is a q-ideal, it follows that $J \subset I$ and consequently $J = I$. We conclude that Q_j is a redundant component in the primary decomposition of I.

For the converse, we assume that $I = \cap_i Q_i$ and that no $\mathcal{V}_{Q_i}$ lies in the zero set of q. Then, for every i, no power of q can lie in Q_i, hence, since Q_i is primary,

$$pq \in I \Longrightarrow pq \in Q_i \Longrightarrow p \in Q_i.$$

We conclude that $p \in I$ and thus I is a q-ideal. ♠

(3.5) Corollary. *A q-ideal can be decomposed into primary q-ideals.*

The following two corollaries will be used in the sequel:

(3.6) Corollary. *If I is a q-ideal, then V in (2.4)Corollary can be chosen from $\mathcal{V}_I^q$. In particular, if I is an E-ideal, V can be chosen from $\mathcal{V}_I^* \subset \mathbf{C}_*^s$.*

(3.7) Corollary. *Assume $\mathcal{V}_I^q$ is finite. Then I is a q-ideal if and only if $\mathcal{V}_I = \mathcal{V}_I^q$.*

Proof: If $\mathcal{V}_I = \mathcal{V}_I^q$, then I is a q-ideal by (3.4)Theorem, since q vanishes nowhere on $\mathcal{V}_I$. Conversely, if $\mathcal{V}_I \backslash \mathcal{V}_I^q$ is not empty, it contains a maximal prime component of $\mathcal{V}_I$ which lies entirely in the zero set of q, which means that there exists a primary ideal Q which appears in every primary decomposition of I and whose variety lies entirely in the zero set of q. Consequently, by (3.4)Theorem, I is not a q-ideal. ♠

4. Spectral synthesis in $\mathcal{C}$

The following lemma is the technical link between ideal theory and spectral synthesis in $\mathcal{C}$. It uses the **normalized factorial function** $[]^\alpha$ defined by

$$[x]^\alpha := \prod_j [x(j)]^{\alpha(j)}, \quad \text{with } [t]^n := t(t-1)\cdots(t-n+1)/n!.$$

This function's chief virtue lies in the fact that $\Delta^\alpha[]^\beta = []^{\beta-\alpha}$, with Δ the forward difference operator. This provides the pretty identity

$$\Delta p([]) = (Dp)([]), \tag{4.1}$$

in which $p([]) := \sum_\beta []^\beta D^\beta p(0)$, and which is meant to signify that $\Delta^\alpha p([]) = (D^\alpha p)([])$ for all $\alpha \in \mathbb{Z}_+^s$.

(4.2) Lemma. *Let $p \in \pi$, $q \in \mathcal{P}_+$, $v \in \mathbb{C}_*^s$, and let $\theta = \log v$, i.e., $e^{\theta_j} = v_j$, $j = 1, ..., s$. Then $p(vD)q\check{}(v) = 0$ if and only if $\langle q, e_\theta p([])\rangle = 0$.*

Proof: For every $\alpha, \beta \in \mathbb{Z}_+^s$,

$$(vD)^\beta ()^\alpha (v) = \frac{\alpha!}{(\alpha-\beta)!} v^\alpha = \beta! [\alpha]^\beta v^\alpha. \tag{4.3}$$

Hence

$$p(vD)q\check{}(v) = \sum_\alpha q_\alpha p([\alpha]) v^\alpha = \langle q, e_\theta p([])\rangle.$$ ♠

(4.4) Theorem([L]). *Every closed shift-invariant subspace of $\mathcal{C}$ contains a dense exponential subspace of finite spectrum.*

Proof: Let C be the space in question. Then $I := C\perp_+\check{}$ is an E-ideal. By (2.4)Corollary and (3.6)Corollary, there exists $V \subset \mathbb{C}_*^s$ such that

$$C\perp_+\check{} = I = \bigcap_{v \in V} I\perp_v\perp_v. \tag{4.5}$$

We conclude from (4.2)Lemma that, with $\Theta := \log V$,

$$C\perp_+ = \{q \in \mathcal{P}_+ : \langle q, e_\theta r([])\rangle = 0, \ \forall \theta \in \Theta, \ r \in P_\theta\}, \tag{4.6}$$

where $P_\theta = \{p(\cdot/v) : p \in I\perp_v\}$. Since $I\perp_v$ is D-invariant, so is P_θ, and hence $P_\theta([]) := \{p([]) : p \in P_\theta\}$ is shift-invariant by (4.1). This implies that the subspace F of $\mathcal{C}$ defined by $F := \bigoplus_{\theta\in\Theta} e_\theta P_\theta([])$ is shift-invariant, while $C\perp_+ = F\perp_+$ by (4.6). Therefore, an application of (1.5)Proposition shows that C and F have the same closure, and since C is closed, F is dense in C. ♠

The proof just given supports the following corollary:

(4.7) Corollary. *Let C be a closed shift-invariant subspace of $\mathcal{C}$. Let Θ be a subset of $\mathbb{C}^s$. If $e^\Theta := \{e^\theta : \theta \in \Theta\}$ intersects each prime component of $\mathcal{V}_{C\perp_+\check{}}$, then the space of all exponentials in C with spectrum in Θ is dense in C.*

With the aid of (3.7)Corollary, we also conclude

(4.8) Corollary. *A closed shift-invariant subspace C of $\mathcal{C}$ is finite-dimensional if and only if it has finite spectrum.*

Proof: The "only if" claim is trivial. For the converse, we note that if the spectrum of C is finite, then the reduced variety of $C\perp_+{}^\vee$ is finite, hence by (3.7)Corollary, so is $\mathcal{V}_{C\perp_+{}^\vee}$. Now, for an ideal of finite variety, it follows from the Nullstellensatz that each of the multiplicity spaces associated with the variety is finite-dimensional. Application of (4.2)Lemma then yields that the space of all exponentials in C is finite-dimensional, and by virtue of (4.4)Theorem, so is C. ♠

5. Main results

Unless stated otherwise, the exponentials considered in the rest of the paper will always be defined on $\mathbb{Z}^s$, hence the associated spectra are meant in $\mathbf{C}^s/2\pi i\mathbb{Z}^s$.

We prove here (1.2)Theorem, (1.3)Theorem and draw other conclusions from the spectral synthesis in $\mathcal{C}$.

Proof of (1.2)Theorem: Since F is closed and shift-invariant, $(\phi*)^{-1}(F)$ is a closed shift-invariant subspace of $\mathcal{C}$. Now apply (4.4)Theorem. ♠

Proof of (1.3)Theorem: The first part of the theorem follows directly from (1.2)Theorem and the fact that F, being finite-dimensional, contains no proper dense subspaces. To prove the second part, we note that, for every $\alpha \in \mathbb{Z}^s$, E^α is an endomorphism on F, hence it indeed makes sense to consider the spectrum $\sigma(\alpha)$ of $E^\alpha{}_{|F}$.

We now take an arbitrary exponential $g := \sum_{\theta\in\Theta} e_\theta p_\theta$ in the preimage of F (under $\phi*$) and, following the argument of [BR; Prop. 7.1], show that, for every $\vartheta \in \Theta$ for which $e_\vartheta(\alpha) \notin \sigma(\alpha)$ for some $\alpha \in \mathbb{Z}^s$, the summand $e_\vartheta p_\vartheta$ is in the kernel of $\phi*$, hence can be omitted from the sum.

For any α, the characteristic polynomial χ_α of $E^\alpha{}_{|F}$ gives

$$\phi{*}\chi_\alpha(E^\alpha)g = \chi_\alpha(E^\alpha)(\phi{*}g) \in \chi_\alpha(E^\alpha)(F) = \{0\}.$$

For arbitrary $p \in \pi$, $\beta \in \mathbb{Z}^s$ and $\lambda \in \mathbf{C}^s$

$$E^\beta(e_\theta p) - \lambda e_\theta p = e_\theta\,(e_\theta(\beta)E^\beta p - \lambda p),$$

hence $(E^\beta - \lambda)(e_\theta p) = e_\theta q$, with q a polynomial that satisfies

$$\deg q = \deg p \Longleftrightarrow e_\theta(\beta) - \lambda \neq 0.$$

Assume now that $e_\vartheta(\alpha) \notin \sigma(\alpha)$. Then $\chi_\alpha(E^\alpha)$ is 1-1 on $e_\vartheta\pi$. Also, we can find a polynomial q for which $q(E)$ annihilates $e_\theta p_\theta$ for all $\theta \in \Theta\backslash\vartheta$ but is 1-1 on $e_\vartheta\pi$. Consequently,

$$0 = q(E)(\phi{*}\chi_\alpha(E^\alpha)g) =: \phi{*}r(E)(e_\vartheta p_\vartheta). \tag{5.1}$$

Since $r(E)$ is 1-1 on $e_\vartheta\pi$, it carries each $e_\vartheta\pi_k$ onto itself, hence, with $k \ge \deg p_\vartheta$, there is some polynomial s so that $(sr)(E)$ is the identity on $e_\vartheta\pi_k$. Thus, from (5.1), $0 = s(E)0 = \phi{*}(sr)(E)(e_\vartheta p_\vartheta) = \phi{*}e_\vartheta p_\vartheta$, which is what we set out to prove. ♠

To make use of the second part of (1.3)Theorem, one needs to know the spectrum of sufficiently many $E^\alpha{}_{|F}$, a task that might appear to be difficult in general. Yet, if we assume that F is an exponential space and denote its spectrum by Θ, then F contains each e_θ with $\theta \in \Theta$, hence

(5.2) $$\sigma(\alpha) = \{e_\theta(\alpha)\}_{\theta\in\Theta}, \ \forall \alpha \in \mathbb{Z}^s.$$

This implies that the points $\theta \in \Theta$ are the only frequencies that satisfy

(5.3) $$e_\theta(\alpha) \in \sigma(\alpha), \ \forall \alpha \in \mathbb{Z}^s.$$

So we obtain

(5.4) Corollary. *Let H be a shift-invariant exponential subspace of $S(\phi)$ with spectrum $\Theta \subset \mathbb{C}^s$. Then there exists a finite-dimensional shift-invariant exponential space of spectrum $\Theta/2\pi i\mathbb{Z}^s$ which is mapped by $\phi{*}$ onto H.*

Of particular interest is the following

(5.5) Corollary. *For every $\theta \in \mathbb{C}^s$, $S(\phi) \cap e_\theta\pi$ is the image of some finite-dimensional shift-invariant space $C \subset \mathcal{C} \cap e_\theta\pi$ under $\phi{*}$.*

6. An example: box splines

We discuss here an example in which we identify the spectrum of the preimage of $H(\phi)$ for a box spline ϕ. For background about box splines we refer to [BR], from where most of the notations are borrowed.

Let Γ be a finite index set. The (exponential) box spline B_Γ is defined via its Fourier transform as

$$\widehat{B}_\Gamma(x) = \prod_{\gamma\in\Gamma} \frac{e^{\lambda_\gamma - i\langle x_\gamma, x\rangle} - 1}{\lambda_\gamma - i\langle x_\gamma, x\rangle},$$

where for each γ, $\lambda_\gamma \in \mathbb{C}$ and $x_\gamma \in \mathbb{Z}^s\backslash 0$. We assume that $\operatorname{span}\{x_\gamma\}_{\gamma\in\Gamma} = \mathbb{R}^s$.

Since $C_\Gamma := (B_\Gamma *)^{-1}(H(B_\Gamma))$ is shift-invariant, its spectrum coincides (mod $2\pi i\mathbb{Z}^s$) with the set

(6.1) $$\Theta := \{\theta \in \mathbb{C}^s : \ B_\Gamma{*}e_\theta \in H(B_\Gamma)\}.$$

An important subset of Θ was identified in [DM] and [BR] as the set

$$\widetilde{\Theta} := \{\theta \in \mathbb{C}^s : \ \operatorname{span}\{x_\gamma\}_{\gamma\in\widetilde{\Gamma}_\theta} = \mathbb{C}^s\},$$

with

$$\widetilde{\Gamma}_\theta := \{\gamma \in \Gamma : \ \nabla^\gamma(e_\theta) = 0\},$$

and $\nabla^\gamma := 1 - e^{\lambda_\gamma}E^{-x_\gamma}$.

(6.2) Proposition([DM],[BR]). *The set $\widetilde{\Theta}$ is finite mod $2\pi i\mathbb{Z}^s$, and for each $\theta \in \widetilde{\Theta}$*

$$B_\Gamma * e_\theta \in H(B_\Gamma).$$

We therefore conclude that indeed $\widetilde{\Theta} \subset \Theta$. In the following theorem we show that the spectrum of C_Γ is a finite union of linear manifolds, each of which intersects $\widetilde{\Theta}$. For $K \subset \Gamma$, we use here the notations

$$\langle K \rangle := \text{span}\{x_\gamma\}_{\gamma \in K}, \quad K^\perp := \{x \in \mathbb{C}^s : x \perp \langle K \rangle\}.$$

(6.3) Theorem. *For an exponential box spline B_Γ, the spectrum of the space C_Γ of the preimage of the exponential space $H(B_\Gamma)$ is*

$$\bigcup_{\theta,K} \theta + K^\perp, \tag{6.4}$$

where θ runs over $\widetilde{\Theta}$ and, for each θ, K runs over all subsets of Γ which are minimal with respect to the property

$$B_K * e_\theta \in H(B_\Gamma).$$

Proof: We show first that each point in (6.4) lies indeed in the desired spectrum Θ (as given by (6.1)). So assume that $\theta \in \widetilde{\Theta}$, that $B_K * e_\theta \in H(B_\Gamma)$, and K is minimal. Then it is sufficient to prove that $B_K * e_{\theta+\eta} \in H(B_\Gamma)$, for all $\eta \in K^\perp$. By (6.2)Proposition, this is true for $\eta = 0$, and hence there is nothing to prove in case $\langle K \rangle = \mathbb{C}^s$, since then $K^\perp = 0$. Otherwise, since B_K is supported on $\langle K \rangle$, we must have $B_K * e_\theta = 0$. In fact, already $\sum_{\alpha \in \langle K \rangle \cap \mathbb{Z}^s} e_\theta(\alpha) E^{-\alpha} B_K = 0$. Since $e_{\theta+\eta}$ coincides on $\langle K \rangle$ with e_θ, we conclude that indeed $B_K * e_{\theta+\eta} = 0$, and hence the union in (6.4) lies in Θ.

For the converse, assume that $\theta \in \Theta$ and let K be a minimal subset of Γ with respect to the property

$$B_K * e_\theta \in H(B_\Gamma).$$

By the preceding arguments, $\theta + K^\perp \subset \Theta$. In what follows, we show that $\theta + K^\perp$ intersects $\widetilde{\Theta}$, and hence $\theta + K^\perp = \vartheta + K^\perp$ for some $\vartheta \in \widetilde{\Theta}$.

For that we introduce, for each $\gamma \in \Gamma$, the differential operator $D^\gamma := D_{x_\gamma} - \lambda_\gamma$, and note [BR] that $D^\gamma(B_K * e_\theta) = B_{K \backslash \gamma} * \nabla^\gamma(e_\theta)$ for $\gamma \in K$. Since $B_K * e_\theta$ is an exponential, so is $D^\gamma(B_K * e_\theta)$, and thus, since $\nabla^\gamma(e_\theta)$ is a constant multiple of e_θ, the minimality of K shows that $\nabla^\gamma(e_\theta) = 0$, and since $\gamma \in K$ was arbitrary, $\nabla^\gamma(e_\zeta) = \nabla^\gamma(e_\theta) = 0$, for all $\gamma \in K$, $\zeta \in \theta + K^\perp$.

Now, let η be the unique solution in $K^\perp$ of the equations

$$\langle x_\gamma, \theta + ? \rangle = \lambda_\gamma, \quad \forall \gamma \in J,$$

where $J \subset \Gamma \backslash K$ is chosen so that $\#J = \dim K^{\perp}$ and $\langle K \cup J \rangle = \mathbf{C}^s$. Then $\theta + \eta \in \theta + K^{\perp}$, and also $\nabla^{\gamma}(e_{\theta+\eta}) = 0$ for every $\gamma \in K \cup J$, which implies that $\vartheta := \theta + \eta \in \widetilde{\Theta}$, and consequently $\theta + K^{\perp}$ intersects $\widetilde{\Theta}$, as claimed.

Finally, if K is also minimal with respect to the property $B_{M} * e_{\vartheta} \in H(B_{\Gamma})$, then $\theta + K^{\perp} = \vartheta + K^{\perp}$ is one of the sets in (6.4); otherwise, a set of the form $\vartheta + M^{\perp}$ with $M \subset K$ appears in (6.4), and since $K^{\perp} \subset M^{\perp}$, $\theta \in \vartheta + M^{\perp}$, and our claim follows. ♠

With the aid of (4.4)Theorem we conclude the following

(6.5) Corollary. *Let $C_{\theta,K}$ be the closure of the space of all exponentials in C_{Γ} with spectrum in $\theta + K^{\perp}$. Then*

(6.6)
$$C_{\Gamma} = \sum_{\theta,K} C_{\theta,K},$$

where θ and K vary as in (6.3)Theorem.

Proof: Note first that the right hand side of (6.6) is closed, as the sum of finitely many closed spaces. Furthermore, by (6.3)Theorem, this sum contains all the exponentials in C_{Γ}. Now apply (4.4)Theorem. ♠

We conjecture that there is 1-1 correspondence between sets of the form $\theta + K^{\perp}$ and the components of the variety of $C_{\Gamma}{\perp}^{\check{}}$. If so, it will follow that the finite set in (4.4)Theorem can be chosen as $\widetilde{\Theta}/2\pi i \mathbb{Z}^s$.

Combining (6.3)Theorem with (4.8)Corollary, we obtain a result which was proved in [DM] by other means:

(6.7) Corollary. *C_{Γ} if finite dimensional if and only if its spectrum is $\widetilde{\Theta}/2\pi i \mathbb{Z}^s$.*

References

[BR] A. Ben-Artzi and A. Ron, Translates of exponential box splines and their related spaces, Trans. Amer. Math. Soc. **309** (1988), 683–710.

[DM] W. Dahmen and C. A. Micchelli, Multivariate E-splines, Advances in Math., to appear.

[K] W. Krull, *Idealtheorie*, Ergebnisse der Math. **iv**, no.3, (1935), pp.vii+152.

[L] M. Lefranc, Analyse Spectrale sur Z_n, C. R. Acad. Sc. **246** (1958), 1951-1953.

[N] D. G. Northcott, *Ideal Theory*, Cambridge University Press, 1960.

Carl de Boor & Amos Ron, Center for the Mathematical Sciences, 610 Walnut St., University of Wisconsin-Madison, Madison, WI 53705, U.S.A.

International Series of
Numerical Mathematics, Vol. 90

CARDINAL INTERPOLATION WITH RADIAL BASIS FUNCTIONS: AN INTEGRAL TRANSFORM APPROACH

M. D. Buhmann

Department of Applied Mathematics and Theoretical Physics, University of Cambridge, England.

In this paper we use asymptotic expansions of certain integral transforms in order to derive conditions on a radial basis function $\phi : \mathbf{R}_{\geq 0} \to \mathbf{R}$ that imply the existence of a cardinal function

$$\chi(x) = \sum_{k \in \mathbb{Z}^n} c_k \phi(\|x-k\|), \qquad x \in \mathbf{R}^n,$$

which satisfies $\chi(l) = \delta_{0l}$ for all $l \in \mathbb{Z}^n$. We also study the rate of decay of $|\chi(x)|$ for large $\|x\|$ and the polynomial recovery of interpolation on $\mathbb{Z}^n$ using this cardinal function. The conditions hold for many important examples of radial basis functions, such as the multiquadrics and related radial functions, and in contrast to some earlier work by the author they are expressed in terms of asymptotic properties of ϕ rather than in terms of its Fourier transform.

1. Introduction and Statement of Results

In some recent work, the author (1989a–1989c) has developed a theory of cardinal interpolation with radial basis functions that, among other things, provides sufficient conditions on a continuous function $\phi : \mathbf{R}_{\geq 0} \to \mathbf{R}$ such that there exists a bounded and continuous function

$$\chi(x) = \sum_{k \in \mathbb{Z}^n} c_k \phi(\|x-k\|), \qquad x \in \mathbf{R}^n, \tag{1.1}$$

the $\{c_k\}_{k \in \mathbb{Z}^n}$ being suitable real coefficients, which satisfies $\chi(l) = \delta_{0l}$ for all $l \in \mathbb{Z}^n$. Here $\|\cdot\|$ denotes the Euclidean norm. In this context, ϕ is called a "radial basis function" and we call χ a cardinal function associated with ϕ. Thus ϕ admits cardinal interpolation

$$If(x) = \sum_{j \in \mathbb{Z}^n} f(j)\chi(x-j), \qquad x \in \mathbf{R}^n, \tag{1.2}$$

on the integer grid $\mathbb{Z}^n$ to functions $f : \mathbf{R}^n \to \mathbf{R}$ that grow sufficiently slowly so as to render (1.2) an absolutely convergent sum for all $x \in \mathbf{R}^n$.

The said sufficient conditions are expressed essentially in terms of requirements on the generalized Fourier transform of $\phi(\|\cdot\|) : \mathbf{R}^n \to \mathbf{R}$ which we shall denote by $\widehat{\phi}(\|\cdot\|) : \mathbf{R}^n \setminus \{0\} \to \mathbf{R}$ (see, for instance,

JONES, 1982, for an exposition of the notion of generalized Fourier transforms). A suitable set of conditions that implies the existence of a cardinal function is as follows:

A1: $\hat{\phi} \in C^{m+n}(\mathbb{R}_{>0})$ for some positive integer m,

A2: $|\hat{\phi}^{(\varrho)}(r)| = O(r^{-n-\delta})$ as $r \to \infty$ for all $\varrho \le m+n$, where δ is a positive constant,

A3: for some constant μ satisfying $0 < \mu \le m$ and some nonzero multiplier $A_{-\mu}$

$$\hat{\phi}(r) = A_{-\mu} r^{-\mu}\{1 + h_\phi(r)\}, \qquad r > 0,$$

where h_ϕ, which is defined by this equation, satisfies $|h_\phi^{(\varrho)}(r)| = O(r^{1-\varrho})$ near the origin for all $\varrho \le m+n$,

A4: $\hat{\phi}$ has no zero, and finally

A5: $|\phi(r)| \le A(1+r)^{\bar{\mu}}$ for all r, where A denotes a generic positive constant and where $\bar{\mu}$ is a constant that satisfies $0 \le \bar{\mu} < \mu$.

These conditions are obtained, for example, by the radial basis functions

$$\phi(r) = (r^2 + c^2)^{\beta/2}, \qquad r \ge 0, \tag{1.3}$$

where β and c are real parameters which satisfy $\beta > -n$ when $c \ne 0$ while $\beta > 0$ when $c = 0$. Further, β must not be an even nonnegative integer. The choice $\beta = 1$ provides the well-known multiquadric radial basis function while the choice $\beta = -1$ gives the inverse multiquadric radial basis function which is also mentioned frequently in the literature. It is easy to verify that the said radial basis functions satisfy the conditions by noting that, according to JONES (1982), these functions have the transforms

$$\hat{\phi}(r) = 2^{n+\beta}\pi^{n/2}\frac{\Gamma(\frac{1}{2}n + \frac{1}{2}\beta)}{\Gamma(-\frac{1}{2}\beta)} r^{-n-\beta}, \qquad r > 0,$$

when c is zero and

$$\hat{\phi}(r) = \frac{2\pi^{n/2}}{\Gamma(-\frac{1}{2}\beta)} K_{(n+\beta)/2}(cr)\left(\tfrac{1}{2}r/c\right)^{-(n+\beta)/2}, \qquad r > 0,$$

when c is nonzero. Here K_ν is the ν-th modified Bessel function which is infinitely differentiable on $\mathbb{R}_{>0}$, decays exponentially for large argument, is always positive, and satisfies for all nonnegative integers ϱ and for some real coefficients A_ϱ

$$K_\nu^{(\varrho)}(z) = A_\varrho z^{-\nu-\varrho} + O(z^{-\nu-\varrho+1}), \qquad z \to 0,$$

cf. ABRAMOWITZ AND STEGUN (1970). Therefore, A1 and A2 hold for arbitrarily large m and for $\delta = \beta$ when β is positive while any positive δ suffices when β is nonpositive. Moreover, we have $\mu = n + \beta$ in condition A3 and $\bar{\mu} = \max(0, \beta)$ in A5. Finally, A4 holds by virtue of the positivity of both $\{r^{-\nu} \mid r > 0\}$ and $\{K_\nu(z) \mid z > 0\}$ for all positive ν.

As is shown in BUHMANN (1989b, 1989c), the conditions A1–A5 are also sufficient to prove that $|\chi(x)|$ decays fast enough for large $\|x\|$ to admit polynomials $f \in \mathbb{P}_n^k$ into (1.2) for all $k < \mu$. Here $\mathbb{P}_n^k$ denotes the linear space of polynomials in n unknowns and of total order no more than k. In fact, (1.2) is exact for these polynomials, that is $If \equiv f$ for all $f \in \mathbf{P}_n^k$ with $k < \mu$. Moreover, the order of polynomial recovery of the cardinal interpolant (1.2) yields convergence orders of scaled cardinal interpolation

$$I_h f(x) = \sum_{j \in \mathbb{Z}^n} f(jh)\chi(x/h - j), \qquad x \in \mathbf{R}^n,$$

to suitably differentiable $f : \mathbf{R}^n \to \mathbf{R}$ as $h \to 0$ (see the aforementioned work by the author). We will not, however, study convergence orders in this paper.

Some of these remarks are summarised in the following theorem:

Theorem 1. *Let ϕ be such that A1–A5 hold. Then there is a cardinal function* (1.1) *that is bounded by*

$$|\chi(x)| \leq A(1 + \|x\|)^{-n-\mu}, \qquad x \in \mathbf{R}^n.$$

Therefore (1.2) *is well-defined for all f that satisfy*

$$|f(x)| \leq A(1 + \|x\|)^{\widehat{\mu}}, \qquad x \in \mathbf{R}^n,$$

$\widehat{\mu}$ being less than μ. Moreover, (1.2) *is exact for all polynomials f in n unknowns of total degree less than μ.* ■

We outline the principal steps of the proof of this theorem because they will be of importance later. The first step is to define a function

$$B(t) := \frac{\widehat{\phi}(\|t\|)}{\sum_{l \in \mathbb{Z}^n} \widehat{\phi}(\|t + 2\pi l\|)}, \qquad t \in \mathbf{R}^n,$$

which is, in view of the assumptions A1–A4, a continuous integrable function. Its inverse Fourier transform

$$C(x) := \frac{1}{(2\pi)^n} \int_{\mathbf{R}^n} e^{i(x,t)} B(t)\, dt, \qquad x \in \mathbf{R}^n, \tag{1.4}$$

is then, solely on account of the fact that $\widehat{\phi}$ yields A1–A4, shown to be a function which satisfies $C(l) = \delta_{0l}$ for all $l \in \mathbb{Z}^n$ and which satisfies the statements Theorem 1 makes about the decay of χ and the polynomial recovery of (1.2), i.e. it satisfies the bound

$$|C(x)| \leq A(1 + \|x\|)^{-n-\mu}, \qquad x \in \mathbf{R}^n,$$

and it also supplies

$$\sum_{j \in \mathbb{Z}^n} f(j)C(x - j) \equiv f(x), \qquad \forall\, f \in \mathbf{P}_n^k,\ k < \mu.$$

It is important to note that these statements do not mention the fact that $\widehat{\phi}$ is the generalized Fourier transform of ϕ. Therefore any rotationally invariant function that provides the conditions A1–A4 can be used to construct a cardinal function that has the said decay and polynomial recovery properties. Only in the final step we use the definition of $\widehat{\phi}$ and condition A5 to show that C is actually of the form (1.1), the coefficients being the Fourier coefficients

$$c_k = \frac{1}{(2\pi)^n} \int_{[-\pi,\pi]^n} \frac{e^{i(k,t)}}{\sum_{l\in\mathbb{Z}^n} \widehat{\phi}(\|t+2\pi l\|)}\, dt, \qquad k \in \mathbb{Z}^n. \tag{1.5}$$

Theorem 1 follows.

Another result of this kind, which is more specific than Theorem 1 and that will be required later, is the following theorem (Buhmann, 1989b, 1989c). Here $\sum'_{l\in\mathbb{Z}^n}$ denotes $\sum_{l\in\mathbb{Z}^n\setminus\{0\}}$.

Theorem 2. *Assume ϕ yields* A1, A2, A4, A5, *and the specific form*

$$\widehat{\phi}(r) = A_{-\mu} r^{-\mu} + A_{-\mu+2} r^{-\mu+2} + \cdots + A_{2(Q-1)} r^{2(Q-1)} + (A_{2Q} + B_{2Q}\log r) r^{2Q}\{1 + h^*_\phi(r)\}, \tag{1.6}$$

of A3, *where $\frac{1}{2}\mu \in \mathbb{N}$, where $Q > -\frac{1}{2}\mu$ is an integer, where $m = 2\mu + 2Q$ in* A1 *and* A2, *and where $|h^{*\,(\varrho)}_\phi(r)| = O(r^{1-\varrho})$ near zero for $\varrho \le 2\mu + 2Q + n$. Then there is a cardinal function* (1.1) *that satisfies*

$$|\chi(x)| \le A(1 + \|x\|)^{-n-2\mu-2Q}, \qquad x \in \mathbb{R}^n.$$

Specifically, we have for large $\|x\|$

$$\chi(x) = \frac{(-4)^{\mu+Q} B_{2Q} \Gamma(\frac{1}{2}n + \mu + Q)(\mu+Q)!}{2A^2_{-\mu}\pi^{n/2}} \sum_{l\in\mathbb{Z}^n}{}' (\cos\langle x, 2\pi l\rangle - 1)\widehat{\phi}(\|2\pi l\|)\|x\|^{-n-2\mu-2Q} + $$
$$+ o(\|x\|^{-n-2\mu-2Q}), \tag{1.7}$$

and the coefficients (1.5) *satisfy*

$$c_k = \frac{(-4)^{\mu+Q} B_{2Q} \Gamma(\frac{1}{2}n + \mu + Q)(\mu+Q)!}{2A^2_{-\mu}\pi^{n/2}} \|k\|^{-n-2\mu-2Q} + o(\|k\|^{-n-2\mu-2Q}) \tag{1.8}$$

for large $\|k\|$. Moreover, (1.2) *is exact for all polynomials f in n unknowns of total degree less than μ.* ∎

Again, Theorem 2 is proved by showing first that, by virtue of the conditions on $\widehat{\phi}$, the function (1.4) has the asymptotic expansion on the right-hand side of (1.7) and provides polynomial recovery for $f \in \mathbb{P}^k_n$, $k < \mu$, and that the asymptotic expansion (1.8) of the Fourier coefficients (1.5) holds. It is then shown that the definition of $\widehat{\phi}$ and A5 are sufficient to imply that C is actually of the form (1.1) with the coefficients (1.5).

We note that the class of radial basis functions (1.3) satisfies the conditions of Theorem 2 if $n + \beta$ is an even positive integer, because $z^{-\nu}K_\nu(z)$ can be expanded as a series

$$z^{-\nu}K_\nu(z) = a_{-2\nu}z^{-2\nu} + a_{-2\nu+2}z^{-2\nu+2} + \cdots + a_{-2}z^{-2} + (a_0 + b_0\log z) + (a_2 + b_2 \log z)z^2 + \cdots, \quad z > 0,$$

whenever ν is a positive integer.

Buhmann and Micchelli (1989) provide conditions on ϕ that imply the assertions of Theorem 1 without mentioning the generalized Fourier transform $\widehat{\phi}$. The purpose of this paper is to use asymptotic properties of certain integral transforms, which will be made specific in the next section, to derive conditions on the radial basis function ϕ that are sufficient for the assertions of Theorem 2, again without mentioning $\widehat{\phi}$. The following notion is crucial to this work.

Definition 1. *Given an integer $\lambda > 1$, a function $\xi \in C^{\lambda-2}(\mathbb{R}_{>0})$ is said to be* λ-times monotone *if $(-1)^j \xi^{(j)}$ is nonnegative, nonincreasing and convex for all $j = 0, 1, 2, \ldots, \lambda - 2$. If $\xi \in C(\mathbb{R}_{>0})$ is nonnegative and nonincreasing, it is said to be* once monotone.

The result of Buhmann and Micchelli is as follows:

Theorem 3. *Let κ and $\lambda > 3\kappa + \frac{1}{2}(5n+1)$ be nonnegative integers and assume $\phi \in C(\mathbb{R}_{\geq 0}) \cap C^{\kappa+\lambda}(\mathbb{R}_{>0})$. Suppose the function*

$$\xi(t) = \frac{d^\kappa}{dt^\kappa}\phi(\sqrt{t}), \qquad t > 0, \tag{1.9}$$

is λ-times monotone. Further, we require

$$\xi^{(\lambda)}(t) = a_0 t^{e_0} + o(t^{e_0}), \qquad t \to 0, \tag{1.10}$$

and

$$\xi^{(\lambda)}(t) = p_0 t^{-r_0} + o(t^{-r_0}), \qquad t \to \infty, \tag{1.11}$$

where e_0, r_0 and p_0 are constants that satisfy $e_0 > -\lambda - \kappa$, $\lambda < r_0 < \frac{1}{2}n + \lambda + \min(\kappa, 1)$ and $p_0 \neq 0$. Suppose finally that

$$(-1)^\lambda \beta^{\lambda+\kappa+n/2-3/2} \xi^{(\lambda)}(\beta^2), \qquad \beta > 0, \tag{1.12}$$

is twice monotone. Then the assertions of Theorem 1 *hold for $\mu = 2\kappa + 2\lambda - 2r_0 + n$.* ∎

It is straightforward to verify that these assumptions are satisfied by the radial basis functions (1.3).

The main result of this paper, which is analogous to Theorem 2, is as follows. It is proved in Section 2 by a method that is similar to the one in Buhmann and Micchelli's paper.

Theorem 4. *Let κ, λ and q be nonnegative integers and assume $\phi \in C(\mathbb{R}_{\geq 0}) \cap C^{\kappa+\lambda+q}(\mathbb{R}_{>0})$. Suppose the function (1.9) is λ-times monotone and satisfies*

$$\xi^{(\lambda+\varrho)}(t) = a_0 \frac{d^\varrho t^{e_0}}{dt^\varrho} + O(t^{e_1-\varrho}), \qquad t \to 0, \ \ \varrho \leq q, \tag{1.13}$$

where $e_1 > e_0 > -\lambda - \kappa$. Further, suppose that there are an integer $K > 1$ and reals $\{p_j\}_{j=0}^{K-1}$ and $r_0 < r_1 < r_2 < \cdots < r_K$ such that

$$\xi^{(\lambda+\varrho)}(t) = \frac{d^\varrho}{dt^\varrho} \sum_{j=0}^{K-1} p_j t^{-r_j} + O(t^{-r_K-\varrho}), \qquad t \to \infty, \ \ \varrho \leq q, \tag{1.14}$$

where $p_0 \neq 0$, where $r_K > -e_0$, and where all $r_j - \frac{1}{2}n$ are integers that satisfy $\{r_j - \frac{1}{2}n < \lambda + \kappa : j = 0, 1, \ldots, K-1\}$ and $\max(-e_1, \lambda) < r_0 < \frac{1}{2}n + \lambda + \min(\kappa, 1)$. We also require that (1.12) be twice *monotone and the conditions* $q \geq 2(\lambda + e_1)$ *and* $\lambda \geq 5\kappa + 2Q + \frac{1}{2}(7n+2)$*, where* Q *is the nonnegative integer* $r_{K-1} - \frac{1}{2}n - \lambda - \kappa$*. Then the conclusions of* Theorem 2 *hold for this* Q *with* $\mu = 2\kappa + 2\lambda - 2r_0 + n$.

2. Proof of Theorem 4

The central idea of our approach is to define a function $\widetilde{\phi}(\|\cdot\|) : \mathbf{R}^n \setminus \{0\} \to \mathbf{R}$, depending on (1.9), that satisfies, by virtue of the theorem's assumptions about ξ, the conditions that were imposed on $\widehat{\phi}(\|\cdot\|) : \mathbf{R}^n \setminus \{0\} \to \mathbf{R}$ in Theorem 2. Consequently, we deduce that the function $C : \mathbf{R}^n \to \mathbf{R}$, which we define as the inverse Fourier transform (1.4) of the continuous and integrable function

$$B(t) := \frac{\widetilde{\phi}(\|t\|)}{\sum_{l \in \mathbf{Z}^n} \widetilde{\phi}(\|t + 2\pi l\|)}, \qquad t \in \mathbf{R}^n,$$

is a cardinal function that satisfies the asymptotic expansion which appears on the right-hand side of (1.7) and yields polynomial recovery for $f \in \mathbf{P}_n^k$, $k < \mu$. We deduce at the same time that the Fourier coefficients of the periodic function

$$\frac{1}{\sum_{l \in \mathbf{Z}^n} \widetilde{\phi}(\|t + 2\pi l\|)}, \qquad t \in \mathbf{R}^n,$$

satisfy the asymptotic estimate (1.8). We then show additionally that C is indeed of the form (1.1), where the coefficients are the aforementioned Fourier coefficients.

We will next specify the function $\widetilde{\phi}$, the main purpose of the rest of the section being to show that our conditions on ξ are appropriate such that $\widetilde{\phi}$ has the properties that are stated in the previous paragraph. We let $\widetilde{\phi}(\|\cdot\|) : \mathbf{R}^n \setminus \{0\} \to \mathbf{R}$ be the integral transform

$$\widetilde{\phi}(r) := r^{-\nu-1/2} \int_0^\infty h(r\beta) f(\beta)\, d\beta, \qquad r > 0, \tag{2.1}$$

where here and throughout this section $\nu := \lambda + \kappa + \frac{1}{2}n - 1$, where $h(t) := J_\nu(t)\sqrt{t}$ for all positive reals t, J_ν being the ν-th Bessel function (ABRAMOWITZ AND STEGUN, 1970, pages 355ff.), and where

$$f(\beta) := 2^{\nu+1}(-1)^{\lambda+\kappa}\pi^{n/2}\beta^{\nu+1/2}\xi^{(\lambda)}(\beta^2), \qquad \beta > 0. \tag{2.2}$$

The integral (2.1) is often called a Hankel transform, and it is this integral transform that gives the present paper its name. Observing that (1.13) and (1.14) imply the estimates

$$|\xi^{(\lambda)}(t)| = O(t^{e_0}), \qquad t \to 0, \tag{2.3}$$

and

$$|\xi^{(\lambda)}(t)| = O(t^{-r_0}), \qquad t \to \infty, \tag{2.4}$$

respectively, we use the theorem's conditions on e_0 and r_0 to show that (2.1) is well-defined for all positive r: By equations (9.1.7) and (9.2.1) of ABRAMOWITZ AND STEGUN (1970), we have $|J_\nu(t)| = O(t^{-1/2})$ for large positive t and $|J_\nu(t)| = O(t^\nu)$ for small positive t. Therefore $|h(r\beta)|$ is uniformly bounded for all β and $|h(r\beta)| = O(\beta^{\nu+1/2})$ near the origin for any fixed positive r. Furthermore (2.3) and (2.4) imply

$$|f(\beta)| = O(\beta^{\nu+1/2-2r_0}), \qquad \beta \to \infty, \tag{2.5}$$

and

$$|f(\beta)| = O(\beta^{\nu+1/2+2e_0}), \qquad \beta \to 0. \tag{2.6}$$

We conclude that the integral (2.1) converges absolutely for all positive r because the theorem's conditions $r_0 > \lambda$ and $\lambda \geq 5\kappa + 2Q + \frac{1}{2}(7n+2)$ imply that we have in particular $r_0 > \frac{1}{2}\nu + \frac{3}{4}$ and because $e_0 > -\lambda - \kappa$ implies that we also have $e_0 > -\nu - 1$.

We will now prove that, assuming at first that $\widetilde{\phi}$ already satisfies Theorem 2's specific form of the conditions A1–A4, the assumptions of Theorem 4 imply that C is of the form (1.1). After that, it will suffice to show that $\widetilde{\phi}$ satisfies the conditions of Theorem 2 on $\widehat{\phi}$ in order to prove Theorem 4, because, as we have remarked earlier, the conclusions of Theorem 2 have been proved by showing first that its assumptions on $\widehat{\phi}$ imply that the function C satisfies all its assertions about asymptotic behaviour and polynomial recovery and by showing then that C is in fact of the form (1.1).

We use the following result of WILLIAMSON (1956) which characterizes multiply monotone functions in full:

Theorem 5. *The function $\xi : \mathbb{R}_{>0} \to \mathbb{R}$ is λ-times monotone if and only if it has the form*

$$\xi(\tau) = \int_0^\infty (1-\tau\beta)_+^{\lambda-1}\, d\gamma(\beta), \qquad \tau > 0, \tag{2.7}$$

where γ is a nondecreasing measure that is bounded below. Moreover, the representation of a multiply monotone function in this way is unique in the sense that γ is determined by

$$\gamma(\beta) = \frac{(-1)^{\lambda-1}}{\Gamma(\lambda)} \int_0^\beta x^{1-\lambda}\, d\xi^{(\lambda-1)}(x^{-1}) + \xi(\infty), \qquad \beta > 0, \tag{2.8}$$

at all its points of continuity. ■

Theorem 5 allows us to write ξ in the representation (2.7) which will in turn allow us to write $\phi(\|\cdot\|) : \mathbb{R}^n \to \mathbb{R}$, and consequently (1.1), in a form that is suitable for relating (1.1) to the function C. To this end we note first of all that the requirement $r_0 > \lambda$, together with (2.4), shows that ξ vanishes at infinity. We thus observe that Theorem 5 implies that the representation (2.7) holds with γ being defined by (2.8), that is

$$d\gamma(\beta) = \frac{(-1)^{\lambda-1}}{\Gamma(\lambda)} \beta^{1-\lambda}\, d\xi^{(\lambda-1)}(\beta^{-1}) = \frac{(-1)^{\lambda}}{\Gamma(\lambda)} \beta^{-1-\lambda} \xi^{(\lambda)}(\beta^{-1})\, d\beta, \qquad \beta > 0. \tag{2.9}$$

Thus

$$\xi(\tau) = \int_0^\infty (1-\tau\beta)_+^{\lambda-1} f^*(\beta)\, d\beta, \qquad \tau > 0, \tag{2.10}$$

where

$$f^*(\beta) := \frac{(-1)^\lambda}{\Gamma(\lambda)} \beta^{-1-\lambda} \xi^{(\lambda)}(\beta^{-1}), \qquad \beta > 0, \tag{2.11}$$

in view of (2.9). Obtaining a representation for $\phi(\|\cdot\|) : \mathbf{R}^n \to \mathbf{R}$ is done by κ-fold integration of (2.10) when κ is positive. Specifically, we integrate (2.10) κ-times between $\tau = t$ and $\tau = 1$. We then substitute $t = \|x\|^2$ to obtain

$$\phi(\|x\|) = p(\|x\|^2) + \frac{(-1)^\kappa}{(\lambda)_\kappa} \int_0^\infty \{(1 - \|x\|^2\beta)_+^{\lambda+\kappa-1} - q_\beta(\|x\|^2)\} \frac{f^*(\beta)\, d\beta}{\beta^\kappa}, \qquad x \in \mathbf{R}^n, \tag{2.12}$$

where p and q_β are in $\mathbf{P}_1^{\kappa-1}$ and where $(\lambda)_\kappa$ is the Pochhammer symbol, that is $(\lambda)_\kappa = \lambda(\lambda+1)\cdots(\lambda+\kappa-1)$ and $(\lambda)_0 = 1$. In fact, q_β is the $(\kappa-1)$-st order polynomial of the Taylor expansion of $(1-\tau\beta)_+^{\lambda+\kappa-1}$ about $\tau = 1$. Thus, for every $\|x\|$, q_β is such that the modulus of the bracketed term in the integrand of (2.12) is $O(\beta^\kappa)$ near $\beta = 0$, while it remains bounded for large β. By the estimate (2.4), (2.11) supplies

$$|f^*(\beta)| = O(\beta^{-1-\lambda+r_0}), \qquad \beta \to 0.$$

Also, by the estimate (2.3),

$$|f^*(\beta)| = O(\beta^{-1-\lambda-e_0}), \qquad \beta \to \infty.$$

Thus, we see that the assumption $r_0 > \lambda$ and the assumption $e_0 > -\lambda - \kappa$ imply (2.12) is well-defined and hence the κ-fold integration of (2.10) is valid. It is also valid for $\kappa = 0$ in which case p and q_β are zero-polynomials.

Having obtained the representation (2.12), we want to express (1.1) in a similar fashion. Firstly, we prove that (1.1) is absolutely convergent when we define the coefficients $\{c_k\}_{k\in\mathbf{Z}^n}$ to be the Fourier coefficients

$$c_k = \frac{1}{(2\pi)^n} \int_{Q^n} \frac{e^{i(k,t)}\, dt}{\sum_{l\in\mathbf{Z}^n} \widetilde{\phi}(\|t + 2\pi l\|)}, \qquad k \in \mathbf{Z}^n. \tag{2.13}$$

We recall that the coefficients (2.13) satisfy the asymptotic estimate (1.8) as soon as $\widetilde{\phi}$ satisfies the conditions of Theorem 2 on $\widehat{\phi}$.

We observe that the order of decay of (2.10) at infinity is $O(t^{\lambda-r_0})$ by virtue of (2.4) and $r_0 > \lambda$. Hence, because we have integrated (2.10) κ-times in order to arrive at the expression (2.12), we have

$$|\phi(r)| = O(r^{2\max[\kappa-1,\kappa+\lambda-r_0]} \log r), \qquad r \to \infty.$$

Hence we derive absolute convergence of the sum (1.1) from (1.8), from the upper bound on r_0, and from the definition of μ, because $r_0 < \frac{1}{2}n + \lambda + 1$ and $\mu = 2\kappa + 2\lambda - 2r_0 + n$ imply that the constant μ, and so in particular the constant $2\mu + 2Q$, is larger than $2\max(\kappa + \lambda - r_0, \kappa - 1)$. Therefore, using the coefficients (2.13), we deduce

$$\begin{aligned} \chi(x) &= \sum_{k\in\mathbf{Z}^n} c_k \phi(\|x-k\|) \\ &= \sum_{k\in\mathbf{Z}^n} c_k p(\|x-k\|^2) + \frac{(-1)^\kappa}{(\lambda)_\kappa} \sum_{k\in\mathbf{Z}^n} c_k \int_0^\infty \{(1 - \|x-k\|^2\beta)_+^{\lambda+\kappa-1} - q_\beta(\|x-k\|^2)\} \frac{f^*(\beta)\, d\beta}{\beta^\kappa} \\ &= \frac{(-1)^\kappa}{(\lambda)_\kappa} \sum_{k\in\mathbf{Z}^n} c_k \int_0^\infty \{(1 - \|x-k\|^2\beta)_+^{\lambda+\kappa-1} - q_\beta(\|x-k\|^2)\} \frac{f^*(\beta)\, d\beta}{\beta^\kappa}, \end{aligned} \tag{2.14}$$

where the last line depends on the moment properties of the coefficients $\{c_k\}_{k\in\mathbb{Z}^n}$: namely, the requirement A3 implies that

$$\frac{1}{\sum_{l\in\mathbb{Z}^n}\tilde{\phi}(\|t+2\pi l\|)}=\frac{\|t\|^\mu}{A_{-\mu}}+o(\|t\|^\mu),\qquad \|t\|\to 0,$$

and therefore, by the definition of the coefficients (2.13),

$$\sum_{k\in\mathbb{Z}^n} c_k k^p\equiv 0,\qquad \forall\, p\in\mathbb{Z}_+^n,\ |p|<\mu,$$

which means in particular

$$\sum_{k\in\mathbb{Z}^n} c_k p(\|x-k\|^2)\equiv 0, \tag{2.15}$$

since $p\in\mathbf{P}_1^{\kappa-1}$ and $2(\kappa-1)<\mu$.

Next, we compare (2.14) with the function C. To this end we consider the function

$$\frac{(-1)^\kappa}{(\lambda)_\kappa}\int_a^b\sum_{k\in\mathbb{Z}^n} c_k(1-\|x-k\|^2\beta)_+^{\lambda+\kappa-1}\frac{f^*(\beta)\,d\beta}{\beta^\kappa},\qquad x\in\mathbf{R}^n, \tag{2.16}$$

where a and b are constants that satisfy $0<a<b<\infty$, which avoids the $\beta^{-\kappa}$ singularity. This function of x is absolutely integrable because there is an upper bound on the integral of $(1-\|\cdot-k\|^2\beta)_+^{\lambda+\kappa-1}:\mathbf{R}^n\to\mathbf{R}$ that depends on a but that is independent of k and $\beta\geq a$, and because (1.8) implies $\sum_{k\in\mathbb{Z}^n}|c_k|<\infty$. Therefore (2.16) has a Fourier transform which we derive as follows. The Fourier transform of the radially symmetric function

$$(1-\|x\|^2\beta)_+^{\lambda+\kappa-1},\qquad x\in\mathbf{R}^n,$$

is the Bessel transform (see, e.g., STEIN AND WEISS, 1971, page 171)

$$\frac{(2\pi)^{n/2}}{\|x\|^{n/2-1}}\int_0^{1/\sqrt{\beta}}(1-s^2\beta)^{\lambda+\kappa-1}s^{n/2}J_{n/2-1}(s\|x\|)\,ds,\qquad x\in\mathbf{R}^n,$$

that, through a change of variable and an application of equation (11.4.10) of ABRAMOWITZ AND STEGUN (1970), can be manipulated to become

$$2^\nu\pi^{n/2}\Gamma(\lambda+\kappa)\frac{J_\nu(\|x\|/\sqrt{\beta})}{\|x\|^\nu}\beta^{(\lambda+\kappa-n/2-1)/2},\qquad x\in\mathbf{R}^n.$$

Therefore the Fourier transform of the function

$$\frac{(-1)^\kappa}{(\lambda)_\kappa}(1-\|x-k\|^2\beta)_+^{\lambda+\kappa-1}\frac{f^*(\beta)}{\beta^\kappa},\qquad x\in\mathbf{R}^n,$$

is the function

$$(-1)^\kappa 2^\nu\pi^{n/2}\Gamma(\lambda)e^{-i(x,k)}\frac{J_\nu(\|x\|/\sqrt{\beta})}{\|x\|^\nu}\beta^{\lambda-\nu/2-1}f^*(\beta),\qquad x\in\mathbf{R}^n,$$

so it follows from the values (2.13) that the Fourier transform of (2.16) is

$$\begin{aligned}&(-1)^\kappa 2^\nu\pi^{n/2}\Gamma(\lambda)\int_a^b\sum_{k\in\mathbb{Z}^n}c_k e^{-i(x,k)}\frac{J_\nu(\|x\|/\sqrt{\beta})}{\|x\|^\nu}\beta^{\lambda-\nu/2-1}f^*(\beta)d\beta\\ &=(-1)^\kappa 2^\nu\pi^{n/2}\Gamma(\lambda)\int_a^b\frac{J_\nu(\|x\|/\sqrt{\beta})}{\|x\|^\nu\sum_{l\in\mathbb{Z}^n}\tilde{\phi}(\|x+2\pi l\|)}\beta^{\lambda-\nu/2-1}f^*(\beta)d\beta\\ &=\int_{1/\sqrt{b}}^{1/\sqrt{a}}h(\|x\|\beta)f(\beta)\,d\beta\|x\|^{-\nu-1/2}\Big/\sum_{l\in\mathbb{Z}^n}\tilde{\phi}(\|x+2\pi l\|),\end{aligned} \tag{2.17}$$

h being defined just after equation (2.1). Therefore, making use of the analogue of (2.15) for q_β instead of p, of (2.17), and of the Parseval identity for Fourier transforms (see, for instance, STEIN AND WEISS, 1971, page 8), we see that for every testfunction η in the space

$$\mathcal{D} := \left\{ \varrho \in C^\infty(\mathbb{R}^n) \middle| \|x\|^k \frac{\partial^{|p|}\varrho(x)}{\partial x_1^{p_1}\partial x_2^{p_2}\cdots\partial x_n^{p_n}} \to 0,\ \|x\| \to \infty,\ \forall\, k \in \mathbb{Z},\ p \in \mathbb{Z}_+^n \right\}$$

of rapidly decaying smooth testfunctions we have

$$\begin{aligned}
&\frac{(-1)^\kappa}{(\lambda)_\kappa} \int_{\mathbb{R}^n} \widehat{\eta}(x) \sum_{k\in\mathbb{Z}^n} c_k \int_a^b \{(1-\|x-k\|^2\beta)_+^{\lambda+\kappa-1} - q_\beta(\|x-k\|^2)\} \frac{f^*(\beta)\,d\beta}{\beta^\kappa}\,dx \\
&= \frac{(-1)^\kappa}{(\lambda)_\kappa} \int_{\mathbb{R}^n} \widehat{\eta}(x) \int_a^b \sum_{k\in\mathbb{Z}^n} c_k \{(1-\|x-k\|^2\beta)_+^{\lambda+\kappa-1} - q_\beta(\|x-k\|^2)\} \frac{f^*(\beta)\,d\beta}{\beta^\kappa}\,dx \\
&= \frac{(-1)^\kappa}{(\lambda)_\kappa} \int_{\mathbb{R}^n} \widehat{\eta}(x) \int_a^b \sum_{k\in\mathbb{Z}^n} c_k (1-\|x-k\|^2\beta)_+^{\lambda+\kappa-1} \frac{f^*(\beta)\,d\beta}{\beta^\kappa}\,dx \\
&= \int_{\mathbb{R}^n} \eta(x) \int_{1/\sqrt{b}}^{1/\sqrt{a}} \frac{h(\|x\|\beta) f(\beta)\,d\beta\,dx}{\|x\|^{\nu+1/2} \sum_{l\in\mathbb{Z}^n} \widetilde{\phi}(\|x+2\pi l\|)}.
\end{aligned}$$

We pass to the limits $a \to 0$ and $b \to \infty$, which is permitted by the dominated convergence theorem because (2.14) is of at most polynomial growth and because we assume that $\widetilde{\phi}$ satisfies conditions A1–A4. Thus we deduce from (2.1), from (2.14), from the definition of C, and from the Parseval formula for Fourier transforms, that

$$\int_{\mathbb{R}^n} \widehat{\eta}(x)\chi(x)\,dx = \int_{\mathbb{R}^n} \eta(x)\widehat{C}(x)\,dx = \int_{\mathbb{R}^n} \widehat{\eta}(x)C(x)\,dx.$$

Since χ and C are both in $C(\mathbb{R}^n)$ and since η is any function in $\mathcal{D}$, it follows from LERCH's Theorem (Acta Mathematica **27**, 339 (1903)), for instance, that $\chi \equiv C$.

Assuming that $\widetilde{\phi}$ satisfies Theorem 2's form of conditions A1–A4, we have now proved that C has the form (1.1), the coefficients being (2.13).

Next, we prove that the assumptions of Theorem 4 imply that condition A4 is indeed satisfied by $\widetilde{\phi}$. To verify this assertion, we state a proposition:

Proposition 6. *Let g be a twice monotone function that is not identically zero. Then for any $\nu \geq \frac{3}{2}$ the function*

$$\int_0^\infty J_\nu(r\beta)\sqrt{r\beta}\,g(\beta)\beta\,d\beta, \qquad r > 0, \tag{2.18}$$

is positive provided that this integral is absolutely convergent for all positive r.

Proof. It is proved by GASPER (1975), page 412, that for $\nu \geq \frac{3}{2}$, for positive σ and positive x the inequality

$$\int_0^\infty (1-\sigma t)_+ t^{3/2} J_\nu(xt)\,dt > 0$$

is satisfied. Therefore, expressing g in the Williamson form

$$g(\beta) = \int_0^\infty (1-\sigma\beta)_+\,d\alpha(\sigma), \qquad \beta > 0,$$

for nondecreasing α that is bounded below, we have that (2.18) is the same as

$$\sqrt{r}\int_0^\infty\int_0^\infty (1-\sigma\beta)_+\beta^{3/2}J_\nu(r\beta)\,d\beta\,d\alpha(\sigma)>0,$$

for positive r and $\nu \geq \frac{3}{2}$, which completes the proof. ■

Setting g to be (1.12), it follows from (2.1) and (2.2) that $\widetilde{\phi}$ is always of one sign because (1.14) and $p_0 \neq 0$ imply that g is not identically zero and the lower bound on λ implies $\nu \geq \frac{3}{2}$.

The conditions of Theorem 4 also imply that $\widetilde{\phi}$ satisfies A1 with $m = 2\mu + 2Q$. In order to ascertain this claim, we shall prove that the lower bound on λ in the theorem suffices for $\widetilde{\phi} \in C^{4\kappa+3n+2Q}(\mathbb{R}_{>0})$. This in turn implies $\widetilde{\phi} \in C^{n+m}(\mathbb{R}_{>0})$ since $\mu = 2\kappa + 2\lambda - 2r_0 + n < 2\kappa + n$ on account of the condition $r_0 > \lambda$ and therefore $m < 4\kappa + 2n + 2Q$.

We find in Abramowitz and Stegun (1970), equation (9.1.27), that the Bessel functions satisfy

$$\frac{dJ_\nu(t)}{dt} = J_{\nu-1}(t) - \tfrac{\nu}{t}J_\nu(t), \tag{2.19}$$

and so we have the relation

$$\frac{dh(r\beta)}{dr} = r^{-1}\{J_{\nu-1}(r\beta)(r\beta)^{3/2} - (\nu-\tfrac{1}{2})h(r\beta)\}, \qquad r>0. \tag{2.20}$$

Inductively we deduce from (2.19) and (2.20) that, for every $\varrho \leq \nu$ and every positive r, $d^\varrho h(r\beta)/dr^\varrho$ is a linear combination of terms

$$r^{-\varrho}J_{\nu-\vartheta}(r\beta)(r\beta)^{\vartheta+1/2}, \qquad r>0, \tag{2.21}$$

where $\vartheta \leq \varrho \leq \nu$. Thus equations (9.1.7) and (9.2.1) of Abramowitz and Stegun show that for all positive reals r

$$\left|\frac{d^\varrho h(r\beta)}{dr^\varrho}\right| = O(\beta^{\nu+1/2}), \qquad \beta\to 0,\ \varrho\leq\nu,$$

and

$$\left|\frac{d^\varrho h(r\beta)}{dr^\varrho}\right| = O(\beta^{\varrho}), \qquad \beta\to \infty,\ \varrho\leq\nu.$$

These two bounds, and (2.5) and (2.6), imply that we have the bounds

$$\left|\frac{d^\varrho h(r\beta)}{dr^\varrho}f(\beta)\right| = O(\beta^{2\nu+1+2e_0}), \qquad \beta\to 0,\ \varrho\leq\nu,$$

and

$$\left|\frac{d^\varrho h(r\beta)}{dr^\varrho}f(\beta)\right| = O(\beta^{\nu+1/2+\varrho-2r_0}), \qquad \beta\to \infty,\ \varrho\leq\nu.$$

From these bounds we see that (2.1) is $(4\kappa+3n+2Q)$-times continuously differentiable on $\mathbb{R}_{>0}$, because the lower bound on λ and the lower bound $r_0 > \lambda$ imply $\nu > 4\kappa + 3n + 2Q$ and $\nu + \frac{1}{2} + \varrho - 2r_0 < -1$ for all $\varrho \leq 4\kappa + 3n + 2Q$, and because $e_0 > -\lambda - \kappa$.

What remains to prove in order to establish Theorem 4 is that $\widetilde{\phi}$ satisfies requirements A2 and the specific form of A3 required in Theorem 2. In order to do this, we require the following lemma on asymptotic expansions of Hankel transforms. We denote the real part of $z \in \mathbb{C}$ by $\Re z$.

Lemma 7. *Suppose that for $\lambda, q \in \mathbb{N}$ it is true that $\xi \in C^{\lambda+q}(\mathbb{R}_{>0})$, and suppose that for $\nu \in \mathbb{R}_{>0}$ and $J, K \in \mathbb{N}$ we have the asymptotic expansions*

$$\xi^{(\lambda+\varrho)}(t) = \frac{d^\varrho}{dt^\varrho} \sum_{j=0}^{J-1} a_j t^{e_j} + O(t^{e_J-\varrho}), \qquad t \to 0, \;\; \varrho \le q,$$

with real numbers $\{a_j\}_{j=0}^{J-1}$ and reals $e_0 < e_1 < \cdots < e_J$, where $e_0 > -\nu - 1$, $q \ge 2e_J + \nu + 2$, and

$$\xi^{(\lambda+\varrho)}(t) = \frac{d^\varrho}{dt^\varrho} \sum_{j=0}^{K-1} p_j t^{-r_j} + O(t^{-r_K-\varrho}), \qquad t \to \infty, \;\; \varrho \le q,$$

with reals $\{p_j\}_{j=0}^{K-1}$ and $r_0 < r_1 < \cdots < r_K$, where $r_0 > \max(\frac{1}{2}\nu + 1, -e_J)$, and where $r_K > -e_0$. Then the Hankel transform (2.1)

(i) satisfies for any $0 < \varepsilon < 2\min(e_0 + \nu + 1, e_J - e_{J-1}, \frac{1}{2}\nu)$ the asymptotic expansion

$$\widetilde{\phi}(r) = (-1)^{\lambda+\kappa} \pi^{n/2} \sum_{j=0}^{J-1} \frac{\Gamma(\nu + e_j + 1) a_j}{\Gamma(-e_j)} \left(\tfrac{1}{2}r\right)^{-2e_j-2\nu-2} + O(r^{-2e_J-2\nu-2+\varepsilon}), \qquad r \to \infty, \tag{2.22}$$

(ii) satisfies for any $0 < \varepsilon < 2\min(r_0 - \frac{1}{2}\nu - 1, r_K - r_{K-1}, \frac{1}{2}\nu)$ the asymptotic expansion

$$\widetilde{\phi}(r) = (-1)^{\lambda+\kappa} \pi^{n/2} \sum_{j=0}^{K-1} \frac{\Gamma(\nu - r_j + 1) p_j}{\Gamma(r_j)} \left(\tfrac{1}{2}r\right)^{2r_j-2\nu-2} \tag{2.23}$$

$$+ 2(-1)^{\lambda+\kappa} \pi^{n/2} \sum_{\substack{j=0,1,2,\ldots \\ j < r_K - \nu - 1}} \frac{(-1)^j \{\int_0^1 t^{2\nu+2j+1} \xi^{(\lambda)}(t^2)\, dt + H(2\nu + 2j + 1)\}}{j!\Gamma(\nu + j + 1)} \left(\tfrac{1}{2}r\right)^{2j} \tag{2.24}$$

$$+ O(r^{2r_K-2\nu-2-\varepsilon}), \qquad r \to 0,$$

where H is the continuation of the holomorphic function $\{\int_1^\infty t^z \xi^{(\lambda)}(t^2) dt \mid \Re z < 2r_0 - 1\}$ as a meromorphic function to $\{z \mid \Re z < 2r_K - 1\}$ which has poles only at $2r_j - 1$ $(j < K)$, and whenever for $j' < K$ and $j'' \in \mathbb{Z}_+$ we have $r_{j'} - \nu - 1 = j''$, then the terms for $j = j'$ and for $j = j''$ in (2.23) and (2.24), respectively, must be omitted and replaced by the sum of expressions

$$\frac{2(-1)^{\lambda+\kappa+j''+1} \pi^{n/2} p_{j'} \left(\tfrac{1}{2}r\right)^{2j''} \log r}{j''!\Gamma(\nu + j'' + 1)} + \frac{2(-1)^{\lambda+\kappa+j''} \pi^{n/2} \left(\tfrac{1}{2}r\right)^{2j''} \int_0^1 t^{2j''+1+2\nu} \xi^{(\lambda)}(t^2) dt}{j''!\Gamma(\nu + j'' + 1)} \tag{2.25}$$

and

$$(-1)^{\lambda+\kappa} \pi^{n/2} \left(\tfrac{1}{2}r\right)^{2j''} \lim_{z \to j''} \frac{d}{dz} \left[\frac{p_{j'} \Gamma(-z)(z - j'')}{4^{z-j''} \Gamma(z + \nu + 1)} + \frac{2(-1)^{j''} H(2z + 2\nu + 1)(z - j'')}{j''!\Gamma(\nu + j'' + 1)} \right]. \tag{2.26}$$

We note that the integral that occurs in (2.24) and (2.25) is absolutely convergent on account of the estimate $|\xi^{(\lambda)}(t)| = O(t^{e_0})$ near zero, e_0 being greater than $-\nu-1$, and therefore for any nonnegative integer j we have $|t^{2j+1+2\nu} \xi^{(\lambda)}(t^2)| = O(t^{2j+1+2\nu+2e_0}) = O(t^{2j-1+\delta})$ near zero where $\delta = 2(e_0 + \nu + 1)$ is positive. Moreover we remark that H is holomorphic on $\{z \mid \Re z < 2r_0 - 1\}$ because on that domain the integral defining it converges absolutely. We also note that the limit in (2.26) exists because both $\Gamma(-\cdot)$ and $H(2 \cdot + 2\nu + 1)$

are, as we shall see in the proof of Lemma 7, meromorphic in neighbourhoods of j'' and have *simple* poles at j'' when j'' is a nonnegative integer.

We have already pointed out that the theorem's requirements imply $e_0 > -\nu - 1$. Moreover, because the lower bound $r_0 > \lambda$ and the lower bound on λ imply $r_0 > \frac{1}{2}\nu + 1$, because the lower bound on q and the lower bound on λ imply $q \geq 2e_1 + \nu + 2$, and because $e_1 > -r_0$ and $r_K > -e_0$ have also been required in the statement of Theorem 4, we may apply Lemma 7 to (2.1) for $J = 1$ and K as in the statement of the theorem.

We observe that the lemma shows in its part (i) that, in particular, $|\widetilde{\phi}(r)| = O(r^{-n-\delta})$ for large r with $\delta = 2(e_0 + \lambda + \kappa)$ which is positive because of the lower bound on e_0. Moreover, part (ii) of the lemma implies the expansion (1.6) for $\widetilde{\phi}$, where $\mu = 2\nu + 2 - 2r_0$, and where

$$A_{-\mu} = \frac{(-1)^{\lambda+\kappa} 4^{1-r_0+\nu} \pi^{n/2} \Gamma(\nu - r_0 + 1) p_0}{\Gamma(r_0)}.$$

$A_{-\mu}$ is finite and nonzero by virtue of the permitted range of r_0 and by the condition that p_0 be nonzero. Therefore requirement A2 and Theorem 4's specific form of A3 hold as conditions on $\widetilde{\phi}$ whereas we still have to verify the requirements on the derivatives of $\widetilde{\phi}$. This is assisted by our previous observation that $d^{\varrho} h(r\beta)/dr^{\varrho}$ is a linear combination of terms (2.21) for $\vartheta \leq \varrho$. Hence, as long as $\varrho \leq 4\kappa + 3n + 2Q$, $\widetilde{\phi}^{(\varrho)}$ is a linear combination of products of

$$\widetilde{\phi}_{\vartheta}(r) = r^{-\nu-1/2+\vartheta} \int_0^{\infty} J_{\nu-\vartheta}(r\beta) \sqrt{r\beta} \beta^{\vartheta} f(\beta)\, d\beta, \qquad r > 0,$$

with $r^{-\varrho}$ where $\vartheta \leq \varrho$. We now employ the fact that as long as $\vartheta \leq \varrho \leq 4\kappa + 3n + 2Q$, it is possible to apply Lemma 7 to each $\widetilde{\phi}_{\vartheta}$ instead of $\widetilde{\phi}$. We find that each $\widetilde{\phi}_{\vartheta}$ obeys the same asymptotic expansions at zero and at infinity as $\widetilde{\phi}$ does, except that the coefficients in the expansions may of course not be the same. Combining this with the observation that $\widetilde{\phi}^{(\varrho)}(r)$ is a linear combination of the $\widetilde{\phi}_{\vartheta}(r)$ times $r^{-\varrho}$ settles the required conditions. Therefore Theorem 4 becomes a consequence of Lemma 7.

We prove Lemma 7. The book by BLEISTEIN AND HANDELSMAN (1986) is an important source of results we will use for the analysis we wish to perform. One main notion used in this text is that of the *Mellin transform* of a function. (In the sequel the letter z will be reserved for the generic complex number $z = x + iy \in \mathbf{C}$ where x—the real part $\Re z$ of z—and y—the imaginary part $\Im z$ of z—are real numbers, and $i^2 = -1$.) The Mellin transform of a function $g : \mathbf{R}_{>0} \to \mathbf{R}$ is defined to be

$$\mathcal{M}[g, z] = \int_0^{\infty} t^{z-1} g(t)\, dt$$

wherever in the complex plane this integral exists. More specifically, if g is continuous (we assume continuity but local integrability on the positive reals would suffice) then $\mathcal{M}[g, \cdot]$ is holomorphic on the vertical strip $\{z \mid \alpha < x < \beta\}$ where

$$\alpha = \inf\{\alpha^* \mid g(t) = O(t^{-\alpha^*}),\ t \to 0\},$$

$$\beta = \sup\{\beta^* \mid g(t) = O(t^{-\beta^*}),\ t \to \infty\},$$

and under circumstances to be discussed in much detail later on, it may be continued to a meromorphic function on a larger domain (see also BLEISTEIN AND HANDELSMAN, 1986, pages 106f.).

Our analysis to prove the asymptotic expansions that are given in (i) and (ii) is based on generalizations of Theorems 4.5 and 4.6 of BLEISTEIN AND HANDELSMAN (1986). We shall now state and prove Theorems 4.5 and 4.6 of BLEISTEIN AND HANDELSMAN in a form that suits our analysis. We write, given any continuous functions $f, h : \mathbf{R}_{>0} \to \mathbf{R}$,

$$f_1(t) := \begin{cases} f(t) & \text{if } t < 1, \\ 0 & \text{otherwise,} \end{cases} \qquad t > 0,$$

$$f_2(t) := \begin{cases} 0 & \text{if } t < 1, \\ f(t) & \text{otherwise,} \end{cases} \qquad t > 0,$$

and $G_j := \mathcal{M}[h, \cdot]\mathcal{M}[f_j, 1 - \cdot]$, $K_j := G_j(1 - \cdot)$, $G := G_1 + G_2$, $K := K_1 + K_2$. We also let

$$I(r) := \int_0^\infty h(r\beta) f(\beta)\, d\beta, \qquad r > 0. \tag{2.27}$$

Finally, the residue of a function g, which is meromorphic on a domain $\Omega \subset \mathbf{C}$, at $z \in \Omega$ will be denoted by $\operatorname{res}\{g(z)\}$. Therefore, if the singular part of the Laurent expansion of g about z is $\sum_{k=1}^{\infty} c_{-k}(\cdot - z)^{-k}$, then $\operatorname{res}\{g(z)\} = c_{-1}$.

Theorem 8. *Let $f, h : \mathbf{R}_{>0} \to \mathbf{R}$ be continuous and such that (2.27) converges absolutely for all positive r and such that the* Parseval formulæ for Mellin transforms

$$I_j(r) := \int_0^\infty h(r\beta) f_j(\beta)\, d\beta = \frac{1}{2\pi i} \int_{\varrho_j - i\infty}^{\varrho_j + i\infty} r^{-z} G_j(z)\, dz, \qquad j = 1, 2, \tag{2.28}$$

hold where we assume that $\varrho_j \in \mathbf{R}$, $\varrho_1 < \varrho_2$, $\int_{-\infty}^{\infty} |G_j(\varrho_j + iy)|\, dy < \infty$ and also that the G_j are holomorphic in vertical strips which contain $\varrho_j + i\mathbf{R}$. Suppose also that

(a) $\lim_{y \to \pm\infty} G_1(z) = 0$ for all $\varrho_1 \le x \le \varrho_2$,

(b) $\lim_{y \to \pm\infty} G(z) = 0$ for all $\varrho_2 \le x \le R$, and

(c) $\int_{-\infty}^{\infty} |G(R + iy)|\, dy$ is finite,

for some $R > \varrho_2$. Then the asymptotic expansion

$$I(r) = \sum_{\varrho_1 < x < \varrho_2} \operatorname{res}\{-r^{-z} G_1(z)\} + \sum_{\varrho_2 < x < R} \operatorname{res}\{-r^{-z} G(z)\} + O(r^{-R}), \qquad r \to \infty, \tag{2.29}$$

holds if, in addition to the assumptions already made, the G_j are meromorphic in vertical strips that contain $\{z \mid \varrho_j < x < R\}$ and holomorphic in vertical strips that contain $R + i\mathbf{R}$ while G_1 has no pole along $\varrho_2 + i\mathbf{R}$ and $\int_{-\infty}^{\infty} |G_1(\varrho_2 + iy)|\, dy < \infty$.

Proof. Assumption (a) and the assumptions about the domains where G_1 has to be holomorphic and where it has to be meromorphic imply that we can displace the contour of integration of the integral

$$\frac{1}{2\pi i} \int_{\varrho_1 - i\infty}^{\varrho_1 + i\infty} r^{-z} G_1(z)\, dz,$$

which is the same as $I_1(r)$ by (2.28), to the right until it coincides with $\varrho_2 + i\mathbf{R}$ so as to obtain by the Residue Theorem

$$\begin{aligned} I(r) &= I_1(r) + I_2(r) \\ &= \sum_{\varrho_1 < x < \varrho_2} \operatorname{res}\{-r^{-z} G_1(z)\} + \frac{1}{2\pi i} \int_{\varrho_2 - i\infty}^{\varrho_2 + i\infty} r^{-z} G_1(z)\, dz + I_2(r) \\ &= \sum_{\varrho_1 < x < \varrho_2} \operatorname{res}\{-r^{-z} G_1(z)\} + \frac{1}{2\pi i} \int_{\varrho_2 - i\infty}^{\varrho_2 + i\infty} r^{-z} G(z)\, dz, \end{aligned}$$

where we have used (2.28) again, now for $j = 2$. All the integrals in the expression above are well-defined by our integrability assumptions.

Supposition (b) and the assumptions we have made about the domains where both G_j have to be meromorphic and holomorphic respectively imply that we can displace the contour of integration in the above identity even further to the right to obtain (2.29) where we also make use of the fact that (c) implies

$$\left| \int_{R-i\infty}^{R+i\infty} r^{-z} G(z)\, dz \right| = O(r^{-R})$$

for large r. ■

Theorem 9. *Let $f, h : \mathbf{R}_{>0} \to \mathbf{R}$ be continuous and such that (2.27) converges absolutely for all positive r and such that the* Parseval formulæ for Mellin transforms

$$I_j(r) := \int_0^\infty h(r\beta) f_j(\beta)\, d\beta = \frac{1}{2\pi i} \int_{\varrho_j' - i\infty}^{\varrho_j' + i\infty} r^{z-1} K_j(z)\, dz, \qquad j = 1, 2, \tag{2.30}$$

hold where we assume that $\varrho_j' \in \mathbf{R}$, $\varrho_2' < \varrho_1'$, $\int_{-\infty}^{\infty} |K_j(\varrho_j' + iy)|\, dy < \infty$ and the K_j are holomorphic in vertical strips which contain $\varrho_j' + i\mathbf{R}$. Suppose also that

(a) $\lim_{y \to \pm\infty} K_2(z) = 0$ for all $\varrho_2' \le x \le \varrho_1'$,

(b) $\lim_{y \to \pm\infty} K(z) = 0$ for all $\varrho_1' \le x \le R'$, and

(c) $\int_{-\infty}^{\infty} |K(R' + iy)|\, dy$ is finite,

for some $R' > \varrho_1'$. Then we have the asymptotic expansion

$$I(r) = \sum_{\varrho_2' < x < \varrho_1'} \operatorname{res}\{-r^{z-1} K_2(z)\} + \sum_{\varrho_1' < x < R'} \operatorname{res}\{-r^{z-1} K(z)\} + O(r^{R'-1}), \qquad r \to 0, \tag{2.31}$$

if also the K_j are meromorphic in vertical strips that contain $\{z \mid \varrho_j' < x < R'\}$ and holomorphic in strips that contain $R' + i\mathbf{R}$ while K_2 has no pole along $\varrho_1' + i\mathbf{R}$ and $\int_{-\infty}^{\infty} |K_2(\varrho_1' + iy)|\, dy < \infty$.

Proof. We apply the same arguments as in the previous proof. ■

We note that Bleistein and Handelsman formulate the above two results only for the event when infinite expansions of f and h near the origin and for large argument are available.

In order to apply Theorems 8 and 9 to our f and h defined in and just before (2.2) respectively, we essentially have to identify the functions G_j and G and their domains of analyticity and their poles, and we have to identify the asymptotic behaviour of $G_j(z)$ and $G(z)$ as y tends to $\pm\infty$. This will allow us to find the ϱ_j, ϱ_j', R and R' so that the assumptions of the theorems, that is in particular the Parseval formulæ and conditions (a)–(c), hold. Consequently we will be in a position to deduce (2.22)–(2.26) from (2.29) and (2.31) by finding the residua of the functions that occur.

We firstly need to collect properties of the Mellin transform of $h = J_\nu\sqrt{\cdot}$: BLEISTEIN AND HANDELSMAN (1986) give in equation (4.4.37) the Mellin transform of h as

$$\mathcal{M}[h, z] = \frac{2^{z-1/2}\Gamma(\frac{1}{4}(2\nu + 2z + 1))}{\Gamma(\frac{1}{4}(2\nu - 2z + 3))},$$

and $\mathcal{M}[h, \cdot]$ is meromorphic in the whole complex plane with simple poles that are only at $-\nu - \frac{1}{2} - 2j$, $j = 0, 1, 2, \ldots$, because Γ is meromorphic in the complex plane and has no zeros but has simple poles at all nonpositive integers (cf. ABRAMOWITZ AND STEGUN, 1970, page 255). We denote the set of these singular points by T. In particular, the Mellin transform of h is holomorphic in $B = \{z \mid x > -\nu - \frac{1}{2}\}$. We note for later reference that by ABRAMOWITZ AND STEGUN (1970), equation (6.1.45), we have the bound

$$|\mathcal{M}[h, z]| = O(|y|^{x-1/2}), \qquad y \to \pm\infty, \tag{2.32}$$

and this estimate is valid for all $x \in \mathbf{R}$.

Having identified the Mellin transform of h as a meromorphic function on the whole complex plane, it remains to identify the domains where the $\mathcal{M}[f_j, 1 - \cdot]$ are holomorphic and to identify their poles, in order to find these domains and poles for the G_j and G. The idea in doing this will be to split each of the Mellin transforms $\mathcal{M}[f_j, 1 - \cdot]$ into the sum of two parts, one of which is meromorphic in the complex plane with easily identifiable poles, and the other one is holomorphic in a vertical strip whose size depends on e_J and r_K. Consequently we combine these observations with the results of the previous paragraph to find the domains of analyticity and the poles of G_j and G.

We expand f asymptotically near the origin as

$$f(t) = \sum_{j=0}^{J-1} b_j t^{d_j} + O(t^{d_J}), \qquad t \to 0.$$

Here $b_j = 2^{\nu+1}(-1)^{\lambda+\kappa}\pi^{n/2}a_j$ and $d_j = 2e_j + \nu + \frac{1}{2}$. For any $\iota \gg d_J - d_0 > 0$ we let

$$f_{1,\iota}(t) = \exp(-t^\iota)\sum_{j=0}^{J-1} b_j t^{d_j}, \qquad t > 0,$$

and

$$r_{1,\iota}(t) = f_1(t) - f_{1,\iota}(t), \qquad t > 0.$$

We observe that by a change of variable

$$\mathcal{M}[f_{1,\iota}, 1 - z] = \sum_{j=0}^{J-1} b_j \int_0^\infty t^{-z}\exp(-t^\iota)t^{d_j}\, dt$$

$$= \iota^{-1} \sum_{j=0}^{J-1} b_j \int_0^\infty e^{-t} t^{(d_j+1-z-\iota)/\iota}\, dt$$
$$= \iota^{-1} \sum_{j=0}^{J-1} b_j \Gamma((d_j + 1 - z)/\iota). \tag{2.33}$$

As the Γ-function is meromorphic on the whole complex plane with simple poles which are only at the nonpositive integers, (2.33) is a meromorphic function with simple poles only on $\{1+d_j+\iota l \mid j = 0, 1, \ldots, J-1,\ l = 0, 1, 2, \ldots\}$. The set of poles that occur in the set $\{z \mid x < 1 + d_J\}$ is restricted to $\{1 + d_j \mid j = 0, 1, \ldots, J - 1\}$ by our choice of ι. We note for later reference that by ABRAMOWITZ AND STEGUN (1970), equation (6.1.45) which shows that $|\Gamma(z)|$ decays exponentially for $y \to \pm\infty$, $|\mathcal{M}[f_{1,\iota}, 1 - z]|$ decays exponentially as $y \to \pm\infty$ for any fixed x. Because $|r_{1,\iota}(t)| = O(t^{d_J})$ near the origin, the Mellin transform

$$\mathcal{M}[r_{1,\iota}, 1 - z] = \int_0^\infty t^{-z} r_{1,\iota}(t)\, dt$$
$$= \int_{-\infty}^\infty \exp(-iyt) \exp((1 - x)t) r_{1,\iota}(e^t)\, dt \tag{2.34}$$

is absolutely convergent whenever $x < 1+d_J$. Hence $\mathcal{M}[r_{1,\iota}, 1- \cdot]$ is holomorphic on $A_1 = \{z \mid x < 1+d_J\}$.

The Mellin transform $\mathcal{M}[f_1, 1 - \cdot]$ is a holomorpic function on $C_1 = \{z \mid x < 1 + d_0\}$. Now, however, letting $\mathcal{M}[f_1, 1-z]$ be for each $z \in A_1$ the sum $\mathcal{M}[f_{1,\iota}, 1-z] + \mathcal{M}[r_{1,\iota}, 1-z]$ provides a continuation of it as a meromorphic function on A_1 which has poles in A_1 that are simple and only at $1+d_j$, $j = 0, 1, \ldots, J-1$.

If $f_{2,\iota}$ and $r_{2,\iota}$ are defined by

$$f_{2,\iota}(t) = \exp(-t^{-\iota}) \sum_{j=0}^{K-1} q_j t^{-s_j}, \qquad t > 0,$$

and

$$r_{2,\iota}(t) = f_2(t) - f_{2,\iota}(t), \qquad t > 0,$$

with $s_j = 2r_j - \nu - \frac{1}{2}$ and $q_j = 2^{\nu+1}(-1)^{\lambda+\kappa}\pi^{n/2}p_j$ respectively, and if we choose $\iota \gg s_K - s_0 > 0$, we can continue the function $\mathcal{M}[f_2, 1 - \cdot]$ which is holomorphic on $C_2 = \{z \mid x > 1 - s_0\}$, in an analogous way as we did with $\mathcal{M}[f_1, 1- \cdot]$ above, to a meromorphic function on $A_2 = \{z \mid x > 1-s_K\}$. Its poles in A_2 are all simple and only at $1-s_j$, $j = 0, 1, \ldots, K-1$. We denote the set of singularities $\mathcal{M}[f_1, 1- \cdot] + \mathcal{M}[f_2, 1- \cdot]$ has on A, which we define to be $A_1 \cap A_2$, by S. So the G_j are holomorphic on $A_j \setminus (S \cup T)$ and on $D_j = C_j \cap B$ and meromorphic on A_j. Moreover, G is meromorphic on A. D_1 is not empty because we have imposed the lower bound $e_0 > -\nu - 1$ and A is not empty because of the bounds $-r_K < -r_0 < e_J$.

We now investigate $G(z)$'s behaviour when $y \to \pm\infty$. Define $r_\iota = r_{1,\iota} + r_{2,\iota}$ and $f_\iota = f_{1,\iota} + f_{2,\iota}$. Thus in particular

$$\mathcal{M}[r_\iota, 1 - z] = \int_0^\infty t^{-z} r_\iota(t)\, dt$$
$$= \int_{-\infty}^\infty \exp(-iyt) \exp((1 - x)t) r_\iota(e^t)\, dt$$

and this is absolutely convergent if $x \in A \cap \mathbf{R}$. Our assumptions about the asymptotic behaviour of $\xi^{(\lambda+\varrho)}$ in the statement of the lemma imply for $\varrho \leq q$

$$\left|\frac{d^\varrho}{dt^\varrho} r_\iota(t)\right| = \left|\frac{d^\varrho}{dt^\varrho} f(t) - \frac{d^\varrho}{dt^\varrho} f_\iota(t)\right| = \begin{cases} O(t^{d_J-\varrho}) & \text{as } t \to 0, \\ O(t^{-s_K-\varrho}) & \text{as } t \to \infty. \end{cases} \tag{2.35}$$

Because all derivatives of the q-times continuously differentiable function $\exp((1-x)\cdot)r_\iota(e^{\cdot}) : \mathbf{R} \to \mathbf{R}$ vanish at infinity when x is in the designated region and because (2.35) implies that for all $\varrho \leq q$ and $x \in A \cap \mathbf{R}$

$$\int_{-\infty}^{\infty} \left|\frac{d^\varrho}{dt^\varrho}\{\exp((1-x)t)r_\iota(e^t)\}\right| dt < \infty,$$

we use standard estimates for Fourier transforms to conclude for $x \in A \cap \mathbf{R}$

$$|\mathcal{M}[r_\iota, 1-z]| = o(|y|^{-q}), \qquad y \to \pm\infty.$$

The Mellin transform $\mathcal{M}[f_\iota, 1-z]$ decays exponentially for $y \to \pm\infty$ and all $x \in \mathbf{R}$ because both $\mathcal{M}[f_{j,\iota}, 1-z]$ do. We see that the function $\mathcal{M}[f_\iota, 1-\cdot] + \mathcal{M}[r_\iota, 1-\cdot]$ satisfies the bound

$$|\mathcal{M}[f_\iota, 1-z] + \mathcal{M}[r_\iota, 1-z]| = o(|y|^{-q}), \qquad y \to \pm\infty, \tag{2.36}$$

for every $x \in A \cap \mathbf{R}$. And for the same range of x it is true that

$$\begin{aligned} \mathcal{M}[f_1, 1-z] + \mathcal{M}[f_2, 1-z] &= \mathcal{M}[f_{1,\iota}, 1-z] + \mathcal{M}[f_{2,\iota}, 1-z] + \mathcal{M}[r_{1,\iota}, 1-z] + \mathcal{M}[r_{2,\iota}, 1-z] \\ &= \mathcal{M}[f_\iota, 1-z] + \mathcal{M}[r_\iota, 1-z]. \end{aligned}$$

So from estimates (2.32) and (2.36), we see that the function G satisfies the estimate

$$|G(z)| = o(|y|^{x-1/2-q}), \qquad y \to \pm\infty, \tag{2.37}$$

for every $x \in A \cap \mathbf{R}$. Let us assume $q = \frac{3}{2} + d_J$. If $q > \frac{3}{2} + d_J$, we replace q by $\frac{3}{2} + d_J$. Therefore $x < q - \frac{1}{2}$ if $x \in A \cap \mathbf{R}$. Thus the bound (2.37) implies for all $x \in A \cap \mathbf{R}$

$$\lim_{y \to \pm\infty} G(z) = 0 \tag{2.38}$$

and for all $x \in A \cap \mathbf{R} \setminus (T \cup S)$

$$\int_{-\infty}^{\infty} |G(z)|\, dy < \infty \tag{2.39}$$

which follows for the designated choice of x because the contour of integration avoids all singularities of the meromorphic function G. (2.38) and (2.39) will be used to find ϱ_2 and R to satisfy conditions (b) and (c) of Theorem 8.

We now proceed to deriving the Parseval identities for Mellin transforms in the form needed in Theorem 8. This will also involve identifying the asymptotic behaviour of the $G_j(z)$ as $y \to \pm\infty$, which we need, in particular, to find ϱ_j to satisfy condition (a) of Theorem 8. We argue formally at first and then give suitable conditions on the ϱ_j that validate the steps we took to derive the Parseval identities. Therefore suppose that for $j = 1, 2$, each integral

$$\int_{\varrho_j - i\infty}^{\varrho_j + i\infty} G_j(z)\, dz \tag{2.40}$$

is well-defined. Then, using the definition of the Mellin transform, we can write

$$\frac{1}{2\pi i}\int_{\varrho_j - i\infty}^{\varrho_j + i\infty} G_j(z)\, dz = \frac{1}{2\pi i}\int_{\varrho_j - i\infty}^{\varrho_j + i\infty} \mathcal{M}[h, z] \int_0^\infty f_j(t) t^{-z}\, dt\, dz. \tag{2.41}$$

Let us suppose that not only the integral (2.40) is well-defined but that we also may interchange the order of integration in identity (2.41). We then obtain

$$\frac{1}{2\pi i}\int_{\varrho_j - i\infty}^{\varrho_j + i\infty} G_j(z)\, dz = \frac{1}{2\pi i}\int_0^\infty f_j(t) \int_{\varrho_j - i\infty}^{\varrho_j + i\infty} \mathcal{M}[h, z] t^{-z}\, dz\, dt.$$

This, upon using the inversion formula for Mellin transforms

$$h(t) = \frac{1}{2\pi i}\int_{\varrho_j - i\infty}^{\varrho_j + i\infty} \mathcal{M}[h, z] t^{-z}\, dz$$

which is valid at all points of continuity of h whenever the Mellin transform of h is holomorphic along the contour of integration (see, for instance, Bleistein and Handelsman, 1986, page 107), gives

$$\int_0^\infty f_j(t) h(t)\, dt = \frac{1}{2\pi i}\int_{\varrho_j - i\infty}^{\varrho_j + i\infty} G_j(z)\, dz. \tag{2.42}$$

By noting that the inversion formula for Mellin transforms also implies, by a simple change of variable,

$$h(r\beta) = \frac{1}{2\pi i}\int_{\varrho_j - i\infty}^{\varrho_j + i\infty} r^{-z} \mathcal{M}[h, z] \beta^{-z}\, dz$$

we see that formula (2.28) follows at once if we can just show that (2.42) holds. In order to validate identity (2.42) we must now justify our usage of the inversion formula for Mellin transforms, we must justify the interchange in the order of integration in identity (2.41), and we must ensure the absolute convergence of the integral (2.40). We do all this by stating suitable sufficient conditions on the ϱ_j. To begin with, applying the inversion formula for Mellin transforms is valid if we require $\varrho_j \in B \cap \mathbf{R}$, since the contour of integration in the inversion formula hence lies in the domain B where the Mellin transform of h is holomorphic, and since h is continuous throughout. For justifying the interchange in the order of integration in (2.41), it suffices that both $\mathcal{M}[h, \varrho_j + i\,\cdot] : \mathbf{R} \to \mathbf{C}$ and $\cdot^{-\varrho_j} f_j : \mathbf{R}_{>0} \to \mathbf{R}$ are absolutely integrable: then the interchange in (2.41) is justified by absolute convergence. Because of the bound (2.32), this is true whenever each $\varrho_j \in D_j \cap \mathbf{R}$ and satisfies additionally $\varrho_j < -\frac{1}{2}$, and these two conditions can be satisfied simultaneously for both j because $r_0 > \frac{1}{2}\nu + 1$ and $\nu > 0$.

Both $\mathcal{M}[f_j, 1 - z]$ satisfy for all $x \in A_j \cap \mathbf{R}$

$$\lim_{y \to \pm\infty} \mathcal{M}[f_j, 1 - z] = 0. \tag{2.43}$$

This we can verify by recalling that each $\mathcal{M}[f_j, 1-\cdot]$ is the sum $\mathcal{M}[f_{j,\iota}, 1-\cdot] + \mathcal{M}[r_{j,\iota}, 1-\cdot]$ and that in this sum the first term decays exponentially in y because it is a linear combination of Γ-functions which decay exponentially along lines that are parallel to the imaginary axis, and because the second term is $o(1)$ as $y \to \pm\infty$ (by the Riemann-Lebesgue Lemma). In particular, the bound (2.32) and the limit (2.43) imply that if $\varrho_j \in D_j \cap E$, where $E := \{t \in \mathbf{R} \mid t < -\frac{1}{2}\}$, then

$$\int_{-\infty}^{\infty} |G_j(\varrho_j + iy)| \, dy < \infty.$$

The absolute convergence of the integral (2.40) is thus ensured whenever $\varrho_j \in D_j \cap E$. Thus the required Parseval identities hold whenever $\varrho_j \in D_j \cap E$.

Additionally, using the bound (2.32) and (2.43) again,

$$\int_{-\infty}^{\infty} |G_1(\varrho_2 + iy)| \, dy < \infty,$$

if $\varrho_2 \in D_2 \cap E \cap A_1 \setminus S$, because then there is no pole of G_1 on the contour of integration in the above expression. Here we make use of the fact that $-r_0 < e_J$ implies $D_2 \cap A_1$ is not empty. And finally, by the bound (2.32) and by (2.43) we have for every $x \in A_j \cap E$

$$\lim_{y \to \pm\infty} G_j(z) = 0. \tag{2.44}$$

We see that for $\varrho_j \in D_j \cap E$ and $\varrho_1 < \varrho_2 < R < q - \frac{1}{2}$, while ϱ_2 and R must not be in S,

1. the Parseval identities for Mellin transforms (2.28) hold, in particular each $\int_{-\infty}^{\infty} |G_j(\varrho_j + iy)| \, dy$ is finite and the G_j are holomorphic in strips that contain $\varrho_j + i\mathbf{R}$,
2. $\lim_{y \to \pm\infty} G_1(z) = 0$ for all $\varrho_1 \leq x \leq \varrho_2$ (by expression (2.44)),
3. $\lim_{y \to \pm\infty} G(z) = 0$ for all $\varrho_2 \leq x \leq R$ (by expression (2.38)),
4. $\int_{-\infty}^{\infty} |G(R + iy)| \, dy$ is finite (by expression (2.39)),
5. the G_j are meromorphic in $A_j \supset \{z \mid \varrho_j < x < R\}$ and holomorphic in strips that contain $R + i\mathbf{R}$. Finally G_1 has no pole along $\varrho_2 + i\mathbf{R}$ and $\int_{-\infty}^{\infty} |G_1(\varrho_2 + iy)| \, dy$ is finite.

Conclusions 1–5 show that we can apply Theorem 8 for our choice of f and h when we choose the ϱ_j and R to satisfy the conditions above. Because the Mellin transform of h is holomorphic in the right half-plane B which contains the right half-plane $\{z \mid x > \varrho_1\}$ and $\mathcal{M}[f_2, 1-\cdot]$ is holomorphic in the right half-plane C_2 which contains the right half-plane $\{z \mid x > \varrho_2\}$, all residua that occur in the expansion (2.29) must come from poles of $\mathcal{M}[f_1, 1-\cdot]$. Hence the expansion (2.29) implies

$$I(r) = \sum_{\varrho_1 < x < R} \operatorname{res}\{-r^{-z} G_1(z)\} + O(r^{-R}), \quad r \to \infty.$$

The singular part of the Laurent expansion of $\mathcal{M}[f_1, 1-\cdot]$ about each of its simple poles at $d_j + 1$ is given by $b_j/(d_j + 1 - \cdot)$. This we can conclude from the expression (2.33) of $\mathcal{M}[f_{1,\iota}, 1-\cdot]$ as a sum of Γ-functions in the following way: because the Γ-function has a simple pole at the origin with residue one, we see that $\iota^{-1}\Gamma((d_j+1-\cdot)/\iota)$ has a Laurent expansion about d_j+1 with singular part $(d_j+1-\cdot)^{-1}$. Its residue at the pole at d_j+1 is therefore -1. Because no pole of $\mathcal{M}[f_1, 1-\cdot]$ can be inherited from the term (2.34) (this term is holomorphic on $A_1 \supset \{z \mid \varrho_1 < x < R\}$), we see that the claim we made at the beginning of this paragraph is true, and moreover the residue of $\mathcal{M}[f_1, 1-\cdot]$ at d_j+1 is $-b_j$. Now we employ the observation that $\operatorname{res}\{g_1(z)g_2(z)\} = g_1(z)\operatorname{res}\{g_2(z)\}$ whenever g_1 is holomorphic in a neighbourhood of z while g_2 is meromorphic in a neighbourhood of z and has a simple pole at z. Therefore the residue of G_1 at each d_j+1 is $-b_j\mathcal{M}[h, 1+d_j]$ and the residue $\operatorname{res}\{-r^{-z}G_1(z)\}$ is $b_j r^{-d_j-1}\mathcal{M}[h, 1+d_j]$. Consequently, the expansion (2.29) implies that for all $0 < \varepsilon < 2\min(e_0+\nu+1, e_J - e_{J-1}, \frac{1}{2}\nu)$ and $\varrho_1 = -\nu - \frac{1}{2} + \varepsilon$ and $R = 1 + d_J - \varepsilon$,

$$
\begin{aligned}
I(r) &= \sum_{\varrho_1 < d_j+1 < R} b_j r^{-d_j-1}\mathcal{M}[h, 1+d_j] + O(r^{-R}) \\
&= \sum_{j=0}^{J-1} \frac{(-1)^{\lambda+\kappa}4^{e_j+\nu+1}\pi^{n/2}\Gamma(\nu+e_j+1)a_j}{\Gamma(-e_j)} r^{-2e_j-\nu-3/2} + O(r^{-2e_J-\nu-3/2+\varepsilon}), \qquad r \to \infty.
\end{aligned}
$$

This yields expansion (2.22) by multiplication with $r^{-\nu-1/2}$ as required.

The analysis for proving the assertions of part (ii) is similar. Here for any $\varrho_j' \in (1-D_j)\cap(1-E)$ and R' such that $\varrho_2' < \varrho_1' < R' < s_K$, while ϱ_1' and R' must not be in $(1-S)\cup(1-T)$,

1. the Parseval identities for Mellin transforms (2.30) hold and in particular each $\int_{-\infty}^{\infty} |K_j(\varrho_j' + iy)|\,dy$ is finite and the K_j are holomorphic along $\varrho_j' + i\mathbf{R}$,
2. $\lim_{y\to\pm\infty} K_2(z) = 0$ for all $\varrho_2' \le x \le \varrho_1'$,
3. $\lim_{y\to\pm\infty} K(z) = 0$ for all $\varrho_1' \le x \le R'$,
4. $\int_{-\infty}^{\infty} |K(R'+iy)|\,dy$ is finite,
5. the K_j are meromorphic in $1 - A_j \supset \{z \mid \varrho_j' < x < R'\}$ and holomorphic in strips covering $R' + i\mathbf{R}$. Finally K_2 has no pole along $\varrho_1' + i\mathbf{R}$ and $\int_{-\infty}^{\infty} |K_2(\varrho_1' + iy)|\,dy$ is finite.

These are conditions sufficient to conclude expansion (2.31). The residua can come either from the poles of $\mathcal{M}[f_2, \cdot]$ or from the poles of $\mathcal{M}[h, 1-\cdot]$ since the Mellin transform of f_1 is holomorphic in the right half-plane $1 - C_1$ which contains the right half-plane $\{z \mid x > \varrho_1'\}$. The (simple) poles of the Mellin transform of f_2 in the set $1 - A_2 \supset \{z \mid \varrho_2' < x < R'\}$ only lie at s_j, $j = 0, 1, 2, \ldots, K-1$, with the singular part of the Laurent expansions about these points being $q_j/(s_j - \cdot)$, that is the residue at each of these points is $-q_j$. Therefore each residue of K_2 at s_j is $-q_j\mathcal{M}[h, 1-s_j]$ provided that $\mathcal{M}[h, 1-\cdot]$ does not have a pole at the point s_j itself, and under these circumstances $\operatorname{res}\{-r^{s_j-1}K_2(s_j)\} = q_j r^{s_j-1}\mathcal{M}[h, 1-s_j]$.

Next, we investigate the poles of the Mellin transform $\mathcal{M}[h, 1-\cdot]$: because

$$
\mathcal{M}[h, 1-z] = \frac{2^{1/2-z}\Gamma(\frac{1}{4}(2\nu - 2z + 3))}{\Gamma(\frac{1}{4}(2\nu + 2z + 1))}, \tag{2.45}
$$

the poles of $\mathcal{M}[h, 1-\cdot]$ are all simple and lie at $\nu + \frac{3}{2} + 2j$, $j = 0, 1, 2, \ldots$, with the singular part of the Laurent expansions being

$$
\frac{(-1)^j}{2^{\nu+2j} j!\,\Gamma(\nu+j+1)(\nu + \frac{3}{2} + 2j - \cdot)}.
$$

Therefore the residue at each of these poles is

$$\frac{(-1)^{j+1}}{2^{\nu+2j}j!\Gamma(\nu+j+1)}.$$

We note that $\nu+\frac{3}{2}+2j>\varrho_1'$ for all nonnegative integers j since $\varrho_1'\in 1-D_1\subset 1-B$. Therefore poles of $\mathcal{M}[h,1-\cdot]$ can only occur in the second term in the expansion (2.31). Since we have identified all the poles of the Mellin transform of f_2 in the previous paragraph, we therefore have found all poles and residua that contribute to the first term of the expansion (2.31).

The residue of K at each of the poles of $\mathcal{M}[h,1-\cdot]$ is

$$\frac{(-1)^{j+1}\{\mathcal{M}[f_1,\nu+\frac{3}{2}+2j]+\mathcal{M}[f_2,\nu+\frac{3}{2}+2j]\}}{2^{\nu+2j}j!\Gamma(\nu+j+1)},$$

provided that the Mellin transform of f_2 does not have a pole at the point $\nu+\frac{3}{2}+2j$ too. We first assume that indeed none of the poles of $\mathcal{M}[f_2,\cdot]$ and of $\mathcal{M}[h,1-\cdot]$ coincide. Then we obtain from expansion (2.31), taking $0<\varepsilon<2\min(r_K-r_{K-1},r_0-\frac{1}{2}\nu-1,\frac{1}{2}\nu)$ and $\varrho_2'=\frac{3}{2}+\varepsilon$, $R'=s_K-\varepsilon$, where ε must be such that $R'\notin\nu+\frac{3}{2}+2\mathbb{Z}_+$,

$$I(r)=\sum_{\varrho_2'<s_j<R'} q_j r^{s_j-1}\mathcal{M}[h,1-s_j] \tag{2.46}$$

$$+\sum_{\nu+3/2\le\nu+3/2+2j<R'}\frac{(-1)^j\{\mathcal{M}[f_1,\nu+\frac{3}{2}+2j]+\mathcal{M}[f_2,\nu+\frac{3}{2}+2j]\}}{2^{\nu+2j}j!\Gamma(\nu+j+1)}r^{\nu+1/2+2j} \tag{2.47}$$

$$+O(r^{R'-1}),\qquad r\to 0.$$

By applying (2.45), the definitions of s_j, q_j and of the Mellin transform of f_1, and by applying the fact that the definition of H in the statement of the lemma relates H to the Mellin transform of f_2 by the identity

$$H(z)=2^{-\nu-1}(-1)^{\lambda+\kappa}\pi^{-n/2}\mathcal{M}[f_2,z-\nu+\tfrac{1}{2}],$$

expressions (2.46) and (2.47) can be reformulated to become

$$I(r)=\sum_{j=0}^{K-1}\frac{(-1)^{\lambda+\kappa}4^{1-r_j+\nu}\pi^{n/2}\Gamma(\nu-r_j+1)p_j}{\Gamma(r_j)}r^{2r_j-\nu-3/2} \tag{2.48}$$

$$+\sum_{\substack{j=0,1,2,\ldots\\ j<r_K-\nu-1}}\frac{(-1)^{\lambda+\kappa+j}\pi^{n/2}\{\int_0^1 t^{2\nu+1+2j}\xi^{(\lambda)}(t^2)dt+H(2\nu+2j+1)\}}{2^{2j-1}j!\Gamma(\nu+j+1)}r^{\nu+1/2+2j} \tag{2.49}$$

$$+O(r^{2r_K-\nu-3/2-\varepsilon}),\qquad r\to 0.$$

Here, H is meromorphic on $\{z\mid x<2r_K-1\}$ with poles that are simple and only at $2r_j-1$, $j=0,1,\ldots,K-1$, because the Mellin transform of f_2 is meromorphic on $1-A_2$ with poles which are simple and only at s_j, $j=0,1,\ldots,K-1$. Identities (2.48) and (2.49) imply (2.23) and (2.24) by multiplication with $r^{-\nu-1/2}$.

We now attend to the case when poles of $\mathcal{M}[f_2, \cdot]$ and of $\mathcal{M}[h, 1-\cdot]$ coincide. We make use of the fact that if g_1 is holomorphic in a neighbourhood of $\widehat{z}$, g_2 and g_3 are meromorphic in a neighbourhood of $\widehat{z}$ and have simple poles at $\widehat{z}$, then

$$\begin{aligned}\operatorname{res}\{g_1(\widehat{z})g_2(\widehat{z})g_3(\widehat{z})\} &= g_1'(\widehat{z})\operatorname{res}\{g_2(\widehat{z})\}\operatorname{res}\{g_3(\widehat{z})\} + \\ &+ g_1(\widehat{z})\lim_{z\to\widehat{z}}\Big\{\operatorname{res}\{g_2(\widehat{z})\}\big[(\cdot-\widehat{z})g_3\big]'(z) + \operatorname{res}\{g_3(\widehat{z})\}\big[(\cdot-\widehat{z})g_2\big]'(z)\Big\}.\end{aligned}$$

Here $g_1'(\widehat{z})$ denotes the complex derivative $\frac{d}{dz}g_1(\widetilde{z})$ evaluated at $\widetilde{z}=\widehat{z}$ and $\big[(\cdot-\widehat{z})g_j\big]'(z)$ denotes the complex derivative $\frac{d}{dz}\big[(\widetilde{z}-\widehat{z})g_j(\widetilde{z})\big]$ evaluated at $\widetilde{z}=z$.

We see that whenever for j' and j'' we have $s_{j'} = \nu + \frac{3}{2} + 2j''$, i.e. poles of the Mellin transform of f_2 and poles of $\mathcal{M}[h, 1-\cdot]$ coincide, then the terms for $j=j'$ and for $j=j''$ in the first sum (2.48) and the second sum (2.49) respectively have to be replaced by the sum of the expressions

$$-\frac{(-1)^{j''}q_{j'}}{2^{\nu+2j''}j''!\Gamma(\nu+j''+1)}r^{\nu+1/2+2j''}\log r = \frac{(-1)^{\lambda+\kappa+j''+1}\pi^{n/2}p_{j'}}{2^{2j''-1}j''!\Gamma(\nu+j''+1)}r^{\nu+1/2+2j''}\log r \tag{2.50}$$

and the limit

$$\lim_{z\to s_{j'}}\frac{d}{dz}\left\{(z-s_{j'})\left[\frac{(-1)^{j''}\{\mathcal{M}[f_1,z]+\mathcal{M}[f_2,z]\}}{2^{\nu+2j''}j''!\Gamma(\nu+j''+1)} + q_{j'}\mathcal{M}[h,1-z]\right]\right\}r^{\nu+1/2+2j''}. \tag{2.51}$$

Identity (2.50) gives the first term of expression (2.25) by multiplication with $r^{-\nu-1/2}$.

Considering expression (2.51) we recall that the Mellin transform of f_1 has no pole at $s_{j'}$. Therefore $\mathcal{M}[f_1, z]$ can be evaluated at $z = s_{j'}$, and we take the relevant term outside the limit. Thus expression (2.51) becomes the sum

$$\begin{aligned}&\frac{(-1)^{j''}\mathcal{M}[f_1,s_{j'}]}{2^{\nu+2j''}j''!\Gamma(\nu+j''+1)}r^{\nu+1/2+2j''} + \\ &\quad + \lim_{z\to s_{j'}}\frac{d}{dz}\left\{(z-s_{j'})\left[\frac{(-1)^{j''}\mathcal{M}[f_2,z]}{2^{\nu+2j''}j''!\Gamma(\nu+j''+1)} + q_{j'}\mathcal{M}[h,1-z]\right]\right\}r^{\nu+1/2+2j''}.\end{aligned}$$

Recalling $s_{j'} = \nu + \frac{3}{2} + 2j''$ we therefore express (2.51) as the sum of

$$\frac{(-1)^{j''}\mathcal{M}[f_1,\nu+\frac{3}{2}+2j'']}{2^{\nu+2j''}j''!\Gamma(\nu+j''+1)}r^{\nu+1/2+2j''} = \frac{(-1)^{\lambda+\kappa+j''}\pi^{n/2}\int_0^1 t^{2j''+1+2\nu}\xi^{(\lambda)}(t^2)dt}{2^{2j''-1}j''!\Gamma(\nu+j''+1)}r^{\nu+1/2+2j''} \tag{2.52}$$

and the limit

$$\begin{aligned}&\lim_{z\to 2j''+\nu+3/2}\frac{d}{dz}\Big\{(z-2j''-\nu-\tfrac{3}{2})\times \\ &\quad\times\left[\frac{(-1)^{j''}\mathcal{M}[f_2,z]}{2^{\nu+2j''}j''!\Gamma(\nu+j''+1)} + 2^{\nu+1}(-1)^{\lambda+\kappa}\pi^{n/2}p_{j'}\mathcal{M}[h,1-z]\right]\Big\}r^{\nu+1/2+2j''}.\end{aligned} \tag{2.53}$$

We get the second term of expression (2.25) by multiplying (2.52) with $r^{-\nu-1/2}$. By using (2.45), by a change of variable, by expressing $\mathcal{M}[f_2,z]$ in terms of H and by multiplication with $r^{-\nu-1/2}$, (2.53) gives expression (2.26). Lemma 7 is proved. ∎

3. References

Abramowitz, M. and Stegun, I.A. (1970) Handbook of mathematical functions (Dover Publications, New York).

Bleistein, N. and Handelsman, R.A. (1986) Asymptotic expansions of integrals (Dover Publications, New York).

Buhmann, M.D. (1989a) Multivariate interpolation in odd-dimensional Euclidean spaces using multiquadrics, Constructive Approximation, in print.

Buhmann, M.D. (1989b) Multivariate cardinal interpolation with radial-basis functions, Constructive Approximation, in print.

Buhmann, M.D. (1989c) Multivariable interpolation using radial basis functions, Ph.D. Dissertation, University of Cambridge.

Buhmann, M.D. and Micchelli, C.A. (1989) Multiply monotone functions for cardinal interpolation, preprint.

Gasper, G. (1975) Positivity and special functions, in The theory and applications of special functions, ed. R. Askey (Academic Press, New York), 375–434.

Jones, D.S. (1982) The theory of generalised functions (Cambridge University Press, Cambridge).

Stein, E.M. and Weiss, G. (1971) Introduction to Fourier analysis on Euclidean spaces (Princeton University Press, Princeton).

Williamson, R.E. (1956) Multiply monotone functions and their Laplace transforms, Duke Journal **23**, 189–207.

M.D. Buhmann, Department of Applied Mathematics and Theoretical Physics, University of Cambridge, Silver Street, Cambridge CB3 9EW, England.

International Series of
Numerical Mathematics, Vol. 90

ON THE EVALUATION OF MULTIVARIATE LAGRANGE FORMULAE

Jesús M. Carnicer, Mariano Gasca
Departamento de Matemática Aplicada, Universidad de Zaragoza

1. Evaluation of polynomials.

In [1] we have given an extension of Horner's algorithm for the evaluation of m-variate polynomials and their derivatives. The schemes of computation were represented graphically by trees. In this paper we present a short description of the algorithm and give further examples of application.

Let $K[X]$ be the ring of m-variate polynomials over a field K and $P \subset K[X]$ be the set of polynomials of exact total degree 1. Our aim is to evaluate polynomials $p_0 \in K[X]$ written in the form

$$p_0 = a_0 + \sum_{h=1}^{n} f_h p_h \text{ with } p_h \in K[X],\ a_0 \in K,\ f_h \in P\ (h = 1, \ldots, n) \tag{1.1}$$

in terms of the evaluation of p_h $h = 1, 2, \ldots n$, and to extend the algorithm to the evaluation of directional derivatives of p_0 in the same way.

It is well known that Horner's algorithm for the evaluation of a univariate polynomial

$$p_0(x) = \sum_{i=0}^{n} a_i x^i \tag{1.2}$$

is based upon the representation of p in a nested form

$$p_0(x) = a_0 + x\,(a_1 + x\,(a_2 + \ldots + x\,(a_{n-1} + x\,(a_n))\ldots)) \tag{1.3}$$

which allows the computation of $p_0(x)$ recursively by

$$\begin{aligned} p_n(x) &= a_n \\ p_i(x) &= a_i + x p_{i+1}(x) \quad i = n-1, \ldots, 0 \end{aligned} \tag{1.4}$$

Let us consider a m-variate polynomial (1.1) where each p_h can be written again in a form similar to (1.1) and so on. For example

$$p_0 = a_0 + f_1 p_1 + f_2 p_2 + f_3 p_3 \tag{1.5}$$

where

$$\begin{array}{llll} p_1 = a_1 + f_{11} p_{11} + f_{12} p_{12} & p_2 = a_2 + f_{21} p_{21} + f_{22} p_{22} & & p_3 = a_3 \\ p_{11} = a_{11} \quad p_{12} = a_{12} & p_{21} = a_{21} + f_{211} p_{211} & p_{22} = a_{22} & \\ & p_{211} = a_{211} & & \end{array} \tag{1.6}$$

with the a's $\in K$ and the f's m-variate polynomials of exact total degree 1. Similarly to (1.3) p_0 can be written

$$(1.7)\qquad \begin{aligned} p_0 = a_0 + f_1 \cdot (a_1 + f_{11} \cdot (a_{11}) + f_{12} \cdot (a_{12})) + \\ + f_2 \cdot (a_2 + f_{21} \cdot (a_{21} + f_{211} \cdot (a_{211})) + f_{22} \cdot (a_{22})) + f_3 \cdot (a_3) \end{aligned}$$

The computation of p_0 is then described graphically by blocks

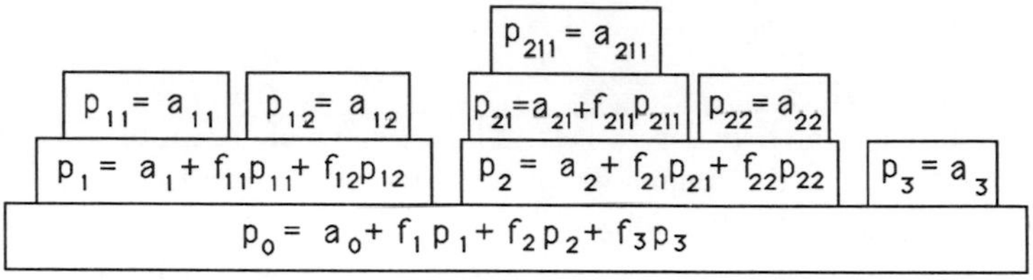

where, similarly to(1.4) a block can be computed only if the blocks supported by it have been previously computed.

Another way to visualize the order of the computations is by trees (see figure 1).

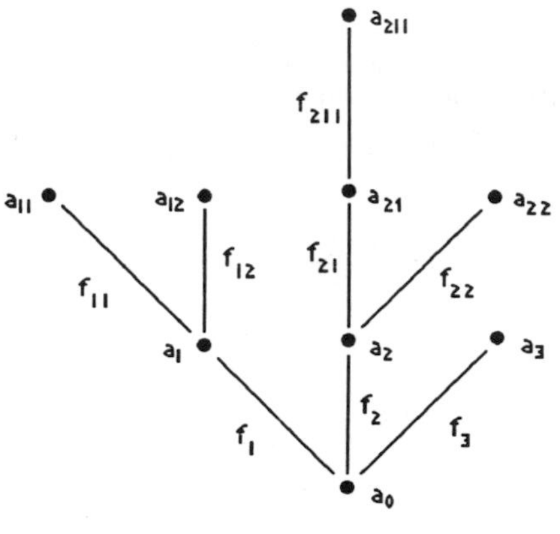

Figure 1

A polynomial of degree 1 is associated to each arc of the tree and a scalar value to each knot (or vertex). See [3] for a more detailed introduction to these types of graphs.

2. Evaluation of derivatives.

Let $\rho^{(j)} = \left(\rho_1^{(j)}, \ldots, \rho_m^{(j)}\right) \in K^m, \quad j = 1, 2, \ldots, n$, be n vectors, not necessarily linearly independent. Denote by

$$(2.1)\qquad D_j p = \frac{\partial p}{\partial x_1}\rho_1^{(j)} + \frac{\partial p}{\partial x_2}\rho_2^{(j)} + \ldots + \frac{\partial p}{\partial x_m}\rho_m^{(j)}$$

the derivative of p in the direction $\rho^{(j)}$, and by $D_j p(u)$ the value of $D_j p$ at $u \in K^m$.

Given any multiindex $t = (t_1, t_2, \ldots, t_n) \in N_0^n$, we write

$$|t| = t_1 + t_2 + \ldots + t_n \tag{2.2}$$

$$D^t = D_1^{t_1} D_2^{t_2} \ldots D_n^{t_n} \tag{2.3}$$

and

$$E^t = \frac{1}{t!} D^t = \frac{1}{t_1! t_2! \ldots t_n!} D_1^{t_1} D_2^{t_2} \ldots D_n^{t_n}. \tag{2.4}$$

By Leibniz's rule [1] for a polynomial p_0 given by (1.1) we have

$$E^t p_0(u) = b_0^t + \sum_{h=1}^{n} f_h(u) \cdot E^t p_h(u) \tag{2.5}$$

with

$$b_0^t = \sum_{h=1}^{n} \left(\sum_{j=1}^{k} D_j f_h \cdot E^{t-e_j} p_h(u) \right) \tag{2.6}$$

where e_j is the j-th canonical vector.

Formula (2.5) suggests a computation similar to that of (1.1) because it has the same structure, with a_0 replaced by b_0^t, which is easily computed from the evaluation of the derivatives of the linear polynomials f_h and the evaluation of derivatives of lower order of the polynomials p_h.

Since p_h is written again in a form similar to (1.1) then $E^t p_h$ can also be described by similar formulae to (2.5) (2.6). In general, the evaluation of a derivative of a polynomial is always reduced to computations which involve simpler polynomials and derivatives of lower order, leading to a recursive process (See [1])

3. Some examples of application: Lagrange representations.

3.1 Lagrange representation of univariate polynomials

The above idea was applied in [1] to two examples one of them being the polynomial

$$p_{00} = \sum_{i=0}^{r} \sum_{j=0}^{m_i} a_{ij} \varphi_0 \ldots \varphi_{i-1} \varphi_{i0} \ldots \varphi_{ij-1} \tag{3.1}$$

with φ_i, φ_{ij} m-variate polynomials of degree 1.

In the bivariate case it could be called the Newton representation of a polynomial (see [2]). However, the univariate Lagrange representation of a polynomial

$$p(x) = \sum_{i=0}^{n} A_i \prod_{\substack{j=0 \\ j \neq i}}^{n} (x - x_j) \tag{3.2}$$

with

$$A_i = \frac{f(x_i)}{\prod_{\substack{j=0 \\ j \neq i}}^{n} (x_i - x_j)} \tag{3.3}$$

is of this type, making the corresponding identifications

$$\begin{aligned} & r = n = m_i \\ & a_{ij} = 0 \qquad \text{if} \quad i + j \neq n \\ & a_{in-i} = A_i \qquad i = 0, 1, \ldots, n \end{aligned} \tag{3.4}$$

Thus (3.2) can be represented by the following tree:

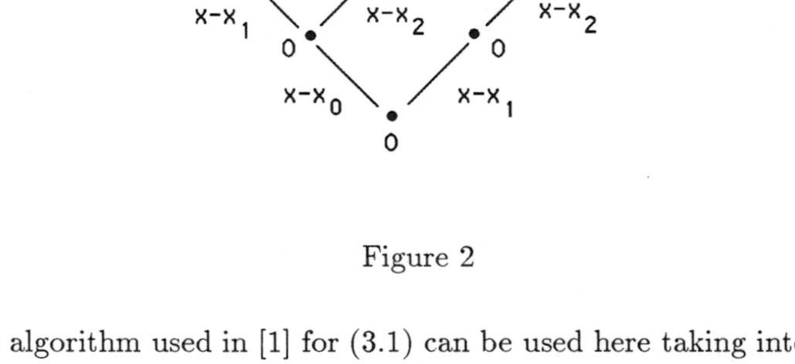

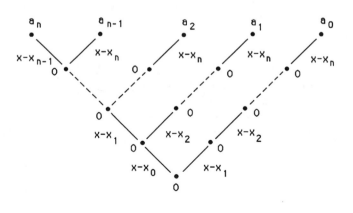

Figure 2

and the same algorithm used in [1] for (3.1) can be used here taking into account (3.4)

Algorithm 3.1.- Evaluation of $D^k p(\xi) = \left.\frac{d^k p}{dx^k}\right|_{x=k}$ for $0 \le k \le t$

```
begin
  for k = 0 to t
    for i = n to 0 step -1
      for j = n - i to 0 step -1
        if k = 0
          if i + j = n
            a_ij^(0) = a_i
          else
            a_ij^(0) = 0
          end if
        else
          if j = 0
            a_i0^(k) = p_i+10^(k)(ξ) + p_i1^(k-1)(ξ)
          else
            a_ij^(k) = p_ij+1^(k-1)(ξ)
          end if
        end if
        if j = 0
          p_i0^(k)(ξ) = a_i0^(k) + (ξ - x_i+1) p_i1^(k)(ξ) + (ξ - x_i) p_i+10^(k)(ξ)
        else
          p_ij^(k)(ξ) = a_ij^(k) + (ξ - x_i+j+1) p_ij+1^(k)(ξ)
        end if
      next j
    next i
  next k
end.
```

3.2 Lagrange representation of bivariate polynomials

To deal with Lagrange representations of bivariate polynomials, it is convenient to begin with polynomials written in the form

$$p = \sum_{i=0}^{m} \sum_{j=0}^{n_i} \sum_{h=0}^{l_{ij}} a_{ijh} \varphi_0 \cdots \varphi_{i-1} \cdot \varphi_{i0} \cdots \varphi_{ij-1} \cdot \varphi_{ij0} \cdots \varphi_{ijh-1} \tag{3.5}$$

Analogously to the algorithm for (3.1) (see [1]) the evaluation of a bidirectional derivative

$$E^{(t,s)} = \frac{1}{t!s!} D_1^t D_2^s \tag{3.6}$$

can be done by the following algorithm, where $p_{000}^{(t,s)}$ denotes $E^{(t,s)} p(\xi, \eta)$

Algorithm 3.2.-

```
begin
  for k = 0 to t + s
    for v = max(0, k - s) to min(k, t)
      w = k - v
      for i = m to 0 step -1
        for j = n_i to 0 step -1
          for h = l_ij to 0 step -1
            if k = 0
              a_ijk^(0,0) = a_ijk
            else
              if h = 0
                if j = 0
                  a_i00^(v,w) = D1 φ_i · p_i+100^(v-1,w)(ξ,η) + D2 φ_i · p_i+100^(v,w-1)(ξ,η)+
                        + D1 φ_i0 · p_i10^(v-1,w)(ξ,η) + D2 φ_i0 · p_i10^(v,w-1)(ξ,η)+
                        + D1 φ_i00 · p_i01^(v-1,w)(ξ,η) + D2 φ_i00 · p_i01^(v,w-1)(ξ,η)
                else
                  a_ij0^(v,w) = D1 φ_ij · p_ij+10^(v-1,w)(ξ,η) + D2 φ_ij · p_ij+10^(v,w-1)(ξ,η)+
                        + D1 φ_ij0 · p_ij1^(v-1,w)(ξ,η) + D2 φ_ij0 · p_ij1^(v,w-1)(ξ,η)
                end if
              else
                a_ijh^(v,w) = D1 φ_ijh · p_ijh+1^(v-1,w)(ξ,η) + D2 φ_ijh · p_ijh+1^(v,w-1)(ξ,η)
              end if
            end if
            if h = 0
              if j = 0
                p_i00^(v,w)(ξ,η) = a_i00^(v,w) + φ_i(ξ,η) · p_i+100^(v,w)(ξ,η)+
                      + φ_i0(ξ,η) · p_i10^(v,w)(ξ,η) + φ_i00(ξ,η) · p_i01^(v,w)(ξ,η)
              else
                p_ij0^(v,w)(ξ,η) = a_ij0^(v,w) + φ_ij(ξ,η) · p_ij+10^(v,w)(ξ,η)+
                      + φ_ij0(ξ,η) · p_ij1^(v,w)(ξ,η)
              end if
            else
              p_ijh^(v,w)(ξ,η) = a_ijh^(v,w) + φ_ijh(ξ,η) · p_ijh+1^(v,w)(ξ,η)
            end if
          next j
        next h
      next i
    nextv
  next k
end.
```

Let us illustrate with an example, how representation (3.5) and Algorithm 3.2 can be useful in order to compute bivariate Lagrange representations.

Consider the interpolation problem where the interpolation points are the intersection of n straight lines in $\mathbb{R}^2$ (see for example [4]) such that:

1) any two of them intersects at exactly one point
2) different pairs of straight lines give different intersection points.

It is a particular case of Chung & Yao "GC condition" and of Gasca-Maeztu "interpolation systems" of order n-2 (see [2]). For the case n=6 we have

$$\{r_0, r_1, r_2, r_3, r_4, r_5\}, \qquad 15 \text{ different points} \quad P_{ij} = r_i \cap r_j \in \mathbb{R}^2$$

$$\text{Lagrange Basis : } \left\{ L_{ij} = \prod_{\substack{k=0 \\ k\neq i,j}}^{5} \frac{r_k(X)}{r_k(P_{ij})} \quad i = 0,1,\ldots,4;\ j > i :\ X = (x,y) \right\}$$

$$p = \sum_{i=0}^{4} \sum_{j=i+1}^{5} a_{ij} \prod_{\substack{k=0 \\ k\neq i,j}}^{5} r_k$$

This form of writing the polynomial can be represented by a tree, as Figure 3 shows

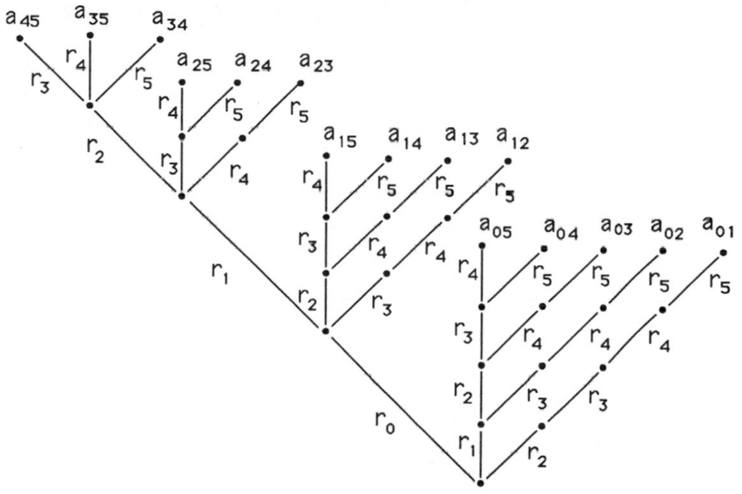

Figure 3

Now we can apply Algorithm 3.2, making the following identifications:

$$m = 4, \quad n_i = 4 - i, \quad l_{ij} = 4 - i - j$$

$$(3.7) \qquad a_{ijh}^{(0,0)} = \begin{cases} a_{ii+j+1} & \text{if } i + j + h = 4 \\ 0 & \text{otherwise} \end{cases}$$

$$\varphi_i = r_i, \quad \varphi_{ij} = r_{i+j+1}, \quad \varphi_{ijh} = r_{i+j+h+2}$$

A second interesting example of the use of the representation (3.5) for bivariate Lagrange formulas are principal lattices (geometric meshes, or different names for other authors). They can be described by 3 sets of equidistant parallel lines: $\{r_{1i}\}, \{r_{2j}\}, \{r_{3k}\}$ $0 \le i, j, k \le n$.

For $n = 4$ the set of intersection pointsm the Lagrange basis and the interpolant can be written respectively

$$P_{ij} = r_{1i} \cap r_{2j} \cap r_{34-i-j} \qquad (i + j \le 4) \tag{3.8}$$

$$L_{ij} = \frac{\prod_{h=0}^{i-1} r_{1h} \prod_{k=0}^{j-1} r_{2k} \prod_{l=0}^{3-i-j} r_{3l}}{\prod_{h=0}^{i-1} r_{1h}(P_{ij}) \prod_{k=0}^{j-1} r_{2k}(P_{ij}) \prod_{l=0}^{3-i-j} r_{3l}(P_{ij})} \qquad (i + j \le 4) \tag{3.9}$$

$$p = \sum_{i=0}^{4} \sum_{i=0}^{4-i} a_{ij} \prod_{h=0}^{i-1} r_{1h} \prod_{k=0}^{j-1} r_{2k} \prod_{l=0}^{3-i-j} r_{3l} \tag{3.10}$$

This polynomial p is associated to a tree isomorphic to the tree shown in Figure 3. So Algorithm 3.2 can be directly applied making the following identification:

$$\begin{aligned} &m = 4, \quad n_i = 4 - i, \quad l_{ij} = 4 - i - j \\ &a_{ijh}^{(0,0)} = \begin{cases} a_{ii+j+1} & \text{if } i + j + h = 4 \\ 0 & \text{otherwise} \end{cases} \\ &\varphi_i = r_{1i}, \quad \varphi_{ij} = r_{2j}, \quad \varphi_{ijh} = r_{3h} \end{aligned} \tag{3.11}$$

REFERENCES

[1] Carnicer, J. M.; Gasca, M. : "Evaluation of multivariate polynomials and their derivatives". To appear in *Mathematics of Computation* January 1990

[2] Gasca, M.; Maeztu, J. I. : "On Lagrange and Hermite interpolation in R^n". *Numerische Mathematik* 39 (1982), 1-14.

[3] Knuth, D.: *The art of computer programming*.Addison-Wesley , 1975.

[4] Micchelli, C. A.: "Algebraic aspects of interpolation.". *Approximation Theory* P.S.A.M. vol 36, C. de Boor editor, Amer. Math. Soc. 1986.

Prof. Dr. M. Gasca, Departamento de Matemática Aplicada, Facultad de Ciencias, 50009 Zaragoza, Spain

Supported by C.I.C.Y.T. Research Grant

International Series of
Numerical Mathematics, Vol. 90

ASYMPTOTICALLY OPTIMAL SAMPLING SCHEMES FOR PERIODIC FUNCTIONS II: THE MULTIVARIATE CASE

Han-lin Chen, Charles K. Chui, and Charles A. Micchelli

1. Introduction

We continue with the theme studied in [2] and examine certain questions pertaining to best methods to recover classes of periodic functions from function evaluations. The main feature that distinguishes this work from [2] is that we are concerned with functions of more than one variable, and this leads us to difficulties not encountered in [2]. We treat periodic function classes similar to those studied in [2], which, because of their greater generality, include those bivariate spaces appearing in [7]. Nevertheless, we follow [7] and [3,4,1] and show how blending interpolation operators yield better error estimates, per function evaluation, than the available tensor product methods. Surprisingly, however, we will also demonstrate that tensor products of equally spaced sampling schemes are optimal in a wide variety of cases. Outstanding unresolved problems remain in determining optimal sampling schemes even for standard spaces of periodic functions. This will be mentioned at the end of the paper.

2. Background

A general setting for the problem we are interested in is a compact Hausdorff space K. On K, we consider the space of continuous functions $C(K)$, and let X be a Banach space contained in $C(K)$ in which convergence on X implies pointwise convergence on K. Also, in X we have a centrally symmetric convex body $\mathcal{F}$, and we wish to compare two quantities which measure the error in estimating $\mathcal{F}$ from n linear observations. The first, which we call the n-th *information* of $\mathcal{F}$ in X, is defined by

$$i_n(F) = \inf_{A,I} \sup_{f \in \mathcal{F}} \|f - A(If)\| \tag{2.1}$$

where the infimum is taken over all mappings A from $\mathbb{R}^n$ into X and all bounded linear mappings I from X into $\mathbb{R}^n$. This quantity represents the intrinsic error in recovering the class $\mathcal{F}$ by n observations. Any linear mapping I_o which achieves the minimum in (2.1) yields n optimal observations for $\mathcal{F}$, and any A_o which together with I_o simultaneously minimizes (2.1) provides an optimal algorithm for recovering F.

We compare $i_n(\mathcal{F})$ to the *n-sampling number*,

$$s_n(\mathcal{T}) := \inf_{\Delta} E(\mathcal{F}, \Delta) \tag{2.2}$$

where $\Delta = \{x^1, \cdots, x^n\}$ is any subset of K consisting of at most n distinct points and

$$E(\mathcal{F}; \Delta) := \inf_{A} \sup_{f \in \mathcal{F}} \|f - A(I^{\Delta} f)\| \tag{2.3}$$

with

$$I^{\Delta} f := (f(x^1), \cdots, f(x^n)).$$

Thus $i_n(\mathcal{F}) \leq s_n(\mathcal{F})$ and our concern is to identify function classes for which

$$\overline{\lim_{n \to \infty}} \frac{s_n(\mathcal{F})}{i_n(\mathcal{F})} < \infty. \tag{2.4}$$

3. Optimal Sampling for Periodic Functions

The function classes $\mathcal{T}$ that we consider have the form

$$\mathcal{F} = \mathcal{F}_{\Phi} := \{\Phi * H : \|H\|_s \leq 1\} \tag{3.1}$$

where $\Phi, H \in \mathcal{L}_s^2$; that is, they are Borel measurable functions on $\mathbb{R}^s$ which are one-periodic in each of their coordinates having finite $L^2(C_s)$ norm

$$\|H\|_s^2 := \int_{C_s} |H(x)|^2 dx \tag{3.2}$$

where $C_s = [0,1]^s$ and $*$ denotes the convolution operation. We also require that Φ which generates the class $\mathcal{F}_{\Phi}$ is continuous.

As an important concrete example of such a function class, we consider for any polynomial p of degree k, the function

$$\Theta(x) := \sum_{\alpha \notin Z_p} \frac{e^{2\pi i \alpha \cdot x}}{p(2\pi i \alpha)} \tag{3.3}$$

where $Z_p := \{\alpha : \alpha \in \mathbb{Z}^s, p(2\pi i \alpha) = 0\}$. This function is continuous and one-periodic, provided that

$$\sum_{\alpha \notin Z_p} |p(2\pi i \alpha)|^{-1} < \infty. \tag{3.4}$$

Moreover, in this case the space $\mathcal{F}_\Theta$ can be described as all $F \in \mathcal{L}_s^2$ such that $p(D)F \in \mathcal{L}_s^2$

$$\widehat{F}(\alpha) := \int_{C_s} F(x)e^{2\pi i\alpha\cdot x}dx = 0, \qquad \alpha \in Z_p. \tag{3.5}$$

This fact follows from the integral identity

$$F(x) = \int_{C_s} \Theta(x-y)(p(D)F)(y)dy, \qquad x \in C_s, \tag{3.6}$$

valid whenever F, $p(D)F \in \mathcal{L}_s^2$ and F satisfies (3.5).

More specifically, when p is a real homogeneous polynomial of degree $k > s$ which vanishes on $\mathbb{R}^s$ only at $x = 0$, there exists a constant $b > 0$ such that

$$\begin{aligned} b\|x\|_2^k &\le |p(2\pi i x)|, \quad x \in \mathbb{R}^s \\ \|x\|_2^2 &:= \sum_{i=1}^s x_i^2. \end{aligned} \tag{3.7}$$

Thus, we have

$$\begin{aligned} \sum_{\alpha\in\mathbb{Z}^s\backslash\{0\}} |p(2\pi i\alpha)|^{-1} &\le b(2\pi)^{-k} \sum_{\alpha\in\mathbb{Z}^s\backslash\{0\}} \|\alpha\|_2^{-k} \\ &\le b(2\pi)^{-k} \sum_{\alpha\in\mathbb{Z}^s\backslash\{0\}} \left(\Pi_{i=1}^s|\alpha_i|^{k/s}\right)^{-1} \\ &= b(2\pi)^{-k}\left(\sum_{j\in\mathbb{Z}\backslash\{0\}} |j|^{-k/s}\right)^s < \infty, \end{aligned}$$

since $\Pi_{j=1}^s|x_j| \le \|x\|^s, x \in \mathbb{R}^s$.

We now consider some simple sets of sampling points in C_s. For any positive integer n we set

$$\delta_n := \left\{\frac{j}{n} : 0 \le j < n\right\}$$

and for $N := (n_1, \cdots, n_s)$ let

$$\Delta_N := \delta_{n_1} \times \cdots \times \delta_{n_s} = \left\{\left(\frac{\alpha_1}{n_1}, \cdots, \frac{\alpha_s}{n_s}\right) : 0 \le \alpha_\ell < n_\ell, \ell = 1, \cdots, s\right\}.$$

When $n_1 = \cdots = n_s = n$ we abbreviate $\Delta(n, \cdots, n)$ as Δ_n. Note that Δ_n contains n^s distinct points; that is, $|\Delta_n| = n^s$.

Our first theorem will give sufficient conditions on Φ so that the set of points Δ_n yields an asymptotically optimal sampling scheme for $\mathcal{F}_\Phi$. For this purpose, the following notion is useful. Let B be a compact convex centrally symmetric body in $\mathbb{R}^s$. Every such B has an associated Minkowski norm, $|\cdot|$, so that $B = \{x : |x| \le 1\}$. We say B is integer-free provided that for every nonnegative integer m, the set $\{x : m < |x| < m+1\}$ is disjoint from $\mathbb{Z}^s$. For instance, the ℓ^1 and ℓ^∞ norms on $\mathbb{R}^s$ have this property.

Theorem 3.1. *Let B be an integer-free compact convex centrally symmetric body in $\mathbb{R}^s$ with corresponding Minkowski norm, $|\cdot|$. Suppose there is a positive increasing function $\psi(t), t \geq 0$, and positive constants L, U, V, such that*

$$|\widehat{\Phi}(\alpha)|^2 \psi(|\alpha|) \leq U, \qquad \alpha \in \mathbb{Z}^s, \tag{3.8}$$

$$0 < L \leq |\widehat{\Phi}(\alpha)|^2 \psi(\|\alpha\|_\infty), \qquad \alpha \in \mathbb{Z}^s, \tag{3.9}$$

$$\|\alpha\|_\infty := \max_{1 \leq j \leq s} |\alpha_j|, \qquad \alpha = (\alpha_1, \ldots, \alpha_s),$$

and

$$\overline{\lim_{k \to \infty}} \left(\psi(k) \sum_{\alpha \in \mathbb{Z}^s \setminus \{0\}} \psi^{-1}(k|\alpha|) \right) = V. \tag{3.10}$$

Then

$$\overline{\lim_{n \to \infty}} \frac{E(\mathcal{F}_\Phi; \Delta_n)}{i_{n^s}(\mathcal{F}_\Phi)} < \infty.$$

Remark 3.1. The case $s = 1$ of this result was proved in [2]. The general case proceeds along similar lines; as some of the concepts and techniques will be used later it is important to elaborate on the details of our general Theorem 3.1.

Essential in the proof is the use of *attenuation operators*, given by

$$(T_{\Lambda,\Phi,N} F)(x) := \sum_{\alpha \in \Lambda} \gamma_\alpha \widehat{F}_N(\alpha) e^{2\pi i \alpha \cdot x}. \tag{3.11}$$

Here, $\widehat{F}_N(\alpha)$ is the *discrete* Fourier transform

$$\widehat{F}_N(\alpha) := \frac{1}{n_1 \cdots n_s} \sum_{x \in \Delta_N} F(x) e^{-2\pi i \alpha \cdot x}, \qquad \alpha \in \mathbb{Z}^s$$

and

$$\gamma_\alpha := |\Phi(\alpha)|^2 \Big/ \sum_{\beta \in G_{N,\alpha}} \left|\widehat{\Phi}(\beta)\right|^2, \qquad \alpha \in \mathbb{Z}^s,$$

where

$$G_{n,\alpha} = \{\beta : \beta \in \mathbb{Z}^s, \beta_i = \alpha_i (\text{mod } n_i), i = 1, \cdots, s\} \tag{3.12}$$

(as consistent with previous notation, $G_{n,\alpha}$ is an abbreviation of $G_{(n,\cdots,n),\alpha}$). Also, the set Λ in (3.11) is any finite subset of $\mathbb{Z}^s$ which will be chosen shortly.

Note that the operator $T_{\Lambda,\Phi,N}$ depends only on the information I^{Δ_N} and so is suitable for bounding $E(\mathcal{F}_\Phi; \Delta_N)$ from above. Specifically, we have

Lemma 3.1. *For any set* $\Lambda \subseteq \mathbb{Z}^s$

$$(E(\mathcal{F}_\Phi;\Delta_N))^2 \le \max_{\alpha\in\Lambda} \sum_{\beta\in G_{N,\alpha}\setminus\{\alpha\}} \left|\widehat{\Phi}(\beta)\right|^2 + \max_{\alpha\notin\Lambda}\left|\widehat{\Phi}(\alpha)\right|^2. \tag{3.13}$$

Proof: Critical in the proof is the fact that for $R = T_{\Lambda,\Phi,N}F$

$$\widehat{R} = \gamma_\alpha \widehat{F}_N(\alpha) = \gamma_\alpha \sum_{\beta\in G_{N,\alpha}} \widehat{F}(\beta), \qquad \alpha\in\mathbb{Z}^s.$$

Hence we get for $F = \Phi * H \in \mathcal{F}_\Phi$

$$\begin{aligned}\|F - T_{\Lambda,\Phi,N}F\|^2 &= \sum_{\alpha\in\Lambda}\left|\widehat{\Phi}(\alpha)\widehat{H}(\alpha) - \gamma_\alpha \sum_{\beta\in G_{N,\alpha}} \widehat{\Phi}(\beta)\widehat{H}(\beta)\right|^2 \\ &\quad + \sum_{\alpha\notin\Lambda}\left|\widehat{\Phi}(\alpha)\widehat{H}(\alpha)\right|^2 \\ &= \sum_{\alpha\in\Lambda}\left|(1-\gamma_\alpha)\widehat{\Phi}(\alpha)\widehat{H}(\alpha) - \gamma_\alpha \sum_{\beta\in G_{N,\alpha}\setminus\{\alpha\}} \widehat{\Phi}(\beta)\widehat{H}(\beta)\right|^2 \\ &\quad + \sum_{\alpha\notin\Lambda}\left|\widehat{\Phi}(\alpha)\widehat{H}(\alpha)\right|^2.\end{aligned}$$

This quantity is bounded above by

$$\begin{aligned}&\max_{\alpha\in\Lambda}\left((1-\gamma_\alpha)^2|\widehat{\Phi}(\alpha)|^2 + \gamma_\alpha^2 \sum_{\beta\in G_{N,\alpha}\setminus\{\alpha\}} \left|\widehat{\Phi}(\beta)\right|^2\right) + \max_{\alpha\notin\Lambda}|\widehat{\Phi}(\alpha)|^2 \\ &= \max_{\alpha\in\Lambda} \frac{|\widehat{\Phi}(\alpha)|^2}{\sum_{\beta\in G_{N,\alpha}}\left|\widehat{\Phi}(\beta)\right|^2} \sum_{\beta\in G_{N,\alpha}\setminus\{\alpha\}} \left|\widehat{\Phi}(\beta)\right|^2 + \max_{\alpha\notin\Lambda}\left|\widehat{\Phi}(\alpha)\right|^2\end{aligned}$$

which proves the lemma.

As it will appear several times later we will denote the right-hand side of inequality (3.13) by $M(\Lambda,\Phi,N)$ with our usual convention that $M(\Lambda,\Phi,(n,\cdots,n))$ will be written as $M(\Lambda,\Phi,n)$.

We use this lemma as follows: Let $B = \{x : |x| \le 1\}$ be an integer-free centrally symmetric convex compact body in $\mathbb{R}^s$ and suppose Φ satifies (3.8) for some positive constant U and increasing function ψ. Then choose $\Lambda = W_n$ where

$$W_n := \left\{\alpha : |\alpha| \le \left\lfloor\frac{n}{2}\right\rfloor\right\}$$

($\lfloor x \rfloor$ is the greatest integer $\leq x$ and $\lceil x \rceil$ is the least integer $\geq x$) and proceed to bound $M(\Lambda, \Phi, n)$ from above.

For every $\alpha \in W_n$ and $\beta = n\gamma + \alpha \in G_{n,\alpha} \backslash \{\alpha\}$ we have $|\gamma| \geq 1$ (since B is integer free) and so

$$\begin{aligned} |\beta| &\geq n|\gamma| - |\alpha| = \left\lceil \frac{n}{2} \right\rceil |\gamma| + \left\lfloor \frac{n}{2} \right\rfloor |\gamma| - |\alpha| \\ &\geq \left\lceil \frac{n}{2} \right\rceil |\gamma| + \left\lfloor \frac{n}{2} \right\rfloor - |\alpha| \geq \left\lceil \frac{n}{2} \right\rceil |\gamma|. \end{aligned}$$

Consequently, using (3.8) we get

$$\max_{\alpha \in W_n} \sum_{\beta \in G_{n,\alpha} \backslash \{\alpha\}} \left| \widehat{\Phi}(\beta) \right|^2 \leq U \sum_{\gamma \in \mathbb{Z}^s \backslash \{0\}} \psi^{-1} \left(\left\lceil \frac{n}{2} \right\rceil |\gamma| \right)$$

and similarly for $\alpha \notin W_n$ we have $|\alpha| \geq \lceil \frac{n}{2} \rceil$ (since B is integer-free) and so again (3.8) gives us

$$\max_{\alpha \notin W_n} \left| \widehat{\Phi}(\alpha) \right| \leq U \psi^{-1} \left(\left\lceil \frac{n}{2} \right\rceil \right)$$

and therefore

$$M(W_n, \Phi, n) \leq U \psi^{-1} \left(\left\lceil \frac{n}{2} \right\rceil \right) \left\{ \psi \left(\left\lceil \frac{n}{2} \right\rceil \right) \sum_{\gamma \in \mathbb{Z}^s \backslash \{0\}} \psi^{-1} \left(\left\lceil \frac{n}{2} \right\rceil |\gamma| \right) + 1 \right\}. \tag{3.14}$$

On the other hand, it can be proved just as in [2] for the case $s = 1$ that for any Δ with $|\Delta| > n$,

$$i_n(\mathcal{F}_\Phi) \geq \min_{\alpha \in \Lambda} \left| \widehat{\Phi}(\alpha) \right|. \tag{3.15}$$

Our choice for Λ in (3.15) for the case at hand is $\Lambda_1 := \{\alpha : \|\alpha\|_\infty \leq \lceil \frac{n}{2} \rceil\}$. Since $|\Lambda_1| > n^s$, we obtain by (3.9) the inequality

$$\begin{aligned} i_{n^s}(\mathcal{F}_\Phi) &\geq L \min_{\alpha \in \Lambda_1} \psi^{-1} \left(\|\alpha\|_\infty \right) \\ &= L \psi^{-1} \left(\left\lceil \frac{n}{2} \right\rceil \right). \end{aligned} \tag{3.16}$$

Combining inequalities (3.14) and (3.16) with Lemma 3.1 proves

$$\overline{\lim_{n \to \infty}} \frac{E(\mathcal{F}_\Phi, \Delta_n)}{i_{n^s}(\mathcal{F})} \leq \left[\frac{U}{L}(V+1) \right]^{\frac{1}{2}} < \infty.$$

Thus we have established Theorem 3.1.

There is a wide class of functions Φ which satisfy the hypothesis of Theorem 3.1. We will not dwell upon this point here. For some information pertaining to this issue see [2]. However, let us point out that the function Θ, defined by (3.3), satisfies the hypothesis of Theorem 3.1 when p is a real homogeneous polynomial of degree $k > \frac{s}{2}$ which vanishes on $\mathbb{R}^s$ only at $x = 0$. To see this, if we choose $|x| := \|x\|_\infty$ and $\psi(t) := t^{2k}$, then clearly (3.8) and (3.9) are satisfied. As for (3.10), we only have to recall that

$$\sum_{\alpha \in \mathbb{Z}^s} \|\alpha\|_\infty^{-2k} \leq s^{-k} \sum_{\alpha \in \mathbb{Z}^s} \|\alpha\|_2^{-2k} < \infty$$

for $2k > s$ has already been verified.

For later use, we note another consequence resulting from the proof of Theorem 3.1 which we will use later. We let $\mathcal{D}_q$ where $q > s/2$ be the class of all continuous functions in $\mathcal{L}_s^2$ such that

$$\sup\left\{|\widehat{\Phi}(\alpha)|\ \|\alpha\|_\infty^q : \alpha \in \mathbb{Z}^s\right\} < \infty.$$

Every $\Phi \in \mathcal{D}_q$ satisfies (3.8) for the $\psi(t) = t^q$ and for that choice (3.10) is valid. Hence for the attenuation operators (mapping $\mathcal{L}_s^2$ into $\mathcal{L}_s^2$)

$$T_{n,\Phi} := T_{W_n,\Phi,n} \tag{3.17}$$

and the error operator

$$E_{n,\Phi} f := f - T_{n,\Phi}, \tag{3.18}$$

there exists a constant b depending on s and Φ, but not n, such that

$$\|E_{n,\Phi}\| \leq b n^{-q}, \qquad \Phi \in \mathcal{D}_q. \tag{3.19}$$

Here $\|\cdot\|$ is the operator norm induced by $\mathcal{L}_s^2$.

4. Sampling Schemes Based on Blending

In this section we will exclusively be concerned with the case that Φ is a tensor product of univariate one-periodic functions. Thus we require that Φ has the form

$$\Phi(x_1, \cdots, x_s) = \phi_1(x_1) \cdots \phi_s(x_s), \qquad x = (x_1, \cdots, x_s) \tag{4.1}$$

where each ϕ_ℓ is a continuous one-periodic function. Note that in this case $\mathcal{F}_\Phi$ can be identified with the closure in $\mathcal{L}_s^2$ of $\otimes_{k=1}^s \mathcal{F}_{\phi_k} = \mathcal{F}_{\phi_1} \otimes \cdots \otimes \mathcal{F}_{\phi_s}$.

We begin with this situation by noting certain necessary conditions on a sequence of sampling schemes $\Gamma^n = \{x^{n,1}, \cdots, x^{n,n}\} \subseteq C_s, |\Gamma^n| = n$, to be asymptotically optimal in the sense that

$$\overline{\lim_{n\to\infty}} \frac{E(\mathcal{F}_\Phi; \Gamma^n)}{i_n(\mathcal{T}_\Phi)} < \infty,$$

for Φ of the form (4.1). This will allow us to highlight the problem of applying Theorem 3.1 in the case of tensor product functions Φ.

For this purpose, we introduce for any given sampling scheme $\Gamma = \{x^1, \cdots, x^n\}$ the univariate projected schemes

$$\mathrm{proj}_\ell \Gamma := \{x_\ell^1, \cdots, x_\ell^n\}, \qquad \ell = 1, \cdots, s.$$

Theorem 4.1. *Suppose $\phi_1, \cdots, \phi_s$ are nontrivial one-periodic continuous functions on $[0,1]$. Then there exists a positive constant μ_Φ, depending only on $\Phi = \otimes_{\ell=1}^s \phi_\ell$ such that*

$$E(\mathcal{F}_\Phi; \Gamma) \geq \mu_\Phi \max_{1\leq \ell \leq s} E(\mathcal{F}_{\phi_\ell}; \mathrm{proj}_\ell \Gamma).$$

Proof: Choose $\alpha = (\alpha_1, \cdots, \alpha_s) \in \mathbb{Z}^s$ such that $\widehat{\Phi}(\alpha) \neq 0$ and set

$$\mu_\Phi := \min_{1\leq \ell\leq s} \left| \Pi_{j\neq \ell} \widehat{\phi}_j(\alpha_j) \right|.$$

For any ℓ, and any $f_\ell \in \mathcal{F}_{\phi_\ell}, f_\ell = \phi_\ell * h_\ell$, where $h_\ell \in \mathcal{L}_1^2, \|h_\ell\|_1 = 1$, we define $F^* = \Phi * H$ where

$$H(x) := h_\ell(x_\ell) \prod_{j\neq \ell} e^{2\pi i x_j \alpha_j}, \qquad x = (x_1, \cdots, x_s).$$

Thus,

$$F^*(x_1, \cdots, x_s) = f_\ell(x_\ell) \prod_{j\neq\ell} \widehat{\phi}_j(\alpha_j) \prod_{j\neq\ell} e^{2\pi i x_j \alpha_j}$$

and so $\|F^*\|_s \geq \mu_\Phi \|f_\ell\|_1$. Moreover, whenever $f_\ell(x_\ell^r) = 0, r = 1, \cdots, n$ we have $F^*(x^r) = 0, r = 1 \cdots, n$. Using the fact that

$$\text{(4.2)} \qquad E(\mathcal{F}_\Phi; \Gamma) = \max\{\|F\|_s : F \in \mathcal{F}_\Phi, F(x^r) = 0, r = 1, \cdots, n\}$$

(see [6]), we get for any $f_\ell \in \mathcal{F}_{\phi_\ell},\ f_\ell(x_\ell^r) = 0,\ r = 1, \cdots, n,$

$$E(\mathcal{F}_\Phi; \Gamma) \geq \|F^*\|_s \geq \mu_\phi \|f_\ell\|_1$$

and so the result follows again by appealing to (4.2), when $s = 1$.

As an upper bound we have the following

Theroem 4.2. *Let $\Gamma_1, \cdots, \Gamma_s$ be any finite subsets of $[0,1]$ and $\phi_1, \cdots \phi_s$ continuous one-periodic functions. Then there exists a constant ν_Φ depending only on $\Phi = \otimes_{\ell=1}^s \phi_\ell$ such that for $N = (n_1, \cdots, n_s) \in \mathbb{N}^s$*

$$(E(\mathcal{F}_\Phi; \Delta_N))^2 \le \nu_\Phi \sum_{\ell=1}^{s} M(\Gamma_\ell, \phi_\ell, n_\ell). \tag{4.3}$$

Proof: For the proof, we use Lemma 3.1, which states that for *any* finite set $\Gamma \subseteq C_s$

$$E^2(\mathcal{F}_\Phi; \Delta_N) \le \max_{\alpha \in \Gamma} \sum_{\beta \in G_{N,\alpha} \setminus \{\alpha\}} \left|\widehat{\Phi}(\beta)\right|^2 + \max_{\alpha \notin \Gamma} \left|\widehat{\Phi}(\alpha)\right|^2. \tag{4.4}$$

Choosing $\Gamma = \Gamma_1 \times \cdots \times \Gamma_s$ in (4.4) above, we get

$$\begin{aligned} \max_{\alpha \in \Gamma} \sum_{\beta \in G_{N,\alpha} \setminus \{\alpha\}} \left|\widehat{\Phi}(\beta)\right|^2 &= \prod_{\ell=1}^{s} \max_{k \in \Gamma_\ell} \sum_{j \neq 0} \left|\widehat{\phi}_\ell(n_\ell j + k)\right|^2 \\ &\le \max_{1 \le \ell \le s} \|\phi_\ell\|_1^{2s-2} \sum_{\ell=1}^{s} \max_{k \in \Gamma_\ell} \sum_{j \neq 0} \left|\widehat{\phi}_\ell(n_\ell j + k)\right|^2 \end{aligned}$$

and also

$$\begin{aligned} \max_{\alpha \notin \Gamma} \left|\widehat{\Phi}(\alpha)\right|^2 &\le \sum_{\ell=1}^{s} \|\phi_\ell\|_1^{2s-2} \max_{k \notin \Gamma_\ell} \left|\widehat{\phi}_\ell(k)\right|^2 \\ &\le \max_{1 \le \ell \le s} \|\phi_\ell\|_1^{2s-2} \sum_{\ell=1}^{s} \max_{k \notin \Gamma_\ell} \left|\widehat{\phi}_\ell(k)\right|^2. \end{aligned}$$

Thus the choice $\nu_\Phi := \max_{1 \le \ell \le s} \|\phi_\ell\|_1^{2s-2}$ proves the result.

To give an idea about the consequence of these results we will apply them to the class $\mathcal{F}_\Phi$ corresponding to the periodic function

$$\Phi := \Omega_q = w_{q_1} \otimes \cdots \otimes w_{q_s}, \qquad Q = (q_1, \cdots, q_s) \in \mathbb{N}^s, \qquad q_i \ge 2.$$

where

$$w_q(t) := \sum_{k \neq 0} \frac{e^{2\pi i k t}}{(2\pi i k)^q}, \qquad q = 1, \cdots, s.$$

First, we note the following

Proposition 4.1. *There exists positive constants $\underline{c}$ and $\overline{c}$ such that for all n and $\Omega_q := \Omega(q, \cdots, q)$, $\underline{c} n^{-q} \le E(\mathcal{F}_{\Omega_q}, \Delta_n) \le \overline{c} n^{-q}$.*

Remark 4.1. Note the fact that the asymptotic decay of the sampling points Δ_n is *independent* of the spatial dimension even though the number of points of Δ_n grows with s as n^s. Thus Proposition 4.1 implies that

$$E(\mathcal{F}_{\Delta_q}; \Delta_n) \sim c \Delta_n^{q/s}$$

for some constant depending on s and q but not n. Theorem 3.1 specialized to $\phi = w_d$, for $s = 1$, shows Δ_n is asymptotically optimal. However, as it turns out this fails for $s \geq 2$.

Proof: For the upper bound we use Theorem 4.2 and the fact already pointed out in the derivation of (3.20) that (3.14) gives $O(n^{-2q})$ as an upper bound for $M(W_n, \Phi, n)$. Hence choosing $\Gamma_1 = \cdots = \Gamma_s = W_n$ proves the upper bound. For the lower bound we can proceed in a few ways. For instance, the lower bound follows from the fact that for $s = 1, i_n(\mathcal{F}_{w_q}) = O(n^{-q})$, see Lemma 4.1 below or the proof of Theorem 4.1 (when $s = 1$). Alternatively, we can bound $E(\mathcal{F}_{w_q}, \mathcal{S}_n)$ (observe $\text{proj}_\ell \Delta_n = \delta_n, \ell = 1, \cdots, s$) from below as follows: the function $f(x) = n^{-q} \sin \pi n x$ vanishes on δ_n and moreover can be expressed as $f = w_q * h$ for some $h \in \mathcal{L}_1^2$, independent of n. Thus

$$E\left(\mathcal{F}_{w_q}; \delta_n\right) \geq \|f\|_1 \Big/ \|h\|_1 = n^{-q} \Big/ \|h\|_1^h$$

and the lower bound follows from Theorem 4.1.

Before we discuss how to obtain better sampling schemes we will first point out

Lemma 4.1. *There exists positive constants $\underline{c}, \overline{c}$ such that for all n*

$$\underline{c}\left(\frac{(\ln n)^{s-1}}{n}\right)^q \leq i_n\left(\mathcal{F}_{\Omega_q}\right) \leq \overline{c}\left(\frac{(\ln n)^{s-1}}{n}\right)^q.$$

Proof: In general, it can be shown just as in [2] for the case $s = 1$ that

$$i_n\left(\mathcal{F}_\Phi\right) = \max_{|\Lambda| = n+1} \min_{\alpha \in \Lambda} \left|\widehat{\Phi}(\alpha)\right| = \tau_n$$

where $\tau_0 \geq \tau_1 \geq \cdots$ is the decreasing rearrangement of the sequence

$$\left\{\left|\widehat{\Phi}(\alpha)\right| : \alpha \in \mathbb{Z}^s\right\}.$$

In our case we have

$$i_n\left(\mathcal{F}_{\Omega_q}\right) = \mu_n^q$$

where $\mu_0 \leq \mu_1 \leq \cdots$ is the increasing rearrangement of the sequence

$$\left\{(2\pi)^{qs} |\alpha_1| \cdots |\alpha_s| : \alpha = (\alpha_1, \cdots, \alpha_s) \in \mathbb{Z}^s\right\}.$$

It is known that

$$\mu_n^{-1} \sim \frac{(\log n)^{s-1}}{n}, \qquad n \to \infty,$$

(cf. [5] for even more general results of this type).

As a corollary we obtain the following necessary condition for a sequence of sampling schemes to be optimal for Ω_q.

Proposition 4.2. *Let Γ^n be any sequence of points in C_s such that $|\Gamma^n| \to \infty$ as $n \to \infty$ and*

$$\overline{\lim_{n\to\infty}} \frac{E\left(\mathcal{F}_{\Omega_q};\Gamma^n\right)}{i_{|\Gamma^n|}\left(\mathcal{F}_{\Omega_q}\right)} < \infty. \tag{4.5}$$

Then for every $\ell, 1 \le \ell \le s$,

$$\underline{\lim_{n\to\infty}} |\mathrm{proj}_\ell \Gamma^n| \frac{(\ln|\Gamma^n|)^{s-1}}{|\Gamma^n|} > 0. \tag{4.6}$$

Proof: Using our hypothesis (4.5) and Lemma 4.1 we conclude that there is a positive constant $\underline{c} > 0$ such that for n sufficiently large

$$E\left(\mathcal{F}_{\Omega_q};\Gamma^n\right) \le \underline{c}\left(\frac{\ln|\Gamma^n|^{s-1}}{|\Gamma^n|}\right)^q.$$

Appealing to Theorem 4.1 and Lemma 4.1 (for $s = 1$) we get for each $\ell, 1 \le \ell \le s$, a positive constant $c_\ell > 0$ such that for n sufficiently large

$$\left(\frac{1}{|\mathrm{proj}_\ell \Gamma^n|}\right)^q \le c_\ell \left(\frac{\ln|\Gamma^n|^{s-1}}{|\Gamma^n|}\right)^q$$

which proves the proposition.

Remark 4.2. Observe that Proposition 4.1 shows that $\Gamma^n = \Delta_n$ is far from being asymptotically optimal, since $|\Delta_n| = n^s$ and $|\mathrm{proj}_\ell \Delta_n| = n$; hence, (4.6) is obviously false for $s \ge 2$.

The next theorem improves upon this result. Let $\phi_1, \cdots, \phi_s$ be continuous one-periodic functions in $\mathcal{D}_q$. Then we have

Theorem 4.3. *For every integer ℓ there exists a constant a depending only on ℓ and s such that there exists a set of sampling points Δ_n^ℓ, $|\Delta_n^\ell| \to \infty$ as $n \to \infty$, in C_s satisfying*

$$E(\mathcal{F}_\Phi;\Delta_n^\ell) \le a|\Delta_n^\ell|^{-\left(\frac{\ell+1}{\ell+s}\right)q}, \qquad \Phi = \otimes_{i=1}^s \phi_i.$$

The proof of this theorem uses blending function methods. First we appeal to a fact from [6] which states that for any set $\Delta = \{x_1, \cdots, x_r\} \subseteq [0,1]$, there is linear operator T_Δ such that $(T_\Delta f)(x_j) = f(x_j)$, $1 \le j \le r$, and

$$\|E_\Delta f\|_1 := \max_{f\in\mathcal{F}_\Phi} \|E_\Delta f\|_1 = E(\mathcal{F}_\Phi;\Delta)$$
$$E_\Delta f := f - T_\Delta f.$$

$T_\Delta f$ is constructed as $\phi * Qh$ where $f = \phi * h$ and Q is the orthogonal projection of $\mathcal{L}_1^2$ onto the range of the information operator $I^\Delta(\phi * h)$.

Because T_Δ is constructed as a minimal norm interpolant, it follows directly that $T_{\Delta_1}T_{\Delta_2} = T_{\Delta_2}$, where $\Delta_2 \subset \Delta_1$. Each T_Δ can be extended parametrically to s variables for each $1 \le \ell \le s$ and integer $k \ge 1$ by its action on the ℓ-th variable only. We let $T_{\ell,k}$ be the parametric extension of T_Δ for

$$\Delta = \left\{ \frac{j}{n^k} : 0 \le j < n^k \right\}.$$

This family of operators have for each $\ell, 1 \le \ell \le n$, the following properties:

$$\|E_{\ell,k}\|_s := \max_{F \in \mathcal{F}_\Phi} \|E_{\ell,k}F\|_s = O(n^{-kq}).$$

This follows because the attenuation operator gives such a convergence rate. (Here, we replace n by n^k in (3.20).) The commutativity relation

$$T_{\ell,r}T_{m,r} = T_{m,r}T_{\ell,r} \tag{4.7}$$

follows because the operators are parametrically defined as acting on separate variables. Also,

$$T_{\ell,k}T_{\ell,r} = T_{\ell,r}\ , \qquad \text{if } r \le k. \tag{4.8}$$

This property is a consequence of the minimal norm construction of operators as has already been pointed out. In algebraic language, for each $\ell, 1 \le \ell \le k$, the operators $\{T_{\ell,k} : k = 1, 2, \cdots\}$ form a chain in the sense of [3]. Next we introduce the *Tensor-product operators*:

$$T_\alpha := T_{1,\alpha_1} \cdots, T_{s,\alpha_s}, \quad \alpha = (\alpha_1, \cdots \alpha_s) \in \mathbb{Z}^s, \quad \alpha_i \ge 1, \quad i = 1, \cdots s.$$

Then $T_\alpha F$ depends on the values of F on the set

$$\Delta^\alpha = \left\{ \left(\frac{j_1}{n^{\alpha_1}}, \cdots, \frac{j_s}{n^{\alpha_s}} \right) : 0 \le j_r < n^{\alpha_r}, r = 1, \cdots, s \right\}.$$

We now define for every $\ell \ge 0$ the operator

$$Q_\ell := \oplus_{|\alpha| = \ell + s} T_\alpha, \qquad |\alpha| = \alpha_1 + \cdots + \alpha_s. \tag{4.9}$$

Here $P \oplus Q$ denotes the Boolean sum of the operators P and Q defined by

$$P \oplus Q = P + Q - PQ. \tag{4.10}$$

The first observation is that $Q_\ell F$ depends only on F on the set

$$\Delta_n^\ell := \bigcup_{|\alpha|=\ell+s} \Delta_\alpha.$$

To see this we appeal to Lemma 2 of [3] which states that

$$Q_\ell = \sum_{j=0}^{s-1} (-1)^j \binom{s-1}{j} \sum_{|\alpha|=\ell+s-j} T_\alpha. \tag{4.11}$$

Clearly,

$$\begin{aligned} |\Delta_n^\ell| \le \sum_{|\alpha|=\ell+s} |\Delta_\alpha| &= n^{\ell+s} \sum_{|\alpha|=\ell+s} 1 \\ &= \binom{\ell+s-1}{s-1} n^{\ell+s}. \end{aligned}$$

To complete the proof we use another formula from the theory of Boolean sums: For this purpose we use P^c for the error operator $P^c F = F - PF$. Then according to [1] we have

$$Q_\ell^c := \sum_{j=1}^{s} \sum_{k=j}^{s} (-1)^{j-1} \binom{k-1}{j-1} \sum_{1 \le \gamma_1 < \cdots < \gamma_k \le s} \sum_{\substack{i_{\nu_1}+\cdots+i_{\nu_k}=\ell+j \\ i_{\nu_1} \ge 1, \ldots, i_{\nu_k} \ge 1}} T^c_{\nu_1, i_{\nu_1}} \cdots T^c_{\nu_k, i_{\nu_k}}. \tag{4.12}$$

Since $\|E_{\nu_1,i_{\nu_1}} \cdots E_{\nu_k,i_{\nu_k}}\| = O(n^{-\ell-j})$, if $i_{\nu_1} + \cdots + i_{\nu_k} = \ell + j$, we see by (4.6) the biggest error term (asymptotically in n) obtained from (4.12) occurs when $j = 1$, so that

$$\|Q_\ell^c\|_s = O\left(n^{-\ell-1}\right),$$

and this completes the proof of the theorem.

We remark that in Theorem 4.3 we have not made a point to determine the dependence of the constant on the integer ℓ. Clearly, the exponent of decay in the estimate given in Theorem 4.3 improves with ℓ. However, it still remains an open problem to determine optimal sampling schemes for $\mathcal{F}_\Phi$ under the conditions of Theorem 4.3. Even in one dimension, optimal sampling schemes have not been found for $\mathcal{F}_\Phi$ in general.

Acknowledgement: We wish to thank G. Baszenski and F. J. Delvos for helpful conversations concerning the interesting formulas (4.11), (4.12), their proof of those formulas, as well as the reference [1]. The research of this work was supported by NSF under Grant No. INT-8712424.

References

1. G. Baszenski and F. J. Delvos, Boolean methods in Fourier approximation, in *Topics in Multivariate Approximation*, C. K. Chui, L. L. Schumaker, and F. Utreras (eds.), Academic Press, N.Y., 1989.
2. W. Dahmen, C. A. Micchelli, and P. W. Smith, Asymptotically optimal sampling schemes for periodic functions, Math. Proc. Camb. Phil. Soc., **99** (1986), 171-177.
3. F. J. Delvos, d-Variate Boolean interpolation, J. Approx Theory, **34** (1982), 99-114.
4. F. J. Delvos and H. Posdorf, N^{th} order blending, in *Constructive Theory of Functions of Several Variables*, W. Schempp and K. Zeller (eds.), Springer Verlag, Heidelberg, 1976.
5. Dinh Dung, Number of integral points in a certain set and the approximation of functions of several variables, Math. Notes, **36** (1984), 736-744.
6. C. A. Micchelli and T. J. Rivlin, A survey of optimal recovery, in *Optimal Estimation in Approximation Theory*, C. A. Micchelli and T. J. Rivlin (eds.), Plenum Press, 1976.
7. G. Wahba, Interpolating surfaces: High order convergence rates and their associated designs, with application to X-ray image reconstruction, Report #523, Univ. of Wisconsin Stat., Madison, 1978.

Han-lin Chen, Institute of Mathematics, Academia Sinica, Beijing, P.R.C.

Charles K. Chui, Department of Mathematics, Texas A&M University, College Station, TX, 77843, USA.

Charles A. Micchelli, IBM T. J. Watson Research Center, Yorktown Heights, NY 10598

International Series of
Numerical Mathematics, Vol. 90

GENERALIZED BOCHNER-RIESZ MEANS OF FOURIER INTEGRALS

Tianping Chen
Department of Mathematics
Fudan University, Shanghai, P.R.China

In this paper, almost everywhere approximation order to a function in Bessel Potential space by generalized Bochner-Riesz means is given.

Suppose $f(x)\ L^2(R^n)$, $\hat{f}$ is it's Fourier Transform, generalized Bochner-Riesz Means is defined as

$$B_R^{a,b}(f)(x)=\int_{R^n}\hat{f}(u)(1-R^{-b}|u^b|)_+^a e^{iux}du.$$

We say $f\in B^r(r>0)$, the Bessel Potential Space of order r, if both $\hat{f}$ and $|x|^r\hat{f}(x)$ belong to $L^2(R^n)$.

The main result of this paper is

Theorem. If $f(x)\in B^r$, and $a>0$, then

$$B_R^{a,b}(f)(x)-f(x)=o(R^{-r}),\ \text{if } b>r,$$

$$B_R^{a,b}(f)(x)-f(x)=O(R^{-r}),\ \text{if } b\geq r$$

hold almost everywhere in R^n.

The proof of the theorem is very complicated, and we divide it into several lemmas.

Lemma 1. If $a>\frac{n-1}{2}+r$, then

$$B_R^{a,2}(f)(x)-f(x)=o(R^{-r}), \text{ a.e., } 0<r<2.$$

Proof. If $f\in B^r$, $0<r<2$, then for almost every $x\in R^n$, the limit

$$\lim_{t\to 0}\int_{|y|>t}\frac{f(x-y)-f(x)}{|y|^{n+r}}\,dy \tag{1}$$

exists, and so

$$\int_{|u|<t}[f(x-u)-f(x)]\,du=o(t^{n+r}), \quad \text{a.e.} \tag{2}$$

By the Bochner's formula

$$B_R^{a,2}(f)(x)-f(x)=\int_{R^n}[f(x-y)-f(x)]\,B_R^a(y)\,dy$$

where

$$B_R^a(y)=\frac{2^a\,(a+1)\,J_{n/2+a}(R|y|)}{(2\pi)^{n/2}(R|y|)^{n/2+a}}R^n$$

and J is Bessel function.

Integrating by parts, using (2) and asymptotic behavior of Bessel function near zero and infinity, we reach the conclussion.

Lemma 2. If $f\in B^r$, define

$$G_r^{a,b}(f)(x)=\left(\int_0^\infty |B_R^{a,b}(f)(x)-B_R^{a+1,b}(f)(x)|^2R^{2r-1}dR\right)^{1/2}$$

then

$$\|G_r^{a,2}(f)(x)\|_{L^2(R^n)}\le C\|f^r\|_{L^2(R^n)},$$

if $b>r, a>-1/2$.

Proof. Parseval Equality and change of integration order lead to the Lemma.

Direct calculation shows

$$B_R^{(a+c),b}(f)(x)=CR^{-b(a+c)}\int_0^R(R^b-t^b)^{c-1}t^{b(a+1)-1}B_t^{a,b}(t)\,dt.$$

Lemma 3. If $f\in B^r$, define

$$N^{a,b}(f)(x)=\sup_{R>0}\left|B_R^{a,b}(f)(x)-B_R^{a+1,b}(f)(x)\right|R^r$$

then

$$\|N^{a,b}(f)(x)\|_{L^2(R^n)}\leqslant C\left\|f^r\right\|_{L^2(R^n)}$$

if $b>2r$, $a>0$.

Proof. Writing $a=c+d$, where $c>-1/2$ and $d>1/2$, then

$$B_R^{a,b}(f)(x)-B_R^{a+1,b}(f)(x)=B_R^{c+d,b}(f)(x)-B_R^{c+d+1,b}(f)(x)$$
$$=R^{-b(c+d)}\int_0^R(R^b-t^b)^{d-1}t^{b(c+1)-1}\left[B_t^{c,b}(f)(x)-B_t^{c+1,b}(f)(x)\right]dt,$$

by Schwartz Inequality, we have

$$\left|B_R^{a,b}(f)(x)-B_R^{a+1,b}(f)(x)\right|\leqslant C(\ (R^b-t^b)^{2(d-1)}t^{2b(c+1)-2r-1}dt)^{1/2}$$
$$(\int_0^R\left|t^{2r-1}\ B_t^{c,b}(f)(x)-B_t^{c+1,b}(f)(x)\right|^2dt)^{1/2}R^{-b(c+d)}\leqslant CR^{-r}G_R^{a,b}(x).$$

Combining Lemma 2 gives Lemma 3.

Lemma 4. If $f\in B^r$ and $b>2r$, $a>0$, then

$$B_R^{a,b}(f)(x)-B_R^{a+1,b}(f)(x)=o(R^{-r})$$

holds almost everywhere.

Summing up previous Lemmas, we have

Theorem 1. If $f(x)\in B^r$, $0<r<1$, and $a>0$, then

$$B_R^{a,2}(f)(x)-f(x)=o(R^{-r}).$$

Now, We shall fill up the gap $1<r\leqslant 2$, and extend the result to the general case $b>0$.

Lemma 5. If $f\in B^r$, and $b,c>r$, then

$$B_R^{1,b}(f)(x)-f(x)=o(R^{-r})$$

iff

$$B_R^{1,c}(f)(x)-f(x)=o(R^{-r}).$$

Lemma 6. If $f\in B^r$, $r<b/2$, $0<b<2$, then

$$B_R^{a,b}(f)(x)-f(x)=o(R^{-r}) \qquad \text{if } a>0.$$

Proff. Theorem 1 shows

$$B_R^{1,2}(f)(x)-f(x)=o(R^{-r}), \qquad \text{a.e.}$$

by Lemma 5,
$$B_R^{1,b}(f)(x)-f(x)=o(R^{-r}) \qquad \text{a.e.}$$

by theorem of consistency for Riesz Means (see [2]), we have

$$B_R^{1+a}(f)(x)-f(x)=o(R^{-r})$$

and by Lemma 4, we have

$$B_R^{a,b}(f)(x)-f(x)=o(R^{-r}) \qquad \text{a.e..}$$

We need more facts on Riesz Means.

If g(x) is integrable, define

$$S_R^{a,b}(g)=\int_{|u|<R} g(u)(1-|uR^{-1}|^b)^a du$$

$$S_R^{a,b}(g^b)=\int_{|u|<R} |u|^b g(u)(1-|uR^{-1}|)^a du$$

then
$$\frac{1}{a+1}S_R^{a,b}(g^b)=\frac{R^b}{a+1}S_R^{a,b}(g)-bR^{-ab}\int_0^R t^{b(1+a)-1}S_t^{a,b}(g)dt,$$

$$S_R^{a,b}(g)=R^{-b}S_R^{a,b}(g^b)+(1+a)\int_0^R t^{-(b+1)}S_t^{a,b}(g^b)dt.$$

From these equalities, it is easy to prove

Theorem 2. There is a real number u, such that

$$S_R^{a,b}(g)-u=\begin{cases} o(R^{-r}) & 0<r<b \\ O(R^{-r}) & 0<r\leq b \end{cases}$$

iff

$$S_R^{a,b}(g^b)=\begin{cases} o(R^{b-r}) & 0<r<b \\ O(R^{b-r}) & 0<r\leq b; \end{cases}$$

$$B_R^{a,b}(f)(x)-f(x)=o(R^{-r}) \text{ a.e., if } r<b,$$

$$B_R^{a,b}(f)(x)-f(x)=-R^{-b}af_b(x)+o(R^{-b}) \text{ a.e., if } r=b.$$

Proof. In case of $b=2$, the proof has been given above. As for $0<b<2$, the proof is similar.

Theorem 4. Suppose $f\in B^r$, $2<b\leq 4$, $a>0$, then the Main Theorem is true.

Proof. We only prove the Theorem for $b=4$, and the proof is similar for $2<b<4$.

If $0<r<2$, then

$$B_R^{1,2}(f)(x)-f(x)=o(R^{-r}) \text{ a.e. (Theorem 3)},$$

Combining with Theorem 2, we have

$$B_R^{1,4}(f)(x)-f(x)=o(R^{-r}) \text{ a.e..}$$

By consistency theorem for Riesz Means,

$$B_R^{1+a}(f)(x)-f(x)=o(R^{-r}) \text{ a.e.,}$$

and using Lemma 4,

$$B_R^{a}(f)(x)-f(x)=o(R^{-r}) \text{ a.e.}$$

if $a>0$.

What remains is the case $2\leq r$. If $r\geq 2$, then $f_2\in B^{r-2}$, and

$$B_R^{1,2}(f_2)(x)-f(x)=o(R^{-r+2}) \text{ a.e.}$$

Using Theorem 2, we have

$$f(x)-B_R^{1,2}(f)(x)=R^{-2}f_2(x)+o(R^{-r}).\text{a.e.}$$

Direct calculation shows

$$B_R^{1,4}(f)(x)=B_R^{1,2}(f)(x)+R^{-2}B_R^{1,2}(f_2)(x)$$

If $S_R^{a,b}(g^b)-s=o(R^{-r})$, $0<r<b$, then there exists u, such that

$$u-S_R^{a,b}(g)=asR^{-b}+o(R^{-r-b}).$$

Now, we assume $1<r<3/2$, then $0<r-1<1/2$. Define $\hat{f}_d=|x|^d\hat{f}(x)$. By previous results, we have

$$S_R^{a,1}(f_1)(x)-f_1(x)=o(R^{-(r-1)}) \text{ a.e. (Lemma 6)},$$

$$S_R^{a,1}(f_2)(x)=o(R^{-r+2}) \text{ a.e. (Theore 2)},$$

$$S_R^{a,2}(f_2)(x)=o(R^{-r+2}) \text{ a.e. (Hardy's Theore, see [2])}$$

$$S_R^{a,2}(f)(x)-f(x)=o(R^{-r}) \text{ a.e. (again Theorem 2)}.$$

By a similar procedure, we can prove that if $f\in B^r$, $0<r<3/4$, then

$$S_R^{a,1}(f)(x)-f(x)=o(R^{-r}) \text{ a.e.}.$$

Repeating previous reasons, we are led to

$$S_R^{a,2}(f)(x)-f(x)=o(R^{-r}) \text{ a.e.},$$

if $0<r<7/4$, and $r=1$.

Reasoning in this way more and more, we reach the conclusion

$$S_R^{a,2}(f)(x)-f(x)=o(R^{-r}) \text{ a.e.}$$

if $f\in B$, $0<r<2$, and $r=1$.

As for the case $r=1$, take any $1<b<2$, as did previous, we have

$$S_R^{a,b}(f)(x)-f(x)=o(R^{-1}) \text{ a.e.},$$

$$S_R^{a,2}(f)(x)-f(x)=o(R^{-1}) \text{ a.e.}.$$

If $f\in B^2$, then as it is well known (see [1]) that if $a<0$,

$$S_R^{a,2}(f_2)(x)-f_2(x)=o(1), \text{ a.e.},$$

$$f(x)-B_R^{a,2}(f)(x)=af_2(x)R^{-2}+o(R^{-2}) \text{ a.e.}$$

Theorem 3. Suppose $f\in B^r$, $0<b<2$, $a<0$, then

and so

$$B_R^{1,4}(f)(x)=f(x)+o(R^{-r}) \text{ a.e..}$$

By consistency property for Riesz Means, if a 0, then

$$B_R^{1+a}(f)(x)-f(x)=o(R^{-r}) \text{ a.e.}$$

and using Lemma 4 and the reasoning procedure above, we will get

$$B_R^{a,4}(f)(x)-f(x)=o(R^{-r}) \text{ a.e.,}$$

if $a>0$, and $r<4$.

If $r=4$, then

$$B_R^{a,4}(f)(x)-f_4(x)=o(1) \text{ a.e.,}$$

and so

$$f(x)-B_R^{a,4}(f)(x)=af_4'(x)R^{-4}+o(R^{-4}) \text{ a.e.}$$

The proof of the Theorem is complete.

Proof of the main theorem. We have proved the theorem for $0<b<4$. Proceed as did in the proof of the theorem 4, we can extend the results obtained to the case $0<b<8$, and then extend to $0<b<16$. Repeat this procees, we can extend the result to the case $0<b<2^m$, where $m=1,2,\cdots$. The main theorem is proved completely.

Remark. If $f(x)$ and $|x|^r f(x)$ are Fourier Transforms of functions in $L^p(R^n)$, we say $f\in B_p^r$, then if a $(n-1)|1/2-1/p|$, then the main theorem is still true.

References

1 . ELIAS M. STEIN and GUIDO WEISS (1971) Fourier analysis on euclidean spaces. Princeton, New Jersey, Princeton University Press.

2 . K. CHANDRASEKHARAN and S.MINAKSHISUNDARAM (1952) Typical means, Oxford University Press.

Tian-Ping Chen
Department of Mathematics
Fudan University
Shanghai
People's Republic of China

International Series of
Numerical Mathematics, Vol. 90

An Algorithm for Best Approximating Algebraic Polynomials in L^p Over a Simplex

Z. Ciesielski

Polish Academy of Sciences

1. Introduction. The set of all algebraic polynomials of of degree m over R^d is denoted by Π_m. For the standard simplex in R^d, we use the letter Q i.e.:

$$Q = \{(x_1, \dots, x_d) \in R^d : x_1 + \dots + x_d \leq 1,\ x_1 \geq 0, \dots,\ x_d \geq 0\}.$$

For $f \in L^p(Q)$ define

$$E_{m,p}(f) = \inf\{\|f - P\|_p : P \in \Pi_m\}, \tag{1.1}$$

where

$$\|f\|_p = \left(\frac{1}{|Q|}\int_Q |f(x)|^p\,dx\right)^{\frac{1}{p}}, \quad 1 \leq p < \infty,$$

and $\|f\|_\infty = \text{ess sup}\{|f(x)| : x \in Q\}$.

In this note we treate problem (1.1) for $f \in L^p(Q)$ if $p < \infty$ and for $f \in C(Q)$ if $p = \infty$. For each such f there is at least one $P_f \in \Pi_m$ such that

$$E_{m,p}(f) = \{\|f - P_f\|_p. \tag{1.2}$$

Our aim is to present an algorithm for computing P_f. The Bernstein basis in Π_m is given as follows

$$N_{\alpha,m}(x) = \frac{m!}{\alpha_0!\alpha!} x_0^{\alpha_0} x^\alpha, \qquad |\alpha| \leq m, \tag{1.3}$$

where $x = (x_1, \dots, x_d)$, $\alpha = (\alpha_1, \dots, \alpha_d)$, $\alpha_j \in N_0 = \{0, 1, \dots\}$, $|\alpha| = \alpha_1 + \dots + \alpha_d$, $\alpha_0 = m - |\alpha|$, $x_0 = 1 - (x_1 + \dots + x_d)$ and $x^\alpha = x_1^{\alpha_1} \cdots x_d^{\alpha_d}$, $\alpha! = \alpha_1! \cdots \alpha_d!$. Thus, we have

$$\Pi_m = \text{span}\{N_{\alpha,m} : \ |\alpha| \leq m\}. \tag{1.4}$$

We also consider the *dual basis* in Π_m with respect to the scalar product

$$(f, g) = \int_Q f(x) g(x)\,dx. \tag{1.5}$$

It is well known that there is unique set of polynomials $\{N^\star_{\alpha,m},\ |\alpha| \leq m\}$ in Π_m such that:

$$(N_{\alpha,m}, N^\star_{\beta,m}) = \delta_{\alpha,\beta} \quad \text{for} \quad |\alpha| \leq m,\ |\beta| \leq m. \tag{1.6}$$

Using the dual basis $\{N^{\star}_{\alpha,m},\ |\alpha| \le m\}$ we reduce the problem (1.1) to a sequence of problems indexed by $k \ge m$ for solving convex minimalization problems in R^s with $s = \binom{m+d}{d}$. To each solution to the k-th problem there corresponds a $P_k \in \Pi_m$. An algorithm for P_k and for $E_{m,p}(f)$ will be given. In case of unique P_f it will be shown that $\|P_f - P_k\|_p \to 0$ as $n \to \infty$.

2. The Appell and Bernstein bases and their duals. For later use we introduce

$$M_{\alpha,m} = (m+d)_d N_{\alpha,m}, \quad |\alpha| \le m. \tag{2.1}$$

The normalization is such that

$$\int_Q M_{\alpha,m}(x)\,dx = 1, \quad |\alpha| \le m. \tag{2.2}$$

Essential role in later dicussion is played by (see [2])

PROPOSITION 2.3. *For $\alpha, \beta \in N_0^d$, $|\alpha| \le m$, $|\beta| \le m$, we have*

$$(x^\beta, M_{\alpha,m}) = \frac{m!(m+d)_d(\alpha+\beta)_\beta}{(m+d+|\beta|)!}, \tag{2.4}$$
$$(x^\beta, N^{\star}_{\alpha,m}) = \frac{(\alpha)_\beta}{(m)_{|\beta|}},$$

where $(\alpha)_\beta = (\alpha_1)_{\beta_1} \cdots (\alpha_d)_{\beta_d}$ and $(n)_j = n(n-1)\cdots(n-j+1)$ for natural n and j.

In the space $L^2(Q)$ we have a basis, namely the Appell [1] polynomials

$$N_\alpha(x) = \frac{1}{\alpha!}D^\alpha(x_0^{|\alpha|}x^\alpha) \tag{2.5}$$
$$= \frac{|\alpha|!}{(2|\alpha|)!}D^\alpha N_{\alpha,2|\alpha|}(x), \quad \alpha \in N_0^d,$$

where $D^\alpha = D_1^{\alpha_1}\cdots D_d^{\alpha_d}$ with $D_j = \frac{\partial}{\partial x_j}$. Introducing the orthogonal decomposition

$$L^2(Q) = \bigoplus_0^\infty L_n \tag{2.6}$$

with $L_0 = \mathrm{span}\{1\}$ and L_n being the orthogonal complement of Π_{n-1} in Π_n, one can state the known fact

$$L_n = \mathrm{span}\{N_\alpha :\ |\alpha| = n\}.$$

The Appell system has a dual $\{N^{\star}_\alpha,\ \alpha \in N_0^d\}$ with respect to (1.5) i.e. $N^{\star}_\alpha \in \Pi_{|\alpha|}$ and

$$(N_\alpha, N^{\star}_\beta) = \delta_{\alpha,\beta}. \tag{2.7}$$

This dual system is explicitly given in [3]. Namely,

$$N^*_\alpha = \frac{1}{|Q|} \quad \text{for} \quad \alpha = (0, \ldots, 0) \in R^d \tag{2.8}$$

$$N^*_\alpha = N^*_{\alpha,|\alpha|} - \frac{1}{|\alpha|}\sum_{j=1}^{d} \alpha_j N^*_{\alpha - e_j, |\alpha|-1} \quad \text{for} \quad |\alpha| > 0,$$

with the understanding that $N^*_{\alpha-e_j,|\alpha|-1} = 0$ whenever $\alpha_j = 0$, where e_j is the j-th unit vector in R^d. To the definition (2.8) one arrives by the well known formula for Bernstein polynomials *for artificial lifting of degree*

$$N_{\alpha,m} = \sum_{j=0}^{d} \frac{\alpha_j + 1}{m+1} N_{\alpha+e_j,m+1}, \quad |\alpha| \leq m,$$

where $e_0 = (0, \ldots, 0) \in R^d$. The following *means* will be used to approximate the norm in the space $L^p(Q)$

$$\mathcal{M}_{m,p}(f) = \left(\frac{1}{\binom{m+d}{d}} \sum_{|\alpha| \leq m} |(f, M_{\alpha,m})|^p \right)^{\frac{1}{p}}. \tag{2.10}$$

We need also *Bernstein-Durrmeyer* polynomial operator

$$\mathcal{R}_m(f) = \sum_{|\alpha| \leq m} (f, M_{\alpha,m}) N_{\alpha,m}. \tag{2.11}$$

Now, (2.9), (2.10) and (2.11) imply (cf.[2])

Proposition 2.12. *For $f \in L^p(Q)$, $1 \leq p \leq \infty$, we have*

$$\|\mathcal{R}_k(f)\|_p \leq \mathcal{M}_{k,p}(f) \leq \mathcal{M}_{k+1,p}(f) \leq \|f\|_p. \tag{2.13}$$

Moreover, we know by [4],[3] that for $f \in L^p(Q)$ if $1 \leq p < \infty$ and for $f \in C(Q)$ if $p = \infty$ the Bernstein-Durrmeyer operators approximate f i.e.

$$\|f - \mathcal{R}_k(f)\|_p \to 0 \quad \text{as} \quad k \to \infty. \tag{2.15}$$

In particular,

$$\|\mathcal{R}_k(f)\|_p \to \|f\|_p$$

and consequently by (2.13) we get

$$\mathcal{M}_{k,p}(f) \nearrow \|f\|_p \quad \text{as} \quad k \nearrow \infty. \tag{2.16}$$

3. Descrite analogue of the Appell polynomials. For fixed degree m denote by Q_m the *standard descrete simplex* in N_0^d

$$Q_m = \{\alpha \in N_0^d : |\alpha| \leq m\}. \tag{3.1}$$

For given $w = \{w(\alpha) : \alpha \in Q_m\}$ and $v = \{v(\alpha) : \alpha \in Q_m\}$ define the scalar product

$$(v, w)_m = \sum_{|\alpha| \leq m} v(\alpha)w(\alpha). \tag{3.2}$$

For given β, m, $|\beta| \leq m$, we define $\{C_{\beta,m}(\alpha),\ |\alpha| \leq m\}$ by formula

$$N_\beta = \sum_{|\alpha| \leq m} C_{\beta,m}(\alpha) N_{\alpha,m}, \tag{3.3}$$

and similarly $\{C^*_{\beta,m}(\alpha),\ |\alpha| \leq m\}$ by formula

$$N^*_\beta = \sum_{|\alpha| \leq m} C^*_{\beta,m}(\alpha) N^*_{\alpha,m}. \tag{3.4}$$

THEOREM 3.5. *Let $m \in N$ be given. Then, for each β, $|\beta| \leq m$, we have that $C_{\beta,m}$, $C^*_{\beta,m} \in \Pi_{|\beta|}$. Moreover,*

$$(C_{\beta,m}, C^*_{\alpha,m}) = \delta_{\alpha,\beta}, \quad |\alpha|, |\beta| \leq m. \tag{3.6}$$

PROOF: According to definiotions (2.5) and (2.8) we have that N_β, $N^*_\beta \in \Pi_{|\beta|}$. Moreover, we find by (3.3) and (3.4) that

$$C_{\beta,m}(\alpha) = (N_\beta, N^*_{\alpha,m}) \quad \text{and} \quad C^*_{\beta,m}(\alpha) = (N^*_\beta, N_{\alpha,m}).$$

Thus, Proposition 2.3 implies that $C_{\beta,m}$, $C^*_{\beta,m} \in \Pi_{|\beta|}$. The biorthogonality ralation (3.6) follows immediately from (2.7).

The construction in Theorem 3.5 is related to the considerations in [2] leading to less constructive orthogonal systems of polynomials on stadard simpleces.

4. The main construction. We assume that $f \in L^p(Q)$ if $1 \leq p < \infty$ and $f \in C(Q)$ in case $p = \infty$. The m is fixed and it is reserved for the degree of the best approximating polynomials. For $k \in N$ we have by (2.13)

$$\mathcal{M}_{k,p}(f - P_k) \leq \mathcal{M}_{k+1,p}(f - P_{k+1}) \leq \|f - P_f\|_p, \tag{4.1}$$

where $P_k \in \Pi_m$ and it is such that

$$\inf_{P \in \Pi_m} \mathcal{M}_{k,p}(f - P) = \mathcal{M}_{k,p}(f - P_k). \tag{4.2}$$

Our aim is to give a prescription for constructing P_k and then to describe the convergence of P_k to P_f as $k \to \infty$. This will be done under the

HYPOTHESIS. *For arbitrarly large k anf for $|\alpha| \leq k$, we are given the numbers $f_k(\alpha) = (f, M_{\alpha,m})$.*

PROPOSITION 4.3. *Let $k \geq m$. Then (4.2) is equivalent to finding*

$$\inf_{r \in R^s} \sum_{|\alpha| \leq k} |f_k(\alpha) - \sum_{|\beta| \leq m} r(\beta) C_{\beta,m}(\alpha)|^p, \tag{4.4}$$

where $s = \binom{m+d}{d}$.

PROOF: Define $R(\alpha) = (P, M_{\alpha,k})$ for $|\alpha| \leq k$ and for given $P \in \Pi_m$. It is a consquence of Proposition 2.3 that $R \in \Pi_m$. Thus, R can be represented uniquely in any descrete basis in Π_m over Q_m e.g. in the basis $\{C_{\beta,m}, |\beta| \leq m\}$. Suppose now, that the solution to (4.4) is given by $r_k \in R^s$. Then we define $R_k \in \Pi_m$ by formula

$$R_k(\alpha) = \sum_{|\beta| \leq m} r_k(\beta) C_{\beta,m}(\alpha). \tag{4.5}$$

Next step is to find $P_k \in \Pi_m$ such that $R_k(\alpha) = (P_k, M_{\alpha,k})$. Using the normalization (2.1) and the definition of the dual basis we find that

$$P_k = \frac{1}{(k+d)_d} \sum_{|\alpha| \leq k} R_k(\alpha) N^{\star}_{\alpha,k}. \tag{4.6}$$

Thus, the extremal solution for (4.2) is given by (4.6) and (4.5) where r_k is a solution to (4.4).

Since $R_k \in \Pi_m$ and k may be very large relatively to m it is clear that formula (4.6) is not economic. It would be natural to have a construction of P_k in terms of $\{R_k(\alpha), |\alpha| \leq m\}$. To this end define

$$P_k^{\star} = \frac{1}{(m+d)_d} \sum_{|\alpha| \leq m} R_k(\alpha) N^{\star}_{\alpha,m}. \tag{4.7}$$

It follows that $P_k^{\star} \in \Pi_m$ and that

$$R_k(\alpha) = (P_k^{\star}, M_{\alpha,m}), \quad |\alpha| \leq m. \tag{4.8}$$

Writing for $P_k^{\star}$ the power basis representation

$$P_k^{\star}(x) = \sum_{|\alpha| \leq m} p_{\beta,k}\, x^{\beta} \tag{4.9}$$

we find by formula (2.4) relation

$$(x^{\beta}, M_{\alpha,m}) = \lambda_{\beta,m,k}\, (x^{\beta}, M_{\alpha,k}), \tag{4.10}$$

where

$$\lambda_{\beta,m,k} = \frac{\binom{k+d+|\beta|}{|\beta|}}{\binom{m+d+|\beta|}{|\beta|}}. \tag{4.11}$$

Now, (4.8), (4.9) and (4.10) give

$$R_k(\alpha) = (P_k, M_{\alpha,k}), \quad |\alpha| \le m \tag{4.12}$$

with

$$P_k(x) = \sum_{|\alpha|\le m} \lambda_{\beta,m,k}\; p_{\beta,k}\; x^\beta. \tag{4.13}$$

Since both sides in (4.12) are polynomials of degree m in α it follows that the relation is satisfied for all $\alpha : |\alpha| \le k$.

THE MAIN THEOREM. *Let $f \in L^p(Q)$ for some p, $1 \le p < \infty$ or let $f \in C(Q)$. Then,*

(i)
$$\mathcal{M}_{k,p}(f - P_k) \nearrow \|f - P_f\|_p, \quad as \quad k \nearrow \infty$$

and if P_f is unique, then

(ii)
$$\|P_k - P_f\|_p \to 0 \qquad as \qquad k \to \infty.$$

PROOF: It follows by the definition of P_k that

$$\mathcal{M}_{k,p}(f - P_k) \le \mathcal{M}_{k,p}(f),$$

whence by (2.13) for $k \ge m$ we have

$$\mathcal{M}_{m,p}(P_k) \le \mathcal{M}_{k,p}(P_k) \le 2\mathcal{M}_{k,p}(f) \le 2\|f\|_p.$$

This implies that for some constant $C_m < \infty$ we have

$$\|P_k\|_p \le C_m \|f\|_p \quad \text{for} \quad k \ge m.$$

Thus $\{P_k,\ k \ge m\}$ is compact in $L^p(Q)$. The same inequalities (2.13) imply that the family of semi-norms $\{\mathcal{M}_{k,p},\ k \ge m\}$ is equicontinuous. Now, suppose that $k_i < k_{i+1}$ and that $P_{k_i} \to P_0$ in $L^p(Q)$ as $i \to \infty$. Then by (4.1) and by the equicontinuity we find that

$$\mathcal{M}_{k_i,p}(f - P_{k_i}) \nearrow \|f - P_0\|_p \le \|f - P_f\|_p.$$

Since always $\|f - P_0\|_p \ge \|f - P_f\|_p$ we get (i). In case of unique P_f we have that $P_f = P_0$ and consequently (ii) follows.

5. The algorithm. We assume that we are given a function $f \in L^p(Q)$ for some finite p or in $C(Q)$. We do discribe below the algorithm for a sequence $(P_k) \subset \Pi_m$ such that property (i) in the main Theorem holds. The polynomials P_k can be obtained in the following steps:
1°. Find a solution $r_k \in R^s$ to (4.4).
2°. Compute $R_k(\alpha)$ for $|\alpha| \leq m$ by (4.5).
3°. Write P_k^* defined in (4.7) in the form (4.9).
4°. Transform P_k^* into P_k by formula (4.13).

For this algorithm we need the bases $\{C_{\beta,m}, \ |\beta| \leq m\}$ and $\{N^*_{\beta,m}, \ |\beta| \leq m\}$. To describe the first basis we introduce suitable difference operators acting on $g : Q_m \to R$. We assume that g is defined outside of Q_m where it takes on the value zero. Thus,

$$\nabla_{e_i} g(\beta) = g(\beta - e_i) - g(\beta),$$
$$\nabla_{e_i}^{\alpha_i} g(\beta) = \nabla_{e_i}^{\alpha_i - 1}(\nabla_{e_i} g(\beta)),$$
$$\nabla^{\alpha} g(\beta) = \nabla_{e_d}^{\alpha_d} \dots \nabla_{e_1}^{\alpha_1} g(\beta).$$

Now, since

$$D_i N_{\alpha,k} = k(N_{\alpha-e_i,k-1} - N_{\alpha,k-1}) \tag{5.1}$$

(2.5) takes the form

$$N_{\alpha} = \nabla^{\alpha} N_{\alpha,n} \quad \text{with} \quad n = |\alpha|, \tag{5.2}$$

whence $C_{\alpha,|\alpha|}$ can be computed. To compute $C_{\alpha,|\alpha|+1}, \dots, C_{\alpha,m}$ for $|\alpha| \leq m$ we apply formula (2.9).

For the second basis we have formula

$$N^*_{\beta,m} = \sum_{|\alpha| \leq m} A_{\alpha,\beta} N_{\alpha,m}, \tag{5.3}$$

where $\mathbf{A} = [A_{\alpha,\beta}, \ |\alpha| \leq m, \ |\beta| \leq m]$, is the inverse matrix to the Gram matrix

$$\mathbf{A}^{-1} = [(N_{\alpha,m}, N_{\beta,m}), \ |\alpha| \leq m, \ |\beta| \leq m], \tag{5.4}$$

which can be computed explicitly with the help of beta and gamma functions.

Acknowledgments. The author is very much indepted to the University and to I.N.S.A. for inviting him to Rennes. His thanks are extended to Christian Coatmelec, Marie Madeleine Derriennic and Paul Sablonnierre for helpful discussions. He also likes to thank to Janine Martin and Evelyne Martinez for patience during typing the manuscript.

References

[1] P. Appell, *Sur les fonctions hypergéométric de plusieurs variables*, Mem. des Sci. Math. Acad. Sc. Paris (1925), 43-51.

[2] Z. Ciesielski, *Approximation by algebraic polynomials on simpleces*, Usp. Matem. Nauk 40 (1985), 212-214.

[3] Z. Ciesielski, *Biorthogonal system of polynomials on the standard simplex*, pp. 116-119 in: International Series od Numerical Mathematics 75 (1985), Birkhäuser Verlag Basel.

[4] Marie Madeleine Derriennic, *On multivariate Approximation by Bernstein-Type Polynomials*, J. of Approx. Theory 45 (1985), 155-166.

Instytut Matematyczny PAN
Oddział w Gdańsku
ul. Abrahama 18
81-825 Sopot, POLAND

International Series of
Numerical Mathematics, Vol. 90

RATIONAL AND ALGEBRAIC APPROXIMATION FOR INITIAL- AND BOUNDARY-VALUE-PROBLEMS

Lothar Collatz
Institut für Angewandte Mathematik der Universität Hamburg

Abstract: There are boundary value problems with unbounded domains for which it is better to approximate the wanted solution by rational functions than by polynomials. Sometimes it may be necessary to use even more complicated approximations, for instance algebraic approximations. In simple cases it is possible to give guaranteeable inclusions for the solutions if monotonicity principles are valued. Some numerical examples are given.

1. Algebraic Approximation for a Blow-up-Problem

Rational approximations have been considered since long time. HELMUT WERNER 1962 used rational approximations for functions in the neighbourhood of poles even in cases in which the location of the pole is not known a priori. He chose the example of an initial value problem with an ordinary differential equation for an unknown function $y(x)$

$$y'(x) = q(x) + \sum_{v=0}^{s} p_v(x)[y(x)]^v, \quad y(x_0) = y_0$$

with given continuous functions $p_v(x)$ with $p_k(x) > 0, q(x) \geq 0, p_v(x) \geq 0$ for $v = 0, 1, \cdots, k-1$ in $x_0 \leq x < \infty$ and a given positive constant y_0 and $k \geq 2$. Then the solution $y(x)$ has a pole at a finite $x = \xi$ (with $x_0 < \xi < \infty$) or even more complicated singularities.

Example Here we will use "algebraic approximation".

$$Ty = y'(x) - x - [y(x)]^3 = 0; \qquad y(0) = 1.$$

The operator T is of "monotonic type" in the space S of nonnegative differentiable functions $z(x)$ with $z(0) = 1$. That means: From $Tf \leq Tg,\ f, g \in S$ follows $f \leq g$. The ordering $\varphi \leq \psi$ means $\varphi(x) \leq \psi(x)$ pointwise for all x of the considered domain with the classical ordering of real numbers: We are looking for a value $x = \hat{x}$ with

$$y(x) > 0 \quad \text{for} \quad 0 \leq x \leq \hat{x} \quad \text{and} \quad \lim_{x \to \hat{x}} y(x) = \infty.$$

I. We try to use a function $\nu[x] = \frac{1}{1-cx}$ with $c > 0$ and with a pole at $x = 1/c$; we get $T\nu = \frac{c}{(1-cx)^2} - x - \frac{1}{(1-cx)^3}$.

For $c = 2$ we have $T\left(\frac{1}{1-2x}\right) \leq 0$ for $0 \leq x < \frac{1}{2}$. Therefore $y(x) \geq \nu(x)$ for $0 \leq x < \hat{x}$, $0 < \hat{x} \leq \frac{1}{2}$, Fig. 1.

Now we wish to get also a lower bound for $\hat{x}$. But we cannot reach $T\nu \geq 0$ in (1) for any c, because $1/(1-cx)^3$ tends to ∞ for $x \to 1/c$.

Therefore we have to look more on the type of the singularity of $y(x)$ at $x = \hat{x}$. We try to approximate $y(x) \approx \nu(x) = A\cdot(x-\hat{x})^m$; we have $\nu'(x) = mA(x-\hat{x})^{m-1}$ and $\nu^3(x) = A^3(x-\hat{x})^{3m}$; $m - 1 = 3m$ or $m = -\frac{1}{2}$. We choose the algebraic function for approximation

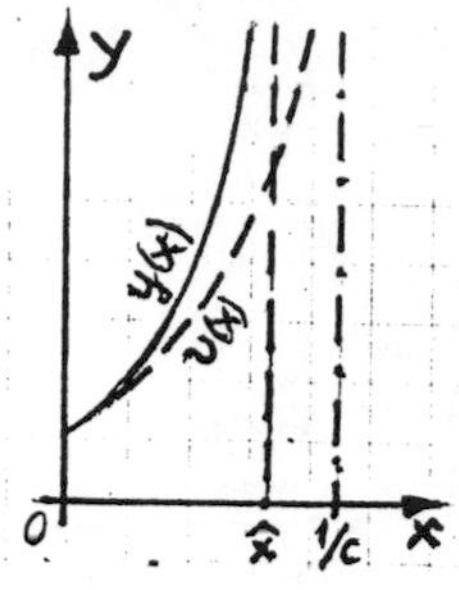

Fig. 1

$$\nu(x) = \nu(a,x) = \frac{1}{\sqrt{(1-2ax)}}, \quad T\nu(ax) = \frac{a-1}{\sqrt{(1-2ax)}^3} - x.$$

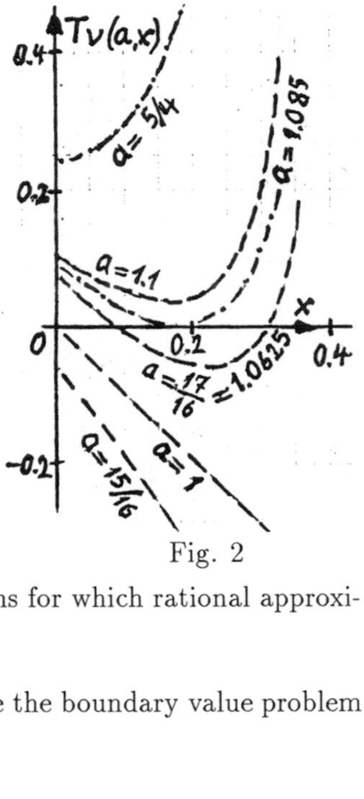

Fig. 2

Fig. 2 shows $T\nu(a,x)$ for some values of a; we observe

for $a = 1 : T\nu(1,x) = -x \leq 0$,
or $\nu(1,x) \leq y(x)$, $\hat{x} \leq \frac{1}{2} = 0.5$ as above;
for $a = 1.085 : T\nu(1.085,x) \geq 0$,
or $\nu(1.085,x) \geq y(x)$, $\hat{x} \geq 1/2.17 \approx 0.460$

Of course one can improve the accuracy.

2. Ideal flow over ground. There are many types of problems for which rational approximation is useful. We mention some problems:

Let us consider in an unbounded domain B of a $x-y$--plane the boundary value problem for a function $u(x,y)$:

$$\begin{aligned}
\Delta u &= \frac{\partial^2 u}{\partial x^2} + \frac{\partial^2 u}{\partial y^2} = 0 \text{ in } B = \{(x,y), y > h(x))\\
u(x,y) &= h(x) \text{ on } C = \{(x,y), y = h(x)\}, \text{ Fig. 3}\\
\lim_{|x|\to\infty} h(x) &= 0.
\end{aligned}$$

The curves $\hat{u} = u - y = \text{const.}$ may be interpreted as streamlines of an ideal flow of a liquid over the contour C.

One can approximate $u(x,y)$ by $\nu(x,y)$:

$$\nu(x,y) = \sum_{p=1}^{m} \alpha_\rho \left(\frac{y-\eta_\rho}{(x-\xi_\rho)^2+(y-\eta_\rho)^2} \right)$$

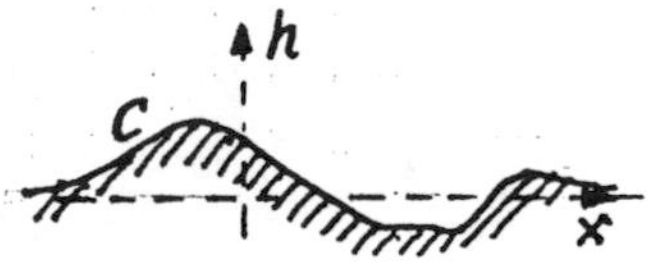

Fig. 3

The poles (ξ_ν, η_ν) with $\eta_\nu < h(\xi_\nu)$ are not known a priori; using Chebychev-approximation, one has the error bound for the error $\varepsilon = \nu - u$:

From $|\nu - u| \leq \delta$ on C follows $|\nu - u| \leq \delta$ in B.

The approximation problem is rational and highly nonlinear. Many examples have been calculated numerically, f.i. Collatz 1981, 1988).

3. Outer-space-Problems

B may be a connected closed bounded domain in the $x-y-z$--space $\mathbb{R}^3$ with the surface $\partial B; \psi(x,y,z)$ may be a continuous function and $\psi = 0$ may describe ∂B, and $\psi > 0$ may be the outer space $\hat{R} = \mathbb{R}^3 \setminus B$. The origin $x = y = z = 0$ may be an inner point of B.

We consider the boundary value problem

$$\begin{aligned} \Delta u &= \frac{\partial^2 u}{\partial x^2} + \frac{\partial^2 u}{\partial y^2} + \frac{\partial^2 u}{\partial z^2} = 0 \quad \text{in} \quad \hat{R} \quad (\text{for} \quad \psi > 0) \\ u &= f(x,y,z) \quad \text{on} \quad \partial B \quad (\text{for} \quad \psi = 0) \lim_{r\to\infty} u = 0 \quad (\text{with} \quad r^2 = x^2 + y^2 + z^2). \end{aligned}$$

u may be interpreted as stationary distribution of the temperature with prescribed temperature on the boundary.
$w = \frac{1}{r}$ is a solution of $\Delta w = 0$. Let $P_v, (v = 1, \cdots, k)$ inner point of B and with coordinates $x^{(v)}, y^{(v)}, z^{(v)}$ and $r^{(j)}$ the distance of a point

$P = (x,y,z)$ from P_j; $\quad r_j^2 = (x^{(j)} - x)^2 + (y^{(j)} - y)^2 + (z^{(j)} - z)^2$.

Then we try to approximate u by ν:

$$u(x,y,z) \approx \nu(x,y,z) = \sum_{j<01}^{k} a_j / r_j.$$

As before we have here the bound for the error $\varepsilon = \nu - u$:

From $|\nu - u| \leq \delta$ on ∂B follows $|\nu - u| \leq \delta$ in $\hat{R}$.

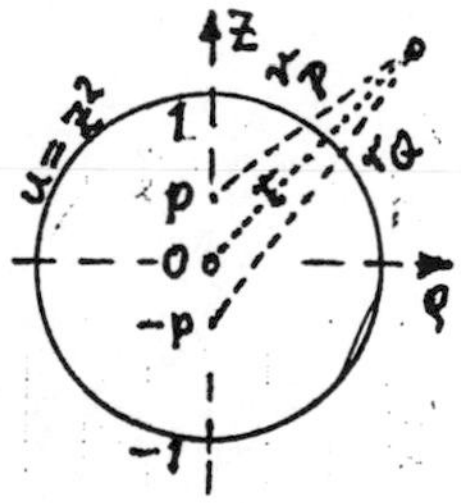

Fig. 4

One tries to determine the $a_j, x^{(j)}, y^{(j)}, z^{(j)}$ so, that δ becomes a minimum. Again we have a highly nonlinear rational approximation problem.

Example: A sphere B with $r \leq 1$ is heated near the "poles" $x = y = 0, z = \pm 1$, Fig. 4. The surface temperature may be given by $u(x,y,z) = z^2$ on $r = 1$ with $r^2 = \rho^2 + z^2$, $\rho^2 = x^2 + y^2$. We approximate u by ν: $u \approx \nu(x,y,z) = a_1 w_1 + a_2 w_2$,
$w_1 = \frac{2}{r}; w_2 = \frac{1}{r_P} + \frac{1}{r_Q}$, $r_P^2 = \rho^2 + (z-p)^2$; $r_Q^2 = \rho^2 + (z+p)^2$.

I thank Mr. Thomas Schiemann, Hamburg, for numerical calculation on a computer; he got the result:
$a_1 = -3333.027756; a_2 = 3333.194421; p = 0.01$, and the error bound
$|\varepsilon| = |\nu - u| \leq 0.000038$.

4. An outer-space problem with algebraic approximation.

The surface ∂B of the ellipsoid B

$$\psi = x^2 + y^2 + \frac{z^2}{2} - 1 = 0$$

may have the constant temperature
$u(x,y,z) = 1$ for $\psi = 0$.
We have $\frac{1}{r} = \frac{1}{\sqrt{1+\frac{1}{2}z^2}}$ on ∂B, Fig. 5,

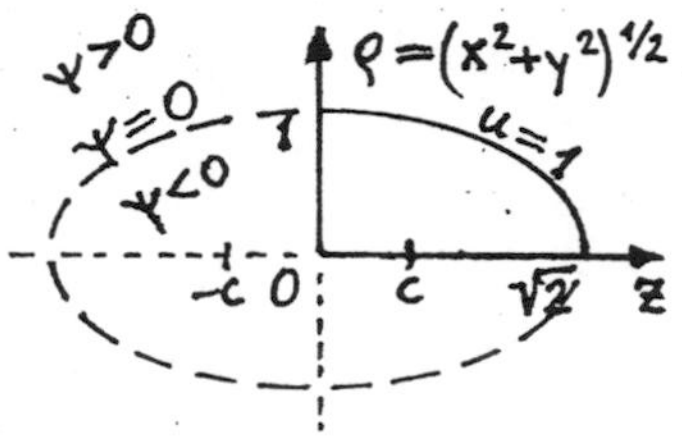

Fig. 5

and we come to the algebraic approximation on the interval $0 \leq z \leq \sqrt{2}$

$$u \approx v = \sum_{j=1}^{k} a_j v_j$$

and

$$v_1 = \frac{1}{\sqrt{1+\frac{1}{2}z^2}}; \quad v_{2,3} = \frac{1}{\sqrt{1 - c^2 + \frac{1}{2}(z \pm 2c)^2}}$$

I thank Mr. Jan Modersitzki, Hamburg, for numerical calculation with $k = 3$.

He got for $c = 0.785$, $a_1 = 0.5050$, $a_2 = 0.3142$ the bound $|\nu - u| \leq 0.0053$.

Prof. Dr. L. Collatz
Institut für Angewandte Mathematik
Bundesstraße 55
D-2000 Hamburg 13
Federal Republic of Germany

References

L. Collatz (1981): Anwendung von Monotoniesätzen zur Einschliessung der Lösungen von Gleichungen. Jahrbuch Überblicke der Mathem., 189-225.

L. Collatz (1988): Inclusion of solutions of some singular boundary value problems in two and three dimensions. Intern. Ser. Numer. Mathem., Vol. 86, Birkhäuser, 115-125.

G. Meinardus (1967): Approximation of functions, theory and numerical methods, Springer, 198 p.

J. Schröder (1980): Operator inequalitites, Acad. Press. 367 p.

H. Werner (1962): Konstruktive Ermittlung der Tschebyscheff-Approximierenden im Bereich der rationalen Funktionen. Arch. Rat. Mech. Anal. 11, 368-384.

International Series of
Numerical Mathematics, Vol. 90

R-TH ORDER BLENDING RECTANGLE RULES

Franz-J. Delvos

Abstract: This paper is concerned with numerical integration over the unit square U^2 of continuous functions which are periodic in both variables. The concept of r-th order blending rectangle rule is introduced by carrying over the idea from Boolean interpolation. Error bounds are developed, and it is shown that r-th order blending rectangle rules are comparable with number-theoretic cubature rules.

1. Bivariate rectangle rules

The problem we consider is the numerical evaluation of integrals of the form

$$\mathfrak{I}(f) \quad = \quad \int_0^1 \int_0^1 f(x,y)\, dx\, dy \quad . \tag{1.1}$$

where f is a continuous function on the unit square $U^2 = [0,1]^2$. Moreover we assume that f satisfies the periodicity conditions

$$f(x,0) = f(x,1) \quad , \quad f(0,y) = f(1,y) \quad (0 \le x,y \le 1) . \tag{1.2}$$

The inner product of $f,g \in L^2(U^2)$ is

$$(f,g) \quad = \quad \int_0^1 \int_0^1 f(x,y)\, \overline{g(x,y)}\, dx\, dy \quad .$$

We introduce the notations

$$e_k(x) = \exp(i2\pi kx) \quad (k \in \mathbb{Z}) ,$$

$$e_{k,l}(x,y) = e_k(x)\cdot e_l(y) \quad (k,l \in \mathbb{Z})$$

where $x,y \in U$. The functions $e_{k,l}$ ($k,l \in \mathbb{Z}$) form an orthonormal basis of the Hilbert space $L^2(U^2)$. We denote by $A(U^2)$ the Wiener algebra of those functions $f \in L^2(U^2)$ with the property that the Fourier series of f is absolutely convergent:

$$\sum_{k=-\infty}^{\infty} \sum_{l=-\infty}^{\infty} |(f,e_{k,l})| < \infty . \tag{1.3}$$

Let $\mathcal{C}(U^2)$ denote the subspace of those functions $f \in L^2(U^2)$ which are continuous on U^2. Moreover $\mathcal{C}_0(U^2)$ denotes the subspace of those functions $f \in \mathcal{C}(U^2)$ which satisfy the periodicity conditions (1.2). It follows from relation (1.3) that

$$A(U^2) \subseteq \mathcal{C}_0(U^2)$$

and

$$f(x,y) = \sum_{k=-\infty}^{\infty} \sum_{l=-\infty}^{\infty} (f,e_{k,l})\cdot e_{k,l}(x,y) \quad (x,y \in U) . \tag{1.4}$$

Let m and n be positive integers. The most obvious cubature formula is the *bivariate rectangle rule* :

$$\mathfrak{J}_{m,n}(f) = \frac{1}{m\cdot n} \sum_{j=0}^{m-1} \sum_{k=0}^{n-1} f(\tfrac{j}{m},\tfrac{k}{n}) .$$

The bivariate rectangle rule is not an efficient cubature formula in view of the large number of function evaluations. On the other hand $\mathfrak{J}_{m,n}(f)$ is a basic tool in constructing the more sophisticated cubature formula of r-th order blending rectangle rule. For this reason we will briefly derive a convenient remainder formula for $\mathfrak{J}_{m,n}(f)$.

Proposition 1. *If* $f \in A(U^2)$, *then*

$$\mathfrak{I}_{m,n}(f) = \sum_{u=-\infty}^{\infty} \sum_{v=-\infty}^{\infty} (f, e_{um,vn}) \quad . \tag{1.5}$$

Proof: Taking into account relation (1.4) we can conclude

$$\begin{aligned}\mathfrak{I}_{m,n}(f) &= \frac{1}{m \cdot n} \sum_{j=0}^{m-1} \sum_{k=0}^{n-1} f(\tfrac{j}{m}, \tfrac{k}{n}) \\ &= \sum_{r=-\infty}^{\infty} \sum_{s=-\infty}^{\infty} (f, e_{r,s}) \frac{1}{m \cdot n} \sum_{j=0}^{m-1} e_r(\tfrac{j}{m}) \sum_{k=0}^{n-1} e_s(\tfrac{k}{n}) \\ &= \sum_{u=-\infty}^{\infty} \sum_{v=-\infty}^{\infty} (f, e_{um,vn})\end{aligned}$$

which completes the proof of Proposition 1.

It is useful to define the series

$$R_{m,\infty}(f) = \sum_{u \neq 0} (f, e_{um,0}) \quad , \quad R_{\infty,n}(f) = \sum_{v \neq 0} (f, e_{0,vn}) \quad ,$$

$$R_{m,n}(f) = \sum_{u \neq 0} \sum_{v \neq 0} (f, e_{um,vn0}) \quad .$$

Proposition 2. *If* $f \in A(U^2)$, *then the error in the bivariate rectangle rule is*

$$\mathfrak{I}_{m,n}(f) - \mathfrak{I}(f) = R_{m,\infty}(f) + R_{\infty,n}(f) + R_{m,n}(f) \quad . \tag{1.6}$$

Proof: It follows from relation (1.5) that

$$\mathfrak{I}_{m,n}(f) = (f, e_{0,0}) + R_{m,\infty}(f) + R_{\infty,n}(f) + R_{m,n}(f) \quad .$$

Since $\mathfrak{I}(f) = (f, e_{0,0})$, the proof of Proposition 2 is complete.

Following Korobov, we define, for each $a \geq 1$, the linear space

$$E^a(U^2) = \{ f \in L^2(U^2) : (f, e_{m,n}) = \mathcal{O}((\bar{m}\cdot\bar{n})^{-a}) \quad (m,n \to \infty) \},$$

where $\bar{m} = \max\{1, |m|\}$ $(m \in \mathbb{Z})$. It is easily seen that

$$E^a(U^2) \subseteq A(U^2) \quad (a > 1) . \tag{1.7}$$

We denote by $\mathcal{C}^{p,p}(U^2)$ the linear subspace of $\mathcal{C}(U^2)$ of those functions f with the property that the partial derivatives of f satisfy

$$D^{k,l}f \in \mathcal{C}(U^2) \quad (0 \leq k, l \leq p)$$

where $p \in \mathbb{Z}_+$. Similarly, $\mathcal{C}_0^{p,p}(U^2)$ is the linear subspace of $\mathcal{C}_0(U^2)$ of those functions with the property that the partial derivatives of f satisfy

$$D^{k,l}f \in \mathcal{C}_0(U^2) \quad (0 \leq k, l \leq p)$$

where $p \in \mathbb{Z}_+$. It was shown in Baszenski - Delvos [1] that

$$\mathcal{C}_0^{q-1,q-1}(U^2) \cap \mathcal{C}^{q+1,q+1}(U^2) \subseteq E^{q+1}(U^2) \quad (q \in \mathbb{N}) . \tag{1.8}$$

Proposition 3. *If* $f \in E^a(U^2)$ *with* $a > 1$, *then the error in the bivariate rectangle rule satisfies*

$$\mathfrak{J}_{m,n}(f) - \mathfrak{J}(f) = \mathcal{O}(m^{-a} + n^{-a}) \quad (m,n \to \infty) . \tag{1.9}$$

Proof: Since $f \in E^a(U^2)$, we have

$$R_{m,\infty}(f) = \mathcal{O}(m^{-a}) , \quad R_{\infty,n}(f) = \mathcal{O}(n^{-a}) , \tag{1.10}$$

$$R_{m,n}(f) = \mathcal{O}(m^{-a}\cdot n^{-a}) \quad (m,n \to \infty) .$$

Taking into account Proposition 2 we obtain the asymptotic error relation (1.9) which completes the proof of Proposition 3.

2. R-th order blending rectangle rules

We introduce the r-th order sum of bivariate rectangle rules

$$\mathbf{S}_r^2(f) = \sum_{m=1}^{r} \mathfrak{I}_{2^m,2^{r+1-m}}(f) \quad (r \in \mathbb{Z}_+) \quad . \tag{2.1}$$

Then the *r-th order blending rectangle rule* $\mathfrak{I}_r^2(f)$ is

$$\mathfrak{I}_r^2(f) = \mathbf{S}_r^2(f) - \mathbf{S}_{r-1}^2(f) \tag{2.2}$$

where $r \in \mathbb{N}$ and $r > 1$. The construction principle of the r-th order blending rectangle rule is similar to the explicit formula of the interpolation projector of r-th order blending (Delvos - Posdorf [3] and Delvos [2]) . The *cubature points* of $\mathfrak{I}_r^2(f)$ are mainly determined by the points occuring in $\mathbf{S}_r^2(f)$:

$$\bigcup_{m=1}^{r} \{ (j\cdot 2^{-m}, k\cdot 2^{-r-1+m}) : 0 \le j < 2^m , 0 \le k < 2^{r+1-m} \} \quad . \tag{2.3}$$

Its number is given by

$$n_r = (r+1)\cdot 2^r \quad . \tag{2.4}$$

Next we will determine a remainder formula for the r-th order blending rectangle rule.

Proposition 4. *If* $f \in A(U^2)$ *, then the error in the r-th order blending rectangle rule is*

$$\mathfrak{I}_r^2(f) - \mathfrak{I}(f) = R_{2^r,\infty}(f) + R_{\infty,2^r}(f) + \sum_{m=1}^{r} R_{2^m,2^{r+1-m}}(f) - \sum_{m=1}^{r-1} R_{2^m,2^{r-m}}(f). \tag{2.5}$$

Proof: Taking into account relation (1.6) we can conclude

$$\mathfrak{I}_r^2(f) - \mathfrak{I}(f)$$

$$= \sum_{m=1}^{r} (\mathfrak{I}_{2^m,2^{r+1-m}}(f) - \mathfrak{I}(f)) - \sum_{m=1}^{r-1} (\mathfrak{I}_{2^m,2^{r-m}}(f) - \mathfrak{I}(f))$$

$$= \sum_{m=1}^{r} (R_{2^m,2^{r+1-m}}(f) + R_{2^m,\infty}(f) + R_{\infty,2^m}(f))$$

$$- \sum_{m=1}^{r-1} (R_{2^m,2^{r-m}}(f) + R_{2^m,\infty}(f) + R_{\infty,2^m}(f))$$

$$= R_{2^r,\infty}(f) + R_{\infty,2^r}(f) + \sum_{m=1}^{r} R_{2^m,2^{r+1-m}}(f) - \sum_{m=1}^{r-1} R_{2^m,2^{r-m}}(f) .$$

This completes the proof of Proposition 4.

Proposition 5. *If* $f \in E^a(U^2)$ *with* $a > 1$, *then the error in the r-th order rectangle rule is*

$$\mathfrak{I}_r^2(f) - \mathfrak{I}(f) = \mathcal{O}(r\cdot(2^r)^{-a}) \quad (r \to \infty) . \tag{2.6}$$

Proof: It follows from the relations (1.10) that

$$R_{2^r,\infty}(f) = \mathcal{O}((2^r)^{-a}) , \quad R_{\infty,2^r}(f) = \mathcal{O}((2^r)^{-a}) \quad (r \to \infty) ,$$

$$R_{2^m,2^{r+1-m}}(f) = \mathcal{O}((2^{r+1})^{-a}) \quad (1 \le m \le r , r \to \infty) ,$$

$$R_{2^m,2^{r-m}}(f) = \mathcal{O}((2^r)^{-a}) \quad (1 \le m < r , r \to \infty) .$$

Now relation (2.6) follows from the remainder formula (2.5). This completes the proof of Proposition 5.

Remark 1. Recall that the number of cubature points of the r-th order blending rectangle rule $\mathfrak{I}_r^2(f)$ is bounded by $n_r = (r+1)\cdot 2^r$.
It is easily seen that the error relation (2.6) of the r-th order blending rectangle rule obtains the form

$$\mathfrak{I}_r^2(f) - \mathfrak{I}(f) = \mathcal{O}(\log(n_r)^{a+1}\cdot(n_r)^{-a}) \quad (r \to \infty)$$

where $f \in E^a(U^2)$ with $a > 1$. Thus, the r-th order blending rectangle rule is comparable with the bivariate number-theoretic "good-lattice" rules (see Sloan [5]). The attractive feature of the r-th order blending rectangle rule is its easy computation based on the relations (2.1) and (2.2) .

3. A numerical example

We consider the double integral

$$\mathfrak{I}(f) \quad = \quad \int_0^1 \int_0^1 f(x,y)\, dx\, dy$$

with the function

$$f(x,y) \quad = \quad \frac{x + y}{1 + x \cdot y} \qquad (x,y \in U) \quad .$$

The function f is an element of the Korobov space $E^1(U^2)$. Following Hua and Wang [4] we introduce the function

$$g(x,y) \quad = \quad \frac{1}{4}(f(x,y) + f(x,1-y)\ f(1-x,y) + f(1-x,1-y)) \quad .$$

It is easily seen that

$$\mathfrak{I}(g) \quad = \quad \mathfrak{I}(f) \quad = \quad 2 \cdot (\log(4) - 1)$$

and

$$g \in \mathcal{C}_0^{0,0}(U^2) \cap \mathcal{C}^{2,2}(U^2) \quad .$$

It follows from relation (1.8) that Proposition 3 and Proposition 6 are applicable to g with $a = 2$. We have computed the following table.

r	$(r+1)\cdot 2^r$	$\mathfrak{I}_r^2(g) - \mathfrak{I}(g)$	2^{2r}	$\mathfrak{I}_{2^r,2^r}(g) - \mathfrak{I}(g)$
1	4	0.01009	4	0.01009
2	12	0.00365	16	0.00282
3	32	0.00120	64	0.00072
4	80	0.00037	256	0.00018
5	192	0.00011	1024	0.00005
6	448	0.00003	4096	0.00001

References

1 **G. Baszenski** and **F.-J. Delvos** : Boolean methods in Fourier approximation. In "**Topics in Multivariate Approximation**" (C. K. Chui, L. L. Schumaker, F. Utreras , Eds.), Academic Press **1987** , 1-11.

2 **F.-J. Delvos** : d-variate Boolean interpolation . Journal of Approximation Theory **34** (1982), 99-114.

3 **F.-J. Delvos** and **H. Posdorf** : N-th order blending. In "**Constructive Theory of Functions of Several Variables**" (W. Schempp, K. Zeller, Eds.) , Lecture Notes in Mathematics **571** (1977) , 53-64.

4 **Hua Loo Keng** and **Wang Yuan** : "**Applications of Number Theory to Numerical Analysis**" , Springer Verlag **1981** .

5 **I. K. Sloan** : Lattice methods for multiple integration. Journal of Computional and Applied Mathematics **12-13** (1985), 131-143.

Prof. Dr. Franz-Jürgen **Delvos**
Lehrstuhl für Mathematik I, Universität GH Siegen
Hölderlin-Str. 3
D-5900 Siegen (W. Germany)

International Series of
Numerical Mathematics, Vol. 90

A TRIVARIATE BOOLEAN CUBATURE SCHEME

Franz-Jürgen DELVOS and *Helmut NIENHAUS*
University of Siegen

Abstract. The objective of this paper is the numerical integration of smooth periodic functions in three dimensions. Using parametric extensions of the univariate trapezoidal rule, we construct a cubature scheme of interpolatory type that is related to the concept of discrete blending function interpolation (cf. [**1**], [**3**], [**4**]). Besides an explicit representation formula we will derive an error estimation for functions of the Korobov space E_3^α being comparible with those of the number theoretic 'good lattice methods' (cf. [**5**], [**7**]).

1. Univariate Periodic Trapezoidal Rule

We first reduce the problem to one dimension. Let $n_k = 2^k$, $k \in \mathbf{N}$, and $\mathcal{C}_1([0,1])$ the space of continuous 1-periodic functions. A well-known method for the numerical integration of a function $f \in \mathcal{C}_1([0,1])$ over $[0,1]$ is the n_k-point *trapezoidal rule*

$$T^k(f) = \frac{1}{n_k} \sum_{m=0}^{n_k-1} f(\frac{m}{n_k}), \qquad k \in \mathbf{N}, \qquad f \in \mathcal{C}_1[0,1]. \tag{1-1}$$

This easy quadrature formula gives surprisingly good results especially for smooth periodic functions. If the integrand has an absolutely convergent Fourier expansion

$$f(x) = \sum_{m \in \mathbf{Z}} a(m)\, e^{2\pi i m x}, \qquad x \in \mathbf{R}, \tag{1-2}$$

an application of the cyclotomic equation leads to the error representation

$$R^k(f) = T^k(f) - \int_0^1 f(x)\,dx = {\sum_{m \in \mathbf{Z}}}' a(m\, n_k), \tag{1-3}$$

where the prime indicates that the $m = 0$ term is to be omitted from the sum. The identity (1-3) implies that the univariate Korobov-space

$$E_1^\alpha = \{f : a(m) = \mathcal{O}(|m|^{-\alpha}),\ |m| \to \infty\}, \qquad \alpha > 1, \tag{1-4}$$

seems to be the appropriate class of testing functions for the above quadrature scheme. Under this assumption the remainder is of the order

$$R^k(f) = \mathcal{O}(N^{-\alpha}), \qquad N = 2^k \to \infty. \tag{1-5}$$

Another reason for the wide propagation of the trapezoidal rule is the fact that it can be computed recursively:

$$T^{k+1}(f) = \frac{1}{2}T^k(f) + \frac{1}{n_{k+1}}\sum_{m=0}^{n_k-1} f(\frac{2m+1}{n_{k+1}}), \qquad k \in \mathbf{N}. \tag{1-6}$$

The reduction formula suggests to introduce the univariate *midpoint sums*

$$\begin{aligned} M^1(f) &= f(0) + f(1/2), \\ M^{k+1}(f) &= \sum_{m=0}^{n_k} f(\frac{2m+1}{n_{k+1}}), \qquad k \in \mathbf{N}. \end{aligned} \tag{1-7}$$

Then one obtains directly from (1-6) that the n_k-point trapezoidal rule possesses a representation in terms of the first k midpoint sums:

$$T^k(f) = \frac{1}{n_k}\sum_{m=1}^{k} M^m(f), \qquad k \in \mathbf{N}. \tag{1-8}$$

Finally it should be noticed that different midpoint sums have pairwise different evaluation points.

2. Tensor Product Trapezoidal Rule

The univariate trapezoidal rule is, in a general sense, of interpolatory type. It can be interpreted as the integral

$$T^k(f) = \int_0^1 Q^k(f)(x)\,dx, \qquad k \in \mathbf{N}, \qquad f \in \mathcal{C}_1([0,1]),$$

where $Q^k(f) \in S_1(t_0,\ldots,t_{n_k})$ is the interpolating 1-periodic linear spline with spline and interpolation nodes $t_m = m/n_k$, $m = 0,1,\ldots,n_k$.

In order to construct trivariate cubature formulas of interpolatory type we briefely recall the concept of trivariate blending function interpolation (cf. **[1]**, **[3]**, **[4]**). It is a simple but essential fact that the spline projectors $Q^k : \mathcal{C}_1([0,1]) \to S_1(t_0,\ldots,t_{n_k})$ commute:

$$Q^kQ^m(f) = Q^mQ^k(f) = Q^{\min\{k,m\}}(f), \qquad k,m \in \mathbf{N}, \qquad f \in \mathcal{C}_1([0,1]).$$

By the method of parametric extension we define the projectors

$$Q_1^k := Q^k \otimes I \otimes I, \qquad Q_2^k := I \otimes Q^k \otimes I, \qquad Q_3^k := I \otimes I \otimes Q^k, \qquad k \in \mathbf{N},$$

with the univarite identity-projector I. They generate a distributive lattice Λ of commuting interpolation projectors with respect to the projector product PQ and the

Boolean sum $P \oplus Q = P + Q - PQ$, $P, Q \in \Lambda$. A special element of the lattice Λ is the tensor product projector

$$Q_1^k Q_2^l Q_3^m : \mathcal{C}_1([0,1]^3) \to S_1(t_0,\dots,t_{n_k}) \otimes S_1(t_0,\dots,t_{n_l}) \otimes S_1(t_0,\dots,t_{n_m}), \quad k,l,m \in \mathbf{N},$$

where $\mathcal{C}_1([0,1]^3)$ denotes the space of continuous trivariate functions with period 1 with respect to each coordinate seperately.

The integration of the trivariate spline $Q_1^k Q_2^l Q_3^m(f)$ over the unit cube U leads to the *tensor product trapezoidal rule* being the most obvious generalization of the corresponding univariate quadrature scheme:

$$T_1^k T_2^l T_3^m(f) = \frac{1}{n_k n_l n_m} \sum_{r=0}^{n_k} \sum_{s=0}^{n_l} \sum_{t=0}^{n_m} f\left(\frac{r}{n_k}, \frac{s}{n_l}, \frac{t}{n_m}\right), \quad k,l,m \in \mathbf{N}, \quad f \in \mathcal{C}_1(U). \tag{2-1}$$

Under the condition that the function f has an absolutely convergent Fourier series

$$f(x,y,z) = \sum_{k,l,m \in \mathbf{Z}} a(k,l,m) e^{2\pi i(kx+ly+mz)}, \qquad (x,y,z) \in \mathbf{R}^3, \tag{2-2}$$

we obtain similar to the univariate case an error representation in terms of the Fourier coefficients of the integrand:

$$R^{k,l,m}(f) = T_1^k T_2^l T_3^m(f) - I_3(f) = \sum_{r,s,t \in \mathbf{Z}} a(rn_k, sn_l, tn_m) - a(0,0,0), \tag{2-3}$$

where $I_3(f)$ denotes the exact value of the integral. In order to have a closer look at the asymtotic behavior of the cubature remainder, we split it into

$$\begin{aligned} R^{k,l,m}(f) &= R_1^k(f) + R_2^l(f) + R_3^m(f) \\ &+ R_1^k R_2^l(f) + R_1^k R_3^m(f) + R_2^l R_3^m(f) \\ &+ R_1^k R_2^l R_3^m(f) \end{aligned} \tag{2-4}$$

with the abbreviations

$$R_1^k(f) = \sum_{r \in \mathbf{Z}}{}' a(rn_k, 0, 0), \qquad R_2^k(f) = \sum_{r \in \mathbf{Z}}{}' a(0, rn_k, 0),$$

$$R_3^k(f) = \sum_{r \in \mathbf{Z}}{}' a(0, 0, rn_k),$$

$$R_1^k R_2^l(f) = \sum_{r,s \in \mathbf{Z}}{}' a(rn_k, sn_l, 0), \qquad R_1^k R_3^l(f) = \sum_{r,s \in \mathbf{Z}}{}' a(rn_k, 0, sn_l),$$

$$R_2^k R_3^l(f) = \sum_{r,s \in \mathbf{Z}}{}' a(0, rn_k, sn_l),$$

$$R_1^k R_2^l R_3^m(f) = \sum_{r,s,t \in \mathbf{Z}}{}' a(rn_k, sn_l, tn_m). \tag{2-5}$$

The reason for this division becomes obvious if we consider functions of the trivariate Korobov-space

$$E_3^\alpha = \{f : a(r,s,t) = \mathcal{O}(|r\,s\,t|^{-\alpha}),\ |r|,|s|,|t| \to \infty\}, \qquad \alpha > 1. \tag{2-6}$$

Then the above sums are of the order

$$\begin{aligned} R_i^k(f) &= \mathcal{O}(2^{-k\alpha}), && k \to \infty, && i \in \{1,2,3\}, \\ R_i^k R_j^l(f) &= \mathcal{O}(2^{-(k+l)\alpha}), && k,l \to \infty, && i,j \in \{1,2,3\}, \\ R_1^k R_2^l R_2^m(f) &= \mathcal{O}(2^{-(k+l+m)\alpha}), && k,l,n \to \infty. && \end{aligned} \tag{2-7}$$

Thus, only the first three sums in (2-4) determine the rate of convergence of the tensor product trapezoidal rule and we get the known result (cf. [**5**]) :

Proposition 1. *Assume that* $f \in E_3^\alpha$, $\alpha > 1$. *Then the error of the* N*-point tensor product trapezoidal rule is of the order*

$$R^{k,k,k}(f) = \mathcal{O}(N^{-\frac{\alpha}{3}}), \qquad N = 2^{3k} \to \infty. \tag{2-8}$$

3. A Boolean 'Good Lattice' Rule

Proposition 1 shows that the trivariate product trapezoidal rule suffers badly from the 'curse of dimensionality'. Therefore we change the underlying interpolation scheme and consider instead of the tensor product projector the Boolean sum projector

$$D_3^q = \bigoplus_{k+l+m=q} Q_1^k Q_2^l Q_3^m \in \Lambda, \qquad q \geq 3, \tag{3-1}$$

with the sum representation

$$D_3^q = \sum_{k+l+m=q} Q_1^k Q_2^l Q_3^m - 2 \sum_{k+l+m=q-1} Q_1^k Q_2^l Q_3^m + \sum_{k+l+m=q-2} Q_1^k Q_2^l Q_3^m, \tag{3-2}$$

first established in [**3**]. The integration of the trivariate spline $D_3^q(f)$ over the unit cube is the motivation for the following definition.

Definition 2. *Let* $f \in C_1(U)$ *and* $q \geq 3$ *a natural number. The trivariate Boolean cubature scheme* H_3^q *is defined by*

$$\begin{aligned} H_3^q(f) = &\sum_{k+l+m=q} T_1^k T_2^l T_3^m(f) - 2 \sum_{k+l+m=q-1} T_1^k T_2^l T_3^m(f) \\ &+ \sum_{k+l+m=q-2} T_1^k T_2^l T_3^m(f). \end{aligned} \tag{3-3}$$

The above representation of $H_3^q(f)$ is not suitable for the practical use because the occuring tensor product schemes may have common evaluation points. Therefore they will be substituted by

$$T_1^k T_2^l T_3^m(f) = \frac{1}{n_k n_l n_m} \sum_{r=1}^{k} \sum_{s=1}^{l} \sum_{t=1}^{m} M_1^r M_2^s M_3^t(f), \qquad k,l,m \in \mathbf{N}, \tag{3-4}$$

where M_i^r is the r-the midpoint sum with respect to the i-the coordinate (cf. (1-7)). The reason for this substitution is the fact that tensor products of different midpoint sums have pairwise different evaluation points. Taking into account the combinatorial identity

$$\sum_{k+l+m=q} \sum_{r=1}^{k} \sum_{s=1}^{l} \sum_{t=1}^{m} x^r y^s z^t = \sum_{k=3}^{q} \binom{q-k+2}{2} \sum_{r+s+t=k} x^r y^s z^t, \qquad q \geq 3, \tag{3-5}$$

that can be proofed recursively from the 1-dimensional analogue and regrouping the terms yields the

Theorem 3. *Let $f \in \mathcal{C}_1(U)$ and $q \geq 3$ a natural number. The trivariate cubature rule H_3^q possesses the explicit representation*

$$H_3^q(f) = \frac{1}{2^{q+1}} \sum_{k=3}^{q} a(q-k)\, S_3^k(f) \tag{3-6}$$

with the weights

$$a(l) = l^2 - 5l + 2, \qquad 0 \leq l \leq q-3, \tag{3-7}$$

and the sums

$$S_3^k(f) = \sum_{r+s+t=k} M_1^r M_2^s M_3^t(f), \qquad 3 \leq k \leq q. \tag{3-8}$$

To determine the number $N(q)$ of evaluation points of $H_3^q(f)$ we first count the number $n(k)$ of points of the sum $S_3^k(f)$, $3 \leq k \leq q$. Since the first midpoint sum needs $N^1 = 2$ and the m-th $N^m = 2^{m-1}$, $m \geq 2$, function evaluations one gets from (3-8):

$$\begin{aligned} n(k) &= \sum_{m_1+m_2+m_3=k} N^{m_1} N^{m_2} N^{m_3} \\ &= \sum_{l=0}^{2} \binom{3}{l} 2^l \sum_{\substack{m_1+\cdots+m_{3-l}=k-l \\ m_1,\ldots,m_{3-l} \geq 2}} N^{m_1} \cdots N^{m_{3-l}} \\ &= 2^k \sum_{l=1}^{3} 2^{-l} \binom{3}{l} \binom{k-4}{l-1} \\ &= 2^{k-4}(k^2+3k-4), \qquad k \geq 4. \end{aligned} \tag{3-9}$$

Trivially, $n(3) = 8$ holds. Summing up $n(k)$ from 3 to q finally leads to

Proposition 4. *The total number of points of the cubature rule $H_3^q(f)$ has the value*

$$N(q) \;=\; 2^{q-3}\,(q^2+q-4)\,, \qquad q \geq 3\,. \tag{3-10}$$

Nevertheless, only $n(q) = 2^{q-4}\,(q^2+3q-4)$ new function evaluations have to be carried out if we increase the parameter from $q-1$ to q.

Our next objective is to derive the rate of convergence of the Boolean cubature scheme. Since $\binom{q-1}{2} - 2\binom{q-2}{2} + \binom{q-3}{2} = 1$, $q \geq 3$, the cubature remainder can be expressed by a combination of errors of certain tensor product trapezoidal rules:

$$\begin{aligned} R_3^q(f) &= H_3^q(f) - I_3(f) \\ &= \sum_{k+l+m=q} \{T_1^k T_2^l T_3^m(f) - I_3(f)\} - 2 \sum_{k+l+m=q-1} \{T_1^k T_2^l T_3^m(f) - I_3(f)\} \\ &\qquad + \sum_{k+l+m=q-2} \{T_1^k T_2^l T_3^m(f) - I_3(f)\} \\ &= \sum_{k+l+m=q} R^{k,l,m}(f) - 2 \sum_{k+l+m=q-1} R^{k,l,m}(f) + \sum_{k+l+m=q-2} R^{k,l,m}(f)\,. \end{aligned} \tag{3-11}$$

Again assume that the integrand is an element of the Korobov-space E_3^α, $\alpha > 1$. Corresponding to (2-4) and (2-5) we substitute the tensor product trapezoidal rule errors by sums of known asymptotic behavior:

$$\begin{aligned} R_3^q(f) &= \sum_{k=1}^{q-2} (q-k-1)[R_1^k(f) + R_2^k(f) + R_3^k(f)] \\ &+ \sum_{k=1}^{q-2} \sum_{l+m=q-k} [R_1^l R_2^m(f) + R_1^l R_3^m(f) + R_2^l R_3^m(f)] + \sum_{k+l+m=q} R_1^k R_2^l R_3^m(f) \\ &- 2\sum_{k=1}^{q-3} (q-k-2)[R_1^k(f) + R_2^k(f) + R_3^k(f)] \\ &- 2\sum_{k=1}^{q-3} \sum_{l+m=q-1-k} [R_1^l R_2^m(f) + R_1^l R_3^m(f) + R_2^l R_3^m(f)] - 2 \sum_{k+l+m=q-1} R_1^k R_2^l R_3^m(f) \\ &+ \sum_{k=1}^{q-4} (q-k-3)[R_1^k(f) + R_2^k(f) + R_3^k(f)] \\ &+ \sum_{k=1}^{q-4} \sum_{l+m=q-2-k} [R_1^l R_2^m(f) + R_1^l R_3^m(f) + R_2^l R_3^m(f)] + \sum_{k+l+m=q-2} R_1^k R_2^l R_3^m(f)\,. \end{aligned}$$

Regrouping the terms finally yields the cubature error representation

$$\begin{aligned}
R_3^q(f) &= R_1^{q-2}(f) + R_2^{q-2}(f) + R_3^{q-2}(f) \\
&\quad + \sum_{k+l=q-1} [R_1^k R_2^l(f) + R_1^k R_3^l(f) + R_2^k R_3^l(f)] \\
&\quad - \sum_{k+l=q-2} [R_1^k R_2^l(f) + R_1^k R_3^l(f) + R_2^k R_3^l(f)] \\
&\quad + \sum_{k+l+m=q} R_1^k R_2^l R_3^m(f) - 2 \sum_{k+l+m=q-1} R_1^k R_2^l R_3^m(f) \\
&\quad + \sum_{k+l+m=q-2} R_1^k R_2^l R_3^m(f) .
\end{aligned} \tag{3-12}$$

It follows from the asymptotic behavior of $R_i^k(f)$, $R_i^k R_j^l(f)$ and $R_1^k R_2^l R_3^m(f)$ in (2-7) that

$$\begin{aligned}
R_i^{q-2}(f) &= \mathcal{O}(2^{-q\alpha}) &&= \mathcal{O}(\frac{\ln(N)^{2\alpha}}{N^\alpha}), && i = 1,2,3, \\
\sum_{k+l=q-r} R_i^k R_j^l(f) &= \mathcal{O}(q 2^{-q\alpha}) &&= \mathcal{O}(\frac{\ln(N)^{2\alpha+1}}{N^\alpha}), && i,j = 1,2,3, \quad r = 1,2, \\
\sum_{k+l+m=q-r} R_1^k R_2^l R_3^m(f) &= \mathcal{O}(q^2 2^{-q\alpha}) &&= \mathcal{O}(\frac{\ln(N)^{2\alpha+2}}{N^\alpha}), && r = 0,1,2,
\end{aligned}$$

if $N = 2^{q-3}(q^2 + q - 4)$ tends to infinity. Thus, only the last three sums in (3-12) determine the rate of convergence of the Boolean cubature scheme and we get

Theorem 5. *Let f be an element of the trivariate Korobov-space E_3^α, $\alpha > 1$. Then the error of the N-point Boolean cubature rule $H_3^q(f)$ is of the order*

$$R_3^q(f) = \mathcal{O}(\frac{\ln(N)^{2\alpha+2}}{N^\alpha}), \qquad N \to \infty. \tag{3-12}$$

References

1. DELVOS, F.-J.: On Discrete Trivariate Blending Interpolation, in: *"Multivariate Approximation Theory II"*, (ed. by W. Schempp and K. Zeller), ISNM **61**, Birkhäuser Verlag, Stuttgart, 1982, 89–106.
2. DELVOS, F.-J.: A Boolean lattice rule, in: *"Multivariate Approximation Theory IV"*, (ed. by C. K. Chui, W. Schempp and K. Zeller), Birkhäuser Verlag, Stuttgart, 1989.

3. DELVOS, F.-J., POSDORF, H.: Boolean trivariate interpolation, in: *"Proceedings of the international conference on functions, series, operators"*, Colloquia Mathematica Societatis Janos Bolyai, Budapest, 1980, 361-374.
4. GORDON, W. J.: Distributive lattices and the approximation of multivariate functions, in: *"Approximation with special emphasis on spline functions"*, (ed. by I. J. Schoenberg), Academic Press, New York, 1969, 223–277.
5. HUA, L. K., WANG, Y.: *Applications of Number Theory to Numerical Analysis*, Springer, Berlin, 1981.
6. NIENHAUS, H.: Numerical integration of trivariate periodic functions to appear in: *Approximation Theory VI*, (ed. by C. K. Chui, L. L. Schumaker and J. D. Ward), Academic Press, New York, 1989.
7. SLOAN, I. H., KACHOYAN, P. J.: Lattice Methods for Multiple Integration: Theory, Error Analysis and Examples, SIAM J. Numer. Anal. **24** (1987), 116–128.

Franz-Jürgen DELVOS, Helmut NIENHAUS
Lehrstuhl für Mathematik I
Universität Siegen
Hölderlinstraße 3
D-5900 Siegen, West-Germany

International Series of
Numerical Mathematics, Vol. 90

MULTIVARIATE BAND-LIMITED FUNCTIONS: SAMPLING REPRESENTATION AND APPROXIMATION

Dinh-Dung (Din' Zung)

Institute of Computer Science and Cybernetics
Hanoi, Vietnam

1. Introduction

Let G be an arbitrary subset of R^n. A tempered distribution $f \in S'(R^n)$ is said to be band-limited to G if the support of the Fourier transform of f is contained in G. In several aspects of the harmonic approximation for functions defined on R^n, functions which are band-limited to G play a basic role as multivariate trigonometric polynomials for multivariate periodic functions (cf. [3,4,5,6,7]). Here G may be of various shape and usually has finite measure. Let us consider a simple example. Let W be the set of all those functions defined on R^2 such that the mixed derivatives $\partial^3 f/\partial xy^2$ and $\partial^3 f/\partial x^2 y$ are L_2-bounded with 1. Then the so-called smooth hyperbolic cross $G(t) = \{ (x,y) \in R^2 : \max (|xy^2|, |x^2 y|) \le t \}$, meas $G(t) = N$, is optimal for the best L_2-approximation of W by sets $B_{G,2}$ of functions $f \in L_2(R^2)$ which are band-limited to G, where meas G is not greater than N. This is one side of background of our paper.

An other side is the famous Whittaker-Kotelnikov-Shannon sampling theorem which has origin from communication theory. It states that every signal function $f \in L_2(R)$ which is band-limited to $[-\sigma,\sigma]$ can be completely reconstructed from its sample values f(hk), $h = \pi/\sigma$, by means of the series

$$(1) \qquad f(x) = \sum_{k \in Z} f(hk)\, D(\sigma(x-hk)) ,$$

where $D(x) := x^{-1}\sin x$ for $x = 0$ and $D(0) := 1$ (cf. [1,8]). Discovering the information sence of this formular KOTELNIKOV [10] first noted that the quantity of information necessary for recovering in the time interval $[-T,T]$ the signal function f is approximately equal to the quantity of information necessary for determining $2T\sigma/\pi$ real numbers for T large enough. SHANNON [13] had a similar idea for random processes.

Let V is a subset of C(R). Taking basic idea of Kotelnikov and Shannon KOLMOGOROV [9] introduced the inferior and superior ε-entropies per length unit $H^i_\varepsilon(V)$ and $H^s_\varepsilon(V)$, $\varepsilon > 0$, as the inferior and superior limits of $(2T)^{-1} H^T_\varepsilon(V)$, where $H^T_\varepsilon(V)$ is the ε-entropy of V in the space $C([-T,T])$. From (1) one can expect that the ε-entropies per length unit of the set of functions which are bounded with 1 and band-limited to $[-\sigma,\sigma]$ would be approximately equal to the product of bandwidth 2σ and $(2\pi)^{-1} \log_2 1/\varepsilon$. A precise form of this assertion was proved by TIKHOMIROV [14] . Later on, he introduced the mean ε-dimension which is based on the same idea, but the role of the ε-entropy is replaced by the ε-dimension which is inverse to the well-known m-width (cf. [3,4,7]). The ε-entropies per length unit and mean ε-dimension were studied in [8,14,3,4,5, 7,11] for some sets of smooth functions, of analytic functions and of band-limited functions, in particular, of functions which are band-limited to unbounded sets [3,4,5,7,11] .

These quantities are suitable for expression of the corresponding methods of approximation of functions on R^n only in the case when the ε-entropy or ε-dimension of the set V^T of restrictions on the cube $[-T,T]^n$ of functions $f \in V$ is approximately proportional to the volume of this cube. However, this property does not hold, in general, for many function sets. We suggest a new approach to the study of the ε-entropy and ε-dimension of sets of functions defined on R^n.

Let X be a normed linear space of functions defined on R^n. Let us suppose that for every $f \in X$ the product of f and the characteristic function of the set $Q_T := \{x \in R^n : |x_i| \leq T_i, i = 1, \ldots, n\}$, $x = (x_1, \ldots, x_n)$, $T = (T_1, \ldots, T_n)$, also belongs to X. For a function set V let V^T be the set of restrictions on Q_T of functions from V, in particular, X^T is the normed linear space with the norm induced from the norm of X. Our hypothesis is that the ε-entropy and ε-dimension of V^T in the space X^T have asymptotic order $(\mathrm{vol}\ Q_T)^s\ F(\varepsilon, V, X)$, $s > 0$, as T tends to infinity. Morever, the power s can be defined as function of V and X, and equal to 1, smaller than 1 and greater than 1 depending, in some sence, on propertities of V as well as its relation with the space X. In this paper we formulate some precise assertions of the hypothesis for sets of band-limited functions and of smooth functions, and the space $X = L_q(R^n)$, $1 \leq q \leq \infty$. We shall be also concerned with a multivariate modification of the classical sampling theorem, the truncation L_q^T-approximation of band-limited functions by finite sampling sums, an analogue of Marcinkiewicz' theorem on equivalence of norms for band-limited functions and other related problems.

2. ε-dimension and ε-entropy

2.1 ε-dimension. Let X be a normed linear space, A be a compact subset of X. Denote by M_k the set of linear manifolds of dimension at most k. The quantity

$$K_\varepsilon(A,X) := \inf \{k : \exists L \in M_k : \sup_{x \in A} \inf_{y \in L} \| x-y \| \leq \varepsilon\},$$

$\varepsilon > 0$, is called the ε-dimension of A in X (cf. [4,7]). This approximation characteristic expresses the necessary dimension of a linear manifold for the approximation of A within to ε.

As usual, $L_p(G)$, $1 \leq p \leq \infty$, $G \subset R^n$, is the normed linear space of functions defined on G with the pth integral norm $\| f \|_{L_p(G)}$ (with the corresponding modification for $p = \infty$). If $G = R^n$, then $L_p(G) := L_p$ and $\| f \|_{L_p} := \| f \|_p$. Denote by $B_{G,p}$ the set of allthose functions $f \in L_p$ which are band-limited to G, and denote by $SB_{G,p}$ the intersection of $B_{G,p}$ with the unit ball of L_p. Put $B_{G,p} = B_{\sigma,p}$ for $G = Q_\sigma$, $\sigma \in R^n_+$, where $R^n_+ = \{ x \in R^n : x_i > 0,\ i = 1,\dots,n \}$, x_i is the ith coordinate of $x \in R^n$. According to Schwartz' theorem $B_{\sigma,p}$ coinsides with the class of functions from L_p which can be continued analytically to entire functions of exponential type σ.

Put $K_\varepsilon(G,T) = K_\varepsilon((SB_{G,p})^T, L^T_q)$ for fixed $1 \leq p,q \leq \infty$. Note that if G is bounded, then $(SB_{G,p})^T$ is a compact subset of L^T_q for any pair p,q. Denote by meas G the Lebesgue measure of measurable $G \subset R^n$. We say that $T \to \infty$ if $T \in R^n_+$ and $T_i \to \infty$ for $i = 1,\dots,n$.

Theorem 1. Let $1 \leq p,q \leq \infty$, $0 < \varepsilon < 1$, and G be a bounded Jordan-measurable subset of R^n. Then

$$\limsup_{T\to\infty} (\mathrm{vol}\ Q_T)^{-1} K_\varepsilon(G,T) \le (2\pi)^{-n} \mathrm{meas}\ G .$$

Theorem 1 shows that the necessary dimensions per "volume unit" of a linear manifold for the L_q^T-approximation of $(SB_{G,p})^T$ within to arbitrary ε are not asymptotically greater than $(2\pi)^{-n}$ vol Q_T meas G for any pair p,q , as $T\to\infty$. The three following theorems sharpen this fact.

Theorem 2. Under the hypotheses of Theorem 1 let $p \ge q$. Then

$$\lim_{T\to\infty} (\mathrm{vol}\ Q_T)^{-1} K_\varepsilon(G,T) = (2\pi)^{-n} \mathrm{meas}\ G .$$

Theorem 3. Under the hypotheses of Theorem 1 let $p < q \le 2$. Then there exists a positive constant $c = c(p,q)$ such that

$$\liminf_{T\to\infty} (\mathrm{vol}\ Q_T)^{-1} K_\varepsilon(G,T) \ge c\ \mathrm{meas}\ G .$$

Theorem 4. Let $1 \le p < q \le \infty$, $q > 2$, $0 < \varepsilon < \varepsilon_0 < 1$. Suppose that $G = Q_\sigma$. Then there exist positive constants $c = c(p,q)$ and $c' = c'(p,q)$ such that

$$c\varepsilon^{-d}(\mathrm{meas}\ G)^\nu \le \liminf_{T\to\infty} (\mathrm{vol}\ Q_T)^{-s} K_\varepsilon(G,T)$$

$$\limsup_{T\to\infty} (\mathrm{vol}\ Q_T)^{-s} K_\varepsilon(G,T) \le c'\varepsilon^{-d}(\mathrm{meas}\ G)^\nu ,$$

where $s = 2/q$, $d = 2 \max\{1, (1/2 - 1/q)/(1/p - 1/q)\}$, $\nu = \max(1, 2/q)$.

Let $W_p^m := \{ f \in L_p :\ \|f\|_p + \sum_{|k|\le m} \|f^{(k)}\|_p \le 1\}$, $m \in N$, $k \in Z_+^n$, be the Sobolev class of functions, where $f^{(k)}$ is the mixed derivative of order k, $|k| = k_1 + \dots + k_n$.

Theorem 5. Let $1 \leq p,q \leq \infty$, $m > 1/p$, $0 < \varepsilon < \varepsilon_0 < 1$. Then there exist positive constants $c = c(p,q,m)$ and $c' = c'(p,q,m)$ such that

$$c\varepsilon^{-r} \leq \liminf_{T \to \infty} (\text{vol } Q_T)^{-s} K_\varepsilon((W_p^m)^T, L_q^T)$$

$$\limsup_{T \to \infty} (\text{vol } Q_T)^{-s} K_\varepsilon((W_p^m)^T, L_q^T) \leq c'\varepsilon^{-r},$$

where r and s are defined by the table

Table I.

p,q	r = r(p,q,m)	s = s(p,q,m)	
$p = q$	$1/m$	1	
$p > q$	$1/m$	$1 + r(1/q - 1/p)$	(> 1)
$p < q \leq 2$	$1/m - 1/p + 1/q$	1	
$p < 2 < q$	$1/m - 1/p + 1/2$	$1 - r(1/2 - 1/q)$	(< 1)
$2 \leq p < q$	$1/m$	$1 - r(1/p - 1/q)$	(< 1)

Let A be a finite subset of R^n. Denote by W_p^A the set of all those functions defined on R^n such that $\|f^{(k)}\|_p \leq 1$, $k \in A$, where $f^{(k)}$ is the Weyl fractional derivative of order k. Let co A be the convex hull of A; $\langle x,y \rangle = x_1y_1 + \ldots + x_ny_n$, $e = (1,1,\ldots,1) \in R^n$.

Theorem 6. Let $1 < p < \infty$, $0 \in \text{int co } A$. Then there exist positive constants $c = c(p,A)$ and $c' = c'(p,A)$ such that

$$c\varepsilon^{-\theta}\log_2{}^r 1/\varepsilon \leq \liminf_{T \to \infty} (\text{vol } Q_T)^{-1} K_\varepsilon((W_p^A)^T, L_q^T)$$

$$\leq \limsup_{T\to\infty} (\text{vol } Q_T)^{-1} K_\varepsilon((W_p^A)^T, L_q^T) \leq c'\varepsilon^{-\theta} \log_2{}^r 1/\varepsilon ,$$

Where θ and r are the value and linear dimension of the set of solutions of the following linear programming problem

$$\langle e,x\rangle \to \sup \quad ; \quad x\in R^n , \langle k,x\rangle \leq 1 , k\in A .$$

In the proof of Theorem 6 the approximation of functions from W_p^A by band-limited functions from $B_{G(t),p}$ and the inequality of Bernstein type $\max_{k\in A} \|f^{(k)}\|_p \leq ct^{-1} \|f\|_p$ for $f\in B_{G(t),p}$ (cf. [7]), the asymptotic degree meas $G(t) \asymp t^\theta \log_2{}^r 1/\varepsilon$, with respect to t tending to infinity and Theorem 2 are used. Here the values θ and r are defined in Theorem 6 and the set $G(t):= \{x\in R^n : \prod_{i=1}^n |x_i|^{k_i} \leq t , k\in A\}$, $t > 0$, is so-called hyperbolic cross which has a close relation with the bets approximations of functions of mixed smoothness (cf. [3,5,6,7]) The condition $0\in \text{int co } A$ in Theorem 6 guarantees the boundedness of G(t).

<u>2.2 ε-entropy</u>. Let X be a metric space and A be a compact subset of X. Denote by $N_\varepsilon(A,X)$, $\varepsilon > 0$, the minimal number of elements of an ε-net of A. Then the quantity $H_\varepsilon(A,X) = \log_2 N_\varepsilon(A,X)$ is called the ε-entropy of A in X (cf. [9]). It expresses the necessary number of bits for the binary recovering the "information" set A within to ε. Put $H_\varepsilon(G,T) = H_\varepsilon((SB_{G,p})^T, L_q^T)$ for fixed $1 \leq p,q \leq \infty$.

<u>Theorem 7</u>. Under the hypotheses of Theorem 1 let p =q. Then

$$\lim_{\varepsilon\to 0} \liminf_{T\to\infty} \log_2^{-1} 1/\varepsilon \, (\text{vol } Q_T)^{-1} H_\varepsilon(G,T)$$

$$= \lim_{\varepsilon \to 0} \limsup_{T \to \infty} \log_2^{-1} 1/\varepsilon \ (\mathrm{vol}\ Q_T)^{-1} H_\varepsilon(G,T)$$

$$= (2\pi)^{-n} \ \mathrm{meas}\ G \ .$$

Theorem 8. Under the hypotheses of Theorem 3 one has

$$\lim_{\varepsilon \to 0} \limsup_{T \to \infty} \log_2^{-1} 1/\varepsilon \ (\mathrm{vol}\ Q_T)^{-1} H_\varepsilon(G,T)$$

$$\leq (2\pi)^{-n} \ \mathrm{meas}\ G \ .$$

Theorem 9. Under the hypotheses and notation of Theorem 4 there exists a positive constant $c = c(p,q)$ such that

$$\lim_{\varepsilon \to 0} \limsup_{T \to \infty} \varepsilon^d \log_2^{-1} 1/\varepsilon \ (\mathrm{vol}\ Q_T)^{-s} H_\varepsilon(G,T)$$

$$\leq c(\mathrm{meas}\ G)^{\nu} .$$

Theorem 10. Under the hypotheses and notation of Theorem 6 one has

$$c \leq \lim_{\varepsilon \to 0} \liminf_{T \to \infty} \varepsilon^\theta \log_2^{-r-1} 1/\varepsilon \,(\mathrm{vol}\ Q_T)^{-1} H_\varepsilon((W_p^A)^T, L_p^T)$$

$$\lim_{\varepsilon \to 0} \limsup_{T \to \infty} \varepsilon^\theta \log_2^{-r-1} 1/\varepsilon \,(\mathrm{vol}\ Q_T)^{-1} H_\varepsilon((W_p^A)^T, L_p^T) \leq c' \ .$$

We call Theorem 7 Kotelnikov-Shannon formular to pay honour to their idea. This Theorem in the one-dimensional case with $p = q = \infty$, $G = [-\sigma, \sigma]$ was proved in [14]. Note that for functions of one variable the statement of Theorem 10 is also true in the case $p = \infty$.

3. Sampling representation and equivalence of norms

3.1 Sampling representation. Put $D_\sigma(x) := \prod_{i=1}^{n} D(\sigma_i x_i)$, $x \in R^n$ for $\sigma \in R_+^n$. It is easy to prove that every $f \in B_{\sigma,2}$ can be represented by the series

$$f(x) = \sum_{k \in Z^n} f(hk)\, D_\sigma(x - hk)$$

converging uniformly on R^n where $hk = (\pi k_1/\sigma_1, \ldots, \pi k_n/\sigma_n)$.

There exist other sampling interpolation representations which are more satisfactory in various problems concerning band-limited functions. In proofs of Theorems 1-10 the following representation plays a central role. Let $\varrho, \delta \in R_+^n$. Denote by $F(\varrho,\delta)$ the set of all those functions g such that $g(x) = D_\varrho(x)V(x)$, $x \in R^n$, where $V \in B_{\delta,2}$ and $V(0) = 1$. One can verify that the function $g(x) = D_\varrho(x)D_\delta^m(x/m)$, $m \in N$, belongs to $F(\varrho,\delta)$.

Theorem 11. Let $1 \le p \le \infty$, $\sigma, \delta \in R_+^n$, $\varrho = \sigma + \delta$. Let $g \in F(\varrho,\delta)$ Then every function $f \in B_{\sigma,p}$ can be represented by the series

$$f(x) = \sum_{k \in Z^n} f(hk)\, g(x - hk) \tag{2}$$

converging uniformly on R^n for $p < \infty$ and on any compact subset of R^n for $p = \infty$ where $hk = (\pi k_1/\varrho_1, \ldots, \pi k_n/\varrho_n)$.

Theorem 11 without the uniform convergence was proved by CARTWRIGHT [2] in the one-dimensional case (n = 1) with $p = \infty$ and $g(x) = \sin \varrho x \sin \delta x / \varrho \delta x^2$.

3.2 Analogue of Marcinkiewicz' theorem. Marcinkiewicz' theorem establishes the equivalence of the L_p-norm and discrete l_p^{2m+1}-norm for trigonometric polynomials of order at most m (cf. [15]) There is an analogue of this theorem for band-limited functions For a sequence $\{a_k\}_{k \in Z^n}$ of real numbers we define the norm (with the corresponding modification for $p = \infty$)

$$\|\{a_k\}\|_p = \Big(\sum_{k \in Z^n} |a_k|^p \Big)^{1/p} .$$

Theorem 12. Let $1 \leq p \leq \infty$, $\varepsilon > 0$. Then there exist positive constants $c = c(p,\varepsilon)$ and $c' = c'(p,\varepsilon)$ such that

$$cA_p(\sigma) \;\|\{f(hk)\}\|_p \leq \|f\|_p \leq c'A_p(\sigma) \;\|\{f(hk)\}\|_p$$

for every $f \in B_{\sigma,p}$ where $A_p(\sigma) = \prod_{i=1}^{n} \sigma_i^{-1/p}$, $hk = (\pi k_1/z_1,\ldots,\pi k_n/z_n)$, $z = (1+\varepsilon)\sigma$.

The left-hand inequality in Theorem 12 was proved in [12] .

4. Truncation L_q^T-approximation by finite sums

Let $\sigma \in R_+^n$. Consider the function $g(x) = D_\rho(x)D_\delta^m(x/m)$ from $F(\rho,\delta)$ where $\delta \in R_+^n$, $\rho = \sigma + \delta$. For $f \in B_{\sigma,p}$ we define the finite sampling sum $S_M f$, $M \in R_+^n$, from the series (2) as follows

$$S_M f(x) = \sum_{k \in Q_M \cap Z^n} f(hk)\; g(x - hk) .$$

To establish estimates of the ε-dimension and ε-entropy in Theorems 1-10 the L_q^T-approximation by sums $S_M f$ and estimate of the L_p^T-norm of these sums are employed. Set $\|f\|_{p,T} = \|f\|_{L_p^T}$. The following theorems are proved:

Theorem 13. Let $1 \leq p,q \leq \infty$, $b > 1/m$. For any $T \in R_+^n$ define $M \in R_+^n$ by $M_i h_i = T_i + T_i^b$, $i = 1,\dots,n$. Then $\|f - S_M f\|_{q,T}$ converges to 0 uniformly in $SB_{6,p}$, as $T \to \infty$.

Theorem 14. Let $1 \leq p \leq \infty$, $1/m < b < 1$. For any $T \in R_+^n$ define $M \in R_+^n$ by $M_i h_i = T_i - T_i^b$, $i = 1,\dots,n$. Then $\|S_M f\|_{p,T}$ converges to $\|S_M f\|_p$ uniformly in $SB_{6,p}$, as $T \to \infty$.

References

1. Butzer, P.L., Splettstosser, W. and Stens, R.L. (1988) The sampling theorem and linear prediction in signal analysis. Jber. d. Math.- Verein 90, 1-70.

2. Cartwright, M.L. (1936) On certain integral function of order 1. Quart. J. Math., Oxf. Ser. 7, 46-55.

3. Din' Zung (1979) Some approximation characteristics of the classes of smooth functions of several variables in the metric of L_2. Uspekhi Mat. Nauk 34, 189-190.

4. Din' Zung (1980) Mean ε-dimension of the function class $B_{G,p}$. Mat. Zametki 28, 727-736.

5. Din' Zung (1985) Approximation of smooth functions of several variables by means of harmonic analysis, Doctor's Dissertation (Moscow State Univ.).

6. Din' Zung (1986) Approximation by trigonometric polynomials

of functions of several variables on torus. Mat. Sb. 131, 251-271.

7. Din' Zung and Magaril-Il'jaev, G.G. (1979) Problems of Bernstein and Farvard type and the mean ε-dimension of some classes of functions. Dokl. Akad. Nauk SSSR 249, 783-786.

8. Kolmogorov, A.N. (1987) Information theory and theory of algorithms (Nauka, Moscow).

9. Kolmogorov, A.N. and Tikhomirov, V.M. (1959) ε-entropy and ε-capacity of sets in function spaces. Uspekhi Mat. Nauk 14, 3-86.

10. Kotelnikov, V.A. (1933) On the truncation capacity of " either" and wire in electrocommunications, In: " Material for the First All-Union Conference on Questions of Communications (Moscow).

11. Le Truong Tung (1980) The mean ε-dimension of the class of functions whose Fourier trnsform have the support contained in a preassigned set. Vestnik of Moscow State Univ., Ser Math. Mech. 5, 44-49.

12. Nikolskii, S.M. (1975) Approximation of fucntions of several variables and imbedding theorems (Springer-Verlag, Berlin-Heidelberg- New York).

13. Shannon, C.E. (1949) Communication in the presence of noise. Proc. IRE 37, 10-21.

14. Tikhomirov, V.M. (1957) On ε-entropy of some classes of analytic functions. Dokl. Akad. Nauk SSSR 117, 191-194.

15. Zygmund, A. (1958) Trigonometric series, II (Cambridge Univ. Press).

Dinh-Dung

Institute of Computer Science and Cybernetics
Lieu Giai, Ba Dinh, Hanoi, Vietnam

International Series of
Numerical Mathematics, Vol. 90

MULTIDIMENSIONAL IRREGULAR SAMPLING OF BAND-LIMITED FUNCTIONS IN L^p-SPACES

Hans G. Feichtinger
Institut für Mathematik
Universität Wien

Karlheinz Gröchenig
Department of Mathematics, U-9
University of Connecticut

It is the purpose of this note to present a qualitative approach to irregular variants of the so-called Sampling theorem for band-limited functions on $\mathbb{R}^m$. *The basic assertion is the following: Given a compact subset* $\Omega \subseteq \mathbb{R}^m$ *there is critical sampling rate* $\delta_0 = \delta_0(\Omega) > 0$ *such thatany band-limited* $f \in L^p(\mathbb{R}^m)$ *with spec* $f \subseteq \Omega$ *can be completely reconstructed from the sampling values* $(f(x_i)_{i \in I}$ *at any* δ_0*-dense discrete family of points* $X = (x_i)_{i \in I}$. *The reconstruction will be obtained by an iterative procedure yielding a sequence of smooth approximations of f, convergent to f in the* L^p*-sense for* $1 \leq p < \infty$.

1. Introduction.

One of the most important mathematical results for information theory and digital signal processing is the famous sampling theorem (due to Shannon, Whittacker, Kotel'nikov and others, cf. [1] and the references given there). It states that an important class of smooth functions - the so-called band-limited functions - can be completely recovered from the sampling values on a sufficiently fine regular lattice by means of the cardinal series. On the other hand the Theorem of Plancherel-Polya (cf.[7]) states that the discrete ℓ^p-sum of the sampling values $(f(x_i)_{i\in I})$ defines an equivalent norm on the band-limited L^p-function under suitable conditions. Thus f is uniquely determined by its sampling values (cf. also [8]); however, no method of reconstruction is provided and this result has no practical consequences.

As a positive answer to this problem, which is also of interest for digital signal processing, we presented in a series of recent papers (cf. [3],[4],[5]) a very general method to reconstruct band-limited functions from their irregular sampling values. The result given so far use spline-type approximation operators, followed by convolutions (filters) with band-limited auxiliary functions. In the present note a new elegant approach is taken, avoiding the use of an auxiliary function. It also allows touse more general filters (including many, which are not band-limited), which yields much better decay properties, hence better localization properties of the iterative procedure, which is of interest if one thinks of parallel processing.

2. Notations

In order to present the basic ideas of our approach as clear as possible (involving some features not present in the more detailed and quantitative presentations obtained earlier) we restrict our discussion to band-limited functions in $L^p(\mathbb{R}^m)$ for $1 \le p < \infty$. More precisely, we shall consider for a fixed compact set $\Omega \subseteq \mathbb{R}^m$ and p as above the space

$$B^p(\Omega) := \{ f \in L^p(\mathbb{R}^m),\ \text{supp}\ \hat{f} \subseteq \Omega \},$$

where supp $\hat{f}$ has to be understood as the support of the Fourier transform of f in the sense of tempered distributions (at least for p>2). The p-norm of f is written as $\|f\|_p := (\int_{\mathbb{R}^m} |f(x)|^p dx)^{1/p}$. We recall that convolution on $\mathcal{K}(\mathbb{R}^m) :=$ { f, complex-valued, continuous, supp f compact } is given pointwise for $f,g \in \mathcal{K}(\mathbb{R}^m)$ through the formula

$$f * g(x) := \int_{\mathbb{R}^m} f(y-x)g(y)dy,$$

and satisfies $\|f * g\|_p \le \|g\|_1 \|f\|_p$ for $p \ge 1$. In particular, $(L^1, \|\ \|_1)$ is a Banach algebra with respect to convolution. The translation operators are given by $T_x f(z) := f(z-x)$ for $f \in \mathcal{K}(\mathbb{R}^m)$.

3. Local Properties of Band-limited Functions.

In the course of our discussions the following two auxiliary functions, associated in a canonical way to any locally bounded (hence any continuous) function will be important (we write $B_\delta(x)$ for the ball of radius δ around $x \in \mathbb{R}^m$, $B(x)$ for $B_1(x)$; $U \subseteq B(0)$ denotes an arbitrary neighborhood of zero).

3.1. Definition. The local maximal function associated to f is given by

$$f^{\#}(x) := \sup_{z \in B(x)} |f(z)| . \tag{3.1}$$

The local U-oscillation of f is given by

$$\text{osc}_U f(x) := \sup_{z,y \in x+U} |f(z)-f(y)| . \tag{3.2}$$

We shall use the symbol $\text{osc}_\delta f$ if $U = B_\delta(0)$. With the help of these notations we may introduce a family of new spaces by

$C^p(\mathbb{R}^m) :=$ { f continuous, complex-valued on $\mathbb{R}^m$, $f^{\#} \in L^p(\mathbb{R}^m)$ } for $1 \le p < \infty$.

It is left to the reader to verify that one has

3.2. Lemma. i) For $1 \le p < \infty$ the spaces $C^p(\mathbb{R}^m)$ are Banach spaces with respect to their natural norm $f \longmapsto \|f^{\#}\|_p$;

ii) For $1 \le p \le q < \infty$ there is a continuous embedding $C^p(\mathbb{R}^m) \hookrightarrow C^q(\mathbb{R}^m)$;

iii) The space $\mathcal{K}(\mathbb{R}^m)$ is dense in $C^p(\mathbb{R}^m)$ for $1 \le p < \infty$. In particular, the spaces $C^p(\mathbb{R}^m)$ are continuously embedded into $(C^0(\mathbb{R}^m), \| \ \|_\infty)$, the space of continuous complex-valued functions vanishing at infinity, with the sup-norm.

iv) $C^1(\mathbb{R}^m) \hookrightarrow L^1 \cap C^0(\mathbb{R}^m) \hookrightarrow L^r(\mathbb{R}^m)$ for any $r \geq 1$.

The following facts will be relevant for our proofs:

3.3. Proposition. i) The following inequality holds pointwise:

$$(f * g)^{\#} \leq |f| * g^{\#}; \tag{3.3}$$

ii) Therefore the following convolution relations hold true (together with corresponding norm estimates):

$$L^1 * C^p \subseteq C^p \tag{3.4}$$

$$L^p * C^1 \subseteq C^p \tag{3.5}$$

for $1 \leq p < \infty$.

Proof. The verification of i) is left to the reader, and (3.4) follows therefrom, the continuity of the convolution product resulting from the inclusion $C^p \subseteq C^0$ which gives $L^1 * C^p \subseteq C^0$. (3.5) follows in a similar way, using now the fact that $L^p * C^1 \subseteq L^p * L^{p'} \subseteq C^0(\mathbb{R}^m)$, where $1/p' + 1/p = 1$.

As a consequence for band-limited functions we obtain the following

3.4. Proposition. i) For any compact set $\Omega \subseteq \mathbb{R}^m$ one has $B^p(\Omega) \hookrightarrow C^p(\mathbb{R}^m)$, i.e. there exists a constant $C_\Omega > 0$ such that

$$\|f^{\#}\|_p \leq C_\Omega \|f\|_p \quad \text{for all } f \in B^p(\Omega) \tag{3.6}$$

Proof. It is sufficient to choose some $h \in C^1$ such that $\hat{h}(t) \equiv 1$ on Ω (e.g. h may be taken to be the inverse Fourier transform of a convolution product of two characteristic functions of rectangles in $\mathbb{R}^m$, or of some function g in the Schwartz space $\mathcal{S}(\mathbb{R}^m)$ with $g(t) \equiv 1$ on Ω.). It follows that $f = h * f$ for all $f \in B^p(\Omega)$, and thus by (3.3) $\|f^{\#}\|_p \leq \|h^{\#}\|_1 \|f\|_p$, q.e.d. .

Similar assertions can be made with respect to the oscillation.

3.5. Proposition. i) The following pointwise inequality holds true:

$$\mathrm{osc}_U(f * h) \leq |f| * \mathrm{osc}_U h ; \tag{3.7}$$

ii) For any compact set $\Omega \subseteq \mathbb{R}^m$ there exists $C^1_\Omega > 0$ such that

$$\|\mathrm{osc}_\delta(f)\|_p \leq \delta \cdot C^1_\Omega \cdot \|f\|_p \quad \text{for all } f \in B^p(\Omega). \tag{3.8}$$

Proof. The verification of i) is left to the reader. In order to prove ii) it is then sufficient to show for some $h \in C^1(\mathbb{R}^m)$ (as in the proof of Prop.3.4) that one has $\|\mathrm{osc}_\delta(h)\|_1 \leq \delta \cdot C^1_\Omega$. For the one-dimensional case this is verified by observing that the mean value theorem implies

$$|h(z)-h(y)| \le 2\delta|h'(\xi)| \text{ for some } \xi \text{ between } z \text{ and } y, \text{ hence}$$

$$|osc_\delta(h)| \le 2\delta(h')^{\#} \quad \text{for } h \in C^1(\mathbb{R}) .$$

In the general m-dimensional setting the same kind of estimate can be obtained by replacing the simple derivative by the absolute value (norm) of the gradient of h (cf. [4] for details). The desired estimate is then obtained for any h satisfying $|grad|^{\#} \in L^1(\mathbb{R}^m)$ (e.g. for $h \in \mathcal{S}(\mathbb{R}^m)$).

Before we can prove a version of the Plancherel-Polya theorem with these ingredients we have to describe more precisely the discrete sets $X = (x_i)_{i\in I}$ of interest in this context.

3.6. Definition. Given a compact neighborhood U of zero a family X is called U-dense in $\mathbb{R}^m$ if the family $(x_i+U)_{i\in I}$ covers $\mathbb{R}^m$ (in the case $U = B_\delta(x)$ we speak of δ-density) . It is called relatively separated if there is a uniform bound C_d for the number of points x_i in any of the balls $B(x)$ (independent of x). It is called well-spread if it is δ-dense (for some $\delta>0$) and relatively separated.

We shall only consider neighborhoods $U \subseteq B(0)$ in the sequel.

3.7. Theorem. i) For any relatively separated family $X = (x_i)_{i\in I}$ in $\mathbb{R}^m$ there exists a constant $C = C(C_d)$ such that

(3.9) $$(\Sigma_{i\in I}|f(x_i)|^p)^{1/p} \le C\cdot\|f^{\#}\|_p \quad \text{for all } f \in C^p(\mathbb{R}^m).$$

ii) For any compact set $\Omega \subseteq \mathbb{R}^m$ there exists a neighborhood $\delta_o > 0$ such that for any relatively separated and δ_o-dense family X in $\mathbb{R}^m$ the expression $(\Sigma_{i\in I}|f(x_i)|^p)^{1/p}$ defines an equivalent norm on $B^p(\Omega)$.

Proof. o) We start with the general observation that for any $\delta>0$ the expression $(\Sigma_{i\in I}\ |f(x_i)|^p)^{1/p}$ defines a norm equivalent to $\|\Sigma_{i\in I}\ |f(x_i)|\chi_{B_\delta(x_i)}\|_p$ in the given situation (where χ_M denotes the indicator-function of the set M). In fact, if the family X has the property that $(B(x_i))_{i\in I}$ defines a family of pairwise disjoint sets $(\Sigma_{i\in I}|f(x_i)|^p)^{1/p}$ can be interpreted, up to some constant, as the L^p-norm of the function $f_X := \Sigma_{i\in I}|f(x_i)|\chi_{B_\delta(x_i)}$. For arbitrary relatively separated sets X the same estimate (up the constant depending only on C_d) is obtained, splitting X into a finite union of discrete sets X^k, $1 \le k \le k_o$ of the above type.

i) Since we have the pointwise inequality $|f_X| \leq C \cdot f^{\#}$ it follows

$$\|f_X\|_p \leq \|f^{\#}\|_p \,.$$

ii) The relevant estimate from below is based on the following inequality: $|f(x)| \leq |f(x_i)| + osc_U f(x_i)$ for all $x \in x_i + U$; upon summation we obtain

$$\sum_{i\in I} |f(x_i)|\chi_{x_i+U} \geq \sum_{i\in I} (|f|\chi_{x_i+U} - osc_U f(x_i)\chi_{x_i+U}) \;;$$

Taking p-norms on both sides this gives

$$\| \sum_{i\in I} |f(x_i)|\chi_{x_i+U}\|_p \geq \|\sum_{i\in I} |f|\chi_{x_i+U}\|_p - \|\sum_{i\in I} osc_U f(x_i)\chi_{x_i+U}\|_p \geq$$

$$\geq \|f\|_p - \|\sum_{i\in I} osc_U f(x_i)\chi_{x_i+U}\|_p \quad \text{(because } X \text{ is } \delta\text{-dense)} := *).$$

But $\|\sum_{i\in I} osc_U f(x_i)\chi_{x_i+U}\|_p \leq \|osc_U(f)^{\#}\|_p \leq \delta \cdot C^2 \|f\|_p$ (by a modification of 3.5.). For a suitable choice of U_o we may ensure that for any $U \subseteq U_o$ the above estimate may be continued by $*) \geq \|f\|_p - 0.5 \cdot \|f\|_p = 0.5 \cdot \|f\|_p$, as was required.

As an immediate consequence we have the following uniqueness theorem:

3.8. Corollary. In the situation of Theorem 3.7. the complete vanishing of a band-limited function f at all points $(x_i)_{i\in I}$ of any U_o-dense family X implies that f is identically zero.

It is an interesting consequence of the theory of *frames* (as developed in [2]; cf. also [8] for a treatment on nonharmonic Fourier series) that in the L^2-case the norm equivalence allows at least on the analytic level to reconstruct f completely from its sampling values. In fact, denoting for a moment by g the function $\mathcal{F}^{-1}\chi_\Omega$ (thus $\hat{g}$ equals the indicator function of Ω), the norm equivalence can be reinterpreted as the fact that the operator $\mathcal{D}$: $f \longmapsto \sum_{i\in I} f(x_i) L_{x_i} g$ is positive and satisfies the following inequality:

$$A \cdot Id \leq \mathcal{D} \leq B \cdot Id \quad \text{for suitable values } A,B > 0.$$

It follows that $Id - B^{-1} \cdot \mathcal{D} \leq B^{-1}(A-B) \cdot Id$, hence $\mathcal{D}$ is invertible (by the usual Neumann series) and $\mathcal{D}^{-1} = B \cdot \sum_{n=1}^{\infty} (Id - B^{-1} \cdot \mathcal{D})^n$. Hence

$$f = \mathcal{D}^{-1} \circ \mathcal{D}(f) = \sum_{i\in I} f(x_i) \mathcal{D}^{-1}(L_{x_i} g) \;,$$

This reconstruction, however, is only of theoretical importance because it has the same drawbacks as the classical sampling cardinal series. The kernel g in the series $\sum_{i\in I} f(x_i) \cdot L_{x_i} g$ has as poor decay properties as the sinc-function. Thus this reconstruction has a rather bad stability behavior and it is useless for numerical analysis.

4. A Reconstruction Algorithm

The last remark raises the problem of finding efficient reconstruction algorithms. We present such a method in this section, with the following desirable properties: a) good localization; b) good stability with respect to numerical errors; c) great generality, going far beyond the Hilbert space case. Since our space is limited here we present the qualitative theory in the setting of L^p-spaces, which does not require too many technical details.

In the first step of the approximation we need the simple fact, that step functions are reasonable good approximations for smooth functions.

<u>4.1. Lemma.</u> Given a family $X = (x_i)_{i\in I}$ in $\mathbb{R}^m$ we denote by $\mathcal{V}_X f$ the most natural step function associated to the family $(f(x_i))_{i\in I}$, given by

(4.1) $$\mathcal{V}_X f(x) = \sum_{i\in I} f(x_i)\cdot\chi_{V_i} ,$$

where V_i is the so-called Voronoi region of nearest neighbors,

$$V_i := \{ x|\ |x-x_j| < |x-x_i| \text{ for all } j \neq i \} .$$

Then one has for any U-dense family $X = (x_i)_{i\in I}$:

(4.2) $$|\mathcal{V}_X f-f| \le \mathrm{osc}_\delta f \ ;$$

and

(4.3) $$|\mathcal{V}_X f| \le f^{\#} .$$

In particular $\|\mathcal{V}_X f-f\|_p \le \|\mathrm{osc}_U f\|_p \longrightarrow 0$ for $U \longrightarrow \{0\}$, for any $f \in C^p$.

The following theorem is the *main result* of this paper. It gives (in the proof) an algorithm which allows to reconstruct the band-limited function from its sampling values.

<u>4.2. Theorem.</u> Let Ω be a compact subset of $\mathbb{R}^m$ and $h \in C^1(\mathbb{R}^m)$ with $\hat{h}(t) \equiv 1$ on Ω be given. Then there exists some compact neighborhood U of the origin and $C = C(h,U)$ such that the following is true: Given any family $X=(x_i)_{i\in I}$ which is U-dense in $\mathbb{R}^m$ there is a bounded linear operator $\mathcal{B}$ on $C^p(\mathbb{R}^m)$ with

(4.4) $$f = \mathcal{B}(V_X f * h) \text{ for all } f \in B^p(\Omega),$$

and $|||\mathcal{B}||| \le C$ (for all p, $1 \le p < \infty$). In particular, complete reconstruction of $f \in B(\Omega)$ from its sampling values is possible.

<u>Proof.</u> Our first observation concerns the fact that we have $f = f * h$ for $f \in B^p(\Omega)$, and therefore $\mathcal{V}_X f * h$ appears as a reasonable and smooth approximation to f. In fact, the "remainder" operator $\mathcal{R}$: $f \longmapsto (f-\mathcal{V}_X f) * h$ will be very useful for us. It is bounded on $C^p(\mathbb{R}^m)$, since by (3.3) and (4.3)

(4.5) $$|\mathcal{R}f|^{\#} = |((f-\mathcal{V}_X f) * h)^{\#}| \le |f-\mathcal{V}_X f| * h^{\#} \le 2\cdot f^{\#} * h^{\#}$$

which implies upon taking norms

(4.6) $$\|\mathcal{R}f\|_{C^p} = \|\mathcal{R}f^{\#}\|_p \leq 2\cdot\|f^{\#}\|_p\cdot\|h^{\#}\|_1 = (2\|h^{\#}\|_1)\cdot\|f\|_{C^p} .$$

Another pointwise estimate based on (4.2) is even more important:

(4.7) $$|\mathcal{R}f| \leq |f-\mathcal{V}_X f| * |h| \leq osc_\delta(f) * |h| .$$

It allows us to verify that $\mathcal{R}^2$ is a contraction on C^p (given sufficient density of the family X only). Applying (4.6) to $\mathcal{R}f$ and using (3.3) yields

(4.8) $$(\mathcal{R}^2 f)^{\#} \leq (osc_U(\mathcal{R}f) * h)^{\#} \leq ocs_U(\mathcal{R}f) * h^{\#},$$

which gives together with the following estimate (involving (3.7) and (4.3))

(4.9) $$osc_U(\mathcal{R}f) \leq |f-\mathcal{V}_X f| * osc_U(h) \leq 2f^{\#} * osc_U(h)$$

the following combined estimate

(4.10) $$(\mathcal{R}^2 f)^{\#} \leq f^{\#} * (2\cdot h^{\#} * osc_U(h)) .$$

Taking p-norms on both sides we obtain the decisive estimate

(4.11) $$\|\mathcal{R}^2 f\|_{C^p} = \|(\mathcal{R}^2 f)^{\#}\|_p \leq \|f\|_{C^p}\cdot 2\|h^{\#} * osc_U(h)\|_1 .$$

Since $\|osc_U(h)\|_1 \longrightarrow 0$ for $U \longrightarrow \{0\}$ for any $h \in C^1$ it is now clear that $\mathcal{R}^2$ is a contraction, i.e. $|||\mathcal{R}^2||| \leq \gamma < 1$ for U small enough.

The decisive step is the following identity which holds true for $n \geq 0$:

(4.12) $$f = \mathcal{R}^{n+1} f + (\textstyle\sum_{k=0}^{n} \mathcal{R}^k)(\mathcal{V}_X f * h) .$$

It is proved by induction. Since it is true for n=0 by the definition of $\mathcal{R}$ we assume that it is true for 1,...n−1. Using the identity $f = f * h$ we obtain

(4.13) $$\mathcal{R}^n f = \mathcal{R}^n(f * h) = \mathcal{R}^n(\mathcal{V}_X f * h + (f-\mathcal{V}_X f) * h) = \mathcal{R}^n(\mathcal{V}_X f * h) + \mathcal{R}^{n+1} f ,$$

showing that the inductive step can be verified.

Since we now already that $|||\mathcal{R}^{2n}||| \leq \gamma^n$ and thus by (4.6) $|||\mathcal{R}^{2n+1}||| \leq$ $\leq 2\|h^{\#}\|_1\cdot\gamma^n$ for U small enough it follows that the series $\mathcal{B} := \sum_{k=0}^{\infty} \mathcal{R}^k$ is convergent (on the operator algebra over C^p for any $p \geq 1$) and

(4.14) $$|||\mathcal{B}||| \leq (1-\gamma)^{-1}(1+2\|h^{\#}\|_1) =: C .$$

Finally we obtain (4.4) by taking limits in (4.12):

$$f = (\textstyle\sum_{k=0}^{\infty} \mathcal{R}^k)(\mathcal{V}_X f * h) = \mathcal{B}(\mathcal{V}_X f * h),$$ and our proof is complete.

<u>4.3. Corollary.</u> In the above situation there exists a bounded family $(e_i)_{i \in I}$ in C^1 such that any $f \in B^p(\Omega)$, $1 \leq p < \infty$, can be written as

(4.15) $$f = \textstyle\sum_{i \in I} f(x_i)\cdot e_i ,$$

with unconditional convergence in $C^p(\mathbb{R}^m)$, hence locally uniformly and in L^p.

<u>Proof.</u> Recall that $V_X f = \sum_{i\in I} f(x_i)\chi_{V_i}$ (with unconditional convergence in L^p, i.e. as limit of partial sums over finite subsets of the index set I). Using now (3.5) we observe that $V_X f * h$ is well defined and coincides with the series $\sum_{i\in I} f(x_i)\chi_{V_i} * h$, which converges in C^p $(1\le p<\infty)$. Applying now the operator $\mathcal{B}$ (which acts boundedly on C^p) we observe that

$$\mathcal{B}(V_X f * h) = \sum_{i\in I} f(x_i)\cdot\mathcal{B}(\chi_{V_i} * h) .$$

Thus setting $e_i := \mathcal{B}(\chi_{V_i} * h)$ we have proved the desired result, since boundedness in C^1 follows from the estimate

$$\|e_i\|_{C^1} = \|\mathcal{B}(\chi_{V_i} * h)\|_{C^1} \le |||\mathcal{B}||| \; \|(\chi_{V_i} * h)^{\#}\|_1 \le \qquad C\cdot\|\chi_{V_i}\|_1 \; \|h^{\#}\|_1 \le C\cdot|U|\cdot\|h^{\#}\|_1$$

for all $i \in I$. This completes the proof.

<u>4.4. Remark.</u> The last result is of particular interest in the case of periodic sampling, i.e. if there is a finite set $F \subseteq \mathbb{R}^m$ and same lattice Λ such that X is of the form $X = F + \Lambda$. In that case it is only necessary to calculate explicitly a finite collection of e_i's (the other ones being of the form $T_\lambda e_i$ for some $\lambda \in \Lambda$).

5. References

[1] Butzer,P. W.Splettstößer and R.L.Stens (1988): The sampling theorem and linear prediction in signal analysis. Jber.d.Dt.Math.-Ver. **90**, 1-70.

[2] Duffin,R; and A.Schaeffer (1952): A class of nonharmonic Fourier series. Trans. Amer.Math.Soc. 72, 341-366.

[3] Feichtinger, H.G. (1988): Discretization of convolution and reconstruction of band-limited functions from irregular sampling. To appear.

[4] Feichtinger, H.G. and K.Gröchenig (1989): Reconstruction of band-limited functions from irregular sampling values. To appear.

[5] Feichtinger, H.G. and K.Gröchenig (1989): Irregular sampling theorems and series expansions of band-limited functions. To appear.

[6] Marvasti, F.A. (1987): A unified approach to zero-crossing and nonuniform sampling of single and multi-dimensional systems. Nonuniform. P.O.Box 1505, Oak Park, IL 60304.

[7] Triebel,H. (1983): Theory of Function spaces. Akad.Verlagsges.,Leipzig 1983.

[8] Walker,W.J. (1987): The separation of zeros for entire functions of exponential type, J.Math.Anal.Appl. 122, 257-259.

[9] Young, R: An Introduction to Nonharmonic Fourier Series. Acad.Press, New York, 1980.

More hints on existing literature are given in the above references.

International Series of
Numerical Mathematics, Vol. 90

L^2-Synthesis by Ambiguity Functions

Ephraim Feig and Charles A. Micchelli
IBM Research Division
Thomas J. Watson Research Center
P. O. Box 218
Yorktown Heights, New York 10598

Abstract

A class of operators on $L^2(\mathcal{R}^2)$ are introduced which, when acting on rank-one tensors, yield ambiguity functions and their generalizations. The L^2- synthesis problem by functions in the range of these operators is solved. The same approach applied to functions whose Fourier transforms are rank-one tensors yields analogous results for wideband ambiguity functions (wavelet transforms).

1 Introduction

For any complex-valued functions $f, g \in L^2(\mathcal{R})$, their cross-ambiguity function is defined by Woodward [28] as

$$A(f,g)(u,v) = \int_{-\infty}^{\infty} f\left(t+\frac{u}{2}\right)\bar{g}\left(t-\frac{u}{2}\right) e^{2\pi i v t}\, dt\,. \tag{1}$$

The ambiguity function and its related variants (such as the Wigner transform) play major roles in several areas of physical science and electrical engineering. In quantum mechanics it is known as the mixed Wigner quasi- probability distribution, where it is useful in the mathematical theory of the uncertainty principle, [25]. In radar detection theory, the ambiguity function gives a measurement of the ability to determine both target range and radial velocity from a single radar pulse and its echoes. It combines the effect of time delays and Doppler shifts resulting from the transmitted pulse and its reflections from various targets [7,8,15,26,28]. The auto-ambiguity function (the case when $f = g$) plays a similar role in signal processing techniques for sonar detection as well as in theoretical optics, where it is sometimes referred to as the indeterminacy or spread function [2,12].

There has been a great deal of interest in the mathematical and computational problems associated with the ambiguity function. The major effort of this work seems to be directed towards two issues. In radar detection, ambiguity surfaces yield important information about target speed and location. Unfortunately, computing the ambiguity function is a time consuming and expensive numerical procedure. In [5,6,24] this problem is addressed and new methods for computing the discrete ambiguity surface are discussed. On the other hand, the relationship between the ambiguity function and nilpotent harmonic analysis has been realized by Schempp [16,17,18,19] and has been actively investigated [1,20,21,22].

Our motivation for this paper comes from a question posed by Woodward [28], and discussed by Wilcox [26], Sussman [23], Wolf, et al [27], and Auslander and Tolimieri [1]. They were concerned with how to recognize whether or not a given surface is an ambiguity function and how to approximate given surfaces with ambiguity functions. This is the inversion problem and we will address this issue here.

One approach to this problem is to measure the discrepancy between a given surface and an arbitrary ambiguity function. Then ambiguity surfaces are characterized by having zero distance to the manifold of all ambiguity surfaces. The choice of the distance function is critical. As it turns out, a fortuitous choice is the L^2 norm on $\mathcal{R}^2$. In this case, there is an elegant solution to the L^2-synthesis problem because of a simple operator theoretic decomposition of the ambiguity operator, which we describe below. The problem in other norms remains to be solved, especially in the important case of the L^∞-synthesis problem.

Our original work on this problem is, in fact, several years old and was done before we were aware of [26]. We have decided to describe them now in light of the recent interest in wideband ambiguity functions [14] and wavelet transforms [3,4,10,11,13]. More details and further develpoments can be found in [9].

2 Generalized Ambiguity Functions

We will adhere to the notational convention of using lower case letters for functions in $L^2(\mathcal{R})$ and upper case letters for functions in $L^2(\mathcal{R}^2)$. For linear operators acting on either $L^2(\mathcal{R})$ or $L^2(\mathcal{R}^2)$ we use script letters. The inner product on $L^2(\mathcal{R})$ is denoted by

$$(f,g) := \int_{-\infty}^{\infty} f(t)\, \bar{g}(t)\, dt$$

while for $K, T \in L^2(\mathcal{R}^2)$ we use

$$< K, T > := \int_{-\infty}^{\infty}\int_{-\infty}^{\infty} K(u,v)\, \bar{T}(u,v)\, du\, dv\, .$$

The corresponding norms are denoted by $\|f\|$ and $|K|$, respectively.

Let $SL(2;\mathcal{R})$ denote the algebra of 2×2 matrices with determinant ± 1. Every $B \in SL(2;\mathcal{R})$ defines a unitary operator $\mathcal{S}_B$ by means of the composition

$$\mathcal{S}_B K := K \circ B\, .$$

Thus, for $B = \begin{pmatrix} a & b \\ c & d \end{pmatrix} \in SL(2;\mathcal{R})$ we have

$$(\mathcal{S}_B K)(u,v) := K(au+bv, cu+dv)\, .$$

We also introduce the one-dimensional Fourier transforms operating on $L^2(\mathcal{R}^2)$

$$(\mathcal{F}_1 K)(u,v) = \int_{-\infty}^{\infty} K(t,v)\, e^{2\pi i t u}\, dt$$

and

$$(\mathcal{F}_2 K)(u,v) = \int_{-\infty}^{\infty} K(u,t)\, e^{2\pi i t v}\, dt\, .$$

Note that $\mathcal{F}_1$ and $\mathcal{F}_2$ are also unitary operators. The following identities are easily established:

$$\mathcal{F} = \mathcal{F}_1\mathcal{F}_2 = \mathcal{F}_2\mathcal{F}_1 \tag{2}$$

$$\mathcal{F}_1 = \mathcal{S}_E \mathcal{F}_2 \, \mathcal{S}_E \,, \qquad E = \begin{pmatrix} 0 & 1 \\ 1 & 0 \end{pmatrix}, \tag{3}$$

$$\mathcal{F}_2{}^2 = \mathcal{S}_D \,, \qquad D = \begin{pmatrix} 1 & 0 \\ 0 & -1 \end{pmatrix} \tag{4}$$

$$\mathcal{S}_B \, \mathcal{S}_C = \mathcal{S}_{CB} \qquad B, C \in SL(2; \mathcal{R}) \,. \tag{5}$$

We also have the adjoint operators

$$\mathcal{S}_B{}^\star = \mathcal{S}_{B^{-1}} \tag{6}$$

and

$$\mathcal{F}_2{}^\star = \mathcal{S}_D \mathcal{F}_2 = \mathcal{F}_2 \, \mathcal{S}_D \,. \tag{7}$$

For $B \in SL(2; \mathcal{R})$ we define the unitary operator

$$\mathcal{U}_B = \mathcal{S}_B \mathcal{F}_2 \,. \tag{8}$$

Its adjoint is

$$\mathcal{U}_B^\star = \mathcal{F}_2{}^\star \, \mathcal{S}_B{}^\star = \mathcal{F}_2 \, \mathcal{S}_D \, \mathcal{S}_{B^{-1}} = \mathcal{F}_2 \, \mathcal{S}_{B^{-1}D} \tag{9}$$

which, when written out explicitly, is given by the formula

$$\mathcal{U}_B^\star(K)(u,v) = \int_{-\infty}^{\infty} K\left(\frac{du+bt}{ad-bc}, \frac{-cu-at}{ad-bc}\right) e^{2\pi i v t} \, dt \,. \tag{10}$$

For $A = \begin{pmatrix} 1 & -1 \\ -\frac{1}{2} & -\frac{1}{2} \end{pmatrix}$, we have

$$\mathcal{U}_A^\star(f \otimes g) = A(f,g) \,, \tag{11}$$

where $(f \otimes g)(x,y) = f(x)\bar{g}(y)$. Thus, $\mathcal{U}_B^\star$ can be thought of as a generalized ambiguity function. Different choices of matrices will yield, for example, the assymmetric ambiguity function or the Wigner transform.

We list below some useful observations about the generalized ambiguity function.

Theorem 2.1 *For any $B \in SL(2; \mathcal{R})$*

1. $< \mathcal{U}_B^\star(f,g), K > = (f, \mathcal{U}_B(K)g)$.
2. $< \mathcal{U}_B^\star(f,g) \,,\, \mathcal{U}_B^\star(h,k) > = (f,g)(h,k)$.
3. $|\mathcal{U}_B^\star(f,g)|^2 = \|f\|^2 \, \|g\|^2$.
4. *If $f_n \to f$ and $g_n \to g$ in $L^2(\mathcal{R})$ then*

$$\lim_{n\to\infty} \mathcal{U}_B^\star(f_n, g_n) = \mathcal{U}_B^\star(f,g) \in L^2(\mathcal{R}^2) \,.$$

5. $\mathcal{U}_B^\star(f,g) = 0$ *if and only if either* $f = 0$ *or* $g = 0$.
6. $\mathcal{U}_B^\star(f,g) = \mathcal{U}_B^\star(h,k)$ *where both* $f \neq 0$ *and* $g \neq 0$ *if and only if* $f = \alpha h$ *and* $g = \beta h$ *for some constants* α, β *with* $\alpha\bar{\beta} = 1$.
7. *The linear span of* $\{\mathcal{U}_B^\star(f,f) \, : \, f \in L^2(\mathcal{R})\}$ *is dense in* $L^2(\mathcal{R}^2)$.
8. $\mathcal{U}_B^\star(f,g)(u,v)$ *is a continuous function of* $(u,v) \in \mathcal{R}^2$ *which achieves its maximum at the origin.*

Proof: The first seven assertions hold for the sesquilinear form $f \otimes g$, and since they are preserved under a unitary transformation, they also hold for $\mathcal{U}_B^\star$. The last assertion is proved by using the Cauchy-Schwartz inequality and the Lebesque dominated convergence theorem. □

3 Approximations by Ambiguity Functions

In this section we consider the problem of approximating $K \in L^2(\mathcal{R}^2)$ by generalized ambiguity functions. We begin by noting the following simple lemma.

Lemma 3.1 *For any elements* $x, y \neq 0$ *in a Hilbert space, we have*

$$min\{ \, ||x - \alpha y||^2 \, : \, \alpha \in \mathcal{R}_+ \, \} \; = \; ||x||^2 \; - \; \frac{(Re(x,y)_+)^2}{||y||^2} \tag{12}$$

where $t_+ = max\,(t, 0)$. *Also*

$$min\{ \, ||x - \alpha y||^2 \, : \, \alpha \in \mathcal{R} \, \} \; = \; ||x||^2 \; - \; \frac{(Re(x,y))^2}{||y||^2} \tag{13}$$

and

$$min\{ \, ||x - \alpha y||^2 \, : \, \alpha \in \mathcal{C} \, \} \; = \; ||x||^2 \; - \; \frac{|(x,y)|^2}{||y||^2} \, . \tag{14}$$

Proof: Clearly (14) follows from (13) and (13) from (12). To prove (12) we note that the quadratic $||x - \alpha y||^2$ has a minimum at $Re(x,y) \, / \, ||y||^2$. □

Every $K \in L^2(\mathcal{R}^2)$ acts on $L^2(\mathcal{R})$ as a Hilbert-Schmidt operator

$$\mathcal{K}(f)(t) \; := \; \int_{-\infty}^{\infty} K(t,s) f(s) \, ds \, .$$

Denote by $\sigma_1(K) \geq \sigma_2(K) \geq \cdots$ the singular values of $\mathcal{K}$, so that for some orthonormal sequence $\phi_1, \phi_2, \cdots$ in $L^2(\mathcal{R})$ we have

$$\begin{aligned} \mathcal{K}^\star \mathcal{K} \phi_i &= \sigma_i \phi_i \\ (\phi_i, \phi_j) &= \delta_{ij} \, . \end{aligned}$$

Then

$$|K|^2 = trace\,(\mathcal{K}^\star\mathcal{K}) = \sum_{i=1}^{\infty} \sigma_i(\mathcal{K})\,.$$

For K Hermitian, i.e., $\bar{K}(v,u) = K(u,v)$, let $\lambda_1(K)$ denote the largest positive eigenvalue of its induced operator $\mathcal{K}$ and f_1 the corresponding normalized eigenfunction,

$$\mathcal{K}f_1 = \lambda_1 f_1\,, \qquad (f_1, f_1) = 1\,. \tag{15}$$

Theorem 3.2 *For any $K \in L^2(\mathcal{R}^2)$ and any $B \in SL(2;\mathcal{R})$, we let K_B be the kernel representing $\mathcal{K}_B := \mathcal{U}_B(\mathcal{K})$. Then we have*

(i) $min\,\{\,|K - \mathcal{U}_B^\star(f,f)|^2 \;:\; f \in L^2(\mathcal{R})\,\}$

$$= \begin{cases} |K_B|^2\,, & \textit{if } \mathcal{K}_B \textit{ is negative semi-definite} \\ |K_B|^2 - {\lambda_1}^2\left(\frac{\mathcal{K}_B + \mathcal{K}_B^\star}{2}\right), & \textit{otherwise} \end{cases}$$

Moreover, in the latter case, equality is achieved for $f_{opt} := Re(\mathcal{K}_B f_1, f_1) f_1$ *where* $\frac{1}{2}(\mathcal{K}_B + \mathcal{K}_B^\star)f_1 = \lambda_1\left(\frac{\mathcal{K}_B+\mathcal{K}_B^\star}{2}\right) f_1$ *and* $\|f_1\| = 1$.

(ii) Define $|\alpha_0| = 1$ *by the equation* $\max_{|\alpha|=1} \lambda_1(\alpha\mathcal{K}_B + \bar{\alpha}\mathcal{K}_B^\star) = \lambda_1(\alpha_0\mathcal{K}_B + \bar{\alpha_0}\mathcal{K}_B^\star)$. *Then*

$$min\,\{\,|K - \alpha\mathcal{U}_B^\star(f,f)|^2 \;:\; f \in L^2(\mathcal{R})\,,\, |\alpha| = 1\} = |K_B|^2 - {\lambda_1}^2\left(\frac{\alpha_0\mathcal{K}_B + \bar{\alpha_0}\mathcal{K}_B^\star}{2}\right)$$

and equality is achieved for $f_{opt} := Re\;\alpha_0(\mathcal{K}_B f_1, f_1) f_1$ *where* $\frac{1}{2}(\alpha_0\mathcal{K}_B + \bar{\alpha_0}\mathcal{K}_B^\star)f_1 = \lambda_1\left(\frac{\alpha_0\mathcal{K}_B+\bar{\alpha_0}\mathcal{K}_B^\star}{2}\right) f_1$ *and* $\|f_1\|^2 = 1$.

(iii) $min\,\{\,|K - \mathcal{U}_B^\star(f,g)|^2 \;:\; f,g \in L^2(\mathcal{R})\,\} = \sum_{i=2}^{\infty} \sigma_i(\mathcal{K}_B)$ *; equality is achieved for* $f_{opt} := (\mathcal{K}_B\phi_1, \phi_1)\phi_1$ *and* $g_{opt} := \mathcal{K}_B\phi_1$*, where* $\mathcal{K}_B^\star\mathcal{K}_B\phi_1 = \sigma_1(\mathcal{K}_B)\phi_1$.

Proof: Using the fact that $\mathcal{K}_B$ is a unitary operator on $L^2(\mathcal{R}^2)$ and Lemma 3.1, we have for (i)

$$\begin{aligned} & min\{|K - \mathcal{U}_B^\star(f,f)|^2 \;:\; f \in L^2(\mathcal{R})\} \\ = \;& min\{|K_B - \alpha(f \otimes f)|^2 \;:\; \|f\| = 1, \alpha \in \mathcal{R}_+\} \\ = \;& min\{|K_B|^2 - (Re(\mathcal{K}_B f, f)_+)^2 \;:\; \|f\| = 1\} \\ = \;& |K_B|^2 - max\{(\tfrac{1}{2}(\mathcal{K}_B + \mathcal{K}_B^\star)f, f)_+ \;:\; \|f\| = 1\}^2 \end{aligned}$$

from which (i) follows. To prove (ii) we see that

$$\begin{aligned}
& min\{|K - \alpha\mathcal{U}_B^\star(f,f)|^2 \ : |\alpha| = 1,\ f \in L^2(\mathcal{R})\} \\
= \ & min\{|K_B - \alpha(f \otimes f)|^2 \ : \ \|f\| = 1, \alpha \in \mathcal{C}\} \\
= \ & |K_B|^2 - max\{|(\mathcal{K}_B f, f)| \ : \ \|f\| = 1\}^2 \\
= \ & |K_B|^2 - max\{|Re\alpha(\mathcal{K}_B f, f)| \ : \ |\alpha| = 1,\ \|f\| = 1\}^2 \\
= \ & |K_B|^2 - max\left\{\left(\tfrac{1}{2}(\alpha\mathcal{K}_B + \bar{\alpha}\mathcal{K}_B^\star)f\ ,\ f\right) \ : \ |\alpha| = 1,\ \|f\| = 1\right\}^2 .
\end{aligned}$$

Finally, we have for (iii)

$$\begin{aligned}
& min\{|K - \mathcal{U}_B^\star(f,g)|^2 \ : \ f,g \in L^2(\mathcal{R})\} \\
= \ & min\{|K_B - \alpha(f \otimes g)|^2 \ : \alpha \in \mathcal{C},\ \|f\| = 1,\ f,g \in L^2(\mathcal{R})\} \\
= \ & |K_B|^2 - max\left\{\tfrac{|(\mathcal{K}_B f,g)|^2}{\|g\|^2} \ : \ \|f\| = 1,\ f,g \in L^2(\mathcal{R})\right\} \\
= \ & |K_B|^2 - max\{(\mathcal{K}_B^\star\mathcal{K}_B f, f) \ : \ \|f\| = 1\}^2 ,
\end{aligned}$$

which completes the proof of the theorem because $|K|^2 = \sum_{i=1}^{\infty} \sigma_i(K)$. □

Remark 3.1 For K_B symmetric and positive definite, the minimization by cross-ambiguity functions is achieved by an auto-ambiguity function (that is, $f = g$).

Our methods can be used to solve the approximation problems in Theorem 3.2 with the additional constraint that both f and g are bandlimited. As an example, we indicate how Theorem 1 part (iii) can be modified to accommodate the constraint $\hat{f}(x) = 0$ for $|x| > \tau$. In this case we have as before

$$min\{|K - \mathcal{U}_B^\star(f,g)|^2 \ : \ f,g \in L^2(\mathcal{R})\} \tag{16}$$

$$= \ |K_B|^2 - max\left\{\tfrac{|(\mathcal{K}_B f,g)|^2}{\|g\|^2} \ : \ \|f\| = 1,\ f,g \in L^2(\mathcal{R})\right\} \tag{17}$$

By Parseval's theorem, the last expression equals

$$|K_B|^2 - max\left\{(\mathcal{J}_B\hat{f},\hat{g})_{L^2(-\tau,\tau)} \ : \ \|\hat{f}\|_{L^2(-\tau,\tau)} = 1,\ \hat{g} \in L^2(-\tau,\tau)\right\}^2 , \tag{18}$$

where $\mathcal{J}_B \ : \ L^2(-\tau,\tau) \rightarrow L^2(-\tau,\tau)$ is the integral operator representing the kernel $\mathcal{J}_B := \mathcal{F}_1(K_B)$. Now we can use, as in Theorem 1, the eigenvalues and corresponding eigenfunctions of the operator $\mathcal{J}_B^\star\mathcal{J}_B$ on $(-\tau,\tau)$ to compute the value of (17). An optimal choice for f and g in (17) are then found by Fourier inversion using the requirement that $\hat{f}$ and $\hat{g}$ vanish outside $(-\tau,\tau)$.

Example 3.1 Consider the Gaussian kernel $K(x,y) = e^{-ax^2-by^2}$ where $a,b > 0$. Then

$$\int_{-\infty}^{\infty} K(x,t)\, e^{2\pi i y t} = \sqrt{\frac{\pi}{b}}\, e^{-ax^2-\pi^2/by^2}$$

and therefore

$$K_A(x,y) = \sqrt{\frac{\pi}{b}}\, e^{-\left(a+\frac{\pi^2}{4b}\right)x^2 + 2\left(a-\frac{\pi^2}{4b}\right)xy - \left(a+\frac{\pi^2}{4b}\right)y^2}$$

which is a symmetric function of x and y. Set

$$\alpha = a + \frac{\pi^2}{4b} \qquad \beta = a - \frac{\pi^2}{4b} \qquad \gamma = \pi\sqrt{\frac{a}{b}}\,.$$

One can check by direct calculation that for every polynomial p,

$$\int_{-\infty}^{\infty} K_A(x,y)\, e^{-\gamma y^2}\, p(y)\, dy = \sqrt{\frac{\pi}{b}}\, e^{-\gamma x^2} \int_{-\infty}^{\infty} e^{-(\alpha+\gamma)y^2}\, p\left(y + \frac{\beta}{\alpha+\gamma}x\right) dy\,.$$

Hence, the eigenvalues of $K_A(x,y)$ are given by

$$\lambda_n = \sqrt{\frac{\pi}{b}} \left(\frac{\beta}{\alpha+\gamma}\right)^n \sqrt{\frac{\pi}{\alpha+\gamma}}\,, \qquad n = 0,1,2,\cdots\,.$$

Consequently, Theorem 3.2 implies that the error in approximating the function by a cross-amibugity function is

$$\sqrt{\sum_{j=2}^{\infty} \lambda_j^2} = \frac{\pi\beta^2}{\sqrt{b(\alpha+\gamma)^3}\,\sqrt{(\alpha+\gamma)^2-\beta^2}}\,.$$

When β is non-negative, or equivalently $ab \geq \frac{\pi^2}{4}$, then K_A is also positive definite, and as we have remarked, the solution to the L^2-synthesis problem by cross ambiguity functions is achieved by an auto ambiguity function. Observe that the condition for positive definiteness is precisely the inequality that relates to the uncertainty principle.

4 Wideband Ambiguity Functions

We will use the notation $\mathcal{R}_+ = \{u : u > 0\}$ and $\mathcal{R}_- = \{u : u < 0\}$. The wideband ambiguity operator is defined by the formula

$$W(f,g)(u,v) := \sqrt{v} \int_{-\infty}^{\infty} f(v(t-u))\, \bar{g}(t)\, dt\,, \qquad u \in \mathcal{R},\ v \in \mathcal{R}_+\,, \tag{19}$$

which, by Parseval's formula, also takes the form

$$W(f,g)(u,v) = \frac{1}{\sqrt{v}} \int_{-\infty}^{\infty} \hat{f}\left(\frac{s}{v}\right) \bar{\hat{g}}(s)\, e^{2\pi i s u}\, ds\,. \tag{20}$$

We will discuss only the problem of approximating a given kernel K on $\mathcal{R} \times \mathcal{R}_+$ by $W(f,g)$ in $L^2(\mathcal{R} \times \mathcal{R}_+)$ relative to Lebesque measure; that is, we minimize

$$\int_0^{\infty} \int_{-\infty}^{\infty} |K(u,v) - W(f,g)(u,v)|^2\, du\, dv \tag{21}$$

over a suitable class of functions f and g to be described below.

To draw an analogy with the material in Section 2, we introduce the operator

$$(\mathcal{E}K)(u,v) := \frac{1}{\sqrt{v}} K\left(\frac{u}{v}, u\right)\,.$$

Then we have

$$W(f,g) = \mathcal{F}_1 \mathcal{E}(\hat{f} \otimes \hat{g})\,,$$

which compares to our definition for $\mathcal{U}_B^\star\,(f \otimes g)$. Using Parseval's theorem on (21) in the first variable, we obtain

$$\int_0^{\infty} \int_{-\infty}^{\infty} |K(u,v) - W(f,g)(u,v)|^2\, du\, dv$$

$$= \int_0^{\infty} \int_{-\infty}^{\infty} \left|K_1(u,v) - \frac{1}{\sqrt{v}} \hat{f}\left(\frac{u}{v}\right) \bar{\hat{g}}(u)\right|^2 du\, dv\,,$$

where K_1 denotes the Fourier transform in the first variable. We introduce the change of variables

$$(x,y) := \Phi(u,v) := \left(\frac{u}{v}, u\right)\,,$$

whose inverse is

$$\Phi^{-1}(x,y) = \left(y, \frac{y}{x}\right)\,.$$

Φ takes $\mathcal{R} \times \mathcal{R}_+$ onto $\mathcal{R}_-{}^2 \cup \mathcal{R}_+{}^2 \cup \{0\}$, and the Jacobian of its inverse is

$$|J_{\Phi^{-1}}(x,y)| = \frac{y}{x} \frac{1}{|x|}\,.$$

Thus we get

$$\int_0^{\infty} \int_{-\infty}^{\infty} |K(u,v) - W(f,g)(u,v)|^2\, du\, dv \tag{22}$$

$$= \int_0^{\infty} \int_0^{\infty} |T(x,y) - \hat{f}(x)\bar{\hat{g}}(y)|^2\, \tfrac{dx\, dy}{|x|} + \int_{-\infty}^{0} \int_{-\infty}^{0} |T(x,y) - \hat{f}(x)\bar{\hat{g}}(y)|^2\, \tfrac{dx\, dy}{|x|}\,,$$

where $T(x,y) := \sqrt{y/x}K_1(y,y/x)$, $(x,y) \in \mathcal{R}_-{}^2 \cup \mathcal{R}_+{}^2$. Similarly, one derives

$$\int_0^\infty \int_{-\infty}^\infty |K(u,v) - W(f,g)(u,v)|^2 \tfrac{|u|}{v}\, du\, dv \tag{23}$$

$$= \int_0^\infty \int_0^\infty |T(x,y) - \hat{f}(x)\bar{\hat{g}}(y)|^2\, dx\, dy + \int_{-\infty}^0 \int_{-\infty}^0 |T(x,y) - \hat{f}(x)\bar{\hat{g}}(y)|^2\, dx\, dy\,.$$

It is convenient to split T as $T = (T_-, T_+)$, where T_-, T_+ are respectively its restricitions to $\mathcal{R}_-^2$ and $\mathcal{R}_+^2$. Each kernel induces an integral operator

$$(\mathcal{T}_- f)(x) = \int_{-\infty}^0 T_-(x,y)\, f(y)\, dy\,, \qquad x \in \mathcal{R}_- \tag{24}$$

$$(\mathcal{T}_+ f)(x) = \int_0^\infty T_+(x,y)\, f(y)\, dy\,, \qquad x \in \mathcal{R}_+\,. \tag{25}$$

To specify the domains of these operators we also split f in the Hilbert space $L^2(\mathcal{R}, \frac{dx}{|x|})$ in two parts as $f = (f_-, f_+)$, where $f_\pm \in L^2(\mathcal{R}_\pm, \frac{dx}{|x|})$. In other words, these spaces provide the decomposition

$$L^2(\mathcal{R}, \tfrac{dx}{|x|}) = L^2(\mathcal{R}_-, \tfrac{dx}{|x|}) \times L^2(\mathcal{R}_+, \tfrac{dx}{|x|})\,.$$

We similarly split $L^2(\mathcal{R}, dx)$ into $L^2(\mathcal{R}_\pm, dx)$ and consider $\mathcal{T}_\pm$ as maps from $L^2(\mathcal{R}_\pm, dx)$ into $L^2(\mathcal{R}_\pm, \frac{dx}{|x|})$. Equivalently, we can think of $\mathcal{T}_-$ and $\mathcal{T}_+$ as defined by the formula

$$\begin{aligned}(\mathcal{T}_\pm g, f)_{L^2(\mathcal{R}_\pm, \frac{dx}{|x|})} &= (T_\pm, f \otimes g)_{L^2(\mathcal{R}_\pm^2, \frac{dx\,dy}{|x|})} \\ &= \int_{-\infty}^\infty \int_{-\infty \mathcal{R}_\pm{}^2}^\infty T_\pm(x,y)\,(f \otimes g)(x,y)\, \frac{dx\, dy}{|x|}\,.\end{aligned}$$

Hence, if we assume that $K \in L^2(\mathcal{R} \times \mathcal{R}_+, dx\, dy)$, then

$$|T|_{L^2(\mathcal{R}_-{}^2 \cup \mathcal{R}_+{}^2, \frac{dx\,dy}{|x|})} = |K|_{L^2(\mathcal{R} \times \mathcal{R}_+, dx\, dy)} < \infty\,.$$

It follows that $\mathcal{T}_\pm$ are compact operators from $L^2(\mathcal{R}_\pm, dx)$ into $L^2(\mathcal{R}_\pm, \frac{dx}{|x|})$. We let $\sigma_\pm^1 \geq \sigma_\pm^2 \geq \cdots$ be the singular values of $\mathcal{T}_\pm$.

Returning to our basic formula (21), we observe that it is natural to minimize (21) over f, g so that $\hat{f} \in L^2(\mathcal{R}, \frac{dx}{|x|})$ and $\hat{g} \in L^2(\mathcal{R})$. In fact, note that from (22) when $K = 0$,

$$|W(f,g)|^2_{L^2(\mathcal{R} \times \mathcal{R}_+, dx\, dy)} = |\hat{f}_+|^2_{L^2(\mathcal{R}_+, \frac{dx}{|x|})} |\hat{g}_+|^2_{L^2(\mathcal{R}_+, dx)} + |\hat{f}_-|^2_{L^2(\mathcal{R}_-, \frac{dx}{|x|})} |\hat{g}_-|^2_{L^2(\mathcal{R}_-, dx)}\,,$$

and so when $\hat{g} \in L^2(\mathcal{R}, dx)$ and $\hat{f} \in L^2(\mathcal{R}, \frac{dx}{|x|}) \cap L^2(\mathcal{R}, dx)$, we get $W(f,g) \in L^2(\mathcal{R} \times \mathcal{R}_+, dx\, dy)$; see also [3,10,13].

Next, we now use this information and proceed as in Section 3,

$$\min_{f,g} |K - W(f,g)|^2_{L^2(\mathcal{R}\times\mathcal{R}_+, dx\, dy)}$$

$$= |K|^2_{L^2(\mathcal{R}\times\mathcal{R}_+, dx\, dy)} - \min_{f_-, g_-} \left\{ \frac{(\mathcal{T}_- g, f)^2_{L^2(\mathcal{R}_-, \frac{dx}{|x|})}}{|g|^2_{L^2(\mathcal{R}_-, dx)} |f|^2_{L^2(\mathcal{R}_-, \frac{dx}{|x|})}} \right\}$$

$$- \min_{f_+, g_+} \left\{ \frac{(\mathcal{T}_+ g, f)^2_{L^2(\mathcal{R}_+, \frac{dx}{|x|})}}{|g|^2_{L^2(\mathcal{R}_+, dx)} |f|^2_{L^2(\mathcal{R}_+, \frac{dx}{|x|})}} \right\}$$

$$\leq \sum_{k+2}^{\infty} \sigma_+^k + \sum_{k+2}^{\infty} \sigma_-^k .$$

Equality above is achieved for $f = h = (h_-, h_+)$, $g = k = (k_-, k_+)$ given by

$$\mathcal{T}_\pm{}^* \mathcal{T}_\pm k_\pm = \sigma^1_\pm k_\pm \qquad , |k|_{L^2_\pm(\mathcal{R}_\pm, dx)} = 1 \tag{26}$$

$$h_\pm = \mathcal{T}_\pm k_\pm . \tag{27}$$

By construction, $h_\pm \in L^2(\mathcal{R}_\pm, \frac{dx}{|x|})$. If we also assume that $T \in L^2(\mathcal{R}_-{}^2 \cup \mathcal{R}_+{}^2, dx\, dy)$, then by formulas (24) and (25) we have also that $h_\pm \in L^2(\mathcal{R}_\pm, dx)$. This last hypothesis means, by setting $f = g = 0$ in (23), that

$$\int_0^\infty \int_{-\infty}^\infty |K(u,v)|^2 \frac{|u|}{v}\, du\, dv < \infty .$$

We summarize the results of this section in the following theorem.

Theorem 4.1 *Let $K(x,y)$ be any function on $\mathcal{R} \times \mathcal{R}_+$ such that*

$$\int_0^\infty \int_{-\infty}^\infty |K(u,v)|^2\, du\, dv < \infty$$

and

$$\int_0^\infty \int_{-\infty}^\infty |K(u,v)|^2 \frac{|u|}{v}\, du\, dv < \infty .$$

Then the integral operators $\mathcal{T}_\pm$ given by (24) and (25) are compact operators mapping $L^2(\mathcal{R}_\pm, dx)$ into $L^2(\mathcal{R}_\pm, \frac{dx}{|x|})$. The minimum of (21) over $\hat{g} \in L^2(\mathcal{R}, dx)$, $\hat{f} \in L^2(\mathcal{R}, \frac{dx}{|x|}) \cap$

$L^2(\mathcal{R}, dx)$ is given by $\hat{f} = h$, $\hat{g} = k$ defined by (26) and (27) and the error squared is given by

$$\sum_{k=2}^{\infty} \sigma_+^k + \sum_{k=2}^{\infty} \sigma_-^k ,$$

where $\sigma_\pm^1 \geq \sigma_\pm^2 \geq \cdots$ are the singular values of $\mathcal{T}_\pm$.

References

[1] Auslander, L., Tolimieri, R., Radar ambiguity functions and group theory, SIAM J. Math. Anal., Vol. 16 No. 3, (1985), pp. 577-601.

[2] Bastians, M. J., The Wigner distribution function applied to optical signals and systems, Optics Comm. No.25, (1978), pp. 26-30.

[3] Daubechies, I., The wavelet transform, time-frequency localization and signal analysis, to appear in IEEE Trans. Information Theory.

[4] Daubechies, I., Orthonormal bases of compactly supported wavelets, Comm. Pure and Applied Math, Vol. 41 (1988), pp. 909-996.

[5] Feig, E., Computational methods with the ambiguity function, IBM RC 13140 (1987).

[6] Feig, E., Estimating interesting portions of ambiguity functions, Workshop on Signal Processing, Institute for Mathematics and its Applications, Minneapolis, Minnesota, (1988).

[7] Feig, E. and Greenleaf, F., Inversion of an integral transform associated with tomography in radar detection, Inverse Problems vol 2, (1986), pp. 405-411.

[8] Feig, E. and Grünbaum, F. A., Tomographic methods in range-Doppler radar, Inverse Problems Vol. 2, (1986), pp. 185-195.

[9] Feig, E. and Micchelli, C. A., Least-squares synthesis by Generalized Ambiguity Functions, IBM RC, (1989).

[10] Grossmann, A. and Morlet, J., Decomposition of Hardy functions into square integrable wavelets of constant shape, SIAM J. Math. Anal. 15, (1984), pp. 723-736.

[11] Grossmann, A. , Morlet, J. and Paul, T., Transforms associated to square integrable group representations, I, General results, J. Math. Physics 26, (1985), pp. 2473-2479.

[12] Knight, W. C., Pridham, R. G., and Kay, S. M., Digital signal processing for sonar, Proc. IEEE 69, (1982), pp. 1451-1506.

[13] Meyer, Y., Principe d'incertitude, bases hilbertiennes et algébres d'operateurs, Seminaire Bourbaki 662, (1985-86).

[14] Naparst, H., Radar signal processing for a dense target environment, PhD thesis, U. California, Berkeley, (1988).

[15] Rihaczek, A. W., *Principles of High Resolution Radar*, McGraw-Hill, (1962).

[16] Schempp, W., Radar reception and nilpotent harmonic analysis I., C. R. Math. Rep. Acad. Sci. Canada 4, (1982), pp. 43-48.

[17] Schempp, W., Radar reception and nilpotent harmonic analysis II., C. R. Math. Rep. Acad. Sci. Canada 4, (1982), pp. 139-144.

[18] Schempp, W., Radar reception and nilpotent harmonic analysis III., C. R. Math. Rep. Acad. Sci. Canada 4, (1982), pp. 219-224.

[19] Schempp, W., Radar reception and nilpotent harmonic analysis IV., C. R. Math. Rep. Acad. Sci. Canada 4, (1982), pp. 287-292.

[20] Schempp, W., On the Wigner quasi-probability distribution function I, C. R. Math Rep. Acad. Sci. Canada 4, (1982), pp. 353-358.

[21] Schempp, W., On the Wigner quasi-probability distribution function II, C. R. Math Rep. Acad. Sci. Canada, 5, (1983) pp. 3-8.

[22] Schempp, W., On the Wigner quasi-probability distribution function III, C. R. Math Rep. Acad. Sci. Canada, 5, (1983) pp. 35-40.

[23] Sussman, S. M., Least squares synthesis of radar ambiguity functions, IRE Trans. Information Th., (1962) pp. 246-254.

[24] Tolimieri, R., Winograd, S., Computing the ambiguity surface, IEEE-ASSP 33, No. 5, (1985), pp. 1239-1245.

[25] Wigner, E. P., On the quantum correction for thermodynamics and equilibrium, Physics Rev. 40, (1932), pp. 749-759.

[26] Wilcox, C. H. The synthesis problem for radar ambiguity functions, MRC Technical Report 157, Mathematics Research Center, U. S. Army, University of Wisconsin (1960).

[27] Wolf, J. D., Lee, G. M., and Suyo, C. E., Radar waveform synthesis by mean-squared optimization techniques, IEEE Trans. Aerospace and Elect. Systems, (1969) pp. 611-619.

[28] Woodward, P. M., *Probability and Information Theory with Applications to Radar*, New York-London, Pergamon Press (1953).

International Series of
Numerical Mathematics, Vol. 90

VECTOR SPHERICAL SPLINE INTERPOLATION

Willi Freeden, Theo Gervens

Rheinisch-Westfälische TH Aachen, F.R.G.

Abstract:

Vector spherical splines are introduced in analogy to the well-known scalar theory. The main tool is the theory of vector spherical harmonics.

Introduction.

Numerous papers concerned with the scalar interpolation theory by splines have appeared in the last decade (cf. e.g. [4], [5], [6]) and the references therein. Scalar spherical splines (s.s.s.) are found to be natural generalizations of polynomials, i.e., spherical harmonics, having desirable characteristics as interpolating functions. S.s.s. can be recommended for the numerical solution of various interpolating and best approximating problems in geophysics or geodesy. In particular, s.s.s. are best suited for the macro - and micro modelling of the earth's gravitational field from discretely given data on the earth's surface (cf. e.g. [3], [4]).

In this paper we are interested in generalizing the scalar spherical spline theory to a vectorial concept. It turns out that interpolation by vector spherical splines (v.s.s.) essentially amounts to solving a well - posed problem of minimizing a suitable (semi -) norm under interpolating constraints. Essential tool is the theory of vector spherical harmonics [7]. Vector spherical theory actually provides approximation theory with an intrinsic concept of multivariate spline ready for vectorial use in discrete problems on the sphere. Because of their conceptual structure v.s.s. seem to be adequate settings for a fundamental problem in geophysics, viz. the deformation analysis of the earth's surface.

The layout of the paper is as follows: Sect. 1 contains some basic definitions and notations. In Sect. 2 we introduce the scalar spherical harmonics as the regular eigenfunctions of the Beltrami operator Δ^* . Correspondingly, in Sect. 3, we define the vector spherical harmonics as regular vector eigenfunctions to the vectorial analogue $\boldsymbol{\Delta}^*$ of the Beltrami operator. Based on these preliminaries we finally give the theory of vector spherical splines in Sect. 4.

1. Definitions and Notations

Let us use $x, y, \ldots$ to represent the elements of Euclidean space $\mathbb{R}^3$. For all $x \in \mathbb{R}^3$, $x = (x_1, x_2, x_3)'$, different from the origin, we have

$$x = r\xi , \qquad r = |x| = \sqrt{x_1^2 + x_2^2 + x_3^2} , \tag{1.1}$$

where $\xi = (\xi_1, \xi_2, \xi_3)'$ is the uniquely determined directional (unit) vector of $x \in \mathbb{R}^3$. The unit sphere in $\mathbb{R}^3$ will be denoted by Ω. If the vectors $\varepsilon^{(1)}, \varepsilon^{(2)}, \varepsilon^{(3)}$ form the canonical basis in $\mathbb{R}^3$, we may represent the points $\xi \in \Omega$ by

$$\begin{aligned} \xi = \ & t\,\varepsilon^{(3)} + \sqrt{1-t^2}\,(\cos\phi\,\varepsilon^{(1)} + \sin\phi\,\varepsilon^{(2)}) \\ & -1 \le t \le 1 , \quad 0 \le \phi < 2\pi , \quad t = \cos\theta . \end{aligned} \tag{1.2}$$

Usually scalar-, vector- and dyadic products of the two vectors $x, y \in \mathbb{R}^3$ are defined by

$$x \cdot y = \sum_{i=1}^{3} x_i\, y_i , \tag{1.3}$$

$$x \wedge y = (x_2y_3 - x_3y_2,\ x_3y_1 - x_1y_3,\ x_1y_2 - x_2y_1)' , \tag{1.4}$$

$$x \otimes y = \begin{pmatrix} x_1y_1 & x_1y_2 & x_1y_3 \\ x_2y_1 & x_2y_2 & x_2y_3 \\ x_3y_1 & x_3y_2 & x_3y_3 \end{pmatrix} . \tag{1.5}$$

In terms of the polar coordinates (1.2) the gradient ∇ in $\mathbb{R}^3$ reads

$$\nabla = \frac{\partial}{\partial r}\,\xi + \frac{1}{r}\,\nabla^* , \tag{1.6}$$

where ∇^* is the surface gradient of the unit sphere Ω. Moreover, the Laplace operator $\Delta = \nabla\nabla$ in $\mathbb{R}^3$ has the representation

$$\Delta = (\frac{\partial}{\partial r})^2 + \frac{2}{r}\frac{\partial}{\partial r} + \frac{1}{r^2}\Delta^* , \tag{1.7}$$

where Δ^* is the Beltrami operator of the unit sphere Ω

$$\Delta^* = \frac{\partial}{\partial t}(1-t^2)\frac{\partial}{\partial t} + \frac{1}{1-t^2}(\frac{\partial}{\partial \varphi})^2 . \tag{1.8}$$

Obviously,

$$\Delta^* = \nabla^*\,\nabla^* . \tag{1.9}$$

Furthermore, we define the differential operator $\mathbf{\Delta}^*$ by

$$\mathbf{\Delta}^* f \; := \; \Delta^* f \; - \; 2\,(\xi \wedge \nabla) \wedge f \; - \; 2f \; , \tag{1.10}$$

acting on suitable vector functions $f : \Omega \rightarrow I\!R^3$.

2. Scalar Spherical Harmonics

As usual, the spherical harmonics K_n of order n are defined as the everywhere on Ω infinitely differentiable eigenfunctions corresponding to the eigenvalues $d_n = n(n+1)$, $n = 0, 1, 2...$ of the Beltrami-operator Δ^*, i.e.,

$$(-\Delta^*_\xi - d_n)\; K_n(\xi) = 0 \;,\; \xi \in \Omega \;. \tag{2.1}$$

As is well-known, the functions $H_n : I\!R^3 \rightarrow I\!R$ defined by $H_n(x) = r^n\, K_n(\xi)$ are polynomials in rectangular coordinates which satisfy the Laplace equation $\Delta^* H_n(x) = 0, x \in I\!R$, and are homogeneous of degree n. Conversely, every homogeneous harmonic polynomial of degree n restricted to the unit sphere Ω is a spherical harmonic of order n.

The Legendre polynomials $P_n \; : \; [-1,1] \; \rightarrow \; I\!R$

$$P_n(t) = \sum_{s=0}^{[\frac{n}{2}]} (-1)^s \frac{(2n-2s)!}{2^n (n-2s)!(n-s)!s!} t^{n-2s} \;,\; t \in [-1,1], \tag{2.2}$$

are the only everywhere on $[-1,1]$ infinitely differentiable eigenfunctions of the Legendre-operator, i. e.,

$$((1-t^2)(\frac{d}{dt})^2 - 2t\frac{d}{dt} \; + \; d_n \;)P_n(t) = 0 \;,\; t \in [-1,+1] \;, \tag{2.3}$$

which in $t = 1$ satisfy $P_n(1) = 1$. Apart from a constant factor, the Legendre functions $P_n(\varepsilon^{(3)}\cdot) : \Omega \; \rightarrow \; I\!R, \; \xi \; \mapsto \; P_n(\varepsilon^{(3)}\xi)$ $,\xi \in \Omega$ are the only spherical harmonics which are invariant under orthogonal transformations.

The linear space Σ_n of all spherical harmonics of order n is of dimension $2n+1$. Thus there are $2n+1$ linearly independent spherical harmonics $K_{n,1}, ..., K_{n,2n+1}$. We assume this system to be orthonormalized in the sense of the L_2 - inner product

$$(K_{n,j}, K_{m,k})_{L_2} \; = \; \int_\Omega K_{n,j}(\eta)\; K_{m,k}(\eta)\; d\omega(\eta) \; = \; \delta_{j,k}\; \delta_{n,m} \tag{2.4}$$

($d\omega$: surface element). For any two vectors $\xi, \eta \in \Omega$ the sum

$$F_n(\xi,\eta) = \sum_{j=1}^{2n+1} K_{n,j}(\xi) K_{n,j}(\eta) \tag{2.5}$$

is invariant under all orthogonal transformations A, i.e., $F_n(A\xi, A\eta) = F_n(\xi,\eta)$. For fixed $\xi \in \Omega$, $F_n(\xi,\cdot) : \Omega \rightarrow \mathbb{R}$ is a spherical harmonic of order n. $F_n(\xi,\eta)$ is symmetric in ξ and η and depends only on the scalar product of ξ and η . Thus, apart from a multiplicative constant a_n, we have

$$F_n(\xi,\eta) = a_n \; P_n(\xi\eta) \; . \tag{2.6}$$

In order to evaluate a_n we set $\xi = \eta$. Then we find

$$F_n(\xi,\xi) = a_n \; P_n(1) = a_n \; . \tag{2.7}$$

Integration over Ω yields $2n+1 = 4\pi \; a_n$. Therefore we finally obtain the *addition theorem* (cf. [8])

$$\frac{2n+1}{4\pi} \; P_n(\xi\eta) = \sum_{j=1}^{2n+1} K_{n,j}(\xi) K_{n,j}(\eta) \; . \tag{2.8}$$

For $\xi = \eta$ we get the formula

$$\sum_{j=1}^{2n+1} (K_{n,j}(\xi))^2 = \frac{2n+1}{4\pi} \tag{2.9}$$

and the inequality

$$|K_{n,j}(\xi)| \leq \sqrt{\frac{2n+1}{4\pi}} \; , \quad j = 1, 2, ..., 2n+1 \; . \tag{2.10}$$

Let g be a function of class $C([-1,1])$. Then, for any spherical harmonic K_n of order n, Hecke's formula gives

$$\int\limits_{\Omega} g(\xi\eta) \; K_n(\eta) \; d\omega(\eta) = b_n \; K_n(\xi) \; , \tag{2.11}$$

where

$$b_n = 2\pi \int\limits_{-1}^{1} g(t) \; P_n(t) \; dt \; . \tag{2.12}$$

This formula establishes the close connection between the orthogonal invariance of the sphere and the addition theorem.

The space $\Sigma_{0,\ldots,m}$ of all spherical harmonics of order m or less has the dimension

$$M = \sum_{n=0}^{m} (2n+1) = (m+1)^2 . \tag{2.13}$$

With respect to the inner product $(.,.)_{L_2}$ we have the orthogonal decomposition

$$\Sigma_{0,\ldots,m} = \Sigma_0 \otimes \ldots \otimes \Sigma_m . \tag{2.14}$$

Every $P \in \Sigma_{0,\ldots,m}$ can be expressed uniquely with a vector $c \in \mathbb{R}^M$,
$c = (c_{0,1}, \ldots, c_{m,1}, \ldots, c_{m,2m+1})'$ as a linear combination

$$P(\xi) = \sum_{n=0}^{m} \sum_{j=1}^{2n+1} c_{n,j}\, K_{n,j}(\xi) \ , \ \xi \in \Omega . \tag{2.15}$$

A set $X_M = \{\eta_1, \ldots, \eta_M\}$ of M points on Ω is called $\Sigma_{0,\ldots,m}$ - unisolvent, if the rank of the (M, M) - matrix

$$\begin{pmatrix} K_{0,1}(\eta_1) & \ldots & K_{0,1}(\eta_M) \\ \vdots & & \vdots \\ K_{m,1}(\eta_1) & \ldots & K_{m,1}(\eta_M) \\ \vdots & & \vdots \\ K_{m,2m+1}(\eta_1) & \ldots & K_{m,2m+1}(\eta_M) \end{pmatrix} \tag{2.16}$$

is equal to M. According to the addition theorem, a set X_M is $\Sigma_{0,\ldots,m}$ - unisolvent if the rank of the (M, M) - matrix

$$\left(\sum_{n=0}^{m} \frac{2n+1}{4\pi} P_n(\eta_j \eta_k) \right)_{k=1,\ldots,M;\ j=1,\ldots,M} \tag{2.17}$$

is equal to M. If X_M is a $\Sigma_{0,\ldots,m}$ - unisolvent set, then we are able to interpolate given real numbers $y_1, \ldots, y_M$ by a unique $P \in \Sigma_{0,\ldots m}$, i.e. $P(\eta_k) = y_k$, $k = 1, \ldots, M$.

A set $X_N = \{\eta_1, \ldots, \eta_N\}$ of $N \geq M$ points on Ω is called $\Sigma_{0,\ldots,m}$ - admissible, if the first M elements $\eta_1, \ldots, \eta_M$ form a $\Sigma_{0,\ldots,m}$ - unisolvent set.

Given a function P of the form (2.15). Then, for every $\Sigma_{0,\dots,m}$ - admissible set $X_N = \{\eta_1, \dots, \eta_N\}$ and all solutions $a \in \mathbb{R}^N$, $a = (a_1, \dots, a_N)'$, of the linear system

$$\sum_{k=1}^{N} a_k \, K_{n,j}(\eta_k) = c_{n,j} \, , \quad n = 0, \dots, m, \; j = 1, \dots, 2n+1, \tag{2.18}$$

we have

$$P(\xi) = \sum_{k=1}^{N} a_k \sum_{n=0}^{m} \sum_{j=1}^{2n+1} K_{n,j}(\eta_k) \, K_{n,j}(\xi) \, , \; \xi \in \Omega \, . \tag{2.19}$$

3. Vector Spherical Harmonics

In the following a brief introduction of vector spherical harmonics will be given. For more details and explicit proofs the reader is referred to the thesis [7].
In analogy to the scalar case vector spherical harmonics $\mathbf{K}_n$ of order n are defined as the everywhere on Ω infinitely differentiable eigenfunctions of the operator $\mathbf{\Delta}^*$ corresponding to the eigenvalues $d_n = n(n+1)$

$$(- \mathbf{\Delta}^*_\xi - d_n) \, \mathbf{K}_n(\xi) = 0 \, , \quad \xi \in \Omega \, . \tag{3.1}$$

If K_n is a scalar spherical harmonic of order n, we can distinguish three kinds of vector spherical harmonics of order n, namely,

$$\begin{aligned} \mathbf{K}_n^{(1)}(\xi) &= \xi \, K_n(\xi) \quad &, \; n \geq 0 \, , \\ \mathbf{K}_n^{(2)}(\xi) &= \nabla^* K_n(\xi) \quad &, \; n \geq 1 \, , \\ \mathbf{K}_n^{(3)}(\xi) &= \xi \wedge \nabla^* K_n(\xi) \quad &, \; n \geq 1 \, , \end{aligned} \tag{3.2}$$

and $\mathbf{K}_0^{(2)}(\xi) = \mathbf{K}_0^{(3)}(\xi) = 0$, by definition. This set of vector spherical harmonics is orthogonal on the sphere Ω and has purely normal and tangential components. We notice that $\xi \wedge \mathbf{K}_n^{(3)}(\xi) = \mathbf{K}_n^{(2)}(\xi)$, $\xi \wedge \mathbf{K}_n^{(2)}(\xi) = -\mathbf{K}_n^{(3)}(\xi)$, $\nabla^*(\xi \wedge \mathbf{K}_n^{(2)}(\xi)) = 0$, $\nabla^* \mathbf{K}_n^{(3)}(\xi) = 0$.

The linear space $\mathbf{\Sigma}_n$ of all vector spherical harmonics of order n ($n \geq 1$) possesses the dimension $3(2n+1)$ (dim $\mathbf{\Sigma}_0 = 1$) ; an orthonormal basis is given by

$$\begin{aligned} \mathbf{K}_{n,j}^{(1)}(\xi) &= \xi \, K_{n,j}(\xi) \, , \\ \mathbf{K}_{n,j}^{(2)}(\xi) &= \frac{1}{\sqrt{n(n+1)}} \, \nabla^* K_{n,j}(\xi) \, , \\ \mathbf{K}_{n,j}^{(3)}(\xi) &= \frac{1}{\sqrt{n(n+1)}} \, \xi \wedge \nabla^* K_{n,j}(\xi) \, , \end{aligned} \tag{3.3}$$

i.e.

$$\int_{\Omega} \mathbf{K}^{(i)}_{n,j}(\xi)\, \mathbf{K}^{(l)}_{m,k}(\xi)\, d\omega(\xi) \;=\; \delta_{i,l}\delta_{j,k}\delta_{n,m} \,. \tag{3.4}$$

In analogy to (2.5) we consider the following sum of dyadic products (i=1,2,3):

$$\mathbf{\Pi}^{(i)}_n(\xi,\eta) \;=\; \sum_{j=1}^{2n+1} \mathbf{K}^{(i)}_{n,j}(\xi) \,\otimes\, \mathbf{K}^{(i)}_{n,j}(\eta) \;, \quad \xi,\eta \in \Omega \,. \tag{3.5}$$

$\mathbf{\Pi}^{(i)}_n(\xi,\eta)$ is a 3-by-3 matrix and for every vector spherical harmonic $\mathbf{K}^{(i)}_n(\xi)$ of order n and kind i we find the reproducing property:

$$\int_{\Omega} \mathbf{\Pi}^{(i)}_n(\xi,\eta)\, \mathbf{K}^{(i)}_n(\eta)\, d\omega(\eta) \;=\; \mathbf{K}^{(i)}_n(\xi) \,. \tag{3.6}$$

Let A be an orthogonal transformation. Then it follows that

$$\mathbf{\Pi}^{(i)}_n(A\xi, A\eta) \;=\; A\, \mathbf{\Pi}^{(i)}_n(\xi,\eta) A' \tag{3.7}$$

for any pair of unit vectors ξ,η and i=1,2,3. Therefore, $\mathbf{\Pi}^{(i)}_n(\xi,\eta)$ is an invariant matrix under orthogonal transformations.

Furthermore, for twice continuously differentiable functions $f : \Omega \times \Omega \;\rightarrow\; I\!R$, we define the matrix operators $\left(O^{(i)}\right)$, $i = 1,2,3$ by

$$\begin{aligned}
\left(O^{(1)}\right)_{k,l} &= (\xi \otimes \eta)_{k,l} \;=\; (\varepsilon^{(k)}\xi)\,(\varepsilon^{(l)}\eta) \\
\left(O^{(2)}\right)_{k,l} &= (\nabla^*_\xi \otimes \nabla^*_\eta)_{k,l} \;=\; \left(\nabla^*_\xi((\nabla^*_\eta \cdot\,)\varepsilon^{(k)})\right)\varepsilon^{(l)} \\
\left(O^{(3)}\right)_{k,l} &= (\xi \wedge \nabla^*_\xi \otimes \eta \wedge \nabla^*_\eta)_{k,l} \;=\; \left(\xi \wedge \nabla^*_\xi((\eta \wedge \nabla^*_\eta \cdot\,)\varepsilon^{(k)})\right)\varepsilon^{(l)}
\end{aligned} \tag{3.8}$$

for $k,l \in \{1,2,3\}$ and $\xi,\eta \in \Omega,\; \xi \neq \pm\eta$.
Then (3.5) can be rewritten by the addition theorem (2.8) as follows

$$\begin{aligned}
\mathbf{\Pi}^{(1)}_n(\xi,\eta) &= \frac{2n+1}{4\pi}\, O^{(1)}\left(P_n(\xi\eta)\right) , \\
\mathbf{\Pi}^{(2)}_n(\xi,\eta) &= \frac{2n+1}{4\pi n(n+1)}\, O^{(2)}\left(P_n(\xi\eta)\right) , \\
\mathbf{\Pi}^{(3)}_n(\xi,\eta) &= \frac{2n+1}{4\pi n(n+1)}\, O^{(3)}\left(P_n(\xi\eta)\right)
\end{aligned} \tag{3.9}$$

for $\xi \neq \pm\eta$. By performing a straightforward calculation and observing the structure of the tensor product, we may show the following *vectorial analogue of the addition theorem of spherical harmonics* ($\xi, \eta \in \Omega$) :

$$\begin{aligned}
\mathbf{\Pi}_n^{(1)}(\xi,\eta) &= \frac{2n+1}{4\pi} P_n(\xi\eta)\ \xi \otimes \eta \\
\mathbf{\Pi}_n^{(2)}(\xi,\eta) &= \frac{2n+1}{4\pi n(n+1)} \Big[P_n''(\xi\eta)\ (\eta - (\xi\eta)\xi) \otimes (\xi - (\xi\eta)\eta) \\
&+ P_n'(\xi\eta) \Big(I - \xi \otimes \xi - (\eta - (\xi\eta)\xi) \otimes \eta \Big) \Big] \qquad (3.10) \\
\mathbf{\Pi}_n^{(3)}(\xi,\eta) &= \frac{2n+1}{4\pi n(n+1)} \Big[P_n''(\xi\eta)\ \xi \wedge \eta \otimes \eta \wedge \xi \\
&+ P_n'(\xi\eta) \Big((\xi\eta) I - \eta \otimes \xi \Big) \Big] ,
\end{aligned}$$

where I denotes the unit matrix. Especially, by computing the matrix trace for $\xi = \eta$, we get the formula

$$\sum_{j=1}^{2n+1} (\ \mathbf{K}_{n,j}^{(i)}(\xi)\ )^2 = \frac{2n+1}{4\pi} , \quad \xi \in \Omega , \qquad (3.11)$$

so that

$$\sup_{\xi\, \in\, \Omega} |\mathbf{K}_{n,j}^{(i)}(\xi)\ | \leq \left(\frac{2n+1}{4\pi} \right)^{\frac{1}{2}} , \ j = 1, 2, ..., 2n+1 . \qquad (3.12)$$

Let $v:\ \Omega \to \mathbb{R}^3$ be a continuous vector function. We call v invariant under orthogonal transformations with respect to η, if for all orthogonal transformations A , which leaves $\eta \in \Omega$ fixed, the relationship

$$v(A\xi) = A\ v(\xi) \qquad (3.13)$$

is satisfied. Apart from a multiplicative constant, the only vector spherical harmonics of order n, which are invariant under orthogonal transformations with $\eta \in \Omega$ fixed, are given by

$$\begin{aligned}
\mathbf{P}_n^{(1)}(\xi,\eta) &= \xi P_n(\xi\eta) , \\
\mathbf{P}_n^{(2)}(\xi,\eta) &= \nabla_\xi^* P_n(\xi\eta) , \qquad (3.14) \\
\mathbf{P}_n^{(3)}(\xi,\eta) &= \xi \wedge \nabla_\xi^* P_n(\xi\eta) .
\end{aligned}$$

Notice, that $\xi\ \mathbf{P}_n^{(1)}(\xi,\xi) = 1$, $(\nabla^*\mathbf{P}_n^{(2)})(\xi,\xi) = -n(n+1)$, $\nabla^*(\xi \wedge \mathbf{P}_n^{(3)})(\xi,\xi) = n(n+1)$.

Now let $w : \Omega \times \Omega \rightarrow I\!R^3$ be a continuous vector function satisfying the relation

$$w(A\xi, A\eta) \ = \ Aw(\xi,\eta) \ \ , \ \xi,\eta \in \Omega \ , \tag{3.15}$$

for all orthogonal transformations A. Then for fixed η, $w(\cdot,\eta)$ is invariant under orthogonal transformations with respect to η.
In analogy to the well-known formula of Funk and Hecke (2.11) we may show that

$$\int_\Omega \mathbf{\Pi}_n^{(i)}(\xi,\eta)\ w(\eta,\beta)\ d\omega(\eta) \ = \ \lambda^{(i)}\ \mathbf{P}_n^{(i)}(\xi,\beta)\ , \ \ \xi,\beta \in \Omega \ , \tag{3.16}$$

where

$$\begin{aligned} \lambda^{(1)} &= \frac{2n+1}{2} \int_{-1}^{1} P_n(t)\Phi_1(t)\ dt \ , \\ \lambda^{(2)} &= \frac{2n+1}{2} \int_{-1}^{1} P_n'(t)\ \Phi_2(t)\sqrt{1-t^2}\ dt \ , \\ \lambda^{(3)} &= \frac{2n+1}{2} \int_{-1}^{1} P_n'(t)\ \Phi_3(t)\sqrt{1-t^2}\ dt \ , \end{aligned}$$

and

$$\begin{aligned} \Phi_1(t) &= \Phi_1(e_3\eta) \ = \ \eta\ w(\eta,e_3)\ , \\ \sqrt{1-t^2}\ \Phi_2(t) &= \sqrt{1-(e_3\eta)^2}\ \Phi_2(e_3\eta) \ = \ (e_3-(e_3\eta)\eta)\ w(\eta,e_3)\ , \\ \sqrt{1-t^2}\ \Phi_3(t) &= \sqrt{1-(e_3\eta)^2}\ \Phi_3(e_3\eta) \ = \ e_3 \wedge \eta\ w(\eta,e_3)\ \ . \end{aligned}$$

The linear space $\mathbf{\Sigma}_{0,\ldots,m}$ of all vector spherical harmonics of order m or less has the dimension

$$\widetilde{M} \ = \ 1 \ + \ \sum_{n=1}^{m} 3(2n+1) \ = \ 3M-2\ , \tag{3.17}$$

and corresponding to the inner product $(.,.)_{L_2}$ we have the orthogonal decomposition

$$\mathbf{\Sigma}_{0,\ldots,m} \ = \mathbf{\Sigma}_0 \otimes \mathbf{\Sigma}_1 \otimes \ \ldots \ \otimes \mathbf{\Sigma}_m \ . \tag{3.18}$$

Every $\mathbf{P} \in \mathbf{\Sigma}_{0,\ldots,m}$ can be expressed uniquely as a linear combination

$$\mathbf{P}(\xi) \ = \ \sum_{n=0}^{m} \sum_{j=1}^{2n+1} \sum_{i=1}^{3} c_{n,j}^{(i)} \mathbf{K}_{n,j}^{(i)}(\xi)\ , \ \xi \in \Omega, \tag{3.19}$$

with real numbers $c_{n,j}^{(i)}$.

Let $X_N = \{\eta_1, ..., \eta_N\}$ be a $\Sigma_{0,...,m}$ - admissible set of N points on Ω . Then for all solutions $a_k^{(i)} \in I\!R^3$, $k = 1, ..., N$, $i = 1,2,3$ of the linear systems (i=1,2,3)

$$\sum_{k=1}^{N} \mathbf{K}_{n,j}^{(i)}(\eta_k)\, a_k^{(i)} = c_{n,j}^{(i)} , \quad n = 0, ..., m, \; j = 1, ..., 2n+1 , \tag{3.20}$$

we have the following representation

$$\begin{aligned} \mathbf{P}(\xi) &= \sum_{k=1}^{N} \sum_{i=1}^{3} (a_k^{(i)})' \sum_{n=0}^{m} \sum_{j=1}^{2n+1} \mathbf{K}_{n,j}^{(i)}(\eta_k) \otimes \mathbf{K}_{n,j}^{(i)}(\xi) \\ &= \sum_{k=1}^{N} \sum_{i=1}^{3} \sum_{n=0}^{m} \mathbf{\Pi}_n^{(i)}(\xi, \eta_k)\, a_k^{(i)} . \end{aligned} \tag{3.21}$$

4. Spline - Interpolation

A sequence $q = (q_n)$ of real numbers q_n, n=0,1,2,... is called admissible if it satisfies the following properties:

$$(i) \quad |q_n| \neq 0 ,$$

$$(ii) \quad \sum_{n=0}^{\infty} \frac{2n+1}{4\pi} |q_n|^{-2} < \infty .$$

Consider the series expansion

$$F(\xi) = \sum_{n=0}^{\infty} \sum_{j=1}^{2n+1} \sum_{i=1}^{3} q_n^{-1} (f, \mathbf{K}_{n,j}^{(i)})_{L_2(\Omega)} \mathbf{K}_{n,j}^{(i)}(\xi) , \quad \xi \in \Omega , \tag{4.1}$$

for an arbitrarily given vector function $f \in L_2(\Omega)$. Then, by virtue of the Cauchy-Schwarz inequality and (3.11), we get for all $\xi \in \Omega$

$$|F(\xi)| \leq \left(3 \sum_{n=0}^{\infty} \frac{2n+1}{4\pi} |q_n|^{-2} \right)^{\frac{1}{2}} \|f\|_{L_2(\Omega)} . \tag{4.2}$$

In other words, the space $\mathcal{H} = \mathcal{H}(q; \Omega)$ defined by

$$\mathcal{H} = \{F | F = \sum_{n=0}^{\infty} \sum_{j=1}^{2n+1} \sum_{i=1}^{3} q_n^{-1} (f, \mathbf{K}_{n,j}^{(i)})_{L_2(\Omega)} \mathbf{K}_{n,j}^{(i)}(\xi) , \quad f \in L_2(\Omega) \} \tag{4.3}$$

is a linear subspace of $C(\Omega)$ on which we are able to define the structure of a separable Hilbert space by introducing the inner product of the elements (cf. e.g. [1], chapt. 6)

$$F = \sum_{n=0}^{\infty} \sum_{j=1}^{2n+1} \sum_{i=1}^{3} q_n^{-1} (f, \mathbf{K}_{n,j}^{(i)})_{L_2(\Omega)} \, \mathbf{K}_{n,j}^{(i)} \quad , \; f \in L_2(\Omega) \tag{4.4}$$

$$G = \sum_{n=0}^{\infty} \sum_{j=1}^{2n+1} \sum_{i=1}^{3} q_n^{-1} (g, \mathbf{K}_{n,j}^{(i)})_{L_2(\Omega)} \, \mathbf{K}_{n,j}^{(i)} \quad , \; g \in L_2(\Omega) \tag{4.5}$$

by

$$(F,G)_{\mathcal{H}} = \sum_{n=0}^{\infty} \sum_{j=1}^{2n+1} \sum_{i=1}^{3} (f, \mathbf{K}_{n,j}^{(i)})_{L_2(\Omega)} \, (g, \mathbf{K}_{n,j}^{(i)})_{L_2(\Omega)} = (f,g)_{L_2(\Omega)} \, . \tag{4.6}$$

__Theorem 1:__ The space $\mathcal{H} = \mathcal{H}(q;\Omega)$, defined by (4.3) and (4.6), is a Hilbert subspace of $C(\Omega)$, $\mathcal{H}$ has the reproducing kernel

$$K(\xi,\eta) = K(q;\xi,\eta) = \sum_{n=0}^{\infty} \sum_{j=1}^{2n+1} \sum_{i=1}^{3} |q_n|^{-2} \, \mathbf{K}_{n,j}^{(i)}(\xi) \otimes \mathbf{K}_{n,j}^{(i)}(\eta) \, , \quad \xi,\eta \in \Omega, \tag{4.7}$$

in the sense that the following properties are satisfied

(i) for fixed $\xi \in \Omega$, each vector function $K(.,\xi)\varepsilon^{(l)}$, $l = 1,2,3$ given by

$$K(.,\xi)\varepsilon^{(l)} = \sum_{n=0}^{\infty} \sum_{j=1}^{2n+1} \sum_{i=1}^{3} q_n^{-2} \left(\mathbf{K}_{n,j}^{(i)}(\xi)\varepsilon^{(l)}\right) \mathbf{K}_{n,j}^{(i)} \tag{4.8}$$

is an element of $\mathcal{H}$

(ii) for every $F \in \mathcal{H}$ and every $\xi \in \Omega$ the reproducing property

$$F(\xi) = \sum_{l=1}^{3} \left(K(.,\xi)\varepsilon^{(l)}, F\right)_{\mathcal{H}} \varepsilon^{(l)} \tag{4.9}$$

holds true.

Proof. $|K(\xi,\xi)\varepsilon^{(l)}|$ is bounded uniformly as to $\xi \in \Omega$, $l = 1,2,3$

$$|K(\xi,\xi)\varepsilon^{(l)}| \leq 3 \sum_{n=0}^{\infty} \frac{2n+1}{4\pi} \, |q_n|^{-2} \, .$$

Thus a necessary and sufficient condition that $\mathcal{H}$ have a reproducing kernel is fulfilled (cf. [1]). ∎

$\mathcal{H}$ is naturally equipped with the semi-inner product $(.,.)_{\mathcal{H}_m}$ corresponding to the seminorm

$$\|F\|^2_{\mathcal{H}_m} = \sum_{n=m+1}^{\infty} \sum_{j=1}^{2n+1} \sum_{i=1}^{3} |q_n|^2 \left(F, \mathbf{K}^{(i)}_{n,j}\right)^2_{L_2(\Omega)} . \tag{4.10}$$

The kernel of this seminorm $\| \, . \, \|_{\mathcal{H}_m}$ is the linear space $\mathbf{\Sigma}_{0,...,m}$. The seminormed space $(\mathcal{H}, \| \, . \, \|_{\mathcal{H}_m})$ is a functional semi - Hilbert subspace of $C(\Omega)$.

Clearly, for every $F \in \mathcal{H}$ and every $\xi \in \Omega$ the reprostructure in $\mathcal{H}$ enables us to see that for l=1,2,3

$$\left(K(.,\xi)\, \varepsilon^{(l)}, F\right)_{\mathcal{H}_m} = \left(\sum_{i=1}^{3} J^{(i)}_m(.,\xi)\, \varepsilon^{(l)}, F\right)_{\mathcal{H}_m} \tag{4.11}$$

where the kernel $J_m(.,.) : \Omega \times \Omega \to \mathbb{R}^3$ is given by

$$K(\xi,\eta) = \sum_{i=1}^{3}\left(I^{(i)}_m(\xi,\eta) + J^{(i)}_m(\xi,\eta)\right) , \quad \xi,\eta \in \Omega , \tag{4.12}$$

with

$$I^{(i)}_m(\xi,\eta) = \sum_{n=0}^{m} \sum_{j=1}^{2n+1} |q_n|^{-2} \mathbf{K}^{(i)}_{n,j}(\xi) \otimes \mathbf{K}^{(i)}_{n,j}(\eta) , \tag{4.13}$$

$$J^{(i)}_m(\xi,\eta) = \sum_{n=m+1}^{\infty} \sum_{j=1}^{2n+1} |q_n|^{-2} \mathbf{K}^{(i)}_{n,j}(\xi) \otimes \mathbf{K}^{(i)}_{n,j}(\eta) . \tag{4.14}$$

Our purpose now is to define vector spherical splines (v.s.s.) as members of the seminormed space $\mathcal{H}$ equipped with the semistructure induced by $\| \, . \, \|_{\mathcal{H}_m}$ (for the scalar case the reader is referred to [5], [6]).

Definition 1: Given a system $X_N = \{\eta_1, ..., \eta_N\}$ of N points $\eta_1, ..., \eta_N \in \Omega$. Then any $S \in \mathcal{H}$ of the form

$$S(\xi) = P(\xi) + \sum_{k=1}^{N} \sum_{i=1}^{3} J^{(i)}_m(\xi,\eta_k) a^{(i)}_k , \quad P \in \mathbf{\Sigma}_{0,...,m},\ a^{(i)}_k \in \mathbb{R}^3,\ \xi \in \Omega , \tag{4.15}$$

is called $\mathbf{\Sigma}_{0,...,m}$- vector spherical spline (v.s.s.) in $\mathcal{H}$ relative to the knots $\eta_1, ..., \eta_N$. The class of all $\mathbf{\Sigma}_{0,...,m}$- v.s.s. relative to the knots $\eta_1, ..., \eta_N$ is denoted by $\mathcal{S}_m(X_N)$.

Definition 2: Given a $\Sigma_{0,...,m}$−admissible system of N points $\eta_1, ..., \eta_N \in \Omega$. Then any $S \in \mathcal{S}_m(X_N)$ of the form (4.15) is called natural $\mathbf{\Sigma}_{0,...,m}$- v.s.s. in $\mathcal{H}$ relative to the knots $\eta_1, ..., \eta_N$, if $a^{(i)} = (a_1^{(i)}, ...a_N^{(i)})$ satisfies the linear system

$$\sum_{k=1}^{N} a_k^{(i)} \; \mathbf{K}_{n,j}^{(i)}(\eta_k) \; = \; 0 \; , \tag{4.16}$$

$n = 0, ..., m,\ j = 1, ..., 2n+1,\ i = 1,2,3$. The class of all natural $\mathcal{H}$ - v.s.s. relative to the knots $\eta_1, ..., \eta_N$ is denoted by $\mathcal{N}_m(X_N)$. (Evidently $\mathcal{N}_m(X_N)$ contains the class $\mathbf{\Sigma}_{0,...,m}$.)

Let there be given now N presented data points $(\eta_i, y_i) \in \Omega \times I\!R^3, i = 1, ..., N$ corresponding to a $\Sigma_{0,...,m}$-admissible system $X_N = \{\eta_1, ..., \eta_N\}$. We consider the spline problem of finding the "$\mathcal{H}_m$ - smallest norm interpolant " to the prescribed data:

$$\|S\|_{\mathcal{H}_m} \; = \; \inf_{F \,\in\, \mathcal{I}_N(y)} \|F\|_{\mathcal{H}_m} \tag{4.17}$$

where

$$\mathcal{I}_N(y) \; = \; \{F \in \mathcal{H} | F(\eta_i) = y_i, \; i = 1, ..., N\}. \tag{4.18}$$

Lemma 1: If $F \in \mathcal{I}_N(y)$ and $S \in \mathcal{N}_m(X_N)$, then

$$(S, F)_{\mathcal{H}_m} \; = \; \sum_{k=1}^{N} \sum_{i=1}^{3} a_k^{(i)} \; F(\eta_k) \, .$$

Proof: First it follows that

$$(S, F)_{\mathcal{H}_m} \; = \; \sum_{k=1}^{N} \sum_{i=1}^{3} \left(J_m^{(i)}(\cdot, \eta_k) \; a_k^{(i)}, F \right)_{\mathcal{H}_m} .$$

According to our assumption about $a^{(i)}$ we have

$$\sum_{k=1}^{N} I_m^{(i)}(\cdot, \eta_k) \; a_k^{(i)} \; = \; 0$$

for i=1,2,3. Therefore we obtain using the reprostructure in $\mathcal{H}$

$$(S, F)_{\mathcal{H}_m} = \sum_{k=1}^{N} \sum_{i=1}^{3} \left(\left(I_m^{(i)}(\cdot, \eta_k) + J_m^{(i)}(\cdot, \eta_k)\right) \; a_k^{(i)}, F \right)_{\mathcal{H}_m} .$$

This proves Lemma 1. ■

__Lemma 2:__ For given $y = (y_1, ..., y_N)$, there exists an unique $S \in \mathcal{N}_m(X_N) \cap \mathcal{I}_N(y)$ (denoted briefly by S_N).

Proof: $S(\eta_k) = y_k,\ k = 1, ..., N$, gives N vectorial linear equations

$$\sum_{l=1}^{N}\sum_{i=1}^{3} J_m^{(i)}(\eta_k, \eta_l)\, a_l^{(i)} + \sum_{n=0}^{m}\sum_{j=1}^{2n+1}\sum_{i=1}^{3} c_{n,j}^{(i)}\mathbf{K}_{n,j}^{(i)}(\eta_k) = y_k\,. \tag{4.19}$$

The linear system

$$\sum_{k=1}^{N} a_k^{(i)}\mathbf{K}_{n,j}^{(i)}(\eta_k) = 0\,, \quad n = 0, ..., m,\ j = 1, ..., 2n+1,\ i = 1, 2, 3, \tag{4.20}$$

provides $\widetilde{M}$ further equations. Lemma will be proved if it can be shown that the overall linear system is nonsingular. This will be established if it can be proved that the corresponding homogeneous system has only the trivial solution in which all coefficients vanish. Equivalently we have to verify that the only $\widetilde{S} \in \mathcal{N}_m(X_N) \cap \mathcal{I}_N(0)$ is the trivial one. To show this we obtain from Lemma 1 that $\|\widetilde{S}\|_{\mathcal{H}_m} = 0$, i.e. $\widetilde{S} \in \mathbf{\Sigma}_{0,...,m} \cap \mathcal{I}_N(0)$. Consequently, because of the assumption imposed on X_N, $\widetilde{S} = 0$, as required. ■

__Lemma 3:__ If $F \in \mathcal{I}_N(y)$, then

$$\|F\|^2_{\mathcal{H}_m} = \|S_N\|^2_{\mathcal{H}_m} + \|S_N - F\|^2_{\mathcal{H}_m}\,.$$

__Lemma 4:__ If $F \in \mathcal{I}_N(y)$, then

$$\|S - F\|^2_{\mathcal{H}_m} = \|S_N - F\|^2_{\mathcal{H}_m} + \|S - S_N\|^2_{\mathcal{H}_m}$$

for every $S \in \mathcal{N}_m(X_N)$.

The proof of the lemmata stated above can be given by straightforward calculation.

__Theorem 2:__ The vectorial spline interpolation problem

$$\|S_N\|_{\mathcal{H}_m} = \inf_{F \,\in\, \mathcal{I}_N(y)} \|F\|_{\mathcal{H}_m}$$

is well-posed in the sense that its solution exists, is unique and depends continuously on the data $y_1, ..., y_N$.

The uniquely determined solution S_N is given in the explicit form

$$S_N = \sum_{n=0}^{m} \sum_{j=1}^{2n+1} \sum_{i=1}^{3} c_{n,j}^{(i)} \mathbf{K}_{n,j}^{(i)} + \sum_{k=1}^{N} \sum_{i=1}^{3} J_m^{(i)}(\cdot, \eta_k)\, a_k^{(i)} , \tag{4.21}$$

where the coefficients $c_{n,j}^{(i)}, a_k^{(i)}$ satisfy the linear equations (4.19) and (4.20).

In a forthcoming paper the choice of the semi-norm $\| \cdot \|_{\mathcal{H}_m}$ and the numerical solution process of vector spherical spline interpolation will be discussed in detail.

References:

[1] Dieudonné, J.: (1969) Foundations of Modern Analysis. Academic Press. New York-London.

[2] Euler, H.J., Groten, E., Hausch,W., Stock, B.: (1985) Precise Geoid Computation at Mountaineous Coastlines in View of Vertical Datum Determinations. Veröff. Zentralinst. für Physik der Erde, Akad. der Wiss. der DDR, 81, Teil I, 109-139.

[3] Euler, H.J., Groten, E., Hausch, W., Kling, Th.: (1986) New results obtained for Detailed Geoid Approximations. Bolletino di geodesica e scienze affini, 4.

[4] Freeden, W.: (1978) Eine Klasse von Integralformeln der mathematischen Geodäsie. Veröff. Geod. Inst. RWTH Aachen, 27.

[5] Freeden, W.: (1981) On Spherical Spline Interpolation and Approximation. Math. Meth. in the Appl. Sciences, 3, 551-575.

[6] Freeden, W., Hermann, P.: (1986) Uniform Approximation by Spherical Spline Interpolation. Math. Z., 193, 265-275.

[7] Gervens, T.: (1989) Vektorkugelfunktionen mit Anwendungen in der Theorie der elastischen Verformungen für die Kugel. Diss. RWTH Aachen.

[8] Müller, Cl.: (1966) Spherical Harmonics. Lecture Notes in Mathematics, 17, Berlin-Heidelberg-New York, Springer Verlag.

Prof. Dr. W. Freeden
RWTH Aachen
Institut für Reine und Angewandte Mathematik
Templergraben 55
D-5100 Aachen
Federal Republic of Germany

Dr. T. Gervens
RWTH Aachen
Institut für Mathematik
Templergraben 55
D-5100 Aachen
Federal Republic of Germany

International Series of
Numerical Mathematics, Vol. 90

SIMULTANEOUS APPROXIMATION BY GENERALIZED n-th ORDER BLENDING OPERATORS

Heinz H. Gonska

Fachbereich Mathematik, Universität Duisburg, FRG

1. Introduction

The present note deals with various aspects concerning n-th order blending operators as introduced by Delvos and Posdorf in [2]. These operators constitute a generalization of the well-known technique of discrete blending interpolation as discussed in [6], among others. The motivation of our contribution is two-fold. First, we stress the fact that applications of this technique should not be restricted to those cases in which the univariate building blocks are projectors. To this end, we introduce so-called generalized n-th order blending operators which share many relevant properties of the classical n-th order blending operators, including their potential for data reduction. Secondly, we shall show that quite elegant upper bounds for the approximation error can be given using mixed moduli of smoothness of appropriate orders and some previous results of the present author. Two applications are added in order to illustrate our more general approach.

2. Basic Definitions and Previous Results

Definition 2.1. Let $I, J \subset \mathbb{R}$ be compact intervals of the real axis, G and H be real vector spaces of functions defined on I and J, respectively, and $L : G \to \mathbb{R}^I$, $M : H \to \mathbb{R}^J$ be operators. Consider $f : I \times J \to \mathbb{R}$ with $f(\cdot,y) \in G$ for all $y \in J$. Then the parametric extension L' of L is given by

$$L'(f;x,y) := L(f(\cdot,y);x).$$

Likewise, M'' is defined by

$$M''(f;x,y) := M(f(x,\cdot);y).$$

n-th order blending operators as considered in [2] are a special instance of the following (informal)

<u>Definition 2.2.</u> Let $P_1, \ldots, P_n : G \to \mathbb{R}^I$, $Q_1, \ldots, Q_n : H \to \mathbb{R}^J$ be linear operators so that the parametric extensions, sums and products below are defined. Then, for $n \in \mathbb{N}$, an <u>n-th order blending operator</u> B_n is given by

$$B_n := P'_1 Q''_n \oplus P'_2 Q''_{n-1} \oplus \ldots \oplus P'_n Q''_1 .$$

Here, $A \oplus B = A + B - AB$ is the Boolean sum of A and B.

<u>Example 2.3.</u> For the case $n = 1$ one obtains a tensor product of parametric extensions. For $n = 2$ we get certain operators including Boolean sums of parametric extensions (for $P_2 = Q_2 = \mathrm{Id}$ (identity)). Considering the operator B_3 leads to the explicit representation

$$\begin{aligned} B_3 = P'_1 Q''_3 + P'_2 Q''_2 - P'_1 Q''_3 P'_2 Q''_2 + P'_3 Q''_1 - P'_1 Q''_3 P'_3 Q''_1 \\ - P'_2 Q''_2 P'_3 Q''_1 + P'_1 Q''_3 P'_2 Q''_2 P'_3 Q''_1 . \end{aligned}$$

This is too complex for computational purposes. The method used in earlier papers to reduce expressions of this type is described in

<u>Remark 2.4.</u> If P'_k and Q''_ℓ, $1 \le k, \ell \le n$, commute, and if absorption conditions of the type

$$P'_{k_2} P'_{k_1} = P'_{k_1} P'_{k_2} = P'_{k_1} \quad (k_1 \le k_2),$$

$$Q''_{\ell_2} Q''_{\ell_1} = Q''_{\ell_1} Q''_{\ell_2} = Q''_{\ell_1} \quad (\ell_1 \le \ell_2)$$

hold, then the above expressions simplify. For example, for $n = 2$ one gets $B_2 = P'_1 Q''_2 + P'_2 Q''_1 - P'_1 Q''_1$, which includes so-called 'discrete spline blending operators'. For $n = 3$ we obtain

$$B_3 = (P'_1 - 0)Q''_3 + (P'_2 - P'_1)Q''_2 + (P'_3 - P'_2)Q''_1 .$$

Clearly, the latter representation of B_3 is much simpler than the former in that it involves only three operator multiplications instead of 17.

Examples of operators satisfying the assumptions of Remark 2.4 are given by the parametric extensions of suitable interpolation projectors. See, e.g., [1] and [8] for a discussion of some special cases.

The following representation of B_n is a slight generalization of Satz 2.5 in [8] (see also Lemma 2.2 in [2]).

Theorem 2.5. Let P_k, Q_k, $1 \le k \le n$, be given as above, so that P'_k and Q''_ℓ commute for $1 \le k, \ell \le n$, and absorption conditions of the kind described in Remark 2.4 hold. Then

$$B_n = \sum_{k=1}^{n} P'_k Q''_{n+1-k} - \sum_{k=1}^{n-1} P'_k Q''_{n-k} = \sum_{k=0}^{n-1} (P'_{k+1} - P'_k) Q''_{n-k}, \quad \text{where } P_0 = 0.$$

The proof of Theorem 2.5 requires the same operations as employed in [2].

It is the latter form of the operation B_n which was used in [2] to derive error representations, etc. It was then of no significance that the B_n's were originally derived from an n-fold Boolean sum. Indeed, this background is too restrictive in the sense that it prevents one from using sequences of operators which do not have the absorption properties from Remark 2.4. This observation is our motivation for introducing generalized n-th order blending operators.

3. The Generalized n-th Order Blending Operator

Definition 3.1. Let $P_1, \ldots, P_n : G \to \mathbb{R}^I$, $Q_1, \ldots, Q_n : H \to \mathbb{R}^J$ be given as in Definition 2.2. Then, for $n \in \mathbb{N}$, the generalized n-th order blending operator G_n is defined by

$$G_n = \sum_{k=0}^{n-1} (P'_{k+1} - P'_k) Q''_{n-k}, \quad \text{where } P_0 = 0.$$

A useful error representation for $Id - G_n$ is provided by the following theorem which generalizes Lemma A1 in [6]. See also the proof of Theorem 2 in [7].

Theorem 3.2. Let P_k, Q_k, $1 \le k \le n$, and G_n be given as in Definition 3.1. Then

$$Id - G_n = (Id - P'_n) + (Id - Q''_n) + \sum_{k=1}^{n-1} (Id - P'_k \oplus Q''_{n-k}) - \sum_{k=1}^{n} (Id - P'_k \oplus Q''_{n+1-k}).$$

Remark 3.3. The decomposition of Theorem 3.2 shows that the error $I - G_n$ consists basically of two components. The first two terms are errors for so-called "lofting operators", while the remaining expression is a sum of errors for Boolean sums of parametric extensions. The latter have been studied to some extent in several recent papers (see, e.g., [5] and the references cited there).

4. Error Estimates for Generalized n-th Order Blending

The estimates of this section will be given in terms of Marchaud's mixed moduli of smoothness of order (r,s). These are defined for $r, s \in \mathbb{N}_0$, $f \in C(I \times J)$ and $\delta_1, \delta_2 \geq 0$ by

$$\omega_{r,s}(f;\delta_1,\delta_2) := \sup \{ |{}_x\Delta_{h_1}^{r} \circ {}_y\Delta_{h_2}^{s} f(x,y)| : (x,y), (x+rh_1, y+sh_2) \in I \times J, |h_i| \leq \delta_i, i=1,2 \}.$$

Here,

$${}_x\Delta_{h_1}^{r} \circ {}_y\Delta_{h_2}^{s} f(x,y) := \sum_{\rho=0}^{r} \sum_{\sigma=0}^{s} (-1)^{r+s-\rho-\sigma} \binom{r}{\rho} \binom{s}{\sigma} f(x+\rho h_1, y+\sigma h_2)$$

is a mixed difference of order (r,s) with increment h_1 with respect to x and increment h_2 with respect to y. See [9, p. 516ff] and [4] for further details. For $r = 0, s \geq 1$, or $r \geq 1, s = 0$, one obtains the well-known partial moduli of smoothness.

In the sequel, the operators P_k and Q_k figuring in the definition of G_n will be such that $P_k : C^p(I) \to C^{p'}(I)$ and $Q_k : C^q(J) \to C^{q'}(J)$. Furthermore, we shall assume that they satisfy inequalities of the following type involving univariate moduli of smoothness (of higher orders) and bounded real-valued functions $\Gamma\ldots$ and $\Lambda\ldots$:

$$\begin{aligned} |(g - P_k g)^{(\kappa)}(x)| &\leq \Gamma_{r,\kappa,P_k}(x) \cdot \omega_r(g^{(p)}; \Lambda_{r,P_k}(x)) \\ &\qquad \text{for } 0 \leq \kappa \leq p^* = \min\{p,p'\}, \text{ and} \\ |(h - Q_k h)^{(\lambda)}(x)| &\leq \Gamma_{s,\lambda,Q_k}(y) \cdot \omega_s(h^{(q)}; \Lambda_{s,Q_k}(y)) \\ &\qquad \text{for } 0 \leq \lambda \leq q^* = \min\{q,q'\}. \end{aligned} \tag{4.1}$$

Making these assumptions the following is obtained.

<u>Theorem 4.1.</u> Let the generalized n-th order blending operator G_n be given as in Definition 3.1, and such that the operators P_k and Q_k satisfy the conditions (4.1). Then for $f \in C^{p,q}(I \times J)$, $(x,y) \in I \times J$ and $(0,0) \leq (\kappa,\lambda) \leq (p^*,q^*)$

$$\begin{aligned} &|D^{(\kappa,\lambda)} \circ (Id - G_n)(f;x,y)| \\ &\quad \leq \Gamma_{r,\kappa,P_n}(x) \cdot \omega_{r,0}(f^{(p,\lambda)}; \Lambda_{r,P_n}(x), 0) \end{aligned}$$

$$+\Gamma_{s,\lambda,Q_n}(y)\cdot\omega_{0,s}(f^{(\kappa,q)};0,\Lambda_{s,Q_n}(y))$$

$$+\sum_{k=1}^{n-1}\Gamma_{r,\kappa,P_k}(x)\cdot\Gamma_{s,\lambda,Q_{n-k}}(y)\cdot\omega_{r,s}(f^{(p,q)};\Lambda_{r,P_k}(x),\Lambda_{s,Q_{n-k}}(y))$$

$$+\sum_{k=1}^{n}\Gamma_{r,\kappa,P_k}(x)\cdot\Gamma_{s,\lambda,Q_{n+1-k}}(y)\cdot\omega_{r,s}(f^{(p,q)};\Lambda_{r,P_k}(x),\Lambda_{s,Q_{n+1-k}}(y)).$$

Proof. Write the difference $I-G_n$ as suggested by Theorem 3.2 and apply the mixed partial differentiation operator $D^{(\kappa,\lambda)}$ to both sides of the resulting equality. Thus,

$$|D^{(\kappa,\lambda)}\circ(Id-G_n)(f;x,y)|$$

$$\leq|D^{(\kappa,\lambda)}\circ(Id-P_n')(f;x,y)|+|D^{(\kappa,\lambda)}\circ(Id-Q_n'')(f;x,y)|$$

$$+\sum_{k=1}^{n-1}|D^{(\kappa,\lambda)}\circ(Id-P_k'\oplus Q_{n-k}'')(f;x,y)|$$

$$+\sum_{k=1}^{n}|D^{(\kappa,\lambda)}\circ(Id-P_k'\oplus Q_{n+1-k}'')(f;x,y)|.$$

The various terms of the upper bound can now be estimated using the same techniques as in the proof of Theorem 5.2 (for the lofting operators P_n' and Q_n'') and with the aid of Theorem 2.2 (for the terms involving Boolean sums) of our paper [5]. The assumptions (4.1) on the operators P_k and Q_k then yield the claim of Theorem 4.1. □

For the case $n = 1$ Theorem 4.1 provides us with compact upper bounds for tensor product approximation by $G_1 = P_1' Q_1''$. However, for higher order generalized blending ($n \geq 2$) the upper bound of Theorem 4.1 becomes quite complex. If we restrict ourselves to the consideration of sequences $P_1, \ldots, P_n$ satisfying compatibility conditions of the form

$$\Gamma_{r,\kappa,P_i}(x)\leq\Gamma_{r,\kappa,P_j}(x),\qquad i\geq j,$$

and

$$\Lambda_{r,P_i}(x)\leq\Lambda_{r,P_j}(x),\qquad i\geq j, \tag{4.2}$$

and assume analogous conditions to hold for the sequence $Q_1, \ldots, Q_n$, the estimate simplifies to the one of

Corollary 4.2. Suppose $n \geq 2$ and that the operators P_k, Q_k, $1 \leq k \leq n$, satisfy inequalities of the types (4.1) and (4.2). Then

$$
\begin{aligned}
&|D^{(\kappa,\lambda)}\circ(Id - G_n)(f;x,y)| \\
&\quad \le \Gamma_{r,\kappa,P_n}(x)\cdot\omega_{r,0}(f^{(p,\lambda)};\Lambda_{r,P_n}(x),0) + \Gamma_{s,\lambda,Q_n}(y)\cdot\omega_{0,s}(f^{(\kappa,q)};0,\Lambda_{s,Q_n}(y)) \\
&\quad + 3\cdot\sum_{k=1}^{n-1}\Gamma_{r,\kappa,P_k}(x)\cdot\Gamma_{s,\lambda,Q_{n-k}}(y)\cdot\omega_{r,s}(f^{(p,q)};\Lambda_{r,P_k}(x),\Lambda_{s,Q_{n-k}}(y)).
\end{aligned}
$$

Example 4.3. Under the conditions of Corollary 4.2, for the case $n = 2$ we obtain the upper bound

$$
\begin{aligned}
&\Gamma_{r,\kappa,P_2}(x)\cdot\omega_{r,0}(f^{(p,\lambda)};\Lambda_{r,P_2}(x),0) + \Gamma_{s,\lambda,Q_2}(y)\cdot\omega_{0,s}(f^{(\kappa,q)};0,\Lambda_{s,Q_2}(y)) \\
&\quad + 3\cdot\Gamma_{r,\kappa,P_1}(x)\cdot\Gamma_{s,\lambda,Q_1}(y)\cdot\omega_{r,s}(f^{(p,q)};\Lambda_{r,P_1}(x),\Lambda_{s,Q_1}(y)).
\end{aligned}
$$

This includes, for example, an estimate for discrete blending interpolation (approximation) operators, as given in [5]. □

5. Applications

5.1 n-th Order Polynomial Spline Blending

Consider the case $I = J = [a,b]$. For the clamped cubic spline interpolation operator $S_{\Delta_m} : C^p(I) \to C^2(I)$, $p = 1, 2, 3$ or 4, with mesh

$$
\Delta_m : a = x_0 < \dots < x_m = b
$$

and gauge $\varepsilon := \max_{0\le i\le m-1} (x_{i+1} - x_i) < 1$, Theorem 3.4 of [5] shows that, for $g \in C^p(I)$,

$$
\|(S_{\Delta_m} g - g)^{(\kappa)}\|_\infty \le c(p,\kappa)\cdot\varepsilon^{p-\kappa}\cdot\omega_{4-p}(g^{(p)};\varepsilon),\ 0 \le \kappa \le p^* = \min\{p,2\}.
$$

Choose $P_k = Q_k$ to be a cubic spline operator from above w.r.t. a mesh with gauge δ^k, $1 \le k \le n$, so that

$$
\|(P_k g - g)^{(\kappa)}\|_\infty \le c\cdot(\delta^k)^{p-\kappa}\cdot\omega_{4-p}(g^{(p)};\delta^k),\ 0 \le \kappa \le p^*,\ 1 \le k \le n.
$$

Here, $c := \max\{c(p,\kappa) : 1 \le p \le 4, 0 \le \kappa \le 2\}$.

The same inequality holds for each Q_k. Thus, for $G_n : C^{p,p}(I\times I) \to C^{2,2}(I\times I)$, by Corollary 4.2 we have

$$\|D^{(\kappa,\lambda)} \circ (Id - G_n)f\|_\infty$$
$$\leq c \cdot (\delta^n)^{p-\kappa} \cdot \omega_{4-p,0}(f^{(p,\lambda)};\delta^n,0) + c \cdot (\delta^n)^{p-\lambda} \cdot \omega_{0,4-p}(f^{(\kappa,p)};0,\delta^n)$$
$$+ 3c^2 \cdot \sum_{k=1}^{n-1} (\delta^k)^{p-\kappa} \cdot (\delta^{n-k})^{p-\lambda} \cdot \omega_{4-p,4-p}(f^{(p,p)};\delta^k,\delta^{n-k}).$$

For example, for $\kappa = \lambda = 0$, $p = q = 4$ and n fixed,

$$\|(Id - G_n)f\|_\infty = O(\delta^{4n}), \quad \delta \to 0.$$

Similar results can be obtained for the so-called complete interpolation schemes discussed in [1].

5.2 n-th Order Blending of Bernstein Operators

The major motivation to investigate n-th order blending schemes B_n based upon suitable interpolation projectors was the fact that they have the general advantage of preserving an asymptotic interpolation error as compared to the corresponding tensor product interpolation but with a reduced number of data. This is also the case for the generalized operators G_n. For them, however, it is not necessary that the univariate building blocks be projectors. It suffices instead to assume that, in the case of discretely defined operators, the sets A_k of evaluation points for the univariate operators P_k (and Q_k) are such that $A_\kappa \subset A_\lambda$ for $\kappa \leq \lambda$. We illustrate this by considering the classical Bernstein operators $S_m : C[0,1] \to C[0,1]$. For them one has (see [3])

$$|(g - S_m g)(x)| \leq 4 \cdot \omega_2(g, \sqrt{\frac{x(1-x)}{m}}), \quad m \geq 1, \quad x \in [0,1], \; g \in C[0,1].$$

Choose $P_0 = 0$ and, for $1 \leq k \leq n$, $P_k = Q_k = S_{m^k}$, $m \geq 2$.
Then for the generalized n-th order blending operator

$$G_n = S'_m S''_{m^n} + \sum_{k=1}^{n-1} (S'_{m^{k+1}} - S'_{m^k}) S''_{m^{n-k}}, \quad n \geq 2,$$

Corollary 4.2 yields

$$|(Id - G_n)(f;x,y)| \leq 4 \cdot \omega_{2,0}\left(f; \sqrt{\frac{x(1-x)}{m^n}}, 0\right) + 4 \cdot \omega_{0,2}\left(f; 0, \sqrt{\frac{y(1-y)}{m^n}}\right)$$
$$+ 48 \cdot \sum_{k=1}^{n-1} \omega_{2,2}\left(f; \sqrt{\frac{x(1-x)}{m^k}}, \sqrt{\frac{y(1-y)}{m^{n-k}}}\right).$$

If $f \in C^{2,2}([0,1]^2)$, it follows that

$$\|(Id - G_n)f\|_\infty = O(\frac{1}{m^n}), \ m \to \infty.$$

The same asymptotic approximation error is obtained for the tensor product operator $S'_{m^n} S''_{m^n}$ which requires a larger amount of data from the function f. A more detailed analysis of this phenomenon leads to results analogous to those in Remark 3.8b of [1].

References

[1] Baszenski, G. (1985) n-th order polynomial spline blending, in: "Multivariate Approximation III"; ed. by W. Schempp and K. Zeller, 35-46 (Birkhäuser, Basel).
[2] Delvos, F.J. and Posdorf, H. (1977) N-th order blending, in: "Constructive Theory of Functions of Several Variables"; ed. by W. Schempp and K. Zeller, 53-64 (Springer, Berlin-Heidelberg-New York).
[3] Gonska, H.H. (1985) On approximation by linear operators: Improved estimates. Anal. Numér. Théor. Approx. 14, 7-32.
[4] Gonska, H.H. (1985) Quantitative Approximation in C(X), Habilitationsschrift (Universität Duisburg).
[5] Gonska, H.H. Degree of simultaneous approximation of bivariate functions by Gordon operators. To appear in J. Approx. Theory.
[6] Gordon, W.J. (1969) Distributive lattices and the approximation of multivariate functions, in: "Approximation with Special Emphasis on Spline Functions"; ed. by I.J. Schoenberg, 223-277 (Acad. Press, New York).
[7] Hall, C.A. (1976) Transfinite interpolation and applications to engineering problems, in: "Theory of Approximation with Applications"; ed. by A.G. Law and B.N. Sahney, 308-331 (Acad. Press, New York).
[8] Posdorf, H. (1977) Boolesche Methoden bei zweidimensionaler Interpolation, Dissertation (Universität Siegen).
[9] Schumaker, L.L. (1981) Spline functions: Basic theory (J. Wiley, New York).

Heinz H. Gonska
Fachbereich Mathematik
Universität Duisburg
D-4100 Duisburg 1
FRG

International Series of
Numerical Mathematics, Vol. 90

SOME RESULTS ON QUADRATIC SPLINES OF THREE (AND MORE) VARIABLES

Gerhard Heindl

University of Wuppertal, FRG

Summary

This paper is devoted to the following problem: Given an n-dimensional simplicial complex K, find a refinement K' of K with the property: For arbitrary data $w_x \in \mathbb{R}, \beta_x \in \mathbb{R}^n$ associated with the vertices x of K, there is a unique quadratic spline function φ with respect to K', satisfying the Hermite interpolation conditions $\varphi(x)=w_x$ and $\operatorname{grad}\varphi(x)=\beta_x$ for all vertices x of K. It is shown how to solve this problem in the 3-dimensional case, if there exists a certain dual cell complex of K. The underlying concepts however are independent of the number of variables.

Notations and preliminary remarks

With the exception that a complex K may be also locally finite (as defined in [1] p.129) instead of finite, we will use the notations introduced in [4].

We are interested in the solutions of the following problem: Given a complex K, find a refinement K' of K with the property: For arbitrary data $w_x \in \mathbb{R}, \beta_x \in \mathbb{R}^n$ associated with the vertices x of K, there is a unique $\varphi \in P_2(K')$ satisfying the Hermite interpolation conditions

$$\text{(H)} \qquad \begin{aligned} \varphi(x) &= w_x \\ \operatorname{grad} \varphi(x) &= \beta_x \end{aligned} \qquad \text{for all vertices } x \text{ of } K.$$

A technique for constructing refinements with this property, suggested and successfully used in [3],[4] und [2]*), is based on the simple but useful

Lemma 1

Given a complex K' and data $w_x \in \mathbb{R}, \beta_x \in \mathbb{R}^n$ for all vertices x of K', then there is a (unique and constructible) $\varphi \in P_2(K')$ satisfying the interpolation conditions

$$\text{(H')} \qquad \begin{aligned} \varphi(x) &= w_x \\ \operatorname{grad} \varphi(x) &= \beta_x \end{aligned} \qquad \text{for all vertices } x \in K',$$

if and only if for every edge

$$\langle x,y \rangle \in K'$$

the edge condition

$$\text{(EC)} \qquad 2w_x + \beta_x^T(y-x) = 2w_y + \beta_y^T(x-y)$$

holds.

Lemma 1 was proved in [3] for the two dimensional case. But, as mentioned in [4], an extension of the proof to the n-dimensional case is trivial. A generalization of Lemma 1 to more complicated Hermite interpolation problems for spline functions of higher degree was obtained by H.J. BUHL in [2]. As he has shown, (EC) has to be replaced in these cases by conditions for certain higher dimensional faces of the n-simplexes of K' (Randsimplexbeziehungen).

Fundamentals of basic constructions

As the examples considered in [3] and [4] show, refinements with the desired property were always obtained by applying certain basic constructions. They and additional ones can be derived from the next two lemmas and their corollaries, which were used already in [3],[4] and [2], at least in special cases.

Lemma 2

Given a subset $\{x_0,\dots,x_k\}$ of $\mathbb{R}^n (k \geq 1)$,

$$z = \sum_{i=0}^{k} \lambda_i x_i \notin \{x_0,\dots,x_k\} \text{ such that } \sum_{i=0}^{k} \lambda_i = 1$$

---

*) As I have seen later, the triangular elements constructed in [3] and [4] were already obtained by POWELL and SABIN in [5].

and data $w_{x_i} \in \mathbb{R}$, $\beta_{x_i} \in \mathbb{R}^n$, $i=0,\dots,k$, $w_z \in \mathbb{R}$, $\beta_z \in \mathbb{R}^n$, then the edge conditions

$$2w_z+\beta_z^T(x_i-z) = 2w_{x_i}+\beta_{x_i}^T(z-x_i) \ , i=0,\dots,k.$$

are satisfied if and only if

(1) $$w_z = \frac{1}{2}\sum_{i=0}^{k} \lambda_i(2w_{x_i}+\beta_{x_i}^T(z-x_i)) \quad \text{and}$$

(2) $$\beta_z^T(x_i-x_0) = 2(w_{x_i}-w_{x_0})+\beta_{x_i}^T(z-x_i)-\beta_{x_0}^T(z-x_0), \quad i=1,\dots,k.$$

Proof: We assume first, that the edge conditions are satisfied. Then (1) is a consequence of the identity

$$\sum_{i=0}^{k} \lambda_i(2w_z+\beta_z^T(x_i-z)) = \sum_{i=0}^{k} \lambda_i(2w_{x_i}+\beta_{x_i}^T(z-x_i)),$$

since the left hand side evaluates to $2w_z$. (2) is obtained by subtracting the first edge condition from the remaining ones. Assume now, that (1) and (2) are satisfied. Then we obtain first

$$2w_{x_0}+\beta_{x_0}^T(z-x_0) = \sum_{i=0}^{k} \lambda_i(2w_{x_i}+\beta_{x_i}^T(z-x_i))$$
$$-\sum_{i=0}^{k} \lambda_i(2w_{x_i}+\beta_{x_i}^T(z-x_i)-(2w_{x_0}+\beta_{x_0}^T(z-x_0))) =$$
$$2w_z-\sum_{i=0}^{k} \lambda_i\beta_z^T(x_i-x_0) = 2w_z+\beta_z^T(x_0-z).$$

The remaining edge conditions are satisfied since

$$2w_{x_i}+\beta_{x_i}^T(z-x_i) = 2w_{x_0}+\beta_{x_0}^T(z-x_0)+\beta_z^T(x_i-x_0)$$
$$= 2w_z+\beta_z^T(x_0-z)+\beta_z^T(x_i-x_0)$$
$$= 2w_z+\beta_z^T(x_i-z), \quad i=1,\dots,k.$$

Corollary

Given affinely independent points $x_0,\dots,x_k \in \mathbb{R}^n (k\geq 1)$, a basis $(v_1,\dots,v_n)$ of $\mathbb{R}^n$ such that $v_i=x_i-x_0$, $i=1,\dots,k$, data $w_{x_i} \in \mathbb{R}$, $\beta_{x_i} \in \mathbb{R}^n$, $i=0,\dots,k$, and, if $k<n$, $\gamma_i \in \mathbb{R}$, $i=k+1,\dots,n$. Then for any

$$z = \sum_{i=0}^{k} \lambda_i x_i \notin \{x_0,\dots,x_k\} \quad \text{such that} \quad \sum_{i=0}^{k} \lambda_i = 1$$

there is a unique $w_z \in \mathbb{R}$ and a unique $\beta_z \in \mathbb{R}^n$ such that

(1) (EC) is satisfied for all edges

$<z,x_i>$, $i=0,\ldots,k$.

(2) $\beta_z^T v_i = \gamma_i$, $i=k+1,\ldots,n$, if $k<n$.

w_z and β_z can be computed form the equations

$$w_z = \frac{1}{2}\sum_{i=0}^{k} \lambda_i(2w_{x_i}+\beta_{x_i}^T(z-x_i))$$

$$\beta_z^T v_i = 2(w_{x_i}-w_{x_0})+\beta_{x_i}^T(z-x_i)-\beta_{x_0}^T(z-x_0),\ i=1,\ldots,k,$$

$$\beta_z^T v_i = \gamma_i,\ i=k+1,\ldots,n,\ \text{if } k<n.$$

Lemma 3

Let $\{x,x_0,\ldots,x_k\}$ be a subset of $\mathbb{R}^n (k\geq 1)$ and $w_x \in \mathbb{R}, \beta_x \in \mathbb{R}^n, w_{x_i} \in \mathbb{R}, \beta_{x_i} \in \mathbb{R}^n$, $i=0,\ldots,k$, data such that (EC) holds for the edges $<x,x_i>$, $i=0,\ldots,k$. Then for any

$$z = \sum_{i=0}^{k} \lambda_i x_i \notin \{x,x_0,\ldots,x_k\} \text{ such that } \sum_{i=0}^{k} \lambda_i = 1$$

we have the identity

$$2w_x+\beta_x^T(z-x) = 2w_z+(\sum_{i=0}^{k} \lambda_i \beta_{x_i})^T(x-z),$$

where

$$w_z = \frac{1}{2}\sum_{i=0}^{k} \lambda_i(2w_{x_i}+\beta_{x_i}^T(z-x_i)).$$

Proof:

$$2(w_x-w_z)+\beta_x^T(z-x) =$$

$$\sum_{i=0}^{k} \lambda_i 2w_x+\beta_x^T(\sum_{i=0}^{k} \lambda_i(x_i-x))-2w_z =$$

$$\sum_{i=0}^{k} \lambda_i(2w_x+\beta_x^T(x_i-x))-2w_z =$$

$$\sum_{i=0}^{k} \lambda_i(2w_{x_i}+\beta_{x_i}^T(x-x_i)) - \sum_{i=0}^{k} \lambda_i(2w_{x_i}+\beta_{x_i}^T(z-x_i)) =$$

$$(\sum_{i=0}^{k} \lambda_i \beta_{x_i})^T(x-z).$$

Corollary

Let U and V be complementary subspaces of $\mathbb{R}^n$ ($\mathbb{R}^n = U \oplus V$), $z \in \mathbb{R}^n$, $\{x_0,\dots,x_k,\dots,x_s\} \subset (z+U)\setminus\{z\}$ such that $(x_1-x_0,\dots,x_k-x_0)$ is a basis of U, $\{y_0,\dots,y_l,\dots,y_t\} \subset (z+V)\setminus\{z\}$ such that $(y_1-y_0,\dots,y_l-y_0)$ is a basis of V. Then there is a unique $(\lambda_0,\dots,\lambda_k) \in \mathbb{R}^{k+1}$ such that

$$z = \sum_{i=0}^{k} \lambda_i x_i \quad \text{and} \quad \sum_{i=0}^{k} \lambda_i = 1$$

and a unique $(\mu_o,\dots,\mu_l) \in \mathbb{R}^{l+1}$ such that

$$z = \sum_{j=0}^{l} \mu_j y_j \quad \text{and} \quad \sum_{j=0}^{l} \mu_j = 1.$$

In addition assume, that there are given data $w_{x_i} \in \mathbb{R}, \beta_{x_i} \in \mathbb{R}^n$, $i=0,\dots,s$, $w_{y_j} \in \mathbb{R}$, $\beta_{y_j} \in \mathbb{R}^n$, $j=0,\dots,t$, such that (EC) holds for the edges

$\langle x_i, y_j \rangle$, $i=0,\dots,k$, $j=0,\dots,l$,

$\langle x_i, y_j \rangle$, $i=0,\dots,k$, $j=l+1,\dots,t$,

$\langle x_i, y_j \rangle$, $i=k+1,\dots,s$, $j=0,\dots,l$.

Then there is a unique $w_z \in \mathbb{R}$ and a unique $\beta_z \in \mathbb{R}^n$ such that (EC) holds for the edges

$\langle z, x_i \rangle$, $i=0,\dots,s$, and

$\langle z, y_j \rangle$, $j=0,\dots,t$.

w_z can be computed from

(I) $$w_z = \frac{1}{2}\sum_{i=0}^{k} \lambda_i (2w_{x_i} + \beta_{x_i}^T (z-x_i)) \text{ or}$$

(I') $$w_z = \frac{1}{2}\sum_{j=0}^{l} \mu_j (2w_{y_j} + \beta_{y_j}^T (z-y_j)),$$

β_z from the n linear equations

(II_1) $$\beta_z^T (x_i - x_0) = \Big(\sum_{j=0}^{l} \mu_j \beta_{y_j}\Big)^T (x_i - x_0), \quad i=1,\dots,k,$$

(II_2) $$\beta_z^T (y_j - y_0) = \Big(\sum_{i=0}^{k} \lambda_i \beta_{x_i}\Big)^T (y_j - y_0), \quad j=1,\dots,l.$$

Proof: Let w_z be defined by (I) and β_z by (II_1) and (II_2). Since (EC) holds for the edges

$$\langle y_j, x_i \rangle,\ i=0,\dots,k,\ j=0,\dots,t,$$

we can conclude from Lemma 3 that the equations

$$(*)\qquad 2w_{y_j}+\beta_{y_j}^T(z-y_j) = 2w_z+\beta_1^T(y_j-z),\ j=0,\dots,t,$$

are satisfied, where

$$\beta_1 = \sum_{i=0}^{k} \lambda_i \beta_{x_i}.$$

Since $(y_1-y_0,\dots,y_k-y_0)$ is a basis of V, (II_2) implies

$$\beta_z^T v = \beta_1^T v \quad \text{for all } v \in V,$$

and therefore

$$(**)\qquad \beta_z^T(y_j-z) = \beta_1^T(y_j-z),\ j=0,\dots,t.$$

But (*) and (**) show that (EC) holds for the edges

$$\langle z, y_j \rangle,\ j=0,\dots,t.$$

Now, as a consequence of Lemma 2 we have

$$w_z = \frac{1}{2}\sum_{j=0}^{1} \mu_j(2w_{y_j}+\beta_{y_j}^T(z-y_j)).$$

Since (EC) holds for the edges

$$\langle x_i, y_j \rangle,\ j=0,\dots,1,\ i=0,\dots,s,$$

we can conclude from Lemma 3 that the equations

$$(*')\qquad 2w_{x_i}+\beta_{x_i}^T(z-x_i) = 2w_z+\beta_2^T(x_i-z),\ i=0,\dots,s,$$

are satisfied, where

$$\beta_2 = \sum_{j=0}^{1} \mu_j \beta_{y_j}.$$

Since $(x_1-x_0,\dots,x_k-x_0)$ is a basis of U, (II_1) implies

$$\beta_z^T u = \beta_2^T u \quad \text{for all } u \in U,$$

and therefore

$$(**')\qquad \beta_z^T(x_i-z) = \beta_2^T(x_i-z),\ i=0,\dots,s.$$

But (*') and (**') show that (EC) holds for the edges

$<z,x_i>$, $i=0,\ldots,s$.

The uniqueness of w_z and β_z is a consequence of the corollary of Lemma 2.

An application

We consider a 3-dimensional complex K with the following property
(D): In any 3-simplex s of K there can be chosen an interior point z_s such that the following conditions are satisfied:

(I) If s and s' have a common 2-face σ, then there is a (unique)

$$z_\sigma \in <z_s, z_{s'}> \cap \text{relint } \sigma.$$

(II) If e is any edge of K, then all z_s such that e is an edge of s, are in a plane H_e intersecting relint e, say in z_e.

(III) If $\sigma=<x_0,x_1,x_2>$ is a face of only one 3-simplex of K, then there is a (unique) z_σ in the intersection of relint σ, $H_{<x_0,x_1>}$, $H_{<x_1,x_2>}$ and $H_{<x_2,x_0>}$.

Remarks: Obviously K has property (D) if for any $s\in K$ (with dim $s\geq 2$) the centre of its circumsphere is in relint s. Choosing the centres of the 3-simplexes of K as the points z_s, (D) is satisfied. (III) is vacuous if $|K|$ is an open subset of $\mathbb{R}^3$, especially if K is space filling ($|K|=\mathbb{R}^3$). A simple example of a space filling K with property (D) can be constructed as follows.

$\mathbb{R}^3$ is divided first into the unit-cubes with vertices in $\mathbb{Z}^3$. Then two adjacent cubes are divided into simplexes as shown in Fig. 1.

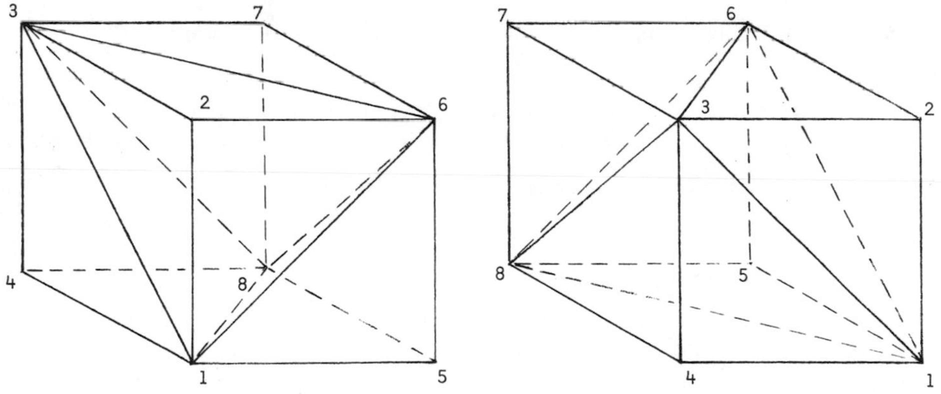

Fig. 1

That the resulting complex has property (D) is easily seen by choosing the points z_s as the points δ,2',4',5',7' as indicated in Fig. 2.

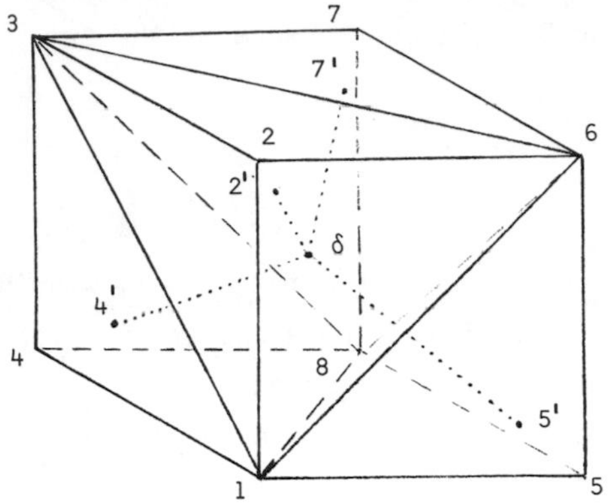

Fig. 2

δ is the barycentre of the interior simplex,

$$j' = \delta+\varepsilon(j-\delta), \quad j=2,4,5,7,$$

where $\frac{1}{3}<\varepsilon<1$. If $\varepsilon=\frac{1}{2}$, then for every 3-simplex s of K, z_s is the barycentre of s. If an edge e of K is an edge of a cube, it is the common edge of exactly four 3-simplexes $s_i \in K$, $i=1,\dots,4$. The z_{s_i} constitute a square orthogonal to e. The midpoint of this square is in relint e. Any other edge e of K is a diagonal of a common face of two cubes. It is the common edge of exactly six 3-simplexes $s_i \in K$, $i=1,\dots,6$. The z_{s_i} constitute a convex hexagon orthogonal to e and containing the midpoint of e. Therefore the points z_s are vertices of a cell partition of $\mathbb{R}^3$, dual to the given simplicial partition K (in the sense of [1] p.427). On the contrary it is easily seen, that a simplicial partition K of $\mathbb{R}^3$ has property (D) if there exists a cell partition of $\mathbb{R}^3$ dual to K.

Now let us describe a solution of our initial problem for 3-dimensional complexes K with property (D). A refinement K' of K with the desired interpolation property can be constructed in three steps.

Step 1

For any 3-simplex $s=\langle x_0,x_1,x_2,x_3\rangle \in K$ introduce z_s as an additional vertex and $\langle z_s,x_i\rangle$, $i=0,\dots,3$, as additional edges. Replace s by the 3 simplexes

$$\langle z_s,x_1,x_2,x_3\rangle, \langle x_0,z_s,x_2,x_3\rangle, \langle x_0,x_1,z_s,x_3\rangle, \langle x_0,x_1,x_2,z_s\rangle.$$

Step 2

For any 2-simplex $\sigma=\langle x_0,x_1,x_2\rangle\in K$ introduce z_σ as an additional vertex and $\langle z_\sigma,x_i\rangle$, $i=0,1,2$, as additional edges. Then for any $s\in K$ such that σ is a face of s, introduce $\langle z_\sigma,z_s\rangle$ as a new edge and replace $\langle x_0,x_1,x_2,z_s\rangle$ by the 3-simplexes

$$\langle z_\sigma,x_1,x_2,z_s\rangle,\langle x_0,z_\sigma,x_2,z_s\rangle,\langle x_0,x_1,z_\sigma,z_s\rangle.$$

Step 3

For any edge $e=\langle x_0,x_1\rangle\in K$ first introduce z_e as an additional vertex. Then for any 2-simplex $\sigma=\langle x_0,x_1,x_2\rangle\in K$ (such that e is an edge of σ) first introduce $\langle z_e,z_\sigma\rangle$ as an additional edge. Then for any 3-simplex $s=\langle x_0,x_1,x_2,x_3\rangle\in K$ (such that σ is an edge of s) introduce the additional edge $\langle z_e,z_s\rangle$ and replace the 3-simplex $\langle x_0,x_1,z_\sigma,z_s\rangle$ by the simplexes

$$\langle z_e,x_1,z_\sigma,z_s\rangle \text{ and } \langle x_0,z_e,z_\sigma,z_s\rangle.$$

In order to show that the resulting refinement K' of K solves our problem, let $w_x\in\mathbb{R},\beta_x\in\mathbb{R}^3$ be arbitrary data associated with the vertices x of K. From the corollary of Lemma 2 we can conclude:

1. For any 3-simplex $s=\langle x_0,x_1,x_2,x_3\rangle\in K$ there are unique artificial data $w_{z_s}\in\mathbb{R},\beta_{z_s}\in\mathbb{R}^3$ such that (EC) holds for the edges $\langle z_s,x_i\rangle$, $i=0,1,2,3$. If λ_i, $i=0,1,2,3$, denote the barycentric coordinates of z_s with respect to the vertices x_i of s, then

$$w_z = \frac{1}{2}\sum_{i=0}^{3}\lambda_i(2w_{x_i}+\beta_{x_i}^T(z_s-x_i)).$$

β_{z_s} can be computed from the linear equations

$$\beta_{z_s}^T(x_i-x_0) = 2(w_{x_i}-w_{x_0})+\beta_{x_i}^T(z_s-x_i)-\beta_{x_0}^T(z_s-x_0),$$

$i=1,2,3$.

2. For any 2-simplex $\sigma=\langle x_0,x_1,x_2\rangle\in K$ which is the face of only one 3-simplex $s\in K$ there are unique artificial data $w_{z_\sigma}\in\mathbb{R},\beta_{z_\sigma}\in\mathbb{R}^3$ such that (EC) holds for the edges $\langle z_\sigma,x_i\rangle$, $i=0,1,2$, and $\langle z_\sigma,z_s\rangle$. If λ_i, $i=0,1,2$, denote the barycentric coordinates of z_σ with respect to the vertices x_i of σ, then

$$w_{z_\sigma} = \frac{1}{2}\sum_{i=0}^{2}\lambda_i(2w_{x_i}+\beta_{x_i}^T(z_\sigma-x_i),$$

and Lemma 3 shows, that β_{z_σ} can be computed from the linear equations

$$\beta_{z_\sigma}^T(x_i-x_0) = 2(w_{x_i}-w_{x_0})+\beta_{x_i}^T(z_\sigma-x_i)-\beta_{x_0}^T(z_\sigma-x_0) \quad i=1,2,$$

and

$$\beta_{z_\sigma}^T(z_s-z_\sigma) = (\sum_{i=0}^{2}\lambda_i\beta_{x_i})^T(z_s-z_\sigma).$$

From the corollary of Lemma 3 we can conclude:

1. For any 2-simplex $\sigma=<x_o,x_1,x_2>\in K$ which is the face of two 3-simplexes s_0 and s_1 of K, there are unique (artificial) data $w_{z_\sigma}\in\mathbb{R},\beta_{z_\sigma}\in\mathbb{R}^3$, that (EC) holds for the edges $<z_\sigma,x_i>$, $i=0,1,2$, $<z_\sigma,z_{s_j}>$, $j=0,1$. w_{z_σ} and β_{z_σ} can be computed as in the case when σ is a face of only one 3-simplex of K. But we can make use of the following relations too.

Let μ_0,μ_1 denote the barycentric coordinates of z_σ with respect to z_{s_0},z_{s_1}, $\lambda_0,\lambda_1,\lambda_2$ the barycentric coordinates of z_σ with respect to x_0,x_1,x_2. Then

$$w_{z_\sigma} = \frac{1}{2}\sum_{j=0}^{1}\mu_j(2w_{z_{s_j}}+\beta_{z_{s_j}}^T(z_\sigma-z_{s_j})),$$

$$\beta_{z_\sigma}^T u = (\sum_{j=0}^{1}\mu_j\beta_{z_{s_j}})^T u \quad \text{for all } u\in\text{span}\{x_1-x_0,x_2-x_0\},$$

$$\beta_{z_\sigma}^T v = (\sum_{i=0}^{2}\lambda_i\beta_{x_i})^T v \quad \text{for all } v\in\text{span}\{z_{s_1}-z_{s_0}\}.$$

2. For any edge $e=<x_o,x_1>\in K$ there are unique (artificial) data $w_{z_e}\in\mathbb{R},\beta_{z_e}\in\mathbb{R}^3$ that (EC) holds for $<z_e,x_i>$, $i=0,1$, and any $<z_e,z_s>,<z_e,z_\sigma>$, if e is an edge of s and σ. If λ_0,λ_1 denote the barycentric coordinates of z_e with respect to x_0,x_1 then

$$w_{z_e} = \frac{1}{2}\sum_{i=0}^{1}\lambda_i(2w_{x_i}+\beta_{x_i}^T(z_e-x_i))$$

and β_{z_e} can be computed from the linear equation

$$\beta_{z_e}^T(x_1-x_0) = 2(w_{x_1}-w_{x_0})+\beta_{x_1}^T(z_e-x_1)-\beta_{x_0}^T(z_e-x_0)$$

and the relation

$$\beta_{z_e}^T v = (\sum_{i=0}^{1}\lambda_i\beta_{x_i})^T v \quad \text{for all } v\in H_e-z_e.$$

If all these artificial data are introduced, then (EC) holds for all edges of K'. Now Lemma 1 shows, that there is a unique $\varphi\in P_2(K')$, satisfying (H'), and especially (H). Since there is no freedom in choosing the artificial data, φ is the only function in $P_2(K')$ with property (H).

Remark: Applying the described refinement procedure to the space filling complex considered in the example, a macro element can be derived, that seems to be a natural generalization of the quadrangular element indicated in Fig.9 of [4].

References

1. Alexandroff, P. and Hopf, H. (1935) Topologie (Springer, Berlin).

2. Buhl, H.J. (1987) Stückweise quadratische C^1-Interpolation und ihr Einsatz bei der Galerkindiskretisierung im Raume $H^2(\Omega)$, Dissertation (Fachbereich Mathematik der Universität Wuppertal (D-468)).

3. Heindl, G. (1979) Interpolation and Approximation by Piecewise Quadratic C^1-Functions of two Variables. Multivariate Approximation Theory, ed. by W. Schempp and K. Zeller, ISNM Vol. 51 (Birkhäuser, Basel).

4. Heindl, G. (1985) Construction and Applications of Hermite interpolating Spline Functions of two and three Variables. Multivariate Approximation Theory III, ed. by W. Schempp and K. Zeller, ISNM Vol. 75 (Birkhäuser, Basel).

5. Powell, M.J.D. and Sabin M.A. (1977) Piecewise Quadratic Approximations on Triangles, ACM Transactions on Mathematical Software, Vol. 3, No. 4, 316-325.

Note

Carl de Boor told me, that there will appear a paper by Andrew Worsey also concerned with the construction of interpolating quadratic spline functions of more than two variables.

Prof. Dr. Gerhard Heindl, Fachbereich Mathematik der Universität Wuppertal, 5600 Wuppertal 1, BRD.

International Series of
Numerical Mathematics, Vol. 90

ON ITERATES OF LINEAR VARIATION DIMINISHING OPERATORS AND CHARACTERIZATION OF BERNSTEIN-TYPE POLYNOMIALS

Ying-Sheng Hu
Institute of Mathematics, Academia Sinica, Beijing, China

1. Introduction

As we all know, Bernstein approximation of a smooth function on $[a,b]$ preserves the signs of function itself and its higher order derivatives. This beautiful property, in one hand, wins important and wide applications, but on the other hand, has to pay a precious price--very slow convergence. It is interesting to notice that the similar situation appear, more or less, in some other wellknown approximations, for instance, the Modified Bernstein-Durrmeyer operator and Schoenberg variation diminishing operator (see[1]).

In the paper[2], Berens & Devore introduced an operator class L, each $L_n \in L$ satisfying

(a) $L_n f \in P_n$, for all $f \in C[0,1]$;

(b) $L_n(l_x)=l_x$, for $l_x \in P_1$;

(c) $[L_n(f)]^{(j)} \geq 0$ if $f^{(j)} \geq 0$, $j=0,1,\ldots,n$.

Class L contains Bernstein operator as a distinct member. Since L_n is positive,

$$\sup_{f\in B} \| f-L_n(f)\|_\infty = \frac{1}{2} \| L_n((\cdot-x)^2, x)\|_\infty \qquad (1)$$

where $B=\{f:\ f'\text{ a.c.},\ \|f''\|_\infty=1\}$. It is shown in [2] that

$$\inf_{L_n\in L} L_n((\cdot-x)^2, x) = \frac{x(1-x)}{n} \quad \text{on } [0,1] \qquad (2)$$

The best approximation order for L is $O(\frac{1}{n})$. Thus (c) and (2) show again the contradiction between aapproximation order and shape-preserving property.

In this paper, we take a point of view of linear variation diminishing operator,using iterate method to study and characterize this contradictious phynomenon in Bernstein-tynpe approximations.

2.Iterates of variation diminishing operators

The study on the topic has been developed by Kelisky & Revlin [3], Nagel [4][5],Micchelli [6] and others. The significance of these results is the (piecewise) linearality of limiting functions. For instance,

1. $\lim_{k\to\infty}(B_n)^k(f)(x) = L(f)(x)$ on [0,1] ([3])

where $L(f)(x)=f(0)(1-x)+f(1)x$.

2 $\lim_{k\to\infty}(S_m)^k(f)(x)=\underline{L}(f)(x)$ on [0,1] ([7],[8])

where $\underline{L}$: $C[0,1] \to \text{Span}\{1,x,(x-x_i)_+,i=1,...,r\}$; x_i,the knots with multiplicity of m or m-1. S_m stands for Schoenberg operator.

In general,we have

Theorem 1: Let T be any linear variation diminishing operator reproducing the linears on X=C[0,1]. For r≥0, if there exists at most a finite set of points,$\{t_i\}$,in (0,1),such that $T(f)(t_i)=f(t_i)$ i=1,...,r for all $f\in X$. Then the sequence of operator $\{T^n\}$ converges stronly to L_r,which is the projection from X to $\text{Span}\{1,x,(x-x_i)_+$ i=1,..,r} satisfying

$$L_rf(t_i) = f(t_i)\ ,\ i=0,1,...,r+1 \text{ with convention } t_0=0\ ,t_{r+1}=1$$

Proof:

The V.D. and reproducing (the linears) properties of T imply that $\text{Range}(Tf) \subseteq \text{Range}(f)$.It turns out that T is positive and $\|T^n\|$ is bounded(≤1 for all n).

According to the Banach-Steinhaus Theorem $T^n \to L_r$ if and only if $\lim_{n\to\infty} T^n Y_s = L_rY_s$ for some closed sequence $\{Y_s\}$ in X.

Denote,by *E*, the set of fixed points of T. So *E* contains all piecewise linear functions with knots at t_i ,i=1,...,r.from the assumption.

Now set $Y_s(x)=x^s$, $s=0,1,\ldots$ and show $T^n Y_s \to L_r Y_s$ for all s. It is obviously true that $T^n Y_s = Y_s = L_r Y_s$, for $s=0,1$ and all n. For $s \geq 2$, Y_s convex ,and so is $T^n Y_s$; moreover, $T^n Y_s \geq T^{n-1} Y_s$ for all n, due to reproducing the linears and variation diminishing properties of T. Hence, $T^n Y_s$ converges monotone pointwisely to a function, namely Y, which is also convex and hence continous on [0,1]. According to Dini's Theorem, the convergence is uniform: $T^n Y_s \to Y$. It turns out that

$$TY = \lim_{n\to\infty} T(T^n Y_s) = \lim_{n\to\infty} T^{n+1} Y_s = Y$$

i.e. $Y \in E$. and $Y = L_r Y_s$ for all $s \geq 2$.

Corollary: For any linear variation diminishing operator satisfying the assumptions in Theorem 1, its spherical spectrum contains only real number 1.

3. Asymptotic variation diminishing

The variation diminishing property of T results the (piecewise) linearality of limiting function of sequence $T^n f, f \in X$ as $n \to \infty$. Meanwhile, the procedure that $T^n f \to L_r f$ as $n \to \infty$, is a good disply for the V.D. behavior of T . For this reason, we introduce in the following, so called asymptoic variation diminishing property and regard the speed of the convergence of T^n as a kind of measurement of the V.D. property of T.

Definition: A linear positive operator on X, P , is called A.V.D., if it meets the following two conditions:

(a) $P(1_x) = 1_x$, $1_x \in P_1$;

(b) For $f \in X$, $\lim_{n\to\infty} P^n f = L_r f$, L_r as described in Theorem 1.

The first example of A.V.D. operator, besides of all linear V.D. operators on X, is Bernstein polynomials on simplex S_m.

$$B_{n,m}(f)(x) = \sum_{\substack{k_1,\ldots,k_m=0 \\ 0\leq|k|\leq n}}^{n}{}' f\left(\frac{k_1}{n},\ldots,\frac{k_m}{n}\right) b_{n,k_1,\ldots,k_m}(x) \qquad x \in S_m$$

where $b_{n,k_1,\dots k_m}(x) = \binom{n}{k_1,\dots,k_m} x_1^{k_1}\dots x_m^{k_m}(1-\sum_0^m x_i)^{n-|k|}$, $|k| = k_1+\dots+k_m$

<u>Proposition 2:</u>

$$\lim_{N\to\infty} (B_{n,m})^N(f)(x) = a_0 + a^T x$$

where $a^T = (a_1,\dots,a_m)^T$, $a_0=f(0,\dots,0)$, $a_i=f(0,\dots,1,0,\dots,0)-f(0,\dots,0)$

([9]-[11])

For the polynomial operator class *L*, introduced by Berens & Devore [2], we have

<u>Proposition 3</u> All $L_n \in L$ are A.V.D..

<u>Proof</u> $L_n \in L$, positive and can be represented by

$$L_n(f,x) = \sum_0^n a_k(f)P_{n,k}(x)$$

where $P_{n,k}(x)=\binom{n}{k}x^k(1-x)^{n-k}$; $a_k(f)=\int_0^1 f\,du_k$, du_k-Borel measure

Now let's consider the expression of the restriction of L_n on P_n under the basis $\{1,x,x^2,\dots,x^n\}$

$$L_n \sim R = \begin{bmatrix} 1 & & & & \\ 0 & 1 & & & \\ r_{20} & r_{21} & r_{22} & & \\ \vdots & \vdots & \vdots & \ddots & \\ r_{n0} & r_{n1} & r_{n2} & \dots & r_{nn} \end{bmatrix} \tag{3}$$

According to 1.(a)-(c) and the fact that $du_0=d\delta_0$ & $du_n=d\delta_1$ ([2]), (here $d\delta_t$,the Dirac measure with unit mass at t),which leads

$$L_n(f)(0)=f(0) \;,\quad L_n(f)(1)=f(1) \qquad \text{for all } f\in X \tag{4}$$

We incorporate, in the following, some properties of R :

(a) $r_{jk} \geq 0$,for all (j,k);

(b) $\sum_{k=0}^n r_{jk} = 1$ and $r_{j0} = 0$,j=1,2,...,n ,since

$$1 = x^j(1)=L_n(t^j)(1)=\sum_{k=0}^n r_{jk} \;,\quad 0 = x^j(0)=L_n(t^j)(0)=r_{j0},\; j=1,\dots,n$$

(c) $1>r_{22}\geq r_{33}\geq\dots\geq r_{nn}\geq 0$. Here notice $r_{22}<1$, otherwise R would reduce to I,the identity, by Krovkin Theorem.

Thus R can be regarded as probability transition matrix of a Markov chain with n+1 states and two absorbing walls,corresponding to two "1" eigenvalues.Since R has no eigenvalue in the form $e^{i\alpha}$, $\alpha\neq 0$, $\lim_{m\to\infty} R^m$ exists and equals to

$$R^* = \begin{bmatrix} 1 & & & & \\ 0 & 1 & & & \\ 0 & 1 & 0 & & \\ \vdots & \vdots & \vdots & \ddots & \\ 0 & 1 & 0 & \dots & 0 \end{bmatrix}$$

Therefore $\lim_{m\to\infty}(L_n)^m(p_n) = L^*(p_n)$ for all $p_n \in P_n$, where $L^* \sim R^*$. The convergence persists on whole X. Denote $v(\frac{k}{n}) = a_k(f)$ and $A_k = \Delta^k_{\frac{1}{n}} v(0)\binom{n}{k}$ ($\Delta^k_{\frac{1}{n}}$-foreward difference of degree k with step $\frac{1}{n}$), we have

$$L_n(f)(x) = \sum_0^n a_k(f)p_{nk}(x) = \sum_0^n A_k x^k = (A_0, A_1, \dots, A_n)(1, x, x^2, \dots, x^n)^T \tag{5}$$

and for all m,

$$(L_n)^m(f)(x) = (A_0, A_1, \dots, A_n)\, R^{m-1}(1, x, \dots, x^n)^T \tag{6}$$

Hence $\lim_{m\to\infty}(L_n)^m(f)(x) = (A_0, A_1, \dots, A_n)R^*(1, x, \dots, x^n)^T$ for all $f \in X$. but $A_0 = a_0(f) = f(0)$, and $A_0 + A_1 + \cdots + A_n = L_n(f)(1) = f(1)$ from (4)&(5). This gives

$$\begin{aligned}\lim_{m\to\infty}(L_n)^m(f)(x) &= (A_0, A_1, \dots, A_n)(1, x, x, \dots, x)^T\\ &= A_0 + x(A_1 + \cdots + A_n) = f(0) + (f(1) - f(0))x\\ &= L(f)(x)\end{aligned}$$

where the convergence is uniform and L is seen as extension of L^*.

An observation on the speed of $(L_n)^m \to L$ from (3), is made as $O(r^{m-1})$, or equivalently $O(\lambda_2^{m-1})$, λ_2 is the largest eigenvalue less than 1 of L_n. Using the Popoviciu mean value Theorem, we have the following precise assertion.

<u>Theorem2:</u> For $f \in X$, there exist $0 < s_0 < s_1 < s_2 < 1$, such that

$$(L(f) - L_n^m(f))(x) = f(s_0, s_1, s_2)\, \lambda_2^m x(1-x), \qquad x \in [0,1] \tag{7}$$

<u>Proof:</u> Let $F = L_n^m - L$, $g(x) = x(1-x)$.

g(x) is strictly concave, according to Popoviciu mean value Theorem for any $f \in X$, there exist $0 < s_0 < s_1 < s_2 < 1$, s.t.

$$F(f)(x) = \frac{f(s_0, s_1, s_2)}{g(s_0, s_1, s_2)} F(g)(x) \qquad \text{for } x \in [0,1]$$

here $F(g)(x) = ((L_n^m)g - Lg)(x) = L(\cdot)^2(x) - (L_n)(\cdot)^2(x) = x - (L_n)(\cdot)^2(x)$ but frorm (3),

$$L_n(\cdot)^2(x) = r_{21}x + r_{22}x^2 = (1 - r_{22})x + r_{22}x^2 = (1 - \lambda_2)x + \lambda_2 x^2$$

and $(L_n^m)(\cdot)^2(x) = (1 - \lambda_2^m)x + \lambda_2^m x^2$, by a direct calculation. Hence $F(g)(x) = \lambda_2^m x(1-x)$ and (7) is obtained immediately.

Now, compare $\sup_{f\in B} \| f-L_n(f)\|_\infty = \frac{1}{2} \| L_n((\ -x)^2,x)\|_\infty$ & $L_n((\ -x)^2,x) = (1-\lambda_2(L_n))x(1-x)$ (frorm (1)&(3)) with $(L(f)-L_n^m(f))(x) = C\lambda_2^m x(1-x)$ we conclude

COROLLARY: Both of approximation property and V.D. property of L_n depend on $\lambda_2(L_n)$, but in an opposite way.

Remark:

A similar characterization for Schoenberg operator in terms of λ_2 and $g_2(x)$, the corresponding eigenfunction, can be made. (see the auther's forthcomming paper)

4. Example of L :

$$M_n(f) = \sum_{k=0}^{n} C_{n,k}(f)p_{nk}(x)$$

where

$$C_{n,k}(f) = \int_0^1 f\, du_k = \begin{cases} f(0) & k=0 \\ (n-1)\int_0^1 f(u)p_{n-2,k-1}(u)du_k & k=1,..,n-1 \\ f(1) & k=n \end{cases}$$

is called the modified Bernstein-Durrmeyer operator due to its reproducing property:

$$M_n(1)(x)=1 \qquad \text{and} \qquad M_n(t)(x)=x \tag{8}$$

(see W.Z.Chen [13]). In this section, we show $M_n \in L$

Proposition 4: $[M_n(f)]^{(j)} \geq 0$, if $f^{(j)} \geq 0$, $j=0,1,...,n$.

Proof:

Denote S_k= { s:polynomial of degee k with positive leading coefficient }

The proposition follows the next assertions:

(a) M_n maps S_j into S_j , j=0,1,..,n;

(b) $V^-(M_n(f)) \leq V^-(f)$ if $V^-(f) \leq n$.

Let $A_j(k)=C_{nk}(t^j)=\int_0^1 t^j\, du_k$, clearly $A_j(0)=0$ and $A_j(n)=1$. It is elementary to show that

$$A_j(k)=\frac{k(k+1)\cdots(k+j-1)}{n(n+1)\cdots(n+j-1)}$$

So that

$$M_n(t^j)(x) = \sum_{k=0}^{n} \Delta^k A_j(0) \binom{n}{k} x^k = \sum_{k=0}^{n} a_{jk} x^k \quad \text{with}$$

$a_{jk} \geq 0$ for all (j,k); $a_{jk}=0$ for $k>j$;

$$A_{jj} = \frac{(n-1)(n-2)\cdots(n-j+1)}{(n+1)(n+2)\cdots(n+j-1)} > 0.$$

To prove (b), set $Z=\frac{x}{1-x}$, $0<x<1$. Thus

$$M_n(f)(x) = (1-x)^n \sum_{k=0}^{n} C_{nk}(f) \binom{n}{k} Z^k$$

From the Descartes' sign principle, we know

$$\underset{0<x<1}{V^-}(M_n(f)) \leqslant \underset{0<x<1}{Z}(M_n(f)) \leqslant V^-\{C_{nk}(f), K=0,..,n\} \leqslant V^-\{J_k(f), k=0,..,n\} \quad (9)$$

where $\{J_k(f)\}=\{f(0), \int_0^1 P_{n-2,k-1}(u) f(u) du, f(1)\}$.

It should be noted that $p_{m,k}(x)=N_{k-m,m+1}(x)$, $k=0,..,m$, where $\{N_{j,m+1}(x), j=-m,..,0\}$ is the B-spline basis of order m+1 on the mesh $\{x_{-m}=...=x_0=0, x_1=...=x_{m+1}=1\}$ so $\{p_{m,k}(x), k=0,..,,m\}$ forms a weak Chebyshev system.It turns out,from Th.3.1 of Karlin[12],that

$$V^-\{J_k(f), K=0,..,n\} \leqslant V^-(f)$$

Combine (a),(b)is desired.

It is wellknown that for any $h \in C^j[a,b]$, $h^{(j)} \geqslant 0$ if and only if h convex of order j, i.e. $V^-(h-g) \leqslant j$, for all $g \in S_{j-1}$, and when"=" happens, a "+" sign concludes the sequence of sign changes in $h(y)-g(y)$ as y runs from a to b.

From (b),$[M_n(f)]^{(j)}$ doesn't change sign on [0,1] when $f^{(j)} \geqslant 0$. Now, we confirm $[M_n(f)]^{(j)} \geqslant 0$.

For any $q \in S_{j-1}$, there exists $q^* \in S_{j-1}$, s.t. $q=F_n q^*$ (by (a)). If $V^-(f-q^*) \leqslant j \leqslant n$, then

$$V^-(F_n f-q) = V^-(F_n(f-q^*)) \leqslant V^-(f-q^*) \quad (10)$$

from (b).Particularly,$V^-(F_n f-q)=V^-(f-q^*)=j$ holds when $V^-(F_n f-q)=j$. Since M_n is positive, $c_0(f)$ is positive as well. From (1),$\int_0^1 du_0 = 1$, $\int_0^1 t\,du_0=0$ and $\int_0^1 t^2 du_0=0$, therefore $du_0 = d\delta_0$.Similarly,we have $du_n=d\delta_1$.This is equivalent to $M_n(f)(0)=f(0)$ and $M_n(f)(1)=f(1)$ for all $f \in C[0,1]$. Hence

$$M_n(f)(1)-q(1)=M_n(f)(1)-M_n(q^*)(1)=f(1)-q^*(1) \quad (11)$$

Thus two sequences of sign change in $f(y)-q^*(y)$ and $M_n(f)(y)-q(y)$ as y tranveses [0,1] coincide. Q.E.D.

Acknowledgement:
It is the author's pleasure to show her sincere appreciation to Prof.H.Berens, who read the original manuscript and gave several valuable suggestions.

References:

1. Y.S.Hu, A Note on the Piecewise-Comonotonic Property of the V.D Spline, written in Oslo, Spring 1982.(unpublished)
2. H.Berens & R.Devore, A Chaaracterization of Bernstein Polynomials,in Approxition Theory III, Proc.Int.Symp.Austin 1980,ed. by E.W.Cheney.
3. R.P.Kelisky & T.J.Revlin, Iterates of Bernstein-Polynomials, Pacific J.Math.21(3)1967.
4. J.Nagel,Asymptotic Properties of Powers of Kantorovic Operators J.A.T.32,1982.
5. J.Nagel,Asymptotic Properties of Powers of Bernstein Operators, J.A.T.29,1980.
6. C.A.Micchelli,The Saturation Class and Iterates of the Bernstein Polynomials, J.A.T.8(1983).
7. Y.S.Hu & S.X.Xu, The Iterative Limit for a Kind of Variation Diminishing Operators I, Acta Mathematical Applacatae Sinica Vol.1,No.3,1978.
8. Y.S.Hu & S.X.Xu, The Iterative Limit for a Kind of Variation Diminishing Operators II, Acta Mathematics Sinica Vol.22,No.3 (1979).
9. G.Z.Chang, Generalized Bernstein Polynomials,J.Computational Math.Vol.1,No.4. 1983.
10. Y.S.Hu, Iterates of Bernstein Polynomials on Triangle,Report. Vol.3.No.6.1987,Inst.of Math. Academia Sinica, Beijing.
11. Y.S.Hu, On Bernstein Polynomials in Multivariables,Report,Vol.3 No.5.1987,Inst.of Math.Academia Sinica,Beijing.
12. S.Karlin,Total Positivity,Vol.1.Stanford Univ.Press.1968.
13. W.Z.Chen, On the Modified Bernstein-Durrmeyer Operator,Report on the Fifth Chinese Conference on Approx.Theory,Zhen Zhou, China,May 1987.

International Series of
Numerical Mathematics, Vol. 90

METHODEN DER FOURIER-TRANSFORMATION BEI DER KARDINALEN INTERPOLATION PERIODISCHER DATEN

Kurt Jetter und Peter Koch

Zusammenfassung

Wir beschreiben einen Algorithmus, der z.B. bei der graphischen Bildverarbeitung eingesetzt werden kann. Hierbei gehen wir davon aus, daß die darzustellende bivariate, 1-periodische Funktion auf dem (groben) Gitter $h_1\mathbb{Z}^2$ bekannt ist. Die Fourierkoeffizienten der interpolierenden Box-Spline-Reihe ergeben sich dann unter Verwendung von Abminderungsfaktoren, und die Auswertung der Reihe auf einem (feinen) Gitter $h_2\mathbb{Z}^2$ kann effizient mit schneller Fourier-Transformation erfolgen.

1. Einleitung

Wir gehen aus von N–periodischen Daten ($N \in \mathbb{N}$)

$$d = (d_\alpha)_{\alpha \in \mathbb{Z}^2},$$

$d_{\alpha+N\beta} = d_\alpha$ für $\alpha, \beta \in \mathbb{Z}^2$, und einer N-periodischen Funktion vom Typ

$$s(x) = \sum_{\alpha \in \mathbb{Z}^2} c_\alpha \phi(x - \alpha) \tag{1}$$

mit festem $\phi \in C_0(\mathbb{R}^2)$, die diese Daten auf dem Gitter $\mathbb{Z}^2$ interpoliert,

$$s(\alpha) = d_\alpha, \quad \alpha \in \mathbb{Z}^2. \tag{2}$$

Als Aufgabe geben wir uns vor, die Funktion s auf einem feinen Gitter $h\mathbb{Z}^2$ auszuwerten. Als typische Situation stelle man sich z.B. vor, daß eine 1-periodische Funktion f gemäß $d_\alpha = f(\frac{1}{N}\alpha), \alpha \in \mathbb{Z}^2$, die Daten liefert und die Werte

$$s_\beta = s\left(\frac{N}{n}\beta\right), \quad \beta \in \mathbb{Z}^2, \tag{3}$$

mit $n = \nu N$ (z.B. $\nu = 8$ oder $\nu = 16$) gesucht sind; dabei kann man sich in (2) bzw. (3) auf $\alpha \in B_N$ und $\beta \in B_n$ beschränken, wenn

$$B_k = \left\{(\gamma_1, \gamma_2) \in \mathbb{Z}^2 \; ; \; -\tfrac{k}{2} \leq \gamma_i < \tfrac{k}{2}, \; i = 1, 2\right\} \tag{4}$$

für $k \in \mathbb{N}$ gesetzt wird.

In unseren Betrachtungen ist $\phi = M_{k,l,m}$ ein 3-Richtungs- Box-Spline, dessen Fourier-Transformierte bekanntlich die einfache Produktform

$$\phi\hat{}(\xi_1, \xi_2) = (\text{sinc } \tfrac{1}{2}\xi_1)^k (\text{sinc } \tfrac{1}{2}\xi_2)^l (\text{sinc } \tfrac{1}{2}(\xi_1 + \xi_2))^m \tag{5}$$

(mit $\text{sinc } t = (\sin \; t)/t$) besitzt. $\phi\hat{}(\xi)$ geht für $|\ \xi\ | \to \infty$ sehr rasch gegen Null, und das zu ϕ gehörende trigonometrische Polynom

$$\phi^{\sim}(\xi) = \sum_{\alpha \in \mathbb{Z}^2} \phi(\alpha) e^{-i\alpha \cdot \xi} \tag{6}$$

ist für $\xi \in \mathbb{R}^2$ strikt positiv (de Boor, Höllig, Riemenschneider [2]); insbesondere existiert zu d genau eine N-periodische Folge $c = (c_\alpha)_{\alpha \in Z^2}$, so daß die Box-Spline-Reihe (1) das Interpolationsproblem (2) löst. Man könnte deshalb daran denken, zunächst die diskrete Faltungsgleichung (2) nach c aufzulösen und dann die Reihe (1) mit den üblichen kürzlich diskutierten Algorithmen (Subdivision, line averaging, Bernstein- Bezier-Techniken, vgl. Chui [3, Kap. 7]) auszuwerten. Wir glauben, daß unser Problem wirksamer mit Methoden der Fourier-Transformation behandelt werden kann.

2. Der Algorithmus

Da der Operator $d \to s$ vom Faltungstyp ist, können die Fourierkoeffizienten von s mittels Abminderungsfaktoren bestimmt werden. Dies ist für Probleme in einer Variablen hinlänglich bekannt (Gautschi [5], Henrici [7], Locher [8]); der mehrdimensionale Fall (unter Verwendung von Box-Splines) wurde kürzlich von Gutknecht [6] und von terMorsche [9] diskutiert.

Wir setzen $h = \frac{2\pi}{N}$ und benützen die folgenden Bezeichnungen:

$$s_N\hat{}(\alpha) = \frac{1}{N^2} \int\limits_{[0,N]^2} s(x)\; e^{-ih\alpha \cdot x}\; dx, \quad \alpha \in \mathbb{Z}^2, \tag{7}$$

für die Fourier-Koeffizienten von s, und $\mathcal{F}_N d$ mit

$$(\mathcal{F}_N d)_\alpha = \frac{1}{N^2} \sum_{\beta \in B_N} d_\beta \; e^{-ih\alpha \cdot \beta}, \quad \alpha \in \mathbb{Z}^2, \tag{8}$$

für die diskrete Fourier-Transformierte von d, mit B_N wie in (4). Es ist bekanntlich $\mathcal{F}_N^{-1} = N^2 R \mathcal{F}_N$ unter Verwendung des Spiegelungsoperators $(Rc)_\alpha = c_{-\alpha}$, also

$$(\mathcal{F}_N^{-1} d)_\alpha = \sum_{\beta \in B_N} d_\beta \, e^{+ih\alpha \cdot \beta}, \quad \alpha \in \mathbb{Z}^2.$$

Theorem 1. *Gilt (1), (2) mit einer N-periodischen Folge c und* $\phi \in C_0(\mathbb{R}^2)$ *mit* $supp(\phi) \subseteq [-\frac{N}{2}, +\frac{N}{2}]^2$, *so folgt für* $h = \frac{2\pi}{N}$:

$$\phi^\sim(h\alpha) s_N\hat{}(\alpha) = \phi\hat{}(h\alpha)(\mathcal{F}_N d)_\alpha, \quad \alpha \in \mathbb{Z}^2.$$

Für den Fall, daß $\phi^\sim$ keine Nullstelle hat, ist dieses Theorem bei terMorsche [9] bewiesen; der allgemeine Fall folgt mit analoger Argumentation. Für $\phi = M_{k,l,m}$ ist der Träger $supp(\phi)$ durch das Sechseck gegeben, das sich als konvexe Hülle der Punkte $\frac{1}{2}(\varepsilon_1 k e_1 + \varepsilon_2 l e_2 + \varepsilon_3 m(e_1 + e_2))$ mit $\varepsilon_i \in \{-1, +1\}$ und $e_1 = (1,0)$, $e_2 = (0,1)$ ergibt.

Aufgrund von Theorem 1 ergibt sich folgender Algorithmus zur Berechnung von Näherungen $\tilde{s}(\frac{N}{n}\beta)$ für $s(\frac{N}{n}\beta)$:

Algorithmus. *Für* $N \in \mathbb{N}$, $\phi \in C_0(\mathbb{R}^2)$ *mit* $supp(\phi) \subseteq [-\frac{N}{2}, +\frac{N}{2}]^2$ *und* $n = \nu N$ *setze* $h = \frac{2\pi}{N}$ *und* $h' = \frac{2\pi}{n}$.

1. Schritt: Berechne $\phi^\sim(h\alpha)$, $\alpha \in B_N$, *und* $\phi\hat{}(h\alpha)$, $\alpha \in B_n$.

2. Schritt: Berechne $(\mathcal{F}_N d)_\alpha = \frac{1}{N^2} \sum_{\beta \in B_N} d_\beta e^{-ih\alpha \cdot \beta}, \quad \alpha \in B_N$.

3. Schritt: Für $\alpha \in B_n$ *bestimme* $\alpha' \in B_N$ *und* $\beta' \in \mathbb{Z}^2$ *mit* $\alpha = \alpha' + N\beta'$ *und berechne*

$$s_N\hat{}(\alpha) = \phi\hat{}(h\alpha) \frac{(\mathcal{F}_N d)_{\alpha'}}{\phi^\sim(h\alpha')} .$$

4. Schritt: Berechne $\tilde{s}(\frac{N}{n}\beta) = \sum_{\alpha \in B_n} s_N\hat{}(\alpha) e^{ih'\alpha \cdot \beta}, \quad \beta \in B_n$.

Sieht man von der Bereitstellung der Daten für $\phi^\sim$ und $\phi\hat{}$ in Schritt 1 ab, so liegt der Hauptaufwand dieses Algorithmus (wenn z.B. $\nu = 8$ gesetzt wird) in Schritt 4.

Es ist angebracht, wirkungsvolle Hilfsmittel zur Berechnung diskreter Fourier-Transformationen einzusetzen; in unseren Berechnungen haben wir schnelle Fourier-Transformation verwendet. Obwohl das von uns verwendete FORTRAN–Programm die Vorteile der schnellen Fourier-Transformation nicht voll ausnutzt, haben wir kurze Laufzeiten beobachtet. Nach unseren Erfahrungen arbeitet der Algorithmus sehr stabil, sofern das trigonometrische Polynom (6) keine zu kleinen Werte annimmt; dies ist für $\phi = M_{2,2,1}$ gesichert, und unsere Testrechnungen (vgl. hierzu Abschnitt 4) haben zufriedenstellende Ergebnisse geliefert.

3. Fehlerbetrachtung

Bei unseren Anwendungen des Algorithmus war

$$d_\alpha = f(\tfrac{1}{N}\alpha), \quad \alpha \in \mathbb{Z}^2, \tag{9}$$

wobei f die 1-periodische Fortsetzung einer Funktion

$$g : [-1/2, +1/2[^2 \to \mathbb{R} \tag{10}$$

darstellte.

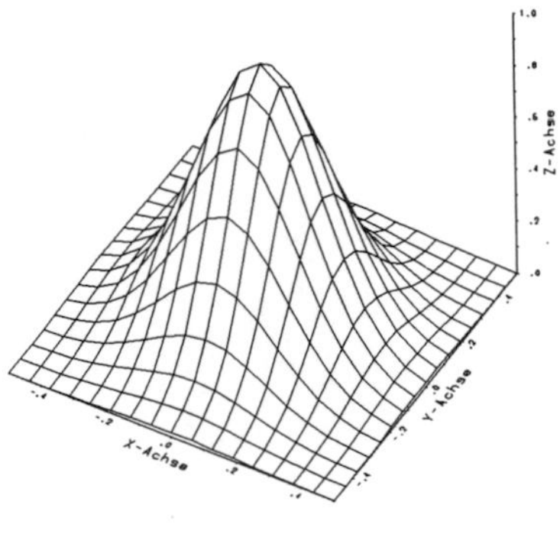

Fig. 1

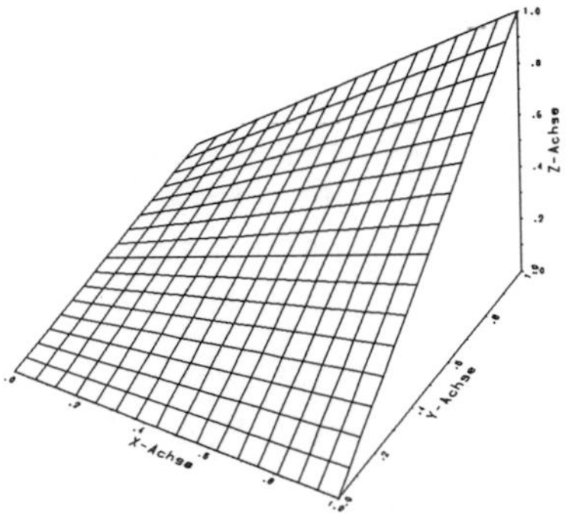

Fig. 2

Sehen wir von Rundungsfehlern ab, so wird der Diskretisierungsfehler

$$ERR = \max\left\{| \, f(\tfrac{1}{n}\beta) - \tilde{s}(\tfrac{N}{n}\beta) \, | \, ; \, \beta \in B_n\right\} \tag{11}$$

auf dem feinen Gitter kontrolliert

– durch den Interpolationsfehler

$$ERR_1 = \sup\left\{| \, f(x) - s(Nx) \, | ; x \in [-\tfrac{1}{2}, +\tfrac{1}{2}[^2\right\} \tag{12}$$

– und durch den Fehler

$$ERR_2 = \max\left\{| \, (s - \tilde{s})(\tfrac{N}{n}\beta) \, | \, ; \, \beta \in B_n\right\}, \tag{13}$$

der durch Abschneiden der Fourier-Reihe entsteht.

Der Interpolationsfehler ist in der Literatur ausführlich diskutiert worden ([9], vgl. auch [4]); entscheidend ist hier, daß die Fortsetzung f der Funktion g hinreichend glatt ist. Beispielsweise erhält man

Theorem 2. *Für $\phi = M_{2,2,1}$ gilt $ERR_1 = O(N^{-\kappa})$ für $N \to \infty$ mit $0 \le \kappa \le 3$, sofern $D^\alpha f$ für alle $\alpha \in \mathbb{N}^2$ mit $| \alpha | \le \kappa$ stetig ist.*

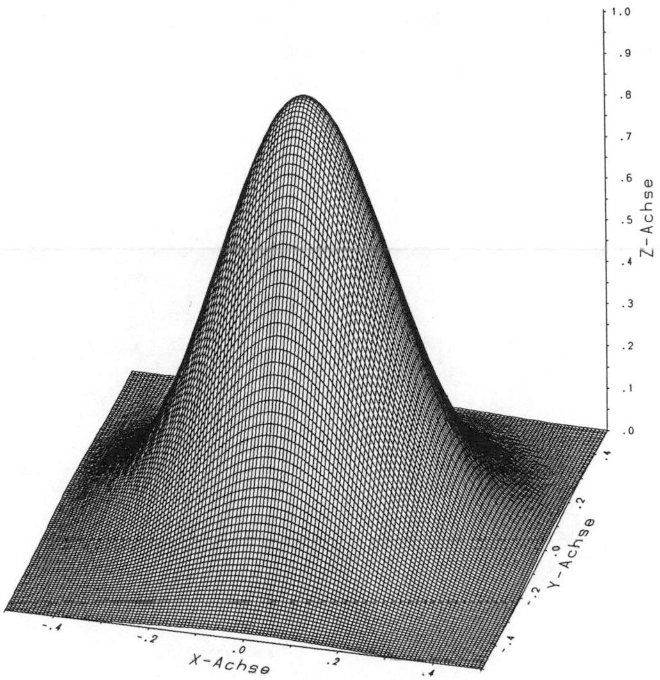

Fig. 3. Interpolant für Beispiel 1

Um ERR_2 zu kontrollieren, beachten wir, daß im Fall $\phi = M_{2,2,1}$ das trigonometrische Polynom (6) bekanntlich die Schranken

$$\frac{1}{3} \leq \phi^{\sim}(\xi) \leq 1$$

besitzt. Zusammen mit der generell gültigen Abschätzung

$$| (\mathcal{F}_N d)_\alpha | \leq \max \{ | d_\beta |; \beta \in B_N \} \leq \|f\|_\infty$$

erhalten wir somit

$$ERR_2 \leq 3 \, \|f\|_\infty \sum_{\alpha \in \mathbb{Z}^2 \setminus B_n} | \phi\hat{~}(h\alpha) |$$

mit $h = \frac{2\pi}{N}$ und $\phi\hat{~}(\xi_1, \xi_2) = (\text{sinc } \frac{1}{2}\xi_1)^2 (\text{sinc } \frac{1}{2}\xi_2)^2 \text{sinc } \frac{1}{2}(\xi_1 + \xi_2)$. Numerische Rechnungen zeigen allerdings, daß diese Schranke sehr grob ist; der tatsächliche Fehler wird in der Regel stark überschätzt.

Andererseits ist s im Fall $\phi = M_{2,2,1}$ eine N-periodische C^1–Funktion, deren Fourier-Koeffizienten $s_N\hat{~}(\alpha)$ für $|\alpha| \to \infty$ dieselbe Asymptotik zeigen wie $\phi\hat{~}(h\alpha)$. Hier mag es angebracht sein, analog zum eindimensionalen Fall (vgl. [1]) auf mehrdimensionale Korobov-Räume Bezug zu nehmen, um bessere Fehlerabschätzungen zu erhalten. Wir werden hierauf an anderer Stelle zurückkommen.

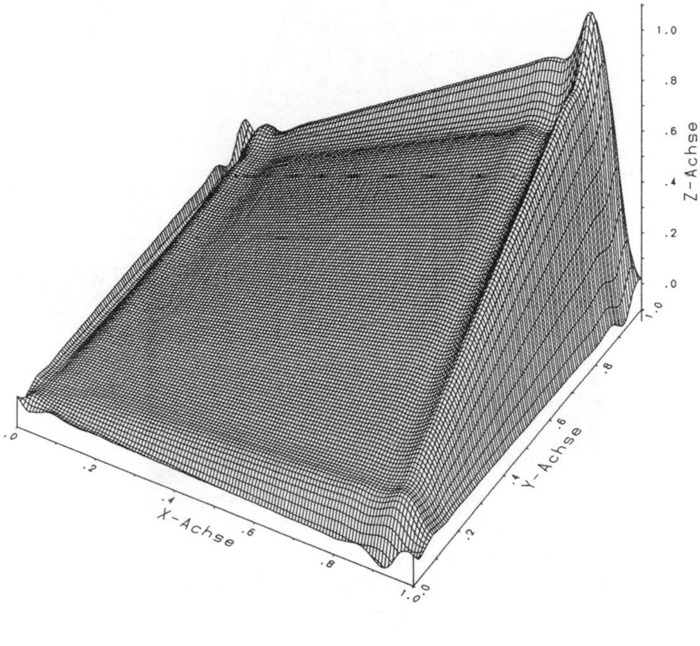

Fig. 4. Interpolant für Beispiel 2

4. Beispiele

Wir demonstrieren die Wirksamkeit des Algorithmus durch zwei Beispiele, die – wie wir meinen – die auftretenden Effekte deutlich genug zeigen. Dabei arbeiten wir generell mit $\phi = M_{2,2,1}$, einem kubischen C^1–Box-Spline (Fall $k = l = 2$ und $m = 1$ in (5)). Die jeweilige Funktion wird auf dem Periodenquadrat der Seitenlänge 1 im äquidistanten Gitter Δ_{h_1} zur Schrittweite $h_1 = \frac{1}{16}$ interpoliert und die Interpolierende anschließend auf dem feinen Gitter Δ_{h_2} mit $h_2 = \frac{1}{128}$ ausgewertet (16384 Gitterpunkte !).

Beispiel 1 behandelt die Funktion $f(x,y) = e^{-16(x^2+y^2)}$ auf $[-\frac{1}{2}, +\frac{1}{2}[^2$, vgl. Fig. 1. Die 1–periodische Fortsetzung dieser Funktion ist stetig, aber nicht stetig differenzierbar;

Theorem 2 liefert also keine nützliche Information. Im Ergebnis (Fig. 3) erkennt man, daß die Funktion zufriedenstellend reproduziert wird; der Absolutfehler auf dem Gitter Δ_{h_2} liegt bei maximal $4 \cdot 10^{-3}$.

Beispiel 2 betrachtet die Funktion $f(x,y) = xy$ auf $[0,1[^2$, vgl. Fig. 2. Die 1–periodische Fortsetzung ist unstetig entlang der Ränder der Periodenquadrate, und im Ergebnis (vgl. Fig. 4) ist deutlich das zu erwartende Gibb'sche Phänomen zu erkennen. Entsprechend liegt der Fehler (vgl. hierzu Fig. 5) entlang des Randes in der Größenordnung der Funktionswerte von f, wobei die Reproduktion im Innern des Intervalls zufriedenstellend ist; z.B. liegt der Absolutfehler im Quadrat $[\frac{1}{4}, \frac{3}{4}]^2$ wieder bei maximal $2.2 \cdot 10^{-3}$.

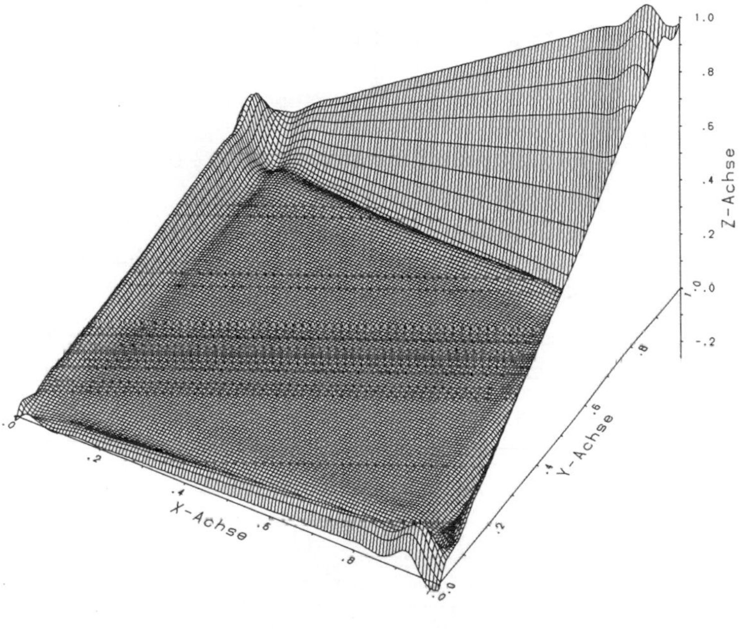

Fig. 5. Fehlerfunktion für Beispiel 2

Abschließend ist zu bemerken, daß die negativen Effekte des Gibb'schen Phänomens generell ausgeschlossen werden können, falls f einer Vorapproximation auf der Basis einer Lanczos–Zerlegung (vgl. [1]) unterworfen wird. Hierbei bestimmt man entlang des Randes des Periodenquadrats eine Blending–Interpolierende f_1 und wendet dann unseren Algorithmus auf $f - f_1$ an. Wegen der stetigen Fortsetzbarkeit von $f - f_1$ ist ein Verhalten wie bei Beispiel 1 zu erwarten.

Literatur

[1] Baszenski, G., Delvos, F.-J. (1987) Boolean methods in Fourier approximation. In: Topics in Multivariate Approximation (C.K. Chui, L.L. Schumaker, F.I. Utreras, Eds.), pp. 1-12 (Academic Press, New York).

[2] de Boor, C., Höllig, K., Riemenschneider, S.D. (1985) Bivariate cardinal interpolation by splines on a three-direction mesh. Illinois J. Math. 29, 533-566.

[3] Chui, C.K. (1988) Multivariate Splines. CBMS-NSF Reg. Conf. Series in Appl. Math., vol. 54 (SIAM, Philadelphia).

[4] Chui, C.K., Jetter, K., Ward, J.D. (1987) Cardinal interpolation by multivariate splines. Math. Comp. 48, 711-724.

[5] Gautschi, W. (1972) Attenuation factors in practical analysis. Numer. Math. 18, 373-400.

[6] Gutknecht, M.H. (1987) Attenuation factors in multivariate Fourier analysis. Numer. Math. 51, 615-629.

[7] Henrici, P. (1979) Fast Fourier methods in computational complex analysis. SIAM Review 21, 481-527.

[8] Locher, F. (1981) Interpolation on uniform meshes by translates of one function and related attenuation factors. Math. Comp. 37, 404-416.

[9] terMorsche, H. (1987) Attenuation factors and multivariate periodic spline interpolation. In: Topics in Multivariate Approximation (C.K. Chui, L.L. Schumaker, F.I. Utreras, Eds.), pp. 165-174 (Academic Press, New York).

Kurt Jetter
Peter Koch
FB Mathematik, Universität Duisburg
D-4100 Duisburg

International Series of
Numerical Mathematics, Vol. 90

DUAL BASES ASSOCIATED WITH BOX SPLINES

R.Q. JIA

Deprtment of Mathematics, Zhejiang University, Hangzhou, Zhejiang, China

1. Introduction

Let E and F be two linear spaces over the field K. A bilinear function $\langle\ ,\ \rangle : (x,y) \mapsto \langle x,y\rangle$ from $E \times F$ to K is called a scalar product if

(i) $\langle x,y\rangle = 0$ for every $y \in F$ implies $x = 0$;

(ii) $\langle x,y\rangle = 0$ for every $x \in E$ implies $y = 0$.

If there is a scalar product between E and F, then E and F will be called dual. Two dual spaces have the same dimension. Let E and F be two dual spaces of dimension $n < \infty$ with respect to the scalar product $\langle\ ,\ \rangle$. Then there is a basis $(x_i)_{1\le i\le n}$ for E, and a basis $(y_j)_{1\le j\le n}$ for F such that $\langle x_i, y_j\rangle = \delta_{ij}$. The two bases $(x_i)_{1\le i\le n}$ and $(y_j)_{1\le j\le n}$ are called dual.

It has been observed recently that dual spaces play an important role in the study of box splines and other related topics. Before illustrating this point, we recall first the definition of box splines (see [2] and [3]). Let $X = (x^1, \ldots, x^n)$ be a family of nonzero vectors in $\mathbb{R}^s$. Then the box spline $B(\cdot|X)$ associated with X is defined to be the linear functional given by

$$\phi \mapsto \int_{[0,1]^n} \phi(\sum_{j=1}^n x^j u_j) du, \quad \phi \in C(\mathbb{R}^s),$$

where $du = du_1 \ldots du_n$. Thus $B(\cdot|X)$ is a distribution supported on

$$[X] := \{\sum_{j=1}^n t_j x^j : 0 \le t_j \le 1, \quad \text{all} \quad j\}.$$

when X spans $\mathbb{R}^s$, $B(\cdot|X)$ is a piecewise polynomial function. Each polynomial piece is in the space $D(X) := \cap\{\ker D_Y : \langle X\backslash Y\rangle \neq \mathbb{R}^s\}$, where $D_Y := \cap_{y\in Y} D_y$, while $D_y f$ denotes the directional derivative of f in the direction y.

It was Dahmer and Micchelli [6] who first computed the dimension of $D(X)$. Their work has stimulated much interest in the algebraic aspects of box spline theory.

For $v \in \mathbb{R}^s$, let $p_v(x) := v \cdot x$, $x \in \mathbb{R}^s$. For $V \subset X$, let $p_V := \prod_{v\in V} p_v$. In the study of linear projectors on the space spanned by a box spline and its translates, the author introduced in [9] the following two spaces:

$$F(X) := \operatorname{span}\{p_V : \langle X\backslash V\rangle = \mathbb{R}^s\},$$

$$G(X) := \{p \in \pi(\mathbb{R}^s) : p(D)B(\cdot|X) \in L^\infty\}.$$

It was shown there that $F(X) = G(X)$, and that with

$$\langle p, f\rangle := p(D)f(0) \quad \text{for} \quad p \in F(X),\ f \in D(X),$$

the bilinear function $\langle\ ,\ \rangle$ is a scalar product between $F(X)$ and $D(X)$. A similar result was also obtained by H. Hakopian independently (see [7]).

In this note we shall investigate the extension of the dual spaces mentioned above and their applications to the box spline theory.

2. Dual Spaces Associated with Exponential Box Splines

The exponential box spline was introduced by Ron [10]. See also [1], [5] and [7] for its properties. Let $X = (x^1, \ldots, x^n) \subset \mathbb{R}^s\backslash\{0\}$ and $\mu = (\mu_1, \ldots, \mu_n) \in \mathbb{C}^n$. If $x = x^j$, we write μ_x for μ_j. The exponential box spline $C_\mu(\cdot|X)$ is the linear functional on $C(\mathbb{R}^s)$ defined by

$$\phi \mapsto \int_{[0,1]^n} e^{-\mu\cdot u}\phi\Big(\sum_{j=1}^n x^j u_j\Big)du, \quad \phi \in C(\mathbb{R}^s).$$

When $\mu = 0, C_\mu(\cdot|X)$ reduces to the box spline $B(\cdot|X)$. For $v \in X$, let $p_{\mu_v,v}(x) := x \cdot v + \mu_v$, $x \in \mathbb{R}^s$. Define, for $V \subset X$, $p_{\mu,V} := \prod_{v\in V} p_{\mu_v,v}$. If X spans $\mathbb{R}^s$, then $C_\mu(\cdot|X)$ is a piecewise exponential polynamial function with each piece in the space

$$D_\mu(X) := \bigcap\{\ker p_{\mu,Y}(D) : Y \subset X, \langle X\backslash Y\rangle \neq \mathbb{R}^s\}.$$

We introduce the following space $F_\mu(X)$:

$$F_\mu(X) := \text{ span}\{p_{\mu,V} : V \subset X, \langle X\backslash V\rangle = \mathbb{R}^s\}.$$

Theorem 2.1. The bilinear function $\langle,\rangle$ given by

$$\langle p, f\rangle := p(D)f(0), \quad p \in F_\mu(X), \quad f \in D_\mu(X)$$

is a scalar product between the spaces $F_\mu(X)$ and $D_\mu(X)$.

Proof. Suppose that $\langle p, f\rangle = 0$ for all $f \in D_\mu(X)$. Since $C_\mu(\cdot|X)$ is a piecewise exponential polynomial function with each piece in the space $D_\mu(X)$, and since $D_\mu(X)$ is translation invariant, we have

$$p(D)C_\mu(\cdot|X) = 0 \quad \text{a.e.}$$

On the other hand, $p(D)C_\mu(\cdot|X) \in L^\infty$. Thus $p(D)C_\mu(\cdot|X) = 0$. Since $C_\mu(\cdot|X)$ is compactly supported, it follows that $p = 0$.

Suppose now that $\langle p, f\rangle = 0$ for all $p \in F_\mu(X)$. We want to prove $f = 0$. This will be done by induction on $\#X$. If $\#X = s$, then $D_\mu(X)$ is spanned by an exponential function $e^{\zeta\cdot()}$ for some $\zeta \in \mathbb{C}^s$. But constants are in $F_\mu(X)$. This implies that $f(0) = 0$ for $f \in D_\mu(X)$. Hence $f = 0$, as desired. Suppose inductively that our claim has been proved for any X' with $\#X' < \#X$, and we want to establish it for X. For $v \in X$, consider $p_{\mu_v,v}(D)f$. We have

$$p_{\mu,V}(D)p_{\mu_v,v}(D)f(0) = 0 \quad \text{for any} \quad V \subset X\backslash v \quad \text{with} \quad \langle X\backslash v\backslash V\rangle = \mathbb{R}^s.$$

Hence by induction hypothesis, $p_{\mu_v,v}(D)f = 0$. This together with the fact $f(0) = 0$ implies $f = 0$, since X contains a basis for $\mathbb{R}^s$. This finishes the induction step.

□

For another proof of this theorem, see Dyn and Ron [5]. There they observed that $F_\mu(X) = F_0(X)$ for any $\mu \in \mathbb{C}^s$. Let $\mathcal{B}(X)$ be the collection of all the bases for $\mathbb{R}^s$ included in X. For $B \in \mathcal{B}(X)$, we denote by $\theta_B \in \mathbb{C}^s$ the unique common zero of all $p_{\mu_v,v}$, $v \in B$. If for any two different bases B_1 and $B_2 \in \mathcal{B}(X)$, the corresponding θ_{B_1} and θ_{B_2} are different, then the defining set (X,μ) is called simple after Ron [10]. It is easily seen that $\dim\big(D_\mu(X)\big) = \#\mathcal{B}(X)$ in the case when (X,μ) is simple. This gives probably the shortest proof for the following fact:

Theorem 2.2. $\dim\big(F_\mu(X)\big) = \dim\big(D_\mu(X)\big) = \#\mathcal{B}(X)$. □

3. Dual Bases Associated with the Polynomial Pieces of a Box Spline

Let $X = (x^1, \dots, x^n)$ be a family of nonzero vectors in $\mathbb{R}^s$ with $\langle X\rangle = \mathbb{R}^s$. Then the box spline $B(\cdot|X)$ is supported on $[X]$. For $Y \subset X, \langle Y\rangle \neq \mathbb{R}^s$, let

$$K_Y := [Y] + \{\sum_{\eta\in X\backslash Y} t_\eta \eta : t_\eta = 0 \quad \text{or} \quad 1\}$$

$$K(X) := \bigcup\{K_Y : Y \subset X, \langle Y\rangle \neq \mathbb{R}^s\}.$$

Denote by $E_1, \dots, E_m$ all the bounded connected components of $\mathbb{R}^2\backslash K(X)$. Then $B(\cdot|X)$ agrees with some $p_j \in D(X)$ on E_j for each $j = 1, \dots, m$. Let $Q(X)$ be the space spanned by $p_1, \dots, p_m$. Then $Q(X) \subseteq D(X)$. Whether $Q(X) = D(X)$ is an interest question.

If $Q(X)$ is translation invariant, then by the same argument as in Theorem 2.1 we see that $\langle\ ,\ \rangle$ is a scalar product between $F(X)$ and $Q(X)$. Hence $\dim\big(Q(X)\big) = \dim\big(F(X)\big) = \dim\big(D(X)\big)$, and it follows that $Q(X) = D(X)$. Thus our task is to verify the translation invariance of $Q(X)$.

For $Y \subset X$, let $u_Y := \sum_{y\in Y} y$. If $Y = \emptyset$, we agree that $u_Y = 0$. Let $U := U(X) := \{u_Y : Y \subset X\}$. First, we prove the following result:

Lemma 3.1. For any $f \in D(X)$, the space $\operatorname{span}\{f(\cdot - u) : u \in U\}$ is D-invariant.

Proof. The proof proceeds with induction on $\#X$. The case when $\#X = s$ is trivial. Suppose that the lemma is true for any X' with $\#X' < \#X$. Let $f \in D(X)$. Then, for any $x \in X$, $\nabla_v f \in D(X\backslash v)$. There is a polynomial q in one variable such that $D_v f = q(D_v)(\nabla_v f)$. By the induction hypothesis, for any polynomial p,

$$p(D)D_v f = p(D)q(D_v)(\nabla_v f)$$

$$\in \operatorname{span}\{\nabla_v f(\cdot - u) : u \in U(X\backslash v)\} \subseteq \operatorname{span}\{f(\cdot - u) : u \in U(X)\}.$$

Since X contains a basis for $\mathbb{R}^s$, any polynomial of positive degree is a linear combination of the polynomials of form $p(D)D_v$. This proves that $\operatorname{span}\{f(\cdot - u) : u \in U(X)\}$ is D-invariant. □

Let us consider the difference operator ∇_X. It can be expanded as $\sum_{u\in U} c_u T_u$, where T_u is the translation operator given by $T_u f := f(\cdot - u)$, and

$$c_u := \sum\{(-1)^{\#Y} : u_Y = u\}.$$

Theorem 3.2. Any polynomial in $D(X)$ is a linear combination of the polynomials in $Q(X)$ and their translates. Moreover, if all $c_u \neq 0, u \in U$, then $Q(X) = D(X)$.

Proof. Without loss of generality, we may assume that 0 is not in the convex hull of X. Let $C(\cdot|X)$ be the cone spline associated with X and let $f_1, \ldots, f_k$ be all the polynomial pieces in $C(\cdot|X)$. Note that $B(\cdot|X) = \nabla_X C(\cdot|X)$. If all $c_u \neq 0$, then $f_j(\cdot - u)$, $j = 1, \ldots, k$, $u \in U$ are in $D(X)$. Hence we have

$$Q(X) = \sum_{j=1}^{k} \operatorname{span}\{f_j(\cdot - u) : u \in U\}.$$

Thus, by Lemma 3.1, $Q(X)$ is D-invariant, as desired. □

4. Dual Bases Associated with an Order-Closed Structure

In this section we consider some extensions of the results in Section 2.

Let X be a set, and $\mathbb{B}(X)$ a collection of subsets of s elements of X. Associated with each $x \in X$ a polynomial p_x in $\pi(\mathbb{C}^s)$. For a subset $Y \subset X$, define $p_Y := \prod_{y\in Y} p_y$. Let

$$\mathbb{K}(X) := \{K \subset X : K \cap B \neq \emptyset, \quad \forall B \in \mathbb{B}(X)\},$$

$$D(X) := \{f \in C^\infty : p_K(D)f = 0, \quad \forall K \in \mathbb{K}(X)\}.$$

We are interested in computing $\dim(D(X))$ (see [4] and [8]).

In Section 2, we demonstrated the usefulness of dual spaces in the study of $D_\mu(X)$. This is also the case when $\mathbb{B}(X)$ has an order-closed structure (see [4]). We impose a (total) order on X. This order induces a partial ordering on $\mathbb{B}(X)$ as follows:

$$(x_1, \ldots, x_s) \le (y_1, \ldots, y_s) \Longleftrightarrow x_j \le y_j, \quad j = 1, \ldots, s,$$

where the elements in the above sequences are arranged in an increasing order. We say that $\mathbb{B}(X)$ is order-closed if $B_1 \in \mathbb{B}(X)$ and $B_2 \le B_1$ imply $B_2 \in \mathbb{B}(X)$. For a subset Y of X, let $\mathbb{B}(Y) := \{B \subset Y : B \in \mathbb{B}(X)\}$. If $\mathbb{B}(X)$ is order-closed, then so is $\mathbb{B}(Y)$. The meaning of the space $D(Y)$ is also clear from $\mathbb{B}(Y)$.

Suppose each p_x is a linear function, and the space $\bigcap_{x\in B} \ker(p_x(D))$ is finitely dimensional for every $B \in \mathbb{B}(X)$. Associate with each $B \in \mathbb{B}(X)$ a set

$$X_B := \{x \in X \backslash B : x < \max\{y : y \in B\}\}.$$

Let $F(X) := \operatorname{span}\{p_{X_B} : B \in \mathbb{B}(X)\}$. It was shown in [4] that $F(X)$ and $D(X)$ are dual spaces with respect to $\langle\ ,\ \rangle$.

Now we extend their result to the case when each p_x is a product of linear functions, say $p_x = p_{x,1} \cdots p_{x,n_x}$ with each $p_{x,j}$ being a linear function, $j = 1, \ldots, n_x$. For a given $B \in \mathbb{B}(X)$, let

$$E_B := \operatorname{span}\{\prod_{x\in B} p_{x,J_x} : J_x \subsetneq \{1, \ldots, n_x\}\}.$$

Then there is a subspace F_B of E_B such that F_B and $D(B)$ are dual spaces with respect to $\langle,\rangle$. Let

$$F(X) := \sum_{B\in\mathbb{B}(X)} p_{X_B} F_B.$$

<u>Theorem 4.1.</u> The spaces $F(X)$ and $D(X)$ are dual with respect to $\langle\ ,\ \rangle$. Con-

sequently,

$$\dim\big(F(X)\big) = \dim\big(D(X)\big) = \sum_{B\in\mathbb{B}(X)} \dim\big(D(B)\big).$$

Proof. Arrange the elements of X in an increasing order:

$$x_1 < x_2 < \cdots < x_n.$$

The proof will proceed with induction on $\#X$. The case $\#X = s$ is trivial. Suppose that the theorem is true for any X' with $\#X' < \#X$. Let $f \in D(X)$. Suppose that $\langle p, f\rangle = 0$ for all $p \in F(X)$. We want to show $f = 0$. If $\mathbb{B}(X)$ is empty, there is noting to prove. If $\mathbb{B}(X)$ is nonempty, then $B_0 := \{x_1, \ldots, x_s\}$ must be in $\mathbb{B}(X)$. Pick $x \in B_0$ and consider $p_x(D)f$. Write Y for $X\backslash\{x\}$. For any $B \in \mathbb{B}(Y)$, we have $X_B = Y_B \cup \{x\}$. Hence, for any $q \in F_B$,

$$p_{Y_B}(D)q(D)\big(p_x(D)f\big)(0) = p_{X_B}(D)q(D)f(0) = 0.$$

By induction hypothesis, $p_x(D)f = 0$ for every $x \in B_0$. This shows $f \in D(B_0)$. Moreover, $X_{B_0} = \emptyset$; therefore for any $q \in F_{B_0}$, $q(D)f(0) = 0$. But F_{B_0} and $D(B_0)$ are dual spaces with respect to $\langle , \rangle$; hence $f = 0$.

Consequently, we have $\dim\big(F(X)\big) \geq \dim\big(D(X)\big)$. However

$$\dim\big(F(X)\big) \leq \sum_{B\in\mathbb{B}(X)} \dim(F_B) = \sum_{B\in\mathbb{B}(X)} \dim\big(D(B)\big).$$

By Theorem (6.6) of [4], we also have

$$\dim\big(D(X)\big) \geq \sum_{B\in\mathbb{B}(X)} \dim\big(D(B)\big).$$

This proves the desired dimension formula. Furthermore, $F(X)$ and $D(X)$ are dual spaces with respect to $\langle\ ,\ \rangle$. □

Acknowledgement

This work was done when the author was invited by Prof. S. Riemenschneider to visit University of Alberta. The research was partially supported by NSERC Grant

#A7687.

References

[1] Ben-Artzi, A. and A. Ron (1988) Translates of exponential box splines and their related spaces, Trans. Amer. Math. Soc. 309, 683-710.

[2] De Boor, C. and R. DeVore (1983) Approximation by smooth multivariate splines, Trans. Amer. Math. Soc. 276, 775-785.

[3] De Boor, C. and K. Höllig (1982/83) B-splines from parallelepipeds, J. Analyse Math. 42, 95-115.

[4] De Boor, C. and A. Ron (1988) On polynomial ideals of finite codimension with applications to box spline theory, CMS Technical Summary Report #889-21, University of Wsconsin-Madison.

[5] Dyn, N. and A. Ron (1988) Local approximation by certain spaces of multivariate exponential polynomials, approximation order of exponential box splines and related interpolation problems, CAT Rep. 160, Texas A& M University.

[6] Dahmen, W. and C.A. Micchelli (1985) On the local linear independence of translates of a box spline, Stud. Math. 82, 243-263.

[7] Dahmen, W. and C.A. Micchelli (1988) Multivariate E-splines, Advances in Math., to appear.

[8] Dahmen, W. and C.A. Micchelli (1988) Local dimension of piecewise polynomial spaces, syzygies, and solutions of systems of partial differential equations, preprint.

[9] Jia, R.Q. (1987) Subspaces invariant under translation and the dual bases for box splines, Chinese Ann. of Math., to appear.

[10] Ron, A. (1988) Exponential box splines, Constr. Approx. 4, 357-378.

Prof. R.Q. Jia, Department of Mathematics, Zhejiang University, Hangzhou, Zhejiang 310013, China.

International Series of
Numerical Mathematics, Vol. 90

SOME POINTWISE NEGATIVE RESULTS IN MULTIVARIATE APPROXIMATION BY CONVOLUTION PROCESSES OF FEJÉR'S TYPE

N. Kirchhoff[1] and R.J. Nessel

Lehrstuhl A für Mathematik, RWTH Aachen

The aim of this note is to apply a nonlinear uniform boundedness principle with rates in connection with the pointwise approximation on the N-dimensional Euclidean space $\mathbb{R}^N$ by convolution processes of Fejér's type.

For a Banach space X with norm $\|\cdot\|$ let X^+ be the set of non-negative functionals T on X which are (absolutely) homogeneous, i.e., $T(af) = |a|Tf$ for all $f \in X$ and scalars a, and lower semicontinuous, i.e., for each $f \in X$, $\varepsilon > 0$ there exists $\delta > 0$ such that $T(f+g) \geq Tf - \varepsilon$ for all $g \in X$ with $\|g\| \leq \delta$. The subset $X^* \subset X^+$ denotes the class of sublinear, bounded functionals, i.e.,

$$T(f+g) \leq Tf + Tg, \qquad T(af) = |a|Tf, \qquad \|T\|_{X^*} := \sup\{Tf : \|f\| \leq 1\} < \infty.$$

Let ω be an (abstract) modulus of continuity with $t/\omega(t) = o(1)$ as $t \to 0+$. Moreover, let $\sigma(t)$ be a (strictly) positive function on $(0,\infty)$ and $\{\varphi_n\}$ be a (strictly) decreasing null-sequence. In these terms there holds true the following nonlinear version of a uniform boundedness principle with rates (cf. [1;2]).

Theorem 1. For $\{T_n\} \subset X^+$ let there exist test elements $g_n \in X$ such that

$$\text{(1)} \qquad \|g_n\| \leq C_1 \qquad (n \in \mathbb{N}),$$

[1] Supported by Deutsche Forschungsgemeinschaft Grant No. IIC4–Ne 171/7–1

(2) $\limsup_{n\to\infty} T_n g_n \geq C_2 > 0.$

Assume that the sequence $\{T_n\}$ is asymptotically lower subadditive on $\text{span}\{g_n\}$ (set of finite linear combinations of test elements) in the sense that

(3) $T_n(p+q) \geq T_n p - T_n q - C_q \varphi_n$ $\quad (p,q \in \text{span}\{g_n\},\ n \in \mathbb{N}).$

If the smoothness measure $\{U_t : t \in (0,\infty)\} \subset X^*$ satisfies

(4) $U_t g_n \leq C_3 \min\{1, \sigma(t)/\varphi_n\}$ $\quad (n \in \mathbb{N}, t > 0),$

then for each modulus ω there exists a counterexample $f_\omega \in X$ such that

(5) $U_t f_\omega = \mathcal{O}(\omega(\sigma(t)))$ $\quad (t \to 0+),$

(6) $\limsup_{n\to\infty} T_n f_\omega / \omega(\varphi_n) \geq 2.$

Thus, if the direct approximation theorem $U_t f = \mathcal{O}(\omega(\sigma(t))) \Rightarrow T_n f = \mathcal{O}(\omega(\varphi_n))$ holds true, then Theorem 1 ensures that the large-$\mathcal{O}$h-error bound cannot be improved to a small-oh-one on the whole smoothness class, described by (5). Conditions (1) and (2) are quite parallel to those in the classical situation which corresponds to $C_2 = \infty$, thus to the resonance version of the uniform boundedness principle. Concerning assumption (3), this kind of asymptotically lower subadditivity is much in the spirit of work of I.S. GÁL (1951) on nonlinear extensions of the classical principle. Also note that the nullsequence $\{\varphi_n\}$ is determined via (3) as a property of the approximation process $\{T_n\}$. The smoothness measure $\{U_t\}$ then has to be chosen appropiately so that the Jackson–Bernstein-type inequality (4) holds true for $\{\varphi_n\}$. Let us also add a remark concerning the proof: One may proceed along a gliding hump method and successively construct a suitable subsequence $\{n_j\}$, delivering the candidate

(7) $$f_\omega = \sum_{j=1}^{\infty} \omega(\varphi_{n_j}) g_{n_j}.$$

This is mentioned since it already indicates that real– or complex–valued test elements g_n imply the counterexample f_ω to be real– or complex–valued, respectively.

The main point here will be to apply the resonance principle of Theorem 1 to a class of convolution processes of Fejér's type, previously employed by H.S. SHAPIRO (cf. [4]). Therefore, in the following, X will always be one of the Banach spaces $C_{2\pi}^{\mathbb{R};\mathbb{C}}(\mathbb{R}^N)$ or $C_0^{\mathbb{R};\mathbb{C}}(\mathbb{R}^N)$ of functions, defined and continuous on $\mathbb{R}^N$, endowed with the usual sup–norm $\|\cdot\|$, which are real– or complex–valued, respectively, and which are 2π–periodic in each variable or vanishing at infinity (i.e., $f(x) = o(1)$ for $|x|\to\infty$), respectively. Let $\mathcal{M}_0(\mathbb{R}^N)$ be the set of real–valued, bounded measures on $\mathbb{R}^N$, satisfying ($<v,u> := \Sigma_{j=1}^N v_j u_j$)

$$(8) \qquad \mu^\wedge(0) = 0, \qquad \mu^\wedge(v) := (2\pi)^{-N} \int_{\mathbb{R}^N} e^{-i<v,u>} d\mu(u).$$

The convolution processes to be considered are then given by ($n \in \mathbb{N}$)

$$(9) \qquad T_n^\mu f(x) := (2\pi)^{-N} \int_{\mathbb{R}^N} f(x-u/n) d\mu(u) = (2\pi)^{-N} \int_{\mathbb{R}^N} f(x-u) d\mu_n(u),$$

where $\mu_n \in \mathcal{M}_0$ is generated by $\mu \in \mathcal{M}_0$ via $\mu_n^\wedge(v) := \mu^\wedge(v/n)$. Note that the normalization (8) then takes care of the fact that in the applications the family $\{\mu_n\}$ will represent the remainders of processes, approximating the identity. Obviously, T_n^μ is a bounded linear operator of X into itself, satisfying ($\bar{z}$:= complex conjugate of $z \in \mathbb{C}$)

$$(10) \qquad T_n^\mu(e^{i<v,\cdot>})(x) = \mu^\wedge(v/n)\, e^{i<v,x>}, \qquad \mu^\wedge(-v) = \overline{\mu^\wedge(v)}.$$

Finally, let r–th (radial) Lipschitz classes be defined by ($r \in \mathbb{N}$)

$$(11) \qquad \mathrm{Lip}_r(\omega,X) := \{f \in X : \omega_r(f,t) = O(\omega(t^r)),\ t\to 0+\},$$

$$\omega_r(f,t) := \sup\{\|\Sigma_{k=0}^r (-1)^{r-k}\tbinom{r}{k} f(x+kh)\| : h \in \mathbb{R}^N,\ |h| \le t\}.$$

In these terms, if for the convolution process (9) there holds true a direct theorem to the effect that $f \in \mathrm{Lip}_r(\omega,X)$ implies $\|T_n^\mu f\| = O(\omega(n^{-r}))$, then an application of Theorem 1 yields the pointwise sharpness of such a uniform estimate on the whole Euclidean space $\mathbb{R}^N$ (for corresponding one–dimensional results see [2;3]). Indeed, starting with the periodic situation, one has

Theorem 2. Let $\mu \in \mathcal{M}_o(\mathbb{R}^N)$ with $\mu\hat{} \not\equiv 0$ be such that

(12) $\quad \mu\hat{}(v) = \mathcal{O}(|v|^r) \qquad (v \to 0)$

for some $r \in \mathbb{N}$. Then for each modulus ω there exists
a) a complex-valued counterexample $f_\omega \in \mathrm{Lip}_r(\omega, C_{2\pi}^{\mathbb{C}}(\mathbb{R}^N))$,
b) a real-valued counterexample $f_\omega \in \mathrm{Lip}_r(\omega, C_{2\pi}^{\mathbb{R}}(\mathbb{R}^N))$
such that simultaneously for each $x \in \mathbb{R}^N$

(13) $\quad \limsup_{n \to \infty} |T_n^\mu f_\omega(x)| / \omega(n^{-r}) \geq 1.$

Thus, in order to apply the abstract Theorem 1, the only point to verify, after all, is condition (12) on the Fourier transform of μ which in fact determines $r \in \mathbb{N}$. Indeed, (12) is easily tested in all the classical examples of convolution processes such as those of, e.g., Bochner–Riesz ($r = 2$), Gauss–Weierstrass ($r = 2$), Cauchy–Poisson ($r = 1$), the corresponding (uniform) direct estimates being well-known.

Proof of Theorem 2a). Since the continuous function $\mu\hat{}$ does not vanish identically, there exists a rational e/a with $e \in \mathbb{Z}^N$ (set of integral lattice points), $a \in \mathbb{N}$ such that $\mu\hat{}(e/a) \neq 0$. Setting $\sigma(t) = t^r$, $\varphi_n = n^{-r}$,

$$g_n(x) = e^{in\langle e,x\rangle}, \qquad T_n f = \inf\{|T_{an}^\mu f(x)| : x \in \mathbb{R}^N\}, \qquad U_t f = \omega_r(f,t),$$

one immediately obtains (1). In view of (cf. (10))

$$T_n g_n = |\mu\hat{}(e/a)| > 0, \qquad \omega_r(g_n,t) \leq \min\{2^r \|g_n\|, t^r \Sigma_{|\tau|=r} \|D^\tau g_n\|\}$$

one also has (2),(4).Moreover, it follows by (12) that for p, $q := \Sigma_{j=1}^m a_j g_j \in \mathrm{span}\{g_n\}$

(14) $\quad T_n(p+q) \geq T_n p - \|T_n^\mu q\| \geq T_n p - \Sigma_{j=1}^m |a_j| \, |\mu\hat{}(\frac{je}{an})| \geq T_n p - C_q \varphi_n.$

Now Theorem 1 yields (13) for a complex-valued (cf.(7)) $f_\omega \in \mathrm{Lip}_r(\omega, C_{2\pi}^{\mathbb{C}})$. □

The real-valued case is somewhat more involved because we are then not allowed to use the complex-valued test elements $e^{in\langle e,x\rangle}$ (cf.(7)). On the other hand, we cannot immediately pass from the complex system to a corresponding real one since in view of common zeros there occur difficulties in establishing the resonance condition (2). Nevertheless, one may proceed via the following two lemmata ($\mathbb{Q}^+ := \mathbb{Q} \cap (0,\infty)$ with $\mathbb{Q} \subset \mathbb{R}$, the set of rational numbers).

Lemma 1. a) If $\mu \in \mathcal{M}_0(\mathbb{R}^N)$ satisfies

$$\mu\hat{}(2ep)\mu\hat{}(eq) = \mu\hat{}(ep)\mu\hat{}(2eq) \qquad (e \in \mathbb{Z}^N,\ p,q \in \mathbb{Q}^+), \tag{15}$$

then necessarily $\mu\hat{} \equiv 0$, i.e., μ is the nullmeasure.

b) Let $e \in \mathbb{R}^N$ be arbitrary, fixed. If $\mu \in \mathcal{M}_0(\mathbb{R}^N)$ satisfies

$$\mu\hat{}(ep)\mu\hat{}(-eq) = \mu\hat{}(-ep)\mu\hat{}(eq) \qquad (p,q \in \mathbb{Q}^+), \tag{16}$$

then there exists $0 \le \vartheta = \vartheta(e) < \pi$ such that

$$\mu\hat{}(-eq) = e^{2i\vartheta}\mu\hat{}(eq) \qquad (q \in \mathbb{Q}^+). \tag{17}$$

Proof. a) Assume that $\mu\hat{} \not\equiv 0$. Then there exist $e_0 \in \mathbb{Z}^N$, $p_0 \in \mathbb{Q}^+$ such that $\mu\hat{}(2e_0p_0) \neq 0$. By (15) one has for any $q \in \mathbb{Q}^+$ that $\mu\hat{}(e_0q) = B\ \mu\hat{}(2e_0q)$ with $B := \mu\hat{}(e_0p_0)/\mu\hat{}(2e_0p_0)$. By induction, $\mu\hat{}(e_0q) = B^n\mu\hat{}(2^ne_0q)$ which implies (cf.(8))

$$0 = \mu\hat{}(0)/\mu\hat{}(2e_0p_0) = \lim_{n\to\infty} \mu\hat{}(2e_0p_0/2^n)/\mu\hat{}(2e_0p_0) = \lim_{n\to\infty} B^n,$$

thus $|B| < 1$. But, since $\mu\hat{}$ is bounded, this leads to the contradiction

$$0 < |\mu\hat{}(2e_0p_0)| = |B|^n|\mu\hat{}(2^{n+1}e_0p_0)| = o(1) \qquad (n\to\infty).$$

b) If $\mu\hat{}(ep) = 0$ for each $p \in \mathbb{Q}^+$, then (17) is trivial. Otherwise, there exists $p_0 \in \mathbb{Q}^+$ such that $\mu\hat{}(ep_0) \neq 0$. In view of (16) one obtains for any $q \in \mathbb{Q}^+$ that $\mu\hat{}(-eq) = B\mu\hat{}(eq)$ with $B := \mu\hat{}(-ep_0)/\mu\hat{}(ep_0)$. Obviously, $|B|=1$ by (10). □

Lemma 2. If $\mu \in \mathcal{M}_0(\mathbb{R}^N)$ with $\mu\hat{} \not\equiv 0$, then there exist $a,b \in \mathbb{N}$, $C_2 > 0$ with

$$|T^{\mu}_{an}h_n(x)| + |T^{\mu}_{bn}h_n(x)| \ge C_2 \qquad (x \in \mathbb{R}^N,\ n \in \mathbb{N}), \tag{18}$$

where $h_n \in C_{2\pi}^{\mathbb{R}}(\mathbb{R}^N)$ are given for some $e \in \mathbb{Z}^N$, $\varepsilon \in \{0,1\}$, $0 \leq \vartheta < \pi$ by

(19) $$h_n(x) := \sin(n<e,x> + \vartheta) + \varepsilon \cdot \cos(2n<e,x> + \vartheta).$$

Proof. Since $\mu\hat{} \not\equiv 0$, by Lemma 1a) there exist $e_0 \in \mathbb{Z}^N$, $a,b \in \mathbb{N}$ such that

(20) $$\mu\hat{}(2e_0/a)\mu\hat{}(e_0/b) \neq \mu\hat{}(e_0/a)\mu\hat{}(2e_0/b).$$

Let us first consider the case that (16) is valid for e_0. With $\varepsilon = 1$ and ϑ according to Lemma 1b) it follows that $F_a(y)$ and $F_b(y)$, where $y := n<e_o,x>$ and

$$F_c(y) := \mu\hat{}(e_0/c)\sin y + \mu\hat{}(2e_0/c)\cos 2y = e^{-i\vartheta}T^{\mu}_{cn}h_n(x),$$

do not have common zeros in view of (20). Therefore (18) for $e = e_0$ and

(21) $$C_2 = \inf\{|F_a(y)| + |F_b(y)|: x \in \mathbb{R}^N\} > 0.$$

On the other hand, if (16) is violated for e_0, there exist $e_1 \in \mathbb{Z}^N$, $a,b \in \mathbb{N}$ with

(22) $$\mu\hat{}(e_1/a)\mu\hat{}(-e_1/b) \neq \mu\hat{}(-e_1/a)\mu\hat{}(e_1/b).$$

In this case set $\vartheta = \varepsilon = 0$. By (22) $F_a(y)$ and $F_b(y)$, where now $y:=n<e_1,x>$ and

$$2F_c(y) := \mu\hat{}(e_1/c)e^{iy} - \mu\hat{}(-e_1/c)e^{-iy} = 2i\, T^{\mu}_{cn}h_n(x),$$

do not have common zeros so that (18) for $e = e_1$ follows with C_2, given by (21). □

Proof of Theorem 2b). With the quantities of Lemma 2 set $\sigma(t) = t^r$, $\varphi_n = n^{-r}$,

$$T_n f = \inf\{|T^{\mu}_{an}f(x)|+|T^{\mu}_{bn}f(x)|: x \in \mathbb{R}^N\}, \qquad U_t f = \omega_r(f,t).$$

Of course, $g_n = h_n$ satisfy (1),(4) as well as (2) by (18). Moreover, one obtains (3) analogously to (14). Now Theorem 1 (cf.(7)) ensures the existence of $f_\omega \in \mathrm{Lip}_r(\omega, C_{2\pi}^{\mathbb{R}})$ with

$$\limsup_{n\to\infty} [|T^{\mu}_{an}f_\omega(x)|+|T^{\mu}_{bn}f_\omega(x)|]/\omega(n^{-r}) \geq 2,$$

simultaneously for each $x \in \mathbb{R}^N$, which finally yields (13). □

Turning to the spaces C_0, we cannot immediately proceed as for Theorem 2, since C_0 does not contain the trigonometric test elements. Indeed, instead of (12) we now make use of the rate of convergence (23) on the subset $C_{00}^{\infty} \subset C_0^{\mathbb{R}}$ of functions, which have compact support and continuous partial derivatives of all orders.

Theorem 3. Let $\mu \in \mathcal{M}_0(\mathbb{R}^N)$ with $\mu^{\wedge} \not\equiv 0$ be such that

$$\|T_n^{\mu} g\| = \mathcal{O}(n^{-r}) \qquad (g \in C_{00}^{\infty}(\mathbb{R}^N)) \tag{23}$$

for some $r \in \mathbb{N}$. Then for each modulus ω there exists a counterexample $f_\omega \in \mathrm{Lip}_r(\omega, C_0^{\mathbb{R};\mathbb{C}}(\mathbb{R}^N))$ such that (13) holds true simultaneously for each $x \in \mathbb{R}^N$.

Proof. Choose $H \in C_{00}^{\infty}$ such that $H(x) = 1$ for $|x| \le 1$ and $0 \le H(x) \le 1$ for $x \in \mathbb{R}^N$, and proceed as for the proof of Theorem 2, but with

$$g_n(x) = H(x/n)h_n(x), \qquad T_n f = \inf\{|T_{an}^{\mu} f(x)| + |T_{bn}^{\mu} f(x)| : |x| \le n-1\},$$

using the quantities of Lemma 2 in order to indicate some details for the, e.g., real–valued case. Then $g_n \in C_{00}^{\infty}$ satisfy (1),(4) as well as (3) in view of (23) (cf.(14)). Concerning (2), let $|x| \le n-1$. Then by (18)

$$|T_{an}^{\mu} g_n(x)| + |T_{bn}^{\mu} g_n(x)| \ge C_2 - 8(2\pi)^{-N} \int_{|u| \ge n} |d\mu(u)| = C_2 - o(1),$$

independent of $|x| \le n-1$. Hence Theorem 1 yields the assertion. □

Finally, let us treat the subclass $\overset{*}{\mathcal{M}}_0(\mathbb{R}^N) \subset \mathcal{M}_0(\mathbb{R}^N)$ of generating measures of product type $\mu = \delta - \bigotimes_{j=1}^{N} \nu$, where δ ist the Dirac measure on $\mathbb{R}^N$, ν is a real–valued, bounded measure on $\mathbb{R}^1$ with $\nu^{\wedge}(0) = 1$, and $\bigotimes_{j=1}^{N} \nu$ denotes the N–dimensional (tensor) product measure of ν on $\mathbb{R}^N$. Correspondingly, smoothness is now measured by the sum of the partial moduli of continuity, thus by

$$\overline{\omega}_r(f,t) := \sum_{j=1}^{N} \sup\{\|\Sigma_{k=0}^{r} (-1)^{r-k}\tbinom{r}{k} f(x_1,..,x_j+kh_j,..,x_N)\| : h_j \in \mathbb{R}, |h_j| \le t\}.$$

Theorem 4. Let $\mu \in \overset{*}{\mathcal{M}}_0(\mathbb{R}^N)$ with $\mu^\wedge \not\equiv 0$ and with associated measure ν, satisfying

$$1 - \nu^\wedge(s) = \mathcal{O}(|s|^r) \qquad (s \in \mathbb{R}, s \to 0) \tag{24}$$

for some $r \in \mathbb{N}$. Then for each modulus ω there exists $f_\omega \in C_{2\pi}^{\mathbb{R};\mathbb{C}}(\mathbb{R}^N)$ with

$$\overline{\omega}_r(f_\omega, t) = \mathcal{O}(\omega(t^r)) \qquad (t \to 0+) \tag{25}$$

for which (13) holds true simultaneously for each $x \in \mathbb{R}^N$.

Proof. Since $1 - \Pi_{j=1}^N a_j = (1-a_1)+a_1(1-a_2)+\ldots+a_1a_2..a_{N-1}(1-a_N)$, by (24)

$$|\mu^\wedge(v_1,..,v_N)| = |1 - \prod_{j=1}^N \nu^\wedge(v_j)| \le \sum_{j=1}^N (\|\nu^\wedge\|+1)^N |1-\nu^\wedge(v_j)| = \mathcal{O}(|v|^r)$$

so that the assumption (12) of Theorem 2 is fulfilled which yields (13) for a counterexample $f_\omega \in \mathrm{Lip}_r(\omega, C_{2\pi}^{\mathbb{R};\mathbb{C}})$. Since $\overline{\omega}_r(f,t) \le N\, \omega_r(f,t)$, one also has (25). □

References

1. Dickmeis,W.,Nessel,R.J.,van Wickeren,E.(1985) On nonlinear condensation principles with rates. Manuscripta Math. 52, 1–20.

2. Dickmeis,W.,Nessel,R.J.,van Wickeren,E.(1986) A nonlinear quantitative resonance principle with applications to pointwise approximation. In: Alfred Haar memorial conference, pp.289–302. J. Szabados and K. Tandori, eds. (North–Holland, Amsterdam).

3. Kirchhoff,N.,Nessel,R.J.,van Wickeren,E. Quantitative condensation of singularities for convolution processes of Fejér–type.(to appear).

4. Shapiro,H.S. (1971) Topics in approximation theory (Springer, Berlin).

N. Kirchhoff, R.J. Nessel, Lehrstuhl A für Mathematik, RWTH Aachen, Templergraben 55, D–5100 Aachen, FRG.

International Series of
Numerical Mathematics, Vol. 90

ON MULTIDIMENSIONAL LEBESGUE-STIELTJES CONVOLUTION OPERATORS

Burkhard Lenze
Fachbereich Mathematik und Informatik, FernUniversität Hagen, FRG

Abstract

In this paper we will construct simple and efficient Lebesgue-Stieltjes type convolution operators for multidimensional approximation of functions of bounded variation. We will work out their basic properties including a sharp result concerning local approximation and will take a look at their behaviour when applied to some special functions.

1. Introduction

Before we can properly motivate the purpose of our approach to multidimensional Lebesgue-Stieltjes convolution operators we need a few introductory definitions dealing with special onedimensional kernel functions.

Definition 1.1. In the following we denote by $(D_\rho)_{\rho\geq\rho_o}$ a family of onedimensional kernel functions satisfying:
(a) Each D_ρ , $\rho \geq \rho_o$, is an even function defined on the whole real line.
(b) Each D_ρ , $\rho \geq \rho_o$, is Lebesgue integrable on $\mathbb{R}$ with $\int_{-\infty}^{\infty} D_\rho(t)dt = 1$.
(c) The family $(D_\rho)_{\rho\geq\rho_o}$ satisfies the approximate identity conditions, i.e., there exists a fixed constant $M > 0$ with $\int_{-\infty}^{\infty} \mid D_\rho(t) \mid dt \leq M$, $\rho \geq \rho_o$, and for each $\epsilon > 0$ we have $\lim_{\rho\to\infty} \int_{|t|>\epsilon} \mid D_\rho(t) \mid dt = 0$.

In connection with the kernel family $(D_\rho)_{\rho\geq\rho_o}$ we also consider the corresponding family $(I_\rho)_{\rho\geq\rho_o}$ of integral functions,

$$I_\rho(x) := \int_0^x D_\rho(t)dt \quad , \quad x \in \mathbb{R} \quad , \quad \rho \geq \rho_o \ . \tag{1.1}$$

Because of the properties of $(D_\rho)_{\rho\geq\rho_o}$ fixed above we immediately obtain for $(I_\rho)_{\rho\geq\rho_o}$:
(a) Each I_ρ , $\rho \geq \rho_o$, is absolutely continuous on $\mathbb{R}$.
(b) Each I_ρ , $\rho \geq \rho_o$, is normalized via $I_\rho(-\infty) = -\frac{1}{2}$ and $I_\rho(\infty) = \frac{1}{2}$, $\rho \geq \rho_o$.
(c) The family $(I_\rho)_{\rho\geq\rho_o}$ satisfies $\lim_{\rho\to\infty} I_\rho(x) = -\frac{1}{2}$, $x < 0$, $I_\rho(0) = 0$, $\rho \geq \rho_o$, and $\lim_{\rho\to\infty} I_\rho(x) = \frac{1}{2}$, $x > 0$.

After these preliminaries we are now able to carry over to our initial problem. It is well-known that in the onedimensional case $(n = 1)$ the family $(D_\rho)_{\rho\geq\rho_o}$ generates a family of operators $(\Lambda_\rho)_{\rho\geq\rho_o}$,

$$\Lambda_\rho(f)(x) := \int_{-\infty}^{\infty} D_\rho(t-x)f(t)dt \quad , \quad x \in \mathbb{R} \quad , \quad \rho \geq \rho_o \ , \tag{1.2}$$

whose approximation properties are almost entirely understood (see for example [13], [4], and [5]). Since in this paper we are only interested in functions of bounded variation we propose $f \in BV(\mathbb{R})$ and may rewrite (1.2) by means of integration by parts as $\Lambda_\rho(f)(x) = \frac{1}{2}(f(-\infty) +$

$f(\infty)) - \int_{-\infty}^{\infty} I_\rho(t-x)df(t)$. We conclude that under the regularity condition $\lim_{x\to-\infty} f(x) = \lim_{x\to\infty} f(x) = 0$ the precise analogue of (1.2) in terms of Lebesgue-Stieltjes convolutions on $BV(\mathbb{R})$ is given by

$$\Omega_\rho(f)(x) := (-1)\int_{-\infty}^{\infty} I_\rho(t-x)df(t) \quad , \quad x \in \mathbb{R} \quad , \quad \rho \geq \rho_o \ . \tag{1.3}$$

While in the onedimensional case there are no difficulties in carrying over to Lebesgue-Stieltjes convolutions, the multidimensional case $(n > 1)$ seems to be more complicated. On the one hand, it is again well-known that in many cases the so-called corresponding radial kernels of $(D_\rho)_{\rho\geq\rho_o}$ generate approximation operators $(\Lambda_\rho)_{\rho\geq\rho_o}$,

$$\Lambda_\rho(f)(x) := (d_\rho^{(n)})^{-1}\int_{\mathbb{R}^n} D_\rho\left(\sqrt{\sum_{k=1}^{n}(t_k - x_k)^2}\right) f(t)dt \quad , \quad x \in \mathbb{R}^n \quad , \quad \rho \geq \rho_o \ , \tag{1.4}$$

with $d_\rho^{(n)} := \int_{\mathbb{R}^n} D_\rho\left(\sqrt{\sum_{k=1}^{n}(t_k)^2}\right) dt$, $\rho \geq \rho_o$, which have nice approximation properties under appropriate assumptions on $f : \mathbb{R}^n \to \mathbb{R}$ (see for example [1], [12], [3], [10], and [2]). However, as far as we know, nothing is known about the canonical counterpart of (1.4) in terms of Lebesgue-Stieltjes convolutions if functions of bounded variation on $\mathbb{R}^n$ are considered. It is the aim of this paper to show that under the regularity condition $\lim_{|x|\to\infty} f(x) = 0$ the "right" analogue of (1.4) in terms of Lebesgue-Stieltjes convolutions on $BV(\mathbb{R}^n)$ is given by

$$\Omega_\rho(f)(x) := (-1)^n 2^{1-n}\int_{\mathbb{R}^n} I_\rho(\prod_{k=1}^{n}(t_k - x_k))df(t) \quad , \quad x \in \mathbb{R}^n \quad , \quad \rho \geq \rho_o \ . \tag{1.5}$$

This result may be read as follows: In case of usual approximation operators of convolution type (1.4) the appropriate argument of the <u>distribution kernels</u> is the <u>radial</u> argument $\sqrt{\sum_{k=1}^{n}(t_k - x_k)^2}$ vanishing precisely at the <u>point</u> $t = x$. In case of approximation operators of Lebesgue-Stieltjes convolution type (1.5) the appropriate argument of the <u>integral kernels</u> is the <u>hyperbolic</u> argument $\prod_{k=1}^{n}(t_k - x_k)$ vanishing precisely on the whole <u>hyperstar</u> $H(x)$,

$$H(x) := \bigcup_{k=1}^{n}\{t \in \mathbb{R}^n \mid t_k = x_k\} \ . \tag{1.6}$$

Therefore, only in case $n = 1$ the arguments have equal absolute value, and point and hyperstar coincide implying the identity between (1.2) and (1.3) while in case $n > 1$ the arguments are essentially different and, therefore, no simple (equality) relation holds between (1.4) and (1.5), any longer.

2. Some facts about $BV(\mathbb{R}^n)$

First of all, we note some well-known facts concerning monotone functions and functions of bounded variation on $\mathbb{R}^n$ and the so-called Lebesgue-Stieltjes integral induced by them (for details we refer to the classical books of KAMKE [7], MCSHANE [9], and SAKS [11]).

For $a, b, x \in \mathbb{R}^n$ with $a \leq b$ (i.e., $a_i \leq b_i$, $1 \leq i \leq n$) we define

$$(a,b) := \{x \in \mathbb{R}^n \mid a_i < x_i < b_i \ , \ 1 \leq i \leq n\} \ , \tag{2.1}$$

$$[a,b] := \{x \in \mathbb{R}^n \mid a_i \leq x_i \leq b_i \ , \ 1 \leq i \leq n\} \ , \tag{2.2}$$

$$Cor[a,b] := \{x \in \mathbb{R}^n \mid x_i = a_i \vee x_i = b_i \ , \ 1 \leq i \leq n\} \ , \tag{2.3}$$

$$\gamma(x,a) := |\{i \in \{1,...,n\} \mid x_i = a_i\}| \ . \tag{2.4}$$

In (2.4) $|\cdot|$ denotes the number of distinct elements of the set under consideration. Now, for a given function $f : \mathbb{R}^n \to \mathbb{R}$ the so-called corresponding interval function $\triangle_f$ of f is defined for all bounded intervals $[a,b] \subset \mathbb{R}^n$ by

$$\triangle_f[a,b] := \sum_{x \in Cor[a,b]} (-1)^{\gamma(x,a)} f(x) \ . \tag{2.5}$$

In case $n = 1$ definition (2.5) reduces to $\triangle_f[a,b] = f(b) - f(a) = f(b_1) - f(a_1)$ and in case $n = 2$ to $\triangle_f[a,b] = f(b_1,b_2) - f(b_1,a_2) - f(a_1,b_2) + f(a_1,a_2)$. Let us note that the interval function $\triangle_f$ is known to be additive, i.e., $[a,b] = [a^{(1)},b^{(1)}] \cup [a^{(2)},b^{(2)}]$, $(a^{(1)},b^{(1)}) \cap (a^{(2)},b^{(2)}) = \emptyset$, implies $\triangle_f[a,b] = \triangle_f[a^{(1)},b^{(1)}] + \triangle_f[a^{(2)},b^{(2)}]$. Now we are prepared to give the following basic definition.

Definition 2.1. A function $f : \mathbb{R}^n \to \mathbb{R}$ is called
- monotone increasing (decreasing) on $\mathbb{R}^n$, if for all $[a,b] \subset \mathbb{R}^n$ we have $\triangle_f[a,b] \geq 0$ (≤ 0) ,
- of (uniform) bounded variation on $\mathbb{R}^n$ (shortly: $f \in BV(\mathbb{R}^n)$), if there exists a constant $K > 0$ such that the interval function $\bar{\triangle}_f$ defined for all $[a,b] \subset \mathbb{R}^n$ by

$$\begin{aligned}\bar{\triangle}_f[a,b] := \sup\Big\{ \sum_{i=1}^{r} |\triangle_f[a^{(i)},b^{(i)}]| : \Big([a^{(i)},b^{(i)}] \subset [a,b], \\ (a^{(i)},b^{(i)}) \cap (a^{(j)},b^{(j)}) = \emptyset, i \neq j\Big) \ , \ 1 \leq i,j \leq r, \ r \in \mathbb{N} \Big\}\end{aligned} \tag{2.6}$$

satisfies the inequality $\sup\{\bar{\triangle}_f[a,b] \mid [a,b] \subset \mathbb{R}^n\} \leq K$.

It can be easily shown that in case of $f \in BV(\mathbb{R}^n)$ the interval function $\bar{\triangle}_f$ defined in (2.6) is additive and nonnegative. Moreover, the same is true for the interval functions $\triangle_{P_f}$ and $\triangle_{N_f}$ induced by f via

$$\triangle_{P_f}[a,b] := \frac{1}{2}(\bar{\triangle}_f[a,b] + \triangle_f[a,b]) \ , \quad [a,b] \subset \mathbb{R}^n \ , \tag{2.7}$$

$$\triangle_{N_f}[a,b] := \frac{1}{2}(\bar{\triangle}_f[a,b] - \triangle_f[a,b]) \ , \quad [a,b] \subset \mathbb{R}^n \ . \tag{2.8}$$

Therefore, we have the so-called Jordan decomposition of $\triangle_f$ into the difference of two nonnegative interval functions $\triangle_{P_f}$ and $\triangle_{N_f}$, $\triangle_f[a,b] = \triangle_{P_f}[a,b] - \triangle_{N_f}[a,b]$, $[a,b] \subset \mathbb{R}^n$.
At this point we remember that any nonnegative additive interval function $\triangle$ implies an outer (Carathéodory) measure $m^*_\triangle$ on $\mathbb{R}^n$ if we define

$$m^*_\triangle(M) := \inf\Big\{ \sum_{i=1}^{r} \triangle[a^{(i)},b^{(i)}] \mid M \subset \bigcup_{i=1}^{r}(a^{(i)},b^{(i)}) \ , \ r \in \mathbb{N} \cup \{\infty\} \Big\} \tag{2.9}$$

for $\emptyset \neq M \subset \mathbb{R}^n$ and $m^*_\triangle(\emptyset) := 0$. As usual, the σ-algebra of sets $M \subset \mathbb{R}^n$ satisfying $m^*_\triangle(N) = m^*_\triangle(N \cap M) + m^*_\triangle(N \setminus M)$, $N \subset \mathbb{R}^n$, is called the set of measurable sets with respect to $m^*_\triangle$ (or $m_\triangle$) and the set function $m_\triangle$ defined for all these sets $M \subset \mathbb{R}^n$ by $m_\triangle(M) := m^*_\triangle(M)$ is refered to as the (Carathéodory) measure induced by $\triangle$. Now, we return to an arbitrary function $f \in BV(\mathbb{R}^n)$. As shown above the (i.g. signed) finite measure m_f ,

$$m_f := m_{\triangle_{P_f}} - m_{\triangle_{N_f}} \ , \tag{2.10}$$

is well-defined on the σ-algebra of sets measurable with respect to $m_{P_f} := m_{\triangle_{P_f}}$ and $m_{N_f} := m_{\triangle_{N_f}}$. The measure m_f is called Lebesgue-Stieltjes measure induced by f and the corresponding integral is refered to as the Lebesgue-Stieltjes integral with respect to f . For any function $g : \mathbb{R}^n \to \mathbb{R}$ integrable with respect to m_f (i.e., with respect to m_{P_f} and m_{N_f}) we define

$$\int_{\mathbb{R}^n} g(t)df(t) := \int_{\mathbb{R}^n} g(t)dm_f(t) := \int_{\mathbb{R}^n} g(t)dm_{P_f}(t) - \int_{\mathbb{R}^n} g(t)dm_{N_f}(t) \quad . \tag{2.11}$$

Now, the Lebesgue-Stieltjes measure and integral induced by $f \in BV(\mathbb{R}^n)$ may be treated by standard measure and integration techniques. We finish our introduction to $BV(\mathbb{R}^n)$ with a Lebesgue-Stieltjes specific result which will be used, later.

Lemma 2.1. Let $f : \mathbb{R}^n \to \mathbb{R}$ be monotone increasing on $\mathbb{R}^n$ and $[a,b] \subset \mathbb{R}^n$. Then we have the inequality $m_f((a,b)) \leq \triangle_f[a,b] \leq m_f([a,b])$.

Proof: Compare [11], p. 68.

□

3. The operators and their basic properties

In the introduction the operators $(\Omega_\rho)_{\rho\geq\rho_o}$ were already defined in (1.5) without having any precise definition of integration with respect to $f \in BV(\mathbb{R}^n)$. Now, as we are familiar with $BV(\mathbb{R}^n)$ and the Lebesgue-Stieltjes integral induced by it we return to (1.5) in a more serious way. In the following $(D_\rho)_{\rho\geq\rho_o}$ and $(I_\rho)_{\rho\geq\rho_o}$ always denote a family of distribution resp. integral kernels satisfying the conditions given in the introduction.

Theorem 3.1. For $f \in BV(\mathbb{R}^n)$ with $\lim_{|t|\to\infty} f(t) = 0$ the operators

$$\Omega_\rho(f)(x) := (-1)^n 2^{1-n} \int_{\mathbb{R}^n} I_\rho\Big(\prod_{k=1}^{n}(t_k - x_k)\Big)df(t) \quad , \quad x \in \mathbb{R}^n \quad , \quad \rho \geq \rho_o \quad , \tag{3.1}$$

are well-defined and map into the space $C(\mathbb{R}^n)$ of continuous functions on $\mathbb{R}^n$. Moreover, they are linear and – with $M > 0$ given by Definition 1.1 (c) – they are bounded via

$$\sup_{x\in\mathbb{R}^n} |\Omega_\rho(f)(x)| \leq 2^{-n}M \sup_{[a,b]\subset\mathbb{R}^n} \bar{\triangle}_f[a,b] \quad . \tag{3.2}$$

Proof: Since the integral kernels $(I_\rho)_{\rho\geq\rho_o}$ are continuous and bounded by $\frac{M}{2}$ it is immediately clear that the operators $(\Omega_\rho)_{\rho\geq\rho_o}$ are well-defined and map into $C(\mathbb{R}^n)$. Moreover, their linearity is an easy consequence of the linearity of the Lebesgue-Stieltjes integral with respect to the integrator function (cf. [7], p. 148 (s), or [9], p. 270, essentially). Finally, their boundedness follows from $|I_\rho(\xi)| \leq \frac{M}{2}$, $\xi \in \mathbb{R}$, $\rho \geq \rho_o$, and [7], p. 141 (a) and p. 142 (g), for example.

□

In the following, we will consider the local approximation properties of the operators $(\Omega_\rho)_{\rho\geq\rho_o}$. To do this, we first of all need some definitions. From now on let

$$z^{(s)} := (z_1^{(s)}, \ldots, z_n^{(s)}) \quad , \quad 1 \leq s \leq 2^n \quad , \tag{3.3}$$

denote the 2^n distinct vectors out of $\mathbb{R}^n$ satisfying

$$\begin{aligned} &|z_k^{(s)}| = 1 \ , \ 1 \leq k \leq n \ , \ \text{and} \ \prod_{k=1}^{n} z_k^{(s)} = 1 \quad , \ 1 \leq s \leq 2^{n-1} \ , \\ &|z_k^{(s)}| = 1 \ , \ 1 \leq k \leq n \ , \ \text{and} \ \prod_{k=1}^{n} z_k^{(s)} = -1 \quad , \ 2^{n-1} < s \leq 2^n \ . \end{aligned} \tag{3.4}$$

For any fixed $x \in \mathbb{R}^n$ we define the open resp. closed quadrants of x with respect to $z^{(s)}$ by

$$\begin{aligned} Q^o(x, z^{(s)}) &:= \{t \in \mathbb{R}^n \mid (t_k - x_k)z_k^{(s)} > 0 \ , \ 1 \leq k \leq n\} \quad , \ 1 \leq s \leq 2^n \ , \\ Q(x, z^{(s)}) &:= \{t \in \mathbb{R}^n \mid (t_k - x_k)z_k^{(s)} \geq 0 \ , \ 1 \leq k \leq n\} \quad , \ 1 \leq s \leq 2^n \ , \end{aligned} \tag{3.5}$$

(see for example [15] in view of definition (3.5)). By means of (3.5) we finally introduce the so-called positive resp. negative open resp. closed sets of quadrants of x by

$$\begin{aligned} Q^o_+(x) &:= \bigcup_{s=1}^{2^{n-1}} Q^o(x, z^{(s)}) \ , \qquad Q_+(x) := \bigcup_{s=1}^{2^{n-1}} Q(x, z^{(s)}) \ , \\ Q^o_-(x) &:= \bigcup_{s=2^{n-1}+1}^{2^n} Q^o(x, z^{(s)}) \ , \quad Q_-(x) := \bigcup_{s=2^{n-1}+1}^{2^n} Q(x, z^{(s)}) \ . \end{aligned} \tag{3.6}$$

Lemma 3.1. Let $f \in BV(\mathbb{R}^n)$ with $\lim_{|t|\to\infty} f(t) = 0$ be given. Then for all $x \in \mathbb{R}^n$ and all $s \in \{1, 2, \ldots, 2^n\}$ we have:

$$\lim_{\substack{t\to x\\ t\in Q^o(x,z^{(s)})}} f(t) = (-1)^n \left(\prod_{k=1}^n z_k^{(s)}\right) m_f(Q^o(x, z^{(s)})) \ . \tag{3.7}$$

Proof: Let $x \in \mathbb{R}^n$ and $s \in \{1, \ldots, 2^n\}$ be given and $m_f = m_{P_f} - m_{N_f}$ the decomposition of m_f according to (2.10). Now, for each $\alpha > 0$ and each $t \in Q^o(x, z^{(s)})$ we consider the cubes

$$W_{s,\alpha}(t) := [\min\{t, t + \alpha z^{(s)}\}, \max\{t, t + \alpha z^{(s)}\}] \tag{3.8}$$

and their interior $W^o_{s,\alpha}(t) = (\min\{t, t + \alpha z^{(s)}\}, \max\{t, t + \alpha z^{(s)}\})$.
By means of the Jordan decomposition of $\triangle_f$ and Lemma 2.1 we immediately get the inequality

$$\begin{aligned} & m_{P_f}(W^o_{s,\alpha}(t)) - m_{N_f}(W_{s,\alpha}(t)) \\ & \quad \le \triangle_f[\min\{t, t + \alpha z^{(s)}\}, \max\{t, t + \alpha z^{(s)}\}] \le \\ & \qquad m_{P_f}(W_{s,\alpha}(t)) - m_{N_f}(W^o_{s,\alpha}(t)) \ . \end{aligned} \tag{3.9}$$

For $\alpha \to \infty$ we have $\lim_{\alpha\to\infty} W_{s,\alpha}(t) = Q(t, z^{(s)})$ and $\lim_{\alpha\to\infty} W^o_{s,\alpha}(t) = Q^o(t, z^{(s)})$. Moreover, since $\lim_{|y|\to\infty} f(y) = 0$ we also get by means of (2.5)

$$\begin{aligned} & \lim_{\alpha\to\infty} \triangle_f[\min\{t, t + \alpha z^{(s)}\}, \max\{t, t + \alpha z^{(s)}\}] \\ & \quad = \lim_{\alpha\to\infty} \sum_{y\in Cor(W_{s,\alpha}(t))} (-1)^{\gamma(y,\min\{t,t+\alpha z^{(s)}\})} f(y) \\ & \quad = (-1)^n \left(\prod_{k=1}^n z_k^{(s)}\right) f(t) \ . \end{aligned} \tag{3.10}$$

Therefore, we conclude from (3.9) for $\alpha \to \infty$:

$$m_{P_f}(Q^o(t, z^{(s)})) - m_{N_f}(Q(t, z^{(s)})) \le (-1)^n \left(\prod_{k=1}^n z_k^{(s)}\right) f(t) \le m_{P_f}(Q(t, z^{(s)})) - m_{N_f}(Q^o(t, z^{(s)})) \ .$$

If we now make use of the set identities

$$\lim_{\substack{t\to x\\ t\in Q^o(x,z^{(s)})}} Q(t, z^{(s)}) = Q^o(x, z^{(s)}) = \lim_{\substack{t\to x\\ t\in Q^o(x,z^{(s)})}} Q^o(t, z^{(s)}) \ , \tag{3.11}$$

we obtain from the above inequality for $t \to x$, $t \in Q^o(x, z^{(s)})$:

$$m_{P_f}(Q^o(x, z^{(s)})) - m_{N_f}(Q^o(x, z^{(s)})) = (-1)^n \left(\prod_{k=1}^n z_k^{(s)}\right) \lim_{\substack{t\to x\\ t\in Q^o(x,z^{(s)})}} f(t) \ , \tag{3.12}$$

which implies (3.7) by means of (2.10).

□

With the help of the above lemma we are now able to compute the Lebesgue-Stieltjes measure of the positive resp. negative open quadrants defined by (3.6).

Lemma 3.2. Let $f \in BV(\mathbb{R}^n)$ with $\lim_{|t|\to\infty} f(t) = 0$ be given. Then for all $x \in \mathbb{R}^n$ we have:

(a)

$$m_f(Q^o_+(x)) = (-1)^n \sum_{s=1}^{2^{n-1}} \lim_{\substack{t\to x \\ t\in Q^o(x,z^{(s)})}} f(t) \ , \tag{3.13}$$

(b)

$$m_f(Q^o_-(x)) = (-1)^{n+1} \sum_{s=2^{n-1}+1}^{2^n} \lim_{\substack{t\to x \\ t\in Q^o(x,z^{(s)})}} f(t) \ . \tag{3.14}$$

Proof: Let $x \in \mathbb{R}^n$ be given. The identities (3.13) and (3.14) follow immediately by means of (3.4) – (3.7) and the additivity of the Lebesgue-Stieltjes measure.

□

Now, we are prepared to return to our operators $(\Omega_\rho)_{\rho\geq\rho_o}$ and to prove the following theorem describing their precise local approximation properties. For the corresponding result in case of usual multivariate convolution operators see [1], p. 191, Theorem 57.

Theorem 3.2. Let $f \in BV(\mathbb{R}^n)$ with $\lim_{|t|\to\infty} f(t) = 0$ be given. Then for all $x \in \mathbb{R}^n$ the operators $(\Omega_\rho)_{\rho\geq\rho_o}$ satisfy

$$\lim_{\rho\to\infty} \Omega_\rho(f)(x) = 2^{-n} \sum_{s=1}^{2^n} \lim_{\substack{t\to x \\ t\in Q^o(x,z^{(s)})}} f(t) \ . \tag{3.15}$$

Especially, if $x \in \mathbb{R}^n$ is a point of continuity of f we have $\lim_{\rho\to\infty} \Omega_\rho(f)(x) = f(x)$.

Proof: Let $x \in \mathbb{R}^n$ be given. By means of the definitions given in the introduction the integral kernels $(I_\rho)_{\rho\geq\rho_o}$ satisfy

$$\lim_{\rho\to\infty} I_\rho(\prod_{k=1}^n (t_k - x_k)) = \left\{ \begin{array}{ccc} \frac{1}{2} & \text{for} & t \in Q^o_+(x) \\ 0 & \text{for} & t \in H(x) \\ -\frac{1}{2} & \text{for} & t \in Q^o_-(x) \end{array} \right\} \ . \tag{3.16}$$

If we now apply the dominated convergence theorem for Lebesgue-Stieltjes integrals (cf. [7], p. 146 (o), for example) we obtain by means of Lemma 3.2:

$$\begin{aligned} \lim_{\rho\to\infty} \Omega_\rho(f)(x) &= \lim_{\rho\to\infty} (-1)^n 2^{1-n} \int_{\mathbb{R}^n} I_\rho(\prod_{k=1}^n (t_k - x_k)) df(t) \\ &= (-1)^n 2^{-n} (m_f(Q^o_+(x)) - m_f(Q^o_-(x))) \\ &= 2^{-n} \sum_{s=1}^{2^n} \lim_{\substack{t\to x \\ t\in Q^o(x,z^{(s)})}} f(t) \ . \end{aligned} \tag{3.17}$$

□

Remarks.

(1) It can be shown that under the given presuppositions (3.15) is equal to $f(x)$ at least for almost all $x \in \mathbb{R}^n$ (for details cf. [8]).

(2) We point to the fact that the condition $\lim_{|t|\to\infty} f(t) = 0$ is essential for $f \in BV(\mathbb{R}^n)$ to have limits as considered in (3.7) (and (3.15)). In fact, there are functions $g \in BV(\mathbb{R}^n)$ not vanishing at infinity for which the limits as considered in (3.7) do not exist at any point $x \in \mathbb{R}^n$ (see also [15] and [8] in this context).

(3) Since Freud's pioneering paper [6] it is well-known that in case of one-sided approximation it is very helpful to have a Jordan typ decomposition of the functions to be approximated. Therefore, it should be possible to develop an applicable strategy for multidimensional one-sided constructive approximation of functions belonging to $BV(\mathbb{R}^n)$. This idea – including local, global, and

saturation type results based on a $BV(\mathbb{R}^n)$-specific hyperbolic-type modulus of smoothness – has been worked out in [8].

4. Examples

In this last section we apply the classical radial Gauß-Weierstraß operators Λ_ρ and the associated hyperbolic Gauß-Weierstraß operators Ω_ρ (set $D_\rho(t) := \sqrt{\frac{\rho}{\pi}} e^{-\rho t^2}$, $\rho \geq 1$) in case $n = 2$ to approximate the radial symmetric sigmoidal function $s(x_1, x_2) := 1 - (1 + 2e^{-3(\sqrt{x_1^2+x_2^2}-6.7)})^{-\frac{1}{2}}$ and the nonsymmetric piecewise bilinear rough model function f as shown below.

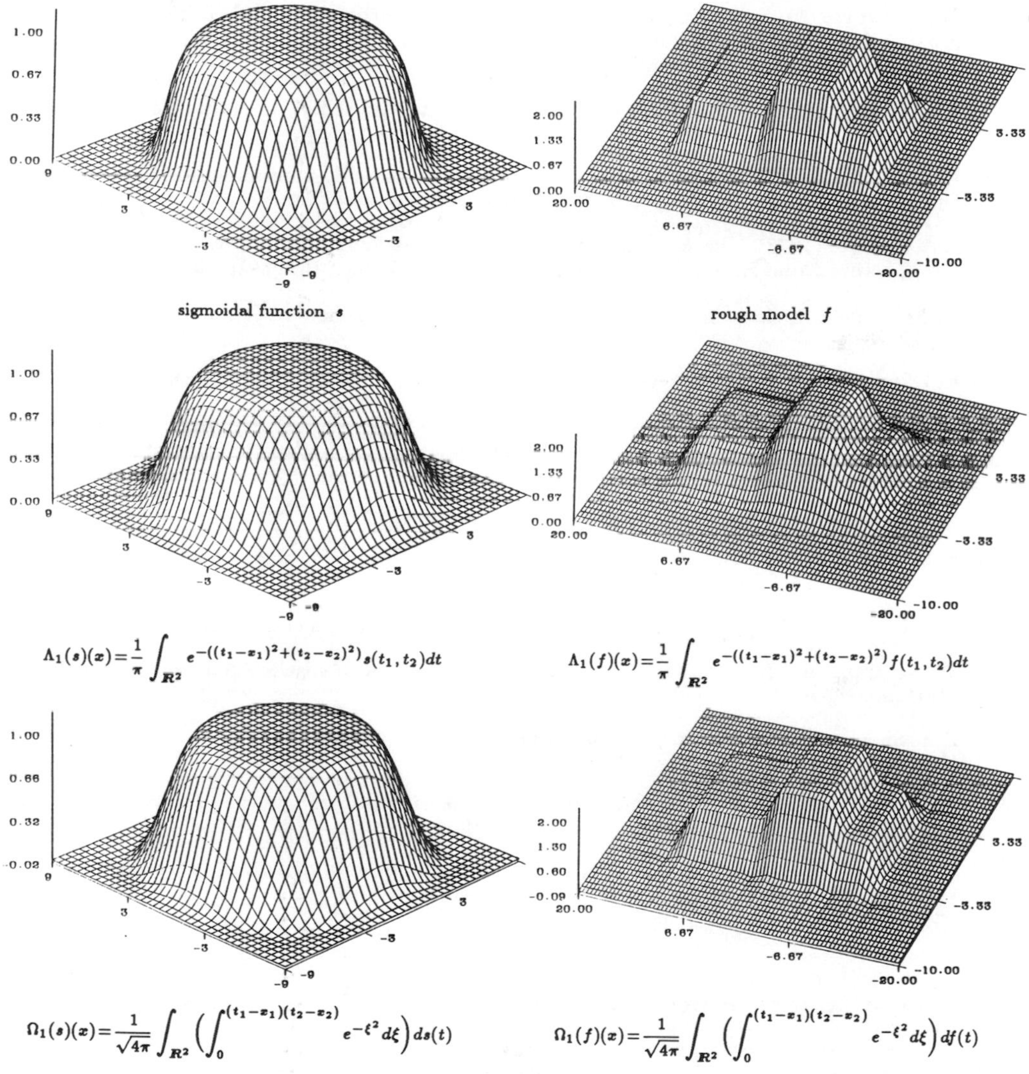

sigmoidal function s — rough model f

$\Lambda_1(s)(x) = \frac{1}{\pi} \int_{\mathbb{R}^2} e^{-((t_1-x_1)^2+(t_2-x_2)^2)} s(t_1, t_2) dt$ — $\Lambda_1(f)(x) = \frac{1}{\pi} \int_{\mathbb{R}^2} e^{-((t_1-x_1)^2+(t_2-x_2)^2)} f(t_1, t_2) dt$

$\Omega_1(s)(x) = \frac{1}{\sqrt{4\pi}} \int_{\mathbb{R}^2} \left(\int_0^{(t_1-x_1)(t_2-x_2)} e^{-\xi^2} d\xi \right) ds(t)$ — $\Omega_1(f)(x) = \frac{1}{\sqrt{4\pi}} \int_{\mathbb{R}^2} \left(\int_0^{(t_1-x_1)(t_2-x_2)} e^{-\xi^2} d\xi \right) df(t)$

Figure 1

Note that we have chosen the approximation parameter ρ equal to 1 and that the hyperbolic operator seems to be almost comparable to the radial operator in case of s while Ω_1 seems to have advantages in comparison with Λ_1 in case of f. We conjecture that the hyperbolic operators in general yield good approximation results when applied to functions with characteristic behaviour with respect to hyperplanes.

REFERENCES

[1] S. Bochner (1932), Vorlesungen über Fouriersche Integrale, Akademische Verlagsgesellschaft, Leipzig.

[2] J. Boman (1971), Saturation problems and distribution theory, published in: Topics in Approximation Theory, Lecture Notes in Mathematics Vol. 187 (Author: H.S. Shapiro), Springer-Verlag, Berlin–Heidelberg–New York, 1971, Appendix I, 249–266.

[3] P.L. Butzer and R.J. Nessel (1966), Contributions to the theory of saturation for singular integrals in several variables I, General Theory, Indag. Math. 28, Ser. A, 515–531.

[4] P.L. Butzer and R.J. Nessel (1971), Fourier Analysis and Approximation, Vol. I, One-Dimensional Theory, Birkhäuser Verlag, Basel–Stuttgart.

[5] R.A. DeVore (1972), The Approximation of Continuous Functions by Positive Linear Operators, Lecture Notes in Mathematics Vol. 293, Springer-Verlag, Berlin–Heidelberg–New York.

[6] G. Freud (1955), Über einseitige Approximation durch Polynome I, Acta Sci. Math. (Szeged) 16, 12–28.

[7] E. Kamke (1956), Das Lebesgue-Stieltjes Integral, B.G. Teubner Verlagsgesellschaft, Leipzig.

[8] B. Lenze (1989), Mehrdimensionale einseitige Approximationsoperatoren, Habilitationsschrift, under consideration at the Department of Mathematics and Computer Sciences of the Fern-University of Hagen.

[9] E.J. McShane (1974), Integration, Princeton University Press, Princeton, eighth edition.

[10] R.J. Nessel (1967), Contributions to the theory of saturation for singular integrals in several variables III, Radial Kernels, Indag. Math. 29, Ser. A, 65–73.

[11] S. Saks (1937), Theory of the Integral, Hafner Publishing Company, New York, second edition.

[12] W. Schempp and B. Dreseler (1980), Einführung in die harmonische Analyse, B.G. Teubner, Stuttgart.

[13] H.S. Shapiro (1969), Smoothing and Approximation of Functions, Van Nostrand Reinholt, New York.

[14] R.L. Wheeden and A. Zygmund (1977), Measure and Integral, Marcel Dekker, Inc., New York–Basel.

[15] W.H. Young and G.C. Young (1923), On the discontinuities of monotone functions of several variables, Proc. London Math. Soc. (2), 22, 124–142.

Dr. Burkhard Lenze, FernUniversität Hagen, Fb. Mathematik & Informatik, D-5800 Hagen, FRG

International Series of
Numerical Mathematics, Vol. 90

THE SINGULARITY OF DISTANCE MATRICES

William A. Light

Mathematics Department
University of Lancaster
Lancaster
England

1 Introduction

There has been a lot of interest recently in the problem of interpolation of data defined on $\mathbb{R}^n$ by radial basis functions. In its most elementary form the problem is as follows. Suppose $x_1, \ldots, x_m$ are given points in $\mathbb{R}^n$, and $\|\cdot\|$ is any norm on $\mathbb{R}^n$. Then a linear subspace of $C(\mathbb{R}^n)$ is defined as the span of the functions $h_i : \mathbb{R}^n \to \mathbb{R}$ where $h_i(x) = \|x - x_i\|$, $1 \leq i \leq m$. The interpolation problem is then to determine conditions on the points x_i such that for any m real numbers $d_1, \ldots, d_m$ there exist unique constants $c_1, \ldots, c_m$ such that

$$\sum_{i=1}^{m} c_i \|x_j - x_i\| = d_j, \quad j = 1, 2, \ldots, m.$$

Of course, the existence of a unique choice of the constants is equivalent to the invertibility of the 'distance' matrix A whose ijth element is $a_{ij} = \|x_i - x_j\|$. The first results in this area known to the author were those of Schoenberg [6], who was interested in the possibility of embedding metric spaces into Hilbert space. This question turns out to have a strong relationship to the question of the invertibility of the distance matrix for the metric space. If the norm is the usual Euclidean norm then Schoenberg proved that the distance matrix A is always invertible under the mild hypothesis that the points $x_1, \ldots, x_m$ are distinct. This result was subsequently greatly improved by Micchelli [5]. Independently, Baxter [1] and Sun [7] have shown that the same result holds for the p-norm when $1 < p < 2$. Baxter has also shown that if $2 < p < \infty$ then there is always a set of points in some space $\mathbb{R}^n$ for which the distance matrix is singular.

Our interest in this paper is the case when the norm is the l_1-norm. The following theorem is already known - see [3] for details of a rather more general version, and [4] for further results in the same vein.

Theorem 1.1 *Let $x_1, x_2, \ldots, x_m$ be distinct points in $\mathbb{R}^n$. Then the following are equivalent:*
(i) the distance matrix A, whose ijth element is $\|x_i - x_j\|_1$, is non-singular
(ii) the functions $\{h_1, h_2, \ldots, h_m\}$, where $h_i(x) = \|x - x_i\|_1$, are linearly independent.

If the points $x_1, x_2, \ldots x_m$ are contained in $\mathbb{R}^2$, then a natural geometric condition can be added to the above result. A *path* in $\mathbb{R}^2$ is an ordered set of points $[y_1, y_2, \ldots, y_r]$ such that the line segments joining consecutive points are of positive length, and are alternately horizontal and vertical. A path is said to be *closed* if $y_r \neq y_1$, and if the line segment joining y_1 with y_2 is perpendicular to the line segment joining y_r with y_1.

Theorem 1.2 *Let $x_1, x_2, \ldots, x_m$ be distinct points in $\mathbb{R}^2$. Then the following are equivalent:*
(i) the distance matrix A, whose ijth element is $\|x_i - x_j\|_1$, is non-singular
(ii) the points $\{x_1, x_2, \ldots, x_m\}$ do not contain a closed path.

This result is also from [3]. The natural question is 'What constitutes the analogue of a closed path in $\mathbb{R}^n$ for $n > 2$?' This paper answers this question, and illustrates this answer by verifying one half of theorem 1.1 for $n > 2$.

2 Multidimensional Paths

A definition of a multidimensional path was given in a completely different context in [2]. If the reader consults that paper carefully, he will find a number of ambiguities and faults in the formulation. Our approach uses the language of trees. We need to define P_j as the jth coordinate projection, so that if $x = (t_1, t_2, \ldots, t_n)$ in $\mathbb{R}^n$, then $P_j x = t_j$, $1 \leq j \leq n$. If e_j denotes the usual jth unit vector in $\mathbb{R}^n$ (all entries of e_j are zero except for a single unit entry at the jth position), then we define $Q_j : \mathbb{R}^n \to \mathbb{R}^n$ by $Q_j x = x - (P_j x) e_j$, $1 \leq j \leq n$.

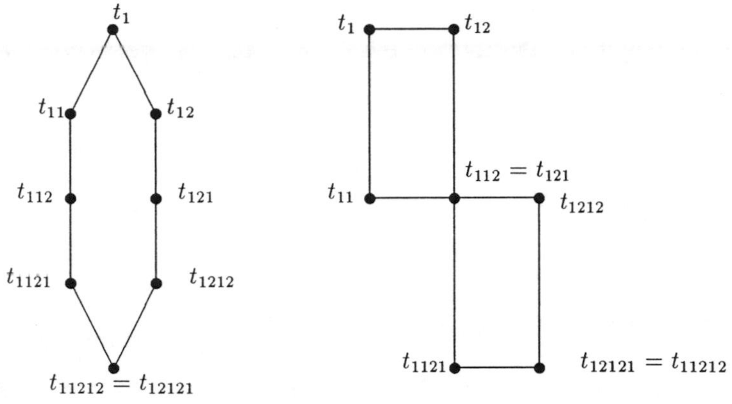

Figure 1: A two dimensional closed path and its corresponding tree.

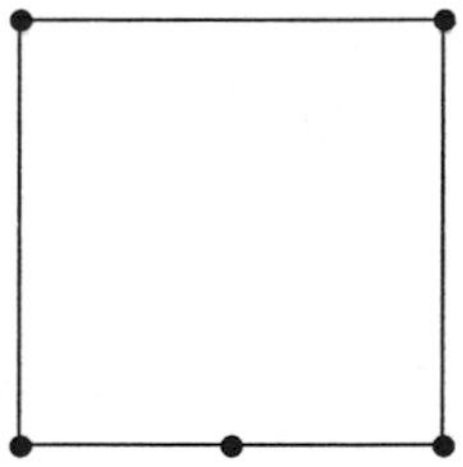

Figure 2: A set of points which does not form a closed path in $\mathbb{R}^2$.

Definition 2.1 *A closed path in $\mathbb{R}^n$ is a partially ordered set of points which can be viewed as a tree in the following way:*

(i) the first level of the tree consists of a single point t_1

(ii) each point in level k of the tree is labelled $t_{i_1,\dots,i_k}$, where $1 \le i_j \le n$ and $1 \le j \le k$

(iii) $Q_{i_k}(t_{i_1,\dots,i_k}) = Q_{i_k}(t_{i_1,\dots,i_{k-1}})$, $k = 2, 3, \dots$

(iv) to each point z in the tree there correspond points $z_1, \dots, z_n$ in either the succeeding or preceding level such that $Q_i z_i = Q_i z$, $1 \le i \le n$. The point z is then joined to each of $z_1, \dots, z_n$ by branches of the tree.

Definition 2.2 *Given a closed path represented by the tree T with r levels, the associated path functional is described by*

$$\Phi_T = \sum_{k=1}^{r} (-1)^k \sum \{\hat{t}_{i_1,\dots,i_k} : t_{i_1,\dots,i_k} \in T\}.$$

Here $\hat{t}_{i_1,\dots,i_k}$ represents the point-evaluation functional at $t_{i_1,\dots,i_k}$.

Before moving on to a discussion of multidimensional paths, we consider two special cases. First of all, the case $n = 2$ is particularly simple. The constraints on the tree for it to represent a closed path mean that each level contains two (not necessarily distinct) points, except for the first and last levels, which each contain one point. An example is illustrated in Figure 1.

Note that Figure 2 does *not* represent a closed path in $\mathbb{R}^2$, since there is no way of ordering the points so that all the conditions are satisfied. It does however, contain a closed path (the four points at the corners of the rectangle). Now suppose $w \in C(\mathbb{R}^2)$ depends only on the first variable and T is a tree representing a closed path in $\mathbb{R}^2$. Then if the tree has r levels,

$$\begin{aligned}\Phi_T(w) = -w(t_1) + w(t_{12}) &+ w(t_{11}) - w(t_{121}) - w(t_{112}) + \dots \\ &+ \dots + (-1)^{r-1}\{w(t_{i_1,\dots,i_{r-1}}) + w(t_{j_1,\dots,j_{r-1}})\} + (-1)^r w(t_{i_1,\dots,i_r}).\end{aligned}$$

where $j_{2k} = 2$, $j_{2k-1} = 1$, $k = 1, 2, \dots$ and $i_1 = 1$, $i_{2k} = 1$, $i_{2k+1} = 2$, $k = 1, 2, \dots$. Suppose for convenience that r is even. Writing $r = 2m$ gives

$$\Phi_T(w) = \sum_{l=1}^{m} [-w(t_{j_1,\dots,j_{2l-1}}) + w(t_{j_1,\dots,j_{2l}})] + \sum_{l=1}^{m-1} [w(t_{i_1,\dots,i_{2l}}) - w(t_{i_1,\dots,i_{2l+1}})].$$

Since $j_{2l} = 2 = i_{2l+1}$, $l = 1, \dots, m$ and w depends only on the first variable,

$$[-w(t_{j_1,\dots,j_{2l-1}}) + w(t_{j_1,\dots,j_{2l}})] = [-w(t_{i_1,\dots,i_{2l}}) + w(t_{i_1,\dots,i_{2l+1}})] = 0,$$

and so $\Phi_T(w) = 0$. A similar argument with a slightly modified rearrangement works if w depends only on the second variable.

In three dimensions, the simplest closed path is a set of points at the eight corners of a rectangular box. Such a path, and its corresponding tree are shown in Figures 3 and 4.

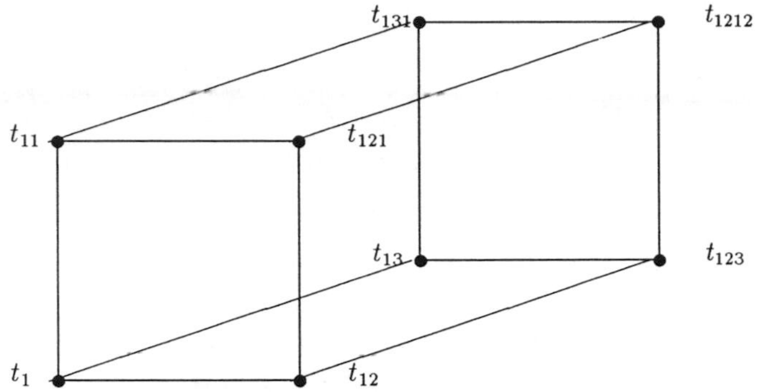

Figure 3: A set in $\mathbb{R}^3$ which forms a closed path.

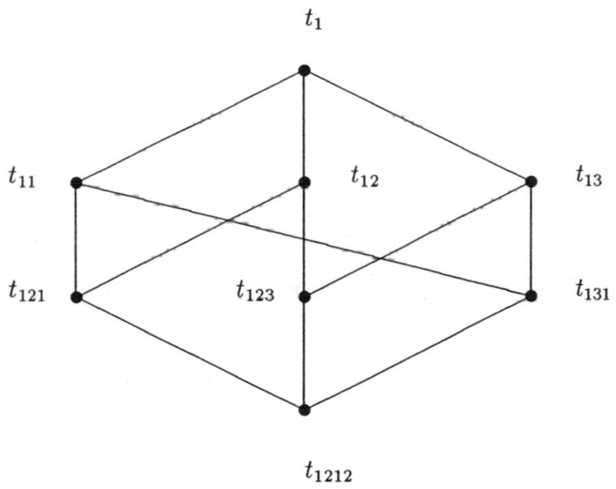

Figure 4: The tree for the above set of points in $\mathbb{R}^3$.

Theorem 2.3 *Let $S_1, \dots, S_n$ be subsets of $\mathbb{R}$ and set $D = S_1 \times S_2 \times \dots \times S_n$. Let W be the subspace of $C(D)$ given by*

$$W = C(S_1) + C(S_2) + \dots + C(S_n).$$

If the tree T represents a closed path in D, then $\Phi_T(w) = 0$ for all w in W.

Proof. The argument centres on induction on the dimension n. The discussions prior to the theorem show that our assertion is true for $n = 2$. Assume now the assertion in the theorem is true for $n = r - 1$, $r \geq 3$, and consider the case $n = r$. Let the tree T represent a closed path in D, and let $w \in C(S_1)$. We make the following construction of a tree T_1:

(i) place t_1 in the first level

(ii) place $t_{12}, \dots, t_{1n}$ in the second level

(iii) for $r = 0, 1, \dots$ until the process fails, place all points in the $(l+1)$th level that have not yet appeared in the tree T_1, are connected in the tree T to points which are in the lth level of T_1, and are not connected by a branch involving Q_1.

It is important to observe that this construction forces points on the $(l+1)$th level of T_1 to be on adjacent levels in T to points on the lth level of T_1. This creates the tree T_1. Begin afresh with the point t_{11} and construct a second tree T_2 in the same manner. This process is continued constructing further trees, starting each new tree with a fresh point in T which is as high as possible in the tree T.

This yields trees $T_1, T_2, \dots, T_p$ which have the property that $T = T_1 \cup T_2 \cup \dots \cup T_p$. Furthermore, $T_i \cap T_j$ is empty if $i \neq j$. Also each set T_i is a tree representing a closed path in $\mathbb{R}^{n-1}$. Thus T has been partitioned into p subtrees. The weights attached to the points in the tree T_i by the path functional described in 2.2 are either all identical with, or all of opposite sign to, the weights attached to those same points when they are regarded as members of T. Thus, if tree T_j has p_j levels,

$$\begin{aligned}\Phi_T(w) &= \sum_{k=1}^{d} (-1)^k \sum \{\hat{t}_{i_1,\dots,i_k} : t_{i_1,\dots,i_k} \in T\} \\ &= \sum_{j=1}^{p} \epsilon_j \sum_{k=1}^{r_j} (-1)^k \sum \{\hat{t}_{i_1,\dots,i_k} : t_{i_1,\dots,i_k} \in T_j\}\end{aligned}$$

where $\epsilon_j = \pm 1$. Hence by the inductive hypothesis,

$$\Phi_T(w) = \sum_{j=1}^{p} \epsilon_j \Phi_{T_j}(w) = 0.$$

Since there is nothing special about the variable s_1, this argument may be carried out for any one of the variable $s_2, \dots, s_n$, and the linearity of Φ is enough to complete the proof. ■

The above result is the key to one half of the promised theorem.

Theorem 2.4 *Let $x_1, \ldots, x_m$ be distinct points in $\mathbb{R}^n$. If this set of points contains a closed path then*
(i) the functions $h_i : \mathbb{R}^n \to \mathbb{R}$ defined by $h_i(x) = \|x - x_i\|_1$, $1 \le i \le m$ are linearly dependent
(ii) the distance matrix A, whose ijth element is $\|x_i - x_j\|_1$, is singular.

Proof. Only assertion (i) needs proof, assertion (ii) being given for the sake of completeness. Suppose the set of points $\{x_1, \ldots, x_m\}$ contains a closed path which is realised in the tree T having d levels. Consider the path functional Φ_T given by

$$\Phi_T = \sum_{k=1}^{r} (-1)^k \sum \{\hat{t}_{i_1,\ldots,i_k} : t_{i_1,\ldots,i_k} \in T\}.$$

Then Φ_T annihilates the subspace $C(S_1) + \ldots + C(S_n)$, where $S_1, \ldots, S_n$ are any compact subsets of $\mathbb{R}$ such that S_i contains $P_i x_j$, $1 \le j \le m$, $1 \le i \le n$. Hence Φ_T annihilates the function $y : \mathbb{R}^n \to \mathbb{R}$ given by

$$y(t_1, \ldots, t_n) = |\tau_1 - t_1| + \ldots + |\tau_n - t_n|,$$

where $(\tau_1, \ldots, \tau_n)$ is any fixed point in $S_1 \times \ldots \times S_n$. Now set

$$t_{i_1,\ldots,i_k} = (s_1^{i_1,\ldots,i_k}, \ldots, s_n^{i_1,\ldots,i_k}).$$

Then

$$\sum_{k=1}^{d} (-1)^k \sum \{|\tau_1 - s_1^{i_1,\ldots,i_k}| + \ldots + |\tau_n - s_n^{i_1,\ldots,i_k}| : t_{i_1,\ldots,i_k} \in T\} = 0.$$

Since this is true for any $\tau = (\tau_1, \ldots, \tau_n)$ in $S_1 \times \ldots \times S_n$, the above equation may be written as

$$\sum_{k=1}^{d} (-1)^k \sum \{y(\tau - t_{i_1,\ldots,i_k}) : t_{i_1,\ldots,i_k} \in T\} = 0,$$

for all $\tau \in S_1 \times \ldots \times S_n$. This gives

$$\sum_{k=1}^{d} (-1)^k \sum \{h_{i_1,\ldots,i_k} : t_{i_1,\ldots,i_k} \in T\} = 0.$$

Thus we have a dependence amongst the functions $h_1, \ldots, h_m$ as required. ∎

References

[1] Baxter, B.J.C. *Conditionally positive functions and p-norm distance matrices*, Department of Applied Mathematics Technical Report, University of Cambridge, DAMTP/1988/NA15, October 1988.

[2] Diliberto, S.P. and Straus, E.G. *On the approximation of a function of several variables by the sum of functions of fewer variables*, Pacific J. Math (1951) **1**, 195-210.

[3] Dyn, N., Light, W.A. and Cheney, E.W. *Interpolation by piecewise-linear radial basis functions*, J. Approx. Th. (to appear).

[4] Dyn, N. and Micchelli, C.A. *Interpolation by sums of radial functions*, IBM Technical Report, 1989.

[5] Micchelli, C.A. *Interpolation of scattered data: distance matrices and conditionally positive definite functions*, Constr. Approx. (1986), **2**, 11-22.

[6] Schoenberg, I.J. *Metric spaces and completely monotone functions*, Ann. of Math., **39**, 522-536.

[7] Sun, X. *On the solvability of some radial basis interpolations*, in *Approximation Theory VI*, to appear.

Dr. William A. Light
Mathematics Department
University of Lancaster
Bailrigg, Lancaster
England.

International Series of
Numerical Mathematics, Vol. 90

Cardinal Interpolation with Polyharmonic Splines

W. R. Madych*

1 Introduction

If k is a positive integer an n-variate *k-harmonic cardinal spline* is a tempered distribution f on R^n such that $\Delta^k f$ is a measure supported on the integer lattice Z^n in R^n. Symbolically

(1) $$\Delta^k f(x) = \sum_{\mathbf{j}\in Z^n} a_{\mathbf{j}}\delta(x-\mathbf{j})$$

where Δ is the n variate Laplacian, $\Delta^k = \Delta\Delta^{k-1}$ for $k > 1$, and $\delta(x)$ is the unit Dirac measure supported at the origin. A *polyharmonic spline* is one which is k-harmonic for some k.

The most important use of these distributions involves the interpolation of data $\{u_{\mathbf{j}}\}$ defined on Z^n to all of R^n. Thus the *cardinal interpolation problem* for k-harmonic splines is the following: given a sequence $\{u_{\mathbf{j}}\}$ defined on Z^n find a k-harmonic spline f such that

(2) $$f(\mathbf{j}) = u_{\mathbf{j}}$$

for all $\mathbf{j}$. Besides the basic questions of existence and uniqueness other meaningful questions concern the behavior of the spline interpolant in terms of the data and the effect of the parameter k.

In the univariate case, $n = 1$, these splines are exactly the polynomial cardinal splines of odd degree and polynomial growth studied by Schoenberg, [20].

It is the purpose of this note to describe the properties of these splines in the general n-variate case. Except for the existence of B-splines, these properties are remarkably similar to those found in the univariate case.

Some of these results were originally announced in [10] and amplified in [11] where motivation and other background is given. Here we only mention that the distributional definition of these splines which is given above is motivated by

*Department of Mathematics, University of Connecticut, Storrs, CT 06268. Partially supported by a grant from the Air Force Office of Scientific Research, AFOSR-86-0145

the facts that it is very convenient and easily allows for the unrestrained use of Fourier transforms. Thus in a certain sense this development may be regarded as an extension of the early work of Schoenberg [19] which used Fourier analysis.

Recall that the classical univariate cardinal splines of degree $2k-1$ and polynomial growth may be viewed as linear combinations of translates of $|x|^{2k-1}$. Similarly the general k-harmonic cardinal spline f may be regarded as a linear combination of translates of the fundamental solution of Δ^k denoted by $E_k(x)$; thus $\Delta^k E_k(x) = \delta(x)$ and

$$f(x) = \sum_{\mathbf{j} \in Z^n} a_{\mathbf{j}} E_k(x - \mathbf{j}) \,. \tag{3}$$

Note that at this point the correspondence between (1) and (3) is merely symbolic; clearly (1) is meaningful in the tempered distribution sense for any sequence $\{a_{\mathbf{j}}\}$ of polynomial growth whereas this is not so apparent for (3).

Interpolation in terms of linear combinations of translates of a fixed function h is certainly very appealing. It arises naturally when the interpolants are solutions of certain variational problems; the general idea goes at least as far back as that of the reproducing kernel Hilbert space, for example see [1,8], but the first meaningful use of the Fourier transform in this context seems to be due to Duchon, [6]; usually in such cases h is the fundamental solution of an appropriate differential or pseudo-differential operator and the interpolant is often further modified in some way to account for various auxiliary conditions and restrictions, for example see [6,7,13,15,17,21] and the appropriate references therein. The classes of positive definite and and conditionally positive definite functions provide a rich collection of examples of h's which can be used for such interpolation; various dilates of the Gaussian $\exp(-|x|^2)$, the so-called multiquadric $\sqrt{1+|x|^2}$, and the fundamental solution $E_k(x)$, $2k \geq n+1$, are specific examples; for for details and more examples see [2,7,13,16]. When the data is given on a lattice the univariate B-splines are perhaps the most popular example of such h's, see [20,18]; the recently developed theory of box splines seems to be an attempt to generalize this concept to the multi-variate case, see [3,5] and the pertinent articles in this volume.

The notation used here is standard, if necessary see [11] for a more detailed explanation. Here we merely remind the reader that there are several common normalizations for the Fourier transform. In this note we use

$$\hat{\psi}(\xi) = (2\pi)^{-n/2} \int_{R^n} \psi(x) e^{-i\langle \xi, x \rangle} dx$$

for the Fourier transform $\hat{\psi}$ of a test function ψ.

2 Basic properties

Suppose f is a k-harmonic cardinal spline. Then f is clearly analytic on $R^n \setminus Z^n$ and, in order to ensure that point evaluation on Z^n is meaningful, we assume that f is continuous on all of R^n. In this case, if $2k < n+1$ it is well known that f must be a k-harmonic polynomial; this follows from the behavior of the corresponding fundamental solution at the origin, see [9] for details. Now, the class of k-harmonic polynomials is too exclusive to interpolate a sufficiently broad class of data $\{u_{\mathbf{j}}\}$ on Z^n. For example, it is not difficult to see that there is no k-harmonic polynomial f such that $f(0) = 1$ and $f(\mathbf{j}) = 0$ for $\mathbf{j}$ in $Z^n \setminus \{0\}$. For this reason we restrict our attention to the case $2k \geq n+1$ in what follows.

Let $SH_k(R^n)$ denote the class of k-harmonic splines on R^n and recall that $C^k(R^n)$ is the class of functions which are k times continuously differentiable on R^n.

Proposition 1 *If $2k \geq n+1$ and f is in $SH_k(R^n)$ then f is in $C^{2k-n-1}(R^n)$.*

Recall that a sequence $\{u_{\mathbf{j}}\}$ is of polynomial growth if there are constants c and p such that

$$|u_{\mathbf{j}}| \leq c(1+|j|)^p \tag{4}$$

holds for all $\mathbf{j}$ in Z^n. The class $\mathcal{Y}^\alpha$ is the collection of those sequences for which (4) holds for $p = \alpha$. Similarly a continuous function f is of polynomial growth if there are constants c and p such that

$$|f(x)| \leq c(1+|x|)^p \tag{5}$$

holds for all x in R^n. The class $SH_k^\alpha(R^n)$ is the collection of those k-harmonic splines for which (5) holds for $p = \alpha$.

Proposition 2 *If $2k \geq n+1$ and f is in $SH_k(R^n)$ then f is of polynomial growth. In other words $SH_k(R^n) = \bigcup SH_k^\alpha(R^n)$ where the union is taken over all $\alpha < \infty$.*

The last proposition implies that in the univariate case the class $SH_k(R)$ is not quite as general as the corresponding class $\mathcal{S}_{2k-1}$ considered by Schoenberg. It fails to contain the subspace of $\mathcal{S}_{2k-1}$ consisting of the null-splines, see [20, Lecture 4, Section 3].

Since the elements of $SH_k(R^n)$ are of polynomial growth it is clear that in order for cardinal interpolation problem to have a solution a necessary requirement on the data sequence is that it also be of polynomial growth. As we shall see this requirement is also sufficient. We begin by first considering the fundamental functions of interpolation.

Consider the distribution L_k which is defined by the formula for its Fourier transform:

$$\hat{L}_k(\xi) = (2\pi)^{-n/2} \frac{|\xi|^{-2k}}{\sum_{\mathbf{j}\in Z^n} |\xi - 2\pi\mathbf{j}|^{-2k}}. \tag{6}$$

If k is an integer such that $2k \geq n+1$ then $L_k(x)$ is well defined as an absolutely convergent integral.

Proposition 3 *Let L_k be defined by the formula for its Fourier transform (6), where k is an integer which satisfies $2k \geq n+1$. Then L_k has the following properties:*

(i) L_k is a k-harmonic cardinal spline.

(ii) For all $\mathbf{j}$ *in* Z^n

(7)
$$L_k(\mathbf{j}) = \begin{cases} 1 & \text{if } \mathbf{j} = 0 \\ 0 & \text{if } \mathbf{j} \neq 0 \end{cases}$$

(iii) There are positive constants A and a, depending on n and k but independent of x, such that

(8)
$$|L_k(x)| \leq A \exp(-a|x|)$$

for all x in R^n.

(iv) L_k has the following representations in terms of E_k:

(9)
$$L_k(x) = \sum_{\mathbf{j} \in Z^n} a_{\mathbf{j}} E_k(x - \mathbf{j})$$

where the $a_{\mathbf{j}}$'s satisfy $|a_{\mathbf{j}}| \leq B\exp(-b|\mathbf{j}|)$ and the positive constants B and b depend only on n and k. The series converges absolutely and uniformly on all compact subsets of R^n.

Item *(i)* is a readily transparent consequence of the definition while item *(ii)* easily follows from the fact that for $\mathbf{j}$ in Z^n

(10)
$$L_k(\mathbf{j}) = \frac{1}{2\pi} \int_{Q^n} e^{i\langle \mathbf{j}, \xi \rangle} d\xi$$

where

$$Q^n = \{\xi = (\xi_1, \ldots, \xi_n) \; : \; -\pi < \xi_j \leq \pi, \; j = 1, \ldots, n\}.$$

The remaining items are consequences of the analyticity of $\hat{L}_k$.

The following theorem concerns the cardinal spline interpolation problem and the nature of its solution. It is essentially a routine consequence of Proposition 3 except for the uniqueness assertion. Details may be found in [11].

Proposition 4 *If $\{u_{\mathbf{j}}\}$, $\mathbf{j}$ in Z^n, is a sequence of polynomial growth and $2k \geq n+1$ then the following is true:*

(i) There is a unique k-harmonic spline f such that $f(\mathbf{j}) = v_{\mathbf{j}}$ for all $\mathbf{j}$.

(ii) If $u_{\mathbf{j}}$ is in $\mathcal{Y}^\alpha$ then f is in $SH_k^\alpha(R^n)$.

(iii) Every k-harmonic spline f has a unique representation in terms of translates of L_k, namely

(11)
$$f(x) = \sum_{\mathbf{j} \in Z^n} f(\mathbf{j}) L_k(x - \mathbf{j}).$$

The expansion (11) converges absolutely and uniformly in every compact subset of R^n.

3 Other Properties

Having given the basic existence and uniqueness result concerning the cardinal interpolation problem for k-harmonic splines we briefly address the following questions:

How is the behavior of the data sequence $\{u_{\mathbf{j}}\}$ reflected in the behavior of its k-harmonic spline interpolant?

Most of the results known in the univariate case have an appropriate analogue in the general case. For example, item *(ii)* of Proposition 4 addresses this question. Other results include appropriate analogues of [4]; namely, if $\{u_{\mathbf{j}}\}$ or certain finite differences of it are in $\ell^p(Z^n)$ the the corresponding k-harmonic spline interpolant or appropriate derivatives are in $L^p(R^n)$.

What about the variational properties of these splines?

The appropriate analogue of results cited in [20, Lecture 6, Section 1] hold in the general case. See [12] for details.

If the data sequence is fixed what is the behavior of the cardinal k-harmonic spline interpolant as $k \to \infty$.

Again, most of the results which hold in the univariate case have an appropriate analogue here. A result which seems to be new even in the univariate case is the following: Suppose f is such that the support of $\hat{f}$ is in Q^n and s_k is its cardinal k-harmonic spline interpolant, namely, $s_k(\mathbf{j}) = f(\mathbf{j})$ for $\mathbf{j}$ in Z^n. Then if $\hat{f}$ satisfies a mild condition in a neighborhood of the boundary of Q^n then

$$\lim_{k \to \infty} s_k(x) = f(x)$$

uniformly on compact subsets of R^n. For some details see [14].

Suppose $s(x)$ is the k-harmonic spline interpolant of f on the dilated lattice aZ^n. What is the degree of approximation in terms of a?

Recall that $s(x)$ reproduces any k-harmonic polynomial; in particular, it reproduces any polynomial of degree $\leq 2k - 1$. This together with routine arguments involving (8) implies that $|s(x) - f(x)| = O(a^{2k})$ as $a \to 0$ whenever f is in $C^{2k}(R^n)$ with bounded derivatives of order $2k$. Similar results hold with L^p norms. Interpolation arguments imply appropriate results for less regular f's. Thus appropriate analogues of all the univariate results hold in the general case.

What about numerical implementations?

The fundamental spline $L_k(x)$ can be easily evaluated quite rapidly and accurately via the fast Fourier transform. See Figures 1 and 2. In view of this the computation of most k-harmonic spline interpolants should should pose no significant difficulties.

What about further generalizations?

There are many directions in which one can extend certain aspects of this theory. For example, by replacing $|\xi|^{-2k}$ and its periodization in formula (6) by an appropriate function ϕ which decays sufficiently fast at ∞ it is readily transparent that the corresponding analogue of L_k, call it L, will be continuous, will certainly satisfy (10), and thus will also satisfy (7). If ϕ is sufficiently regular then L will have corresponding decay properties at ∞. In view of this it is quit natural to consider interpolants of the form

$$f(x) = \sum_{\mathbf{j} \in Z^n} f(\mathbf{j}) L(x - \mathbf{j}) .$$

Typical ϕ's for which the basic properties of the above type interpolants are particularly transparent are $\phi(\xi) = P(\xi)^{-1}$ where $P(\xi)$ is a homogeneous elliptic polynomial of sufficiently high degree and $\phi(\xi) = g(|\xi|^2)$ where $g(\zeta)$ is a is a univariate function which is analytic away from the origin and decays sufficiently fast at ∞ on the real axis. For some details in the second case see [2,7].

Another direction in one could consider extensions is the replacement of the lattice Z^n by a more general discrete set X. The case when X is finite is essentially treated in [6,15,17]. The general infinite case is not so clear.

References

[1] J. H. Ahlberg, E. N. Nilson, and J. L. Walsh, *The Theory of Splines and Their Applications*, Academic Press, New York, 1967.

[2] M. D. Buhmann and M. J. D. Powell, Radial basis function interpolation on an infinite regular grid, preprint 1988, 24p.

[3] C. K. Chui, *Multivariate Splines*, CBMS Vol. 54, SIAM, Philadelphia, 1988.

[4] C. deBoor, How small can one make the derivatives of an interpolating function?, *J. Approx. Theory* 13(1975), 105-116.

[5] C. de Boor, K. Hollig, and S. Riemenschnieder, Bivariate cardinal interpolation on a three-direction mesh, *Ill. J. Math.*, 29 (1985), 533-566.

[6] J. Duchon, Splines minimizing rotation-invariant seminorms in Sobolev spaces, in *Constructive Theory of Functions of Several Variables*, W. Schempp and K. Zeller eds., Springer-Verlag, 1977, 85-100.

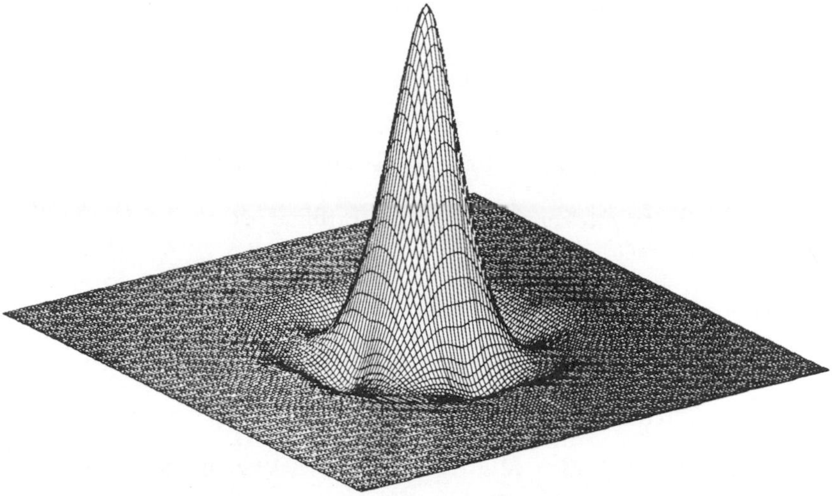

Figure 1: Plot of the surface $z = L_2(x, y)$.

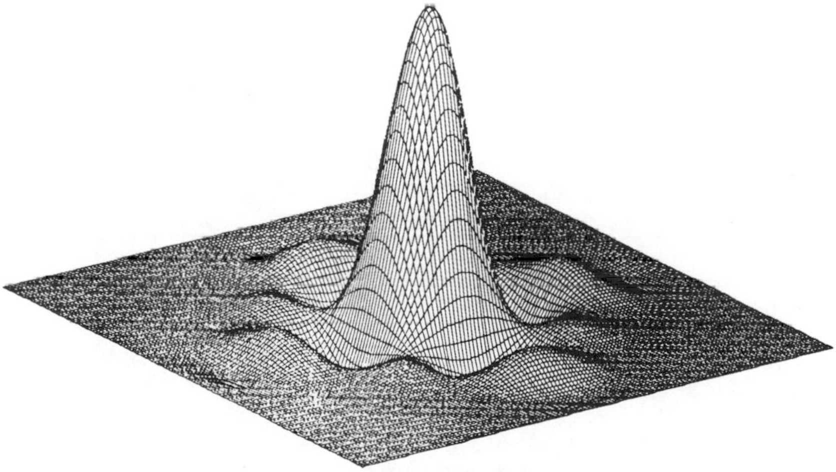

Figure 2: Plot of the surface $z = L_5(x, y)$.

[7] N. Dyn, Survey Lecture, to appear in *Approximation Theory VI*, C. Chui, L. Schumaker, J. Ward, eds., Academic Press, New York, 1989.

[8] M. Golomb and H. F. Weinberger, Optimal approximation and error bounds, in *On Numerical Approximation*, R. E. Langer, ed., Madison, 1959, 117-190.

[9] W. R. Madych, Polyharmonic splines, unpublished preprint 1978, 16p.

[10] W. R. Madych and S. A. Nelson, Polyharmonic cardinal splines, *Abstracts Amer. Math. Soc.* 7(1986), 378.

[11] W. R. Madych and S. A. Nelson, Polyharmonic cardinal splines, to appear in *J. Approx. Theory*.

[12] W. R. Madych and S. A. Nelson, Polyharmonic cardinal splines: a minimization property, technical report, BRC/MATH-TR-89-1.

[13] W. R. Madych and S. A. Nelson, Multivariate interpolation and conditionally positive definite functions II, to appear in *Math. Comp.*

[14] W. R. Madych, Splines and entire functions, technical report, BRC/MATH-TR-89-2.

[15] J. Meinguet, Multivariate interpolation at arbitrary points made simple, *Z. Angew Math. Phys.*, 30(1979), 292-304.

[16] C. A. Micchelli, Interpolation of scattered data: distance matrices and conditionally positive definite functions. *Constr. Approx.*, 2(1986), 11-22.

[17] E. H. Potter, Multivariate Polyharmonic Spline Interpolation, Ph.D. thesis, Iowa State University, 1981.

[18] W. Schempp, *Complex Contour Integral Representation of Cardinal Spline Functions*, Contemporary Mathematics, Vol. 7, Amer. Math. Soc., Providence, 1982.

[19] I. J. Schoenberg, Contributions to the problem of approximation of equidistant data by analytic functions, *Quart. Appl. Math.*, 4 (1946), 45-99.

[20] I. J. Schoenberg, *Cardinal Spline Interpolation*, CBMS Vol. 12, SIAM, Philadelphia, 1973.

[21] G. Wahba, Spline bases, regularization, and generalized cross validation for solving approximation problems with large quantities of noisy data, *Approximation Theory III*, E. W. Cheney, ed., Academic Press, New York, 1980.

International Series of
Numerical Mathematics, Vol. 90

MULTIVARIATE RATIONAL INTERPOLATION
Reconstruction of Rational Functions

H. Michael Möller
Fachbereich Mathematik und Informatik, FernUniversität Hagen, FRG

Abstract

In this paper we consider the problem of reconstructing a multivariate rational function, when only its values at sufficiently many points are known. We use for the reconstruction of bivariate rational functions a bivariate rational interpolation operator investigated by Siemaszko [7] and a new one, compare both by examples in a Computer Algebra system, and present their multivariate generalizations.

1. Introduction

Rimey [5] asked for all solutions (x, y, z) of the system of equations

$$\begin{aligned} \lambda x + \varepsilon yz - x(x^2 + \alpha y^2 + \beta z^2) &= 0, \\ \lambda y + \varepsilon zx - y(y^2 + \alpha z^2 + \beta x^2) &= 0, \\ \lambda z + \varepsilon xy - z(z^2 + \alpha x^2 + \beta y^2) &= 0. \end{aligned} \tag{1.1}$$

Since the solutions depend on the parameters $\alpha, \beta, \lambda, \varepsilon$, no numerical method can be used for showing the dependency of the solutions on the parameters. Rimey derived by nonstandard methods the 27 solutions explicitly and remarked that he could not find them using packages from Computer Algebra Systems (CAS). The components of the solutions can be described by rational functions in the four parameters. And during the performance of the algorithm in the CAS polynomials occur with coefficients which are complicated rational functions in the parameters. This lead in all considered CAS to a break down by storage problems.
Therefore Melenk [4] proposed to specify the parameters to fixed (integer) values and solve then the system 1.1. When sufficiently many values of the solutions are known, the rational functions in $\alpha, \beta, \lambda, \varepsilon$ on which the 27 solutions depend can hopefully be reconstructed.
This rises the more general problem how to reconstruct a multivariate rational function, which is only known to exist and for which at arbitrary points the value can be computed. No a priori informations on numerator and denominator degrees are given. Obviously, in order to solve this problem good methods for computing interpolating rational functions must be available.
In the univariate case the linearized rational interpolation problem is as follows

Find polynomials $p, q \in I\!K[x]$, $I\!K$ a field, with $deg(p) \leq r, deg(q) \leq s$, such that

$$p(t_i) - y_i q(t_i) = 0, i = 1, \ldots, r + s + 1$$

holds, where $t_1, \ldots, t_{r+s+1} \in I\!K$ are given distinct points and $y_1, \ldots, y_{r+s+1} \in I\!K$ are given data. (1.2)

This problem is solvable by a polynomial pair p, q, where not the pair but the rational function p/q is uniquely determined. Therefore we also say in abuse of notation that p/q solves 1.2, if it is solved by the pair p, q. For a survey and for construction methods see for instance [6].
If the data $y_1, \ldots, y_{r+s+1}$ are known to be the values of a rational function P/Q at distinct points $t_1, \ldots, t_{r+s+1}$, then the solution of 1.2 with $y_i := P(t_i)/Q(t_i)$ reconstructs the rational function in question, provided the degrees of P and Q are not too great, in other words, r and s are sufficiently great numbers.
The situation is more difficult in the multivariate case. Here 1.2 reads as follows

$$\text{Find polynomials } p, q \in I\!K[x_1, \ldots, x_n], \text{ with } deg(p) \leq r, deg(q) \leq s, \text{ such that}$$
$$p(t_i) - y_i q(t_i) = 0, i = 1, \ldots, M,$$
$$\text{holds, where } t_1, \ldots, t_M \in I\!K^n \text{ are given distinct points and } y_1, \ldots, y_M \in I\!K \text{ are given data.} \tag{1.3}$$

Again, we call p/q a solution, if the pair p, q solves 1.3. The dependence of M on r and s is not as canonical as in the univariate case, and for the notion of degree we may choose between the total degree (sum of exponents) or the degree by components, i.e. $deg(f) \leq r$ means $r = (r_1, \ldots, r_n)$ and $deg(f, x_i) \leq r_i, i = 1, \ldots, n$. Some methods are known for the construction of a p/q solving 1.3, see [2, 3]. Due to the lack of uniqueness, most of the methods do not reproduce the rational function P/Q as solution of 1.3, when $y_i = P(t_i)/Q(t_i), i = 1, \ldots, M$, even if (the components of) r and s are sufficiently great. When such method is applied to solve problems with increasing degree bounds, in most cases only rational functions with increasing numerator and denominator degrees are produced.
The multivariate reconstruction of a rational function P/Q consists ideally in the construction of a series of rational functions p_M/q_M solving 1.3 where r and s increase with M, such that $p_M/q_M = P/Q$ for all $M \geq M^*$, M^* a fixed constant. For practical reasons, only a finite number of p_M/q_M's can be computed and P/Q is not known. The verification that the guess made for P/Q is in fact equal to P/Q can not be done with the methods presented here. This check can be eventually made in the area, where the reconstruction problem came from.
Therefore, we must be content with the following procedure. First of all let us assume, that we are able to find always the value of a rational function P/Q for all points in question. We select an isotone sequence of finite sets $T_1 \subset T_2 \subset \ldots \subset I\!K^n$. Let $T_k := (t_{1,k}, \ldots, t_{m_k,k})$. Then we select for each $k = 1, 2, \ldots$ a rational interpolation operator $\mathcal{P}_k$, which maps every $(y_1, \ldots, y_{m_k}) \in I\!K^{m_k}$ to a rational function p_k/q_k, such that p and q satisfy

$$p_k(t_{i,k}) - y_i q_k(t_{i,k}) = 0 \quad \text{for} \quad i = 1, \ldots, m_k.$$

(If $\mathcal{P}_k$ is the restriction of $\mathcal{P}_{k+1}$ to T_k, then T_k and $\mathcal{P}_k$ are redundant. We exclude in the following such situations.) Now let P/Q be a rational function and let p_k/q_k be the result of $\mathcal{P}_k$ applied on

$$(P(t_{1,k})/Q(t_{1,k}), \ldots, P(t_{m_k,k})/Q(t_{m_k,k})).$$

If there are an M and an $M^* \geq 1$, such that $p_M/q_M = \ldots = p_{M+M^*}/q_{M+M^*}$, then we accept p_M/q_M as guess for P/Q and terminate the procedure.

Definition 1. We say the described procedure given by the point sets $T_1 \subset T_2 \subset \ldots$, and the corresponding interpolation operators $\mathcal{P}_k, k = 1, 2, \ldots$ has the reproducing property, if it terminates for every rational function P/Q with a guess for P/Q.

In §3, the author was able to show, that a procedure using bivariate rational interpolation operators investigated by Siemaszko [7] has the reproducing property. A new bivariate method based on univariate rational and polynomial interpolation is proposed. It has no reproducing property, but only in degenerate cases, it does not reproduce the rational function in question. This procedure requires the solution of a lesser number of rational interpolation subproblems by employing polynomial interpolation. Hence, as the examples in §3 confirm, it is faster than Siemaszko's already for moderate sized functions and recovers the function when Siemaszko's fails because of storage problems. The multivariate analoga of the two methods are presented in §4.

2. Univariate Rational Interpolation

In the univariate case, rational interpolation methods with reproducing property are easily found. Take $T_m := \{t_1, \ldots, t_m\}$ with distinct points t_i. And take as rational interpolation operator $\mathcal{P}_m$ the operator which maps m-tuples $y_1, \ldots, y_m$ to the rational function p_m/q_m uniquely determined by the interpolation conditions

$$\begin{aligned} p_m(t_i) - y_i q_m(t_i) = 0 \;\text{ for }\; i = 1, \ldots, m, \\ \text{with } deg(p_m) \le r_m \;\text{ and }\; deg(q_m) \le s_m,\; r_m + s_m + 1 = m. \end{aligned} \tag{2.1}$$

Let P/Q be a rational function with $y_i = P(t_i)/Q(t_i)$ for all $i \geq 1$. If both r_m and s_m tend to infinity, when $m \to \infty$, then for sufficiently great m both degree bounds $deg(P) \leq r_m$ and $deg(Q) \leq s_m$ are satisfied, i.e. for sufficiently great m all rational functions p_m/q_m are identical with P/Q. In order to guarantee, that both r_m and s_m tend to infinity for $m \to \infty$, we make the standard assumption

$$r_m := [m/2],\; s_m := [(m-1)/2], \tag{2.2}$$

where $[a]$ means the integer part of a.
Practical algorithms which calculate the p_m/q_m satisfying 2.1 and 2.2 take advantage from the fact, that the rational functions p_m/q_m can be defined recursively. So many quantities computed in previous calculations can be used for abbreviating the calculations for p_m/q_m. The method of Stoer, cf. [2], calculates rational functions p_{ik}/q_{ik} interpolating at $t_i, \ldots, t_{i+k}$ and satisfying the degree bounds corresponding to 2.2,

$$deg(p_{ik}) \leq [(k+1-i)/2],\; deg(q_{ik}) \leq [(k-i)/2].$$

It initializes with $p_{ii}/q_{ii} = P(t_i)/Q(t_i)$ and calculates then iteratively

$$\begin{aligned} p_{ik}(x) &:= \lambda_{ik} \cdot (x - t_i) \cdot p_{i+1,k}(x) + \mu_{ik} \cdot (t_k - x) \cdot p_{i,k-1}(x), \\ q_{ik}(x) &:= \lambda_{ik} \cdot (x - t_i) \cdot q_{i+1,k}(x) + \mu_{ik} \cdot (t_k - x) \cdot q_{i,k-1}(x), \end{aligned} \tag{2.3}$$

where the constants λ_{ik} and μ_{ik} are chosen such that the degree restrictions also hold for p_{ik} and q_{ik}. Then $p_m/q_m := p_{1m}/q_{1m}$ solves 2.1 and 2.2.
Stoer's method requires for the computation of $p_{m+1}/q_{m+1} = p_{1,m+1}/q_{1,m+1}$ the additional computation of the m rational functions $p_{i,m+1}/q_{i,m+1}$ for $i = m+1, m, \ldots, 2$. An alternative method which avoids the computation of polynomials as long as the final guess is not found can be derived from a method which is attributed to Thiele, cf. [2].

Theorem 1. Let inverted divided differences of length 1 be given by

$$\Phi[t_i] := P(t_i)/Q(t_i), i = 1, \ldots, m,$$

and inverted divided differences of length $k+1$ by those of length k,

$$\Phi[t_1, \ldots, t_k, t_i] := \frac{t_i - t_k}{\Phi[t_1, \ldots, t_{k-1}, t_i] - \Phi[t_1, \ldots, t_k]}, k < i \leq m. \tag{2.4}$$

Then the continued fraction

$$\frac{p_m}{q_m} = \frac{P(t_1)}{Q(t_1)} + \frac{x - t_1 |}{|\Phi[t_1, t_2]} + \frac{x - t_2 |}{|\Phi[t_1, t_2, t_3]} + \cdots + \frac{x - t_{m-1} |}{|\Phi[t_1, \ldots, t_m]} \tag{2.5}$$

is a rational function satisfying 2.1 and 2.2, provided the denominator of no $\Phi[t_1, \ldots, t_k]$ vanishes.
If the denominators of $\Phi[t_1, \ldots, t_i], i = 1, \ldots, m-1$ do not vanish, but $\Phi[t_1, \ldots, t_m]$ has a vanishing denominator, then by the definition of continued fractions, $p_{m-1}/q_{m-1} = p_m/q_m$ and p_{m-1}/q_{m-1} interpolates also in t_m. It could mean that we did already reconstruct P/Q by this p_{m-1}/q_{m-1}, but

it could mean a degeneration as well. In order to overcome such degeneration, we may replace t_m by a better suited $t_k, k > m$, i.e. we look for a $\Phi[t_1, \ldots, t_{m-1}, t_k]$ with nonvanishing denominator and replace then t_k by t_m and vice versa. If no such t_k exists, we have by theorem 1 independent of the selection of t_m always p_{m-1}/q_{m-1} as rational function which interpolates at $t_1, \ldots, t_{m-1}$ and at all possible forthcoming $t_k, k \geq m$. In this case p_{m-1}/q_{m-1} is the guess for P/Q. Using this modification for avoiding degenerate situations, the author together with H. Melenk and W. Neun (both from Konrad-Zuse-Zentrum für Informationsbehandlung, Berlin) implemented Thiele's algorithm in the Computer Algebra system REDUCE.
The following complexity analysis explains why we implemented Thiele's and not Stoer's method. These two methods require exact arithmetic. Therefore, we apply the results of [1] for the comparison. In most applications we have in mind (cf. the example in the beginning) the points can be assumed to be integers of moderate length, and the polynomials have integer coefficients. Then, denoting by $L(a)$ the length of an integer a, and assuming, that integer multiplication is performed by Karatsuba's method, we get from [1] for integers a, b

Operation	Complexity
$a+b$	$min\{L(a), L(b)\}$
$a \cdot b$	$max\{L(a), L(b)\}^{log3}$
$quot(a,b)$	$L(b)(L(a) - L(b) - 1)$ (for $L(a) \geq L(b)$)
$gcd(a,b)$	$L(a)L(b)$

And for univariate polynomials p, q with integer coefficients using $L(\Sigma a_i x^i) := max L(a_i)$ simple calculations give for great $L(p), L(q)$, and $L(a)$

Operation	Complexity
$p+q$	$[1 + min\{deg(p), deg(q)\}] min\{L(p), L(q)\}$
$a \cdot p$	$[1 + deg(p)] max\{L(a), L(p)\}^{log3}$
$(x-a)p$	$[1 + deg(p)][max\{L(a), L(p)\}^{log3} + L(a) + L(p)]$
$a(x-x_i)p$	$[1 + deg(p)][max\{L(a), L(p)\}^{log3} + L(p)^{log3}]$ (if $L(x_i) \ll L(p), L(a)$)

If we denote by L_0 the maximum of all numbers $L(P(x_i)), L(Q(x_i))$, then we get in Stoer's method that $L(p_{ik}), L(q_{ik})$ are both approximately $2^{k-i}L_0$. And the complexity for computing p_m/q_m by Stoer's method is then approximatey $\frac{4}{9}m4^m L_0^2 + m3^m L_0^{log3}$. The first summand came from gcd computations for reducing previous p_i/q_i, whereas the second summand could be replaced by a lesser number if we knew that some of the gcd's were non-trivial.
Similarly, in Thiele's method we have that numerator and denominator of any inverted divided difference of length k is approximately $2^{k-1}L_0$. And the complexity for computing all inverted divided differences in question and the combination to obtain the guess p_m/q_m is approximately $\frac{16}{3}4^m L_0^2 + \frac{29}{2}3^m L_0^{log3}$. This is approximately by a factor m less than the computational amount in Stoer's method.

3. Bivariate rational interpolation

Some bivariate rational interpolation operators are presented in [2, 3]. With respect to the better performance of Thiele's method in comparison with Stoer's, we concentrate on interpolation methods which use branched continued fractions, a generalization of continued fractions. However, we got by several examples the impression, that most of these methods are not suited for being used in procedures with the reproducing property, because even for rational functions P/Q with low $deg(P)$ and $deg(Q)$ the branched continued fraction representation of P/Q seemed not to be finite. And finiteness is an essential tool for proving the reproducing property, as we will see in the following.

<u>**Theorem 2.**</u> Let P/Q be a rational function with

$$deg(P,x) \leq [m_1/2], deg(P,y) \leq [m_2/2], deg(Q,x) \leq [(m_1-1)/2], deg(Q,y) \leq [(m_2-1)/2],$$

and let $y_1, \ldots, y_{m_2}$ be different points in $I\!K$. Then there are an $s \leq m_2$ and polynomials $P_k, Q_k \in I\!K[x], k = 0, \ldots, s$, such that $deg(P_k) \leq 2^{k-1}m_1, deg(Q_k) \leq 2^{k-1}m_1$, and

$$\frac{P(x,y)}{Q(x,y)} = \frac{P_0(x)}{Q_0(x)} + \frac{y-y_1 \mid}{|P_1(x)/Q_1(x)} + \ldots + \frac{y-y_s \mid}{|P_s(x)/Q_s(x)}. \tag{3.1}$$

If $y_1, \ldots, y_{m_2}$ are fixed, then s and the P_k/Q_k are uniquely determined.

<u>Remark.</u> The theorem is stated and proved in [7] without the degree bounds for the P_k and Q_k.
<u>Proof.</u> Only the degree bounds for P_k, Q_k must be shown. Let $\rho_s := P_s/Q_s$ and then recursively for $k := s-1, \ldots, 0$ $\rho_k := P_k/Q_k + (y - y_{k+1})/\rho_{k+1}$. It follows that $\rho_0 = P/Q$. Denoting numerator and denominator of ρ_k by A_k and B_k resp., then by definition of ρ_k

$$deg(P_k) \leq deg(A_k(., y_{k+1}) \leq deg(A_k, x), \; deg(Q_k) \leq deg(B_k(., y_{k+1}) \leq deg(B_k, x).$$

Beginning with the estimates

$$deg(P_0) \leq deg(A_0, x) \leq [m_1/2] \leq m_1/2, \; deg(Q_0) \leq deg(B_0, x) \leq [(m_1-1)/2] \leq m_1/2,$$

the recursion

$$A_{k+1}/B_{k+1} = 1/(y - y_{k+1}) \cdot B_k Q_k/(A_k Q_k - B_k P_k)$$

gives by induction $deg(P_k) \leq deg(A_k, x) \leq 2^{k-1}m_1$ and $deg(Q_k) \leq deg(B_k, x) \leq 2^{k-1}m_1$.

□

The bounds for $deg(P_k)$ and $deg(Q_k)$ are in general too pessimistic, since no cancellation of common factors has been assumed. So we have for instance if $y_i := i - 1$ for $i = 1, 2, \ldots$

P/Q	s	$(deg(P_k), deg(Q_k))$ $k = 0, \ldots, s$
$\frac{xy+1}{x+y+2}$	2	(0,1), (2,2), (2,1)
$\frac{3x^2+xy-7y}{y^2+x+3}$	4	(2,1), (2,2), (4,4), (6,6), (4,3)
$\frac{(x-y)^2-2xy}{(x-y)^2+1}$	4	(2,2), (4,3), (6,6), (8,7), (4,4)
$\frac{(x-y)^4-2xy^3}{(x-y)^4+1}$	8	(4,4), (8,5), (10,13), (18,15), (20,23), (28,25), (30,30), (32,31), (16,16)

The rational interpolation operator described in [7] uses a rectangular grid of interpolation points $T_{(k1,k2)} := \{(x_i, y_j) \mid 1 \leq i \leq k1, 1 \leq j \leq k2\}$. If d_{ij} is the interpolation date at (x_i, y_j), then for every fixed x_i the inverted divided differences $\Phi_i[y_1, \ldots, y_k]$ for the continued fraction of the univariate rational function p_i/q_i in y are calculated, which interpolates d_{ij} at $y_j, j = 1, \ldots, k2$. This gives continued fraction representations

$$\frac{p_i}{q_i} = \Phi_i[y_1] + \frac{y-y_1 \mid}{|\Phi_i[y_1,y_2]} + \ldots + \frac{y-y_{s_i-1} \mid}{|\Phi_i[y_1,\ldots,y_{s_i}]}. \tag{3.2}$$

Using for fixed k the quantities $\Phi_i[y_1, \ldots, y_k]$ as interpolation data for the points $x_i, i = 1, \ldots, k1$, then Thiele's method calculates rational functions u_k/v_k in x. This gives then the bivariate rational function

$$\frac{u_1}{v_1} + \frac{y-y_1 \mid}{|u_2/v_2} + \ldots + \frac{y-y_{k2-1} \mid}{|u_{k2}/v_{k2}}, \tag{3.3}$$

which interpolates d_{ij} at (x_i, y_j) for all $(x_i, y_j) \in T_{(k1,k2)}$.
Now let P/Q be a given bivariate rational function and let d_{ij} be the value of P/Q at (x_i, y_j). If $k2 \leq 2 \cdot max\{deg(P,y), deg(Q,y)\}$, then by the uniqueness of the univariate rational interpolation $p_i(y)/q_i(y) = P(x_i, y)/Q(x_i, y)$. Comparing with the continued fraction of P/Q given by thm. 2, we state $\Phi_i[y_1, \ldots, y_k] = P_k(x_i)/Q_k(x_i)$. If $k1$ is at least two times greater than the maximal degree

of all $deg(P_k), deg(Q_k)$, then $u_k/v_k = P_k/Q_k$ again by uniqueness of the univariate problem. Hence for sufficiently great $k1, k2$, P/Q is reproduced, i.e. the procedure of using this bivariate rational interpolation operator on grids increasing in both directions has the reproducing property.
An alternative to this procedure is the following. We interpolate again on a rectangular grid $T_{(k1,k2)} = \{(x_i, y_j) \mid 1 \le i \le k1, 1 \le j \le k2\}$ given data d_{ij}. First we construct for every y_j by Thiele's method the rational function p_j/q_j solving

$$p_j(x_i) - d_{ij}q_j(x_i) = 0, i = 1, \ldots, k1.$$

Let $p_j(x) = \Sigma_{i=0}^m a_{ij}x^i$, and $q_j(x) = \Sigma_{i=0}^n b_{ij}x^i$, where $m \le [k1/2]$ is the maximal degree of all p_j and $n \le [(k1-1)/2]$ that one of all q_j. Cancel all p_j/q_j with $(a_{m,j}, b_{n,j}) = (0,0)$ and renumber the remaining p_l/q_l and renumber the points in $T_{(k1,k2)}$ after removing those with second component $= y_j$ for such j. For simplicity let us assume $(a_{mj}, b_{nj}) \neq (0,0)$ for $j = 1, \ldots, k2$. Then compute by (an easy modification of) Thiele's method a rational function a_m/b_n in y solving

$$b_{nj}a_m(y_j) - a_{mj}b_n(y_j) = 0, j = 1, \ldots, k_2.$$

Let $c_j := a_m(y_j)/a_{mj}$ if $a_{mj} \neq 0$ and $c_j := b_n(y_j)/b_{nj}$ if $a_{mj} = 0$. Then find by polynomial interpolation for every $i \in \{1, \ldots, k1\}$ the lowest degree polynomial a_i satisfying

$$a_i(y_j) = c_j a_{ij}, j = 1, \ldots, k2$$

and the lowest degree polynomial b_i satisfying

$$b_i(y_j) = c_j b_{ij}, j = 1, \ldots, k2.$$

Then the rational function P^*/Q^* defined by

$$P^*(x,y) := \Sigma_{l=0}^m a_l(y)x^l, \; Q^*(x,y) := \Sigma_{l=0}^n b_l(y)x^l$$

satisfies

$$\begin{aligned} P^*(x_i, y_j) - d_{ij}Q^*(x_i, y_j) &= \Sigma_l a_l(y_j)x_i^l - d_{ij}\Sigma_l b_l(y_j)x_i^l \\ &= c_j\Sigma_l a_{lj}x_i^l - c_j d_{ij}\Sigma_l b_{lj}x_i^l = c_j[p_j(x_i) - d_{ij}q_j(x_i)] = 0 \end{aligned} \tag{3.4}$$

If the data d_{ij} are the values of a rational function P/Q evaluated at (x_i, y_j) for $i = 1, \ldots, k1, j = 1, \ldots, k2$, then by construction $P(x, y_j)/Q(x, y_j) = p_j(x)/q_j(x), j = 1, \ldots, k2$, for sufficiently great $k1$. p_j/q_j and P/Q are reduced. Therefore only for degenerate cases $P(., y_j)/Q(., y_j)$ is not reduced. Hence only in these cases $P(x, y_j) = c_j p_j(x)$ and $Q(x, y_j) = c_j q_j(x)$ holds, where c_j is not a constant polynomial. Apart of these degenerations, we have by comparing the coefficients of the powers of x,

$$a_i(y_j) = c_j a_{ij}, \quad b_i(y_j) = c_j b_{ij}, j = 1, \ldots, k2, \tag{3.5}$$

when $P(x,y) = \Sigma a_i(y)x^i, Q(x,y) = \Sigma b_i(y)x^i$ and $p_j(x) = \Sigma a_{ij}x^i, q_j(x) = \Sigma b_{ij}x^i$. By 3.5 the univariate polynomials a_i and b_i are uniquely determined if there are sufficiently many interpolation points y_j, i.e. if $k2$ is sufficiently great, and if c_j is known in advance. But this can be reconstructed by a univariate rational interpolation as described above.
Therefore this new method reconstructs a rational function P/Q, if only for a restricted number of second components y_j of points in all $T_{(k1,k2)}$ the rational function $P(., y_j)/Q(., y_j)$ is reducible or both $deg(P(., y_j))$ and $deg(Q(., y_j))$ are simultaneously less than $deg(P, x)$ and $deg(Q, x)$ resp.
H. Melenk and the author compared the method described by Siemaszko and the new one by some examples. We run the procedures on a CRAY X-MP using REDUCE 3.3 and obtained the following, where x means, that the result was different from the function to be reconstructed.

P/Q	Siemaszko 10 × 10 points	Siemaszko 20 × 20 points	New method 10 × 10 points	New method 20 × 20 points
$\frac{xy+1}{x+y+2}$	1.2 sec	1.1 sec	0.8 sec	3.2 sec
$\frac{3x^2+xy-7y}{y^2+x+3}$	x	6.0 sec	1.2 sec	5.0 sec
$\frac{xy-1}{x+y+2}$	0.8 sec	1.2 sec	0.9 sec	3.2 sec
$\frac{(x-y)^2-2xy}{(x-y)^2+1}$	x	7.0 sec	1.5 sec	5.5 sec
$\frac{(x-y)^4-4xy^3}{(x-y)^4+1}$	x	x	2.2 sec	11.0 sec
$\frac{(x-y)^6-6xy^5}{(x-y)^6+1}$	x	x	x	20.1 sec

The examples show that the method investigated by Siemaszko is only for rational functions of very low numerator and denominator degree (0 or 1) comparable or better than the new method. For moderate degrees the new method gives better results. The reason is that the functions P_k/Q_k depending on P/Q as in 3.1 have unproportionally high (numerator and denominator) degrees. Hence their reconstruction by univariate rational interpolation is very time consuming. And we observed in these P_k/Q_k coefficients of remarkable length (more than 100 digits). So there are also storage problems. On the other hand, the new method interpolates only rational functions or polynomials, where the degrees never surpass the degrees of the rational function P/Q.

4. n-variate rational interpolation

The method described by Siemaszko can be generalized to the n−variate case in the following way. Consider the grid $T_{(k1,\ldots,kn)} := \{(x_{1,i1},\ldots,x_{n,in}) \mid 1 \le i1 \le k1,\ldots,1 \le in \le kn\}$. For every fixed $(i2,\ldots,in)$ calculate by Thiele's method the univariate rational function in x_1

$$\frac{P_{i2,\ldots,in}}{Q_{i2,\ldots,in}} = \frac{P^{(0)}_{i2,\ldots,in}}{Q^{(0}_{i2,\ldots,in}} + \frac{x_1-x_{11} \;|}{|P^{(1)}_{i2,\ldots,in}/Q^{(1)}_{i2,\ldots,in}} + \ldots + \frac{x_1-x_{1s} \;|}{|P^{(s)}_{i2,\ldots,in}/Q^{(s)}_{i2,\ldots,in}} \tag{4.1}$$

interpolating $d_{i1,\ldots,in}$ at $x_{1,i1}, 1 \le i1 \le k1$. s can be assumed to be a global variable, because continued fractions like 4.1 can be extended by adding arbitrary terms of similar type provided the first of them has a denominator $P^{(s+1)}_{i2,\ldots,in}/Q^{(s+1)}_{i2,\ldots,in}$ with $Q^{(s+1)}_{i2,\ldots,in} = 0$. The rational function P/Q which we will reconstruct has a continued fraction

$$\frac{P}{Q} = \frac{P^{(0)}}{Q^{(0)}} + \frac{x_1-x_{11} \;|}{|P^{(1)}/Q^{(1)}} + \ldots + \frac{x_1-x_{1s} \;|}{|P^{(s)}/Q^{(s)}}, \tag{4.2}$$

where $P^{(k)}/Q^{(k)}$ depends on $x_2,\ldots,x_n$. Then the $(n-1)$-variate variant of the method calculates $P^{(k)}/Q^{(k)}$ from the value $P^{(k)}_{i2,\ldots,in}/Q^{(k)}_{i2,\ldots,in}$ at point $(x_{2,i2},\ldots,x_{n,in})$.
The degrees of (numerator and denominator) of the rational functions in the intermediate steps of this method will certainly surpass the degrees of the rational function P/Q, as we already detected in the bivariate case. In addition, one n-variate reconstruction requires roughly $deg(P,x_1) + deg(Q,x_1) + 1$ $(n-1)$-variate reconstructions of rational functions with higher degrees. Therefore we expect an efficient reconstruction by this method only for for rational functions with extremely low numerator and denominator degree. On the other hand, it is a robust method. It always reconstructs the function, if enough time and enough storage is available.
The $n-$ variate generalization of our new method also interpolates on a grid $T_{(k1,\ldots,kn)}$. For every fixed $(i2,\ldots,in)$ calculate the univariate rational function in x_1 $P_{i2,\ldots,in}/Q_{i2,\ldots,in}$ which interpolates $d_{i1,\ldots,in}$ at $x_{1,i1}, 1 \le i1 \le k1$. Let m resp. m' be the maximal degree of all $P_{i2,\ldots,in}$ resp. $Q_{i2,\ldots,in}$ and $a^{(m)}_{i2,\ldots,in}$ resp. $b^{(m')}_{i2,\ldots,in}$ the coefficient of x_1^m in $P_{i2,\ldots,in}$ resp. of $x_1^{m'}$ in $Q_{i2,\ldots,in}$. Reduce now the grid $T_{(k1,\ldots,kn)}$ to a new grid by cancelling point, such that in the new grid always $(a^{(m)}_{i2,\ldots,in}, b^{(m')}_{i2,\ldots,in}) \neq$

$(0,0)$ holds. Let w.l.o.g. $T_{(k1,\ldots,kn)}$ be this grid again. Then solve the $(n-1)$-variate rational interpolation problem

$$P_m(x_{2,i2},\ldots,x_{n,in}) - \frac{a^{(m)}_{i2,\ldots,in}}{b^{(m')}_{i2,\ldots,in}} Q_{m'}(x_{2,i2},\ldots,x_{n,in}) = 0, 1 \le i2 \le k2, \ldots, 1 \le in \le kn. \tag{4.3}$$

Let

$$P_{i2,\ldots,in}(x_1) = \Sigma^m_{i=0} a^{(i)}_{i2,\ldots,in} x_1^i, Q_{i2,\ldots,in}(x_1) = \Sigma^{m'}_{i=0} b^{(i)}_{i2,\ldots,in} x_1^i$$

and

$$c_{i2,\ldots,in} := \begin{cases} P_m(x_{2,i2},\ldots,x_{n,in})/a^{(m)}_{i2,\ldots,in} & \text{if } a^{(m)}_{i2,\ldots,in} \neq 0 \\ Q_{m'}(x_{2,i2},\ldots,x_{n,in})/b^{(m')}_{i2,\ldots,in} & \text{if } a^{(m)}_{i2,\ldots,in} = 0. \end{cases}$$

Then the rational function P/Q which we want to reconstruct is given by

$$P = \Sigma^m_0 P_i(x_2,\ldots,x_n) x_1^i, Q = \Sigma^{m'}_0 Q_i(x_2,\ldots,x_n) x_1^i, \tag{4.4}$$

where P_i and Q_i are determined (in case the grid contains enough points) by the interpolation conditions

$$P_i(x_{2,i2},\ldots,x_{n,in}) = c_{i2,\ldots,in} \cdot a^{(i)}_{i2,\ldots,in}, \quad Q_i(x_{2,i2},\ldots,x_{n,in}) = c_{i2,\ldots,in} \cdot b^{(i)}_{i2,\ldots,in}.$$

The advantage of this method is that no intermediate rational function has unnecessary great degrees, and that only one $(n-1)$-variate variant of this method is needed for the n-variate method. On the other hand, there are degenerate cases, where the rational function reconstruction fails.

REFERENCES

[1] G. E. Collins, M. Mignotte, F. Winkler (1982), Arithmetic in basic algebraic domains. Published in: Computer Algebra – Symbolic and Algebraic Computation (eds.: B. Buchberger, G. E. Collins, R. Loos), Computing Suppl. 4, 189 –220.

[2] A. A. M. Cuyt and B. M. Verdonk (1985), Multivariate rational interpolation. Computing 34, 41 – 61.

[3] Kh. I. Kuchminskaya and W. Siemaszko (1985), Rational approximation and interpolation of functions by branched continued fractions. Published in: Rational Approximation and its Application in Mathematics and Physics, Lecture Notes in Mathematics Vol. 1237 (ed.: J. Gilewicz, M. Pindor, W. Siemaszko), Springer-Verlag, Berlin–Heidelberg–New York, 1987, 24 – 40.

[4] H. Melenk (1988) Private communication.

[5] K. Rimey (1984), A system of polynomial equations and a solution by an unusual method. ACM SIGSAM Bull. 18, Nr.1.

[6] C. Schneider and W. Werner (1986), Some new aspects of rational interpolation. Math. of Comp. 47, Nr. 175, 285 – 299.

[7] W. Siemaszko (1983), Thiele-type branched continued fractions for two-variable functions. J. Comp. and Appl. Math. 9, 137 – 153.

H. M. Möller, FernUniversität Hagen, FB Mathematik & Informatik, D-5800 Hagen, FRG

International Series of
Numerical Mathematics, Vol. 90

ON THE ROLE OF THE EXPONENTIAL EIGEN SPLINES IN TRANSLATION INVARIANT PERIODIC SPLINE SPACES

H.G. ter Morsche
Department of Mathematics
University of Technology
Eindhoven, The Netherlands

1. Introduction

As pointed out by I.J. Schoenberg in his beautiful work on cardinal spline functions (cf. SCHOENBERG [4]) the so-called exponential eigen splines play a fundamental rôle in cardinal spline spaces. The reason is the simple observation that the associated uniform knot distribution is invariant with respect to translation over the mesh size. The eigen functions for the corresponding shift operator are just the exponential eigen splines. In the multivariate setting translation invariance may concern several directions and distances depending on the grid shape. In stead of saying that the grid-partition is translation invariant, we say that the corresponding spline space is translation invariant.

To be more precise and more general a linear space V (over $\mathbb{C}$) of complex- valued functions defined on $\mathbb{R}^n$ is called translation invariant with respect to n independent vectors $v_1, v_2, \cdots, v_n$ in $\mathbb{R}^n$ if and only if

$$T_j(f) \in V \quad (f \in V; j=1,2, \cdots, n).$$

Here T_j is the shift operator:

$$(1.1) \qquad T_j f(x) := f(x+v_j).$$

Now a function s in V is called an (exponential) eigen function corresponding to an n-tuple $z=(z_1, \cdots, z_n) \in \mathbb{C}^n$ of complex numbers if

$$T_j(s) = z_j\, s \quad (j=1,2, \cdots, n).$$

In this note our attention is focussed on the role of the exponential eigen functions in subspaces of V consisting of (multi) periodic functions f for which

$$f(x+N_j v_j) = f(x) \quad (x \in \mathbb{R}^n; j=1,2, \cdots, n),$$

where $N=(N_1, N_2, \cdots, N_n) \in \mathbb{N}^n$.

A function f satisfying this periodicity condition is called an N-periodic function. The linear subspace of V consisting of the N-periodic functions in V is denoted by V^N. An exponential eigen function s based on the n-tuple $(z_1, z_2, \cdots, z_n)$ is N-periodic in case $z_j^{N_j}=1$ $(j=1, \cdots, n)$. Therefore it has the property

$$s(x+v_j)=e^{2\pi i\mu_j/N_j}\,s(x)\quad(x\in \mathbb{R}^n;j=1,\cdots,n),$$

where $\mu=(\mu_1,\cdots,\mu_n)\in\omega_N$ with

$$\omega_N=\left\{\mu\in\mathbb{Z}^n\mid\mu_j\in\{0,1,\cdots,N_j-1\}\right\}.$$

The next section deals with some basic properties of the N-periodic eigen functions. Especially if V^N is supplied with a semi inner product, which is also translation invariant in some sense. In fact, it will be shown in that section that V^N has an orthogonal base consisting of N-periodic eigen functions, which can be used to compute the dimension of V^N. This is illustrated by an example with respect to bivariate periodic splines on a three direction mesh. Section 3 is devoted to an application of the obtained properties to least semi norm interpolation by means of periodic splines on a rectangular mesh.

2. Some basic properties of the N-periodic exponential eigen functions

By E_μ $(\mu\in\omega_N)$ we denote the space of the N-periodic eigen functions corresponding to the n-tuple of "frequencies" $(\mu_1/N_1,\mu_2/N_2,\cdots,\mu_n/N_n)$. Hence, $s\in E_\mu$ if and only if

$$s(x+v_j)=e^{2\pi i\mu_j/N_j}\,s(x)\quad(x\in\mathbb{R}^n;j=1,2,\cdots,n).$$

The first basic property of the N-periodic eigen functions is contained in the following lemma. In this lemma a direct sum of spaces is denoted by $\sum^{\oplus}$.

Lemma 2.1. Let V be a translation invariant space of functions defined on $\mathbb{R}^n$ with respect to the n independent vectors $v_1, v_2,\cdots, v_n$ and let $N=(N_1,N_2,\cdots,N_n)\in\mathbb{N}^n$. Then

$$V^N=\sum_{\mu\in\omega_N}{}^{\oplus}E_\mu.$$

Proof. The DFT (Discrete Fourier Transform) of an N-periodic sequence (a_v), $v\in\mathbb{Z}^n$, of complex numbers ($a_{v+N_je_j}=a_v$ $(j=1,\cdots,n)$) is given by

$$\hat a_\mu=\sum_{v\in\omega_N}a_v\,e^{-2\pi i(\frac{\mu_1v_1}{N_1}+\cdots+\frac{\mu_nv_n}{N_n})}\quad(\mu\in\mathbb{Z}^n).$$

The sequence (a_v) can be recovered by means of the inverse DFT:

$$a_v=\frac{1}{N_1N_2\cdots N_n}\sum_{\mu\in\omega_N}\hat a_\mu\,e^{2\pi i(\frac{\mu_1v_1}{N_1}+\cdots+\frac{\mu_nv_n}{N_n})}.$$

Now let $f\in V^N$. We apply the DFT to the N-periodic sequence

$$a_\mu=f(x-\mu_1v_1-\mu_2v_2-\cdots-\mu_nv_n).$$

It can easily be shown that the function s_μ defined by $s_\mu(x)=\hat a_\mu$ is an N-periodic eigen function corresponding to the frequencies $(\mu_1/N_1,\cdots,\mu_n/N_n)$. Hence, $s_\mu\in E_\mu$. Note that s_μ can be identically zero. By the inverse DFT, we have

$$f(x)=\frac{1}{N_1N_2\cdots N_n}\sum_{\mu\in\omega_N}s_\mu(x).$$

Apparently, every $f \in V^N$ is a linear combination of N-periodic eigen functions. There remains to prove that $E_\mu \cap E_\nu$ consists only of the null function if $\mu, \nu \in \omega_N$ and $\mu \neq \nu$.
So, let $f \in E_\mu \cap E_\nu$. Then

$$e^{2\pi\mu_j/N_j} f(x) = f(x+\nu_j) = e^{2\pi\nu_j/N_j} f(x) \quad (x \in I\!R^n; j=1, \cdots, n).$$

Since $\mu_j \neq \nu_j \pmod{N_j}$ for some j, we conclude that $f(x)=0$. □

It is an immediate consequence of the previous lemma that

$$\text{(2.1)} \qquad \dim V^N = \sum_{\mu \in \omega_n} \dim E_\mu .$$

This formula can be very helpful for computing the dimension of V^N.
As an example we consider the space S_k^ρ of bivariate polynomial splines of degree at most k and global smoothness ρ on the so-called three direction mesh (type–1 triangulation) obtained by drawing in the x_1, x_2 plane the mesh lines $x_1 = \nu_1$, $x_2 = \nu_2$, $x_1 = x_2 + \nu_3$ $(\nu_1, \nu_2, \nu_3 \in \mathbb{Z})$. The space $V = S_k^\rho$ is translation invariant with respect to the unit vectors e_1, e_2. It is shown in TER MORSCHE [3] as a part of a much more general result that for $\rho = 2l$ and $k = 3l+1$ the following formula holds.

$$\dim E_\mu = \begin{cases} 1 & (t=0), \\ l+1 & (t=1), \\ 3l+1 & (t=3), \end{cases}$$

where t is the number of ones in the sequence $(e^{2\pi i\mu_1/N_1}, e^{2\pi i\mu_2/N_2}, e^{2\pi i(\mu_1/N_1+\mu_2/N_2)})$ $(\mu \in \omega_N)$.
From (2.1) we then have

$$\text{(2.2)} \qquad \dim V_N = N_1 N_2 + l(N_1 + N_2 + gcd(N_1, N_2)) \quad (\rho = 2l),$$

In KREBS [1] a similar technique is applied for the computation of the dimension of continuous periodic spline spaces with respect to a uniform hexagon partition of the x_1, x_2 plane.

Let us now return to the general case of the translation invariant space of functions defined on $I\!R^n$ and assume that the subspace V^N is supplied with a semi inner product $<,>$ which is translation invariant in the sense:

$$<T_j f, T_j g> = <f, g> \quad (f, g \in V^N; j=1, \cdots, n).$$

Here T_j is defined in (1.1).
It is a direct consequence of the definition of the eigen function that

$$<f, g> = 0 \quad (f \in E_\mu, g \in E_\nu, \mu, \nu \in \omega_N, \mu \neq \nu).$$

This property and Lemma 2.1 finally lead to the following theorem

Theorem 2.2. Let V be a translation invariant space of functions defined on $\mathbb{R}^n$ with respect to the n independent vectors $v_1, v_2, \cdots, v_n$. Let the subspace V^N $(N \in \mathbb{N}^n)$ be supplied with a translation invariant inner product $<,>$. Then the following holds:
To every $f \in V^N$ there exist N-periodic eigen functions $s_\mu \in E_\mu$ $(\mu \in \omega_N)$ such that

$$\begin{cases} f = \sum\limits_{\mu \in \omega_N} s_\mu , \\ <f, f> = \sum\limits_{\mu \in \omega_N} <s_\mu , s_\mu> . \end{cases}$$

3. Minimum norm interpolation

The interpolation problem we will consider in this note is of cardinal type, which can be formulated in this context as follows.
Let $\alpha \in [0, 1)^n$ and let (y_ν) be an N-periodic sequence of data (complex numbers). The question is to find a function f in a N-periodic space V^N which is translation invariant with respect to the n independent vectors $v_1, v_2, \cdots, v_n$, such that

(3.1) $$f(\alpha+\mu_1 v_1+\mu_2 v_2+\cdots+\mu_n v_n)=y_\mu \quad (\mu\in \mathbb{Z}^n) .$$

Due to the periodicity, we are faced with a total number of $N_1 N_2 \cdots N_n$ interpolation data. It happens frequently in the more dimensional situation that $\dim V^N > N_1 N_2 \cdots N_n$ (cf. (2.2)). In general, we like to have an interpolation problem that is unisolvent, i.e., it has a unique solution for every N-periodic sequence of data. Therefore, some additional conditions are needed. In cardinal spline interpolation. (cf. STÖCKLER [5], TER MORSCHE [2]) one selects a specific $N_1 N_2 \cdots N_n$ dimensional subspace of V^N generated by translates of a fixed function in V. Then the extra condition is that the interpolating function must belong to that subspace.
We propose here to use as a selection for the interpolating functions the solution having a minimal given semi norm among all the possible candidates. Thereby, we assume that the semi norm $\|\cdot\|$ stems from a translation invariant inner product. In fact that means again that the interpolating function is an element of a specific $N_1 N_2 \cdots N_n$ dimensional subspace. First, we have to verify that there exists at least one function in V^N satisfying (3.1). As shown in the next lemma this is controlled by the N-periodic eigen splines.

Lemma 3.1. Let $\alpha \in [0, 1)^n$ be given. Then for every N-periodic sequence of data there exists at least one function f in V^N satisfying (3.1) if and only if there corresponds to every $\mu \in \omega_N$ a function $s_\mu \in E_\mu$ such that

(3.2) $$s_\mu(\alpha) \neq 0 .$$

This lemma can easily be proven by using the DFT. To find a unique minimal norm solution we need a further assumption for the space V^N in combination with the semi inner product. This assumption can entirely be expressed in terms of the N-periodic eigen functions as follows.

(3.3) $$\begin{cases} \text{For every } \mu \in \omega_N \text{ there is a unique } \tilde{s}_\mu \in E_\mu \\ \text{satisfying} \\ \|\tilde{s}_\mu\| = \min \{\|s_\mu\| \mid s_\mu \in E_\mu , s_\mu(\alpha) = 1\} . \end{cases}$$

Note that assumption (3.3) implies that the trivial function $s_\mu = 0$ is the only function satisfying $\|s_\mu\| = 0$, $s_\mu(\alpha) = 0$.

Theorem 3.2. To every N-periodic sequence (y_ν) $(\nu \in \mathbb{Z}^n)$ there corresponds a unique function $f \in V^N$ satisfying (3.1) and having minimal semi norm $\|f\|$ if and only if (3.3) holds. Moreover, the unique solution can be written as

$$f = \frac{1}{N_1 N_2, \cdots, N_n} \sum_{\mu \in \omega_N} \hat{y}_\mu \tilde{s}_\mu .$$

The proof of this theorem follows directly from Theorem 2.2 and properties of the DFT.
As an illustration of the previous theorem we present now a simple example dealing with bivariate polynomial splines on the rectangular mesh defined by the mesh lines $x_1 = \nu_1$, $x_2 = \nu_2$ $(\nu_1, \nu_2 \in \mathbb{Z})$.
The space V is the space of polynomial splines of degree k and global smoothness ρ on the rectangular mesh. This space is translation invariant with respect to the unit vectors e_1 and e_2. Let Δ^m be the m-th iterate of the Laplacian $\Delta = \partial^2_{x_1} + \partial^2_{x_2}$. On the N-periodic subspace V^N of V the following semi inner product is defined.

$$<f, g> = \frac{1}{N_1 N_2} \int_{[0,N_1]\times[0,N_2]} (\Delta^m f)\, \overline{g}\, dx \quad (f, g \in V^N),$$

where $\overline{g}$ is the complex conjugate of g and $2m \leq \rho + 1$.
The interpolation points are taken at the lattice points $\nu \in \mathbb{Z}^2$. Hence $\alpha = 0$.
In order to solve the minimum norm interpolation problem, we need the exponential eigen functions in V^N. For the rectangular mesh the exponential eigen splines can easily be represented by means of the univariate exponential splines $t \to H_l(\lambda, t)$ $(\lambda \in \mathbb{C}, t \in \mathbb{R})$ of degree l, which satisfy the functional relation

$$H_l(\lambda, t+1) = \lambda H_l(\lambda, t) \quad (t \in \mathbb{R}),$$

and which have smoothness $l-1$ if $\lambda \neq 1$ and smoothness $l-2$ if $\lambda = 1$. It is well known that the restriction of $H_l(\lambda, \cdot)$ to the interval $[0, 1]$ corresponds to a generalized Euler-Frobenius polynomial in case $\lambda \neq 1$ or to a Bernoulli polynomial in case $\lambda = 1$ (cf. TER MORSCHE [3]). We normalize $H_l(\lambda, \cdot)$ by requiring that $H_l^{(l)}(\lambda, \cdot) \equiv 1$ on $(0, 1)$. For a given smoothness ρ, the smallest value k for which there exist compactly supported splines in V is given by $k = 2\rho + 2$. From now on we assume that $k = 2\rho + 2$.
The eigen spaces E_μ $(\mu \in \omega_N)$ may be written as a linear span in the following way:

$$E_\mu = \begin{cases} <H_{\rho+1}(z_1, x_1) H_{\rho+1}(z_2, x_2)> & (z_1 \neq 1, z_2 \neq 1), \\ <H_l(z_2, x_2) \mid l = \rho+1, \cdots, 2\rho+2> & (z_1 = 1, z_2 \neq 1), \\ <H_l(z_1, x_1) \mid l = \rho+1, \cdots, 2\rho+2> & (z_1 \neq 1, z_2 = 1), \\ <H_i(1, x_1), H_j(1, x_2) \mid i, j = \rho+2, \cdots, 2\rho+2> & (z_1 = 1, z_2 = 1), \end{cases}$$

where $z_1 = e^{2\pi i \mu_1 / N_1}$ and $z_2 = e^{2\pi i \mu_2 / N_2}$. With help of these representations of E_μ and well-known properties of the univariate exponential eigen splines, we are able to solve the minimum norm interpolation problem in V^N. Due to Theorem 3.2 it suffices to give the functions $\tilde{s}_\mu$. For our interpolation problem we have obtained the following results.

If ρ is even then (3.2) is always satisfied, and

$$\tilde{s}_\mu = \begin{cases} \tilde{H}_{\rho+1}(z_1, x_1)\,\tilde{H}_{\rho+1}(z_2, x_2) & (z_1 \neq 1, z_2 \neq 1)\,, \\ \tilde{H}_{2m-1}(z_2, x_2) & (z_1 = 1, z_2 \neq 1)\,, \\ \tilde{H}_{2m-1}(z_1, x_1) & (z_1 \neq 1, z_2 = 1)\,, \\ 1 & (z_1 = z_2 = 1)\,. \end{cases}$$

Here $\tilde{H}_l(z_1, x) = H_l(z, x) / H_l(z, 0)$.

References

[1] F. Krebs (1988) Periodische Splines auf dem Regelmässigen sechseckgitter. Thesis, Dortmund.

[2] H.G. ter Morsche (1986) Bivariate cubic periodic spline interpolation on a three direction mesh. EUT Report 86-Wsk-02, Eindhoven University of Technology, Eindhoven.

[3] H.G. ter Morsche (1988) On the dimension of bivariate periodic spline spaces : type– 1 triangulation. Reports on Applied and Numerical Analysis (RANA 88-05), Eindhoven University of Technology, Eindhoven

[4] I.J. Schoenberg (1973) Cardinal spline interpolation. Regional conference series in applied mathematics **12**, Siam, Philadelphia.

[5] J. Stöckler (1988) Interpolation mit mehrdimensionalen Bernoulli-Splines und periodischen Box-Splines. Thesis, Duisburg.

H.G. ter Morsche
Department of Mathematics
University of Technology
P.O. Box 513
5600 MB Eindhoven
The Netherlands

International Series of
Numerical Mathematics, Vol. 90

UNIFORM CLOSURE OF TENSOR PRODUCT OF LINEAR SUBSPACES

João B. Prolla

UNICAMP - IMECC, Campinas, SP, Brazil.

1. Introduction

When X is a compact Hausdorff space and E is normed space, $C(X;E)$ denotes the space of all continuous mappigs $f : X \to E$, equipped with the sup-norm

$$\|f\| = \sup\{\|f(x)\|_E \; ; \; x \in X\}.$$

When $E = \mathbb{R}$, we write $C(X) = C(X, \mathbb{R})$.
Suppose now that S and T are two compact Hausdorff spaces, and that two linear subspaces $G \subset C(S)$ and $H \subset C(T)$ are given. We are interested in the following bivariate approximation problem.
Q. Which functions $f \in C(S \times T)$ can be uniformly approximated on $S \times T$ by functions of the form

$$w(s,t) = \sum_{i=1}^{n} g_i(s)h_i(t)$$

where $g_i \in G$, $h_i \in H$, and $n \in \mathbb{N}$ is arbitrary.
Let us denote by $G \otimes H$ the subset of $C(S \times T)$ of such functions $w(s,t)$, and by $G \overline{\otimes} H$ its uniform closure in $C(S \times T)$. Then our problem can be stated as follows:
Q. Characterize those $f \in C(S \times T)$ that belong to $G \overline{\otimes} H$, i.e., characterize the uniform closure in $C(S \times T)$ of the <u>tensor product</u> $G \otimes H$ of the linear subspaces G and H.

2. Slice products

In order to answer this question, let us recall the definition of the slice-product $G \# H$ introduced by EIFLER (1969): a function $f \in C(S \times T)$ belongs to $G \# H$ if, and only if, for every pair (s,t) its sections f_s and f_t belong to H and G respectively, where f_s is the mapping $y \in T \to f(s,y)$, and f_t is the mapping $x \in S \to f(x,t)$. Clearly, the following inclusions hold

$$G \otimes H \subset G \# H \subset \overline{G} \# \overline{H}$$

where $\overline{G}$ (resp. $\overline{H}$) denotes the uniform closure of G (resp. H) in $C(S)$ (resp. $C(T)$). On the other hand, the slice-product of two closed subspaces is closed. Hence

$$G \mathbin{\overline{\otimes}} H \subset \overline{G} \# \overline{H}.$$

Our objective is to find properties of G and H that will make true the equality

$$G \mathbin{\overline{\otimes}} H = \overline{G} \# \overline{H}.$$

If both G and H are unital subalgebras, then $G \otimes H$ is a unital subalgebra of $C(S \times T)$ and the classical Stone-Weierstrass theorem for subalgebras describes $G \mathbin{\overline{\otimes}} H$, and it is easy to prove that $G \mathbin{\overline{\otimes}} H = \overline{G} \# \overline{H}$. But when G or H is not assumed to be an algebra, then that theorem cannot be used because now $G \otimes H$ is not a subalgebra of $C(S \times T)$. However a stronger version of that theorem, namely a vector-valued version for modules solves the problem if G or H is assumed to be a subalgebra. Notice that in this case $G \otimes H$ is a linear subspace of $C(S \times T)$. We state our solution when G is assumed to be a subalgebra, but of course a similar proof establishes the same result when H is assumed to be a subalgebra (and G is arbitrary).

Theorem 1. If G is a subalgebra of $C(S)$ and H is a linear subspace of $C(T)$, then

$$G \mathbin{\overline{\otimes}} H = \overline{G} \# \overline{H}.$$

The proof of Theorem 1 will appear elsewhere. See PROLLA (preprint).

The strong version of the Stone-Weierstrass theorem that is used in the proof of Theorem 1 is the following. See Theorem 1.26, PROLLA (1977).

Theorem 2. Let X be a compact Hausdorff space and let E be a normed space. Let W be a vector subspace of $C(X;E)$ which is an A-module for some subalgebra $A \subset C(X)$, i.e., $AW \subset W$. Then, for each $f \in C(X;E)$, there exists some equivalence class $[x]$ (mod. A) such that $\text{dist}(f;W) = \text{dist}(f[x]; W[x])$.

Let us explain the notation used above. For each $x \in X$, we denote by $[x]$ the equivalence class of x modulo the following equivalence relation:

$$x \equiv y \ (\text{mod. } A) \iff \varphi(x) = \varphi(y) \text{ for all } \varphi \in A.$$

Then $[x] = \{y \in X;\ \varphi(x) = \varphi(y) \text{ for all } \varphi \in A\}$. Notice that $[x]$ is closed in X, and therefore a compact Hausdorff space. For every function $f \in C(X;E)$, we denote by $f[x]$ the restriction of f to $[x]$. Then $f[x]$ belongs to $C([x];E)$. Finally, if $W \subset C(X;E)$ then

$$W[x] := \{g[x];\ g \in W\} \subset C([x];E)$$

and $\text{dist}(f[x]; W[x])$ is measured in the space $C([x];E)$. When $[x]$ is the singleton $[x]$ one identifies $f[x]$ with $f(x)$ and $W[x]$ with the subspace $W(x) = \{g(x);\ g \in W\} \subset E$.

3. Grothendieck's approximation property

The following result shows that to find a closed vector subspace $G \subset C(S)$ such that $G \overline{\otimes} H$ is properly contained in $G \# H$ for some closed vector subspace $H \subset C(T)$ is equivalent to find such a G without Grothendieck's approximation property.

Theorem 3. For a closed vector subspace $G \subset C(S)$, S compact, the following are equivalent:

(a) G has the approximation property;

(b) for every compact Hausdorff space T and every closed vector subspace $H \subset C(T)$, $G \overline{\otimes} H = G \# H$.

Corollary 1. Every closed subalgebra $G \subset C(S)$, S a compact Hausdorff space, has the approximation property.

The proof of Corollary 1 depends on Theorem 3 whose proof uses several tools from Functional Analysis. Hence an elementary direct proof that any closed subalgebra $G \subset C(S)$ has the approximation property is desirable. Let us recall the definition of the metric approximation property. Let $\lambda \geq 1$. We say that a Banach space E has the λ-bounded approximation property (λ- b.a.p. for short) if, for every totally bounded subset $B \subset E$ and every $\varepsilon > 0$, there is a continuous linear operator $T : E \to E$ of finite rank such that $\|x - Tx\| < \varepsilon$, for all $x \in B$, and $\|T\| \leq \lambda$. We say that E has the metric approximation property if it has the λ- b.a.p. for $\lambda = 1$.

Lemma 1. Let $A \subset C(S)$ be a closed subalgebra containing the constants, and let $x \in S$ be given. If $N(x)$ is an open neighborhood of $[x]$ (mod. A), there exists an open neighborhood $W(x)$ of $[x]$, contained in $N(x)$, and such that, for each $0 < \delta < 1$, there is $\varphi \in A$ such that

(1) $0 \leq \varphi(s) \leq 1$, for all $s \in S$;

(2) $\varphi(t) < \delta$, for all $\notin N(x)$;

(3) $\varphi(t) > 1 - \delta$, for all $t \in W(x)$.

Proof. The result follows from Lemma 1, PROLLA (1988).

Lemma 2. Let A be as in Lemma 1. For each $x \in S$, let there be given an open neighborhood $N(x)$ of $[x]$ (mod. A). There exists a finite set $\{x_1,\dots,x_m\} \subset S$ such that, given $0 < \delta < 1$, there are $\varphi_1,\dots,\varphi_m \in A$ such that

(1) $0 \leq \varphi_i \leq 1$, $i = 1,\dots,m$;

(2) $\Sigma_{i=1}^m \varphi_i(x) = 1$, for all $x \in S$;

(3) $0 \leq \varphi_i(t) < \delta$, if $t \notin N(x_i)$, $i = 1,\dots,m$.

Proof. Select $x_1 \in S$ arbitrarily. Let $K = S \setminus N(x_1)$. For each

$x \in K$, select an open neighborhood $W(x)$ by Lemma 1. By compactness of K, there exists a finite set $x_2,\dots,x_m$ in K such that $K \subset W(x_2) \cup \dots \cup W(x_m)$. Let $0 < \delta < 1$ be given. By Lemma 1, there are $\psi_2,\dots,\psi_m$ in A such that $0 \le \psi_i \le 1$ and $\psi_i(t) < \delta$ for all $t \notin N(x_i)$, and $\psi_i(t) > 1 - \delta$ for all $t \in W(x_i)$, $i = 2,\dots,m$. Define $\varphi_2 = \psi_2$, $\varphi_3 = (1 - \psi_2)\psi_3,\dots,\varphi_m = (1-\psi_2)\dots(1-\psi_{m-1})\psi_m$. Clearly, $\varphi_i \in A$ and $0 \le \varphi_i \le 1$ for all $i = 2,\dots,m$. Since

$$\varphi_2 + \dots + \varphi_m = 1 - (1 - \psi_2)(1 - \psi_3)\dots(1 - \psi_m)$$

can be easily verified by induction, let us define $\varphi_1 = (1-\psi_2)(1-\psi_3)\dots(1-\psi_m)$. Then $\varphi_1 \in A$, $0 \le \varphi_1 \le 1$ and $\varphi_1 + \varphi_2 + \dots + \varphi_m = 1$. Hence (1) and (2) are verified. To prove (3), note that for each $i = 2,\dots,m$ we have $\varphi_i(t) \le \psi_i(t) < \delta$ for all $t \notin N(x_i)$. On the other hand, if $t \notin N(x_1)$, then $t \in K$ and for some index $j = 2,\dots,m$, we have $t \in W(x_j)$. Hence $\psi_j(t) > 1 - \delta$ and so $1 - \psi_j(t) < \delta$. Thus

$$\varphi_1(t) = (1 - \psi_j(t)) \prod_{i \ne j} (1 - \psi_i(t)) < \delta.$$

<u>Theorem 4.</u> Let S be a compact Hausdorff space and let $A \subset C(S)$ be a closed subalgebra. Then A has the 2-bounded approximation property. If A contains the constants, it has the metric approximation property.

<u>Proof</u>. Suppose A contains the constants. Let $\varepsilon > 0$ and $B \subset A$ a totally bounded subset be given. There is a finite set $F \subset B$ such that, given $f \in B$ there is some $g \in F$ with $|f(x) - g(x)| < \varepsilon/3$ for all $x \in S$. For each $x \in S$ define

$$N(x) = \{t \in S; |g(t) - g(x)| < \varepsilon/6, \text{ for all } g \in F\}.$$

Since F is finite, $N(x)$ is open. Notice that if $t \in [x]$ (mod. A), then $g(t) = g(x)$. Hence $N(x)$ is an open neighborhood of $[x]$ (mod. A). There exists a finite set $x_1,\dots,x_m \in S$ with the property stated in Lemma 2. Let $M = \max\{\|g\|;\ g \in F\}$ and choose $0 < \delta < 1$ so small that $12\,m\,M\,\delta < \varepsilon$. For this δ there are $\varphi_1,\dots,\varphi_m \in A$ such that (1) - (3) of Lemma 2 are true. Define a linear operator $T : A \to A$ by setting for all $f \in A$ and $x \in S$:

$$(*) \quad (Tf)(x) = \Sigma_{i=1}^{m} \varphi_i(x) f(x_i)$$

Clearly, T is a finite rank operator, and by (1) and (2), $\|T\| \leq 1$. Let $f \in B$. There exists $g \in F$ such that $\|f - g\| < \varepsilon/3$, and for any $x \in S$,

$$\begin{aligned}|f(x) - (Tf)(x)| &= \Big|\sum_{i=1}^{m} \varphi_i(x)(f(x) - f(x_i))\Big| \\ &\leq \sum_{i=1}^{m} \varphi_i(x)|f(x) - f(x_i)| \\ &\leq \sum_{i=1}^{m} \varphi_i(x)[|f(x) - g(x)| + |g(x) - g(x_i)| + |g(x_i) - f(x_i)|] \\ &\leq \frac{\varepsilon}{3} + \frac{\varepsilon}{3} + \sum_{i=1}^{m} \varphi_i(x)|g(x) - g(x_i)|.\end{aligned}$$

Let $I(x) = \{1 \leq i \leq m;\ x \in N(x_i)\}$ and $J(x) = \{1 \leq i \leq m;\ x \notin N(x_i)\}$. For $i \in I(x)$, we have $|g(x) - g(x_i)| < \varepsilon/6$, and therefore

(a) $\quad \Sigma_{i\in I(x)} \varphi_i(x)|g(x) - g(x_i)| < \frac{\varepsilon}{6} \Sigma_{i\in I(x)} \varphi_i(x) \leq \frac{\varepsilon}{6}$.

For $i \in J(x)$, we have $\varphi_i(x) < \delta$, and therefore

(b) $\quad \Sigma_{i\in J(x)} \varphi_i(x)|g(x) - g(x_i)| < \delta\, \Sigma_{i\in J(x)} |g(x) - g(x_i)|$
$\quad \leq \delta m 2M < \varepsilon/6$.

From (a) and (b), $\Sigma_{i=1}^{m} \varphi_i(x)|g(x) - g(x_i)| < \varepsilon/3$, and so $\|f - Tf\| < \varepsilon$.

Suppose now that A does not contain the non-zero constants. By the Stone-Weierstrass Theorem it is equivalent to say that $N \neq \emptyset$, where $N = \{x \in S;\ \varphi(x) = 0$ for all $\varphi \in A\}$. Let $A_e = A \oplus \mathbb{R}$. Hence A_e is a closed subalgebra containing the constants. Let $\varepsilon > 0$ and $B \subset A$ a totally bounded subset be given. Clearly $B \subset A_e$. Apply the first part to $\varepsilon/2$ and B. Let T be the operator defined in (*), which maps A_e into A_e. Each φ_i is of the form $\varphi_i = \psi_i + \lambda_i$, where $\psi_i \in A$ and $0 \leq \lambda_i \leq 1$. Define $U : A \longrightarrow A$ by setting

$$(Uf)(x) = \sum_{i=1}^{m} \psi_i(x) f(x_i)$$

for all $f \in A$ and $x \in S$. Since $\Sigma_{i=1}^{m} \varphi_i(x) = 1$ is true for all $x \in S$, choosing $x \in N$ we see that $\Sigma_{i=1}^{m} \lambda_i = 1$. Hence

$$|(Uf)(x)| \leq |(Tf)(x)| + |\sum_{i=1}^{m} \lambda_i f(x_i)|$$
$$\leq \|Tf\| + \|f\| \sum_{i=1}^{m} \lambda_i \leq 2\|f\| .$$

Hence $\|U\| \leq 2$. Let us $f \in B$. By the definition of T we have $|f(x) - (Tf)(x)| < \varepsilon/2$ for all $x \in S$. Choosing $x \in N$ we see that $|\Sigma_{i=1}^{m} \lambda_i f(x_i)| < \varepsilon/2$. Hence $\|f - Uf\| < \varepsilon$ for all $f \in B$.

4. Semi-algebras and Δ-subspaces

Let us recall the definition of a semi-algebra: a subset $G \subset C(S)$ is a semi-algebra if $G + G \subset G$, $GG \subset G$ and $\lambda G \subset G$, for all $\lambda \geq 0$. Clearly, if $A \subset C(S)$ is a subalgebra, then the set A^+ is a semi-algebra, where $A^+ = \{g \in A;\ g \geq 0\}$.

We shall say that a semi-algebra G is of type V, if $\{g \in G;\ 0 \leq g \leq 1\}$ has property V. For any non-empty subset $X \subset S$, the set G of all $g \in C(S)$ such that $g(x) \geq 0$, for each $x \in X$, is an example of closed semi-algebra of type V. If A is a unital subalgebra of $C(S)$ then $G = A^+ = \{g \in A;\ g \geq 0\}$ is a semi-algebra of type V.

Theorem 5. If $G \subset C^+(S)$ is a semi-algebra of type V, and H is a linear subspace of $C(T)$, then $G \mathbin{\overline{\otimes}} H = \overline{G} \# \overline{H}$.

Let V be a vector subspace of $C(X;E)$. The set G_V is by definition the set of all pairs (x,y) such that either

(1) $f(x) = f(y) = 0$ for all $f \in V$; or

(2) there exists $t \in \mathbb{R}$, $t \neq 0$, such that $f(x) = td(y)$ for all $f \in V$ and $g(x) \neq 0$ for some $g \in V$.

The set G_V is an equivalence relation for X. Define a map $\gamma : G_V \to \mathbb{R}$ as follows: $\gamma(x,y) = 0$ if (1) is true, and $\gamma(x,y) = t$ if (2) is true. The subsets KS_V and WS_V of all pairs $(x,y) \in G_V$ such that $\gamma(x,y) \geq 0$ and $\gamma(x,y) \in \{0,1\}$, respectively, are likewise equivalence relations for X. (The letters G, KS and WS stand for Grothendieck, Kakutani-Stone and Weierstrass-Stone, respectively.) The vector subspace

$$\Delta(V) = \{f \in C(X;E);\ f(x) = \gamma v(x,y) f(y),$$
$$\text{for all } (x,y) \in \Delta_V\}$$

where $\Delta \in \{G,KS,WS\}$, is called the Δ-hull of V. Notice that $\Delta(V)$ is a closed subspace of $C(X;E)$ containing V, and V is called a Δ-subspace, if $\Delta(V) = \overline{V}$.

If $\Delta \in \{G,KS,WS\}$, we denote by $A(\Delta_V)$ the subalgebra of $C(X)$ of all function $\varphi \in C(X)$ that are constant on the equivalence classes modulo Δ_V, where $V \subset C(X;E)$ is given. When no confusion is feared we write simply $A(\Delta) = A(\Delta_V)$.

Theorem 6. Let V be a Δ-subspace of $C(S)$ such that each equivalence class $[x]$ (mod. $A(\Delta)$) is contained in $[x]$ (mod. Δ_V). Then, for all linear subspaces $H \subset C(T)$, $V \overline{\otimes} H = \overline{V} \# \overline{H}$.

5. References

Eifler, L. (1969) The slice product of function algebras. Proc. Amer. Math. Soc. 23, 559-564.

Prolla, J. B. (1977) Approximation of vector valued functions (North-Holland, Amsterdam).

Prolla, J. B. (1988) A generalized Bernstein approximation theorem. Math. Proc. Cambridge Phil. Soc. 104, 317-330.

Prolla, J. B. (preprint) Slice products in bivariate approximation.

Prof. João B. Prolla, UNICAMP-IMECC, Caixa Postal 6065,
13081 Campinas SP, Brazil.

International Series of
Numerical Mathematics, Vol. 90

ON PERIODIC HERMITE-BIRKHOFF INTERPOLATION BY TRANSLATION

Karin von Radziewski

University of Siegen, Lehrstuhl fuer Mathematik I, Siegen, BRD

0. Introduction:

The equidistant periodic Lagrange interpolation in the space

$$V = \text{span}\ \{ T_{x_j} g \mid 0 \le j < N \}$$

spanned by the translates

$$T_{x_j} g(x) := g(x-x_j)$$

of a function $g \in C_{2\pi}$ with the N knots

$$x_j := 2\pi j/N , \quad 0 \le j < N ,$$

as considered in the papers of DELVOS [1], KNAUFF and KRESS [2], LOCHER [3] and PRAGER [4], can be solved with the help of a very easy algorithm: The functions

$$B_t(x)/B_t(0) \in V \quad \text{with} \quad B_t(x) := \sum_{j=0}^{N-1} e_t(x_j)\ T_{x_j} g(x) \quad , \quad 0 \le t < N ,$$

interpolate the exponential functions

$$e_t(x) := e^{itx}$$

at the N knots $x_m = 2\pi m/N$, $0 \le m < N$. The simple summation

$$s_0 = N^{-1} \sum_{t=0}^{N-1} B_t(x)/B_t(0) \in V$$

of these interpolating functions builds the first fundamental function,

$$s_0(x_m) = N^{-1} \sum_{t=0}^{N-1} e^{itx_m} = \delta_{m0} , \quad 0 \le m < N ,$$

whose translates

$$s_j(x) := T_{x_j} s_0(x) := s_0(x-x_j)$$

do the rest of the work:

$$s_j \in V \quad , \quad s_j(x_m) := s_0(x_m - x_j) = \delta_{j,m} \; .$$

The present paper deals with the generalization of this method to Hermite interpolation and to some Hermite-Birkhoff interpolation problems.

1. Generalizations

At first let us consider the 2π-periodic Hermite interpolation problem with N equidistant knots x_m , $0 \le m < N$, of multiplicities $k+1$. Thus for given data

$$f_q(m) \in \mathbb{C} \; , \quad 0 \le q \le k \; , \; 0 \le m < N \; ,$$

we have to compute a sufficiently often differentiable 2π-periodic function s from a modified space V with

$$D^q s(x_m) = f_q(m) \; , \; 0 \le m < N \; \text{ and } \; 0 \le q \le k \; . \tag{1}$$

In order to include some Hermite-Birkhoff interpolation problems we generalize (1) as follows: With $k+1$ given linear functionals L_q we look for $s \in V$ that fulfills

$$L_q(T_{-x_m} s) = f_q(m) \; , \; 0 \le m < N \; \text{ and } \; 0 \le q \le k \; . \tag{2}$$

This includes (1), using the functionals

$$L_q(s) := (D^{v(q)} s)(c_q) \; , \; c_q \in \mathbb{R} \; , \; v(q) \in \mathbb{N}_0 \; , \tag{3}$$

and also permits gaps in the sequence of derivatives and interpolation at shifted knots

$$x_m + c_q \; , \; 0 \le m < N \; .$$

Now we have to expand the N-dimensional interpolation space

$$V = \text{span} \, \{ \, T_{x_j} g \,|\, 0 \le j < N \, \} \quad , \quad g \in C_{2\pi} \; ,$$

of Lagrange interpolation to dimension $N(k+1)$. A first idea would be to use additional translates:

$$\text{span}\ \{ T_{t_j} g \mid 0 \le j < (k+1)N \} \quad , \quad t_j := j\, x_1/(k+1) \ . \tag{4}$$

In this paper we choose the more general space

$$V = \text{span}\ \{ T_{x_j} g_u \mid 0 \le j < N \ , \ 0 \le u \le k \} \ , \tag{5}$$

that uses the translates of additional functions g_u . Of course the functionals L_q , $0 \le q \le k$, must be defined on g_u . The interpolation problem (3) for example requires $g_u \in C^r_{2\pi}$ with $r \ge \max \{v(0),\dots,v(k)\}$.

This space is indeed a generalization of (4) since (4) can be generated by

$$g_u := T_{t_u} g \ , \ 0 \le u \le k \ .$$

Moreover the space (5) fits into the theory of reproducing kernels used in the following chapter.

2. Existence and uniqueness

Theorem 1: The functions

$$g_u = D^{v(u)}\, T_{c_u}\, p \ , \quad c_u \in \mathbb{R} \ , \quad v(u) \le r \ , \quad 0 \le u \le k \ , \tag{a}$$

defined by

$$p := \sum_{j\in\mathbb{Z}} d_j e_j \quad , \quad d_j \ge 0 \quad , \quad e_j(x) := \exp(ix) \ , \tag{b}$$

with

$$\sum_{j\in\mathbb{Z}} j^{2r}\, d_j < \infty \quad , \quad r \in \mathbb{N}_0 \ , \tag{c}$$

and

$$d_j \ne 0 \quad \text{for} \quad m \le j < m + N(k+1) \quad \text{with} \quad m \in \mathbb{Z} \tag{d}$$

yield unique solutions of the interpolation problems (3) with arbitrary data $f_q(m) \in \mathbb{C}$ in the generalized space (5).

Proof:

Here we give only a short sketch of the proof, for more information see the paper [5] of the author.

The conditions (b) and (c) characterize a reproducing kernel function $K(x,y) := p(x-y)$ of some Hilbert space $H \subseteq C^r_{2\pi}$. In H the functions

$$(-1)^{v(u)} T_{x_j} g_u , \quad 0 \le j < N \text{ and } 0 \le u \le k ,$$

that span the interpolation space V, represent the defining functionals $L_q T_{-x_j}$ of the interpolation problem.

Condition (d) guarantees the existence of the HAAR subspace

$$\operatorname{span}\{e_m, e_{m+1}, \ldots, e_{m+N(k+1)-1}\} \subseteq H$$

of the Hilbert space with fitting dimension corresponding to the interpolation problem. The orthogonal projection of the interpolating function in this HAAR space to the specially chosen V retains the interpolating quality, uniqueness is given by dimension properties. ■

In [2] and [4], with $r = k = 0$, $c_0 = 0$, existence and uniqueness are based on the stronger assumption

$$d_j \ne 0 \text{ for all } j \in \mathbb{Z} . \qquad \text{(c')}$$

3. Computation

While Theorem I can be proved for non-equidistant x_m (see [5]), the following algorithm makes essential use of it. The special choice of the interpolation space V and the definition (2) of the interpolation problem provide us the system

$$\left(L_q T_{-x_m}\right)\left(\sum_{u=0}^{k} \sum_{t=0}^{N-1} \alpha_u(t)\, T_{x_t} g_u\right) = f_q(m) , \quad 0 \le q \le k \text{ and } 0 \le m < N , \qquad (6)$$

of linear equations, where the complex coefficients $\alpha_u(t)$ are to be computed.

Equidistance and the 2π-periodicity of the functions g_u cause the N-periodicity in the argument $m-t$ of

$$\mu_{q,u}(m-t) := L_q(T_{x_{t-m}} g_u) \quad , \quad -N < t-m < N . \tag{7}$$

Considering $\alpha_u(t)$, $f_q(m)$ and $\mu_{q,u}(m-t)$ in the formulation

$$\sum_{u=0}^{k} \left(\sum_{t=0}^{N-1} \alpha_u(t) \; \mu_{q,u}(m-t) \right) = f_q(m)$$

of (6) as N-periodic Functions on $\mathbb{Z}$ in the integer parameter in parentheses, we can regard the inner summation as a convolution

$$(\tau*\mu)(m) := \sum_{t=0}^{N-1} \tau(t) \; \mu(m-t) \quad , \; m \in \mathbb{Z} \; ,$$

of N-periodic functions $\tau,\mu : \mathbb{Z} \to \mathbb{R}$, and apply the periodic discrete Fourier transform

$$\tau^{\wedge}(m) := \sum_{t=0}^{N-1} \tau(t) \; e^{-2\pi imt}$$

to the linear system:

$$\left(\sum_{u=0}^{k} \alpha_u * \mu_{q,u} \right)^{\wedge} = \sum_{u=0}^{k} (\alpha_u * \mu_{q,u})^{\wedge} = f_q^{\wedge} . \tag{8}$$

The theorem of convolution belonging to the discrete periodic Fourier transform yields now

$$\sum_{u=0}^{k} \alpha_u^{\wedge}(w) \; \mu_{q,u}^{\wedge}(w) = f_q^{\wedge}(w) \; , \quad 0 \le q \le k \quad , \quad 0 \le w < N \; , \tag{9}$$

and such we can handle each subset of $k+1$ transformed equations with k+1 variables $\alpha_0^{\wedge}(w),\dots,\alpha_k^{\wedge}(w)$ per knot index w separately. This yields

<u>Theorem 2:</u> The system (8) of linear equations in the $N(k+1)$ variables

$$\alpha_u(t) \; , \; 0 \le u \le k, \; 0 \le t \le N-1,$$

has at least (respectively exactly) one solution, if and only if every of the N systems of (9) in the k+1 variables $y_u(w) := \alpha_u^{\wedge}(w)$ has at least (respectively exactly) one solution. The coefficients of (8) compute from the inverse Fourier transform

$$\alpha_u(w) = N^{-1} \sum_{t=0}^{N-1} y_u(t) \; e^{2\pi iwt} . \tag{10}$$

In Lagrange interpolation the transformed system (9) is perfectly separated. Solvability and uniqueness therefore are equivalent to the criterion

$$g^{\wedge}(w) \neq 0 \ , \quad 0 \leq w < N \ ,$$

that can be found in the papers [1] and [3].

Example: Let $C(w)$, $0 \leq w < N$, be the inverse matrices of the coefficient matrices

$$M(w) := \mu_{q,u}{}^{\wedge}(w)$$

belonging to the subsystems of (9). The simple Data

$$f_q(j) = \delta_{q,u}\,\delta_{j,0}$$

of the u-th fundamental functions s_u , $0 \leq u \leq k$, yield the Fourier transforms

$$f_q{}^{\wedge}(j) = \delta_{q,u} \ .$$

Therefore $\alpha_z{}^{\wedge}(w) = (C(w))_{z,u}$, and the inverse Fourier transforms

$$\alpha_z(w) = N^{-1} \sum_{t=0}^{N-1} (C(t))_{z,u}\, e^{2\pi i w t} \ , \quad 0 \leq z \leq k \ ,$$

solve the interpolation problem.

4. Symmetry

Now let us analyze the simplifications caused by symmetry. For simplicity we consider the interpolation problem (3) and assume Theorem 1 to be applicable with a real valued kernel function p . Thus p must be an even function, and in the case $c_u = 0$ the functions

$$\mu_{q,u}(m) = D^{v(q)}(T_{x_{-m}} D^{v(u)}p)(0) = (D^{v(q)+v(u)}p)(x_m)$$

are even functions in respect to the integer variable m for even order $v(q)+v(u)$ of derivatives, odd functions otherwise. Although we want to compute real valued coefficients $\alpha_u(t)$ of the real valued translates, the transformed system of linear equation (9) requires the inversion of complex valued matrices

$$M(w) := (\mu_{q,u}{}^{\wedge}(w))_{0 \leq q,u \leq k} \ , \quad \mu_{q,u}{}^{\wedge}(w) \in \begin{cases} \mathbb{R} & \text{for even } v(u)+v(q) \\ i\mathbb{R} & \text{for odd } v(u)+v(q) \end{cases} .$$

But we can avoid the complex numbers by inverting a simply transformed matrix:

$$\mathrm{diag}(\lambda_0,\dots,\lambda_k)\ M(w)\ \mathrm{diag}(\bar\lambda_0,\dots,\bar\lambda_k) \in \mathbb{R}^{(k+1)\times(k+1)}\ ,\quad \lambda_j := \begin{cases} 1\ , & v(j) \text{ even} \\ i\ , & v(j) \text{ odd} \end{cases} .$$

This transform and its inverse only change signs of some components of the matrix and remove respectively insert i .

A similar matrix transform appears in the equation

$$M(N-w) = \mathrm{diag}(\lambda_0^{\,2},\dots,\lambda_k^{\,2})\ M(w)\ \mathrm{diag}(\lambda_0^{\,2},\dots,\lambda_k^{\,2})\ ,\quad 1 \le w < N\ , \tag{11}$$

and such replaces the second half of the N matrix inversions by simple change of signs in some coefficients:

$$(C(N-w))_{q,u} = (-1)^{v(q)+v(u)}\ (C(w))_{q,u}\ .$$

Since the odd functions $(C(w))_{q,u}$ are the pure imaginary ones and the even functions are real valued, the inverse Fourier transforms yield real and symmetric coefficients for the symmetric fundamental functions s_u and real valued coefficients for arbitrary real valued data.

Moreover, if the data fulfill

$$f_q(j) = (-1)^{v(q)} f_q(N-j)\ ,\quad 0 \le q \le k \text{ and } 1 \le j < N\ ,$$

for example if $f_q(j) := D^{v(q)} f(x_j)$ of some even function f , the coefficients α_u show the same symmetry as g_u :

$$\alpha_u(t) = (-1)^{v(u)}\ \alpha_u(N-t)\ ,\quad 0 \le u \le k \text{ and } 1 \le t < N\ ,$$

and the interpolating function $s \in V$ is even.

If

$$f_q(j) = -(-1)^{v(q)} f_q(N-j)\ ,\quad 0 \le q \le k \text{ and } 1 \le j < N\ ,$$

for example if $f_q(j) := D^{v(q)} f(x_j)$ of some odd function f , the coefficients α_u show the opposite symmetry to g_u :

$$\alpha_u(t) = -\ (-1)^{v(u)}\ \alpha_u(N-t)\ ,\quad 0 \le u \le k \text{ and } 1 \le t < N\ ,$$

and the interpolating function $s \in V$ is odd.

5. References

[1] F.-J. DELVOS, *"Periodic Interpolation on Uniform Meshes"*, Journal of Approximation Theory, Vol 51, No.1, September 1987.

[2] W. KNAUFF und R. KRESS, *"Optimale Approximation linearer Funktionale auf periodischen Funktionen"*, Numer.Math.22, 187-205(1974).

[3] F. LOCHER, *"Interpolation on Uniform Meshes By the Translates of One Function and Related Attenuation Factors"*, Mathematics of Computation, Vol. 37, No.156, October 1981.

[4] M. PRÁGER, *"Universally Optimal Approximation of Functionals"*, Aplikace Matematiky, 1979, 406-420.

[5] K. v. RADZIEWSKI, *"On Periodic Hermite Interpolation by Translation of a Kernel Function and its Derivatives"* ,Approximation Theory VI, Academic Press, 1989.

Dr. Karin von Radziewski
Lehrstuhl fuer Mathematik I
University of Siegen
Hölderlinstrasse 3
D-5900 Siegen
Federal Republic of Germany

International Series of
Numerical Mathematics, Vol. 90

Problems and Results in the Calculation of Extremal Fundamental Systems for Sphere and Ball

Manfred Reimer

Fachbereich Mathematik
Universität Dortmund
Federal Republic of Germany

1. Introduction

Let $\mathbb{P}(D)$ denote any space of real polynomial restrictions onto the compact set $D \subset \mathbb{R}^r$, $r \in \mathbb{N} \setminus \{1\}$ with finite dimension N. The nodes $t_1,...,t_N \in D$ are called a fundamental system (with regard to $\mathbb{P}$) if the corresponding evaluation-functionals are linear independent in $\mathbb{P}'$. In this case the Lagrangians $L_1,...,L_N \in \mathbb{P}$ are well-defined by

$$L_j(t_k) = \delta_{j,k} \quad \text{for} \quad j,k \in \{1,...,N\}.$$

They form an extremal basis in the sense of REIMER 1980, if $\|L_j\|$ is minimal for all j-s in the uniform norm, i. e. if $\|L_j\| = 1$ holds for $j \in \{1,...,N\}$. In this case, the fundamental system itself is called extremal. An extremal fundamental system always exists. A sufficient condition is that the determinant $\det(x_j(t_k))$ attains its maximum value for any basis $x_1,...,x_N$ for $\mathbb{P}$, which will not be available in the beginning. However, if $\mathbb{P}$ is in possess of a reproducing kernel $Q(\cdot,\cdot)$ with respect to any inner product, then $t_1,...,t_N$ are extremal if the determinant

$$\det(Q(t_j,t_k))_{j,k=1,...,N} \tag{1}$$

attains its maximum value on D^N. This is the background on which an exchange algorithm of REIMER-SÜNDERMANN 1986 works. What is necessary is to know $Q(\cdot,\cdot)$ explicitly, which is the case if $D = S^{r-1}$ is the unit-sphere and $\mathbb{P}$ is rotation-invariant, such as the space $\overset{*}{\mathbb{H}}{}^r_\mu(S^{r-1})$ of homogeneous harmonic polynomials and the space $\mathbb{P}^r_\mu(D)$ of all "polynomials" on D with degree μ, $\mu \in \mathbb{N}_0$, if $D = S^{r-1}$. The algorithm should converge (theoretically) if it is initiallized by any fundamental system. However, in the case of the spaces $\overset{*}{\mathbb{H}}{}^3_\mu(S^2)$ the algorithm failed in practice. A possible answer to the questions, why, is given in the next chapter. In the last chapter we discuss positive results for the spaces $\mathbb{P}^3_\mu(B^3)$. We should note that the Lagrangians can always be expressed by

$$L_j(x) = \sum_{k=1}^{N} \langle L_j, L_k \rangle \, Q(t_k, x), \qquad j = 1,\ldots,N, \;\; x \in D,$$

where the matrix

$$(\langle L_j, L_k \rangle) = (Q(t_j, t_k))^{-1}$$

can be calculated in advance by a single inversion of the definite matrix $(Q(t_j,t_k))$.

2. Problems Occuring with $\overset{*}{\mathbb{H}}{}^r_\mu$ – an Example

Let $\mathbb{P}(D) = \overset{*}{\mathbb{H}}{}^r_\mu(S^{r-1})$, $r = 3$, $\mu \in \mathbb{N}_0$. In every step, the exchange-algorithm evaluates

$$\|L_1\|, \|L_2\|, \ldots, \|L_N\|.$$

This is very expensive, except, the norms can be evaluated by the aid of Lagrange's conditions. However, we shall discuss a whole family of fundamental systems where all the L_j-s satisfy the Lagrange-conditions of the first and of the second order in t_j without making the determinant (1) maximum. As a consequence, the algorithm will show the numerical tendency to settle down onto a nodal system, which is not yet extremal. The example is the following:

By the use of polar coordinates

$$x(\varphi,\psi) = (\cos\varphi \sin\psi,\ \sin\varphi \sin\psi,\ \cos\psi),$$

the elements $H \in \overset{*}{\mathbb{H}}{}^2_\mu(S^2)$ can be represented by $H(x(\varphi,\psi)) = h(\varphi,\psi)$,

$$h(\varphi,\psi) = \frac{A_0}{2} P^0_\mu(\cos\psi) + \sum_{\nu=1}^{\mu} [A_\nu \cos\nu\varphi + B_\nu \sin\nu\varphi]\, P^\nu_\mu(\cos\psi) \tag{2}$$

where

$$P^\nu_\mu(\xi) = (1-\xi^2)^{\frac{\nu}{2}} P^{(\nu)}_\mu(\xi) \ , \quad \nu \in \{0,1,\ldots,\mu\},$$

are the generalized Legendre-polynomials (with $P_\mu = C^{\frac{1}{2}}_\mu$). The reproducing kernel is now given by

$$Q(x,y) = P(xy) = \frac{2\mu+1}{4\pi} P_\mu(xy) \ , \quad x,y \in S^2,$$

the dimension is $N = 2\mu+1$. Assume that $t_0,\ldots,t_{2\mu} \in S^2$ are equidistributed on the circle where $\psi = \psi_0 \in (0,\frac{\pi}{2}]$, $t_0 = x(0,\psi_0)$. Then the corresponding matrix (1) is circulant and its eigenvalues are the coefficients in the expansion

$$P(\cos^2\psi_0 + \sin^2\psi_0 \cos\varphi) = \frac{\alpha_0}{2} + \sum_{\nu=1}^{\mu} \alpha_\nu \cos\nu\varphi\ ,$$

where $\alpha_1,\ldots,\alpha_\mu$ occur with multiplicity two and where

$$\alpha_\nu = \gamma_{\mu\nu}\, [P^\nu_\mu(\cos\psi_0)]^2, \qquad \gamma_{\mu\nu} \neq 0\ ,$$

cf. REIMER–SÜNDERMANN 1987. Hence

$$\det(P(t_j t_k)) = \gamma_\mu R_\mu(\cos\psi_0) \qquad \gamma_\mu \neq 0\ , \tag{3}$$

if

$$R_\mu(x) := [P_\mu^0(x)]^2 \prod_{\nu=1}^{\mu} [P_\mu^\nu(x)]^4$$

$$= (1-x^2)^{\mu(\mu+1)/2} [P_\mu(x)]^2 \prod_{\nu=1}^{\mu} [P_\mu^{(\nu)}(x)]^4.$$

By this we see that $t_0,\dots,t_{2\mu}$ are fundamental if and only if

$$R_\mu(\cos\psi_0) \neq 0\,. \tag{4}$$

In what follows (4) is assumed to be valid. Then the Lagrangians are defined. Let

$$\ell_j(\varphi,\psi) := L_j(x(\varphi,\psi))\ , \qquad j = 0,1,\dots,2\mu,$$

compare (2). Obviously $\ell_0(\varphi,\psi_0)$ is a trigonometric Lagrangian belonging to equidistant nodes, hence

$$\ell_0(\varphi,\psi) = \frac{1}{2\mu+1}\left\{\frac{P_\mu^0(\cos\psi)}{P_\mu^0(\cos\psi_0)} + 2\sum_{\nu=1}^{\mu}\frac{P_\mu^\nu(\cos\psi)}{P_\mu^\nu(\cos\psi_0)}\cdot\cos\nu\varphi\right\}, \tag{5}$$

$$\ell_j(\varphi,\psi) = \ell_0\left(\varphi - \frac{2\pi j}{2\mu+1}, \psi_0\right), \qquad j \in \{0,1,\dots,2\mu\}\ , \tag{6}$$

are valid. By this it is obvious that

$$\left[\frac{\partial}{\partial\varphi}\ell_0\right](0,\psi_0) = 0, \tag{7}$$

$$\left[\frac{\partial^2}{\partial\varphi^2}\ell_0\right](0,\psi_0) < 0\ , \qquad \left[\frac{\partial^2}{\partial\varphi\partial\psi}\ell_0\right](0,\psi_0) = 0 \tag{8}$$

hold. Now let $\cos\psi_0$ denote one of the many points where $R(x)$ attains a relative maximum. Then we obtain, in addition,

$$\left[\frac{\partial}{\partial\psi}\ell_0\right](0,\psi_0) = 0\,. \tag{9}$$

Note that this derivative can be expressed by the logarithmic derivative of $R(\cos\psi)$. Finally, by the use of (9) we obtain

$$\left[\frac{\partial^2}{\partial\psi^2}\ell_0\right](0,\psi_0) = \frac{\sin^2\psi_0}{2\mu+1}\left[\frac{D^2P^0_\mu}{P^0_\mu(\cos\psi_0)} + 2\sum_{\nu=1}^{\mu}\frac{D^2P^\nu_\mu}{P^\nu_\mu(\cos\psi_0)}\right]_{\cos\psi_0} .$$

Now let us use the differential equation

$$\sin^2\psi\, D^2P^\nu_\mu - 2\cos\psi\, DP^\nu_\mu + \left\{\mu(\mu+1) - \left[\frac{\nu}{\sin\psi}\right]^2\right\} P^\nu_\mu = 0 \ ,$$

TRICOMI, p. 201, again together with (7). Then we obtain

$$\left[\frac{\partial^2}{\partial\psi^2}\ell_0\right](0,\psi_0) = \frac{\mu(\mu+1)}{3}\left\{\frac{1}{\sin^2\psi_0} - 3\right\} .$$

Hence,

$$\left[\frac{\partial^2}{\partial\psi^2}\ell_0\right](0,\psi_0) < 0 \quad \text{iff} \quad \cos^2\psi_0 < \tfrac{2}{3} . \tag{10}$$

However by (6) and (7) to (10), the maximum points of R_μ, satisfying the right hand inequality of (10), are condensating on the interval $[0,\sqrt{\tfrac{2}{3}}]$, and they are all furnishing Lagrangians L_j with a strict local maximum at t_j. However, by the location of the zeros of R_μ, R_μ attains its absolute maximum in a right-hand neighborhood of zero. Hence, there are fundamental systems which are numerous of order μ^2 and providing L_j-s with a local maximum at t_j, but which do not yield the absolute maximum of $R_\mu(x)$ for $x \in [0,1]$. Note that

$$\cos^2\psi_0 > \tfrac{2}{3}$$

implies by (10), together with (7) to (9), that the L_j-s have a saddle-point at t_j for $j = 0,\dots,2\mu$.

3. Extremal Fundamental Systems for $\mathbb{P}_\mu^3(B^3)$

Next let $\mathbb{P}(D) = \mathbb{P}_\mu^r(B^r)$. This space has been treated by U. LINDE, M. REIMER and B. SÜNDERMANN. However, instead of dealing with the problem directly, which is possible, but not convenient, we treated B^r as the projection of

$$S_+^r := \{(x_1,\dots,x_r,x_{r+1}) \mid x_{r+1} \geq 0\} ,$$

defined by

$$S_+^r \ni (x,x_{r+1}) \to x \in B^r ,$$

which is bijektive. For, if we define

$$\mathbb{G}_\mu^{r+1}(S^r) := \{\tilde{H} \in \mathbb{P}_\mu^{r+1}(S^r) \mid \tilde{H}(\cdot,-x_{r+1}) = \tilde{H}(\cdot,x_{r+1})\}$$

and if we define the mapping

$$\mathbb{G}_\mu^{r+1}(S^r) \ni G \to P \in \mathbb{P}_\mu^r(B^r)$$

by

$$P(x) := G(x,\sqrt{1-x^2}) , \quad x \in B^r ,$$

then this defines an isometric isomorphism. Hence,

$$N := \dim \mathbb{G}_\mu^{r+1}(S^r) = \dim \mathbb{P}_\mu^r(B^r) = \begin{bmatrix}\mu+r \\ r\end{bmatrix} ,$$

and if

$$\tilde{t}_1,\dots,\tilde{t}_N \in S^r \text{ are extremal w. r. to } \mathbb{G}_\mu^{r+1}(S^r)$$

then

$$t_1,\dots,t_N \in B^r \text{ are extremal w. r. to } \mathbb{P}_\mu^r(B^r)$$

where the Lagrangians $\tilde{L}_j$ and L_j with respect to these systems are related by

$$\tilde{L}_j(\tilde{x}) = L_j(x) \;, \qquad j = 1,\dots,N.$$

Now define

$$<\tilde{F},\tilde{G}> := \int_{S^r} \tilde{F}(\tilde{x})\tilde{G}(\tilde{x})d\tilde{x} \qquad \text{for} \quad \tilde{F},\tilde{G} \in \mathbb{P}_\mu^{r+1}(S^r)$$

(surface integral). The space $\mathbb{G}_\mu^{r+1}(S^r)$ is no more rotation-invariant, such that the reproducing kernel has to be determined. But, the space is subspace of the space $\mathbb{P}_\mu^{r+1}(S^{r+1})$, the kernel of which is given by

$$D(\tilde{x}\tilde{y}) = \frac{1}{\omega_{r+1}} \left\{ C_\mu^{\frac{r+1}{2}}(\tilde{x}\tilde{y}) + C_{\mu-1}^{\frac{r+1}{2}}(\tilde{x}\tilde{y}) \right\}$$

where $\omega_{r+1} = <1,1>$. $D(\tilde{x}\tilde{y})$ reproduces also the elements of $\mathbb{G}_\mu^{r+1}(S^r)$, though $D(\tilde{x}\cdot)$ is not contained in this space, in general. But the kernel can be gained from $D(\tilde{x}\tilde{y})$ by symmetrisation, it is given by

$$Q(\tilde{x},\tilde{y}) = \frac{1}{2\omega_{r+1}} \left\{ C_\mu^{\frac{r+1}{2}}(xy + x_{r+1}y_{r+1}) + C_{\mu-1}^{\frac{r+1}{2}}(xy + x_{r+1}y_{r+1}) \right.$$
$$\left. + C_\mu^{\frac{r+1}{2}}(xy - x_{r+1}y_{r+1}) + C_{\mu-1}^{\frac{r+1}{2}}(xy - x_{r+1}y_{r+1}) \right\}.$$

As a consequence, the exchange-algorithm can now be applied. We could calculate an extremal fundamental system in case of $r = 3$, $\mu = 6$, for instance, where the dimension is $N = 84$. This means that we had to deal with an highly non-linear problem with 336 variables. By an eigenvalue-technique the corresponding interpolation-norm (Lebesgue-constant) could be estimated by the value of 26, which is about $N/3$. The weights A_j of the corresponding interpolatory cubature for the integral

$$IF := \int_{x \in B^3} F(x) \frac{dx}{\sqrt{1-x^2}} = \frac{1}{2} \int_{\tilde{x} \in S^r} F(x)d\tilde{x}$$

are given by

$$A_j = \int_{x\in B^r} L_j(x) \frac{dx}{\sqrt{1-x^2}} = \frac{1}{2} \int_{\tilde{x}\in S^r} \tilde{L}_j(\tilde{x}) d\tilde{x}$$

and can be calculated from the matrix

$$(<\tilde{L}_j,\tilde{L}_k>) = (Q(\tilde{t}_j,\tilde{t}_k))^{-1}$$

by the formula

$$A_j = \frac{1}{2} <\tilde{L}_j,1> = \frac{1}{2} \sum_{k=1}^{N} <\tilde{L}_j,\tilde{L}_k> \;,$$

$j = 1,2,\ldots,N$. In case of $r = 3$, $\mu = 6$, the relative error in the cubature is about 10^{-8}, if it is applied to entire functions.

4. References

Linde, U., Reimer, M., Sündermann, B. Numerische Berechnung extremaler Fundamentalsysteme. To appear in Computing.

Reimer, M. (1980) Extremal bases for normed vector spaces. Approximation Theory III (Cheney, E., ed., Academic Press) 727 - 728.

Reimer, M., and Sündermann, B. (1986) A Remez-type algorithm for the calculation of extremal fundamental systems for polynomial spaces over the sphere. Computing 37, 43 - 58.

Reimer, M., and Sündermann, B. (1987) Günstige Knoten für die Interpolation mit homogenen harmonischen Polynomen. Resultate der Mathematik 11, 254 - 266.

Tricomi, F.G. (1955) Vorlesungen über Orthogonalreihen (Springer).

Prof. Dr. Manfred Reimer
Fachbereich Mathematik
Universität Dortmund
Postfach 50 05 00
D-4600 Dortmund 50
Federal Republic of Germany.

International Series of
Numerical Mathematics, Vol. 90

BERNSTEIN QUASI-INTERPOLANTS ON [0,1]

Paul Sablonnière
Laboratoire LANS, INSA Rennes, France

1. INTRODUCTION

Let f be some regular function defined on [0,1] and suppose that we only know its values on the sets $X_n = \{ i/n \; ; \; 0 \le i \le n \}$ for all $n \ge 1$. In order to approximate f in the space $\mathbb{P}_n$ (of polynomials of degree at most n), we can use the two following classical operators :

1) The Lagrange interpolation projector :

$$L_n f = \sum_{i=0}^{n} f(i/n)\, \ell_i^n \quad \text{where } \mathscr{L}_n = \left\{ \ell_i^n(x) = \prod_{j \neq i} \left(\frac{nx-j}{i-j} \right), 0 \le i \le n \right\}$$

is the Lagrange basis of $\mathbb{P}_n$ associated with the uniform partition X_n .

2) The Bernstein (quasi-interpolant) operator :

$$B_n f = \sum_{i=0}^{n} f(i/n)\, b_i^n \quad \text{where } \mathscr{B}_n = \left\{ b_i^n(x) = \binom{n}{i} x^i (1-x)^{n-i}, 0 \le i \le n \right\}$$

is the Bernstein basis of $\mathbb{P}_n$.

Both of them have good and bad properties. L_n is exact on $\mathbb{P}_n$(i.e. $L_n p = p$ for all $p \in \mathbb{P}_n$) , but in general $L_n f$ does not converge to f and the norm of L_n (for the Chebyshev norm on C[0,1]) tends to infinity exponentially. On the contrary, $B_n f$ converges uniformly to f in C[0,1] and its norm is equal to one for all $n \ge 1$ but the convergence is very slow. Various attempts have been made to define quasi–interpolants converging faster, but they are somewhat artificial. The quasi–interpolants defined below seem more natural and easier to compute. We hope that they will be useful in various fields of approximation theory and of computer aided geometric design.

The paper is organized as follows : we first give the definitions of Bernstein quasi–interpolants, then we study some convergence and norm properties. Finally, we show that the same technique is applicable to Bernstein operators defined on squares and triangles (more generaly on hypercubes and simplices) and to other types of quasi–interpolants. The corresponding results will be published in further reports (e.g. [11]). Throughout the paper, we use the notation $X = x(1-x)$ for sake of simplicity.

2. B_n AND ITS INVERSE AS DIFFERENTIAL OPERATORS

B_n is an antomorphism of $\mathbb{P}_n$ because the image of the Lagrange basis $\mathcal{L}_n$ is the Bernstein basis $\mathcal{B}_n$. Therefore B_n and $A_n = B_n^{-1}$ can be considered as linear differential operators.

Theorem 1 :

a) $B_n = \sum_{i=0}^{n} \beta_i^n D^i$, where the polynomials $\beta_i^n \in \mathbb{P}_i$ are defined by the recurrence relation :

$$(1) \quad \begin{cases} \beta_o^n(x) = 1 \ , \ \beta_1^n(x) = 0 \ , \text{ and for } i \geq 1 : \\ n(i+1)\ \beta_{i+1}^n(x) = X\ (\ D\beta_i^n(x) + \beta_{i-1}^n(x)\ ) \end{cases}$$

b) $B_n^{-1} = A_n = \sum_{j=0}^{n} \alpha_j^n D^j$, where the polynomials $\alpha_j^n \in \mathbb{P}_j$, are defined by the recurrence relation :

$$(2) \quad \begin{cases} \alpha_o^n(x) = 1 \ , \ \alpha_1^n(x) = 0 \ , \text{ and for } \ell \geq 2 : \quad \sum_{r=0}^{\ell} \delta_{\ell r}^n\ \alpha_r^n = 0 \ , \\ \text{where : } \delta_{\ell r}^n = \sum_{i=0}^{r} \binom{r}{i} D^i \beta_{i+\ell-r}^n \end{cases}$$

Proof : The proof of (1) can be found e.g. in [7] . To derive (2), compute formally :

$$I = A_n \circ B_n = I + \sum_{\ell \geq 1} \gamma_\ell^n D^\ell, \text{ where } \gamma_\ell^n = \sum_{\ell=0}^{\ell} \delta_{\ell r}^n \alpha_r^n \text{ and } \delta_{\ell r}^n = \sum_{i=0}^{r} \binom{r}{i} D^i \beta_{i+\ell-r}^n .$$

This follows from the Leibniz formula :

$$D^r(\beta_k^n D^k) = \sum_{i=0}^{r} \binom{r}{i} D^i \beta_k^n D^{k+r-i} .$$

Theorem 2 :

a) $B_n^{(k)}$ can be extended to C [0,1] :

$$B_n^{(k)} f = A_n^{(k)} (B_n f) = \sum_{j=0}^{k} \alpha_j^n D^j B_n f .$$

b) $B_n^{[k]}$ can be extended to $C^k[0,1]$:

$$B_n^{[k]} f = B_n (A_n^{[k]} f) = \sum_{r=0}^{n} \left\{ \sum_{j=0}^{k} \alpha_j^n \left(\frac{r}{n}\right) D^i f\left(\frac{r}{n}\right) \right\} b_r^n$$

c) Both of them are exact on $\mathbb{P}_k$, i.e. $B_n^{(k)} p = B_n^{[k]} p = p$ for all $p \in \mathbb{P}_k$.

d) Moreover , $B_n^{(0)} = B_n^{(1)} = B_n$ and $B_n^{(n)} = L_n$.

Proof : It is an obvious consequence of definitions for (a),(b),(c) .
For (d), we know that $b_i^n = B_n \ell_i^n$, therefore $\ell_i^n = A_n b_i^n$ and :

$$B_n^{(n)} f = A_n (B_n f) = \sum_{i=0}^{n} f\left(\frac{i}{n}\right) (A_n b_i^n) = \sum_{i=0}^{n} f\left(\frac{i}{n}\right) \ell_i^n = L_n f .$$

We shall not study here the right operators $B_n^{[k]}$: this will be done elsewhere. Let us give some results on the norms and convergence properties of the left operators $B_n^{(k)}$ which seem easier to construct.

4. NORMS OF THE LEFT QUASI-INTERPOLANTS

Experimental results (see table 2) strongly suggest that, for k fixed, the sequence of norms $\|B_n^{(k)}\|_\infty$ is decreasing and therefore uniformly bounded w.r.t. $n \geq 1$. This result has been proved recently for k=2.

n \ k	2	3	4	5	6	7	8
2	1.25						
3	1.25	1.63					
4	1.25	1.53	2.21				
5	1.20	1.48	2.10	3.10			
6	1.195	1.45	2.04	2.98	4.55		
7	1.19	1.43	1.99	.	.	.	
8	1.18	1.41	.	.	.	.	10.95

Table 2 : Approximate values of norms of the first operators $B_n^{(k)}$

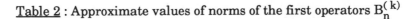

It is easy to show that the coefficient of α_ℓ^n is equal to :

$$\delta_{\ell\ell}^n = \frac{1}{\ell!} D^\ell B_n e_\ell = n^{-\ell} \binom{n}{\ell} \neq 0 \quad (\text{where } e_\ell(x) = x^\ell \text{ for all } \ell \geq 0) .$$

Therefore the polynomials α_ℓ^n can be computed from (2) in an unique way. ∎

Table 1 gives the first values of β_i^n and α_j^n .

k	$k!\ n^{k-1}\ \beta_k^n(x)$	$k(k-2)!\ (n-1)(n-2)...(n-k-1)\ \alpha_k^n(x)$
2	$X = x(1-x)$	$-X$
3	$(1-2x)\,X$	$(1-2x)X$
4	$X\,[1+3(n-2)\,X\,]$	$-X[2-(n+6)\,X\,]$
5	$(1-2x)\,X\,[1+2(5n-6)\,X\,]$	$(1-2x)\,X\,[6-(5n+12)\,X\,]$
6	$X\,[1+5(5n-6)\,X + 5(3n^2-26n+24)X^2\,]$	$-X\,[24-2(13n+60)X + (3n^2+86n+120)X^2]$
7	$(1-2x)X[1+4(14n-15)X + (105n^2-462n + 360)\,X^2]$	

Table 1 : The first coefficient polynomials of B_n and A_n

The following corollary is used in &. 5 for convergence results and is easily derived from the above theorem :

Corollary 1 : We have the following limits when n tends to infinity :

$$\lim n^k \beta_{2k-1}^n = \lim n^k (-1)^k \alpha_{2k-1}^n / 2 = (1-2x)\, X^k / 3.2^{k-1} (k-2)!$$

$$\lim n^k \beta_{2k}^n = \lim n^k (-1)^k \alpha_{2k}^n = X^k / 2^k .\ k!$$

3. LEFT AND RIGHT QUASI–INTERPOLANTS

Definitions :

a) For $0 \leq k \leq n$, let $A_n^{(k)} = A_n^{[k]} = \sum_{j=0}^{k} \alpha_j^n D^j$ the truncated inverse of B_n .

b) The **left Bernstein quasi–interpolant** (LBQI) of order k is defined as :

$$B_n^{(k)} = A_n^{(k)} \circ B_n$$

c) The **right Bernstein quasi–interpolant** (RBQI) or order k is defined as :

$$B_n^{[k]} = B_n \circ A_n^{[k]} .$$

Theorem 3 : (Powell) For all $n \geq 2$, $\|B_n^{(2)}\|_\infty \leq 3$, therefore $B_n^{(2)} f$ converges uniformly to $f \in C[0,1]$.

Proof:

$$B_n^{(2)} f(x) = B_n f(x) - \frac{X}{2(n-1)} D^2 B_n f(x) .$$

Using the fact that, by rearrangement of terms :

$$X^2 D^2 b_j^n (x) = b_j^n(x) \; [\, j(j-1)\,(1-x)^2 - 2j(n-j)\; x(1-x) + (n-j)\,(n-j-1)\; x^2\,]$$

$$= b_j^n(x) \,.\, n^2 \left[\left(x - \frac{j}{n}\right)^2 - \frac{1}{n}(1-x)^2 \frac{j}{n} - \frac{1}{n} x^2 \left(1 - \frac{j}{n}\right) \right]$$

and that $B_n [\, (x-t)^2\,] = X/n$, $B_n\left[\frac{t}{n} (1-x)^2 \right] = x(1-x)^2 /n$

and $B_n\left[\frac{1}{n} (1-t)\, x^2 \right] = x^2(1-x) / n$, we obtain , for $\|f\|_\infty \leq 1$:

$$|B_n^{(2)} f(x)\,| \leq 1 + \frac{n^2}{2(n-1)} \cdot \frac{1}{X} \frac{1}{n} \left[(1-x)\, X + x\, X + X \,\right] = \frac{2n-1}{n-1}$$

therefore $\| B_n^{(2)} \|_\infty \leq 3$ for all $n \geq 2$.

By theorem 4 below, we know that $B_n^{(2)}p$ converges to p for every polynomial p. Using the density of $\mathbb{P}$ in C[0,1] and the uniform boundedness theorem, we get the desired result . ∎

5. CONVERGENCE RESULTS

Theorem 4 :

1/ If the conjecture on norms is true, then $\lim B_n^{(k)} f = f$ in C[0,1] , for all $k \geq 2$ fixed.

2/ When $f \in C^k[0,1]$, $\lim B_n^{(k)} f = f$, moreover when $f \in C^{k+\ell}\,[0,1]$, $\lim D^r B_n^{(k)} f = D^r f$, for $0 \leq r \leq \ell$.

3/ More precisely, we have the following extension of Woronovskaja theorem :

$$\lim n^{\ell+1} [B_n^{(2\ell)} f(x) - f(x)] = (-1)^\ell (1-2x) X^\ell D^{2\ell+1} f(x) / 3.2^{\ell-1}(\ell-1)!$$
$$+ (-1)^\ell X^{\ell+1} D^{2\ell+2} f(x) / 2^{\ell+1} (\ell+1)!$$

$$\lim n^{\ell+1} [B_n^{(2\ell+1)} f(x) - f(x)] = (-1)^\ell X^{\ell+1} D^{2\ell+2} f(x) / 2^{\ell+1}(\ell+1)!$$

when the corresponding derivatives of f exist.

Proof : The proof is easy, but technical and will be given elsewhere : it uses corollary 1 and standard methods as described in Butzer [1] or Lorentz [7]. For the first values of k, we have :

$$\lim n^2 [B_n^{(2)} f(x) - f(x)] = -\frac{1}{3} (1-2x) X D^3 f(x) - \frac{1}{8} X^2 D^4 f(x)$$

$$\lim n^2 [B_n^{(3)} f(x) - f(x)] = -\frac{1}{8} X^2 D^4 f(x)$$

$$\lim n^3 [B_n^{(4)} f(x) - f(x)] = \frac{1}{6} (1-2x) X^2 D^5 f(x) + \frac{1}{24} X^3 D^6 f(x)$$

$$\lim n^3 [B_n^{(5)} f(x) - f(x)] = \frac{1}{24} X^3 D^6 f(x) \quad .$$

These results show that the convergence of $B_n^{(2\ell)}f$ or $B_n^{(2\ell+1)}f$ is a $O(n^{-(\ell+1)})$, therefore it is faster than that of B_n. Moreover some extrapolation methods à la Butzer [1] could be used very efficiently to improve the convergence speed.

6. EXTENSION TO OTHER QUASI-INTERPOLANTS

This extension can be made in many directions : for example to multidimensional Bernstein operators and also to other types of quasi–interpolants (and their own multidimensional extensions). Here are some examples :

6.1/ The extension to Bernstein QI on the square $[0,1]^2$ (or more generally the hypercube) is straightforward, by using standard tensor product techniques.

6.2/ The extension to B.Q.I. on triangles (or more generally simplices) is also easy. Using barycentric coordinates $\lambda = (\lambda_1, \lambda_2, \lambda_3)$ and standard notations for multi–indices, we get a natural extension of theorem 1 to :

$$B_n f = \sum_{|i|=n} f(i/n)\, b_i^n$$

where $i = (i_1, i_2, i_3) \in [0,n]$, $|i| = i_1 + i_2 + i_3 = n$, and :

$$b_i^n(\lambda) = \frac{n!}{i!}\lambda^i = \frac{n!}{i_1!\, i_2!\, i_3!}\lambda_1^{i_1}\lambda_2^{i_2}\lambda_3^{i_3} .$$

Theorem 6 : B_n is a linear differential operator on $\mathbb{P}_n$:

$$B_n = \sum_{0\le |k| \le n} \beta_k^n D^k$$

where the polynomials $\beta_k^n \in \mathbb{P}_r$, $|k| = r$, are defined by the recurrence relation :

$$\beta_0^n = 1 , \beta_k^n = 0 \quad \text{for } |k| = 1 ,$$

then for $1 \le |k| \le n-1$ and $1 \le r,s,t \le 3$, $r \ne s \ne t$:

$$n(k_r+1)\,\beta_{k+\varepsilon_r}^n = \lambda_r\lambda_s\left[D_{\varepsilon_r-\varepsilon_s}\beta_k^n + \beta_{k-\varepsilon_r}^n - \beta_{k-\varepsilon_s}^n\right] + \lambda_r\lambda_s\left[D_{\varepsilon_r-\varepsilon_t}\beta_k^n + \beta_{k-\varepsilon_r}^n - \beta_{k-\varepsilon_t}^n\right]$$

where $\varepsilon_1 = (1,0,0)$, $\varepsilon_2 = (0,1,0)$ and $\varepsilon_3 = (0,0,1)$.

The whole theory developed above for the interval [0,1] can be extended in the same way to this case. (see the forthcoming paper [11]).

6.3/ Durrmeyer–Derriennic Operators and generalizations

Other positive linear operators, like the Durrmeyer–Derriennic operators (see [2, 3, 4, 5]) and their generalizations (see [9, 10]) , the Bernstein–Szasz operators [6] and their generalizations [12], can be interpreted also as differential operators on spaces of polynomials and the same theory will be developed for the univariate and multivariate cases in a series of papers.

Acknowledgements : I thank very much professor Michael J.D. Powell for the proof of theorem 3.

7. REFERENCES

[1] BUTZER P.L., (1953), Linear combinations of Bernstein polynomials. Canad. J. Math. 5 , 559–567.

[2] CIESIELSKI Z., DOMSTA J., (1985), The degenerate B–splines in the space of algebraic polynomials, Ann. Polon. Math 46, 71–79.

[3] DERRIENNIC M.M., (1981), Sur l'approximation de fonctions intégrables sur [0,1] par des polynômes de Bernstein modifiés. J. of Approximation Theory, 31, N°4, 325–343.

[4] DERRIENNIC M.M., (1985), On Multivariate Approximation by Bernstein Type Polynomials. J. of Approximation Theory, 45, N° 2, 155–166.

[5] DURRMEYER J.L., (1967), Une formule d'inversion de la transformée de Laplace. Applications à la théorie des moments. Thèse de 3e cycle, Université de Paris .

[6] GOLOMB M., (1962). Lectures on Theory of Approximation, Argonne National Laboratory.

[7] LORENTZ G.G., (1953), Bersntein Polynomials, University of Toronto Press, Toronto.

[8] POWELL M.J.D., (1981), Approximation Theory and Methods, Cambridge University Press,

[9] SABLONNIERE P., (1981), Opérateurs de Bernstein–Jacobi et de Bernstein. Laguerre, Rapports ANO 37 et 38, Université de Lille 1, (Unpublished).

[10] SABLONNIERE P., (1988), Hahn Polynomials as eigenvectors of positive operators. Second International Symposium on Orthogonal Polynomials and their applications (Segovia, 1986). Monografias de la Academia de Ciencias de Zaragoza , p. 139–146.

[11] SABLONNIERE P., (1989), Bernstein quasi–interpolants on a simplex, to be presented at the Conference Konstruktive Approximations–theorie, Oberwolfach (July 30 – August 5, 1989).

[12] WOOD B., (1989),Uniform Approximation with Positive Linear Operators Generated by Binomial Expansions. J. of Approximation Theory 56, N°1, 48–58.

Prof. Paul SABLONNIERE, Laboratoire L.A.N.S., I.N.S.A., 20, avenue des Buttes de Coësmes, 35043 RENNES Cédex, FRANCE.

International Series of
Numerical Mathematics, Vol. 90

ELEMENTARY HOLOGRAMS, ARTIFICIAL NEURAL NETWORKS, AND THETA - NULL VALUES

Walter Schempp

Our struggles with digital computers have taught us much about how neural computation is not *done; unfortunately, they have taught us relatively little about how it* is *done.*

Carver A. Mead (1989)

ABSTRACT. Based on a unified nilpotent harmonic analysis approach to artificial neural net work models implemented with coherent optical or analog electronic neurocomputer architectures, the paper establishes a new identity for the matching polynomials of complete bichromatic graphs. The key idea is to identify the hologram plane with the three-dimensional Heisenberg nilpotent Lie group quotiented by its one-dimensional center and then to restrict the holographic transform to the holographic lattices located inside the hologram plane. The quantum mechanical treatment of optical holography is also useful in microoptics or amacronics since atoms coherently excited by short laser pulses may be as large as some transistors in microelectronic circuits and the pathways between them inside the VLSI chips.

1. Introduction. Real-time image analysis and processing, computer vision, automatic target recognition in robotics, speech processing and understanding, sensor processing, and other areas of artificial intelligence (AI) need to process extremely large amounts of data with very high velocity. The computational power required exceeds by many orders of magnitude the capabilities of sequential digital computers. The Space Station program's Earth Observing System (Eos) polar orbiting platforms, for instance, require to process data rates up to 1.5 gigabits per second. The problem of large-volume and high-speed computations can be solved by

- o data compression techniques,
- o parallel data processing.

Since their very beginning, artificial neural networks have been considered as massively parallel computing paradigms. The fundamental characteristics of all neurocomputer architectures are the interconnections of arrays of simple processing elements to form a concurrent distributed processing network of extensive connectivity. Large scale (LS) collective systems like artificial neural networks exhibit many properties, including robustness, reliability, and fault tolerance, an ability to deal with ill-posed problems and noisy data, which conventional digital computer architectures do not. Neurobiology provides existence theorem on effectiveness of neural network parallel algorithms on appropriate problems.

For artificial neural networks to become ultimately useful, neuromorphic hardware must be developed. Development efforts in the field of sixth generation computers have concentrated on one of two goals: to build

- o efficient hardware that effectively executes software simulations,
- o actual hardware emulators for specific neural network models.

Examples of the first are the Hecht-Nielsen Neurocomputer (HNC) accelerator board for conventional serial personal computers, and the Delta board by Science Applications International Corporation (SAIC). An important application of the SAIC neural network software simulation is the detection of explosives in checked airline baggage: the luggage is bathed in low energy (thermal) neutrons and the gamma rays resulting from neutron absorption by atomic elements in the luggage are analyzed. The artificial neural network software then searches for specific combinations of atomic elements that characterize explosives including dynamites and water gels.

Examples of the second are arrays of coherent optical processors ([2], [3], [18], [19], [20], [32], [34]) for the implementation of neural network models by holographic interconnections, and neural network analog very large scale integrated (VLSI) chips. For instance, the silicon models of the orientation-selective retina for pattern recognition ([14], [15], [16], [1]), and the analog electronic cochlea for auditory localization ([13], [14], [15]) belong to this category. The retinal and the cochleal VLSI chip are made with a standard complementary MOS (CMOS) process.

Although the implementation of the various neural network models needs to overcome many difficult design problems, their performance is modest compared with the powerful organizing principles found in biological neural wetware. The visual system of a single human being does more image processing than do the entire world's supply of supercomputers, and the nervous system of even a very simple animal like the common house-fly (Musca domestica) contains computing paradigms that are orders of magnitude more effective than are those found in systems made by humans. Presently the most advanced neural network analog VLSI chips model, to a first approximation, the time-frequency domain processing of two highly spectacular biological neural systems: the active auditory localization system of the horseshoe bats (Rhinolophidae), and the passive auditory localization system of the barn owl (Tyto alba) which both produce complete maps of the auditory space from the time-frequency coding pathways. Continuing evolution, however, of technology and of neuromathematics, the highly promising new field of studying how computations can be carried out in extensive networks formed by arrays of heavily interconnected simple processing elements, will create neurocomputers within the next decade which will be able to solve problems intractable for even the largest digital computers.

This paper concentrates on a unified approach to massively parallel coherent optical and analog electronic neurocomputer architectures which is based on harmonic analysis of the three-dimensional Heisenberg nilpotent Lie group G. The key idea is to identify the hologram plane with G quotiented by its one-dimensional center C. As a result, the analysis on G/C provides the Gabor wavelets which form a total family of approximating functions in $L^2(\mathbb{R} \oplus \mathbb{R})$ of correlating and decorrelating code primitives of artificial neural networks. Finally, a series of new identities for theta-null values shows that studies in computational mathematics combined with synthetic neurobiology may have a spin-off in pure mathematics.

2. The holographic transform. Let $\mathcal{S}(\mathbb{R})$ denote the Schwartz space of complex-valued $\mathcal{C}^\infty$ functions on the real line $\mathbb{R}$ rapidly decreasing at infinity. Consider $\mathcal{S}(\mathbb{R})$ as a dense vector subspace of the complex Hilbert space $L^2(\mathbb{R})$ under its natural isometric embedding. In optical holography, a square-law detector encodes in a massively parallel way the optical path length difference $x \in \mathbb{R}$ and the phase difference $y \in \mathbb{R}$ of two coherent signals having the same carrier and their amplitudes ψ in φ in the space $\mathcal{S}(\mathbb{R})$ by simultaneously recording the coordinates (x,y) of the interference pattern written by the two-wave mixing $\psi \otimes \varphi$ into the hologram plane $\mathbb{R} \oplus \mathbb{R}$. The sesquilinear extension to $\mathcal{S}(\mathbb{R}) \otimes \mathcal{S}(\mathbb{R})$ of the mapping

$$\psi \otimes \varphi \mapsto H(\psi,\varphi;x,y) = \int_{\mathbb{R}} \psi(t-x)\overline{\varphi}(t)e^{2\pi iyt}dt$$

describes by coherent superposition the holographic angle encoding: each object to be globally stored by the coherent object signal beam in the hologram is encoded prior to its recording by mixing (or heterodyning) an unfocused linearly polarized coherent non-object-bearing reference signal beam having a particular angle between its wave vector and the normal vector of the hologram plane $\mathbb{R} \oplus \mathbb{R}$. Therefore the sesquilinear mapping $\psi \otimes \varphi \mapsto H(\varphi,\psi;.,.)$ is called the holographic transform of the writing amplitudes ([27], [28], [29]). The method of holography applies to all waves: to electron waves, X rays, light waves, acoustic waves, and seismic waves, providing the waves are coherent enough to form the required interference patterns in the hologram plane ([29]). In radar analysis, H is called the cross-ambiguity function ([23], [7], [21]). In the following it will be convenient to define the auto-ambiguity function by $H(\psi;.,.) := H(\psi,\psi;.,.)$.

Remark 1. High-resolution radar imagery of the terrain and optical holographic imaging are closely related concepts. In fact, airborne and spaceborne synthetic aperture radar (SAR) remote sensing systems use microwave holograms for data storage and can therefore be regarded as optical neurocomputers which implement a Doppler filter bank by a relatively static reflection pattern of the architecture mirror ([29]). The massive parallelism inherent to the optical data processing approach is in large part responsible for the success of SAR imaging.

Remark 2. Since the advent of optical holography or coherent wavefront reconstruction, there has been a strong interest in replacing the lenses used in optical systems by holographic optical elements (HOEs). In particular, optical SAR data processing systems may be realized by optical heads which include HOEs. Many HOEs are fabricated by recording the interference pattern between two mixing laser beams. The use of digital computer-generated hologram (CGH) techniques, however, avoids the technological difficulties involved in the interferometric HOE fabrication. Moreover, one benefit that digital CGHs can offer that is not available with optical holography is the ability to deal with objects that exist only mathematically. High quality digital CGHs may be fabricated with the same technology used in the manufacture of VLSI circuits. A digital computer controlled output device such as an electron-beam high-resolution microlithographic system writes the desired geometric pattern on photoresist, which is subsequently processed to produce the finished transmissive or reflective holographic element. Alternately, digital CGHs may be realized by writing the appropriate pattern on a spatial light modulator (SLM). In any case, digital CGHs are at the base of a technology transfer from microelectronics to microoptics or amacronics and form a bridge between digital computer and optical neurocomputer architectures. Since atoms coherently excited by short laser pulses may be as large as some transistors of VLSI circuits ([35], [36]), the quantum mechanical treatment of optical holography is of particular importance for amacronics.

Remark 3. A vital element of optical neurocomputer architectures is the medium for optical hologram recording because it plays the rôle of a holographic associative memory. Electro-optical photorefractive crystals (PRCs) are known to form reusable holographic storage materials that can be infinitely recycled and do not require additional processing. The crystals of the sillenite family, bismuth silicon oxide $Bi_{12}SiO_{20}$ (BSO), bismuth titanium oxide $Bi_{12}TiO_{20}$ (BTO), and bismuth germanium oxide $Bi_{12}GeO_{20}$ (BGO) exhibit the highest sensitivity to light among presently known PRCs ([33]). Optical holograms are recorded inside PRCs directly by illuminating the crystal with laser light. The light induces a charge redistribution inside the crystal ([8]) and in a certain characteristic time interval a dynamic equilibrium between distributions of the recording light intensity and internal electric charge is established. The electric charge induces an internal electrostatic field that changes the refractive index of the crystal by the electro-optical effect and forms a volume phase hologram. As the interference pattern undergoes changes, a new charge distribution is formed, hence a new optical hologram is recorded. This charge distribution again comes to a dynamic equilibrium with the recording interference pattern. If the period during which the interference pattern changes is sufficiently long, the electro-optical crystal rerecords an optical hologram. Hence the electro-optical PRCs can adapt itself to varying external conditions, such as occasional temperature-induced changes of the phase difference between the writing object signal beam and reference signal beam, or mechanical instabilities. This is an extremely important feature because it allows more reliable storage of scattering objects by almost-real-time holography.

3. The Heisenberg nilpotent Lie group. Let G denote the multiplicative group of all unipotent real matrices

$$\begin{pmatrix} 1 & x & z \\ 0 & 1 & y \\ 0 & 0 & 1 \end{pmatrix} := (x,y,z)$$

Then G is a two-step nilpotent Lie group with one-dimensional center $C = \{(0,0,z) | z \in \mathbb{R}\}$; G is a realization of the three-dimensional Heisenberg group ([23]) with Lie algebra $\mathfrak{g}$ formed by the upper triangular matrices $\{(x,y,z)-(0,0,0) | x,y,z \in \mathbb{R}\}$. For each real number $\nu \neq 0$ the central character χ_ν: $(0,0,z) \mapsto e^{2\pi i\nu z}$ determines up to an isomorphism a unique infinite-dimensional irreducible unitary linear representation U_ν of G in $L^2(\mathbb{R})$ which acts on the vector subspace $\mathcal{S}(\mathbb{R})$ according to the rule

$$U_\nu(x,y,z)\psi(t) = e^{2\pi i\nu(z+yt)}\psi(t-x) \qquad (t \in \mathbb{R}).$$

Let $\bar{U}_\nu$ denote the contragredient representation of U_ν, so that

$$\bar{U}_\nu(x,y,z) = {}^tU_\nu((x,y,z)^{-1})$$

holds for all elements $(x,y,z) \in G$. Obviously

$$U_\nu|C = \chi_\nu, \quad \bar{U}_\nu|C = \chi_{-\nu} \qquad (\nu \in \mathbb{R},\ \nu \neq 0).$$

The flatness of the affine Kirillov coadjoint orbits $\mathcal{O}_\nu$ and $\mathcal{O}_{-\nu}$ associated with U_ν and $\bar{U}_\nu$ in the dual $\mathfrak{g}^*$ of the Heisenberg Lie algebra $\mathfrak{g}$, respectively, is equivalent to the square integrability modulo C of U_ν and $\bar{U}_\nu$. From these facts the central projection G-slice theorem follows:

Theorem 1. *The holographic transform is the coefficient function of the linear Schrödinger representation* U_1 *of the polarized Heisenberg group* G *projected along the center* C *onto* G/C, *i.e., the identities*

$$\begin{cases} H(\psi',\varphi';x,y) = \langle U_1(x,y,0)\psi' \,|\, \varphi' \rangle \\ \overline{H}(\psi,\varphi;x,y) = \langle \overline{U}_1(x,y,0)\overline{\psi} \,|\, \overline{\varphi} \rangle \end{cases}$$

hold for all points $(x,y) \in \mathbb{R} \oplus \mathbb{R}$.

The importance of the preceding result lies in the fact that the hidden symmetries of the holographic transform H can be expressed by the group of automorphisms of the Heisenberg nilpotent Lie group G keeping the center C pointwise fixed. This group, the metaplectic group **Mp**(1,ℝ), forms a twofold cover of the symplectic group **Sp**(1,ℝ) acting on the hologram plane $\mathbb{R} \oplus \mathbb{R}$ ([23]).

4. Readout of optical holograms. In the following, the isomorphic G-manifolds $\mathcal{O}_1 \in \mathfrak{g}^*/\mathrm{CoAd}(G)$, $\mathcal{O}_{-1} \in \mathfrak{g}^*/\mathrm{CoAd}(G)$, and the central projection G-slice G/C will be identified with the hologram plane $\mathbb{R} \oplus \mathbb{R}$. An application of Schur's lemma provides the biorthogonality relations ([23], [22], [31])

$$\iint_{\mathbb{R}\oplus\mathbb{R}} H(\psi',\varphi';x,y)\overline{H}(\psi,\varphi;x,y)\,dxdy = \langle \psi' \otimes \varphi \,|\, \psi \otimes \varphi' \rangle$$

for $\psi',\varphi',\psi,\varphi$ in $\mathcal{S}(\mathbb{R})$. Therefore the dyads

$$\begin{cases} E(\psi',.\,;x,y):\ \varphi' \mapsto H(\psi',\varphi';x,y)\overline{U}_1(x,y,0)\overline{\psi}' \\ \overline{E}(\psi,.\,;x,y):\ \varphi \mapsto \overline{H}(\psi,\varphi;x,y)U_1(x,y,0)\psi \end{cases} \qquad ((x,y) \in \mathbb{R} \oplus \mathbb{R})$$

which embed $\psi' \in \mathcal{S}(\mathbb{R})$ and $\psi \in \mathcal{S}(\mathbb{R})$, respectively, into the Hilbert-Schmidt (HS) operators acting on $L^2(\mathbb{R})$, define a U_1-system $(E(.,.;x,y))_{(x,y)\in\mathbb{R}\oplus\mathbb{R}'}$ and a $\overline{U}_1$-system $(\overline{E}(.,.;x,y))_{(x,y)\in\mathbb{R}\oplus\mathbb{R}}$ of coherent states based on the hologram plane $\mathbb{R} \oplus \mathbb{R}$ ([17]).

Theorem 2. *For all writing amplitudes* $\psi',\varphi',\psi,\varphi$ *in* $\mathcal{S}(\mathbb{R})$ *the gain equations*

$$\iint_{\mathbb{R}\oplus\mathbb{R}} E(\psi',\varphi';x,y)\,dxdy = \|\psi'\|_2\overline{\varphi}'$$

$$\iint_{\mathbb{R}\oplus\mathbb{R}} \overline{E}(\psi,\varphi;x,y)\,dxdy = \|\psi\|_2\varphi$$

hold.

Remark 4. Similar inversion formulas can be established for the affine coherent states defined by the wavelet transform and the square integrable irreducible unitary linear representations of the non-unimodular affine Lie group of the real line $\mathbb{R}$. Wavelets are particularly useful code primitives for voice decomposition ([9]).

Remark 5. Turning from optical holography to computer-aided tomography ([5]), the preceding identities give rise by an application of the theory of the reductive dual pair $(\tilde{\mathbf{Sp}}(1,\mathbb{R}),\tilde{\mathbf{O}}(n,\mathbb{R}))$, ([25], [11]), to the singular value decomposition of the Radon transform $\mathcal{R}$: $\mathcal{S}(\mathbb{R}^n) \to \mathcal{S}(\mathbb{R}\times\mathbf{S}_{n-1})$ acting on functions $f \in \mathcal{S}(\mathbb{R}^n)$ according to

$$\mathcal{R}f(r,\omega) = \int_{\mathbb{R}^n} f(x)\varepsilon_{(r-\langle\omega|x\rangle)}dx.$$

It follows that the inversion problem for the Radon transform $\mathcal{R}$ which underlies computer-aided tomography (CT) is ill-posed. Neurocomputers, however, seem to be more appropriate to solve ill-posed problems than conventional digital computers.

As a special case we obtain from Theorem 2 supra the following result which describes the readout procedure of optical holograms.

Corollary. *Let* $\varphi \in \mathcal{S}(\mathbb{R})$ *and assume that* $\psi \in \mathcal{S}(\mathbb{R})$ *satisfies the normalization condition* $\|\psi\|_2 = 1$. *If* $\mathcal{F}$ *denotes the Fourier transform acting on* $\mathcal{S}(\mathbb{R})$ *then the reproducing scattering integrals of degenerate four-wave mixing*

$$\begin{cases} \displaystyle\iint_{\mathbb{R}\oplus\mathbb{R}} H(\psi,\varphi;x,y)e^{-2\pi iyt}\bar{\psi}(t-x)dxdy = \bar{\varphi}(t) \\ \displaystyle\iint_{\mathbb{R}\oplus\mathbb{R}} H(\psi,\varphi;y,x)e^{2\pi iyt}\mathcal{F}\bar{\psi}(t-x)dydx = \mathcal{F}\bar{\varphi}(t) \end{cases} \qquad (t \in \mathbb{R})$$

hold.

The preceding integral equations prove the holographic reciprocity principle which governs the angle decoding of optical holograms: The amplitude and the phase of the conjugate object signal can be read out simultaneously by illuminating the hologram with the unfocused conjugate reference signal beam.

The pair of reproducing scattering integrals describing the holographic filter bank are also at the basis of optical wavefront conjugation by means of real-time holography ([8]) in electro-optical PRCs. Wavefront conjugate mirrors provide retroreflection and optical tracking novelty filters. Therefore, Theorem 2 is at the basis of neural network models implemented by holographic interconnections in optical neurocomputer architectures ([2], [3], [18], [19], [20], [32]). If the holographic associative memory has net gain comparable with the losses in the resonator cavity, the output will converge to a real image of the globally stored object: the expanded conjugate reference signal beam acts as an optical scanner for readout of the associate information. In case of a linear resonator memory, gain is supplied by the wavefront conjugate mirror which provides regenerative feedback, whereas in case of a loop resonator memory, gain is supplied by an externally pumped electro-optical PRC.

5. Radial isotropy. A writing amplitude $\psi \in \mathcal{S}(\mathbb{R})$ is called radially isotropic if $H(\psi;.,.)$ is a radial function on the hologram plane $\mathbb{R} \oplus \mathbb{R}$, i.e., if $H(\psi;.,.)$ is invariant under the natural action of the orthogonal group $O(2,\mathbb{R})$.

Theorem 3. *The amplitude $\psi \in \mathcal{S}(\mathbb{R})$ is radially isotropic if and only if it admits the form of Hermite-Gaussian eigenmodes*

$$\psi = \zeta_n H_n$$

where $\zeta_n \in \mathbb{C}$ is a constant and $H_n(t) = e^{-t^2/2} h_n(t)$ is the Hermite function of degree $n \geq 0$.

The proof follows by classifying the irreducible unitary linear representations of the diamond solvable Lie group $\mathbb{T} \times G$ having U_ν as their restrictions to G ([24]).

The elementary holograms $(H(H_m, H_n;.,.))_{m\geq 0, n\geq 0}$ form a total orthogonal approximating family in the complex Hilbert space $L^2(\mathbb{R} \oplus \mathbb{R})$, hence a decorrelating family of code primitives. The Hermite-Gaussian eigenmodes $(H_n)_{n\geq 0}$ are crucial for the phenomenon of daydreaming in optical neurocomputers ([3]).

6. Scanout of pixel arrays. The implementation of pixel arrays by holographic optical interconnections ([2], [3], [18], [19], [20], [32], [34]), and analog VLSI wavefront arrays ([14], [15], [16], [1], [13]) suggests to look at restrictions of the holographic transform to lattices inside the hologram plane ([4]). The quadratic lattice $\mathbb{Z} \oplus \mathbb{Z}$ embedded in the hologram plane $\mathbb{R} \oplus \mathbb{R}$ may be considered as the projection onto G/C of the 3-cubic lattice $L_0 := \{(\mu,\nu,\zeta) \mid \mu \in \mathbb{Z},\ \nu \in \mathbb{Z},\ \zeta \in \mathbb{Z}\}$ and the normal subgroup $L := \mathbb{Z} \oplus \mathbb{Z} \oplus C$ inside the three-dimensional Heisenberg nilpotent Lie group G along its center C. Then the compact Heisenberg nilmanifold $L_0\backslash G$ associated to G allows to realize by an application of the Weil-Zak isomorphism

$$w_1 \colon \psi \mapsto ((x,y,z) \mapsto e^{2\pi i z} \sum_{n\in\mathbb{Z}} e^{2\pi i n y}\psi(n-x)) \qquad (\psi \in \mathcal{S}(\mathbb{R}))$$

the linear Schrödinger representation U_1 of G as the linear lattice representation $\delta_1 = \mathrm{Ind}_L^G(\chi_1)$ of G ([23]). It follows

$$H(\psi,\varphi;x,y) = \langle\delta_1(x,y,0)w_1(\psi) \mid w_1(\varphi)\rangle$$

for all points (x,y) of the pixel $]-1/2,+1/2] \times]-1/2,+1/2]$ in the hologram plane $\mathbb{R} \oplus \mathbb{R}$. Therefore the Parseval-Plancherel type pixel identity

$$\sum_{(\mu,\nu)\in\mathbb{Z}\oplus\mathbb{Z}} H(\psi;\mu,\nu)\overline{H}(\varphi;\mu,\nu) = \sum_{(\mu,\nu)\in\mathbb{Z}\oplus\mathbb{Z}} |H(\psi,\varphi;\mu,\nu)|^2$$

holds for writing amplitudes ψ,φ in $\mathcal{S}(\mathbb{R})$. If the Hermite functions H_m and H_n $(m \geq n \geq 0)$ are inserted for ψ and φ, respectively, the radial symmetry of the terms of the left-hand side implies by a trace argument that the associated lattices of pixel arrays in the hologram plane have the crystallographic groups D_k $(k \in \{1,2,3,4,6\})$ of order 2k as their groups of symmetry ([26], [27], [34]). An application of the Weil-Zak isomorphism w_1 to the readout formulae of the Corollary of Theorem 2 supra shows that the scanout of the pixel arrays of the holographic lattices may be performed by a time-multiplexing procedure.

Remark 6. It is a highly remarkable observation of neurophysiology that the presynaptic vesicular grids of the mammalian brain are hexagonal holographic lattices. The thickness of the presynaptic membrane by which the synaptic vesicles emit their specific transmitter substances is about 50 Å whereas the uncertainty of the position of a synaptic vesicle is due to the Heisenberg uncertainty principle about 50 Å per millisecond.

Remark 7. The holographic lattices are at the basis of the detour phase method ([28], [30]) of writing digital CGHs of sampled images by use of the fast Fourier transform (FFT) algorithm. The height and the displacement of a single aperture centered at the sampling points of the holographic lattice are used to encode the amplitude and the phase of the complex wavefront. Thus the actual encoding of detour phase CGHs is performed without the explicit use of a reference beam. The holographic lattice corresponding to the crystallographic group D_6 of twelvefold symmetry offers substantial computational efficiency and a significant reduction of required data storage compared with rectangular sampling: the hexagonal FFT is 25% more efficient than the most efficient rectangular FFT algorithm. The scanout of the wavefront is achieved when the CGH is illuminated with a plane wave and focused with a Fourier-transforming lens.

Remark 8. The compact disks (CDs) may be regarded as one-dimensional digital CGHs that may be scanned out by the holographic optical head of a CD digital audio player. Another point of view is to consider the spin variables of erasable CDs as one-dimensional artificial neural networks.

7. Artificial neural networks. In order to identify explicitly the terms of the Parseval-Plancherel type pixel identity indicated above, we denote by $K_{m,n}$ the complete bichromatic graph of m + n vertices. Define $c(K_{m,n},0) := 1$ and let $c(K_{m,n},l)$ denote the number of choices of $l \geq 1$ disjoint edges in $K_{m,n}$ each linking two vertices of different colours. Then

$$\Phi_{m,n}(X) := \sum_{0\leq l\leq[(m+n)/2]} (-1)^l c(K_{m,n},l) X^{m+n-2l}$$

denotes the matching polynomial ([8]) of variable X associated to the bipartite graph $K_{m,n}$.

Theorem 4. *The coefficients of the matching polynomial* $\Phi_{m,n}(X)$ *are the elementary synaptic weights* $(-1)^l c(K_{m,n},l)$, $0\leq l\leq[(m+n)/2]$, *where* $c(K_{m,n},l)$ *denotes the number of disjoint synaptic interconnections of the neural network* $K_{m,n}$ $(m\geq n\geq 0)$ *activated by l simultaneously firing neurons.*

The next theorem describes the relationship between the elementary holograms and the matching polynomials attenuated by the Gaussian $(H_0 \otimes H_0) \in L^2(\mathbb{R} \oplus \mathbb{R})$ with distance: the farther away an input is from a point in the neural network, the less weight it is given.

<u>**Theorem 5.**</u> *Let* $m \geq n \geq 0$. *Then the elementary holograms admit the form*

$$H(H_m, H_n; x, y) = \frac{(-1)^n}{\sqrt{m!n!}} \, e^{-\pi(x^2+y^2)/2} \, \Phi_{m,n}(\sqrt{\pi}(x+iy))$$

for all pairs $(x,y) \in \mathbb{R} \oplus \mathbb{R}$.

Remark 9. In biological vision, the center-surround receptive field profiles of the retinal neurons ([5]) and the cells of the lateral geniculate nucleus are far from forming an orthogonal family in $L^2(\mathbb{R} \oplus \mathbb{R})$. Therefore the resulting neural representation remains highly correlated. Theorem 2 supra suggests to implement a matching filter bank by an adaptive artificial neural network model which is based on the central projection G-slice orbits

$$G_{(y,y')}: (x,x') \mapsto U_1(x,y,0) \otimes \bar{U}_1(x',y',0)(H_0 \otimes H_0) \qquad ((y,y') \in \mathbb{R} \oplus \mathbb{R})$$

in $L^2(\mathbb{R}\oplus\mathbb{R})$. The approximating family of Gabor wavelets $\{G_{(y,y')} \mid (y,y') \in \mathbb{R}\oplus\mathbb{R}\}$ is total in the complex Hilbert space $L^2(\mathbb{R} \oplus \mathbb{R})$ due to the irreducibility of the linear Schrödinger representation U_1 of G, but non-orthogonal. Early stages of biological visual systems pay for keeping $m = n = 0$ by the non-orthogonality of the center-surround receptive field profiles ([4], [12]). The retina and the lateral geniculate nucleus, however, act as decorrelators of the incoming signals. At the level of the mammalian visual cortex, the introduction of orientation selectivity through localized wave modulation combined with quadrature phase relations among paired cells results in a decorrelated neural representation with optimal image compression performance by the total orthogonal approximating family in $L^2(\mathbb{R} \oplus \mathbb{R})$ of elementary holograms $(H(H_m, H_n; .,.))_{m\geq 0, n\geq 0}$. Signal preprocessing and processing in the auditory parts of the cortex follow similar lines.

Theorem 5 supra implies

Theorem 6. *For* m ≥ n ≥ 0 *the identity*

$$\sum_{(\mu,\nu)\in\mathbb{Z}\oplus\mathbb{Z}} (-1)^{m+n}\, e^{-\pi(\mu^2+\nu^2)} \Phi_{m,m}(\sqrt{\pi}(\mu+i\nu))\Phi_{n,n}(\sqrt{\pi}(\mu+i\nu)) =$$

$$\sum_{(\mu,\nu)\in\mathbb{Z}\oplus\mathbb{Z}} e^{-\pi(\mu^2+\nu^2)} |\Phi_{m,n}(\sqrt{\pi}(\mu+i\nu))|^2$$

holds.

8. Theta-null values. The preceding theorem gives rise to the following special identities for the odd powers of π in terms of theta-null values $\vartheta(0,1) = \sum e^{-\pi\mu^2}$ ([23], [24]) where $\sum := \sum_{\mu\in\mathbb{Z}}$:

m = 1, n = 0

$$\pi = \frac{\sum e^{-\pi\mu^2}}{4 \sum \mu^2 e^{-\pi\mu^2}}$$

m = 2, n = 1

$$\pi^3 = \frac{15 \sum (8\pi^2\mu^4-1)\, e^{-\pi\mu^2}}{32 \sum \mu^6 e^{-\pi\mu^2}}$$

m = 3, n = 2

$$\pi^5 = \frac{45 \sum (16\pi^4\mu^8 - 140\pi^2\mu^4 + 21)\, e^{-\pi\mu^2}}{64 \sum \mu^{10} e^{-\pi\mu^2}}$$

m = 4, n = 3

$$\pi^7 = \frac{91 \sum (256\pi^6\mu^{12} - 15840\pi^4\mu^8 + 166320\pi^2\mu^4 - 25245)\, e^{-\pi\mu^2}}{1024 \sum \mu^{14} e^{-\pi\mu^2}} .$$

Theorem 5 supra shows that the preceding identities for the theta-null values $\vartheta(0,1)$ are of a combinatorial character.

Remark 1o. The univariate impulse response of the ideal lowpass filter admits the Euler factorization

$$\operatorname{sinc} x = \prod_{n\geq 1} \left(1 - \frac{x^2}{n^2}\right) \qquad (x \in \mathbb{R}).$$

Its logarithmic derivative combined with the generating function of the Bernoulli polynomials $B_n(X)$ of degree $n \geq 0$ yields the classical Euler formulae for the even powers of π:

$$\pi^{2n} = (-1)^{n+1} \frac{2(2n)!}{2^{2n}B_{2n}} \zeta(2n) \qquad (n \geq 1),$$

where ζ denotes the Riemann zeta-function and $B_{2n} = B_{2n}(0)$ are the Bernoulli numbers.

Acknowledgments. The author acknowledges the support of the Visiting International Scholar Award 1988/89 from the University of Missouri-Saint Louis. It is his pleasure to thank Professors Gail D.L. Ratcliff and Grant V. Welland (St. Louis) for interesting discussions of these topics.

REFERENCES

1. **T. Allen, C. Mead, F. Faggin, and G. Gribble,** Orientation-selective VLSI retina, Visual Communications and Image Processing '88, T. Russell Hsing, Editor, Proc. SPIE 1001, 1040-1046 (1988).

2. **D.Z. Anderson,** Coherent optical eigenstate memory, Optics Letters 11, 56-58 (1986).

3. **D.Z. Anderson, M.C. Erie,** Resonator memories and optical novelty filters, Optical Engineering 26, 434-444 (1987).

4. **J.G. Daugman,** Relaxation neural network for complete discrete 2-D Gabor transforms, Visual Communications and Image Processing '88, T. Russell Hsing, Editor, Proc. SPIE 1001, 1048-1061 (1988).

5. **J.E. Dowling,** The retina: an approachable part of the brain, The Belknap Press of Harvard University Press, Cambridge, Massachusetts, and London 1987.

6. **N.H. Farhat, C.L. Werner, and T.H. Chu,** Prospects for three-dimensional projective and tomographic imaging radar networks, Radio Science 19, 1347-1355 (1984).

7. **E. Feig, C.A. Micchelli,** L^2-synthesis by ambiguity functions, Multivariate Approximation Theory IV, C.K. Chui, W. Schempp, and K. Zeller, Editors, Birkhäuser Verlag, Basel, Boston, Berlin 1989.

8. **J. Feinberg,** Applications of real-time holography, Holography, Lloyd Huff, Editor, Proc. SPIE 532, 119-135 (1985).

9. **A. Grossmann, J. Morlet,** Decomposition of functions into wavelets of constant shape and related transforms, Mathematics and Physics, Lectures on Recent Results, Vol. 1, L. Streit, Editor, World Scientific, Singapore, Philadelphia 1985.

10. **H. Hosoya,** Matching and symmetry of graphs, Comp. and Maths. with Appls. 12B, 271-290 (1986).

11. **R. Howe,** Dual pairs in physics: Harmonic oscillators, photons, electrons, and singletons, Applications of Group Theory in Physics and Mathematical Physics, M. Flato, P. Sally, and G. Zuckerman, Editors, 179-207, American Mathematical Society, Providence, Rhode Island 1985.

12. **J. Jones, L. Palmer,** An evaluation of the two-dimensional Gabor filter model of simple receptive fields in cat striate cortex, J. of Neurophysiology 58, 1233-1258 (1987).

13. **J. Lazzaro, C.A. Mead,** A silicon model of auditory localization, Neural Computation 1, 47-57 (1989).

14. **C. Mead,** Analog VLSI and neural systems, Addison-Wesley, Reading, Massachusetts 1989.

15. **C. Mead, M. Ismail,** Analog VLSI implementation of neural systems, Kluwer, Norwell, Massachusetts 1989.

16. **C.A. Mead, M.A. Mahowald,** A silicon model of early visual processing, Neural Networks 1, 91-97 (1988).

17. **H. Moscovici,** Coherent state representations of nilpotent Lie groups, Commun. math. Phys. 54, 63-68 (1977).

18. **J. Ohta, M. Takahashi, Y. Nitta, S. Tai, K. Mitsunaga, and K. Kjuma,** A new approach to a GaAs/AlGaAs optical neurochip with three layered structure, Proc. IJCNN International Joint Conference on Neural Networks, II-477-480 (1989).

19. **Y. Owechko, E. Marom, B.H. Soffer, and G. Dunning,** Associative memory in a phase conjugate resonator cavity utilizing a hologram, IOCC-1986 International Optical Computing Conference, J. Shamir, A.A. Friesem, and E. Marom, Editors, Proc. SPIE 700, 296-7300 (1986).

20. **D. Psaltis, D. Brady, X. Gu, and K. Hsu,** Optical implementation of neural computers, Optical Processing and Computing, H. Arsenault, T. Szoplik, and B. Macukow, Editors, Academic Press, Boston, Orlando, San Diego, New York, Austin, London, Sydney, Tokyo, Toronto 1989.

21. **G. Ries,** Rotationssymmetrische Radar-Ambiguity-Funktion, Manuskript, Lehrstuhl für Elektrotechnik VIII - Hochfrequenztechnik, Universität Siegen 1989.

22. **W. Schempp,** Radar ambiguity functions, the Heisenberg group, and holomorphic theta series, Proc. Amer. Math. Soc. 92, 103-110 (1984)

23. **W. Schempp,** Harmonic analysis on the Heisenberg nilpotent Lie group, with applications to signal theory, Pitman Research Notes in Math., Vol. 147, Longman Scientific and Technical, Harlow, Essex, and J. Wiley & Sons, New York 1986.986.

24. **W. Schempp,** Group theoretical methods in approximation theory, elementary number theory, and computational signal geometry, Approximation Theory V, C.K. Chui, L.L. Schumaker, and J.D. Ward, Editors, 129-171, Academic Press, Boston, Orlando, San Diego, New York, Austin, London, Sydney, Tokyo, Toronto 1986.

25. **W. Schempp,** The oscillator representation of the metaplectic group applied to quantum electronics and computerized tomography, Stochastic Processes in Physics and Engineering, S. Albeverio, P. Blanchard, M. Hazewinkel, and L. Streit, Editors, 305-344, D. Reidel, Dordrecht, Boston, Lancaster, Tokyo 1988.

26. **W. Schempp,** Elementary holograms and 3-orbifolds, C.R. Math. Rep. Acad. Sci. Canada 10, 155-160 (1988).

27. **W. Schempp,** Holographic grids, Visual Communications and Image Processing '88, T. Russell Hsing, Editor, Proc. SPIE 1001, 116-120 (1988).

28. **W. Schempp,** The holographic transform, Numerical Methods and Approximation Theory III, G.V. Milovanovič, Editor, 67-91, University of Niš, Niš 1988.

29. **W. Schempp,** Holographic image processing, coherent optical computing, and neural computer architecture for pattern recognition, Lie Methods in Optics II, K.B. Wolf, Editor, Lecture Notes in Physics, Springer-Verlag, Berlin, Heidelberg, New York, Tokyo 1989.

30. **D. Schreier,** Synthetische Holografie, Fachbuchverlag Leipzig 1984.

31. **D.S. Shucker,** Square integrable representations of unimodular groups, Proc. Amer. Math. Soc. 89, 169-172 (1983).

32. **B.H. Soffer, G.J. Dunning, Y. Owechko, and E. Marom,** Associative holographic memory with feedback using phase-conjugate mirrors, Optics Letters 11, 118-120 (1986).

33. **H.J. Tiziani,** Real-time metrology with BSO crystals, Optica Acta 29, 463-470 (1982).

34. **T. Yatagai,** Cellular logic architectures for optical computers, Applied Optics 25, 1571-1577 (1986).

35. **J.A. Yeazell, C.R. Stroud,** Rydberg-atom wave packets localized in the angular variables, Phys. Rev. A 35, 2806-2809 (1987).

36. **J.A. Yeazell, C.R. Stroud,** Observation of spatially localized atomic electron wave packets, Phys. Rev. Lett. 60, 1494-1497 (1988).

LEHRSTUHL FUER MATHEMATIK I
UNIVERSITY OF SIEGEN
D-5900 SIEGEN
GERMANY

International Series of
Numerical Mathematics, Vol. 90

SOME RECENT RESULTS ON COMPLEX INTERPOLATORY APPROXIMATION

Xie-Chang Shen, Department of Mathematics, Peking University, Beijing, China

In this paper some results obtained in last years on complex interpolatory approximation are introduced.

1. The convergence in the mean of interpolating polynomials and rational functions of functions of class $A(|z|\leq 1)$

We denote by $A(|z|\leq 1)$ class of functions analytic in $|z|<1$ and continuous on $|z|\leq 1$. Consider the nth roots of unity as nodes and the Lagrange interpolating polynomials $L_{n-1}(f,z)$ of degree $\leq n-1$ of $f(z)\in A(|z|\leq 1)$.

In 1964 WALSH and SHARMA proved:

$$\lim_{n\to +\infty} \| f(z) - L_{n-1}(f,z) \|_{L^2(|z|=1)} = 0$$

using the orthogonality of Lagrange basic functions $|z|=1$. In 1983 SHARMA and VERTESI generalized the above result to the case $L^p(|z|=1)$, $0<p<+\infty$. Besides, they investigated the interpolation of meromorphic functions (also see SAFF and WALSH).

In 1988 SHEN generalized the Lagrange interpolating polynomials to the rational interpolation. For $|\alpha_i|<1$, $0\leq i\leq n$, consider the Blaschke product:

$$B_{n+1}(z) = \prod_{i=0}^{n} \frac{\alpha_i - z}{1-\bar{\alpha}_i z} \quad \frac{|\alpha_i|}{\alpha_i}$$

Then Shen proved that there exists $n+1$ different points $\{z_k'\}$, $|z_k'|=1$, $|z_{k+1}' - z_k'| \geq \frac{c}{n} > 0$, $0\leq k\leq n$, $z_{n+1}' = z_0'$ satisfying $|B_{n+1}(z)| = 1$. If rational function $R_n(f,z) = (a_n z^n + \cdots + a_0)/\prod_{i=0}^{n}(1-\bar{\alpha}_i z)$ interpolates $f(z)\in A(|z|\leq 1)$ at $\{z_k'\}$, $0\leq k\leq n$, then

$$\| f(z)-R_n(f,z) \|_{L^2(|z|=1)} = O\left(\omega\left(f,\frac{1}{\Sigma_n}\right)\sqrt{\sum_{j=0}^{n} 1/(z_j' B_{n+1}'(z_j'))}\right)$$

where $\Sigma_n = \sum_{i=0}^{n}(1-|\alpha_i|)$. If $|\alpha_i|\leq\rho<1$, $0\leq i\leq n$, then

$$0 < C_2 \ln n \leq \| R_n \|_{C(|z|=1)} \leq C_1 \ln n$$

and

$$\| f(z)-R_n(f,z) \|_{L^2(|z|=1)} = O\left(\omega\left(f, \frac{1}{\Sigma_n}\right)\right).$$

SHEN also extended above result to the case $L^p(|z|=1)$, $0<p<+\infty$.

SHEN also generalized the Lagrange interpolation to the Hermite--Fejer interpolation and obtained the rate of convergence in the mean as $\omega(f, \frac{1}{n})$. Besides, this rate is sharp.

2. The degree of approximation of interpolating polynomials in a Jordan domain

There have been a lot of papers concerning the approximation in a Jordan domain, but only a few of papers are devoted to interpolatory approximation.

SHEN and ZHONG obtained the following result: Let $f(z)\in E^p(D)$, $p>1$, $\partial D\in C^{2+\varepsilon}$, $\varepsilon>0$. Then there exists an interpolation matrix $\{z_{kn}\}$ such that

$$\| f(z)-L_{n-1}(f,z) \|_{L^p(\Gamma)} = O(E_{n,p}(f))=O(\omega(f,\frac{1}{n})_p) ,$$

where $E_{n,p}(f)$ is the best approximation in space $L^p(\Gamma)$ by polynomials of degree $\leq n$. This improved the SEWELL's result, in which more strong condition on ∂D is posed and for $\omega(f,\Gamma)_p \in \mathrm{Lip}\,\alpha$, the degree of approximation is $(\ln n/n)^{\alpha}$.

For Fejer nodes and analytic boundary ∂D CURTISS obtained

$$\lim_{n\to +\infty} \| f(z)-L_{n-1}(f,z) \|_{L^2(\partial D)} = 0 ,$$

where $f(z)\in A(\overline{D})$-class of functions analytic in D and continuous on $\overline{D}$, and for $\partial D\in C^{2+\varepsilon}$, $\varepsilon>0$, AL'PER and KALINOGORSKAJA extended above result to the case $L^p(\partial D)$, $0<p<+\infty$. But in 1988 SHEN and ZHONG obtained

$$\|f(z)-L_{n-1}(f,z)\|_{L^p(\partial D)} = O(\omega(f, \frac{1}{n})), \qquad f\in A(\overline{D})$$

under the condition

$$\int_0 \omega(\Psi', t)|\ln t|^2/t \, dt < +\infty ,$$

where Ψ is the outer mapping function. Besides, this estimate is sharp and the $\omega(f, \frac{1}{n})$ can not be substituted by $\omega(f, \frac{1}{n})_p$.

Recently, CHUI and SHEN considered the approximation by Hermite--Fejer interpolating polynomials in a Jordan domain. For given integer $q\geq 0$ and Fejer nodes $\{z_k\}$, $1\leq k\leq n$ we denote by $\tilde{H}_N(f,z)$, $N=(q+1)n-1$, interpolating polynomials of $f(z)$ $A(\overline{D})$ satisfying

$$\tilde{H}_N(f,z_k)=f(z_k), \quad \tilde{H}_N^{(j)}(f,z_k)=a_k^{(j)}, \ 1\leq k\leq n, \ 1\leq j\leq q,$$

where $\{a_k^{(j)}\}$ are given numbers. If all $a_k^{(j)}=0$, $1 \leq k \leq n$, $1 \leq j \leq q$ then we denote if by $H_N(f,z)$. Suppose ∂D satisfies

$$\int_0 \omega(\Psi'', t)\,|\ln t| \,/\, t \ dt < +\infty ,$$

then

$$\| f(z)-H_N(f,z) \|_{C(\partial D)} = O(\omega(f, \tfrac{1}{n}) \ln n) ,$$

$$\| f(z)-H_N(f,z) \|_{L^p(\partial D)} = O(\omega(f, \tfrac{1}{n})), \quad 0<p<+\infty ,$$

and these two extimates are sharp. Besides, if $\lim\limits_{t \to 0} \omega(f,t)\ln t =0$ and $\max\limits_{1\leq k \leq n} |a_k^{(j)}|=o(n^j/\ln n)$, $1 \leq j \leq q$, then

$$\lim_{n\to +\infty} \| f(z)-\tilde{H}_N(f,z) \|_{C(\partial D)} = 0$$

if $\max\limits_{1\leq k \leq n} |a_k^{(j)}| = o(n^j)$, $1 \leq j \leq n$, then

$$\lim_{n\to +\infty} \| f(z)-\tilde{H}_N(f,z) \|_{L^p(\partial D)} = 0 , \quad 0<p<+\infty .$$

These improved GAIER'S result in which the case $q=1$ and analytic boundary ∂D were considered and the convergence was obtained only on the compact inside D .

3. Birkhoof interpolation

For arbitrary fixed integer $q \geq 0$, the $q+1$ natural numbers

$$0 < m_1 < m_2 < \cdots < m_q$$

are considered. The polynomial $B_N(f,z)$ of degree $\leq N=(q+1)n-1$ satisfying the conditions:

$$B_N^{(m_j)}(f, z_k) = f(z_k)\,\delta_{jo} , \quad 1 \leq k \leq n, \quad 0 \leq j \leq q,$$

is called the $(0, m_1, \cdots, m_q)$ Birkhoof interpolating polynomial of $f(z) \in A(|z| \leq 1)$, where $\{z_k\}$ is the nth roots of unity, δ_{jo} is the knonecker delta.

In 1980 VERTESI mentioned that the uniform convergence on $|z| \leq 1$ is not valid for whole class $A(|z| \leq 1)$. In 1988 SHARMA and SZABADOS obtained the error of approximation on $|z| \leq 1$ as $O(\omega_{m_1}, (f, \frac{1}{n}) + E_{[cn]}(f) \ln n)$, $c>0$.

It is very interesting to investigate the degree of approximation in $L^p(|z|=1)$, $0<p<+\infty$. In 1989 SHEN obtained the estimation

$O(\omega_{m_1}, (f, \frac{1}{n}))$ and

$$\lim_{n \to +\infty} \| f(z) - \tilde{B}_{n-1}(f,z) \|_{L^p(|z|=1)} = 0$$

where polynomial $\tilde{B}_N(f,z)$ of degree $\leq N$ satisfies the conditions:

$$\tilde{B}_N(f, z_k) = f(z_k), \quad \tilde{B}_N^{(m_j)}(f, z_k) = a_k^{(j)}, \quad 1 \leq k \leq n, \quad 1 \leq j \leq q,$$

and $\max_{1 \leq k \leq n} |a_k^{(j)}| = o(n^{m_j})$, $1 \leq j \leq q$. In the proof SHEN first obtained an inequlity: for any polynomial $Q_N(z)$ of degree $N=(q+1)n-1$, $1<p<+\infty$

$$\int_{|z|=1} |Q_N(z)|^p |dz| = O\left(\sum_{k=1}^{n} \sum_{j=0}^{q} |Q_N^{(m_j)}(z_k)|^p / n^{pm_j+1} \right)$$

The results of SZABADOS and VARMA and VARMA are consequences of above results for $p=1$, $q=1$ and $q=1$ respectively. In addition, TURAN's problem 46 is also a very special case $p=2$, $q=1$ and $m_1 = 2$.

References

Al'per, S. Ya. and Kalinogorskaja, G.I. (1969) The Convergence of Lagrange interpolation polynomials in the Complex domain, Izv. Vyss. Ucebn. Zaved Math. 11, 13-23.

Chui, C.K. and Shen, X.C. (1989), The degree of approximation by Hermite-Fejer interpolating polynomials in a Jordan domain, Trans. Amer. Math. Coc. (to be submitted)

Curtiss, J.H. (1965) Convergence of complex Lagrange interpolation polynomials on the locus of the interpolation points, Duke Math. J. 32 187-204.

Gaier, D. (1954) Uber Interpolation in regelmassig verteilten Punkten mit Nebenbedingunger, Math. Zeitschr. 61, 119-133.

Saff, E.B. and Walsh, J.L. (1973) On the convergence of rational function which interpolate in the roots of unity, Pacific J. Math. 45, 639-654.

Sewell, W.E. (1966) Integrated Lipschitz conditions and approximation in the mean by interpolating polynomials, SIAM Num. Anal. 3, 329-343.

Sharma, A. and Szabados, J.(1988) Convergence rates for some lacunary interpolators on the roots of unity, Approx. Theory and its Appl. 4, 41-48.

Sharma, A. and Vertesi, P. (1983) Mean convergence and interpolation in roots of unity, SIAM Math. Anal. 14, 800-806.

Shen, X.C. (1988) On the convergence in the mean of interpolating rational functions, Acta Math. Sinica (to be submitted).

Shen, X.C. (1988) On the convergence of interpolating rational functions in the unite disk, Acta Math. Sinica (to be submitted).

Shen, X.C. (1988) The convergence problem of (0,1,···,q) Hermite--Fejer interpolating polynomials on the roots of unity, Chinese Annals of Math. (to be submitted).

Shen, X.C. (1988) The convergnece problem of (0,1,···,q) Hermite--Fejer interpolating polynomials on the roots of unity II, Chinese Annals of Math. (to be submitted).

Shen, X.C. (1989) On the Approximation in the mean by Birkhoff interpolation on the roots of unity, Approx. Theory III. Edit. by C.K. Chui et. (to be submitted).

Shen, X.C., (1988) Generalization of Marciekiewicz-Zygmund inequlities, Advances in Math. (to be submitted).

Shen, X.C. and Zhong, L.F. (1988), Approximation by interpolating polynomials in $E^p(D)$ spaces, Kexue Tongbao 11 876.

Shen, X.C. and Zhong, L.F. (1988) Approximation in the mean by Lagrange interpolating polynomial in the complex plane, Kexue Tongbao 33, 810-814.

Szabados, J. and Varma, A.K. (1986) On an open problem of P. Turan concerning Birkhoof interpolation based on the roots of unity, J. Approx. Theory 47, 255-264.

Turan, P. (1980) On some open problem of approximation theory, J. Approx, Theory 29, 23-85.

Varma, A.K. (1988) Complex interpolating polynomials, Proceedings Amer. Math. Soc. 103, 125-130.

Vertesi, P. (1980) Linear operators on the roots of unity, Studia Sci. Math. Hungar. 15, 241-245.

Walsh, J.L. and Sharma, A.(1964) Least squares and interpolation in roots of unity, Pacific J. Math. 14, 727-750.

Prof. Xie-Chang Shen, Department of Mathematics, Peking University
Beijing 100871, P.R. of China

International Series of
Numerical Mathematics, Vol. 90

INDEX TRANSFORMS FOR MULTIDIMENSIONAL DISCRETE FOURIER TRANSFORMS

Gabriele Steidl and Manfred Tasche

Wilhelm-Pieck-Universität Rostock, Sektion Mathematik,
Rostock, German Democratic Republic

1. Introduction

Index transforms of m-dimensional arrays into n-dimensional arrays play a significant role in many fast algorithms of multivariate discrete Fourier transforms (DFT's) and cyclic convolutions. Indeed, they provide one of the foundations on which row-column methods or very efficient nesting methods for the fast computation of DFT's or cyclic convolutions are based (such as the prime factor algorithm [6, pp. 127 - 133], the Winograd algorithm [8; 6, pp. 133 - 145] and the Agarwal-Cooley algorithm [1; 6, pp. 43 - 52]). The general computing scheme for many fast m-dimensional DFT algorithms (convolution methods) is based on the following three essential steps:

(1) By an index transform of the input data, the m-dimensional DFT (convolution) is transfered into an n-dimensional DFT (convolution) of "short lengths" $(n > m)$.

(2) By efficient algorithms for one-dimensional DFT's (convolutions) of short lengths, the n-dimensional DFT (convolution) is computed in parallel (cf. [6]).

(3) By an index transform of the output data, the desired result of the m-dimensional DFT (convolution) is obtained.

BURRUS [2], NUSSBAUMER [6] and HEKRDLA [4, 5] dealt with the properties of index transforms for multidimensional DFT's and convolutions in order to decrease the expense for organizing such necessary index transforms.

In this paper, the nature of index transforms is explained from the algebraic point of view. Using known facts from group theory we solve the open problems posed by HEKRDLA [4, 5]. We show in Theorem 1 that every index transform for DFT's is an isomorphism between the corresponding sets of indices considered as abelian groups. It is remarkable that the conditions of existence and construction for index transforms are the same. Furthermore, we use our results to extend the known Chinese Remainder Theorem to the multivariate case and to deduce new index transforms which allow a simplified implementation of input and output data permutations for fast DFT-algorithms or convolution methods.

2. Preliminaries

In the following we use standard notations. Let Z_M be the additive group of all integers modulo $M \in Z$ $(M > 1)$. Further, let G be the additive abelian group

$$(1) \qquad G := \bigoplus_{j=1}^{m} Z_{M_j} \qquad (M_j \in Z,\ M_j > 1)$$

with the character group $G' := \{p_g : g \in G\}$, where $p_g: G \to C$ [3, p. 202] is defined for

$$u = (u_j)_{j=1}^{m},\ g = (g_j)_{j=1}^{m} \in G$$

by

$$p_g(u) := \exp\left(-2\pi i \sum_{j=1}^{m} g_j u_j / M_j\right).$$

Let CG be the set of all formal sums

$$\underline{x} = \sum_{u\in G} x_u u, \quad \underline{y} = \sum_{u\in G} y_u u \quad (x_u, y_u \in C).$$

With the operations

$$\underline{x} + \underline{y} := \sum_{u\in G} (x_u + y_u)u,$$

$$c\underline{x} := \sum_{u\in G} (cx_u)u \quad (c\in C),$$

CG is a vector space over C with basis G. Note that in the representation of $\underline{x}\in CG$ each $u\in G$ can be considered as an pointer. Defining a multiplication in CG as (m-dimensional) cyclic convolution ($*_G$)

$$\underline{x} *_G \underline{y} := \sum_{u\in G} \Big(\sum_{g\in G} x_g\, y_{u-g}\Big)u,$$

CG becomes a group algebra. Finally, the (m-dimensional) <u>discrete Fourier transform</u> (DFT) F_G on CG is defined by

$$F_G\underline{x} := \sum_{g\in G} \Big(\sum_{u\in G} x_u\, p_g(u)\Big)g.$$

Let

$$(2) \qquad H := \bigoplus_{k=1}^{n} Z_{N_k} \qquad (N_k \in Z,\ N_k > 1)$$

be another additive abelian group with character group $H' := \{q_h : h\in H\}$. Similarly as above, the group algebra CH and the (n-dimensional) DFT F_H are explained.

3. Index Transforms for DFT's

Let G and H be given by (1) and (2), respectively. We consider a mapping $\varphi: G \to H$. Then the <u>transformed element</u> $\underline{x}\circ\varphi \in CG$ of $\underline{x}\in CH$ is defined by

$$\underline{x}\circ\varphi := \sum_{u\in G} x_{\varphi(u)}u.$$

Now we seek all mappings of G into H such that the m-dimensional DFT F_G can be computed as n-dimensional DFT F_H. That yields

Problem 1 (cf. [4]). Determine all mappings $\varphi, \psi: G \to H$ satisfying

(3) $$F_G(\underline{x} \circ \varphi) = (F_H \underline{x}) \circ \psi$$

for all $\underline{x} \in CH$, or equivalently

$$\sum_{u \in G} x_{\varphi(u)} \, p_g(u) = \sum_{v \in H} x_v \, q_{\psi(g)}(v)$$

for all $\underline{x} \in CH$ and $g \in G$.

The answer is given by the following theorems, whose proofs (see [7]) are mainly based on properties of characters of abelian groups. Especially, we use that $G \cong G'$.

Theorem 1. Let G and H be given by (1) and (2), respectively. Then there exist $\varphi, \psi: G \to H$ satisfying (3) if and only if $G \cong H$ and φ is an isomorphism. If $G \cong H$, then for each isomorphism $\varphi: G \to H$ there exists a unique isomorphism $\psi: G \to H$ such that (3) holds.

Let $G \cong H$. Then an isomorphism $\varphi: G \to H$ is called an index transform of G onto H.

For any prime power p^a $(a \in Z,\ a > 0)$, we introduce the sets

$$I(p^a) := \{ j \in \{1,\dots,m\} : p^a \mid M_j,\ p^{a+1} \nmid M_j \},$$
$$J(p^a) := \{ k \in \{1,\dots,n\} : p^a \mid N_k,\ p^{a+1} \nmid N_k \}.$$

Then it is well-known that $G \cong H$ if and only if $|I(p^a)| = |J(p^a)|$ for every prime power p^a. Hence, Theorem 1 yields a necessary and sufficient condition for the existence of index transforms fulfilling (3), which is easy to check in practice. One has only to compare the prime factorizations of all M_j $(j = 1,\dots,m)$ and all N_k $(k = 1,\dots,n)$. This solves a recent problem posed by HEKRDLA [4, 5].

Now we construct index transforms of G onto H and their inverses under the assumption $G \cong H$. In the following, we denote by $|x|_N$ the residue of $x \in Z$ modulo N $(N \in Z,\ N > 1)$, i.e. $|x|_N \equiv x \pmod N$ and $0 \leqq |x|_N < N$.

Theorem 2. Let G and H with $G \cong H$ be given by (1) and (2), respectively. Then the index transforms $\varphi, \Psi : G \to H$ fulfil (3) if and only if $\varphi = (\varphi_k)_{k=1}^n$ and $\Psi = (\Psi_k)_{k=1}^n$ with φ_k, $\Psi_k : G \to Z_{N_k}$ are of the form

$$(4)\qquad \begin{aligned} \varphi_k(u) &= \Big|\sum_{s=1}^{m} \frac{N_k}{\gcd(M_s,N_k)}\, \mu_{sk} u_s\Big|_{N_k}, \\ \Psi_k(u) &= \Big|\sum_{s=1}^{m} \frac{N_k}{\gcd(M_s,N_k)}\, \nu_{sk} u_s\Big|_{N_k}, \end{aligned}$$

where $\mu_{sk}, \nu_{sk} \in Z$ $(0 \leqq \mu_{sk}, \nu_{sk} < \gcd(M_s,N_k))$ are solutions of

$$(5)\qquad \sum_{k=1}^{n} \frac{N_k\ M_s}{\gcd(M_j,N_k)\ \gcd(M_s,N_k)}\, \mu_{jk} \nu_{sk} \equiv \delta_{sj} \pmod{M_s}$$

for all $j, s = 1,\dots,m$. In this case, the inverse transforms $\varphi^{-1} = (\varphi_j^{-1})_{j=1}^m$ and $\Psi^{-1} = (\Psi_j^{-1})_{j=1}^m$ with $\varphi_j^{-1}, \Psi_j^{-1} : H \to Z_{M_j}$ are determined by

$$(6)\qquad \begin{aligned} \varphi_j^{-1}(v) &= \Big|\sum_{t=1}^{n} \frac{M_j}{\gcd(M_j,N_t)}\, \nu_{jt} v_t\Big|_{M_j}, \\ \Psi_j^{-1}(v) &= \Big|\sum_{t=1}^{n} \frac{M_j}{\gcd(M_j,N_t)}\, \mu_{jt} v_t\Big|_{M_j}. \end{aligned}$$

Note that there exist solutions μ_{sk}, ν_{sk} $(s = 1,\dots,m;\ k = 1,\dots,n)$ of (5) if and only if $G \cong H$. This answers an open question of HEKRDLA [4, 5].

4. Special Index Transforms

We specify the above results for the important case of DFT's of size $M \times \dots \times M$. Let

$$M_j := M = p_1^{n_1} \dots p_r^{n_r},$$

where P_l are primes $(2 \leq P_1 < \dots < P_r)$, $R_l := M/P_l^{n_l}$ and

$$N_k = Q_l := P_l^{n_l}$$

with $k := (l-1)m + i$ for $l = 1,\dots,r$ and $i = 1,\dots,m$. Further, let

$$(7) \qquad G := \bigoplus_{j=1}^{m} Z_M, \quad H := \bigoplus_{k=1}^{mr} Z_{N_k} = \bigoplus_{l=1}^{r} \Big(\bigoplus_{i=1}^{m} Z_{Q_l} \Big).$$

Set $\mu_{ji}^{(l)} := \mu_{jk}$ and $\nu_{si}^{(l)} := \nu_{sk}$. Then by Theorem 2, two index transforms $\varphi, \psi: G \to H$ with property (3) can be represented in the form (4), where $\mu_{ji}^{(l)}, \nu_{si}^{(l)} \in Z$ $(0 \leq \mu_{ji}^{(l)}, \nu_{si}^{(l)} < Q_l)$ are solutions of the congruences

$$(8) \qquad R_l \sum_{i=1}^{m} \mu_{ji}^{(l)} \nu_{si}^{(l)} \equiv \delta_{sj} \pmod{Q_l}$$

for all $j, s = 1,\dots,m$ and $l = 1,\dots,r$. Then it follows from Theorem 2 that $\varphi: G \to H$ of the form (4) fulfils (3) if and only if $P_l \nmid \det (\mu_{ji}^{(l)})_{j,i=1}^{m}$ for $l = 1,\dots,r$. In this case, the associated index transform ψ of φ can be obtained from (8) by Cramer's rule.

This leads now to a simple construction of $\varphi, \psi: G \to H$ satisfying (3), which can be considered as extension of the Chinese Remainder Theorem to the multivariate case. Setting

$$(\mu_{ji}^{(l)})_{j,i=1}^{m} := (\delta_{ji})_{j,i=1}^{m} \qquad (l = 1,\dots,r),$$

we obtain by (8) that

$$(\nu_{si}^{(l)})_{s,i=1}^{m} = R_l' \, (\delta_{si})_{s,i=1}^{m},$$

where $R_l' \in Z$ $(1 \leq R_l' < Q_l)$ is defined by $R_l R_l' \equiv 1 \pmod{Q_l}$. Then by (4) and (6), the corresponding index transforms φ, ψ: $G \to H$ and their inverses $\varphi^{-1}, \psi^{-1}: H \to G$ read for $u \in G$, $v \in H$ as follows:

$$\varphi_{(l-1)m+i}(u) = |u_i|_{Q_l},$$

$$\Psi_{(l-1)m+i}(u) = |R_l' \, u_i|_{Q_l} \quad (l = 1,\dots,r;\ i = 1,\dots,m),$$

$$\varphi_j^{-1}(v) = \Big|\sum_{l=1}^{r} R_l \, R_l' \, v_{(l-1)m+j}\Big|_M ,$$

$$\Psi_j^{-1}(v) = \Big|\sum_{l=1}^{r} R_l \, v_{(l-1)m+j}\Big|_M \quad (j = 1,\dots,m).$$

For $m = 1$, the above mappings yield the known Chinese Remainder Theorem.

But unfortunately, we have $\varphi \neq \Psi$ in general. Note that we can give necessary and sufficient conditions (see [7]), such that there exists an index transform $\varphi: G \to H$ with

(9) $$F_G(\underline{x} \circ \varphi) = (F_H \underline{x}) \circ \varphi$$

for all $\underline{x} \in CH$. This leads to a simplified computer implementation of fast algorithms for DFT's of size $M \times \dots \times M$ and reduces the required memory capacity to one half. For instance, the one-dimensional DFT of length $M = 900 = 2^2 \cdot 3^2 \cdot 5^2$ can be computed via DFT's of lengths 4, 9 and 25 by the prime factor algorithm or by the Winograd algorithm. The necessary permutations of the input and output data for such DFT's can be arranged by an index transform $\varphi: Z_{900} \to Z_4 \oplus Z_9 \oplus Z_{25}$ with property (9), namely

$$\varphi(u) = (|u|_4,\ |u|_9,\ |4u|_{25}),$$
$$\varphi^{-1}(v) = |225\, v_1 + 100\, v_2 + 144\, v_3|_{900}$$

for $u \in Z_{900}$ and $v = (v_1, v_2, v_3) \in Z_4 \oplus Z_9 \oplus Z_{25}$.

5. Index Transforms for Convolutions

Let G and H be given by (1) and (2), respectively.

Problem 2 (cf. [5]). Determine all mappings $\varphi: G \to H$ satisfying

(10) $(\underline{x} \circ \varphi) *_G (\underline{y} \circ \varphi) = (\underline{x} *_H \underline{y}) \circ \varphi$

for all $\underline{x}, \underline{y} \in CH$.

Theorem 3 (see [7]). Let G and H be given by (1) and (2), respectively. Then there exists a mapping $\varphi: G \to H$ satisfying (10) if and only if $G \cong H$ and φ is an isomorphism.

From mathematical point of view, it is interesting that the conditions for the existence of index transforms for DFT's and convolutions are identical. The index transforms explain the similar structure of efficient algorithms for DFT's and convolutions (cf. [6]).

References

1. Agarwal, R.C., Cooley, J.W. (1977) New algorithms for digital convolution. IEEE Trans. Acoust. Speech Signal Process. 25, 392 - 410.

2. Burrus, C.S. (1977) Index mappings for multidimensional formulation of the DFT and convolution. IEEE Trans. Acoust. Speech Signal Process. 25, 239 - 242.

3. Hasse, H. (1950) Vorlesungen über Zahlentheorie, (Springer, Berlin).

4. Hekrdla, J. (1987) Index transforms for N-dimensional DFT's. Numer. Math. 51, 469 - 480.

5. Hekrdla, J. (1986) Index transforms for multidimensional cyclic convolutions and discrete Fourier transforms. IEEE Trans. Acoust. Speech Signal Process. 34, 996 - 997.

6. Nussbaumer, H.J. (1981) Fast Fourier transform and convolution algorithms, (Springer, Berlin).

7. Steidl, G., Tasche, M. (in print) Index transforms for multidimensional DFT's and convolutions. Numer. Math.

8. Winograd, S. (1978) On computing the discrete Fourier transform. Math. Comp. 32, 175 - 199.

Dr. Gabriele Steidl, Prof. Dr. Manfred Tasche, Wilhelm-Pieck-Universität Rostock, Sektion Mathematik, Universitätsplatz 1, DDR - 2500 Rostock, German Democratic Republic

International Series of
Numerical Mathematics, Vol. 90

MINIMAL PROPERTIES OF PERIODIC BOX-SPLINE INTERPOLATION ON A THREE DIRECTION MESH

Joachim Stöckler

Department of Mathematics, University of Duisburg, West-Germany

1. Introduction

Let ϕ be a piecewise continuous complex valued function on $\mathbb{R}^s$, $s \geq 1$, which is 2π-periodic in each coordinate direction. Given a "meshsize" $h = 2\pi/N$, $N \geq 1$, let $\mathbb{F} := \mathbb{F}_h := h\mathbf{Z}^s \cap [0, 2\pi)^s$ and

$$\mathcal{S}(\phi) := \mathcal{S}_h(\phi) := \Big\{ \sum_{\mathbf{j}\in\mathbb{F}} a_{\mathbf{j}}\phi(\,.\, - \mathbf{j}) \mid a_{\mathbf{j}} \in \mathbb{C} \Big\}.$$

The periodic interpolation problem is to find for any complex data sequence $\{d_{\mathbf{j}} \mid \mathbf{j} \in \mathbb{F}\}$ a uniquely determined function $s = \sum_{\mathbf{j}\in\mathbb{F}} a_{\mathbf{j}}\phi(\,.\, - \mathbf{j}) \in \mathcal{S}(\phi)$ which satisfies

$$(1) \qquad \sum_{\mathbf{j}\in\mathbb{F}} a_{\mathbf{j}}\phi(\mathbf{k} - \mathbf{j}) = d_{\mathbf{k}} \quad \text{for all } \mathbf{k} \in \mathbb{F}.$$

This interpolation problem is closely related to the method of attenuation factors. If the sequence $\{d_{\mathbf{j}} \mid \mathbf{j} \in \mathbb{F}\}$ represents the function values of a periodic continuous function f, i.e. $d_{\mathbf{j}} = f(\mathbf{j})$, then an efficient scheme of estimating the Fourier coefficient $\widehat{f}(\alpha)$ is to compute the Fourier coefficient of the interpolant If in the form

$$(2) \qquad (If)^\wedge(\alpha) = \tau_\alpha \widetilde{f}(\alpha);$$

here $\widetilde{f}(\alpha) := N^{-s}\sum_{\mathbf{j}\in\mathbb{F}} f(\mathbf{j})e^{-i\alpha\cdot\mathbf{j}}$ is the discrete Fourier transform of f, and $\tau_\alpha := \widehat{\phi}(\alpha)/\widetilde{\phi}(\alpha)$ is the attenuation factor.

If ϕ is a periodic B-spline of odd degree in $\mathbb{R}$, a variational characterization of the interpolating spline is well known [1, 5]; furthermore, the method (2) is the optimal approximation of $\widehat{f}(\alpha)$ in the sense of Sard (cf. [4, 8]) in a certain Hilbert space. Recently the interpolation problem (1) was studied using translates of periodic box-splines in $\mathbb{R}^s$, cf. [6, 7]. We restrict our attention to bivariate three directional box-splines for which the poisedness of the interpolation has been established in [2]. For these splines we develop a variational characterization of the interpolating periodic spline comparable to the univariate case.

For further reference we introduce some notations. Let $\xi_1 := (1,0)$, $\xi_2 := (0,1)$, $\xi_3 := (1,1)$, and let X denote the ordered set

$$X = \{\xi_1 : k,\ \xi_2 : l,\ \xi_3 : m\}\,, \qquad k, l, m \geq 1,$$

with each vector ξ_ν repeated the designated number of times. We let $X_\nu := \{\xi \in X \mid \xi \neq \xi_\nu\}$, $1 \leq \nu \leq 3$. Using sinc $x := \sin x/x$, $x \in \mathbb{R}$, we define the periodic three directional box-spline by letting

$$\widehat{M}(\alpha \mid X) := \left(\operatorname{sinc}\frac{h\alpha_1}{2}\right)^k \left(\operatorname{sinc}\frac{h\alpha_2}{2}\right)^l \left(\operatorname{sinc}\frac{h(\alpha_1+\alpha_2)}{2}\right)^m ;$$

hence, $M(\,.\mid X)$ is the periodic extension of the scaled cardinal box-spline M_{klm} studied in [2]. Directional derivatives are denoted by D_ξ, $D_Y := \prod_{\xi\in Y} D_\xi$. Other operators of special interest are the "line averages"

$$P_\nu f(x) := (2\pi)^{-1}\int_0^{2\pi} f(x+s\xi_\nu)\,ds, \quad \nu = 1,2,3,$$

(3) $$S_1 f(x) := N^{-1}\sum_{k=0}^{N-1} f(kh, x_2), \qquad S_2 f(x) := N^{-1}\sum_{k=0}^{N-1} f(x_1, kh),$$

$$S_3 f(x) := N^{-1}\sum_{k=0}^{N-1} f(x_1 - x_2 + kh, kh),$$

and $R_\nu := \prod_{\mu\neq\nu}(id - P_\mu)$. They act on the function space

$$H(X) := \{f \in L^2_{2\pi} \mid D_Y f \in L^2_{2\pi} \text{ for all } Y \subset X\},$$

a multivariate analogue of the space H_m (cf. [5]), on which the variational characterization of univariate splines of degree $2m-1$ is based. $L^2_{2\pi}$ denotes the space of 2π-periodic functions with finite norm $\|f\|_2 := \left((2\pi)^{-2}\int_{(0,2\pi)^2} |f(x)|^2\,dx\right)^{1/2}$.

2. Reproducing kernel on $H(X)$

The function space $H(X)$ is a Hilbert space equipped with the anisotropic Sobolev norm $\|f\| := (\sum_{Y\subset X} \|D_Y f\|_2^2)^{1/2}$, cf. [9]. For computing the reproducing kernel on $H(X)$ we define a different norm on this space.

Lemma 1. *Equivalent to the Sobolev norm on $H(X)$ is the norm*

$$\|f\|_X := \Big(\|D_X f\|_2^2 + \sum_{\nu=1}^{3} \|D_{X_\nu}(S_\nu R_\nu f)\|_2^2 + |\widetilde{f}(0)|^2\Big)^{1/2}, \tag{4}$$

where, as above, $\widetilde{f}(0)$ denotes the discrete Fourier transform of f.

We omit the proof of the lemma which is lead by using the Cauchy Schwarz inequality. Note that in contrast to the Sobolev norm the equivalent norm $\|\,.\,\|_X$ is not translation invariant. However, for any $\mathbf{j} \in \mathbb{F}$ we find $\|f(\,.\,-\mathbf{j})\|_X = \|f\|_X$. This property will be reflected by a certain shift invariance of the reproducing kernel.

Theorem 1. *The Hilbert space $(H(X), \|\,.\,\|_X)$ has the reproducing kernel*

$$K(x;t) = (id - S_3)(id - S_2)(id - S_1)K_0(x;t) + \sum_{\nu=1}^{3}(K_\nu(x;t) - \widetilde{K}_\nu(0;t)) + 1,$$

where the functions $K_\nu(\,.\,;t)$, $0 \le \nu \le 3$, are given by

$$K_0(x;t) = \sum_{\substack{\alpha\in\mathbf{Z}^2 \\ \alpha\cdot\xi_\nu\neq 0 \text{ all } \nu}} c_\alpha(t) \prod_{\xi\in X} |\alpha\cdot\xi|^{-2} e^{i\alpha\cdot x},$$

(5)

$$K_\nu(x;t) = \sum_{0\neq\alpha\perp\xi_\nu} c_\alpha(t) \prod_{\xi\in X_\nu} |\alpha\cdot\xi|^{-2} e^{i\alpha\cdot x}$$

with

$$c_\alpha(t) = e^{-i\alpha\cdot t} - e^{-i\alpha_2 t_2}\chi_1(\alpha) - e^{-i\alpha_1 t_1}\chi_2(\alpha) - e^{-i\alpha_1(t_1-t_2)}\chi_3(\alpha) + \chi_4(\alpha), \tag{6}$$

$$\chi_\nu(\alpha) = \begin{cases} 1 & , \text{ if } \alpha\cdot\xi_\nu \in N\mathbf{Z}\setminus\{0\}, \\ 0 & , \text{ otherwise,} \end{cases} \qquad 1 \le \nu \le 3,$$

$$\chi_4(\alpha) = \begin{cases} 2 & , \text{ if } \alpha\cdot\xi_\nu \in N\mathbf{Z}\setminus\{0\} \text{ for all } 1 \le \nu \le 3, \\ -1 & , \text{ if } \alpha\cdot\xi_\nu = 0 \text{ for one } 1 \le \nu \le 3 \text{ and } \alpha\cdot\xi_\mu \in N\mathbf{Z}\setminus\{0\} \text{ for } \mu\neq\nu, \\ 0 & , \text{ otherwise.} \end{cases}$$

The proof of Theorem 1 is given in Section 4. The above mentioned shift invariance of the norm (4) on $H(X)$ is reflected by the relation

$$K(x;t+\mathbf{j}) = K(x-\mathbf{j};t), \qquad \mathbf{j}\in \mathbb{F}, \tag{7}$$

which can easily be checked using (6). In order to study the linear span of the functions $(K(\,.\,;\mathbf{j}),\ \mathbf{j}\in\mathbb{F})$, we therefore can equivalently deal with the space $\mathcal{S}(K(\,.\,;0)) = \{\sum_{\mathbf{j}\in\mathbb{F}} a_{\mathbf{j}}K(\,.\,-\mathbf{j};0)\mid a_{\mathbf{j}}\in\mathbb{C}\,\}$. Since the definition (5) of $c_\alpha(t)$ simplifies for $t=0$ to

$$c_\alpha(t) = \begin{cases} 0 & \text{, if } \alpha\cdot\xi_\nu \in N\mathbf{Z}\setminus\{0\} \text{ for at least one } 1\le\nu\le 3,\\ e^{-i\alpha\cdot t} & \text{, otherwise,}\end{cases} \tag{8}$$

the space $\mathcal{S}(K(\,.\,;0))$ has a special structure described below.

Theorem 2. *Let $M := M(\,.\mid X\cup X)$ denote the three directional periodic box-spline with direction set $X\cup X$. Then the following relation holds:*

$$\mathcal{S}(K(\,.\,;0)) = \mathcal{S}(M).$$

Proof: By dimension arguments it suffices to prove the containment $\mathcal{S}(K(\,.\,;0))\subset\mathcal{S}(M)$. In order to do this we show $K(\,.\,;0)\in\mathcal{S}(M)$. With $K_0(x;0)$ given in (5) and using (8), we find $\widehat{K}_0(\alpha;0)=0$, if $\alpha\cdot\xi_\nu\in N\mathbf{Z}$ for at least one $1\le\nu\le 3$. It directly follows that $S_\nu K_0(\,.\,;0)=0$ for $1\le\nu\le 3$. Similarly we have $\widetilde{K}_\nu(0;0)=0$, $1\le\nu\le 3$. Hence, the kernel function in $t=0$ has the simpler form

$$K(x;0) = \sum_{\nu=0}^{3} K_\nu(x;0)+1.$$

Again using (8) we can represent the Fourier coefficients of $K_0(\,.\,;0)$ in the form $\widehat{K}_0(\alpha;0) = a_\alpha\widehat{M}(\alpha)$ with the $N-$periodic sequence

$$a_\alpha := \begin{cases} 0 & \text{, if } \alpha\cdot\xi_\nu\in N\mathbf{Z} \text{ for at least one } 1\le\nu\le 3,\\ \prod_{\xi\in X}\left(\frac{2}{h}\operatorname{sinc}\frac{h\alpha\cdot\xi}{2}\right)^{-2} & \text{, otherwise.}\end{cases}$$

A standard argument involving the discrete Fourier transform of (a_α) yields $K_0(\,.\,;0)\in\mathcal{S}(M)$. Similarly it is shown that $K_\nu(\,.\,;0)\in\mathcal{S}(M)$ for $1\le\nu\le 3$, thus completing the proof of the theorem.

3. Periodic Interpolation with $M(\,.\mid X\cup X)$

The classical theory of Hilbert spaces with reproducing kernel yields interesting properties of periodic spline interpolation with translates of the three directional spline $M := M(\,.\mid X\cup X)$. Let I denote the interpolation operator; i.e.

$$I:\; H(X) \longrightarrow \mathcal{S}(M) \quad \text{with} \quad If|_{\mathbb{F}} = f|_{\mathbb{F}}.$$

Theorem 3. *The operator I is the orthogonal projection of $H(X)$ onto $\mathcal{S}(M)$; i.e.*

$$\|f - If\|_X = \inf\{\|f - s\|_X : s \in \mathcal{S}(M)\}. \tag{9}$$

Furthermore, I is uniquely characterized by the following minimal property:

$$\|If\|_X = \inf\{\|g\|_X : g \in H(X) \text{ and } g|_{\mathbb{F}} = f|_{\mathbb{F}}\}. \tag{10}$$

Equations of type (9), (10) are well known for univariate interpolation with splines of odd degree and for tensor product splines with odd degree in each coordinate direction [1]. Following along the lines of [5, 10] we find the exact approximation order for interpolation in $H(X)$ with three directional splines.

Theorem 4. *Let $\varrho := \min\{k+l,\; k+m,\; l+m\}$. Then for any $f \in H(X)$ we have*

$$\|f - If\|_\infty \le C h^{\varrho - 1/2} \|f\|_X$$

with C independent of f and h. The order $\varrho - 1/2$ cannot be increased.

The interpolation scheme $f \mapsto If$ is closely related to the method of attenuation factors $\widehat{f}(\alpha) \sim \tau_\alpha \widetilde{f}(\alpha)$ with

$$\tau_\alpha = \widehat{M}(\alpha \mid X\cup X)/\widetilde{M}(\alpha \mid X\cup X), \tag{11}$$

which was investigated in [6]. Theorem 2 in connection with Sard's theory of optimal approximation [8] directly apply giving

Theorem 5. *The method of attenuation factors (11) is optimal in the following sense: for any $\alpha \in \mathbf{Z}^2$ and any linear operator $L:\; (f(\mathbf{j}),\, \mathbf{j} \in \mathbb{F}) \longrightarrow H(X)$, there is $f \in H(X)$ such that $|\widehat{f}(\alpha) - (Lf)\widehat{\ }(\alpha)| \ge |\widehat{f}(\alpha) - \tau_\alpha \widetilde{f}(\alpha)|$. Furthermore, for any $\alpha \in \mathbf{Z}^2$, $-N/2 \le \alpha_1, \alpha_2 \le N/2$, we have with C independent of f and h*

$$|\widehat{f}(\alpha) - \tau_\alpha \widetilde{f}(\alpha)| \le C h^{\varrho} \|f\|_X. \tag{12}$$

Proof: It is sufficient to prove (12). In [10] the given approximation order was established for periodic interpolation in $H(X)$ with translates of the Bernoulli spline $B(\,.\mid X\cup X)$. Since the underlying norm

$$\|f\|_* := \Big(\|D_X f\|_2^2 + \sum_{\nu=1}^{3}\|D_{X_\nu}P_\nu f\|_2^2 + |\widehat{f}(0)|^2\Big)^{1/2}$$

is equivalent to the norm (4), inequality (12) follows from the optimality assertion.

4. Proof of Theorem 1

We show that for any $f\in H(X)$ the following relation holds:

$$\begin{aligned} f(t) =&(2\pi)^{-2}\int_{(0,2\pi)^2} D_X f(x)\overline{D_X K(x;t)}\,dx+ \\ &(2\pi)^{-2}\sum_{\nu=1}^{3}\int_{(0,2\pi)^2} D_{X_\nu}S_\nu R_\nu f(x)\overline{D_{X_\nu}S_\nu R_\nu K(x;t)}\,dx+ \\ &\widetilde{f}(0)\overline{[K(\,.\,;t)]^{\sim}(0)}. \end{aligned} \tag{13}$$

An easy calculation gives

$$S_\nu f(x) = \sum_{\substack{\alpha\in\mathbf{Z}^2\\ \alpha\cdot\xi_\nu=0}}\sum_{l\in\mathbf{Z}}\widehat{f}(\alpha+Nl\eta_\nu)e^{i\alpha\cdot x}$$

with $\eta_1=(1,0)$, $\eta_2=\eta_3=(0,1)$. Inserting the Fourier series of $K(\,.\,;t)$ we observe that $D_XK(\,.\,;t) = D_XK_0(\,.\,;t)$, $D_{X_\nu}S_\nu R_\nu K(\,.\,;t) = D_{X_\nu}K_\nu(\,.\,;t)$, and $\widetilde{K}(0;t)=1$. Furthermore we find

$$\begin{aligned} (2\pi)^{-2}\int_{(0,2\pi)^2} D_X f(x)\overline{D_X K_0(x;t)}\,dx =& \sum_{\substack{\alpha\in\mathbf{Z}^2\\ \alpha\cdot\xi_\nu\neq 0 \text{ all } \nu}}\widehat{f}(\alpha)\overline{c_\alpha(t)} \\ = g-\sum_{\nu=1}^{3}S_\nu g + 2\widetilde{g}(0) \qquad & \text{with}\quad g(t) = \sum_{\alpha\cdot\xi_\nu\neq 0 \text{ all } \nu}\widehat{f}(\alpha)e^{i\alpha\cdot t}, \end{aligned}$$

$$(2\pi)^{-2}\int_{(0,2\pi)^2} D_{X_\nu}h(x)\overline{D_{X_\nu}K_\nu(x;t)}\,dx = \sum_{0\neq\alpha\perp\xi_\nu}\widehat{h}(\alpha)\overline{c_\alpha(t)}. \tag{14}$$

Letting $h := S_\nu R_\nu f$ in (14) and observing $R_\nu f(t) = g + \sum_{0\neq\alpha\perp\xi_\nu} \widehat{f}(\alpha)e^{i\alpha\cdot t}$, all terms in (13) combine to $\sum_{\alpha\in\mathbf{Z}^2} \widehat{f}(\alpha)e^{i\alpha\cdot t} = f(t)$. This concludes the proof of Theorem 1.

5. Remarks

(i) Typically the characterization in Theorem 3 applies to box-splines $M(\,.\mid X\cup X)$ with each direction having an even multiplicity. Similar results for three directional splines with odd multiplicities can be obtained by using spline histopolation instead of interpolation, cf. [3].

(ii) For constructing the reproducing kernel on $H(X)$ we implicitly needed the "determinant condition"; this means that for any two vectors in X which form a basis of $\mathbb{R}^2$ the corresponding 2×2-matrix is unimodular. With different methods we developed in [9] a reproducing kernel on $H(X)$ whenever each direction in X is relatively prime. This applies, for example, to the four directional case in $\mathbb{R}^2$. However, the constructed norm on $H(X)$ has a much more complicated structure than (4).

References

1. Ahlberg, J. H., Nilson, E. N., Walsh, J. N. (1965) The Theory of Splines and their Applications (Academic Press, New York-London).

2. de Boor, C., Höllig, K., Riemenschneider, S. D. (1985) Bivariate cardinal interpolation by splines on a three direction mesh. Illinois J. Math. 29, 533-566.

3. Delvos, F.-J. (1987) Optimal periodic interpolation in the mean. Preprint.

4. Ehlich, H. (1966) Untersuchungen zur numerischen Fourieranalyse. Math. Z. 91, 380-420.

5. Golomb, M. (1968) Approximation by periodic spline interpolants on uniform meshes. J. Approximation Theory 1, 26-65.

6. Gutknecht, M. H. (1987) Attenuation factors in multivariate Fourier analysis. Numer. Math. 51, 615-629.

7. terMorsche, H. (1987) Attenuation factors and multivariate periodic spline interpolation. In: Topics in Multivariate Approximation, C. Chui, L. Schumaker, F. Utreras, eds. (Academic Press, New York), 165-174.

8. Sard, A. (1967/68) Optimal approximation, J. Funct. Anal. 1, 222-244; 2, 368-369.

9. Stöckler, J. (1988) Interpolation mit mehrdimensionalen Bernoulli-Splines und periodischen Box-Splines. Dissertation, Duisburg.

10. Stöckler, J. (1989) On minimum norm interpolation by multivariate Bernoulli splines. To appear in: Approximation Theory VI, C. Chui, L. Schumaker, J. Ward, eds. (Academic Press, New York).

Joachim Stöckler, Fachbereich Mathematik, Universität Duisburg, Lotharstr. 65, 4100 Duisburg 1, West-Germany

International Series of
Numerical Mathematics, Vol. 90

STRONG UNIFORM APPROXIMATION BY BOCHNER-RIESZ MEANS

Wang Kun-yang
Lehrstuhl für Mathematik I
University of Siegen, D-5900 Siegen (West Germany)

1. Introduction

All those real-valued continuous functions defined on R^n which are periodic in each variable with period 2π compose a Banach space with max-norm. We denote this space by $C(Q^n)$, where $Q^n=\{(x_1,\dots,x_n): -\pi\leq x_j<\pi,\ j=1,\dots,n\}$. Suppose $f\in C(Q^n)$ then the norm of f is

$$\|f\|=\max\{|f(x)|: x\in Q^n\}.$$

The Bochner-Riesz means of f is defined by

$$S_R^{\alpha}(f;x)=\sum_{|m|<R} c_m(f)e^{imx}(1-|m|^2R^{-2})^{\alpha}.$$

where m denotes n-dimensional integers and $mx=m_1x_1+\dots+m_nx_n$ for $x\in R^n$, $|m|=(mm)^{\frac{1}{2}}$. The index α can be any complex number. The symbol $c_m(f)$ denotes the Fourier coefficients of f, i.e.,

$$c_m(f)=|Q^n|^{-1}\int_{Q^n} f(y)e^{-imy}dy,$$

where $|Q^n|$ denotes the Lebesgue measure of Q^n, that is $(2\pi)^n$. The special value $\alpha_0=\frac{1}{2}n-\frac{1}{2}$ of the index is called the critical index. When n=1, $S_R^0(f)$ is just the R-th Fourier sum of f. And for n>1 $S_R^{\alpha_0}$ have many properties similar to that of univariate Fourier sums. So we reasonably look upon the B-R means of critical index $S_R^{\alpha_0}$ as the analogue of the univariate Fourier sums. By this viewpoint we consider the problem of the convergence of the quantity

$$\|R^{-1}\int_0^R |S_r^{\alpha_0}(f)-f|^q dr\| \quad (q>0)$$

as $R\to\infty$, and call it to be the problem of strong uniform approximation.

For a function $f\in C(Q^n)$ we denote by $\omega_2(f;t)$ $(t>0)$ its modulus of continuity of order 2 which is defined by

$$\omega_2(f;t)=\sup\{\|f(\cdot+h)+f(\cdot-h)-2f(\cdot)\|:\ |h|<t\}\ (t>0).$$

In the present paper we will prove the following

<u>Theorem</u> If $\frac{1}{2}n-1<\alpha\leqslant\frac{1}{2}n-\frac{1}{2}$ then there exists a constant $c(n,\alpha)$ depending only on n and α, such that for any $f\in C(Q^n)$ and any R>o

$$\|R^{-1}\int_0^R |S_r^{\alpha}(f)-f|^2 dr\| \leqslant c(n,\alpha)R^{-1}\int_0^R \omega_2(f;r^{-1})^2 dr.$$

2. The integral representation of $R^{-1}\int_0^R\{S_r^{\alpha}(f;x)\}^2 dr$

Suppose $f\in C(Q^n)$, $x\in Q^n$ and R>o are all fixed. For every $\varepsilon\in[0,\frac{3}{4})$ we define a region $S_\varepsilon=\{\alpha=u+iv:\ \varepsilon+\frac{1}{2}n-1<u<\frac{1}{2}n-\frac{1}{4},\ -1<v<1\}$. For a complex number $\alpha\in S_\varepsilon$ we write

$$\alpha=\tfrac{1}{2}n-1+\beta,\quad \delta=\mathrm{Re}\beta\in(\varepsilon,\tfrac{3}{4}).$$

We know, if $\alpha\in S_{\frac{1}{2}}$ then the following Bochner formula ([1]) is valid:

$$S_R^{\alpha}(f;x)=2^{\alpha+1-\frac{1}{2}n}\Gamma(\alpha+1\ \Gamma(\tfrac{1}{2}n)\}^{-1}\int_0^{\infty}f_x(t)\,t^{n-1}r^nV_{\frac{1}{2}n+\alpha}(rt)\,dt$$

where

$$f_x(t)=2^{-1\ -\frac{1}{2}n}\Gamma(\tfrac{1}{2}n)\int_{|y|=1}f(x+ty)\,d\sigma(y),\quad V_{\nu}(z)=z^{-\nu}J_{\nu}(z)$$

and J_{ν} denotes the Bessel function of first kind. From this formula we derive that

$$R^{-1}\int_0^R\{S_r(f;x)\}^2dr=A(n,\alpha)\int_0^{\infty}\int_0^{\infty}f_x(s)f_x(t)(st)^{n-1}\cdot$$

$$\cdot K_R(s,t,\alpha)\,ds\,dt,$$

where

$$A(n,\alpha)=4^{\alpha+1-\frac{1}{2}n}\{\Gamma(\alpha+1)\}^2\{\Gamma(\tfrac{1}{2}n)\}^{-2},$$

$$K_R(s,t,\alpha)=R^{-1}\int_0^R r^{2n}V_{\frac{1}{2}n+\alpha}(sr)V_{\frac{1}{2}n+\alpha}(tr)\,dr.$$

We define a function of α

$$F(\alpha)=A(n,\alpha)\int_0^{\infty}\int_0^{\infty}f_x(s)f_x(t)(st)^{n-1}K_R(s,t,\alpha)\,ds\,dt. \tag{1}$$

Then we see that the equation

$$R^{-1}\int_0^R\{S_r^{\alpha}(f;x)\}^2dr=F(\alpha) \tag{2}$$

is valid when $\alpha\in S_{\frac{1}{2}}$ and F is analytic in $S_{\frac{1}{2}}$. If we are able to prove that F is also well-defined and analytic in S_{ε} for all $\varepsilon\in(0,\frac{1}{2})$, then we can immediately conclude that this equation holds for all $\alpha\in S_0$.

We define four sets as follows:

$$E_1=\{(s,t):0<t<s<R^{-1}\},\quad E_2=\{(s,t):0<t<R^{-1}<s\},$$

$$E_3=\{(s,t):R^{-1}<t<s<t+R^{-1}\},\quad E_4=\{(s,t):R^{-1}<t<s-R^{-1}\}.$$

Then we estimate $K_R(s,t,\alpha)$ on E_k for $k=1,2,3,4$, respectively. By a careful calculation and applying some properties of Bessel function of first kind, which can be found in [2], we get

$$|K_R(s,t,\alpha)|<3R^{2n} \quad \text{if } (s,t)\in E_1,$$

$$|K_R(s,t,\alpha)|<c_n R^{n-1-\delta}s^{-n-1-\delta} \quad \text{if } (s,t)\in E_2,$$

$$|K_R(s,t,\alpha)|<c_n R^{1-2\delta}s^{-2n+1-2\delta} \quad \text{if } (s,t)\in E_3,$$

$$|K_R(s,t,\alpha)|<c_n \varepsilon^{-1}R^{-1}(R^{1-2\delta}+t^{2\delta-1})(st)^{-n+\frac{1}{2}-\delta}(s-t)^{-1}$$

$$\text{if } (s,t)\in E_4.$$

where c_n denotes a constant depending only on n. From these estimates we derive the following lemma.

<u>Lemma</u> If $\varepsilon\in(o,2^{-1})$ and $\alpha\in S_\varepsilon$ then

$$\int_0^\infty\int_0^\infty (st)^{n-1}|K_R(s,t,\alpha)|dsdt<c_n\varepsilon^{-2} \quad (R>o).$$

From this lemma we derive the following proposition.

<u>Proposition</u> If $\alpha>2^{-1}n-1$ then the expression (2) holds for all $f\in C(Q^n)$ at all x, and when $2^{-1}n-1<\alpha<2^{-1}n-4^{-1}$,

$$\sup\{R^{-1}\int_0^R|S_r^\alpha(f;x)|^2dr:R>o,x\in Q^n\}\leqslant c_n(\alpha-\tfrac{1}{2}n+1)^{-2}\|f\|^2. \quad (3)$$

<u>Proof</u> Let $\varepsilon\in(o,2^{-1})$, $\alpha\in S_\varepsilon$ and $f\in C(Q^n)$. We set

$$I_R^\alpha f(x)=|A(n,\alpha)|\int_0^\infty\int_0^\infty|f_x(s)f_x(t)|(st)^{n-1}|K_R(s,t,\alpha)|dsdt.$$

Using Lemma we get

$$I_R^{\alpha} f(x) \leqslant c_n \varepsilon^{-2} \|f\|^2. \tag{4}$$

Hence we conclude that the function $F(\alpha)$, in (1), for $\alpha \in S_\varepsilon$ is well-defined and is analytic. And we have proved that the equation (2) holds for all $\alpha \in S_0$. Now for $\alpha \in (2^{-1}n-1, 2^{-1}n-4^{-1})$ we take ε in (4) such that $o<\varepsilon<\min(\alpha-2^{-1}n+1, 2^{-1})$ and then let ε tend to $\min(\alpha-2^{-1}n+1, 2^{-1})$. Then we get (3). Hence the proof is complete.

3. The proof of the Theorem

Let $2^{-1}n-1<\alpha<2^{-1}(n-1)$, $f \in C(Q^n)$ and $R>o$. Suppose $T_R(x)$ is the R-th trigonometric polynomial of the best approximation of f. Then obviously

$$\int_o^R |S_r^{\alpha}(f)-f|^2 dr \leqslant 4\int_o^R \{ |S_r^{\alpha}(f-T_R)|^2 + |S_r^{\alpha}(T_R)-S_r^{\alpha+1}(T_R)|^2 +$$

$$+ |S_r^{\alpha+1}(T_R)-T_R|^2\} dr + 4|T_R-f|^2, \tag{5}$$

$$\|f-T_R\| \leqslant c_n \omega_2(f;R^{-1}). \tag{6}$$

Applying our Proposition we get

$$\|R^{-1}\int_o^R |S_r^{\alpha}(f-T_R)|^2 dr\| \leqslant c(n,\alpha)|f-T_R|^2 \leqslant c(n,\alpha)\omega_2(f;R^{-1})^2. \tag{7}$$

Noticing $\alpha+1>2^{-1}n>2^{-1}(n-1)$ and applying a result of approximation by B-R means (with the index biger than $2^{-1}(n-1)$) (see [3]) we get for $o<r<R$

$$|S_r^{\alpha+1}(T_R)-T_R\| \leqslant c(n,\alpha)\omega_2(T_R;r^{-1}) \leqslant c(n,\alpha)\omega_2(f;r^{-1}). \tag{8}$$

We denote by Δ the Laplace operator. Then we have

$$S_r^{\alpha}(T_R)-S_r^{\alpha+1}(T_R) = S_r^{\alpha}(-R^{-2}\Delta T_R).$$

Noticing that

$$\|R^{-2}\Delta T_R\| \leqslant c_n \omega_2(f;R^{-1})$$

and applying the Proposition once again we get

$$\|R^{-1}\int_0^R |S_r^{\alpha}(T_R)-S_r^{\alpha+1}(T_R)|^2 dr\| \leqslant c(n,\alpha)\omega_2(f;R^{-1})^2. \qquad (9)$$

Substituting (6)—(9) into (5) we complete the proof.

Acknowledgement

This paper was completed while the author was a visiting scholar at University of Siegen. The author thanks Professor Schempp very much for his kind help.

References

[1] Bochner,S., Summation of multiple Fourier series by spherical means, Trans. AMS, 40(1936), 175-207.

[2] Watson, G.N., Theory of Bessel functions, Cambridge 1952.

[3] Wang Kun-yang, Approximation for continuous periodic function of several variables and its conjugate function by Riesz means on set of total measure, Approximation theory and its applications, Vol.1(1985)No.4, 19-56.

The author's permanent address:

Prof. Dr. Wang Kun-yang, Department of Mathematics, Beijing Normal University, 100875 Beijing, People's Republic of China.